Clashing Views on Controversial

Issues in Anthropology

Selected, Edited, and with Introductions by

Kirk M. Endicott
Dartmouth College

and

Robert L. Welsch
Dartmouth College

McGraw-Hill/Dushkin
A Division of The McGraw-Hill Companies

For Karen and Sarah

Photo Acknowledgment
Cover image: © 2001 by PhotoDisc, Inc.

Cover Art Acknowledgment
Charles Vitelli

Library of Congress Cataloging-in-Publication Data
Main entry under title:
Taking sides: clashing views on controversial issues in anthropology/selected, edited, and with introductions by Kirk M. Endicott and Robert L. Welsch.—1st ed.
Includes bibliographical references and index.
1. Anthropology. I. Endicott, Kirk M., *comp.* II. Welsch, Robert L., *comp.*
306

0-07-238885-4
ISSN: 1530-0757

Printed on Recycled Paper

Preface

Many courses and textbooks present anthropology as a discipline that largely consists of well-established facts. In *Taking Sides: Clashing Views on Controversial Issues in Anthropology* we present the discipline in quite a different light. Here we focus on active controversies that remain unresolved. These issues represent the kind of arguments and debates that have characterized anthropology for more than a century. They show the varied ways that anthropologists approach the subject of their research and the kinds of anthropological evidence needed to bolster an academic argument.

Generally, we have chosen selections that express strongly worded positions on two sides of an issue. For most issues, several other reasonable positions are also possible, and we have suggested some of these in our introductions and postscripts that accompany each issue.

Taking Sides: Clashing Views on Controversial Issues in Anthropology is a tool to encourage and develop critical thinking about anthropological research questions, methods, and evidence. As much as possible, we have attempted to select readings that represent most aspects of what anthropologists study. Another goal of this volume is to provide opportunities for students to explore how anthropologists frame and defend their interpretations of anthropological evidence. We have also chosen issues that raise questions about research methods and the quality or reliability of different kinds of data. All of these complex matters go into shaping the positions that anthropologists debate and defend in their writings. We hope that in discussing these issues students will find opportunities to explore how anthropologists think about the pressing theoretical issues of the day.

Plan of the book This book is made up of 19 issues that deal with topics that have provoked starkly different positions by different anthropologists. We have divided the volume into four Parts reflecting the discipline's three main subfields (Biological Anthropology, Archaeology, and Cultural Anthropology) as well as another Part dealing with Ethics in Anthropology. Each issue begins with an *introduction,* which sets the stage for the debate as argued in the YES and NO selections. Following these two selections is a *postscript* that makes some final observations and points the way to other questions related to the issue. In reading an issue and forming your own opinions, you should remember that there are often alternative perspectives that are not represented in either the YES or NO selections. Most issues have reasonable positions that might appear to be intermediate between the two more extreme viewpoints represented here in the readings. There are also reasonable positions that lie totally outside the scope of the debate presented in these selections, and students should consider all of these possible positions. Each postscript also contains *suggestions for further reading* that will help you find further resources to continue your study of any topic. Students researching any of these issues or related ones for a research paper will find these further readings (as well as their bibliographies) a useful place to begin a more intensive analysis. At the end of the book we have also included a list of all the *contributors to this volume,* which will give you information on the anthropologists and other commentators whose views are debated here. An *On the Internet* page accompanies each part opener. This page gives you Internet site addresses (URLs) that are relevant to the issues discussed in that part of the book. Many of these sites contain links to related sites and bibliographies for further study.

A word to the instructor   An *Instructor's Manual With Test Questions* (multiple-choice and essay) is available through the publisher for the instructor using *Taking Sides* in the classroom. A general guidebook, called *Using Taking Sides in the Classroom,* which discusses methods and techniques for integrating the pro-con approach into any classroom setting, is also available. An online version of *Using Taking Sides in the Classroom* and a correspondence service for Taking Sides adopters can be found at http://www.dushkin.com/usingts/.

Taking Sides: Clashing Views on Controversial Issues in Anthropology is only one title in the Taking Sides series. If you are interested in seeing the table of contents for any of the other titles, please visit the Taking Sides Web site at http://www.dushkin.com/takingsides/.

Acknowledgments   We received many helpful comments and suggestions from many friends and colleagues, including Hoyt Alverson, Cohn Calloway, Dale Eickelman, Samuel B. Fee, Jana Fortier, Alison Galloway, Ridie Ghezzi, Rosemary Gianno, Paul Goldstein, Alberto Gomez, Robert Gordon, Allen Hockley, Judy Hunt, Sergei Kan, Steve Kangas, Kenneth Korey, Christine Kray, Marilyn Lord, Deborah Nichols, Lynn Rainville, Jeanne Shea, Robert Tonkinson, John Watanabe, and Adrienne Zihlman. We also want to thank John Cocklin, Lucinda Hall, Francis X. Oscadal, Cindy Shirkey, and Reinhart Sonnenberg, members of the Baker Library Reference Department, all of whom have helped track down many of the sources we have used. Special thanks go to our student research assistant and Presidential Scholar Lauren Weldon. We also want to thank Ted Knight and Juliana Gribbins at McGraw-Hill/Dushkin for their constant assistance, suggestions, patience, and good humor. We also wish to thank our wives, Karen L. Endicott and Sarah L. Welsch, for their support and encouragement during the preparation of this volume.

Kirk M. Endicott
Dartmouth College

Robert L. Welsch
Dartmouth College

Contents In Brief

Contents

Paleoanthropologist Christopher Stringer and science writer Robin McKie argue that recent analysis of mitochondrial DNA evidence dates the evolution of anatomically modern humans to about 200,000 years ago. They assert that *Homo sapiens* originated from a single African population, which then spread over the rest of that continent and ultimately dispersed to all parts of the Old World, replacing all earlier hominid populations. Paleoanthropologists Alan G. Thorne and Milford H. Wolpoff counter that models derived from mitochondrial DNA evidence do not agree with the fossil and archaeological evidence. They maintain that *Homo erectus* populations had dispersed to all parts of the Old World by one million years ago. As the populations dispersed, they maintained contact and interbred enough so that the populations gradually evolved throughout the Old World to become anatomically modern humans.

Science writer Scott Norris surveys recent osteological, archaeological, and genetic evidence and concludes that the predominance of evidence favors a period of "mixing" between Neanderthals and early modern humans in Europe. Biological anthropologist Ian Tattersall contends that the anatomical and behavioral differences between Neanderthals and early modern humans were too great for them to have been the same species and thus able to interbreed and produce fertile offspring.

Biological anthropologist Jonathan Marks argues that the popular idea of races as discrete categories of people who are similar to each other and different from all members of other races is a cultural—not a biological—concept. Biological and forensic anthropologist George W. Gill contends that races—conceived as populations originating in particular regions—can be distinguished both by external and skeletal features. Furthermore, the notion of race provides a vocabulary for discussing human biological variation and racism.

Issue 4.   Are Humans Inherently Violent?   52

Biological anthropologist Richard Wrangham and science writer Dale Peterson argue that sexual selection, a type of natural selection, has fostered an instinct for male aggression because males who are good fighters mate more frequently and sire more offspring than weaker and less aggressive ones. Biological anthropologist Robert W. Sussman regards the notion that human males are inherently violent as a Western cultural tradition, not a scientifically demonstrated fact.

Issue 5.   Can Apes Learn Language?   74

Psychologist and primate specialist E. S. Savage-Rumbaugh argues that, since the 1960s, attempts to teach chimpanzees and other apes symbol systems similar to human language have resulted in the demonstration of a genuine ability to create new symbolic patterns. Linguist Joel Wallman counters that attempts to teach chimps and other apes sign language or other symbolic systems have demonstrated that apes are very intelligent animals, but up to now these attempts have not shown that apes have any innate capacity for language.

PART 2   ARCHAEOLOGY   91

Issue 6.   Did People First Arrive in the New World After the Last Ice Age?   92

Archaeologist Stuart J. Fiedel supports the traditional view that humans first reached the Americas from Siberia at the end of the last Ice Age. He argues that there are currently no convincing sites dated before that time and is skeptical of claims by other archaeologists who date human occupation of sites significantly earlier. Archaeologist Thomas D. Dillehay asserts that the site he has excavated at Monte Verde proved that humans reached the New World well before the end of the last Ice Age, possibly as early as 30,000 years ago.

Archaeologist John Edward Terrell argues that while all indigenous peoples in the Pacific had ancestors who lived in Southeast Asia in the very distant past, Polynesians represent a local stock, which derives itself biologically, culturally, and linguistically from a cultural melting pot in Melanesia. Archaeologist P. S. Bellwood contends that the Polynesians represent the extreme eastern expansion of the Mongoloid peoples he calls *Austronesians.* He states that Austronesians originally came from Taiwan to Southeast Asia and passed through Melanesia on their way to the Polynesian Islands.

Archaeologist Marija Gimbutas argues that the civilization of pre–Bronze Age "Old Europe" was matriarchal—ruled by women—and that the religion centered on the worship of a single great Goddess. Archaeologist Lynn Meskell considers the belief in a supreme Goddess and a matriarchal society in prehistoric Europe to be an unwarranted projection of some women's utopian longings onto the past.

Archaeologist Richard E. W. Adams argues that while military factors must have played some role in the collapse of the Classic Maya states, a combination of internal factors combined with environmental pressures were more significant. Archaeologist George L. Cowgill agrees that no single factor was responsible for the demise of the Classic Maya civilization, but he contends that military expansion was far more significant than scholars had previously thought.

PART 3 CULTURAL ANTHROPOLOGY 177

Cultural anthropologist Marvin Harris argues that anthropology has always been a science and should continue to be scientific. He contends that anthropology's goal should be to discover general, verifiable laws as in the other natural sciences. Cultural anthropologist Clifford Geertz views anthropology as a science of interpretation. He believes that anthropology's goal should be to generate deeper interpretations of diverse cultural phenomena, using what he calls "thick description," rather than attempting to prove or disprove scientific laws.

Archaeologists James R. Denbow and Edwin N. Wilmsen argue that the San of the Kalahari Desert in southern Africa have been involved in pastoralism, agriculture, and regional trade networks since at least A.D. 800. Cultural anthropologists Jacqueline S. Solway and Richard B. Lee contend that relations between San and other groups are highly variable from place to place. The Dobe !Kung followed an autonomous hunting-and-gathering way of life until their land was overrun by pastoralists in the late 1960s.

Cultural anthropologist Thomas N. Headland contends that tropical rain forests are poor in energy-rich wild foods that are readily accessible to humans, especially starches. Cultural anthropologists Serge Bahuchet and Igor de Garine and biologist Doyle McKey argue that rain forest foragers harvest far fewer wild foods than the forests actually contain, precisely because they now have easy access to cultivated foods.

Cultural anthropologist Maria Lepowsky argues that among the Vanatinai people of Papua New Guinea, the sexes are basically equal, although minor areas of male advantage exist. Sociologist Steven Goldberg contends that in all societies men occupy most high positions in hierarchical organizations and most high-status roles, and they dominate women in interpersonal relations. He believes that this is because men's hormones cause them to compete more strongly than women for high status and dominance.

Anthropologist and sociobiologist Napoleon A. Chagnon argues that the high incidence of violence and warfare he observed among the Yanomamö in the 1960s was directly related to man's inherent drive toward reproductive fitness (i.e., the innate biological drive to have as many offspring as possible). Anthropologist and cultural materialist R. Brian Ferguson counters that the high incidence of warfare and violence observed by Chagnon in the 1960s was a direct result of contact with Westerners at mission and government stations.

Social anthropologist Derek Freeman contends that Margaret Mead went
to Samoa determined to prove anthropologist Franz Boas's cultural determinist agenda and states that Mead was so eager to believe in Samoan
sexual freedom that she was consistently the victim of a hoax perpetrated
by Samoan girls and young women who enjoyed tricking her. Cultural anthropologists Lowell D. Holmes and Ellen Rhoads Holmes contend that
during a restudy of Mead's research, they came to many of the same conclusions that Mead had reached about Samoan sexuality and adolescent
experiences.

Postmodernist anthropologist James Clifford argues that the very act of
removing objects from their ethnographic contexts distorts the meaning
of objects held in museums. Exhibitions misrepresent ethnic communities
by omitting important aspects of contemporary life, especially involvement
with the colonial or Western world. Anthropologist Denis Dutton asserts
that no exhibition can provide a complete context for ethnographic objects,
but that does not mean that museum exhibitions are fundamentally flawed.

PART 4   ETHICS IN ANTHROPOLOGY   337

Assistant professor of justice studies and member of the Pawnee tribe
James Riding In argues that holding Native American skeletons in museums and other repositories represents a sacrilege against Native American dead and, thus, all Indian remains should be reburied. Professor of
anthropology and archaeologist Clement W. Meighan believes that archaeologists have a moral and professional obligation to the archaeological
data with which they work. Such data is held in the public good and must
be protected from destruction, he concludes.

Professor of the history and philosophy of science Merrilee H. Salmon argues that clitoridectomy (female genital mutilation) violates the rights of the women on whom it is performed. Professor of anthropology Elliott P. Skinner accuses feminists who want to abolish clitoridectomy of being ethnocentric. He argues that African women themselves want to participate in the practice, which functions like male initiation, transforming girls into adult women.

Anthropology professor James F. Weiner asserts that anthropologists have a responsibility to defend traditional native cultures, particularly if secret cultural knowledge is involved. Applied anthropologist Ron Brunton argues that even when hired as consultants, anthropologists have a moral and professional responsibility to the truth, whether the gained knowledge is considered by the native community as secret or not.

Introduction

Kirk M. Endicott

Robert L. Welsch

Anthropology is the study of humanity in all its biological, social, cultural, and linguistic diversity. Some of the founders of American anthropology, like Franz Boas, made important contributions to the understanding of human biology, culture, and language. But few such Renaissance men and women can be found today. To master the concepts, methods, and literatures involved in studying the different aspects of human variation, anthropologists have had to specialize. At times it may seem that no two anthropologists actually study the same things, yet they all are working toward a greater understanding of the commonalties and differences that define the human species.

Today, anthropology encompasses three major subdisciplines—biological anthropology, prehistoric archaeology, and cultural anthropology—and several smaller subdisciplines. Controversial issues in each of these subfields are included in the first three parts of this volume.

Biological Anthropology, also called *Physical Anthropology,* concerns the anatomy, physiology, mental capabilities, and genetics of humans and our nearest relatives, the primates. Traditionally, biological anthropologists, like other biologists, have understood human variation in evolutionary terms. Increasingly, as geneticists have introduced new ways of analyzing genetic data encoded in our DNA, biological anthropologists have described and explained human biological variation at the molecular level.

Fundamental questions for biological anthropologists include: How did our species evolve from early non-human primates? When did our species take on attributes that are associated with anatomically modern humans? Where did our species arise? What were the evolutionary forces that contributed to our anatomical and behavioral evolution? How and why did the hominids develop the capacity for culture—socially learned and transmitted patterns of behavior, thought, and feeling?

Paleoanthropologists (students of humankind's ancient ancestors) search for and excavate fossil bone fragments of long-dead primates, reconstruct their skeletons, and make inferences about their behavior patterns from bones, teeth, and other clues. They also use sophisticated dating techniques, computer models, and studies of living primates, both in the laboratory and in their natural environments, to create plausible models of human evolution and the relationships among the different branches of the primate order.

Archaeology, which is also referred to as *Prehistory,* involves documenting, understanding, and explaining the history of human communities and civilizations that existed before written records. Unlike most historians who can turn to documents and papers to detail the life and times of their subjects, archaeologists must usually find evidence for their reconstructions of the past through excavations of sites where people formerly lived or worked.

One issue at the heart of most archaeological controversies is how we can or should interpret these varied kinds of data to reconstruct the ways of life of earlier times. Recurrent questions include: What is the use and meaning of an artifact? To what extent can we use current lifeways of tribal or foraging groups as analogies for how prehistoric communities lived?

A set of questions that archeologists continue to ask is when, why, and how people first settled different parts of the world. They also ask why innovations like agriculture developed at particular times and in particular places. Why did some societies develop into complex civilizations, while others remained village-based societies, free of centralized political authority?

A frequent point of debate among archaeologists concerns the dating of archaeological deposits. Accurate dating, even if only relative to other artifacts in a site, is clearly essential for accurate interpretations, although dating alone does not reveal the processes that led to particular changes in the archaeological record. Stratification—the principle that the lower layers of a deposit are older than the upper layers—is still the most reliable basis for relative dating within a site. Now archaeologists also draw on a wide battery of high-tech absolute dating methods—including carbon 14, potassium-argon, and thermoluminescence dating—which have varying degrees of accuracy for different time spans. Dating always requires interpretation because, for example, carbon samples may be contaminated by more recent organic material like tree roots, and scholars do not always agree on the correct interpretation.

Cultural Anthropology, which is also called *Social Anthropology* in Great Britain or sometimes *Sociocultural Anthropology* in the United States, is concerned with the cultures and societies of living communities. Cultural anthropologists have proposed many different definitions of *culture.* Most emphasize that cultural behavior, thought, and feeling are socially created and learned, rather than generated by biologically transmitted instincts. Anthropologists differ considerably on the relative weight they assign to culture and instincts in explaining human behavior, as some of the issues in this volume show. Because cultures are human creations, they differ from one society to another.

Data for most cultural anthropologists come from observations, informal conversations, and interviews made while living within a study community. The hallmark of cultural anthropology is *fieldwork,* in which the anthropologist lives with another cultural group, learns their language, their customs, and their patterns of interaction. Anthropological fieldwork involves *participant observation*—observing while participating in the life of the community.

As in the other subfields of anthropology, cultural data must be interpreted. Interpretation begins with the creation of the research questions themselves. This reflects what investigators consider as being important to discover and directs their observations and questions in the field. At each step of data collection and analysis, the investigators' theories and interests shape their understanding of other cultures.

Much explanation in cultural anthropology is based on the comparison of cultural features in different societies. Some anthropologists explicitly make cross-cultural comparisons, using statistics to measure the significance of apparent correlations between such things as childrearing practices and adult personalities. Even anthropologists who concentrate on explaining or interpreting features of particular cultures use their knowledge of similar or different features in other societies as a basis for insights.

Like other anthropologists, cultural anthropologists look for uniformities in human behavior as well as variations. Understanding what patterns of human behavior are possible has been at the center of many controversies in cultural anthropology. Questions touched on in this book include: Is gender equality possible? Is violence inevitable? Can small-scale hunting and gathering societies live in contact with more powerful food-producing societies without being dominated by them? Does the amount of sexual freedom offered to adolescents make a difference in their transition to adulthood?

Recently, cultural anthropologists have begun asking questions about possible biases in the ways anthropologists depict and represent other cultures through writing, films, and other media. This movement has been called *post-modern anthropology* or *critical anthropology*. Post-modernists ask, among other things: Do our theories and methods of representation inadvertently portray the people we study as exotic "Others," in exaggerated contrast with Western peoples? This is the question that lies behind Issue 16, "Do Museums Misrepresent Ethnic Communities Around the World?"

Other Subfields Anthropologists sometimes distinguish two other subfields: *Linguistic Anthropology* and *Applied Anthropology*.

Linguistic anthropology includes the study of language and languages, especially non-Western and unwritten languages, and the study of the relationship between language and other aspects of culture. Some anthropologists regard linguistic anthropology as a subdivision of cultural anthropology because language is a part of culture and is the medium by which much of culture is transmitted from one generation to the next.

A classic question for linguistic anthropologists has been: Do the categories of a language shape how humans perceive and understand the world? For example, if a language has terms for certain races, as English does, do speakers actually perceive people as members of those races? (See Issue 3, "Should Anthropology Abandon the Concept of Race?")

Two issues in this volume deal with linguistic questions. The first is Issue 5, "Can Apes Learn Language?" We have included this question with controversial issues in biological anthropology because it focuses directly on the characteristics that distinguish *Homo sapiens* from other primates. The second is Issue 7, "Did Polynesians Descend from Melanesians?" Here the question is whether archaeologists can use linguistic data to reconstruct the cultural history of a people.

In recent years, cultural anthropologists have increasingly been involved in applied anthropology, in which anthropological methods and conclusions are used to solve or address practical problems in particular communities. While applied anthropology is sometimes thought of as a fifth subfield of anthropology, it draws so heavily on the methods and theories of the other subfields that we feel it is unnecessary to include it as a separate part of the book. The work of applied anthropologists, however, has raised a number of important ethical issues in anthropology. For example, Issue 19 asks, "Do Anthropologists Have a Moral Responsibility to Defend the Interests Of 'Less Advantaged' Communities?"

Ethics in Anthropology   Concerns about the ethics of research have become increasingly important in contemporary anthropology. The American Anthropological Association has developed a Code of Ethics covering both research and teaching (see the American Anthropological Association Web site at www. aaanet.org.) It recognizes that researchers sometimes have conflicting obligations to the people and animals studied, host countries, the profession, and the public. One basic principle is that researchers should do nothing that could harm or distress the people or animals they study. Cultural anthropologists must be aware of the possibility of harming the living people with whom they work, but similar considerations also affect archaeologists and biological anthropologists because the artifacts of past communities often represent the ancestors of living communities. Here the interests of anthropologists and native peoples may diverge. In Issue 17 we ask, "Should the Remains of Prehistoric Native Americans Be Reburied Rather Than Studied?" Similarly, we may ask what the ethical responsibilities of Western anthropologists should be when they find certain cultural practices of other peoples abhorrent or unjust. For example, Issue 18 asks, "Should Anthropologists Work to Eliminate the Practice of Female Circumcision?"

Some Basic Questions

On the surface, the issues presented in this book are very diverse. Anthropologists from different subfields tend to focus on their own specialized problems and to work with different kinds of evidence. Most of the controversial issues we have chosen for this volume can be read as very narrow, focused debates within a subfield. But many of the issues that confront anthropologists in one subfield arise in other subfields as well. What has attracted us to the issues presented here is that each raises much broader questions that affect the entire discipline. In this section we briefly describe some of the basic questions lying behind specific issues.

Is Anthropology a Science or a Humanity?

Science is a set of ideas and methods intended to describe and explain phenomena in a naturalistic way, seeing individual things and events as the outcome of discoverable causes and as conforming to general laws. Anthropologists taking a scientific approach are concerned with developing broad theories about the processes that lead to observed patterns of variation in human biology, language, and culture. The humanities, on the other hand, are concerned with understanding people's cultural creations in terms of their meanings to their creators and the motivations behind their creation.

Biological anthropology seeks the reasons for human evolution and biological diversity largely in the processes of the natural world, and it uses the methods of the physical sciences for investigating those phenomena. Archaeology, too, uses natural science concepts and methods of investigation, but it also draws on understandings of human behavior that take account of culturally-influenced motivations, values, and meanings. Cultural anthropologists are divided over whether cultural anthropology should model itself on the natural sciences or on the humanities. Some cultural anthropologists try to discover the causes of particular cultural forms occurring at specific places and times, while others try to interpret the meanings (to the people themselves) of cultural forms in other societies in ways that are intelligible to Western readers. Issue 10, "Should Cultural Anthropology Model Itself on the Natural Sciences?" directly addresses the question of whether anthropology is part of the sciences or humanities.

Is Biology or Culture More Important in Shaping Human Behavior?

Most anthropologists accept that both genetically-transmitted behavioral tendencies (instincts) and cultural ideas and norms influence human behavior, thought, and emotion. However, anthropologists diverge widely over the amount of weight they assign to these two influences. *Biological determinists* believe that all human behavior is ultimately determined by the genes, and culture merely lends distinctive coloration to our genetically-driven behaviors. At the other extreme, *cultural determinists* believe that any instincts humans may have are so weak and malleable that cultural learning easily overcomes them. The conflict between supporters of the two extreme views, called the *nature-nurture debate,* has been going on for many years and shows no sign of being resolved soon.

Several of the issues in this volume deal directly with the nature-nurture question, including Issue 4, "Are Humans Inherently Violent?"; Issue 5, "Can Apes Learn Language?"; Issue 13, "Do Sexually Egalitarian Societies Exist?"; and Issue 14, "Are Yanomamö Violence and Warfare Natural Human Efforts to Maximize Reproductive Fitness?" In addition, Issue 15, about the Margaret Mead–Derek Freeman controversy, concerns two diametrically opposed positions about whether adolescence is shaped more by biology or by culture.

Is the Local Development of Culture or Outside Influence More Important in Shaping Cultures?

In trying to explain the form a particular culture takes, different anthropologists place different amounts of emphasis on the local development of culture and outside influence. Those who favor local development emphasize unique innovations and adaptations to the natural environment, while those favoring outside influences emphasize the borrowing of ideas from neighbors (*diffusion*) and changes forced upon a people by more powerful groups (*acculturation*). Most anthropologists recognize some influence from both sources, but some attribute overriding importance to one or the other.

The debate between proponents of local development of culture and proponents of outside influence plays a major role in several of the issues in this volume, including Issue 7, "Did Polynesians Descend from Melanesians?"; Issue 9, "Were Environmental Factors Responsible for the Mayan Collapse?"; Issue 11, "Are San Hunter-Gatherers Basically Pastoralists Who Have Lost Their Herds?"; Issue 12, "Do Hunter-Gatherers Need Supplemental Food Sources to Live in Tropical Rain Forests?"; and Issue 14, "Are Yanomamö Violence and Warfare Natural Human Efforts to Maximize Reproductive Fitness?"

Is a Feminist Perspective Needed in Anthropology?

Although female anthropologists—like Margaret Mead and Ruth Benedict—have been very influential in the development of anthropology, there was a bias in early anthropological studies toward emphasizing the social and political lives of men. Over the past 30 years feminist anthropologists have argued that these male-biased accounts have overlooked much of what goes on in traditional societies because male anthropologists have been preoccupied with men's activities and the male point of view.

Issue #8, "Was There a Goddess Cult in Prehistoric Europe?" considers one possible male bias in interpreting prehistoric religions. Issue 13, "Do Sexually Egalitarian Societies Exist?" considers whether or not a feminist perspective is needed to recognize sexual equality. Feminist anthropologists have also asserted that male bias affects anthropological methodologies as well. Issue 15, "Was Margaret Mead's Fieldwork on Samoan Adolescents Fundamentally Flawed?" hinges in part on different methods available to male and female researchers.

Some Theoretical Approaches

Anthropologists draw on many theories of widely varying scope and type. We present brief summaries of a number of theoretical approaches used by authors in this book so that you will recognize and understand them when you see them. We have arranged these theories in a rough continuum from most scientific in approach to most humanistic.

Biological evolution   Biological anthropology is based predominantly on the modem theory of biological evolution. This builds upon the ideas that Charles Darwin developed in the mid-nineteenth century. Darwin combined the idea of evolution—the development of species by means of incremental changes in previous species—with the concept of natural selection. Natural selection means that in a variable population those individuals best adapted to the environment are most likely to survive and reproduce, thus passing on their favorable characteristics (called *survival of the fittest*). The modem theory of biological evolution adds an understanding of genetics, including the concepts of *genetic* *drift* (random variation in gene frequencies) and *gene flow* (transmission of genes between populations). Most biological anthropologists today also subscribe to the notion of *punctuated equilibrium,* which states that evolutionary change takes place in fits and starts, rather than at an even pace.

Virtually all biological anthropologists use the modem theory of evolution, so their disagreements arise not over which theory to use, but over interpretations of evidence and questions of how the theory applies to specific cases.

Sociobiology   Sociobiology is a theory that attempts to use evolutionary principles to explain all behavior of animals, including humans. The best-known practitioner is biologist E. O. Wilson, whose book *Sociobiology: The New Synthesis* (Harvard University Press, 1975) sets out the basic concepts. Sociobiologists believe that human behavior is determined by inherited behavioral tendencies. The genes promoting behaviors that lead to survival and successful reproduction are favored by natural selection and thus tend to become more common in a population over the generations. For sociobiologists such behaviors as selfishness, altruism to close kin, violence, and certain patterns of marriage are evolutionarily and biologically determined. They see individual and cultural ideas as mere rationalizations of innate patterns of behavior. In their view, no culture will persist that goes against the "wisdom of the genes."

Cultural evolution   Drawing on an analogy with biological evolution, nineteenth-century cultural anthropologists developed the idea that complex societies evolve out of simpler ones. The unilineal schemes of such cultural evolutionists as Lewis Henry Morgan, E. B. Tylor, and James G. Fraser postulated that all societies pass through a fixed series of stages, from savagery to civilization. They regarded contemporary simple societies, like the tribal peoples of the Amazon, as "survivals" from earlier stages of cultural evolution.

Unilineal schemes of cultural evolution have now been discredited because they were speculative, ignored differences in patterns of culture change in different places, and were blatantly ethnocentric, regarding all non-Western cultures as inferior to those of Europe. But some archaeologists and cultural anthropologists still espouse more sophisticated versions of cultural evolution regarding at least some aspects of culture change.

Cultural ecology   The theory of cultural ecology was developed by cultural anthropologist Julian Steward in the 1930s as a corrective to the overly simple schemes of cultural evolution. Emphasizing the process of adaptation to the physical environment, he postulated that societies in different environments would develop different practices, though the general trend was toward higher levels of complexity, a process he called *multilinear evolution.* His idea of adaptation, like natural selection, explained why some societies and practices succeeded and were perpetuated, while other less well-adapted ones died out.

Many archaeologists and cultural anthropologists use versions of cultural ecology to explain why certain practices exist in certain environments. Marvin Harris's widely-used theory of *cultural materialism* is a further development of cultural ecology. The basic idea behind all versions of cultural ecology is that societies must fulfill their material needs if they are to survive. Therefore those institutions involved with making a living must be well adapted to the environment, while others, like religions, are less constrained by the environment.

Culture history   One of the founders of American cultural anthropology, Franz Boas, rejected the cultural evolution schemes of the nineteenth century, with their fixed stages of cultural development. He pointed out that all societies had unique histories, depending on local innovations and diffusion of ideas from neighboring societies. Also, change is not always toward greater complexity; civilizations crumble as well as rise. Boas advocated recording the particular events and influences that contributed to the makeup of each culture.

World system theory   The world system theory, which has gained great prominence in the social sciences in recent years, asserts that all societies, large and small, are—and long have been—integrated in a single worldwide political-economic system. This approach emphasizes the connections among societies, especially the influence of politically powerful societies over weak ones, as in colonialism, rather than local development of culture.

Cultural interpretation   Humanist anthropologists emphasize their role as interpreters, not explainers, of culture. They focus on the task of describing other cultures in ways that are intelligible to Western readers, making sense of customs that at first glance seem incomprehensible. The most prominent practitioner of cultural interpretation is Clifford Geertz, who coined the term *thick description* for this process. This approach is used especially for dealing with aspects of culture that are products of human imagination, like art and mythology, but even the institutions involved in physical survival, like families and economic processes, have dimensions of meaning that warrant interpretation.

Feminist anthropology   Feminist anthropology began in the 1970s as an approach meant to correct the lack of coverage of women and women's views in earlier anthropology. It has now developed into a thoroughgoing alternative approach to the study of culture and society. Its basic idea is that gender is a cultural construction affecting the roles and meanings of the sexes in particular societies. The aim of feminist anthropology is both to explain the position of women and to convey the meanings surrounding gender. Feminist anthropologists emphasize that all social relations have a gender dimension.

How Anthropologists Reach Conclusions

None of the issues considered in this volume have been resolved, and several are still the subject of heated, and at times, acrimonious debate. The most heated controversies typically arise from the most extreme points of view. When reading these selections students should bear in mind that only two positions are presented formally, although in the introductions and postscripts we raise questions that should guide you to consider other positions as well. We encourage you to question all of the positions offered before coming to any conclusions of your own. Remember, for more than a century anthropology has prided itself on revealing how our own views of the world are culturally biased. Try to be aware of how your own background, upbringing, ethnicity, religion, likes, and dislikes affect your assessments of the arguments presented here.

In our own teaching we have often used controversial issues as a way to help students understand how anthropologists think about research questions. We have found that five questions often help students focus on the most important points in these selections:

1. Who is the author?
2. What are the author's assumptions?
3. What methods and data does an author use?
4. What are the author's conclusions?
5. How does the author reach his or her conclusions from the data?

For each issue we suggest that you consider what school of thought, what sort of training, and what sort of research experience each author has. We often find it useful to ask why this particular author finds the topic worth writing about. Does one or the other author seem to have any sort of bias? What assumptions does each author hold? Do both authors hold the same assumptions?

For any anthropological debate, we also find it useful to ask what methods or analytical strategies each author has used to reach the conclusions he or she presents. For some of the issues presented in this book, authors share many of the same assumptions and are generally working with the same evidence, but disagree as to how this evidence should be analyzed. Some authors disagree most profoundly on what kinds of data are most suitable for answering a particular research question. Some even disagree about what kinds of questions anthropologists should be asking.

Finally, we suggest that you consider how the author has come to his or her conclusions from the available data. Would different data make any difference? Would a different kind of evidence be more appropriate? Would different data likely lead to different conclusions? Would different ways of analyzing the data suggest other conclusions?

If you can answer most of these questions about any pair of selections, you will be thinking about these problems anthropologically and will understand how anthropologists approach controversial research questions. After weighing the various possible positions on an issue you will be able to form sound opinions of your own.

On the Internet . . .   DUSHKIN ONLINE

Human Origins and Evolution in Africa

Jeanne Sept, an anthropology professor at Indiana University who has done fieldwork on the question of human origins in Africa, created this Web site. The site provides information about human evolution in Africa and provides links to related Web sites.

http://www.indiana.edu/~origins/

Fossil Evidence for Human Evolution in China

This site, created by the Center for the Study of Chinese Prehistory, introduces fossil evidence for human evolution in China. It includes a catalog of Chinese human fossil remains; provides links to other sites dealing with paleontology, human evolution, and Chinese prehistory; and includes other resources that may be useful for gaining a better understanding of China's role in the emergence of humankind.

http://www.cruzio.com/~cscp/index.htm

Neanderthals

This site provides information on the differences between Neanderthals and modern humans and on the emergence of modern humans. It also includes links to other sites offering further information on Neanderthals.

http://www.neanderthal.de/e_thal/fs_1.htm

Fossil Hominids: The Evidence for Human Evolution

Created by Jim Foley, this site provides links to recent articles about human evolution and the question of whether or not Neanderthals and early modern humans interbred. A discussion of creationism and the Biblical interpretation of the origins of life is also presented.

http://www.talkorigins.org/faqs/homs/

The Chimpanzee and Human Communication Institute Home Page

The Chimpanzee and Human Communication Institute provides information on this site about current research on teaching American Sign Language to chimpanzees. The site includes information about experiments with chimps as well as links to other sites dealing with the question of whether apes can learn a language.

http://www.cwu.edu/~cwuchci/

PART 1

Biological Anthropology

*B*iological anthropologists, also called physical anthropologists, study the bodies, bones, and genetics of humans and of our nearest relatives, the other primates. Their basic goals are to understand human evolution scientifically and to explain contemporary human diversity. Fundamental questions include: How did our species evolve from early nonhuman primates? When did our species take on attributes that are associated with anatomically modern humans? Where did our species develop as a species, and what were the evolutionary forces that contributed to our anatomical evolution? These questions have traditionally required detailed comparisons of bones from living species and fossilized bones from extinct species. However, increasingly anthropologists asking these kinds of questions are developing new models about evolution from observing and studying living primates either in the laboratory or in their natural environment.

- Did *Homo Sapiens* Originate Only in Africa?

- Did Neanderthals Interbreed With Modern Humans?

- Should Anthropology Abandon the Concept of Race?

- Are Humans Inherently Violent?

- Can Apes Learn Language?

ISSUE 1

Did *Homo Sapiens* Originate Only in Africa?

YES: Christopher Stringer and Robin McKie, from *African Exodus: The Origins of Modern Humanity* (Henry Holt & Company, 1996)

NO: Alan G. Thorne and Milford H. Wolpoff, from "The Multiregional Evolution of Humans," *Scientific American* (April 1992)

ISSUE SUMMARY

YES: Paleoanthropologist Christopher Stringer and science writer Robin McKie argue that recent analysis of mitochondrial DNA evidence dates the evolution of anatomically modern humans to about 200,000 years ago. They assert that *Homo sapiens* originated from a single African population, which then spread over the rest of that continent and ultimately dispersed to all parts of the Old World, replacing all earlier hominid populations.

NO: Paleoanthropologists Alan G. Thorne and Milford H. Wolpoff counter that models derived from mitochondrial DNA evidence do not agree with the fossil and archaeological evidence. They maintain that *Homo erectus* populations had dispersed to all parts of the Old World by one million years ago. As the populations dispersed, they maintained contact and interbred enough so that the populations gradually evolved throughout the Old World to become anatomically modern humans.

$\mathbf{F}$ew debates in biological anthropology have been as heated as the debate concerning when and where anatomically modern humans evolved. At the heart of the debate are two distinct sets of biological data.

The first data set consists of the fossil record of early hominids and associated archaeological evidence of stone tools. Models of human evolution have remained fairly stable in spite of the fact that in recent years the number of fossilized hominid skeletons available to paleoanthropologists for study has increased substantially.

The second data set consists of mitochondrial DNA—genetic material that has only recently been deciphered by molecular biologists. Nuclear DNA from each parent combines at conception so that a child shares half of his or her DNA with each parent. This fact also means that half of the child's DNA differs from that of each parent. In this way nuclear, or recombinant, DNA continues to recombine with each generation so that after five generations, a child shares only a very small part of his or her DNA with each of its 32 great-great-great grandparents. But mitochondrial DNA is different; it comes exclusively from the mother and does not recombine with the father's DNA at all. It is passed on intact from mothers to daughters forming female lineages called matrilines. Mitochondrial DNA changes only through mutation.

In the 1950s early fossil skeletons were discovered along the Rift Valley in Africa by Louis and Mary Leakey. Since then paleoanthropologists have found many *Australopithecus* remains, thus proving that Africa is where our human lineage split off from that of the great apes. This gave rise to Robert Ardrey's book *African Genesis* (Atheneum, 1961), which stated that our first bipedal ancestors originated in Africa. Scholars today accept that *Homo erectus* spread out from Africa to settle in most of the Old World by at least one million years ago. These conclusions about *Homo erectus* have been confirmed by new fossil evidence both within Africa and elsewhere, and no paleoanthropologists or geneticists challenge this theory.

But where and how *Homo erectus* evolved to become *Homo sapiens* has been a fiercely contested matter. Two theories have been put forward: (1) the "out-of-Africa" theory and (2) the "multiregional" theory.

The "out-of-Africa" theory was first proposed in 1987 by a group of geneticists and molecular anthropologists in Berkeley, California. They interpreted their analysis of human mitochondrial DNA as indicating that all humans living today are members of the same mitochondrial DNA matrilineage that originated roughly 200,000 years ago.

In their selection, Christopher Stringer and Robin McKie discuss what is known as the "African Eve." They argue that by calibrating the rate of mutations in mitochondrial DNA, they can date the founding mother of all living human beings.

In the second selection, Alan G. Thorne and Milford H. Wolpoff support the "multiregional" theory. According to this theory, after *Homo erectus* spread across the Old World, the species continued to evolve as a single species to become *Homo sapiens*. The shift from *Homo erectus* to *Homo sapiens* was gradual and at no time were *Homo erectus* and *Homo sapiens* competing for the same resources or ecological niches.

These selections raise a number of questions for anthropologists: How reliable is DNA evidence? What assumptions are built into these DNA models? How can the rates of genetic mutation be calibrated? Does mitochondrial DNA mutate at the same rate as nuclear DNA? How complete is the fossil record? Do paleoanthropologists also have assumptions about how fossils change that might be incorrect? What evidence in the fossil or archaeological record should be found if *Homo sapiens* replaced *Homo erectus*? Can anthropologists find some middle ground between these two models that will account for all of the current data?

Christopher Stringer
and Robin McKie

The Mother of All Humans?

It is not the gorilla, nor the chimpanzee, nor the orangutan, that is unusual.... Each enjoys a normal spectrum of biological variability. It is the human race that is odd. We display remarkable geographical diversity, and yet astonishing genetic unity. This dichotomy is perhaps one of the greatest ironies of our evolution. Our nearest primate relations may be much more differentiated with regard to their genes but today are consigned to living in a band of land across Central Africa, and to the islands of Borneo and Sumatra. We, who are stunningly similar, have conquered the world.

This revelation has provided the unraveling of our African origins with one of its most controversial chapters. And it is not hard to see why. The realization that humans are biologically highly homogeneous has one straightforward implication: that mankind has only recently evolved from one tight little group of ancestors. We simply have not had time to evolve significantly different patterns of genes. Human beings may look dissimilar, but beneath the separate hues of our skins, our various types of hair, and our disparate physiques, our basic biological constitutions are fairly unvarying. We are all members of a very young species, and our genes betray this secret.

It is not this relative genetic conformity per se that has caused the fuss but the results of subsequent calculations which have shown that the common ancestor who gave rise to our tight mitochondrial DNA lineage must have lived about 200,000 years ago. This date, of course, perfectly accords with the idea of a separate recent evolution of *Homo sapiens* shortly before it began its African exodus about 100,000 years ago. In other words, one small group of *Homo sapiens* living 200 millennia ago must have been the source of all our present, only slightly mutated mitochondrial DNA samples—and must therefore be the fount of all humanity. Equally, the studies refute the notion that modern humans have spent the last one million years quietly evolving in different parts of the globe until reaching their present status. Our DNA is too uniform for that to be a realistic concept....

Not surprisingly, such intercessions into the hardened world of the fossil hunter, by scientists trained in the "delicate" arts of molecular biology and genetic manipulation, have not gone down well in certain paleontological circles. The old order has reacted with considerable anger to the interference of these "scientific interlopers." The idea that the living can teach us anything about the past is a reversal of their cherished view that we can best learn about ourselves from studying our prehistory. Many had spent years using fossils to establish their interpretations of human origins, and took an intense dislike to being "elbowed aside by newcomers armed with blood samples and computers," as *The Times* (London) put it. "The fossil record is the real evidence for human evolution," announced Alan Thorne and Milford Wolpoff in one riposte (in *Scientific American*) to the use of mitochondrial DNA to study our origins. "Unlike the genetic data, fossils can be matched to the predictions of theories about the past without relying on a long list of assumptions." Such a clash of forces has, predictably, generated a good many sensational headlines, and triggered some of the most misleading statements that have ever been made about our origins. Scientists have denied that these genetic analyses reveal the fledgling status of the human race. Others have even rejected the possibility of ever re-creating our past by studying our present in this way. Both views are incorrect, as we shall see. Even worse, the multiregionalists have attempted to distort the public's understanding of the Out of Africa theory by deliberately confusing its propositions with the most extreme and controversial of the geneticists' arguments. By tarnishing the latter they hope to diminish the former. This [selection] will counter such propaganda and highlight the wide-ranging support for our African Exodus provided, not just by the molecular biologists, but by others, including those who study the words we speak and who can detect signs of our recent African ancestry there. We shall show not only that the majority of leading evolutionists and biologists believe in such an idea but that their views raise such serious questions about the multiregional hypothesis that its future viability must now be very much in doubt.

Unraveling the history of human migration from our current genetic condition is not an easy business, of course. It is a bit like trying to compile a family tree with only an untitled photograph album to help you. "Our genetic portrait of humankind is necessarily based on recent samplings, [and] it is unavoidably static," says Christopher Wills of the University of San Diego. "Historical records of human migrations cover only a tiny fraction of the history of our species, and we know surprisingly little about how long most aboriginal people have occupied their present homes. We are pretty close to the position of a viewer who tries to infer the entire plot of *Queen Christina* from the final few frames showing Garbo's rapt face."

It is an intriguing image. Nevertheless, biologists are beginning to make a telling impact in unraveling this biological plot and in understanding *Homo sapiens'* African exodus. And they have done this thanks to the development of some extraordinarily powerful techniques for splitting up genes, which are made of stands of DNA (deoxyribonucleic acid) and which control the process of biological inheritance. . . .

[T]his is exactly what Allan Wilson, Rebecca Cann, and Mark Stoneking, working at the University of California, Berkeley, did in 1987. They took specimens from placentas of 147 women from various ethnic groups and analyzed each's mitochondrial DNA. By comparing these in order of affinity, they assembled a giant tree, a vast family network, a sort of chronological chart for mankind, which linked up all the various samples, and therefore the world's races, in a grand, global genealogy.

The study produced three conclusions. First, it revealed that very few mutational differences exist between the mitochondrial DNA of human beings, be they Vietnamese, New Guineans, Scandinavians, or Tongans. Second, when the researchers put their data in a computer and asked it to produce the most likely set of linkages between the different people, graded according to the similarity of their mitochondrial DNA, it created a tree with two main branches. One consisted solely of Africans. The other contained the remaining people of African origin, and everyone else in the world. The limb that connected these two main branches must therefore have been rooted in Africa, the researchers concluded. Lastly, the study showed that African people had slightly more mitochondrial DNA mutations compared to non-Africans, implying their roots are a little older. In total, these results seemed to provide overwhelming support for the idea that mankind arose in Africa, and, according to the researchers' data, very recently. Their arithmetic placed the common ancestor as living between 142,500 and 285,000 years ago, probably about 200,000 years ago. These figures show that the appearance of "modern forms of *Homo sapiens* occurred first in Africa" around this time and "that all present day humans are descendants of that African population," stated Wilson and his team.

The Berkeley paper outlining these findings was published in the journal *Nature* in January 1987, and made headlines round the world, which is not surprising given that Wilson pushed the study's implications right to the limit. He argued that his mitochondrial tree could be traced back, not just to a small group of *Homo sapiens*, but to one woman, a single mother who gave birth to the entire human race. The notion of an alluring fertile female strolling across the grasslands of Africa nourishing our forebears was too much for newspapers and television. She was dubbed "African Eve"—though this one was found, not in scripture, but in DNA. (The honor of so naming this genetic mother figure is generally accorded to Charles Petit, the distinguished science writer of the *San Francisco Chronicle*. Wilson claimed he disliked the title, preferring instead, "Mother of us all" or "One lucky mother.")

The image of this mitochondrial matriarch may seem eccentric but it at least raises the question of how small a number of *Homo sapiens* might have existed 200,000 years ago. In fact, there must have been thousands of women alive at that time. The planet's six billion inhabitants today are descendants of many of these individuals (and their male partners), not just one single super-mother. As we have said, we humans get our main physical and mental characteristics from our nuclear genes, which are a mosaic of contributions from myriad ancestors. We appear to get our mitochondrial genes from only one woman, but that does not mean she is the only mother of all humans.

"Think of it as the female equivalent of passing on family surnames," states Sir Walter Bodmer, the British geneticist. "When women marry they usually lose their surname, and assume their husband's. Now if a man has two children, there is a 25 percent chance both will be daughters. When they marry, they too will change their name, and his surname will disappear. After twenty generations, 90 percent of surnames will vanish this way, and within 10,000 generations—which would take us from the time of 'African Eve' to the present day—there would only be one left." An observer might assume that this vast, single-named clan bore a disproportionately high level of its originator's genes. In fact, it would contain a fairly complete blend of all human genes. And the same effect is true for mitochondrial DNA (except of course it is the man who is "cut out"). The people of the world therefore seem to have basically only one mitochondrial "name." Nevertheless, they carry a mix of all the human genes that must have emanated from that original founding group of *Homo sapiens.* It is a point that Wilson tried, belatedly, to make himself. "She wasn't the literal mother of us all, just the female from whom all our mitochondrial DNA derives." . . .

And there we have it. The blood that courses through our veins, the genes that lie within our cells, the DNA strands that nestle inside our mitochondrial organelles, even the words we speak—all bear testimony to the fact that 100,000 years ago a portion of our species emerged from its African homeland and began its trek to world dominion. (The other part, which stayed behind, was equally successful in diversifying across the huge African continent, of course.) It may seem an exotic, possibly unsettling, tale. Yet there is nothing strange about it. This process of rapid radiation is how species spread. The real difference is just how far we took this process—to the ends of the earth. A species normally evolves in a local ecology that, in some cases, provides a fortuitously fertile ground for honing a capacity for survival. Armed with these newly acquired anatomies, or behavior patterns, it can then take over the niches of other creatures. This is the normal course of evolution. What is abnormal is the supposed evolution of mankind as described by the multiregionalists. They place their faith in a vast global genetic link-up and compare our evolution to individuals paddling in separate corners of a pool. . . . According to this scheme, each person maintains their individuality over time. Nevertheless, they influence one another with the spreading ripples they raise—which are the equivalent of genes flowing between populations.

Let us recall the words of Alan Thorne and Milford Wolpoff. . . .
They state that:

> The dramatic genetic similarities across the entire human race do not reflect a recent common ancestry for all living people. They show the consequences of linkages between people that extend to when our ancestors first populated the Old World, more than a million years ago. They are the results of an ancient history of population connections and mate exchanges that has characterised the human race since its inception. Human evolution happened everywhere because every area was always part of the whole.

Gene flow is therefore crucial to the idea that modern humans evolved separately, for lengthy periods, in different corners of the earth, converging somehow into a now highly homogeneous form. Indeed, the theory cannot survive without this concept—for a simple reason. Evolution is random in action and that means that similar environmental pressures—be they associated with climate change, or disease, or other factors—often generate different genetic responses in separate regions. Consider malaria, a relatively new disease that spread as human populations became more and more dense after the birth of agriculture. Our bodies have generated a profusion of genetic ripostes for protection in the form of a multitude of partially effective inherited blood conditions. And each is unique to the locale in which it arose. In other words, separate areas produced separate DNA reactions. There has been no global human response to malaria.

Nevertheless, multiregionalism maintains that gene flow produces just such a global response. Given enough time gene exchange from neighboring peoples will make an impact, its proponents insist. This phenomenon, they say, has ensured that the world's population has headed towards the same general evolutionary goal, *Homo sapiens;* though it is also claimed that local selective pressure would have produced some distinctive regional physical differences (such as the European's big nose). And if the new dating of early *Homo erectus* in Java is to be believed (as many scientists are prepared to), then we must accept that this web of ancient lineages has been interacting—like some ancient, creaking international telephone exchange—for almost two million years.

Now this is an interesting notion which makes several other key assumptions: that there were enough humans alive at any time in the Old World over that period to sustain interbreeding and to maintain the give and take of genes; that there were no consistent geographical barriers to this mating urge; that the different human groups or even species that existed then would have wished to have shared their genes with one another; and that this rosy vision of different hominids evolving globally towards the same happy goal has some biological precedent.

So let us examine each supposition briefly, starting with the critical question of population density. According to the multiregionalists, genes had to be passed back and forward between the loins of ancient hominids, from South Africa to Indonesia. And this was done, not by rapacious, visiting males spreading their genotype deep into the heart of other species or peoples (a sort of backdoor man school of evolution), but by local interchange. In neighboring groups, most people would have stayed where they were, while some individuals moved back and forward, or on to the next group as they intermarried. In other words, populations essentially sat still while genes passed through them. But this exchange requires sufficient numbers of neighboring men and women to be breeding in the first place. By any standard, hominids—until very recent times—were very thin on the ground. One calculation by Alan Rogers, a geneticist at the University of Utah, in Salt Lake City, and colleagues uses mitochondrial DNA mutations to assess how many females the species possessed as it evolved. The results he produced are striking. "The multiregional model implies that modern humans evolved in a population that spanned several continents, yet the present results imply that this population contained fewer than 7,000 females," he states in *Current Anthropology.* It is therefore implausible, he adds, that a species so thinly spread could have spanned three continents and still have been connected by gene flow.

Then there is the question of geography. To connect humanity throughout the Old World, genes would have had to flow ("fly" might be a better word) back and forth up the entire African continent, across Arabia, over India, and down through Malaysia; contact would therefore have had to have been made through areas of low population density such as mountains and deserts, coupled with some of the worst climatic disruptions recorded in our planet's recent geological past. Over the past 500,000 years, the world was gripped by frequent Ice Ages: giant glaciers would have straddled the Himalayas, Alps, Caucasus Mountains; meltwater would have poured off these ice caps in torrents, swelling inland lakes and seas (such as the Caspian) far beyond their present sizes; while deserts, battered by dust storms, would have spread over larger and larger areas. Vast regions would have been virtually blocked to the passage of humans. At times our planet was extremely inhospitable while these straggling hordes of humans were supposed to be keeping up the very busy business of cozy genetic interaction. "Even under ecologically identical conditions, which is rarely the case in nature, geographically isolated populations will diverge away from each other and eventually become reproductively isolated. . . . It is highly improbable that evolution would take identical paths in this multi-dimensional landscape," writes the Iranian researcher Shahin Rouhani.

[Luca] Cavalli-Sforza agrees: "What is very difficult to conceive is a parallel evolution over such a vast expanse of land, with the limited genetic exchange that there could have been in earlier times." He acknowledges that it is theoretically possible that the genes of west European humans would have been compatible with those of east Asia despite their ancient separation. Barriers to fertility are usually slow to develop: perhaps a million years or more in mammals. However, he adds, "barriers to fertility of a cultural and social nature may be more important than biological ones." Two very different looking sets of people may have been able to interbreed physically but would have considered such action as breaking a gross taboo.

In other words, we are expected to believe that a wafer-thin population of hominids, trudging across continents gripped by Ice Ages, were supposed to be ready to mate with people they would have found extraordinarily odd-looking and who behaved in peculiar ways. Cavalli-Sforza, for one, does not buy this. "Proponents of the multiregional model simply do not understand population genetics," he states. "They use a model that requires continuous exchange of genes, but it requires enormous amounts of time to reach equilibrium. There has been insufficient time in human history to reach that equilibrium." The spread of modern humans over a large fraction of the earth's surface is more in tune with a specific expansion from a nuclear area of origin, he adds.

Now this last point is an important one, for it is frequently presented in the popular press that the Out of Africa theory represents a divergence from the natural flow of biological affairs, that its protagonists are somehow on the fringes of orthodoxy, proposing strange and radical notions. The reverse is true —the large number of scientists quoted [here] indicates the wide intellectual support now accorded the theory. It is a very new idea, admittedly. It is only a little more than a decade since it was first proposed, on the basis of fossils, by scientists like [Gunter] Bräuer and [Chris] Stringer. Yet its precepts now affect many areas of science, and its implications are accepted by their most distinguished practitioners. We are witnessing a rare moment in science, the replacement of a redundant orthodoxy by a formerly heretical vision. Hence the words of Yoel Rak as he staggered from a multiregionalists' symposium in 1991. "I feel like I have just had to sit through a meeting of the Flat Earth Society," he moaned.

Of course, Rak became an African Exodus proselytizer many years ago. A more damning convert, if you are multiregionalist, is that of *Science,* a journal noted for its dispassion and conservatism. "The theory that all modern humans originated in Africa is looking more and more convincing," it announced in March 1995, "and the date of the first human exodus keeps creeping closer to the present . . . the evidence coming out of our genes seems to be sweeping the field."

In fact, the idea that the opposition—the multiregionalists—represent the norm in biological thinking is to present the story of human origins "ass backwards," as Stephen Jay Gould succinctly puts it.

> Multi-regionalism . . . is awfully hard to fathom. Why should populations throughout the world, presumably living in different environments under varying regimes of natural selection, all be moving on the same evolutionary pathway? Besides, most large, successful, and widespread species are stable for most of their history, and do not change in any substantial directional sense at all. For non-human species, we never interpret global distribution as entailing preference for a multiregional view of origins. We have no multiregional theory for the origin of rats or pigeons, two species that match our success and geographical spread. No one envisions proto-rats on all continents evolving together toward improved ratitude. Rather we assume that *Rattus rattus* and *Columbia livia* initially arose in a single place, as an entity or isolated population, and then spread out, eventually to cover the globe. Why uniquely for humans, do we develop a multiregional theory and then even declare it orthodox, in opposition to all standard views about how evolution occurs?

The answer to that critical question has much to do with an outlook that has pervaded and bedeviled science throughout history. We have, at various times, been forced to abandon species-centric scientific notions that we live at the center of the cosmos, and that we were specially created by a supreme being. A last vestige of this urge to self-importance can be seen in multiregionalism, which holds that our brain development is an event of all-consuming global consequence towards which humanity strived in unison for nearly two million years. It argues that *Homo sapiens'* emergence was dictated by a worldwide tendency to evolve large braincases, and share genes and "progress." Humanity is the product of a predictable proclivity for smartness, in other words, so we cannot possibly be the outcome of some local biological struggle. Surely that would demean us. To believe that humanity could be the product of a small, rapidly evolving African population who struck it lucky in the evolution stakes is therefore viewed as being worse than apostasy by these people. Unfortunately for them, there is little proof to support their specialist, global promotion of mankind—as we have seen. Once again we must adopt the simplest scientific explanation (i.e., the one for which the facts best fit) as the superior one. As this [selection] has made clear, there is no good genetic evidence to sustain an argument that places humanity on a plinth of global superiority. To do so is to indulge in mysticism. *Homo sapiens* is not the child of an entire planet, but a creature, like any other, that has its roots in one place and period—in this case with a small group of Africans for whom "time and chance" has only just arrived. Nor is our species diminished in any way by such interpretations. Indeed, we are enriched through explanations that demonstrate our humble origins, for they place us in an appropriate context that, for the first time, permits proper self-evaluation and provides an understanding of the gulf we are crossing from a clever ape to a hominid that can shape a planet to its requirements—if only it could work out what these are.

Alan G. Thorne and
Milford H. Wolpoff

 NO

The Multiregional Evolution of Humans

Two decades ago paleoanthropologists were locked in a debate about the origin of the earliest humans. The disagreement centered on whether the fossil *Ramapithecus* was an early human ancestor or ancestral to both human and ape lineages. Molecular biologists entered that discussion and supported the minority position held by one of us (Wolpoff) and his students that *Ramapithecus* was not a fossil human, as was then commonly believed. Their evidence, however, depended on a date for the chimpanzee-human divergence that was based on a flawed "molecular clock." We therefore had to reject their support.

Today the paleoanthropological community is again engaged in a debate, this time about how, when and where modern humans originated. On one side stand some researchers, such as ourselves, who maintain there is no single home for modern humanity—humans originated in Africa and then slowly developed their modern forms in every area of the Old World. On the other side are workers who claim that Africa alone gave birth to modern humans within the past 200,000 years. Once again the molecular geneticists have entered the fray, attempting to resolve it in favor of the African hypothesis with a molecular clock. Once again their help must be rejected because their reasoning is flawed.

Genetic research has undeniably provided one of the great insights of 20th-century biology: that all living people are extremely closely related. Our DNA similarities are far greater than the disparate anatomic variations of humanity might suggest. Studies of the DNA carried by the cell organelles called mitochondria, which are inherited exclusively from one's mother and are markers for maternal lineages, now play a role in the development of theories about the origin of modern human races.

Nevertheless, mitochondrial DNA is not the only source of information we have on the subject. Fossil remains and artifacts also represent a monumental body of evidence—and, we maintain, a much more reliable one. The singular importance of the mitochondrial DNA studies is that they show one of the origin theories discussed by paleontologists must be incorrect.

With Wu Xinzhi of the Institute of Vertebrate Paleontology and Paleoanthropology in Beijing, we developed an explanation for the pattern of human evolution that we described as multiregional evolution. We learned that some of the features that distinguish major human groups, such as Asians, Australian

Aborigines and Europeans, evolved over a long period, roughly where these peoples are found today.

Multiregional evolution traces all modern populations back to when humans first left Africa at least a million years ago, through an interconnected web of ancient lineages in which the genetic contributions to all living peoples varied regionally and temporally. Today distinctive populations maintain their physical differences despite interbreeding and population movements; this situation has existed ever since humans first colonized Europe and Asia. Modern humanity originated within these widespread populations, and the modernization of our ancestors was an ongoing process.

An alternative theory, developed by the paleontologist William W. Howells of Harvard University as the "Noah's ark" model, posited that modern people arose recently in a single place and that they subsequently spread around the world, replacing other human groups. That replacement, recent proponents of the theory believe, must have been complete. From their genetic analyses, the late Allan C. Wilson and his colleagues at the University of California at Berkeley concluded that the evolutionary record of mitochondrial DNA could be traced back to a single female, dubbed "Eve" in one of his first publications on the issue, who lived in Africa approximately 200,000 years ago. Only mitochondrial DNA that can be traced to Eve, these theorists claim, is found among living people.

❧◈☙

How could this be? If Eve's descendants mixed with other peoples as their population expanded, we would expect to find other mitochondrial DNA lines present today, especially outside Africa, where Eve's descendants were invaders. The most credible explanation for the current absence of other mitochondrial DNA lineages is that none of the local women mixed with the invading modern men from Africa—which means that Eve founded a new species. Wilson's reconstruction of the past demands that over a period of no more than 150,000 years there was a complete replacement of all the preexisting hunter-gatherers in Africa and the rest of the then inhabited world; later, the original African features of the invading human species presumably gave way to the modern racial features we see in other regions.

An analogy can highlight the difference between our multiregional evolution theory and Wilson's Eve theory. According to multiregional evolution, the pattern of modern human origins is like several individuals paddling in separate corners of a pool; although they maintain their individuality over time, they influence one another with the spreading ripples they raise (which are the equivalent of genes flowing between populations). In contrast, the total replacement requirement of the Eve theory dictates that a new swimmer must jump into the pool with such a splash that it drowns all the other swimmers. One of these two views of our origin must be incorrect.

Mitochondrial DNA is useful for guiding the development of theories, but only fossils provide the basis for refuting one idea or the other. At best, the genetic information explains how modern humans might have originated if the assumptions used in interpreting the genes are correct, but one theory cannot be used to test another. The fossil record is the real evidence for human evolution, and it is rich in both human remains and archaeological sites stretching back for a million years. Unlike the genetic data, fossils can be matched to the predictions of theories about the past without relying on a long list of assumptions.

The power of a theory is measured by how much it can explain; the scientific method requires that we try to incorporate all sources of data in an explanatory theory. Our goal is to describe a theory that synthesizes everything known about modern human fossils, archaeology and genes. The Eve theory cannot do so.

The Eve theory makes five predictions that the fossil evidence should corroborate. The first and major premise is that modern humans from Africa must have completely replaced all other human groups. Second, implicit within this idea is that the earliest modern humans appeared in Africa. Third, it also follows that the earliest modern humans in other areas should have African features. Fourth, modern humans and the people they replaced should never have mixed or interbred. Fifth, an anatomic discontinuity should be evident between the human fossils before and after the replacement.

※

We are troubled by the allegations that beginning about 200,000 years ago one group of hunter-gatherers totally replaced all others worldwide. Although it is not uncommon for one animal species to replace another locally in a fairly short time, the claim that a replacement could occur rapidly in every climate and environment is unprecedented.

We would expect native populations to have an adaptive and demographic advantage over newcomers. Yet according to the Eve theory, it was the newcomers who had the upper hand. How much of an advantage is necessary for replacement can be measured by the survival of many hunter-gatherer groups in Australia and the Americas; they have persisted despite invasions by Europeans, who during the past 500 years arrived in large numbers with vastly more complex and destructive technologies.

If a worldwide invasion and complete replacement of all native peoples by Eve's descendants actually took place, we would expect to find at least some archaeological traces of the behaviors that made them successful. Yet examining the archaeology of Asia, we can find none. For instance, whereas the hand ax was a very common artifact in Africa, the technologies of eastern Asia did not include that tool either before or after the Eve period. There is no evidence for the introduction of a novel technology.

Geoffrey G. Pope of the University of Illinois has pointed out that six decades of research on the Asian Paleolithic record have failed to unearth any indication of intrusive cultures or technologies. Types of artifacts found in the earliest Asian Paleolithic assemblages continue to appear into the very late Pleistocene. If invading Africans replaced the local Asian populations, they must have adopted the cultures and technologies of the people they replaced and allowed their own to vanish without a trace.

Archaeological evidence for an invasion is also lacking in western Asia, where Christopher B. Stringer of the Natural History Museum in London and a few other researchers believe the earliest modern humans outside of Africa can be found at the Skhūl and Qafzeh sites in Israel. The superb record at Qafzeh shows, however, that these "modern" people had a culture identical to that of their local Neanderthal contemporaries: they made the same types of stone tools with the same technologies and at the same frequencies; they had the same stylized burial customs, hunted the same game and even used the same butchering procedures. Moreover, no evidence from the time when Eve's descendants are supposed to have left Africa suggests that any new African technology emerged or spread to other continents. All in all, as we understand them, the Asian data refute the archaeological predictions implied by the Eve theory.

Perhaps that refutation explains why Wilson turned to a different advantage, asserting that the invasion was successful because Eve's descendants carried a mitochondrial gene that conferred language ability. This proposal is yet to be widely accepted. Not only does it conflict with paleoneurology about the language abilities of archaic humans, but if it were true, it would violate the assumption of Wilson's clock that mitochondrial mutations are neutral.

The remaining predictions of the Eve theory relate to abrupt anatomic changes and whether the earliest recognizably modern humans resembled earlier regional populations or Africans. With the fossil evidence known at this time, these questions can be unambiguously resolved in at least two and possibly three regions of the world. The most convincing data are from southern and northern Asia.

The hominid fossils from Australasia (Indonesia, New Guinea and Australia) show a continuous anatomic sequence during the Pleistocene that is uninterrupted by African migrants at any time. The distinguishing features of the earliest of these Javan remains, dated to about one million years ago, show they had developed when the region was first inhabited.

Compared with human fossils from other areas, the Javan people have thick skull bones, with strong continuous browridges forming an almost straight bar of bone across their eye sockets and a second well-developed shelf of bone at the back of the skull for the neck muscles. Above and behind the brows, the forehead is flat and retreating. These early Indonesians also have large projecting faces with massive rounded cheekbones. Their teeth are the largest known in archaic humans from that time.

A series of small but important features can be found on the most complete face and on other facial fragments that are preserved. These include such things as a rolled ridge on the lower edge of the eye sockets, a distinctive ridge on the cheekbone and a nasal floor that blends smoothly into the face.

This unique morphology was stable for at least 700,000 years while other modern characteristics continued to evolve in the Javan people. For example, the large fossil series from Ngandong, which recent evidence suggests may be about 100,000 years old, offers striking proof that the Javans of that time had brain sizes in the modern range but were otherwise remarkably similar to much earlier individuals the region.

❦

The first inhabitants of Australia arrived more than 60,000 years ago, and their behavior and anatomy were clearly those of modern human beings. Their skeletons show the Javan complex of features, along with further braincase expansions and other modernizations. Several dozen well-preserved fossils from the late Pleistocene and early Holocene demonstrate that the same combination of features that distinguished those Indonesian people from their contemporaries distinguishes modern Australian Aborigines from other living peoples.

If the earliest Australians were descendants of Africans, as the Eve theory required, the continuity of fossil features would have to be no more than apparent. All the features of the early Javans would need to have evolved a second time in the population of invaders. The repeated evolution of an individual feature would be conceivable but rare; the duplication of an entire set of unrelated features would be unprecedentedly improbable.

Northern Asia also harbors evidence linking its modern and ancient inhabitants. Moreover, because the similarities involve features different from those significant in Australasia, they compound the improbability of the Eve theory by requiring that a second complete set of features was duplicated in a different population.

The very earliest Chinese fossils, about one million years old, differ from their Javan counterparts in many ways that parallel the differences between north Asians and Australians today. Our research with Wu Xinzhi and independent research by Pope demonstrated that the Chinese fossils are less robust, have smaller and more delicately built flat faces, smaller teeth and rounder foreheads separated from their arched browridges. Their noses are less prominent and more flattened at the top. Perhaps the most telling indication of morphological continuity concerns a peculiarity of tooth shapes. Prominently "shoveled" maxillary incisors, which curl inward along their internal edges, are found with unusually high frequency in living east Asians and in all the earlier human remains from that area. Studies by Tracey L. Crummett of the University of Michigan show that the form of prehistoric and living Asian incisors is unique.

This combination of traits is also exhibited at the Zhoukoudian cave area in northern China, where fully a third of all known human remains from the Middle Pleistocene have been found. As Wu Rukang of the Chinese Academy of Sciences has pointed out, even within the 150,000 or more years spanned by the Zhoukoudian individuals, evolutionary changes in the modern direction, including increases in brain size, can be seen. Our examinations of the Chinese specimens found no anatomic evidence that typically African features ever replaced those of the ancient Chinese in these regions. Instead there is a smooth transformation of the ancient populations into the living peoples of east Asia.

Paleontologists have long thought Europe would be the best source of evidence for the replacement of one group, Neanderthals, by more modern humans. Even there, however, the fossil record shows that any influx of new people was neither complete nor without mixture. In fact, the most recent known Neanderthal, from Saint-Césaire in France, apparently had the behavioral characteristics of the people who succeeded the Neanderthals in Europe. The earliest post-Neanderthal Europeans did not have a pattern of either modern or archaic African features. Clearly, the European Neanderthals were not completely replaced by Africans or by people from any other region.

Instead the evidence suggests that Neanderthals either evolved into later humans or interbred with them, or both. David W. Frayer of the University of Kansas and Fred H. Smith of Northern Illinois University have discovered that many allegedly unique Neanderthal features are found in the Europeans who followed the Neanderthals—the Upper Paleolithic, Mesolithic and later peoples. In fact, only a few Neanderthal features completely disappear from the later European skeletal record.

Figure 1

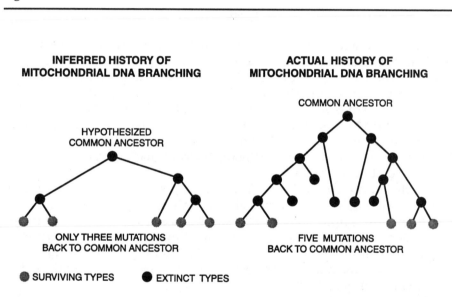

INFERRED HISTORY OF
MITOCHONDRIAL DNA BRANCHING

ACTUAL HISTORY OF
MITOCHONDRIAL DNA BRANCHING

COMMON ANCESTOR

HYPOTHESIZED
COMMON ANCESTOR

ONLY THREE MUTATIONS
BACK TO COMMON ANCESTOR

FIVE MUTATIONS
BACK TO COMMON ANCESTOR

SURVIVING TYPES   EXTINCT TYPES

Maternal lineage reconstructions based solely on the mitochondrial DNA types found today are inherently flawed. A hypothetical tree inferred from only five surviving types (*left*) leaves out the branches and mutational histories of extinct lines (*right*). Consequently, it sets the date for a common ancestor much too recently by presenting evidence of too few mutations.

Features that persist range from highly visible structures, such as the prominent shape and size of the nose of Neanderthals and later Europeans, to much more minute traits, such as the form of the back of the skull and the details of its surface. A good example is the shape of the opening in the mandibular nerve canal, a spot on the inside of the lower jaw where dentists often give a pain-blocking injection. The upper part of the opening is covered by a broad bony bridge in many Neanderthals, but in others the bridge is absent. In European fossils, 53 percent of the known Neanderthals have the bridged form; 44 percent of their earliest Upper Paleolithic successors do, too, but in later Upper Paleolithic, Mesolithic and recent groups, the incidence drops to less than 6 percent.

In contrast, the bridged form is seen only rarely in fossil or modern people from Asia and Australia. In Africa the few jaws that date from the suggested Eve period do not have it. This mandibular trait and a number of others like it on the skull and the rest of the skeleton must have evolved twice in Europe for the Eve theory to be correct.

In sum, the evolutionary patterns of three different regions—Australasia, China and Europe—show that their earliest modern inhabitants do not have the complex of features that characterize Africans. There is no evidence that Africans completely replaced local groups. Contrary to the Eve theory predictions, the evidence points indisputably toward the continuity of various skeletal features between the earliest human populations and living peoples in different regions.

✦❦✦

If Africa really were the "Garden of Eden" from which all living people emerged, one would expect to find evidence for the transition from archaic to modern forms there—and only there. Following the lead of the German worker Reiner Protsch of Goethe University in Frankfurt, some paleontologists did argue that modern *Homo sapiens* originated in Africa because they believed the earliest modern-looking humans were found there and that modern African racial features can be seen in these fossils. But the African evidence is sparse, fragmentary and for the most part poorly dated; it includes materials that do not seem to fit the Eve theory.

Early human remains from Africa, such as the Kabwe skull from Zambia, are extremely rare and are presumed to be at least 150,000 years old. Later transitional fossils from Morocco, Ethiopia, Kenya and South Africa confirm the expectation that local modernization occurred in Africa, as it did everywhere else. No pattern in the fossils, however, indicates the previous emergence of skeletal features that uniquely characterize modern humans generally or even modern Africans in particular.

The evidence for a great antiquity of modern-looking people is based primarily on the interpretation of bones from three sites: the Omo site in Ethiopia and the Klasies River and Border Cave sites in South Africa. Some of the Omo and Border Cave individuals resemble modern humans, but all the remains are fragmentary. Most of the Omo remains were found on the surface, not in datable strata. The estimate of their age, which is based on inappropriate dating techniques, is widely considered to be unreliable. Some of the Border Cave bones, including the most complete cranium, were dug out by local workmen looking for fertilizer and are of unknown antiquity. Other human bones found at a 90,000-year-old level are chemically different from animal bones found there. They may actually be more recent burials dug into the cave.

The best excavated remains are from the Klasies River Mouth Cave and are securely dated to between 80,000 and 100,000 years ago. Some of the skull fragments are small and delicate and are said to "prove" that modern humans were present. Yet a comparative analysis of the entire sample by Rachel Caspari of Albion College showed that others are not modern-looking at all. Two of the four lower jaws do not have chins, so thorough proof of a modern jaw is lacking. The single cheekbone from the site is not only larger than those of living Africans but also larger and more robust than those of both the earlier transitional humans and the archaic humans found in Africa. The claim that this sample contains modern Africans is highly dubious and does not justify the proposal that the earliest modern humans arose in Africa.

~⊙~

With the disproof of the unique African ancestry theory for the living people of most areas and the lack of evidence showing that modern people first appeared in Africa, we conclude that the predictions of the Eve theory cannot be substantiated. We must wonder why the analysis of mitochondrial DNA suggested a theory so contrary to the facts. Perhaps the mitochondrial DNA has been misinterpreted.

The basic difficulty with using mitochondrial DNA to interpret recent evolutionary history stems from the very source of its other advantages: in reproduction, the mitochondrial DNA clones itself instead of recombining. Because mitochondrial DNA is transmitted only through the maternal line, the potential for genetic drift—the accidental loss of lines—is great: some mitochondrial DNA disappears every time a generation fails to have daughters.

The problem is analogous to the way in which family surnames are lost whenever there is a generation without sons. Imagine an immigrant neighborhood in a large city where all the families share a surname. An observer might assume that all these families were descended from a single successful immigrant family that completely replaced its neighbors (just as Eve's descendants are supposed to have replaced all other humans). An alternative explanation is that many families immigrated to the neighborhood and intermarried; over time, all the surnames but one were randomly eliminated through the occasional appearance of families that had no sons to carry on their names. The surviving family name would have come from a single immigrant, but all the immigrants would have contributed to the genes of the modern population. In the same way, generations without daughters could have extinguished some lines of mitochondrial DNA from Eve's descendants and her contemporaries.

Any interpretation of the surviving mitochondrial DNA mutations in populations consequently depends on a knowledge of how the size of the populations has changed over time and how many maternal lines may have vanished. Random losses from genetic drift alter a reconstruction of the tree of human mitochondrial DNA branching by pruning off signs of past divergences. Each uncounted branch is a mutation never taken into account when determining how long ago Eve lived.

Changes in population sizes have been dramatic. In parts of the Northern Hemisphere, some human populations shrank because of climate fluctuations during the Ice Ages. Archaeological evidence from both Africa and Australia suggests that similar population reductions may have taken place there as well. These reductions could have exacerbated genetic drift and the loss of mitochondrial DNA types.

At the end of the Ice Ages, along with the first domestication of animals and plants, some populations expanded explosively throughout a wide band of territory from the Mediterranean to the Pacific coast of Asia. Although the number of people expanded, the number of surviving mitochondrial DNA lines could not—those lost were gone forever.

Human populations with dissimilar demographic histories can therefore be expected to preserve different numbers of mutations since their last common mitochondrial DNA ancestor. They cannot be used together in a model that assumes the lengths of mitochondrial lineages reflect the age of their divergence. One cannot assume, as Wilson does, that all the variation in a population's mitochondrial DNA stems solely from mutations: the history of the population is also important.

⋅◈⋅

A major problem with the Eve theory, therefore, is that it depends on an accurate molecular clock. Its accuracy must be based on mutation rates at many different loci, or gene positions. Yet genes in the mitochondrial DNA cannot recombine as genes in the nucleus do. All the mitochondrial DNA genes are the equivalent of a single locus. The molecular clock based on mitochondrial DNA is consequently unreliable.

Mitochondrial DNA may not be neutral enough to serve as the basis for a molecular clock, because some data suggest that it plays a role in several diseases. Because of random loss and natural selection some vertebrate groups— cichlid fish in Lake Victoria in Africa, American eels, hardhead catfish and redwing blackbirds, for example—have rates of mitochondrial DNA evolution that are dramatically slower than Wilson and his colleagues have claimed for humans. A number of molecular geneticists disagree with Wilson's interpretation of the mitochondrial genetic data.

The molecular clock of Wilson and his colleagues has, we believe, major problems: its rate of ticking has probably been overestimated in some cases and underestimated in others. Rebecca L. Cann of the University of Hawaii at Manoa and Mark Stoneking of Pennsylvania State University, two of Wilson's students, admitted recently that their clock was able to date Eve only to between 50,000 and 500,000 years ago. Because of the uncertainty, we believe that for the past half a million years or more of human evolution, for all intents and purposes, there is no molecular clock.

Putting aside the idea of a clock, one can interpret the genetic data in a much more reasonable way: Eve, the ultimate mitochondrial ancestor of all living humans, lived before the first human migrations from Africa at least one million years ago. The spread of mitochondria would then mark the migration of some early human ancestors into Eurasia when it contained no other hominids. Such an interpretation can fully reconcile the fossil record with the genetic data. We propose that future research might more productively focus on attempts to disprove this hypothesis than on attempts to recalibrate a clock that clearly does not work.

The dramatic genetic similarities across the entire human race do not reflect a recent common ancestry for all living people. They show the consequences of linkages between people that extend to when our ancestors first populated the Old World, more than a million years ago. They are the results of an ancient history of population connections and mate exchanges that has characterized the human race since its inception. Human evolution happened everywhere because every area was always part of the whole.

Neither anatomic nor genetic analyses provide a basis for the Eve theory. Instead the fossil record and the interpretation of mitochondrial DNA variation can be synthesized to form a view of human origins that does fit all the currently known data. This synthetic view combines the best sources of evidence about human evolution by making sense of the archaeological and fossil record and the information locked up in the genetic variation of living people all over the world. The richness of human diversity, which contrasts with the closeness of human genetic relationships, is a direct consequence of evolution. We are literally most alike where it matters, under the skin.

POSTSCRIPT

Did *Homo Sapiens* Originate Only in Africa?

The debate between the "multiregional" and the "out-of-Africa" theorists has not been resolved since these selections were first published. Nor have tensions between proponents of these two positions diminished. This acrimony has been intensified by the fact that some commentators have seen the "multiregional" theory as merely a racist attempt to deny Africa its status as the place of origin for all humankind. It should be noted, however, that the multiregionalists continue to see African origins for *Homo erectus* and earlier hominids, but have argued that *Homo sapiens* evolved more-or-less simultaneously in Africa, Asia, Europe, and Australia. For a discussion of these issues see Milford H. Wolpoff and Rachel Caspari's *Race and Human Evolution: A Fatal Attraction* (Simon & Schuster, 1996).

Another issue separating these two groups of scientists concerns the data used for determining whether anatomically modern humans evolved uniquely in one place or simultaneously in all inhabited places. Either the mitochondrial evidence is poorly interpreted or the analysis of fossils is flawed, since both theories cannot be correct. Currently, our knowledge of mitochondrial DNA evolution is still imperfect, and the use of mitochondrial DNA as a clock for dating the emergence of *Homo sapiens* carries with it some uncertainty. There is now consensus that mitochondrial DNA and nuclear DNA mutate at different rates, but it is still uncertain as to how fast mitochondrial DNA mutates. The debate between the "multiregionalists" and the "out-of-Africa" theorists parallels a similar divide between paleontologists who support a gradualist model and paleontologists who support a punctuated equilibrium model. For a discussion of the paleontological issues see Stephen Jay Gould's *Dinosaur in a Haystack: Reflections in Natural History* (Harmony Books, 1995), pp. 101–107, in which he supports the African origins model of this debate for much the same reasons that he supports a punctuated equilibrium model concerning other species.

For one of the earliest statements framing the "out-of-Africa" theory, see Rebecca L. Cann, Mark Stoneking, and A. C. Wilson's "Mitochondrial DNA and Human Evolution," *Nature* (1987). Also see Allan C. Wilson and Rebecca L. Cann's statement, "The Recent African Genesis of Humans," *Scientific American* (1992). Michael H. Brown's *The Search for Eve* (Harper & Row, 1990) offers a popular account of the early research, while Stringer and McKie's *African Exodus: The Origins of Modern Humanity* (Henry Holt & Company, 1996), from which the Yes-side selection was excerpted, provides a more extended discussion. For background on mitochondrial DNA research, see J. N. Spuhler's paper

"Evolution of Mitochondrial DNA in Monkeys, Apes and Humans," *American Journal of Physical Anthropology Yearbook* (1988).

For an early assessment of the "out-of-Africa" theory and the "multiregional" theory, see Wolpoff and Thorne's article entitled, "The Case Against Eve," *New Scientist* (June 22, 1991); Alan R. Templeton's "The 'Eve' Hypotheses: A Genetic Critique and Reanalysis," *American Anthropologist* (1993); and Leslie C. Aiello's "The Fossil Evidence for Modern Human Origins in Africa: A Revised View," *American Anthropologist* (1993). For background on the "multiregional" theory and the fossil record see Fred H. Smith and Frank Spencer's edited volume, *The Origins of Modern Humans: A World Survey of the Fossil Evidence* (Alan R. Liss, 1984).

Several years after Cann, Stoneking, and Wilson released their findings on mitochondrial DNA, M. F. Hammer reported identifying a single male lineage of Y chromosomes. See his "A Recent Common Ancestry for Human Y Chromosomes," *Nature* (1995) and another paper by M. F. Hammer et al., "The Geographic Distribution of Human Y Chromosome Variation," *Genetics* (1997). Hammer and his colleagues contend that the "African Adam" from whom we all descend lived about 200,000 years ago. Not surprisingly, multiregionalists have raised many of the same issues here as they have with "Eve," arguing that Hammer and his colleagues have incorrect assumptions and weak calibration of the rate at which the Y chromosome mutates. For a recent review of both mitochondrial DNA and Y chromosome research, see Joanna L. Mountain's "Molecular Evolution and Modern Human Origins," *Evolutionary Anthropology* (1998).

ISSUE 2

Did Neanderthals Interbreed With Modern Humans?

YES: Scott Norris, from "Family Secrets," *New Scientist* (June 19, 1999)

NO: Ian Tattersall, from *The Last Neanderthal: The Rise, Success, and Mysterious Extinction of Our Closest Human Relatives*, rev. ed. (Westview Press, 1999)

ISSUE SUMMARY

YES: Science writer Scott Norris surveys recent osteological, archaeological, and genetic evidence and concludes that the predominance of evidence favors a period of "mixing" between Neanderthals and early modern humans in Europe.

NO: Biological anthropologist Ian Tattersall contends that the anatomical and behavioral differences between Neanderthals and early modern humans were too great for them to have been the same species and thus able to interbreed and produce fertile offspring.

The image of Neanderthals has fluctuated widely since the mid-nineteenth century, when scholars first recognized that the fossil bones being unearthed in Europe were those of early humans and not just deformed individuals. The scientists who reconstructed the Neanderthal skeletons were influenced by the theory of evolution introduced by Charles Darwin in his books *Origin of Species* (John Murray, 1859) and *Descent of Man* (John Murray, 1871). Some scientists pictured Neanderthals as the "missing link" between humans and the apes. This view was exemplified by French scientist Marcellin Boule's 1909 analysis of a Neanderthal skeleton from Chapelle-aux-Saints, popularly known as the "Old Man." Classifying Neanderthals as a separate species from humans, Boule illustrated the Chapelle-aux-Saints man in a slouching, bent-kneed posture, which he contrasted with the upright carriage of an Australian Aborigine, then thought to be the most primitive form of modern humans. Other scholars considered Neanderthals the ancestors of Europeans or even of all humanity, positing a "Neanderthal stage" of human evolution. For example, the eminent anatomist Sir Arthur Keith analyzed the same Chapelle-aux-Saints remains and concluded that the Old Man was a full member of the human family. These sharply contrasting images express the enigmatic nature of Neanderthals: they were both like us and not like us.

Evidence accumulated over the last 100 years has partially resolved the question of the status of the Neanderthals. The notions of both a missing link and a global Neanderthal stage of human evolution have been discarded. Today the predominant theories of recent human evolution are the "out of Africa" theory and the "multiregional evolution" theory. According to proponents of the out of Africa theory, Neanderthals were a dead-end branch of humanity, which evolved out of *Homo erectus* in Europe and met its demise when modern humans arrived from Africa and outcompeted or killed the Neanderthals off. Multiregionalists contend that Neanderthals were part of the widespread *Homo erectus* population that evolved as a whole into modern humans. In their view Neanderthals were local variants of the early human species who probably interbred with the incoming variants from Africa and whose genes were eventually mixed into the gene pool of modern Europe. Scientists are now seeking direct evidence of interbreeding in the bones, genes, stone tools, and behavior patterns of Neanderthals and early modern humans in Europe.

Scott Norris discusses the recent find in Portugal of a fossil skeleton of a child, which appears to combine Neanderthal features (e.g., short, thick limb bones) and modern human features (e.g., modern teeth and chin). Norris argues that the sophisticated Châtelperronian stone tool industry shows that Neanderthals independently achieved an Upper Paleolithic level of cultural development. The long period during which both types of humans coexisted in Europe (about 40,000 to 26,000 B.C.) also argues against the idea that early modern humans killed off the Neanderthals.

Ian Tattersall, on the other hand, contends that the anatomical and behavioral differences between Neanderthals and modern humans were too great for them to have been members of the same species. Therefore they could not have interbred. He associates Neanderthals with Mousterian stone tools and asserts humans with Upper Paleolithic tools and asserts that the abrupt transition from the former to the latter in European archaeological sites indicates rapid replacement of Neanderthals by modern humans, most probably by violent conflict. He dismisses the Upper Paleolithic Châtelperronian stone tool industry as a product of Neanderthals copying the more advanced tool technology of modern human immigrants.

Although the evidence available to these two writers is not exactly the same—the possibly mixed child had not yet been found when Tattersall was writing—it is interesting that they do not agree on the significance of some evidence, like the Châtelperronian tools. How convincing do you find the writers' interpretations? Do they reveal any biases in the language they use? What kinds of evidence do you think scholars need to determine whether or not Neanderthals and modern humans interbred? Are there other possible explanations for the disappearance of Neanderthals that these authors do not consider?

Scott Norris  **YES**

Family Secrets

T he bones looked distinctly odd. Unearthed in 1856 by workers at a limestone quarry in the Neander Valley near Düsseldorf, they were strangely curved and thick, and clearly very old. But their significance was far from obvious even to the scientists who examined them. Many accepted the theory that they belonged to a deformed Cossack horseman who had crawled into a cave to die. Then, three years later, Charles Darwin published his ideas, and sparked a debate about human origins. People began to see that our own evolutionary history might be traced in the fossil record, and "Neanderthal Man" was hailed as the first European.

Today we know that Neanderthals dominated Europe and parts of Asia for around 200,000 years. They had large brains—bigger than ours—and they made stone tools, cared for their injured and buried their dead. If a human life span is 70 years, Neanderthals died out only a few hundred lifetimes ago. But time has been hard on the Neanderthals. In popular culture they have become synonymous with stupidity and a lack of sophistication, and most palaeoanthropologists dismiss the old claim that they are our ancestors. Current thinking centres on the "Out of Africa" theory: the idea that all modern humans can trace their origins to a single African population whose descendants, Cro-Magnons, spread across Europe some 40,000 years ago, killing off the Neanderthals. "I think the issue is resolved," says Richard Klein from Stanford University. "You could always imagine how the case could be stronger. But if you accept what I think are reasonable rules of evidence, then the story is finished—the Neanderthals became extinct."

There are, however, some prominent dissenters from this view. They argue that Neanderthals were not replaced, but absorbed through centuries of interbreeding with the larger Cro-Magnon population. The "Neanderthals are us" school of thought was given a huge boost recently by evidence that Neanderthal populations existed in both eastern and western Europe long after modern humans arrived, and by the discovery in Portugal of what looks like the skeleton of a hybrid child.

Alongside these findings has come a renewed focus on some tantalising clues in the archaeological record suggesting that Neanderthals were capable of surprisingly "modern" behaviours. Even researchers who do not consider

Neanderthals to be among our ancestors are starting to acknowledge that interactions between Neanderthals and Cro-Magnons may have been more varied, protracted and complex than they had thought. "The supposed behavioural gap between them and us has narrowed," says Chris Stringer of the Natural History Museum in London, who originated the Out of Africa theory. "This, together with an apparently long period of coexistence in Europe, makes a simple scenario of massive cognitive or technological superiority of [Cro-Magnon] much less plausible."

The current reappraisal of Neanderthals comes only two years after a group of European and American scientists appeared to place them firmly on a dead-end branch of the hominid family tree. They recovered and sequenced a small piece of mitochondrial DNA from the original Neander Valley specimen, and found that the difference between the Neanderthal sequence and an equivalent stretch of modern DNA was three times greater than that between most modern populations. They concluded that Neanderthals were a distinct biological species.

But enthusiasm for the DNA results has waned. "No matter who you sample from before 30,000 years ago, there's a pretty good chance that their mitochondrial DNA wouldn't look like that of anybody alive today," says Klein. Others are even more sceptical. Milford Wolpoff of the University of Michigan, who is a critic of the idea that we are descended from a single population of early humans, says of the DNA finding: "It didn't show that Neanderthals were a separate species, only that they were more different from us than most contemporary human groups are from each other."

Wolpoff's student John Hawkes has developed a computer model that simulates contemporary DNA patterns that might be expected under a range of evolutionary scenarios, involving various degrees of interaction between Neanderthals and Cro-Magnons. "We should not expect to find Neanderthal mitochondrial DNA lineages still around today," he concludes, "even in the case that they were partly ancestral to living people in Europe and elsewhere."

Millennia of Mutations

Wolpoff adds that a comparison between contemporary human and Cro-Magnon DNA might also reveal large differences, due to mutations and other genetic changes over the past 40,000 years. Such a comparison will require the sequencing of more ancient DNA, a task that is proving extraordinarily difficult.

More direct evidence for interbreeding comes from the skeleton discovered in Portugal last year. The bones, from a four-year-old boy, provide a clear indication of hybridisation between Neanderthals and Cro-Magnons, according to João Zilhão, director of the Institute of Archaeology at the University of Lisbon, and Erik Trinkaus of Washington University in St Louis, Missouri. Their preliminary analysis has revealed a mix of anatomical features, including a characteristically modern chin and teeth of Cro-Magnon, together with robust Neanderthal limbs. From the evidence so far, hybridisation "seems to be the best possible explanation", says Zilhão. "It's as certain as any new scientific hypothesis can be."

Perhaps the most intriguing aspect of the discovery is the radiocarbon date from four separate samples of bone and charcoal from the grave site. The child lived 24,500 years ago—several thousand years after the last Neanderthal populations are thought to have disappeared. "The fact that 4000 years later this mosaic of features is still present suggests that hybridisation a few millennia before must have been extensive," says Zilhão.

But Stringer cautions against reading too much into this one discovery. "If the skeleton is that of a hybrid, it [still] cannot answer the questions of how common such matings were, whether hybrids were fertile and whether their genes ever penetrated into early modern populations," he says. And despite recent revelations, the DNA evidence still suggests that interbreeding cannot have been widespread. "The evidence does fit with Neanderthals representing a deep and separate lineage to that of all modern humans," he says.

In other parts of Europe, human fossils from this period generally show more fully developed modern characteristics. Even so, the Portuguese boy may not be a one-off example of hybridisation. Over the years, several sites have yielded human remains—mostly fragmentary—which, to some observers at least, seem to have hybrid or transitional characteristics.

Until now, the strongest evidence has come from the work of David Frayer of the University of Kansas. In a comparative analysis of fossils from various sites in central and eastern Europe, Frayer has found what he says is convincing evidence of biological continuity. His work focuses mainly on detailed features of Neanderthal teeth and jaws, which he says show that "a number of traits present in Neanderthals were also present in the peoples who followed them. It tells us there was gene flow . . . and refutes the argument of total placement."

New chronologies indicate that there may have been plenty of time for interbreeding to occur. Many anthropologists now accept that there were Neanderthal outposts in Portugal and southern Spain as recently as 30,000 years ago. At Zafarraya in southern Spain, for example, it appears that Neanderthals were still around up to 8000 years after the arrival of Cro-Magnons in northern Spain.

More surprising news came in March, when Paul Pettitt from the University of Oxford revealed that Neanderthal fossil remains from the Vindija cave in Croatia have been dated to 29,000 years ago. "These are the youngest dates we have for any Neanderthals," says Fred Smith, an anthropologist from Northern Illinois University who worked on the dating project with Pettitt and Trinkaus. "You begin to wonder if modern humans were coming into Europe as early as we thought," Smith adds. Trinkaus points out the parallel between these new dates and those from Portugal and Spain. "What these late survivals emphasise more than anything else is that the Out of Africa models are grossly simplistic," he says.

These suggestions of side-by-side coexistence of modern and Neanderthal populations over thousands of years are something of a problem for those who still believe that the newcomers quickly drove Neanderthals to extinction. The evidence from Spain, for example, points to a stable, long-term cultural frontier along the valley of the River Ebro, with moderns in the north and Neanderthals in the south. But if modern humans' technological advantage was such that they could replace the original inhabitants of most of Europe, why did it not extend into the south of the Iberian peninsula?

Some anthropologists argue that Neanderthals and moderns may have each been better adapted to conditions in different regions. "As the climates regularly changed... there would have been constant ebbs and flows in both populations, with the Neanderthals gradually losing out," says Stringer. Zilhão notes that a climatic threshold may have been reached around 30,000 years ago, with cooler conditions—to which modern humans may have been better culturally adapted—spreading into the southern-most regions of Europe.

Another idea is that contact came late to Portugal and Spain because of their isolated geographical position. But the same cannot be said of Croatia. "It's on the pathway to the Near East," notes Smith, referring to the route by which modern humans are thought to have spread into Europe.

While some fossil and DNA analysis hints at interbreeding, tools and other artefacts provide evidence of sophisticated cultural production by Neanderthals, during and even before the period of contact with Cro-Magnons. According to conventional archaeology, the arrival of modern humans in Europe is heralded by the appearance of new, more sophisticated stone and bone tools, and by a rapid increase in symbolic representation in the form of portable and cave art. In western Europe, early evidence of this "modern" Upper Palaeolithic culture, known as the Aurignacian, dates back to around 38,000 years ago. The fact that these assemblages often directly overlie Neanderthal fossil and cultural remains has led to the hypothesis that a broad, east-to-west invasion of competitively superior Cro-Magnons caused the Neanderthals' demise.

Some archaeologists, such as Geoffrey Clark of Arizona State University and Lawrence Straus of the University of New Mexico, have long disputed this view. They interpret the evidence as revealing a continuum of change across the Middle and Upper Palaeolithic, particularly the period between 40,000 and 30,000 years ago. "I've always argued that the transition is a mosaic, not a 20th-century-style invasion," says Straus. "The archaeological picture is of pockets of different industries existing contemporaneously with each other. Some things change quickly, some things don't—it depends on where you are in Europe."

Straus says that the new evidence of overlap and interbreeding is consistent with the variability found in the archaeological record. The late Neanderthal remains at Vindija cave, for example, were found alongside several Aurignacian-style stone and bone artefacts, as well as more typical Neanderthal tools. Elsewhere in Europe, the picture is even more complex where different cultural traditions—neither Aurignacian nor typically Neanderthal—have been identified. Most famous is the Châtelperronian culture known from some two dozen sites in France and northern Spain. Châtelperronian artefacts include carefully crafted bone implements and portable art objects. These items were once thought to be the hallmark of a modern Upper Palaeolithic culture, but fossils from Saint-Césaire and Arcy-sur-Cure in France indicate that they were almost certainly produced by Neanderthals. "I think that the Châtelperronian is a big problem," says Klein, "and I don't have an explanation for it."

One possibility is that Neanderthals were merely imitating modern humans they had seen, or were collecting their discarded artefacts. But this idea was rejected in a controversial paper published last year by Zilhão and a group of researchers led by Francesco d'Errico of the University of Bordeaux. D'Errico's team compared Châtelperronian ornaments and bone tools from Arcy-sur-Cure with Aurignacian artefacts from the same site. They found a distinct stylistic difference between the two, as well as differences in production techniques, indicating that the Châtelperronian objects were not the result of imitation. Moreover, says d'Errico, close scrutiny of the Arcy record reveals that the Châtelperronian implements and the by-products of their production were always found in strata below those containing Aurignacian remains.

All this evidence indicates that the Châtelperronian predates the arrival of Cro-Magnons and thus could only have been an independent invention by Neanderthals. "The Châtelperronian reveals that Neanderthals were fully cultural human beings, with symbol-aided communication," says Zilhão. This view is supported by evidence from other locations, including Croatia and Italy. "When they arrived in Europe, moderns met Neanderthal populations that had already accomplished their own Middle-to-Upper Palaeolithic transition." Ultimately, he says, these Neanderthals were absorbed by anatomically modern populations.

Critics argue that it seems rather too much of a coincidence for Neanderthals to have achieved these modern behaviours immediately before the arrival of modern peoples. But is it not equally a coincidence, replies d'Errico, that artistic production by Cro-Magnons appears to flourish only when they enter Europe and come in contact with Neanderthals?

Others go even further, and question whether the Aurignacian itself was really the product of a distinct group of early human immigrants to Europe. "There is no correlation whatsoever between particular 'kinds' of hominids and particular 'kinds' of archaeological assemblages, either in Europe or anywhere else," says Clark. And several researchers stress that the only clearly identifiable hominid fossils from early Aurignacian times are Neanderthal—which certainly leaves room for speculation.

In a recent article in *Science,* Clark argued that our understanding of modern human origins has been hampered by biases and assumptions inherent in the different research traditions involved. "We are in effect consumers of one another's research conclusions, but we pick and choose among them according to our preconceptions," he wrote. Those preconceptions are shaped by 19th-century cultural and taxonomic categories, says Clark, and he believes this makes it difficult for researchers to appreciate the full extent of variation in the archaeological and fossil record.

Stringer agrees that matching the archaeological record with fossil and genetic evidence is tricky. But the combination of approaches should be a source of strength rather than endless debate, he says. "In the end there was only one real history... and ultimately the different approaches should converge on this."

The Last Neanderthal

By little less than 30,000 years ago the Neanderthals had disappeared from the fossil record, after a tenure of 150,000 years or more in a vast region that stretched from the Atlantic to Uzbekistan. What happened to them? They had led hard lives, certainly: virtually none of the Neanderthal fossils known is that of an individual who survived beyond the age of about forty years, and few made it past thirty-five. Degenerative joint disease was common among these people, and many Neanderthal bones show evidence of injury. Yet the Neanderthals had successfully occupied a large area of the world over a long period in which climates fluctuated wildly, and their way of life was evidently flexible enough to cope with changing environmental conditions. Their abrupt demise must thus have been due to an entirely new factor. And that factor, almost certainly, was us.... [T]he extinction of species has been a normal and frequent occurrence throughout biological history.... [O]ur own emergence and evolution took place through unexceptional processes. Nonetheless, the ways in which our complex behaviors contrast with those of the Neanderthals serve to underline the fact that with the arrival of behaviorally modern *Homo sapiens* the world faced an entirely new phenomenon: one from whose impact it is still reeling, and of which the Neanderthals were among the first to bear the brunt.

... Neanderthals and *Homo sapiens* shared the Levant [the region located at the eastern end of the Mediterranean Sea] for an extended period, possibly about 60,000 years or even more. We don't know whether Neanderthals and moderns ever coexisted side by side in the region; the paucity of sites during this long time and the uncertainties of dating make possible arguments both pro and con. One popular idea is that Neanderthals occupied the Levant in cooler phases, during which modern humans withdrew south toward the kinder climates of Africa; when the climate warmed up, the latter moved back in and the Neanderthals retreated northward. Indirect support for this notion comes in the form of modern human body proportions, which suggest a heat-shedding habitus for *Homo sapiens,* in contrast to the heat-conserving proportions of the Neanderthals. But although the fossil record does suggest an African origin for modern humans, and the initial modern penetration of the Levant presumably came from this quarter, our body proportions could be a simple matter of heritage rather than one of specific adaptation in warm climate. This is especially so given modern humans' long-standing mastery of fire and the near certainty that clothing was available to mitigate the effects of cold climate.

What is clear, however, is that during Mousterian [Middle Paleolithic] times, despite possible differences in economic strategies, neither Levantine group was able to outcompete the other in any definitive way. Neanderthals and moderns may have come and gone in the Levant, but both continued to exist somewhere. There is no convincing biological evidence in the region for intermixing of Neanderthal and modern morphologies—and if *Homo neanderthalensis* and *Homo sapiens* were indeed different species, as the anatomical distinctions between them so strongly suggest, they could not have interbred successfully, certainly not over the long term. The two groups thus appear to have been in some sense separate but equal during most of the latest Pleistocene. Only with the arrival of Upper Paleolithic technologies in the Levant do we see the final exit of the Neanderthals. The Upper Paleolithic was fully established in this region by about 45,000 years ago, and the latest Neanderthal date comes from Amud [Cave in Israel], about 40,000 years ago. This general coincidence in time appears to be significant, although the Levantine record is much sparser than one would like.

The record is much denser in Europe, with dozens of sites both of Neanderthals and of Cro-Magnons. And it is made that much better by the fact that the first modern people to enter the subcontinent brought Upper Paleolithic technology with them. The Neanderthals, for their part, remained steadfastly Mousterian, with the minor exception of such short-lived "transitional" industries as the Châtelperronian [characterized by knives with curved backs]. If we assign Upper Paleolithic sites lacking human fossils to *Homo sapiens,* and Mousterian ones to *Homo neanderthalensis,* the record becomes little short of excellent. We've seen that the earliest evidence of Aurignacian [Upper Paleolithic culture that produced finely made artifacts, paintings, and engravings] occupation of Europe dates to about 40,000 years ago both in the far west of Europe (in Spain) and in the east (in Bulgaria). The Mousterian declines rapidly after that time, although final dates come in quite late, about 30,000 years ago or even less. *Homo sapiens* and *Homo neanderthalensis* thus overlapped in Europe for at least 10,000 years, but it's probably more significant that at individual sites the shift between Mousterian and Aurignacian appears to have been abrupt. This pattern starts right at the beginning. At Spain's L'Arbreda Cave, for example, dates for the latest Mousterian industry average 40,400 years ago, and for the earliest Aurignacian 38,500 years ago. These dates are part of a continuous, uninterrupted record, for the sediments yielding them are homogeneous and show no sedimentary break between levels. What's more, the artifact assemblages show no evidence of cultural intermixing.

Biologically, the evidence for intermixing isn't much better. Advocates of "Multiregional Continuity" have claimed that a few crania from Aurignacian strata in eastern Europe show some Neanderthal-like features—for example, a bit of occipital protrusion, or heavy brows. Thus, they claim, these specimens provide putative evidence of interbreeding between Neanderthals and moderns.

This is, however, really no more than a fallback position from the notion, now totally discredited by precise dating (among other things), that Neanderthals gave rise directly to modern Europeans. One ingenious theory supporting the idea that today's Europeans possess at least some "Neanderthal genes" has been the proposition that the "transition" from Neanderthal to modern morphology was essentially a process in which skeletal robustness was reduced. On the assumption that robustness is a function of use (as to some degree it is, especially in the postcranial skeleton), it is thus proposed that Upper Paleolithic cultural innovations reduced demands on the masticatory apparatus. This reduced need would in turn have lightened the build of the face, and such reduction, together with interbreeding among Neanderthals and moderns, would have hastened the rapid and total disappearance of Neanderthal morphology. This smacks heavily of special pleading, however. First, the argument depends on the mistaken assumption that Neanderthals and moderns are variants of the same species. Second, it assumes that at least many of the structural differences between the skulls of Neanderthals and moderns are reflections of use rather than of heritage. Given the scale and the nature of those differences, both assumptions are totally implausible.

What is certain is that there was some kind of interaction between the resident Neanderthals of Europe and the invading moderns. The nature of that interaction is particularly difficult to discern because in the absence of convincing evidence for biological hybridization, all the evidence we can bring to bear on the question is indirect. Contact, we can safely say, was not generally prolonged; the pattern of short-term replacement of the Mousterian by the Upper Paleolithic is too consistent for it to have been otherwise. But if, as by now is widely if not universally accepted, the Châtelperronian was a product of the adoption of Upper Paleolithic technologies by Mousterians, rather than an indigenous development by the latter, there must have been some cultural contact, direct or indirect, between Neanderthals and Cro-Magnons. What's more, that contact cannot have been uniquely destructive; for if it had been, the Châtelperronian would never have developed as a distinctive industry. Nonetheless, it's notable that Châtelperronian sites were much more scattered than the Mousterian ones that preceded them (only a handful are known, over a 4,000-year period), suggesting that Neanderthal populations thinned out considerably during Châtelperronian times.

Exactly what form contact between Neanderthals and Cro-Magnons took thus remains obscure. Maybe the moderns trickled slowly into the areas where the Châtelperronian developed—in which case, occasional interactions between individuals could have been sufficient to transfer some technology. On the one hand, it's quite easy to imagine this happening because the high consistency and craftsmanship of the Mousterian suggests strongly that Neanderthals learned easily by imitation. On the other hand, though, envisioning exactly how beings who differed enormously in their cognitive capacities would have communicated and interacted is difficult. Perhaps it's not too far-fetched to imagine that only the cleverest Neanderthals could have managed such contacts successfully and passed their newfound knowledge on to others. Or maybe, as my colleague Niles Eldredge suggested only half in jest, an exceptionally gifted

Neanderthal stumbled upon the remains of an abandoned Cro-Magnon campsite, recognized the utility of the unfamiliar blade tools and cores lying around, and figured out how to make them. Irrespective of how the idea of making blade tools and bone ornaments was acquired, though, it's clear that it's subsequent spread among the Neanderthals would have been a natural development.

Whatever the nature of those early contacts between Neanderthals and Cro-Magnons, they were clearly not enough to dislodge the former from their homeland immediately. But dislodged they eventually were. Within about 10,000 years of the first arrival of the Aurignacians in Europe, the Neanderthals were gone. Europe, of course, is a big place with many inaccessible mountain fastnesses, and it is highly improbable that a single wave of Aurignacians swept away the Neanderthals before it from east to west. Indeed, the interlayering of Châtelperronian and Aurignacian levels at a couple French sites argues strongly that this was not the case. The complex local geography and the low population levels of hunting-gathering peoples would have combined to make the complete takeover of the subcontinent by *Homo sapiens* a gradual and fragmented process. To what extent the Neanderthals themselves impeded that process is not known. Did they resist the invaders directly? Were their hunting and gathering practices efficient enough to make them effective competitors for ecological space, at least for a while? Did short-term environmental changes cause the balance to shift from one to the other for at least a few millennia? Was there, as some paleoanthropologists still think, a process of peaceful assimilation, the local Neanderthal genes eventually becoming "swamped" by those of the invaders?

We will never know for certain what happened. All we can say with assurance is that in the end, the moderns won out. It may be that despite their species difference, the Neanderthals and moderns were similar enough externally to have elicited the occasional attempt to interbreed—or perhaps more likely, the urge to ravish. It's vanishingly unlikely, however, that peaceful assimilation was an overall option, with groups of the two kinds of humans exchanging members when they met and going their separate ways, or joining forces. More likely, perhaps, if intermixing is to be considered at all, is a scenario of well-equipped and cunning *Homo sapiens* descending on Neanderthal groups, killing the males —through strategy and guile, certainly not through strength—and abducting the females. Yet it's highly improbably that viable offspring could have been produced by the resulting unions; Neanderthal females would hardly have been of much reproductive value to the invaders.

Whatever the details, in view of the ways that invading *Homo sapiens* have tended to treat resident members of their own as well as other species throughout recorded history, encounters between *Homo neanderthalensis* and *Homo sapiens* probably were not often happy ones. Today when we think of the Cro-Magnons we tend to focus on their more admirable achievements, particularly the ethereal art of such sites as Lascaux [in France], Altamira [in Spain], and Font de Gaume [in France]. Like us, however, the Cro-Magnons must have had a darker side. Their arrival in Europe heralded the extinction of a large variety of mammal species. Those that have survived until now are those that managed to adapt to this remarkable new phenomenon on the landscape. The Neanderthals, it seems, could not—which is not surprising, for it is hard to imagine two species so similar, if at the same time so different, sharing the same habitat for long....

One last cautionary note. It is the winners who write history, and this is the story of the Neanderthals written by a member of *Homo sapiens,* for an audience of *Homo sapiens.* In the evolutionary game the Neanderthals were ultimately "losers"—as, in the narrow sense of extinction, all species, like all individuals, must eventually be. But the Neanderthals were highly successful for a long time, longer certainly than we have yet been, and they occupied a unique place in nature. Evolution is not a straight-line process, each successive species bringing its lineage closer to some goal, preordained or otherwise. There are many ways of playing the evolutionary game, and the Neanderthals' strategy simply differed from ours. We may certainly look upon the Neanderthals as a mirror to reflect our own species' position among the almost infinite variety of living things, but it is profoundly misleading to see them simply as an inferior version of ourselves.

POSTSCRIPT

Did Neanderthals Interbreed With Modern Humans?

The debate rages on between those, like Norris, who believe that Neanderthals interbred with early modern humans in Europe and those, like Tattersall, who believe that Neanderthals were a separate species that became extinct. Proponents of interbreeding theories emphasize the similarities between Neanderthals and modern humans. Neanderthals' brains were as large as those of modern humans and appear to have been structurally similar. Evidence of their intelligence includes the making of sophisticated tools, use of fire, use of clothing to protect against the cold, and success at killing large and dangerous animals, including mammoths. These scholars infer that Neanderthals had language from such evidence as their ability to coordinate activities like big-game hunting and to transmit complex tool-making methods to their children. Indications that some Neanderthals recovered from life-threatening injuries suggest that they took care of the injured and elderly. Graves containing remains of food, pollen from flowers, and red ocher pigment may indicate a belief in an afterlife. Proponents of interbreeding imagine Neanderthals as early human, cold-adapted hunter-gatherers living in small groups, much like recent Eskimos in the Arctic.

Those who view Neanderthals as evolutionary dead-ends, however, emphasize the differences between Neanderthals and modern humans. They point to the Neanderthals' flattened skulls, heavy browridges, lack of chins, and unusually short and sturdy bodies and lower limbs compared to those of modern humans. These researchers regard Neanderthal stone tools as less advanced than those of early modern humans, emphasizing the lack of bone and ivory tools in the Neanderthal tool kit, and argue that the most sophisticated Neanderthal tools, the Châtelperronian industry, resulted from Neanderthals copying the techniques of the modern immigrants. These researchers especially emphasize that Neanderthals did not produce art, like the ivory carvings and cave paintings of early modern humans, and cite that as evidence that Neanderthals lacked the capacity for abstract thinking. Of course Neanderthals may have created less durable art, such as body paintings or wood carvings. These researchers also contend that Neanderthals, unlike early modern people, lived in small, isolated groups and did not undertake long-distance trade. Some have argued that Neanderthals did not have language because their larynxes were too high in their throats to produce a full range of vocal sounds.

Resolving whether or not Neanderthals and modern humans interbred will probably require more direct evidence of how the two groups arose from *Homo erectus*—whether or not they formed separate species—and how they interacted when they met in Europe. Fortunately new fossil and archaeological evidence is coming in fast. The discovery of the possibly mixed child in Portugal in 1998 and new fossil evidence of Neanderthals living as recently as 28,000 years ago in Spain and Croatia have given support to the proponents of interbreeding (see *Science News* [October 30, 1999]). But those on the other side contend that the Portuguese child was just an unusually robust Gravettian (modern human) child. A mitochondrial DNA test of Neanderthal bones from central Europe proved similar to earlier results from the Neander Valley specimen, indicating that the earlier results were reliable and that Neanderthals formed a closely related population. But resolving whether or not they were a separate species depends on obtaining mitochondrial DNA profiles of modern humans from the same period for comparison. New evidence of Neanderthal behavior is also appearing. For example, close study of Châtelperronian sites shows Châtelperronian tools consistently underlying Upper Paleolithic Aurignacian tools, suggesting that the former were independently developed by Neanderthals, not copied from early modern humans (see Joao Zilhao, "Fate of the Neanderthals," *Archaeology* [July/August 2000]). A recent excavation contains evidence that some Neanderthals were cannibals (see "Neanderthal Eats Neanderthal," *Discover* [December 1999]). Bones of Neanderthals were found to bear the same marks of butchering as the bones of game animals at the same site. While some commentators see this as shockingly animalistic behavior, others regard it as evidence of a fully human, if unsavory, practice.

There is a huge and rapidly growing literature on Neanderthals. Because new evidence is coming in so fast, students should try to get the most recent possible sources. The Web site of the Neanderthal Museum in Germany, at www.neanderthal.de, is especially useful in this respect. It provides general information, the latest scholarly reports, and links to related sites. Because of the enormous public interest in Neanderthals, most popular science magazines—including *Natural History, Archaeology,* and *Scientific American*—feature regular updates on the Neanderthal controversy. An excellent recent overview of the controversy is Kate Wong's article "Who Were the Neanderthals?" *Scientific American* (April 2000). Detailed and readable descriptions of the discovery of the "mixed" child in Portugal can be found in Robert Kunzig's article "Learning to Love Neanderthals," *Discover,* (August 1999) and Joao Zilhao's article "Fate of the Neanderthals," *Archaeology* (July/August 2000). *Archaeology* magazine promises an opposing view of the fate of the Neanderthals in a forthcoming issue. Recent books arguing against interbreeding theories include Christopher Stringer and Clive Gamble's *In Search of the Neanderthals* (Thames & Hudson, 1993) and Ian Tattersall and Jeffrey H. Schwartz's *Extinct Humans* (Westview Press, 2000). Scholarly journals periodically devote parts of issues to the debate over the Neanderthals. Recent examples include the *Current Anthropology* special supplement, "The Neanderthal Problem and the Evolution of Human Behavior" (vol. 39, 1998) and the *Current Anthropology* Forum on Theory in Anthropology, "The Neanderthal Problem Continued" (vol. 40, no. 3, 1999), in which anthropologists Paul Mellars, Marcel Otte, Laurence Straus, João Zilhão, and Francesco D'Errico present conflicting views of recent Neanderthal evidence.

ISSUE 3

Should Anthropology Abandon the Concept of Race?

YES: Jonathan Marks, from "Black, White, Other," *Natural History* (December 1994)

NO: George W. Gill, from "The Beauty of Race and Races," *Anthropology Newsletter* (March 1998)

ISSUE SUMMARY

YES: Biological anthropologist Jonathan Marks argues that race is not a useful concept because there are no "natural" divisions of the human species. The popular idea of races as discrete categories of people who are similar to each other and different from all members of other races is a cultural—not a biological—concept, he concludes.

NO: Biological and forensic anthropologist George W. Gill contends that we should not scrap the concept of race because races—conceived as populations originating in particular regions—can be distinguished both by external and skeletal features. He states that the concept of race is especially useful in the forensic task of identifying human skeletons. Furthermore, the notion of race provides a vocabulary for discussing human biological variation and racism.

The European idea of humanity being divided into physically distinct types —races—developed after the Age of Exploration in the fifteenth and sixteenth centuries. Before the era of rapid transportation and mass population movements, most people were born, lived, and died without seeing anyone who looked appreciably different from themselves. But when European explorers reached Africa, East Asia, and the Americas, they were confronted with people who were very different from them in appearance and in their ways of life. Europeans tried to understand this unforeseen human diversity in terms of the religious worldview of the time. High councils of the Church debated whether or not particular peoples had souls that missionaries could save. Killing and enslaving colonized peoples was justified by the view that they were inherently inferior beings, not fully human.

By the nineteenth century the idea that populations looked and acted differently because of their different hereditary endowments was widely believed. Scholars viewed different groups as being at different stages of progress on the march to European-style civilization, and those that lagged behind were thought to have been held back by their inferior physical, mental, and moral endowments. The development of cultural evolutionary schemes in the second half of the century, inspired in part by Darwin's theory of the evolution of species, seemed to give a scientific basis for this view. In short, racism and the idea of race developed together. One of the founding figures in American anthropology, Franz Boas, fought a life-long battle against racism and the idea that cultural and psychological characteristics could be explained in terms of biology.

Toward the middle of the twentieth century, biological anthropologists tried to refine the concept of race by separating biological differences from cultural ones and by focusing on populations, rather than individuals, and genetic variations, rather than superficial physical differences like head shape. One intractable problem, however, was that scholars could not agree on how many races there were. For example, was there one African race or many? This uncertainty revealed an underlying problem with the concept: different sets of races resulted depending on the number and nature of the features considered. And no matter how many races were distinguished, there were always some groups that did not fit in.

In his selection, Jonathan Marks distinguishes races as culturally-defined categories—the popular usage—from races as biological subspecies of human beings. Culturally-defined races can be clear-cut because they are based on arbitrary criteria, such as the number of great-grandparents who came from Africa. Marks concludes that there are no clusters of discrete characteristics that could unambiguously distinguish a member of one race from another. Therefore race as a biological concept is meaningless.

George W. Gill argues, on the other hand, that races—understood as populations derived from particular geographical regions—can be distinguished not only through their external characteristics, like skin color, but also by skeletal features. By utilizing a combination of distinctive osteological characteristics, which are found in varying proportions in different geographical races, forensic anthropologists can make highly accurate guesses about the ancestry of the person whose bones are under study.

This issue touches on a number of thorny questions for anthropologists, some scientific and some ethical. What sorts of concepts are needed for discussing and analyzing human hereditary differences? Can geographical races be defined in terms of varying proportions of characteristics that together form a distinctive profile? What is the relationship between individuals and racial categories? Does the very idea of classifying humans into clear-cut categories inherently misrepresent the gradual nature of genetic variation and change? Is the term *race* so loaded with racist connotations that it must be replaced by a more neutral term before dispassionate discussion of human hereditary variation can proceed?

Jonathan Marks

 **YES**

Black, White, Other

While reading the Sunday edition of the *New York Times* one morning last February, my attention was drawn by an editorial inconsistency. The article I was reading was written by attorney Lani Guinier. (Guinier, you may remember, had been President Clinton's nominee to head the civil rights division at the Department of Justice in 1993. Her name was hastily withdrawn amid a blast of criticism over her views on political representation of minorities.) What had distracted me from the main point of the story was a photo caption that described Guinier as being "half-black." In the text of the article, Guinier had described herself simply as "black."

How can a person be black and half black at the same time? In algebraic terms, this would seem to describe a situation where $x = \frac{1}{2}x$, to which the only solution is $x = 0$.

The inconsistency in the *Times* was trivial, but revealing. It encapsulated a longstanding problem in our use of racial categories—namely, a confusion between biological and cultural heredity. When Guinier is described as "half-black," that is a statement of biological ancestry, for one of her two parents is black. And when Guinier describes herself as black, she is using a cultural category, according to which one can either be black or white, but not both.

Race—as the term is commonly used—is inherited, although not in a strictly biological fashion. It is passed down according to a system of folk heredity, an all-or-nothing system that is different from the quantifiable heredity of biology. But the incompatibility of the two notions of race is sometimes starkly evident—as when the state decides that racial differences are so important that interracial marriages must be regulated or outlawed entirely. Miscegenation laws in this country (which stayed on the books in many states through the 1960s) obliged the legal system to define who belonged in what category. The resulting formula stated that anyone with one-eighth or more black ancestry was a "negro." (A similar formula, defining Jews, was promulgated by the Germans in the Nuremberg Laws of the 1930s.)

Applying such formulas led to the biological absurdity that having one black great-grandparent was sufficient to define a person as black, but having seven white great grandparents was insufficient to define a person as white.

Here, race and biology are demonstrably at odds. And the problem is not semantic but conceptual, for race is presented as a category of nature.

Human beings come in a wide variety of sizes, shapes, colors, and forms —or, because we are visually oriented primates, it certainly seems that way. We also come in larger packages called populations; and we are said to belong to even larger and more confusing units, which have long been known as races. The history of the study of human variation is to a large extent the pursuit of those human races—the attempt to identify the small number of fundamentally distinct kinds of people on earth.

This scientific goal stretches back two centuries, to Linnaeus, the father of biological systematics, who radically established *Homo sapiens* as one species within a group of animals he called Primates. Linnaeus's system of naming groups within groups logically implied further breakdown. He consequently sought to establish a number of subspecies within *Homo sapiens*. He identified five: four geographical species (from Europe, Asia, Africa, and America) and one grab-bag subspecies called *monstrosus*. This category was dropped by subsequent researchers (as was Linnaeus's use of criteria such as personality and dress to define his subspecies).

While Linnaeus was not the first to divide humans on the basis of the continents on which they lived, he had given the division a scientific stamp. But in attempting to determine the proper number of subspecies, the heirs of Linnaeus always seemed to find different answers, depending upon the criteria they applied. By the mid-twentieth century, scores of anthropologists—led by Harvard's Earnest Hooton—had expended enormous energy on the problem. But these scholars could not convince one another about the precise nature of the fundamental divisions of our species.

Part of the problem—as with the *Times's* identification of Lani Guinier— was that we humans have two constantly intersecting ways of thinking about the divisions among us. On the one hand, we like to think of "race"—as Linnaeus did—as an objective, biological category. In this sense, being a member of a race is supposed to be the equivalent of being a member of a species or of a phylum—except that race, on the analogy of subspecies, is an even narrower (and presumably more exclusive and precise) biological category.

The other kind of category into which we humans allocate ourselves— when we say "Serb" or "Hutu" or "Jew" or "Chicano" or "Republican" or "Red Sox fan"—is cultural. The label refers to little or nothing in the natural attributes of its members. These members may not live in the same region and may not even know many others like themselves. What they share is neither strictly nature nor strictly community. The groupings are constructions of human social history.

Membership in these *un*biological groupings may mean the difference between life and death, for they are the categories that allow us to be identified (and accepted or vilified) socially. While membership in (or allegiance to) these categories may be assigned or adopted from birth, the differentia that mark members from nonmembers are symbolic and abstract; they serve to distinguish people who cannot be readily distinguished by nature. So important are these symbolic distinctions that some of the strongest animosities are often expressed between very similar-looking peoples. Obvious examples are Bosnian Serbs and Muslims, Irish and English, Huron and Iroquois.

Obvious natural variation is rarely so important as cultural difference. One simply does not hear of a slaughter of the short people at the hands of the tall, the glabrous at the hands of the hairy, the red-haired at the hands of the brown-haired. When we do encounter genocidal violence between different looking peoples, the two groups are invariably socially or culturally distinct as well. Indeed, the tragic frequency of hatred and genocidal violence between biologically indistinguishable peoples implies that biological differences such as skin color are not motivations but, rather, excuses. They allow nature to be invoked to reinforce group identities and antagonisms that would exist without these physical distinctions. But are there any truly "racial" biological distinctions to be found in our species?

Obviously, if you compare two people from different parts of the world (or whose ancestors came from different parts of the world), they will differ physically, but one cannot therefore define three or four or five basically different kinds of people, as a biological notion of race would imply. The anatomical properties that distinguish people—such as pigmentation, eye form, body build —are not clumped in discrete groups, but distributed along geographical gradients, as are nearly all the genetically determined variants detectable in the human gene pool.

These gradients are produced by three forces. Natural selection adapts populations to local circumstances (like climate) and thereby differentiates them from other populations. Genetic drift (random fluctuations in a gene pool) also differentiates populations from one another, but in non-adaptive ways. And gene flow (via intermarriage and other child-producing unions) acts to homogenize neighboring populations.

In practice, the operations of these forces are difficult to discern. A few features, such as body build and the graduated distribution of the sickle cell anemia gene in populations from western Africa, southern Asia, and the Mediterranean can be plausibly related to the effects of selection. Others, such as the graduated distribution of a small deletion in the mitochondrial DNA of some East Asian, Oceanic, and Native American peoples, or the degree of flatness of the face, seem unlikely to be the result of selection and are probably the results of random biohistorical factors. The cause of the distribution of most features, from nose breadth to blood group, is simply unclear.

The overall result of these forces is evident, however. As Johann Friedrich Blumenbach noted in 1775, "you see that all do so run into one another, and that one variety of mankind does so sensibly pass into the other, that you cannot mark out the limits between them." (Posturing as an heir to Linnaeus, he nonetheless attempted to do so.) But from humanity's gradations in appearance, no defined groupings resembling races readily emerge. The racial categories with which we have become so familiar are the result of our imposing arbitrary cultural boundaries in order to partition gradual biological variation.

Unlike graduated biological distinctions, culturally constructed categories are ultrasharp. One can be French or German, but not both; Tutsi or Hutu, but not both; Jew or Catholic, but not both; Bosnian Muslim or Serb, but not both; black or white, but not both. Traditionally, people of "mixed race" have been obliged to choose one and thereby identify themselves unambiguously to census takers and administrative bookkeepers—a practice that is now being widely called into question.

A scientific definition of race would require considerable homogeneity within each group, and reasonably discrete differences between groups, but three kinds of data militate against this view: First, the groups traditionally described as races are not at all homogeneous. Africans and Europeans, for instance, are each a collection of biologically diverse populations. Anthropologists of the 1920s widely recognized *three* European races: Nordic, Alpine, and Mediterranean. This implied that races could exist within races. American anthropologist Carleton Coon identified *ten* European races in 1939. With such protean use, the term race came to have little value in describing actual biological entities within *Homo sapiens*. The scholars were not only grappling with a broad north-south gradient in human appearance across Europe, they were trying to bring the data into line with their belief in profound and fundamental constitutional differences between groups of people.

But there simply isn't one European race to contrast with an African race, nor three, nor ten: the question (as scientists long posed it) fails to recognize the actual patterning of diversity in the human species. Fieldwork revealed, and genetics later quantified, the existence of far more biological diversity within any group than between groups. Fatter and thinner people exist everywhere, as do people with type O and type A blood. What generally varies from one population to the next is the *proportion* of people in these groups expressing the trait or gene. Hair color varies strikingly among Europeans and native Australians, but little among other peoples. To focus on discovering differences between presumptive races, when the vast majority of detectable variants do not help differentiate them, was thus to define a very narrow—if not largely illusory—problem in human biology. (The fact that Africans are biologically more diverse than Europeans, but have rarely been split into so many races, attests to the cultural basis of these categorizations.)

Second, differences between human groups are only evident when contrasting geographical extremes. Noting these extremes, biologists of an earlier era sought to identify representatives of "pure," primordial races presumably located in Norway, Senegal, and Thailand. At no time, however, was our species composed of a few populations within which everyone looked pretty much the same. Ever since some of our ancestors left Africa to spread out through the Old World, we humans have always lived in the "in-between" places. And human populations have also always been in genetic contact with one another. Indeed, for tens of thousands of years, humans have had trade networks; and where goods flow, so do genes. Consequently, we have no basis for considering *extreme* human forms the most pure, or most representative, of some ancient primordial populations. Instead, they represent populations adapted to the most disparate environments.

And third, between each presumptive "major" race are unclassifiable populations and people. Some populations of India, for example, are darkly pigmented (or "black"), have Europeanlike ("Caucasoid") facial features, but inhabit the continent of Asia (which should make them "Asian"). Americans might tend to ignore these "exceptions" to the racial categories, since immigrants to the United States from West Africa, Southeast Asia, and northwest Europe far outnumber those from India. The very existence of unclassifiable peoples undermines the idea that there are just three human biological groups in the Old World. Yet acknowledging the biological distinctiveness of such groups leads to a rapid proliferation of categories. What about Australians? Polynesians? The Ainu of Japan?

Categorizing people is important to any society. It is, at some basic psychological level, probably necessary to have group identity about who and what you are, in contrast to who and what you are not. The concept of race, however, specifically involves the recruitment of biology to validate those categories of self-identity.

Mice don't have to worry about that the way humans do. Consequently, classifying them into subspecies entails less of a responsibility for a scientist than classifying humans into sub-species does. And by the 1960s, most anthropologists realized they could not defend any classification of *Homo sapiens* into biological subspecies or races that could be considered reasonably objective. They therefore stopped doing it, and stopped identifying the endeavor as a central goal of the field. It was a biologically intractable problem—the old square-peg-in-a-round-hole enterprise; and people's lives, or welfares, could well depend on the ostensibly scientific pronouncement. Reflecting on the social history of the twentieth century, that was a burden anthropologists would no longer bear.

This conceptual divorce in anthropology—of cultural from biological phenomena was one of the most fundamental scientific revolutions of our time. And since it affected assumptions so rooted in our everyday experience, and resulted in conclusions so counterintuitive—like the idea that the earth goes around the sun, and not vice-versa—it has been widely underappreciated.

Kurt Vonnegut, in *Slaughterhouse Five*, describes what he remembered being taught about human variation: "At that time, they were teaching that there was absolutely no difference between anybody. They may be teaching that still." Of course there are biological differences between people, and between populations. The question is: How are those differences patterned? And the answer seems to be: Not racially. Populations are the only readily identifiable units of humans, and even they are fairly fluid, biologically similar to populations nearby, and biologically different from populations far away.

In other words, the message of contemporary anthropology is: You may group humans into a small number of races if you want to, but you are denied biology as a support for it.

NO ↩

George W. Gill

The Beauty of Race and Races

What good is a worldview of race and races? To me the major races of humankind are among nature's most beautiful and fascinating creations. Biologically, they are our colorful symbol of success as an ecologically widely adapted species, and they are our hedge against extinction should one or more of these varied habitats disappear. Socially, race is a part of the source of ethnic pride and identity. Finally, forensically race forms one of the 4 cornerstones of personal identity (with sex, age and stature) and thus serves society as a means of reducing the residuum of the unidentified for law enforcement. This, in turn, often leads to the solution and reduction of many forms of serious crime.

Should We Scrap "Race"?

"Race differences," renowned geneticist Theodosius Dobzhansky once said, "are facts of nature which can, given sufficient study, be ascertained objectively." What did he mean by this, and was he correct?

At the time of Dobzhansky's writing, anthropology was at its peak in the revolutionary overhaul of the old typological race concept. Throughout anthropology, we were replacing it rapidly with a populational view, coupled with a realization that many of the curious physical differences among the world's peoples have (or had in the Pleistocene past) definite survival value. On the other hand, with all the new work at that time in blood factor analysis, and other serological trait studies (which seemed to be poorly explained by a "racial model"), the question was, should we just scrap the whole concept and move on?

Over the years, as I became involved in two separate kinds of anthropological activity (forensic anthropology research and casework, and teaching an undergraduate course on human variation), I decided that we should *not* scrap the race concept to describe and study human variation. First, the populational view of race and adaptive value of racial traits seemed to *disconnect race from racism*. After all, how could anyone be a racist as long as they realized that (1) the distinctive traits of each group have real "value" in a Darwinian sense and (2) each major population contains such a wide range of variation for almost any trait, that individuals cannot be judged by their group affinity? For three decades this idea was pervasive in anthropology. The assumption was that we were free to study any aspect of human variation without fearing misuse of the information, at least among educated people. We believed that increased knowledge and dialogue about race and races would help extinguish, not fan, the fires of racism. This position helped not only to breathe new life and vitality into human variation studies, but to promote open dialogue on both race and racism.

It was not until 1990 that the mere word *race* acquired such a social taboo that it could rarely be used in polite company, especially among anthropologists, those who ironically had just spent a century intensively studying the subject of race from practically every angle. The politically correct view has become the position that we should *not* study or even talk about race, first because there is no real biological validity to the concept and second because it clearly leads to racist thinking if we do talk about it. How true are these two assumptions? How does the first (the unreality of races) mesh with Dobzhansky's statements or with the experiences of modern forensic anthropologists? How does the second (that race thinking causes racism) mesh with the experiences of anthropology teachers?

Are Races Real?

For those truly interested in the degree of accuracy attained by human osteologists in determining geographic racial affinities by utilizing various new and traditional osteological methods, a number of pertinent articles are available. Many of these are well-conducted studies designed to test methods objectively for percentage of correct placement. In our 1990 handbook of new methods for forensic anthropologists (*Skeletal Attribution of Race*) Stanley Rhine and I compiled 14 contributions by a number of active forensic anthropologists that present new research. In a 1995 *Journal of Forensic Sciences* article (40(5):783) I also review a number of new methods for discerning American Indians from whites osteologically, as well as for evaluating skeletons of blacks and Polynesians.

These new methods are probably no better than many traditional nonmetric approaches that utilize such things as alveolar prognathism, form of incisors and chin projection but simply have been quantitatively tested and reported in the literature. No osteologist would make a racial assessment in an actual case based on just *one* of these methods. That's why actual racial assessment results in real court cases or law enforcement reports run very close to 100% correct (as do assessments of sex, stature and age). If there is much doubt about any of these assessments, which can happen in the cases of very fragmentary skeletons or some that show a conflicting pattern of skeletal criteria, a board certified forensic anthropologist will not offer a conclusion.

My respected colleague C Loring Brace, who is as skilled as the leading forensic anthropologists at assessing ancestry from bones, does not subscribe to the concept of race. Neither does Norman Sauer, a board certified forensic anthropologist. Some of my students ask, how can these people, who can on a random sample of skeletons given to them out of context and who can classify

Figure 1

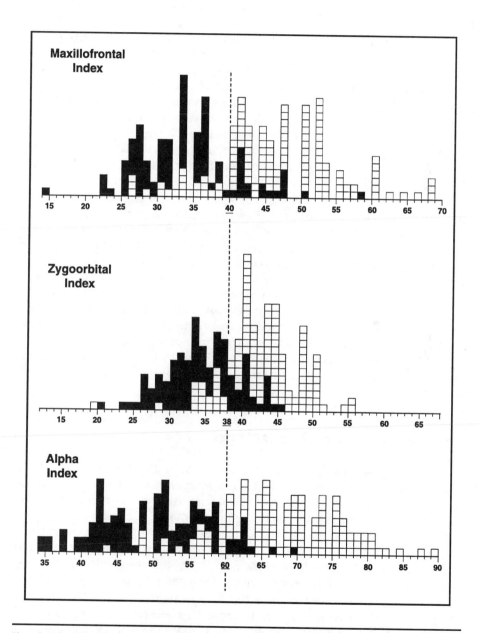

Plot values for black and white Americans, for each of three interorbital indexes. These indexes assess the degree of nasal projection. The same cutoff values (40-38-60) separate North American Indians from whites with approximately the same degree of accuracy. Initial samples in this study were 125 whites, 100 American blacks and 175 North American Indians. Percentages of correct placement are 88.8 for whites, 87.0 for blacks and 87.9 for Amerindians (using all three indexes together). (From G W Gill and B M Gilbert, "Racial Identification from the Mid-Facial Skeleton: American Blacks and Whites," G Gill and S Rhine, eds, *Skeletal Attribution of Race*, 1990)

them accurately by region (or "race" if forced to use this despised "social construct"), claim that they do not believe in race? My answer is that we can often *function* within systems that we do not believe in.

As a middle-aged American, for example, I am not sure that I believe any longer in the chronological "age" categories utilized by osteologists. Certainly some 40-year-olds have portions of their skeletons that look older than parts of some 50-year-olds. If called by law enforcement to provide "age" on a skeleton I can, however, provide an answer that will be proven sufficiently accurate should the decedent eventually be identified. I may not believe in society's "age" categories, but I can be very effective at "aging" skeletons. The next question of course is how "real" is age biologically? My answer is that if biological criteria can be used to assess age with reasonable accuracy, then it has *some* basis in biological reality even if the particular "social construct" that defines its limits might be imperfect. I find this true not only for age and stature estimations but for sex and race identifications.

The "reality of race" therefore depends more on the definition of *reality* than on the definition of *race*. If we choose to accept the system of racial taxonomy established traditionally by physical anthropologists, then human skeletons can be classified within it just as well as can living humans. The bony traits of the nose, mouth, femur and cranium are just as revealing to a good osteologist as skin color, hair form, nose form and lips to the perceptive observer of living humanity. I have been able to prove to myself over the years, in actual legal cases, that I am *more* accurate at assessing race from skeletal remains than from looking at living people standing before me. So those of us in forensic anthropology know that race, whether "real" or not, is just as well reflected (or better) by the skeleton as it is by the superficial soft tissue. The idea that race is "only skin deep," as any reputable forensic anthropologist will affirm, is simply not true.

Does Race Promote Racism?

Does teaching human variation, or discussing it in a framework of racial biology, promote or reduce racism? This is an important question, but one that does not have a simple answer. Most social scientists over the past decade have convinced themselves that it runs the risk of promoting racism in certain quarters. Anthropologists of the 1950s, 1960s and early 1970s, on the other hand, believed that they were *combating* racism by teaching courses on human races and racism. Which approach has worked best? What do the intellectuals among racial minorities believe? How do students react and respond?

Last spring when I served on a NOVA show panel in New York (Debates/ Debates, June 1997) we were given the topic "Is There Such a Thing as Race?" Six of us were chosen, three proponents of the race concept and three antagonists. All had authored books or papers on race. Loring Brace and I were the two anthropologists "facing off" in the debate. The ethnic composition of the panel was three white and three black scholars. As our conversations developed, I was struck by how similar many of my concerns regarding racism were to those of

Figure 2

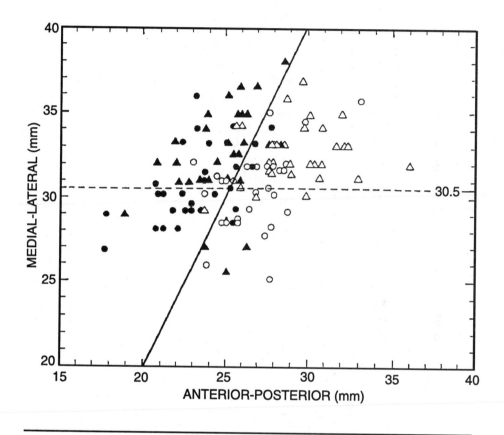

Plot points for North American Indian males and females and North American whites males and females, for two common measurements of the proximal femur. These measurements taken together reveal the degree of platymeria (flatness) of the proximal diaphysis. This method yields a percentage of correct placement of approximately 85% for both North American whites and North American Indians. (From G Gill and S Rhine, eds, *Skeletal Attribution of Race,* 1990)

my two black teammates. Although recognizing that embracing the race concept can have risks attached, we were more fearful of the form of racism likely to emerge if race is denied and dialogue about it lessened. We three fear that the social taboo over the subject of race has served to suppress open discussion over a very important subject in need of dispassionate debate. One of my teammates, an affirmative action lawyer, is afraid that a denial that races exist also serves to encourage a denial that racism exists. He asked, how can we combat racism if no one is willing to talk about race?

My reasons for teaching at least part of my human variation course from the "racial perspective" are many. First, it seems easier to discuss and study the subject of biological variation with nomenclature and structure than without. Cultural anthropologists cannot discuss cultural diversity without names for specific cultures (no matter how arbitrary they might prove to be), nor can archaeologists deal with artifact assemblages without systems of classification. Along the same line, how can paleoanthropologists talk about hominid change through time without erecting taxonomic categories and creating names? Why is it that those who are more interested in the richness and beauty of biological variation among existing human populations (than past ones), or more interested in biological variation than cultural diversity, are denied the tools for communication and study granted all others? Has a focus on race caused more human suffering than a focus on culture or religion? Absolutely not. Infinitely more human suffering has been caused by religious persecution than racial bias, yet we are to celebrate human cultural diversity while carefully containing our enthusiasm for racial variation. I detect a bias based not on truth but on prejudice. Those of us (from all races and walks of life) fascinated by biological variation are greatly outnumbered by those more focused on cultural or "ethnic" variations. Are we a misunderstood minority in need of a political action group?

Who Will Benefit?

Students who have been the strongest supporters of my "racial perspective" on human variation have been almost invariably the minority students. The first black student in my human variation class several years ago came to me at the end of the course and said, "Dr Gill, I really want to thank you for changing my life with this course." He went on to explain that, "My whole life I have wondered about why I am black, and if that is good or bad. Now I know the reasons why I am the way I am and that these traits are useful and good." A human variation course with another perspective would probably have accomplished the same for this student *if* he had ever noticed it. The truth is, innocuous contemporary human variation classes with their politically correct titles and course descriptions do not attract attention of minorities or those other students who could most benefit.

POSTSCRIPT

Should Anthropology Abandon the Concept of Race?

No one denies that variations in hereditary features between individuals and populations exist. The disagreement is over whether or not the concept of race, or subspecies, accurately expresses these variations. Marks argues that distinct races cannot be defined objectively on the basis of biological variations. Among other problems, differences among the members of any defined race are greater than those between races. Indeed, the average differences between traditional races represent only about 10 percent of our total species variation, while 90 percent of that variation is found within races. Gill contends, on the other hand, that combinations of characteristics cluster together, making it possible to distinguish geographical populations as separate races.

The majority of physical anthropologists today hold positions similar to Marks's. The American Anthropological Association (AAA) has created a "Statement on 'Race,'" which expresses the current view of most anthropologists on race and racism. It can be seen on the AAA Web site at www.aaanet.org/stmts/racepp.htm.

But, as Gill implies, the view that races do not exist seems nonsensical to the average American, who has grown up steeped in the idea that humanity is made up of different races. Racial categories are so ingrained in our vocabulary and thought that we identify people by race as readily as by sex or age. We are asked our race on official census forms, and many government policies, such as affirmative action, depend on the reality of race. What is needed, Marks would say, is recognition that this notion of race is a cultural—not a biological—construction.

The literature on race, including the concept of race, is enormous. Informative overviews of the concept of race in anthropology include Michael Banton's book *Racial Theories* (Cambridge University Press, 1987) and Eugenia Shanklin's short book *Anthropology and Race* (Wadsworth Publishing, 1994). Two landmark books in the development of anthropological views of race are Franz Boas's *Race, Language, and Culture* (The Free Press, 1940) and Ashley Montagu's *Man's Most Dangerous Myth: The Fallacy of Race* (Columbia University Press, 1945). Accessible books on forensic anthropology, which continues to use the concept of race, include Douglas Ubelaker and Henry Scammel's *Bones: A Forensic Detective's Casebook* (Edward Burlingame Books, 1992) and Stanley Rhine's *Bone Voyage: A Journey in Forensic Anthropology* (University of New Mexico Press, 1998).

ISSUE 4

Are Humans Inherently Violent?

YES: Richard Wrangham and Dale Peterson, from *Demonic Males: Apes and the Origins of Human Violence* (Houghton Mifflin Company, 1996)

NO: Robert W. Sussman, from "Exploring Our Basic Human Nature," *Anthro Notes* (Fall 1997)

ISSUE SUMMARY

YES: Biological anthropologist Richard Wrangham and science writer Dale Peterson argue that male humans and chimpanzees, our closest nonhuman relatives, have an innate tendency to be aggressive and to defend their territory by violence. They argue that sexual selection, a type of natural selection, has fostered an instinct for male aggression because males who are good fighters mate more frequently and sire more offspring than weaker and less aggressive ones.

NO: Biological anthropologist Robert W. Sussman rejects the theory that human aggression is an inherited propensity, arguing instead that violence is a product of culture and upbringing. He rejects the contention that male chimpanzees routinely commit violent acts against other male chimps. Sussman regards the notion that human males are inherently violent as a Western cultural tradition, not a scientifically demonstrated fact.

$\mathbf{H}$uman history is rife with wars between groups of all types, from clans to nation-states, and interpersonal violence is common enough that all societies attempt to control it. But is violence a part of human nature, or is violence merely one of many human capabilities that may be either encouraged or discouraged by cultures?

The question of whether or not humans have an instinct for aggression has been around since the formative years of anthropology, and it is still being debated today. Some nineteenth-century scholars interpreted Darwin's concepts of "natural selection" and "survival of the fittest" to mean that the strong would kill off the weak. The strongest and most aggressive individuals, therefore, would have the most offspring, and their strength and instinct for aggression would gradually come to predominate in the population.

Most cultural anthropologists from the 1950s onward rejected the explanation of human aggression in terms of instincts, emphasizing instead the social and cultural causes of violence. They pointed out that the amount of aggression tolerated varies widely from one society to another and that individuals can become aggressive or peaceful depending on how they are raised. They held up such groups as the Semai of Malaysia (see Robert K. Dentan, *The Semai: A Nonviolent People of Malaya* [Holt, Rinehart & Winston, 1968]) as proof that culture could create a people who abhorred all forms of aggression and coercion. Whatever instinct for aggression humans might have, they argued, must be very weak indeed.

The question behind this issue concerns the nature of human nature. Have we a set of innate behavioral predispositions which, when set off by certain stimuli, are very likely to be expressed? Or, are any such predispositions at best weak tendencies that can be shaped or even negated by cultural conditioning? Many apparently innate behaviors in humans turn out to be highly variable in their strength and form. While the sucking instinct of babies operates predictably in all newborns, a hypothesized "mothering instinct" seems quite diverse in expression and variable in strength from one woman to another. The question, then, is whether the hypothesized aggression instinct is a powerful drive, which all human males must express in one way or another, or a weak and pliable tendency, which some males may never act upon.

Richard Wrangham and Dale Peterson argue that human wars and interpersonal violence are driven by inherited behavioral tendencies that have evolved under pressure of sexual selection—natural selection of traits that enhance the reproductive success of one sex. Among both humans and chimpanzees, males who are aggressive use their fighting ability to dominate other males and prevent them from mating with the available females. Therefore the genes causing aggression are passed on to succeeding generations in greater numbers than the genes causing nonaggressive behavior.

Robert W. Sussman rejects Wrangham and Peterson's claim that natural selection favors aggressive human males and that aggressiveness is an inherited tendency rather than a result of environment and upbringing. He contends that human hunter-gatherers and most apes are remarkably nonaggressive, as were our earliest human ancestors, the australopithecines. He sees the evidence that chimpanzee males routinely attack other males as weak, and he questions the relevance of chimpanzee behavior for humans.

These selections raise a number of questions with regard to the nature and causes of human aggression. How can we determine whether a person's aggressive act is due to instinct, upbringing, or both? If male aggression in humans is based on instinct, how can scholars explain variations in the amount and type of aggression found in different individuals and cultures? If male aggression is not based on instinct, why is violence between men so widespread? What role did women have in the evolution of an instinct for male violence? To what extent can studies of animal behavior be applied to humans?

Richard Wrangham
and Dale Peterson

 **YES**

Demonic Males: Apes and the Origins of Human Violence

Paradise Lost

The killer ape has long been part of our popular culture: Tarzan had to escape from the bad apes, and King Kong was a murderous gorilla-like monster. But before the Kahama obeservations [in which males of one chimpanzee group killed the males of a neighboring group], few biologists took the idea seriously. The reason was simple. There was so little evidence of animals killing members of their own species that biologists used to think animals killed each other only when something went wrong—an accident, perhaps, or unnatural crowding in zoos. The idea fit with the theories of animal behavior then preeminent, theories that saw animal behavior as designed by evolution for mutual good. Darwinian natural selection was a filter supposed to eliminate murderous violence. Killer apes, like killers in any animal species, were merely a novelist's fantasy to most scientists before the 1970s.

And so the behavior of people seemed very, very different from that of other animals. Killing, of course, is a typical result of human war, so one had to presume that humans somehow broke the rules of nature. Still, war must have come from somewhere. It could have come, for example, from the evolution of brains that happened to be smart enough to think of using tools as weapons, as Konrad Lorenz argued in his famous book, *On Aggression,* published in 1963.

However it may have originated, more generally war was seen as one of the defining marks of humanity: To fight wars meant to be human and apart from nature. This larger presumption was true even of nonscientific theories, such as the biblical concept of an original sin taking humans out of Eden, or the notion that warfare was an idea implanted by aliens, as Arthur C. Clarke imagined in *2001: A Space Odyssey.* In science, in religion, in fiction, violence and humanity were twinned.

The Kahama killings were therefore both a shock and a stimulus to thought. They undermined the explanations for extreme violence in terms of uniquely human attributes, such as culture, brainpower, or the punishment of an angry god. They made credible the idea that our warring tendencies go back into our prehuman past. They made us a little less special.

And yet science has still not grappled closely with the ultimate questions raised by the Kahama killings: Where does human violence come from, and why? Of course, there have been great advances in the way we think about these things. Most importantly, in the 1970s, the same decade as the Kahama killings, a new evolutionary theory emerged, the selfish-gene theory of natural selection, variously called inclusive fitness theory, sociobiology, or more broadly, behavioral ecology. Sweeping through the halls of academe, it revolutionized Darwinian thinking by its insistence that the ultimate explanation of any individual's behavior considers only how the behavior tends to maximize genetic success: to pass that individual's genes into subsequent generations. The new theory, elegantly popularized in Richard Dawkins's *The Selfish Gene,* is now the conventional wisdom in biological science because it explains animal behavior so well. It accounts easily for selfishness, even killing. And it has come to be applied with increasing confidence to human behavior, though the debate is still hot and unsettled. In any case, the general principle that behavior evolves to serve selfish ends has been widely accepted, and the idea that humans might have been favored by natural selection to hate and to kill their enemies has become entirely, if tragically, reasonable.

Those are the general principles, and yet the specifics are lacking. Most animals are nowhere near as violent as humans, so why did such intensely violent behavior evolve particularly in the human line? Why kill the enemy, rather than simply drive him away? Why rape? Why torture and mutilate? Why do we see these patterns both in ourselves and chimpanzees? Those sorts of questions have barely been asked, much less addressed.

Because chimpanzees and humans are each other's closest relatives, such questions carry extraordinary implications, the more so because the study of early human ancestry, unfolding in a fervor as we approach the century's end, is bringing chimpanzees and humans even closer than we ever imagined. Three dramatic recent discoveries speak to the relationship between chimpanzees and humans, and all three point in the same direction: to a past, around 5 million years ago, when chimpanzee ancestors and human ancestors were indistinguishable.

First, fossils recently dug up in Ethiopia indicate that over 4.5 million years ago there walked across African lands a bipedal ancestor of humans with a head strikingly like a chimpanzee's.

Second, laboratories around the world have over the last decade demonstrated chimpanzees to be genetically closer to us than they are even to gorillas, despite the close physical resemblance between chimpanzees and gorillas.

And third, both in the field and in the laboratory, studies of chimpanzee behavior are producing numerous, increasingly clear parallels with human behavior. It's not just that these apes pat each other on the hand to show affection, or kiss each other, or embrace. Not just that they have menopause, develop lifelong friendships, and grieve for their dead babies by carrying them for days or weeks. Nor is it their ability to do sums like 5 plus 4, or to communicate with hand signs. Nor their tool use, or collaboration, or bartering for sexual favors.

Nor even that they hold long-term grudges, deliberately hide their feelings, or bring rivals together to force them to make peace.

No, for us the single most gripping set of facts about chimpanzee behavior is what we have already touched on: the nature of their society. The social world of chimpanzees is a set of individuals who share a communal range; males live forever in the groups where they are born, while females move to neighboring groups at adolescence; and the range is defended, and sometimes extended with aggressive and potentially lethal violence, by groups of males related in a genetically patrilineal kin group.

What makes this social world so extraordinary is comparison. Very few animals live in patrilineal, male-bonded communities wherein females routinely reduce the risks of inbreeding by moving to neighboring groups to mate. And only two animal species are known to do so with a system of intense, male-initiated territorial aggression, including lethal raiding into neighboring communities in search of vulnerable enemies to attack and kill. Out of four thousand mammals and ten million or more other animal species, this suite of behaviors is known only among chimpanzees and humans.

Humans with male-bonded, patrilineal kin groups? Absolutely. *Male bonded* refers to males forming aggressive coalitions with each other in mutual support against others—Hatfields versus McCoys, Montagues versus Capulets, Palestinians versus Israelis, Americans versus Vietcong, Tutsis versus Hutus. Around the world, from the Balkans to the Yanomamö of Venezuela, from Pygmies of Central Africa to the T'ang Dynasty of China, from Australian aborigines to Hawaiian kingdoms, related men routinely fight in defense of their group. This is true even of the villages labeled by anthropologists as "matrilineal" and "matrilocal," where inheritance (from male to male) is figured out according to the mother's line, and where women stay in their natal villages to have children—such villages operate socially as subunits of a larger patrilineal whole. In short, the system of communities defended by related men is a human universal that crosses space and time, so established a pattern that even writers of science fiction rarely think to challenge it.

When it comes to social relationships involving females, chimpanzees and humans are very different. That's unsurprising. Discoveries in animal behavior since the 1960s strongly suggest that animal societies are adapted to their environments in exquisitely detailed ways, and obviously the environments of chimpanzees and humans are a study in contrast. But this just emphasizes our puzzle. Why should male chimpanzees and humans show such similar patterns?

Is it chance? Maybe our human ancestors lived in societies utterly unlike those of chimpanzees. Peaceful matriarchies, for example, somewhat like some of our distant monkey relatives. And then, by a remarkable quirk of evolutionary coincidence, at some time in prehistory human and chimpanzee social behaviors converged on their similar systems for different, unrelated reasons.

Or do they both depend on some other characteristic, like intelligence? Once brains reach a certain level of sophistication, is there some mysterious logic pushing a species toward male coalitionary violence? Perhaps, for instance, only chimpanzees and humans have enough brainpower to realize the advantages of removing the opposition.

Or is there a long-term evolutionary inertia? Perhaps humans have retained an old chimpanzee pattern which, though it was once adaptive, has now acquired a stability and life of its own, resistant even to new environments where other forms of society would be better.

Or are the similarities there, as we believe, because in spite of first appearances, similar evolutionary forces continue to be at work in chimpanzee and human lineages, maintaining and refining a system of intergroup hostility and personal violence that has existed since even before the ancestors of chimpanzees and humans mated for the last time in a drying forest of eastern Africa around 5 million years ago? If so, one must ask, what forces are they? What bred male bonding and lethal raiding in our forebears and keeps it now in chimpanzees and humans? What marks have those ancient evolutionary forces forged onto our twentieth-century psyches? And what do they say about our hopes and fears for the future? . . .

Sexual selection, the evolutionary process that produces sex differences, has a lot to answer for. Without it, males wouldn't possess dangerous bodily weapons and a mindset that sanctions violence. But males who are better fighters can stop other males from mating, and they mate more successfully themselves. Better fighters tend to have more babies. That's the simple, stupid, selfish logic of sexual selection. So, what about us? Is sexual selection ultimately the reason why men brawl in barrooms, form urban gangs, plot guerrilla attacks, and go to war? Has it indeed designed men to be especially aggressive?

Until we have carefully examined the evidence, our answer should be: not necessarily. Because the social, environmental, genetic, and historical circumstances for any single species are so extremely complex, we can't assume a priori that sexual selection has acted in any particular way for any single species. Among the 10 million or more animal species on earth, you can find interesting exceptions to almost every rule. On the one hand, you can find species like spotted hyenas, where such extraordinary ferocity has evolved among females that it outshines even the stark sexual aggression shown by males. And on the other, you will discover the pacifists. . . .

So there is no particular reason to think that human aggression is all cultural, or that our ancestors were as pacific as muriquis [nonaggressive monkeys of South America]. The only way to find out whether sexual selection has shaped human males for aggression is to leave the theory and go back to the evidence. There are two places to look for an answer. We can look at our bodies, and we can think about our minds. The easier part is our bodies.

✦

A biologist from Mars looking at a preserved human male laid out on a slab might find it hard to imagine our species as dangerous. Lined up next to male specimens from the other apes, or from virtually any other mammal species, human males don't look as if they are designed to fight at all. They are rather slender, their bones are light, and they appear to have no bodily weapons.

People don't think of humans in the same way that they think of dangerous animals. That first impression is misleading, however. Humans are indeed designed to fight, although in a different way from most of the other primates.

Here's one clue. Men are a little larger and more heavily muscled than women. For other primate species, larger male size links strongly to male aggression. But with humans, that apparent evidence seems to conflict with the absence of fighting canine teeth. Could it be that humans break the general rule linking larger males to an evolved design for aggression?

Consider our teeth. The upper canines of most primates are longer and sharper than any other tooth. These long teeth are obvious weapons, bright daggers ground to a razor-sharp edge against a special honing surface on a premolar tooth in the lower jaw. Baboons, for example, have canines five to six centimeters long. Male baboons trying to impress each other grind their canines noisily, occasionally showing off their teeth in huge, gaping yawns. When male baboons make those display yawns, they are acting like cowboys twirling their revolvers.

By comparison, human canines seem tiny. They barely extend beyond the other teeth, and in males they are no longer than in females. Those canines may help us bite an apple, we love to imagine them elongated for the Halloween scare, and we unconsciously display them when we sneer, but our canines virtually never help us fight. In fact, the fossil record indicates that ever since the transition from rainforest ape to woodland ape, our ancestors' canines have been markedly smaller than they are in chimpanzees. In the woodlands, those teeth quickly became muriqui-like in appearance—one reason why some people wonder if woodland apes were as pacific as modern muriquis are.

But we should not allow ourselves to become misled by the evidence of canine teeth. The importance of a species' canines depends entirely on how it fights. . . .

Apes can fight with their fists because they have adapted to hanging from their arms, which means that their arms can swing all around their shoulders, the shoulder joint being a flexible multidirectional joint. So chimpanzees and gorillas often hit with their fists when they fight, and they can keep most canine-flashing opponents at bay because their arms are long. If chimpanzees and gorillas find punching effective, then surely the woodland apes, who were standing up high on hind legs, would have fought even better with their arms.

Fists can also grasp invented weapons. Chimpanzees today are close to using hand-held weapons. Throughout the continent, wild chimpanzees will tear off and throw great branches when they are angry or threatened, or they will pick up and throw rocks. Humphrey, when he was the alpha male at Gombe, almost killed me once by sending a melon-size rock whistling less than half a meter from my head. They also hit with big sticks. A celebrated film taken in Guinea shows wild chimpanzees pounding meter-long clubs down on the back of a leopard. (Scientists were able to get that film because the leopard was a stuffed one, placed there by a curious researcher. The chimpanzees were lucky to find a leopard so slow to fight back.) Chimpanzees in West Africa already have a primitive stone tool technology, and there could well be a community of chimpanzees today, waiting to be discovered, who are already using heavy sticks as clubs against each other. Certainly we can reasonably imagine that the woodland apes did some of these things.

... The shoulders of boys and girls are equally broad until adolescence; but at puberty, shoulder cartilage cells respond to testosterone, the male sex hormone newly produced by the testes, by growing. (In an equivalent way, pubertal girls get wider hips when their hip cartilage cells respond to estrogen, the female sex hormone.) The result is a sudden acceleration of shoulder width for boys around the age of fourteen, associated with relative enlargement of the upper arm muscles. In other words, the shoulders and arms of male humans— like the neck muscles of a red deer, the clasping hands of a xenopus frog, or the canine teeth of many other primates—look like the result of sexual selection for fighting. All these examples of male weaponry respond to testosterone by growing. They are specialized features that enlarge for the specific purpose of promoting fighting ability in competition against other males. Small wonder, then, that men show off to each other before fights by hunching their shoulders, expanding their muscles, and otherwise displaying their upper-body strength....

If the bipedal woodland apes fought with fists and sometimes with weapons, those species should have had especially broad shoulders and well-muscled arms, like modern men. We haven't enough fossils yet to know if that's true. Indeed, it is not yet absolutely certain that male woodland apes were larger than females, though most of the current fossil evidence suggests so. If they were, we can confidently imagine that the males were designed for aggression. Perhaps the early development of club-style weapons might also explain why the skulls of our ancestors became strikingly thicker, particularly with *Homo erectus* at 1.6 to 1.8 million years ago. That's a guess, but it's clear in any case that our present bodies carry the same legacy of sexual selection as other mammals whose males fight with their upper bodies. The broad shoulders and powerful, arching torso we so admire in Michelangelo's *David* are the human equivalent of antlers. The mark of Cain appears in our shoulders and arms, not in our teeth.

⋅✦⋅

What about our minds? Has sexual selection shaped our psyches also, in order to make us better fighters? Can sexual selection explain why men are so quick to bristle at insults, and, under the right circumstances, will readily kill? Can our evolutionary past account for modern war?

Inquiry about mental processes is difficult enough when we deal just with humans. Comparison with other species is harder still. The supposed problem is that animals fight with their hearts, so people say, whereas humans fight with their minds. Animal aggression is supposed to happen by instinct, or by emotion, and without reason. Wave a red rag in a bull's face and the bull charges thoughtlessly—that's the model. Human wars, on the other hand, seem to emerge, so Karl von Clausewitz declared, as "the continuation of policy with the admixture of other means." According to historian Michael Howard, human wars "begin with conscious and reasoned decisions based on the calculation, made by both parties, that they can achieve more by going to war than by remaining at peace." The principle seems as true for the measured deliberations on the top floor of the Pentagon as for the whispered councils among the Yanomamö, and it suggests a wholly different set of psychological processes from the supposedly rigid, instinctual, emotional drives of animals. The fact that we possess consciousness and reasoning ability, this theory says, takes us across a chasm into a new world, where the old instincts are no longer important. If there is no connection between these two systems, the rules for each cannot be the same. In other words, aggression based on "conscious and reasoned decisions" can no longer be explained in terms of such evolutionary forces as sexual selection.

The argument sounds fair enough, but it depends on oversimplified thinking, a false distinction between animals acting by emotion (or instinct) and humans acting by reason. Animal behavior is not purely emotional. Nor is human decision-making purely rational. In both cases, the event is a mixture. And new evidence suggests that even though we humans reason much more (analyze past and present context, consider a potential future, and so on) than nonhuman animals, our essential process for making a decision still relies on emotion....

People have always accepted that animals act from emotions; humans ... can never act without them. Suddenly the apparent chasm between the mental processes of chimpanzees and our species is reduced to a comprehensible difference. Humans can reason better, but reason and emotion are linked in parallel ways for both chimpanzees and humans. For both species, emotion sits in the driver's seat, and reason (or calculation) paves the road.

We are now ready to ask what causes aggression. If emotion is the ultimate arbiter of action for both species, then what kinds of emotions underlie violence for both? Clearly there are many. But one stands out. From the raids of chimpanzees at Gombe to wars among human nations, the same emotion looks extraordinarily important, one that we take for granted and describe most simply but that nonetheless takes us deeply back to our animal origins: pride.

Male chimpanzees compete much more aggressively for dominance than females do. If a lower-ranking male refuses to acknowledge his superior with one of the appropriate conventions, such as a soft grunt, the superior will become predictably angry. But females can let such insults pass. Females are certainly capable of being aggressive to each other, and they can be as politically adept as males in using coalitions to achieve a goal. But female chimpanzees act as if they just don't care about their status as much as males do.

By contrast, we exaggerate only barely in saying that a male chimpanzee in his prime organizes his whole life around issues of rank. His attempts to achieve and then maintain alpha status are cunning, persistent, energetic, and time-consuming. They affect whom he travels with, whom he grooms, where he glances, how often he scratches, where he goes, and what time he gets up in the morning....

Eighteenth-century Englishmen used less dramatic tactics than wild chimpanzees, but that acute observer Samuel Johnson thought rank concerns were as pervasive: "No two people can be half an hour together, but one shall acquire an evident superiority over the other." Pride obviously serves as a stimulus for much interpersonal aggression in humans, and we can hypothesize confidently that this emotion evolved during countless generations in which males who achieved high status were able to turn their social success into extra reproduction. Male pride, the source of many a conflict, is reasonably seen as a mental equivalent of broad shoulders. Pride is another legacy of sexual selection....

Our ape ancestors have passed to us a legacy, defined by the power of natural selection and written in the molecular chemistry of DNA. For the most part it is a wonderful inheritance, but one small edge contains destructive elements; and now that we have the weapons of mass destruction, that edge promotes the potential of our own demise. People have long known such things intuitively and so have built civilizations with laws and justice, diplomacy and mediation, ideally keeping always a step ahead of the old demonic principles. And we might hope that men will eventually realize that violence doesn't pay.

The problem is that males are demonic at unconscious and irrational levels. The motivation of a male chimpanzee who challenges another's rank is not that he foresees more matings or better food or a longer life. Those rewards explain why sexual selection has favored the desire for power, but the immediate reason he vies for status is simpler, deeper, and less subject to the vagaries of context. It is simply to dominate his peers. Unconscious of the evolutionary rationale that placed this prideful goal in his temperament, he devises strategies to achieve it that can be complex, original, and maybe conscious. In the same way, the motivation of male chimpanzees on a border patrol is not to gain land or win females. The temperamental goal is to intimidate the opposition, to beat them to a pulp, to erode their ability to challenge. Winning has become an end in itself.

It looks the same with men.

Robert W. Sussman

 **NO**

Exploring Our Basic Human Nature

Are human beings forever doomed to be violent? Is aggression fixed within our genetic code, an inborn action pattern that threatens to destroy us? Or, as asked by Richard Wrangham and Dale Peterson in their recent book, *Demonic Males: Apes and the Origins of Human Violence,* can we get beyond our genes, beyond our essential "human nature"?

Wrangham and Peterson's belief in the importance of violence in the evolution and nature of humans is based on new primate research that they assert demonstrates the continuity of aggression from our great ape ancestors. The authors argue that 20–25 years ago most scholars believed human aggression was unique. Research at that time had shown great apes to be basically non-aggressive gentle creatures. Furthermore, the separation of humans from our ape ancestors was thought to have occurred 15–20 million years ago (Mya). Although Raymond Dart, Sherwood Washburn, Robert Ardrey, E.O. Wilson and others had argued through much of the 20th century that hunting, killing, and extreme aggressive behaviors were biological traits inherited from our earliest hominid hunting ancestors, many anthropologists still believed that patterns of aggression were environmentally determined and culturally learned behaviors, not inherited characteristics.

Demonic Males discusses new evidence that killer instincts are not unique to humans, but rather shared with our nearest relative, the common chimpanzee. The authors argue that it is this inherited propensity for killing that allows hominids and chimps to be such good hunters.

According to Wrangham and Peterson, the split between humans and the common chimpanzee was only 6–8 Mya. Furthermore, humans may have split from the chimpanzee-bonobo line after gorillas, with bonobos *(pygmy chimps)* separating from chimps only 2.5 Mya. Because chimpanzees may be the modern ancestor of all these forms, and because the earliest australopithecines were quite chimpanzee-like, Wrangham speculates (in a separate article) that "chimpanzees are a conservative species and an amazingly good model for the ancestor of hominids" (1995, reprinted in Sussman 1997:106). If modern chimpanzees and modern humans share certain behavioral traits, these traits have "long evolutionary roots" and are likely to be fixed, biologically inherited parts of our basic human nature and not culturally determined.

Wrangham argues that chimpanzees are almost on the brink of human-ness:

> Nut-smashing, root-eating, savannah-using chimpanzees, resembling our ancestors, and capable by the way of extensive bipedalism. Using ant-wands, and sandals, and bowls, meat-sharing, hunting cooperatively. Strange para-dox... a species trembling on the verge of hominization, but so conservative that it has stayed on that edge.... (1997:107).

Wrangham and Peterson (1996:24) claim that only two animal species, chimpanzees and humans, live in patrilineal, male-bonded communities "with intense, male initiated territorial aggression, including lethal raiding into neigh-boring communities in search of vulnerable enemies to attack and kill." Wrang-ham asks:

> Does this mean chimpanzees are naturally violent? Ten years ago it wasn't clear.... In this cultural species, it may turn out that one of the least variable of all chimpanzee behaviors is the intense competition between males, the violent aggression they use against strangers, and their willingness to maim and kill those that frustrate their goals.... As the picture of chimpanzee soci-ety settles into focus, it now includes infanticide, rape and regular battering of females by males (1997:108).

Since humans and chimpanzees share these violent urges, the implication is that human violence has long evolutionary roots. "We are apes of nature, cursed over six million years or more with a rare inheritance, a Dostoyevskyan demon... The coincidence of demonic aggression in ourselves and our closest kin bespeaks its antiquity" (1997: 108–109).

Intellectual Antecedents

From the beginning of Western thought, the theme of human depravity runs deep, related to the idea of humankind's fall from grace and the emergence of original sin. This view continues to pervade modern "scientific" interpretations of the evolution of human behavior. Recognition of the close evolutionary rela-tionship between humans and apes, from the time of Darwin's *Descent of Man* (1874) on, has encouraged theories that look to modern apes for evidence of parallel behaviors reflecting this relationship.

By the early 1950s, large numbers of australopithecine fossils and the dis-covery that the large-brained "fossil" ancestor from Piltdown, in England, was a fraud, led to the realization that our earliest ancestors were more like apes than like modern humans. Accordingly, our earliest ancestors must have behaved much like other non-human primates. This, in turn, led to a great interest in using primate behavior to understand human evolution and the evolutionary basis of human nature. The subdiscipline of primatology was born.

Raymond Dart, discoverer of the first australopithecine fossil some thirty years earlier, was also developing a different view of our earliest ancestors. At first Dart believed that australopithecines were scavengers barely eking out an existence in the harsh savanna environment. But from the fragmented and dam-aged bones found with the australopithecines, together with dents and holes in these early hominid skulls, Dart eventually concluded that this species had used bone, tooth and antler tools to kill, butcher and eat their prey, as well as to kill one another. This hunting hypothesis (Cartmill 1997:511) "was linked from the beginning with a bleak, pessimistic view of human beings and their ancestors as instinctively bloodthirsty and savage." To Dart, the australopithecines were:

> confirmed killers: carnivorous creatures that seized living quarries by violence, battered them to death, tore apart their broken bodies, dismembered them limb from limb, slaking their ravenous thirst with the hot blood of victims and greedily devouring livid writhing flesh (1953:209).

Cartmill, in a recent book (1993), shows that this interpretation of early human morality is reminiscent of earlier Greek and Christian views. Dart's (1953) own treatise begins with a 17th century quote from the Calvinist R. Baxter: "of all the beasts, the man-beast is the worst/ to others and himself the cruellest foe."

Between 1961–1976, Dart's view was picked up and extensively popularized by the playwright Robert Ardrey (*The Territorial Imperative, African Genesis*). Ardrey believed it was the human competitive and killer instinct, acted out in warfare, that made humans what they are today. "It is war and the instinct for territory that has led to the great accomplishments of Western Man. Dreams may have inspired our love of freedom, but only war and weapons have made it ours" (1961: 324).

Man the Hunter

In the 1968 volume *Man the Hunter,* Sherwood Washburn and Chet Lancaster presented a theory of "The evolution of hunting," emphasizing that it is this behavior that shaped human nature and separated early humans from their primate relatives.

> To assert the biological unity of mankind is to affirm the importance of the hunting way of life.... However much conditions and customs may have varied locally, the main selection pressures that forged the species were the same. The biology, psychology and customs that separate us from the apes ... we owe to the hunters of time past ... for those who would understand the origins and nature of human behavior there is no choice but to try to understand "Man the Hunter" (1968:303).

Rather than amassing evidence from modern hunters and gatherers to prove their theory, Washburn and Lancaster (1968:299) use the 19th-century concept of cultural "survivals": behaviors that persist as evidence of an earlier time but are no longer useful in society.

> Men enjoy hunting and killing, and these activities are continued in sports even when they are no longer economically necessary. If a behavior is important to the survival of a species ... then it must be both easily learned and pleasurable (Washburn & Lancaster, p. 299).

Man the Dancer

Using a similar logic for the survival of ancient "learned and pleasurable" behaviors, perhaps it could easily have been our propensity for dancing rather than our desire to hunt that can explain much of human behavior. After all, men and women love to dance; it is a behavior found in all cultures but has even less obvious function today than hunting. Our love of movement and dance might explain, for example, our propensity for face-to-face sex, and even the evolution of bipedalism and the movement of humans out of trees and onto the ground.

Could the first tool have been a stick to beat a dance drum, and the ancient Laetoli footprints evidence of two individuals going out to dance the "Afarensis shuffle"? Although it takes only two to tango, a variety of social interactions and systems might have been encouraged by the complex social dances known in human societies around the globe.

Sociobiology and E.O. Wilson

In the mid-1970s, E.O. Wilson and others described a number of traits as genetically based and therefore human universals, including territoriality, male–female bonds, male dominance over females, and extended maternal care leading to matrilineality. Wilson argued that the genetic basis of these traits was indicated by their relative constancy among our primate relatives and by their persistence throughout human evolution and in human societies. Elsewhere, I have shown that these characteristics are neither general primate traits nor human universals (Sussman 1995). Wilson, however, argued that these were a product of our evolutionary hunting past.

For at least a million years—probably more—Man engaged in a hunting way of life, giving up the practice a mere 10,000 years ago.... Our innate social responses have been fashioned through this life style. With caution, we can compare the most widespread hunter-gatherer qualities with similar behavior displayed by some of the non-human primates that are closely related to Man. Where the same pattern of traits occurs in... most or all of those primates—we can conclude that it has been subject to little evolution. (Wilson 1976, in Sussman 1997: 65–66).

Wilson's theory of sociobiology, the evolution of social behavior, argued that:

1. the goal of living organisms is to pass on one's genes at the expense of all others;
2. an organism should only cooperate with others if:

   (a) they carry some of his/her own genes (kin selection) or
   (b) if at some later date the others might aid you (reciprocal altruism).

To sociobiologists, evolutionary morality is based on an unconscious need to multiply our own genes, to build group cohesion in order to win wars. We should not look down on our warlike, cruel nature but rather understand its success when coupled with "making nice" with *some* other individuals or groups. The genetically driven "making nice" is the basis of human ethics and morality.

> Throughout recorded history the conduct of war has been common... some of the noblest traits of mankind, including team play, altruism, patriotism, bravery... and so forth are the genetic product of warfare (Wilson 1975:572–3).

The evidence for any of these universals or for the tenets of sociobiology is as weak as was the evidence for Dart's, Ardrey's and Washburn and Lancaster's theories of innate aggression. Not only are modern gatherer-hunters and most apes remarkably non-aggressive, but in the 1970s and 1980s studies of fossil bones and artifacts have shown that early humans were not hunters, and that weapons were a later addition to the human repertoire. In fact, C.K. Brain (1981) showed that the holes and dents in Dart's australopithecine skulls matched perfectly with fangs of leopards or with impressions of rocks pressing against the buried fossils. Australopithecines apparently were the hunted, not the hunters (Cartmill, 1993, 1997).

Beyond Our Genes

Wrangham and Peterson's book goes beyond the assertion of human inborn aggression and propensity towards violence. The authors ask the critical question: Are we doomed to be violent forever because this pattern is fixed within our genetic code or can we go beyond our past?—get out of our genes, so to speak.

The authors believe that we can look to the bonobo or pygmy chimpanzee as one potential savior, metaphorically speaking.

Bonobos, although even more closely related to the common chimpanzee than humans, have become a peace-loving, love-making alternative to chimpanzee-human violence. How did this happen? In chimpanzees and humans, females of the species select partners that are violent... "while men have evolved to be demonic males, it seems likely that women have evolved to prefer demonic males... as long as demonic males are the most successful reproducers, any female who mates with them is provided with sons who themselves will likely be good reproducers" (Wrangham and Peterson 1996:239). However, among pygmy chimpanzees females form alliances and have chosen to mate with less aggressive males. So, after all, it is not violent males that have caused humans and chimpanzees to be their inborn, immoral, dehumanized selves, it is rather, poor choices by human and chimpanzee females.

Like Dart, Washburn, and Wilson before them, Wrangham and Peterson believe that killing and violence is inherited from our ancient relatives of the past. However, unlike these earlier theorists, Wrangham and Peterson argue this is not a trait unique to hominids, nor is it a by-product of hunting. In fact, it is just this violent nature and a natural "blood lust" that makes both humans and chimpanzees such good hunters. It is the bonobos that help the authors come to this conclusion. Because bonobos have lost the desire to kill, they also have lost the desire to hunt.

> ... do bonobos tell us that the suppression of personal violence carried with it the suppression of predatory aggression? The strongest hypothesis at the moment is that bonobos came from a chimpanzee-like ancestor that hunted monkeys and hunted one another. As they evolved into bonobos, males lost their demonism, becoming less aggressive to each other. In so doing they lost their lust for hunting monkeys, too... Murder and hunting may be more closely tied together than we are used to thinking (Wrangham and Peterson 1996:219).

The Selfish Gene Theory

Like Ardrey, Wrangham and Peterson believe that blood lust ties killing and hunting tightly together but it is the killing that drives hunting in the latter's argument. This lust to kill is based upon the sociobiological tenet of the selfish gene. "The general principle that behavior evolves to serve selfish ends has been widely accepted; and the idea that humans might have been favored by natural selection to hate and to kill their enemies has become entirely, if tragically, reasonable" (Wrangham and Peterson 1996:23).

As with many of the new sociobiological or evolutionary anthropology theories, I find problems with both the theory itself and with the evidence used to support it. Two arguments that humans and chimpanzees share biologically fixed behaviors are: (1) they are more closely related to each other than chimpanzees are to gorillas; (2) chimpanzees are a good model for our earliest ancestor and retain conservative traits that should be shared by both.

The first of these statements is still hotly debated and, using various genetic evidence, the chimp-gorilla-human triage is so close that it is difficult to tell exact divergence time or pattern among the three. The second statement is just not true. Chimpanzees have been evolving for as long as humans and gorillas, and there is no reason to believe ancestral chimps were similar to present-day chimps. The fossil evidence for the last 5–8 million years is extremely sparse, and it is likely that many forms of apes have become extinct just as have many hominids.

Furthermore, even if the chimpanzee were a good model for the ancestral hominid, and was a conservative representative of this phylogenetic group, this would not mean that humans would necessarily share specific behavioral traits. As even Wrangham and Peterson emphasize, chimps, gorillas, and bonobos all behave very differently from one another in their social behavior and in their willingness to kill conspecifics.

Evidence Against "Demonic Males"

The proof of the "Demonic Male" theory does not rest on any theoretical grounds but must rest solely on the evidence that violence and killing in chimpanzees and in humans are behaviors that are similar in pattern; have ancient, shared evolutionary roots; and are inherited. Besides killing of conspecifics,

Wrangham "includes infanticide, rape, and regular battering of females by males" as a part of this inherited legacy of violent behaviors shared by humans and chimpanzees (1997:108).

Wrangham and Peterson state: "That chimpanzees and humans kill members of neighboring groups of their own species is... a startling exception to the normal rule for animals" (1996:63). "Fighting adults of almost all species normally stop at winning: They don't go on to kill" (1996:155). However, as Wrangham points out there are exceptions, such as lions, wolves, spotted hyenas, and I would add a number of other predators. In fact, most species do not have the weapons to kill one another as adults.

Just how common is conspecific killing in chimpanzees? This is where the real controversy may lie. Jane Goodall described the chimpanzee as a peaceful, non-aggressive species during the first 24 years of study at Gombe (1950–1974). During one year of concentrated study, Goodall observed 284 agonistic encounters: of these 66% were due to competition for introduced bananas, and only 34% "could be regarded as attacks occurring in 'normal' aggressive contexts" (1968:278). Only 10 percent of the 284 attacks were classified as 'violent', and "even attacks that appeared punishing to me often resulted in no discernable injury.... Other attacks consisted merely of brief pounding, hitting or rolling of the individual, after which the aggressor often touched or embraced the other immediately (1968:277).

Chimpanzee aggression before 1974 was considered no different from patterns of aggression seen in many other primate species. In fact, Goodall explains in her 1986 monograph, *The Chimpanzees of Gombe,* that she uses data mainly from after 1975 because the earlier years present a "very different picture of the Gombe chimpanzees" as being "far more peaceable than humans" (1986:3). Other early naturalists' descriptions of chimpanzee behavior were consistent with those of Goodall and confirmed her observations. Even different communities were observed to come together with peaceful, ritualized displays of greeting (Reynolds and Reynolds 1965; Suguyama 1972; Goodall 1968).

Then, between 1974 and 1977, five adult males from one subgroup were attacked and disappeared from the area, presumably dead. Why after 24 years did the patterns of aggression change? Was it because the stronger group saw the weakness of the other and decided to improve their genetic fitness? But surely there were stronger and weaker animals and subgroups before this time. Perhaps we can look to Goodall's own perturbations for an answer. In 1965, Goodall began to provide "restrictive human-controlled feeding." A few years later she realized that

> the constant feeding was having a marked effect on the behavior of the chimps. They were beginning to move about in large groups more often than they had ever done in the old days. Worst of all, the adult males were becoming increasingly aggressive. When we first offered the chimps bananas the males seldom fought over their food;.... now... there was a great deal more fighting than ever before.... (Goodall 1971:143).

The possibility that human interference was a main cause of the unusual behavior of the Gombe chimps was the subject of an excellent, but generally ignored book by Margaret Power (1991). Wrangham and Peterson (1996:19) footnote this book, but as with many other controversies, they essentially ignore its findings, stating that yes, chimpanzee violence might have been unnatural behavior if it weren't for the evidence of similar behavior occurring since 1977 and "elsewhere in Africa" (1996:19).

Further Evidence

What is this evidence from elsewhere in Africa? Wrangham and Peterson provide only four brief examples, none of which is very convincing:

(1) Between 1979–1982, the Gombe group extended its range to the south and conflict with a southern group, Kalande, was suspected. In 1982, a "raiding" party of males reached Goodall's camp. The authors state: "Some of these raids may have been lethal" (1996:19). However, Goodall describes this "raid" as follows: One female "was chased by a Kalande male and mildly attacked. . . . Her four-year-old son . . . encountered a second male—but was only sniffed" (1986:516). Although Wrangham and Peterson imply that these encounters were similar to those between 1974–77, no violence was actually witnessed. The authors also refer to the discovery of the dead body of Humphrey; what they do not mention is Humphrey's age of 35 and that wild chimps rarely live past 33 years!

(2) From 1970 to 1982, six adult males from one community in the Japanese study site of Mahale disappeared, one by one over this 12 year period. None of the animals were observed being attacked or killed, and one was sighted later roaming as a solitary male (Nishida et al., 1985:287–289).

(3) In another site in West Africa, Wrangham and Peterson report that Boesch and Boesch believe "that violent aggression among the chimpanzees is as important as it is in Gombe" (1986:20). However, in the paper referred to, the Boesches simply state that encounters by neighboring chimpanzee communities are more common in their site than in Gombe (one per month vs. 1 every 4 months). There is no mention of violence during these encounters.

(4) At a site that Wrangham began studying in 1984, an adult male was found dead in 1991. Wrangham states: "In the second week of August, Ruizoni was killed. No human saw the big fight" (Wrangham & Peterson 1996:20). Wrangham gives us no indication of what has occurred at this site over the last 6 years.

In fact, this is the total amount of evidence of warfare and male-male killing among chimpanzees after 37 years of research!! The data for infanticide and rape among chimpanzees is even less impressive. In fact, data are so sparse for these behaviors among chimps that Wrangham and Peterson are forced to use examples from the other great apes, gorillas and orangutans. However, just as for killing among chimpanzees, both the evidence and the interpretations are suspect and controversial.

Can We Escape Our Genes?

What if Wrangham and Peterson are correct and we and our chimp cousins are inherently sinners? Are we doomed to be violent forever because this pattern is fixed within our genetic code?

After 5 million years of human evolution and 120,000 or so years of *Homo sapiens* existence, is there a way to rid ourselves of our inborn evils?

> What does it do for us, then, to know the behavior of our closest relatives? Chimpanzees and bonobos are an extraordinary pair. One, I suggest shows us some of the worst aspects of our past and our present; the other shows an escape from it.... Denial of our demons won't make them go away. But even if we're driven to accepting the evidence of a grisly past, we're not forced into thinking it condemns us to an unchanged future (Wrangham 1997:110).

In other words, we can learn how to behave by watching bonobos. But, if we can change our inherited behavior so simply, why haven't we been able to do this before *Demonic Males* enlightened us? Surely, there are variations in the amounts of violence in different human cultures and individuals. If we have the capacity and plasticity to change by learning from example, then our behavior is determined by socialization practices and by our cultural histories and not by our nature! This is true whether the examples come from benevolent bonobos or conscientious objectors.

Conclusion

The theory presented by Wrangham and Peterson, although it also includes chimpanzees as our murdering cousins, is very similar to "man the hunter" theories proposed in the past. It also does not differ greatly from early European and Christian beliefs about human ethics and morality. We are forced to ask:

Are these theories generated by good scientific fact, or are they just "good to think" because they reflect, reinforce, and reiterate our traditional cultural beliefs, our morality and our ethics? Is the theory generated by the data, or are the data manipulated to fit preconceived notions of human morality and ethics?

Since the data in support of these theories have been weak, and yet the stories created have been extremely similar, I am forced to believe that "Man the Hunter" is a myth, that humans are not necessarily prone to violence and aggression, but that this belief will continue to reappear in future writings on human nature. Meanwhile, primatologists must continue their field research, marshaling the actual evidence needed to answer many of the questions raised in Wrangham and Peterson's volume.

References

Ardrey, Robert. 1961. *African Genesis: A Personal Investigation into Animal Origins and Nature of Man.* Atheneum.
_____. *The Territorial Imperative.* Atheneum, 1966.

Brain, C.K. 1981. *The Hunted or the Hunter? An Introduction to African Cave Taphonomy.* Univ. of Chicago.

Dart, Raymond. 1953. "The Predatory Transition from Ape to Man." *International Anthropological and Linguistic Review* 1:201–217.

Darwin, Charles. 1874. *The Descent of Man and Selection in Relation to Sex.* 2nd ed. The Henneberry Co.

Cartmill, Matt 1997. "Hunting Hypothesis of Human Origins." In *History of Physical Anthropology: An Encyclopedia,* ed. F. Spencer, pp. 508–512. Garland.

———. 1993. *A View to a Death in the Morning: Hunting and Nature Through History.* Harvard Univ.

Goodall, Jane. 1986. *The Chimpanzees of Gombe: Patterns of Behavior.* Belknap.

———. 1971. *In the Shadow of Man.* Houghton Mifflin.

Goodall, Jane. 1968. "The Behavior of Free-Living Chimpanzees in the Gombe Stream Reserve." *Animal Behavior Monographs* 1:165–311.

Nishida, T., Hiraiwa-Hasegawa, M., and Takahtat, Y. "Group Extinction and Female Transfer in Wild Chimpanzees in the Mahali Nation Park, Tanzania." *Zeitschrift für Tierpsychologie* 67:281–301.

Power, Margaret. 1991. *The Egalitarian Human and Chimpanzee: An Anthropological View of Social Organization.* Cambridge University.

Reynolds, V. and Reynolds, F. 1965. "Chimpanzees of Budongo Forest." In *Primate Behavior: Field Studies of Monkeys and Apes,* ed. I. DeVore, pp. 368–424. Holt, Rinehart, and Winston.

Suguyama, Y. 1972. "Social Characteristics and Socialization of Wild Chimpanzees." In *Primate Socialization,* ed. F.E. Poirier, pp. 145–163. Random House.

Sussman, R.W., ed. 1997. *The Biological Basis of Human Behavior.* Simon and Schuster.

Sussman, R.W. 1995. "The Nature of Human Universals." *Reviews in Anthropology* 24:1–11.

Washburn, S.L. and Lancaster, C. K. 1968. "The Evolution of Hunting." In *Man the Hunter,* eds. R. B. Lee and I. DeVore, pp. 293–303. Aldine.

Wilson, E. O. 1997. "Sociobiology: A New Approach to Understanding the Basis of Human Nature." *New Scientist* 70(1976):342–345. (Reprinted in R.W. Sussman, 1997.)

———. 1975. Sociobiology: *The New Synthesis.* Cambridge: Harvard University.

Wrangham, R.W. 1995. "Ape, Culture, and Missing Links." *Symbols* (Spring):2–9, 20. (Reprinted in R. W. Sussman, 1997.)

Wrangham, Richard and Peterson, Dale. 1996. *Demonic Males: Apes and the Origins of Human Violence.* Houghton Mifflin.

POSTSCRIPT

Are Humans Inherently Violent?

Wrangham and Peterson's argument that human males have an innate tendency toward aggressive behavior is a classic sociobiological explanation. Sociobiological explanations consist of two basic claims: (1) that all human behavior is ultimately driven by instincts, and (2) that those instincts result from natural selection favoring the behaviors they cause. Sociobiology, which has become very popular in recent years, began in biology and ethology (the study of animal behavior) and spread to the social sciences, including psychology, where it is called "evolutionary psychology." Its popularity is probably due to its attempt to explain many confusing variations in behavior by using a few simple, scientific principles. Any human social behavior—from selfishness to altruism—can be explained by sociobiology. It's all in the genes. Why are human males aggressive? Sociobiology would say it is because natural selection favored our more aggressive ancestors, allowing them to have more children than less aggressive individuals, thus ensuring that the tendency for male aggression increased in our species.

To learn more about sociobiology in general, the best starting point is probably E. O. Wilson's seminal book *Sociobiology: The New Synthesis* (Harvard University Press, 1975). Works explaining the human propensity for violence in terms of instincts include—besides Wrangham and Peterson's book *Demonic Males* (Houghton Mifflin, 1996)—Konrad Lorenz's classic book *On Aggression* (Harcourt, Brace & World, 1967); Martin Daly and Margo Wilson's book *Homicide* (A de Gruyter, 1988); and Michael Ghiglieri's book *The Dark Side of Man: Tracing the Origins of Male Violence* (Perseus Books, 1999). Carrying sociobiological reasoning a step further, Randy Thornhill and Craig T. Palmer argue in their book *A Natural History of Rape: Biological Bases of Sexual Coercion* (MIT Press, 2000) that human males have an instinct for rape because in the evolution of hominids rape was an effective way for males to pass on their genes.

Sussman's argument that human violence is basically a product of social and cultural conditions comes from the tradition of cultural anthropology. He challenges Wrangham and Peterson's assumptions that human behaviors are driven by instincts. Sussman says that the behaviors that Wrangham and Peterson, following E. O. Wilson, attribute to instinct, such as territoriality and male dominance over females, are not in fact universal among humans and lower primates. He also rejects Wrangham and Peterson's contention that an instinct exists if a behavior is universal to the human species, is easy to learn, and is pleasurable to perform. By these criteria, Sussman says, dancing must also be caused by an instinct to dance. Presumably a long list of similar activities, such as playing games and telling jokes, must also have their governing instincts. Sussman also rejects Wrangham and Peterson's contention that aggressive males would have been favored by natural (sexual) selection during hominid evolution. If this were so, he implies, why aren't all males equally aggressive today? How could the genes for nonaggressive behavior have survived countless generations of selection against them? Further, Sussman ridicules the notion that female hominids (or chimpanzees) would deliberately select aggressive males to father their offspring.

Important works challenging the sociobiological explanation of human violence include Ashley Montagu's book *The Nature of Human Aggression* (Oxford University Press, 1976); Richard Lewontin, Leon Kamin, and Stephen Rose's book *Not in Our Genes: Biology, Ideology, and Human Nature* (Pantheon Books, 1984); Kenneth Bock's book *Human Nature and History: A Response to Sociobiology* (Columbia University Press, 1980); and Matt Cartmill's book *A View to a Death in the Morning: Hunting and Nature through History* (Harvard University Press, 1993). For descriptions and analyses of societies in which aggression is minimized, see Leslie E. Sponsel and Thomas A. Gregor's edited volume *The Anthropology of Peace and Nonviolence* (L. Rienner, 1994) and Signe Howell and Roy Willis's volume *Societies at Peace: Anthropological Perspectives* (Routledge, 1989).

ISSUE 5

Can Apes Learn Language?

YES: E. S. Savage-Rumbaugh, from "Language Training of Apes," in Steve Jones, Robert Martin, and David Pilbeam, eds., *The Cambridge Encyclopedia of Human Evolution* (Cambridge University Press, 1999)

NO: Joel Wallman, from *Aping Language* (Cambridge University Press, 1992)

ISSUE SUMMARY

YES: Psychologist and primate specialist E. S. Savage-Rumbaugh argues that, since the 1960s, attempts to teach chimpanzees and other apes symbol systems similar to human language have resulted in the demonstration of a genuine ability to create new symbolic patterns.

NO: Linguist Joel Wallman counters that attempts to teach chimps and other apes sign language or other symbolic systems have demonstrated that apes are very intelligent animals, but up to now these attempts have not shown that apes have any innate capacity for language.

For more than a century anthropologists have generally assumed that humankind's ability to make tools and use language are two characteristics that distinguish humans from other animals. In the 1960s and 1970s Jane Goodall and other primatologists convincingly demonstrated that chimpanzees, our nearest biological relatives, made simple tools, thus narrowing the gap between apes and humans. Beginning in the 1940s a series of other scientists have worked with gorillas, chimps, and most recently the bonobo (or pygmy chimp), attempting to teach these apes simple forms of human-like language.

In the 1950s psychologist B. F. Skinner argued that human children learn natural language through conditioning, such that positive responses to utterances from proud parents and other adults essentially train children to recognize both grammatical patterns and vocabulary. But in the 1960s linguist Noam Chomsky disproved Skinner's theory, showing that human language is so highly complex that it must require some innate biological capability, which he called a "language acquisition device." In several respects, all of the ape-language experiments since then have sought to understand when this biological capacity for language learning evolved in primates.

The early years of the ape-language projects encountered one major difficulty. Try as they might, trainers could not get apes to vocalize human words reliably. This difficulty was a consequence of the fact that a chimp's vocal apparatus simply does not allow the possibility of human utterances.

Since Chomsky's studies of human language, linguists have generally accepted that the manipulation of symbols in systematic grammatical ways, rather than the ability to make utterances, is the most important and complex aspect of human language. Thus, if apes could manipulate symbols in linguistic ways, researchers hoped they could demonstrate that the ability to acquire language is a biological trait shared by at least certain species of the apes and humans.

If true, the ability to learn and use language, the last barrier that separates human beings from our nonhuman primate relatives, has fallen away. This view has its supporters and detractors, many of whom—largely on political or religious grounds—would either like to see humans as just another of the great apes or would prefer to view human beings as unique in the animal kingdom. But at issue is whether or not the long series of ape-language projects has demonstrated that apes can learn to manipulate signs and symbols.

E. S. Savage-Rumbaugh and her husband Duane Rumbaugh have been among the most innovative researchers in their field at the intersection of anthropology, linguistics, and cognitive psychology. They argue that of all the great apes a certain species of pygmy chimps, the bonobo, is biologically closest to *Homo sapiens*. Their recent work with a bonobo named Kanzi has been among the most successful of these ape-language projects. After tracing the history of these projects, Savage-Rumbaugh concludes that Kanzi's ability to use symbols closely resembles similar abilities observed among young human children.

Joel Wallman interprets the evidence very differently from Savage-Rumbaugh. He acknowledges that the various gorillas, chimps, and bonobos are clever animals, which have learned to respond to their trainers. But he argues that these animals have not learned anything resembling human language. However, chimps and bonobos are clever animals, and while they do not have full linguistic abilities, their abilities to use mental abstractions suggest that at least modest versions of these mental processes arose before our branch of the hominoid lineage split off from the lineage of the great apes.

These selections raise a number of questions about the similarities and differences between apes and humans. What kind of linguistic ability do these ape learners exhibit? Do their symbolic strings genuinely parallel early childhood language acquisition? Most importantly, do these ape-language studies show that apes and human beings genuinely share a common ability for language? What are the minimal features that make up any natural language?

E. S. Savage-Rumbaugh

 **YES**

Language Training of Apes

Can apes learn to communicate with human beings? Scientists have been attempting to answer this question since the late 1960s when it was first reported that a young chimpanzee named Washoe in Reno, Nevada had been taught to produce hand signs similar to those used by deaf humans.

Washoe was reared much like a human child. People made signs to her throughout the day and she was given freedom to move about the caravan where she lived. She could even go outdoors to play. She was taught how to make different signs by teachers who moved her hands through the motions of each sign while showing her the object she was learning to 'name'. If she began to make a portion of the hand movement on her own she was quickly rewarded, either with food or with something appropriate to the sign. For example, if she was being taught the sign for 'tickle' her reward was a tickling game.

This training method was termed 'moulding' because it involved the physical placement of Washoe's hands. Little by little, Washoe became able to produce more and more signs on her own. As she grew older, she occasionally even learned to make new signs without moulding. Once Washoe had learned several signs she quickly began to link them together to produce strings of signs such as 'you me out'. Such sequences appeared to her teachers to be simple sentences.

Many biologists were sceptical of the claims made for Washoe. While they agreed that Washoe was able to produce different gestures, they doubted that such signs really served as names. Perhaps, to Washoe, the gestures were just tricks to be used to get the experimenter to give her things she wanted; even though Washoe knew how and when to make signs, she really did not know what words meant in the sense that people do.

The disagreement was more than a scholarly debate among scientists. Decades of previous work had demonstrated that many animals could learn to do complex things to obtain food, without understanding what they were doing. For example, pigeons had been taught to bat a ball back and forth in what looked like a game of ping pong. They were also taught to peck keys with such words as 'Please', 'Thank you', 'Red' and 'Green' printed on them. They did this in a way that made it appear that they were communicating, but they

From E. S. Savage-Rumbaugh, "Language Training of Apes," in Steve Jones, Robert Martin, and David Pilbeam, eds., *The Cambridge Encyclopedia of Human Evolution* (Cambridge University Press, 1999). Copyright © 1999 by Cambridge University Press. Reprinted by permission.

were not; they had simply learned to peck each key when a special signal was given.

This type of learning is called *conditioned discrimination* learning, a term that simply means that an animal can learn to make one set of responses in one group of circumstances and another in different circumstances. Although some aspects of human language can be explained in this way, such as 'Hello', 'Goodbye', 'Please' and 'Thank you', most cannot. Human beings learn more than what to say when: they learn what words stand for.

If Washoe had simply signed 'drink' when someone held up a bottle of soda, there would be little reason to conclude that she was doing anything different from other animals. If, however, Washoe used the sign 'drink' to represent any liquid beverage, then she was doing something very different— something that everyone had previously thought only humans could do.

It was difficult to determine which of these possibilities charcterised her behaviour, as the question of how to distinguish between the 'conditioned response' and a 'word' had not arisen. Before Washoe, the only organisms that used words were human beings, and to determine if a person knew what a word stood for was easy: one simply asked. This was impossible with Washoe, because her use of symbols was not advanced enough to allow her to comprehend complex questions. One- and two-year-old children are also unable to answer questions such as these. However, because children are able to answer such questions later on, the issue of determining how and when a child knows that words have meanings had not until then been seen as critical.

Teaching Syntax

Several scientists attempted to solve this problem by focusing on sentences instead of words. Linguists argue that the essence of human language lies not in learning to use individual words, but rather in an ability to form a large number of word combinations that follow the same set of specific rules. These rules are seen as a genetic endowment unique to humans. If it could be shown that apes learn syntactical rules, then it must be true that they were using symbols to represent things, not just perform tricks.

Three psychologists in the 1970s each used a different method in an attempt to teach apes syntax. One group followed the method used with Washoe and began teaching another chimpanzee, Nim, sign language. Another opted for the use of plastic symbols with the chimpanzee Sarah. Still another used geometric symbols, linked to a computer keyboard, with a chimpanzee named Lana. Both Lana and Sarah were taught a simple syntax, which required them to fill in one blank at a time in a string of words. The number of blanks was slowly increased until the chimpanzee was forming a complete 'sentence'. Nim was asked to produce syntactically correct strings by making signs along with his teacher.

Without help from his teachers, Nim was unable to form sentences that displayed the kind of syntactical rules used by humans. Nim's sign usage could best be interpreted as a series of 'conditioned discriminations' similar to, albeit more complex than, behaviours seen in many less-intelligent animals. This work suggested that Nim, like circus animals but unlike human children, was using words only to obtain rewards.

However, the other attempts to teach sentences to apes arrived at a different conclusion, perhaps because a different training method was used. Both Sarah and Lana learned to fill in the blanks in sentences in ways that suggested they had learned the rules that govern simple sentence construction. Moreover, 6 per cent of Lana's sentences were 'novel' in that they differed from the ones that she had been taught. Many of these sentences, such as 'Please you move coke in cup into room', followed syntactical rules and were appropriate and meaningful communications. Other sentences followed the syntactical rules that Lana had learned, but did not make sense; for example, 'Question you give beancake shut-open'. Thus, apes appeared to be able to learn rules for sentence construction, but they did not generalise these rules in a way that suggested full comprehension of the words.

By 1980, Washoe had matured and given birth. At this time there was great interest in whether or not she would teach her offspring to sign. Unfortunately, her infant died. However, another infant was obtained and given to Washoe. This infant, Loulis, began to imitate many of the hand gestures that Washoe used, though the imitations were often quite imprecise. Washoe made few explicit attempts to mould Loulis's hands. Although Loulis began to make signs, it was not easy to determine why he was making them or what, if anything, he meant. Loulis has not yet received any tests like those that were given to Washoe to determine if he can make the correct sign when shown an object. It is clear that he learned to imitate Washoe, but it is not clear that he learned what the signs meant.

The question of whether or not apes understand words caused many developmental psychologists to study earlier and earlier aspects of language acquisition in children. Their work gave, for the first time, a detailed insight into how children use words during the 'one-word' stage of language learning and showed that children usually learn to understand words before they begin to use them. At the same time, there was a new approach to the investigation of ape language. Instead of teaching names by pairing an object with its sign or symbol and rewarding correct responses, there was a new emphasis on the communicative aspect of symbols. For example, to teach a symbol such as 'key', a desirable item was locked in a box that was given to the chimpanzee. When the chimpanzee failed to open it, he was shown how to ask for and how to use a key. On other occasions, the chimpanzee was asked to retrieve a key for the teacher, so that she might open the box.

This new approach was first used with two chimpanzees named Sherman and Austin. It resulted in a clearer symbolic use of words than that found in animals trained by other methods. In addition, because these chimpanzees were taught comprehension skills, they were able to communicate with one another and not just with the experimenters. Sherman and Austin could use their symbols to tell each other things that could not be conveyed by simple glances or by pointing. For example, they could describe foods they had seen in another room, or the types of tools they needed to solve a problem. Although other apes had been reported to sign in each other's presence, there was no evidence that they were intentionally signing to each other or that they responded to each other's signs.

Most important, Sherman and Austin began to show an aspect of symbol usage that they had not been taught; they used symbols to say what they were going to do *before* they did it. Symbol use by other apes had not included descriptions of intended actions; rather, communications had been begun by a teacher, or limited to simple requests.

Sherman and Austin also began to use symbols to share information about objects that were not present and they passed a particularly demanding test, which required them to look at symbols and answer questions that could be answered only if they knew what each symbol represented. For example, they could look at printed lexigram symbol such as 'key', 'lever', 'stick', 'wrench', 'apple', 'banana', 'pineapple' and 'juice', and state whether each lexigram belonged to the class of 'food' words or 'tool' words. They could do this without ever being told whether these lexigram symbols should be classified as foods or tools. These findings were important, because they revealed that by using symbols an ape can describe what it is about to do.

How Similar Is Ape Language to Human Language?

Even though it was generally agreed that apes could do something far more complex than most other animals, there still remained much disagreement as to whether ape's symbols were identical to human symbols. This uncertainty arose for two reasons: apes did not acquire words in the same manner as children —that is, by observing others use them; and apes did not appear to use true syntactical rules to construct multiple-word utterances.

The first of these differences between ape and child has recently been challenged by a young pygmy chimpanzee or bonobo named Kanzi. Most previous studies had focused on common chimpanzees because pygmy chimpanzees are very rare (they are in great danger of having their habitat destroyed in the coming decade and have no protected parks).

In contrast to other apes, Kanzi learned symbols simply by observing human beings point to them while speaking to him. He did not need to have his arms placed in position, or to be rewarded for using a correct symbol. More important, he did not need to be taught to comprehend symbols or taught that symbols could be used for absent objects as well as those present. Kanzi spontaneously used symbols to announce his actions or intentions and, if his meaning was ambiguous, he often invented gestures to clarify it, as young children do.

Kanzi learned words by listening to speech. He first comprehended certain spoken words, then learned to read the lexigram symbols. This was possible because his caretakers pointed to these symbols as they spoke. For example, Kanzi learned 'strawberries' as he heard people mention the word when they ran across wild strawberries growing in the woods. He soon became able to lead people to strawberries whenever they asked him to do so. He similarly learned the spoken names of many other foods that grew outdoors, such as wild grapes, honeysuckle, privet berries, blackberries and mushrooms, and could take people to any of these foods upon spoken request.

Unlike previous apes reared as human children, Kanzi was reared in a semi-natural woodland. Although he could not produce speech, he understood much of what was said to him. He could appropriately carry out novel spoken requests such as 'Will you take some hamburger to Austin?', 'Can you show your new toy to Kelly?' and 'Would you give Panzee some of your melon?'. There appeared to be no limit to the number of sentences that Kanzi could understand as long as the words in the sentences were in his vocabulary.

During the first 3 or 4 years of his life, Kanzi's comprehension of spoken sentences was limited to things that he heard often. However, when he was 5 years old, he began to respond to novel sentences upon first hearing them. For example, the first time he heard someone talk about throwing a ball in the river, he suddenly turned and threw his ball right in the water, even though he had never done this before. Similarly, when someone suggested, for fun, that he might then try to throw a potato at a turtle that was nearby, he found a potato and tossed it at the turtle. To be certain that Kanzi was not being somehow 'cued' inadvertently by people, he was tested with headphones. In this test he had to listen to a word and point to a picture of the word that he heard. Kanzi did this easily, the first time he took the test.

About this time, Kanzi also began to combine symbols. Unlike other apes, he did not combine symbols ungrammatically to get the experimenter to give something that was purposefully being held back. Kanzi's combinations had a primitive English word order and conveyed novel information. For example, he formed utterances such as 'Ball go group room' to say that he wanted to play with a specific ball—the one he had seen in the group room on the previous day. Because the experimenter was not attempting to get Kanzi to say this, and was indeed far from the group room, such a sentence conveyed something that only Kanzi—not the experimenter—knew before Kanzi spoke.

Thus Kanzi's combinations differed from those of other apes in that they often referred to things or events that were absent and were known only to Kanzi, they contained a primitive grammar and were not imitations of the experimenter. Nor did the experimenter ask rhetorical questions such as 'What is this?' to elicit them, Kanzi's combinations include sentences such as 'Tickle bite', 'Keep-way balloon' and 'Coke chase'. As almost nothing is yet known of how pygmy chimpanzees communicate, they could use a form of simple language in the wild. Kanzi understands spoken English words, so the ability that is reflected in language comprehension is probably an older evolutionary adaptation than is the ability to talk.

Studying ape language presents a serious challenge to the long-held view that only humans can talk and think. Certainly, there is now no doubt that apes communicate in much more complex and abstract ways than dogs, cats and other familiar animals. Similarly, apes that have learned some language skills are also able to do some remarkable non-linguistic tasks. For example, they can recognise themselves on television and even determine whether an image is taped or live. They can also play video games, using a joystick to catch and trap a video villain.

Scientists have only just begun to discover ways of tapping the hidden talents for language and communication of our closest relatives. Sharing 98 per cent of their DNA with human beings, it has long been wondered why African apes seem so much like us at a biological level, but so different when it comes to behaviour. Ape-language studies continue to reveal that apes are more like us than we ever imagined.

Joel Wallman

 **NO**

Aping Language

Experiments carried out over the past two decades... attempted to impart a language, either natural or invented, to an ape. The debate engendered by these projects has been of interest—consuming for some, passing for others—to all of those whose concerns include the enduring questions of human nature, among them anthropologists, psychologists, linguists, biologists, and philosophers.

An adequate treatment of the linguistic capabilities of apes entails consideration of a number of related issues, each of which is an interesting problem in its own right. Continuities in primate mentality, the relationship between language and thought in the individual and in the species, and the origin of language... are themes that... recur throughout this [debate].

... [N]one of the ape-language projects succeeded, despite employing years of tutelage far more intense than that experienced by most children, in implanting in an ape a capacity for language equal to that of a young child, let alone an adult....

Why the Ape-Language Controversy Is a Controversy

All scientific arguments have in common at least these elements: (1) a minimum of two positions regarding the subject in dispute, positions generally held to be irreconcilable, and (2) an intensification of the normal emotional investment of the scientist in his or her position, due in some measure to the contending itself but perhaps also related to the ideological significance of the subject within the larger society. If, in addition, the argument includes suggestions of fraudulent or quasi-fraudulent procedures, the disagreement becomes a controversy. To the extent that this is an accurate characterization of scientific controversies, the ape-language debate is an exemplary one.

The radical opposition of opinion about the achievement of the various ape-language projects is well conveyed by the following quotations:

> [Washoe] learned a natural human language and her early utterances were highly similar to, perhaps indistinguishable from, the early utterances of human children. (Gardner and Gardner 1978, p. 73)

The evidence we have makes it clear that even the brightest ape can acquire not even so much as the weak grammatical system exhibited by very young children. (Premack and Premack 1983, p. 115)

On measures of sign performance (form), sign order (structure), semantic relations (meaning), sign acts (function) and sign acquisition (development), apes appear to be very similar to 2 to 3 year old human children learning sign... Apes also appear to be very similar to 2 to 3 year old human children learning to speak. (Miles 1978, p. 114)

[The experimental chimpanzees] show, after years of training and exposure to signing, not the slightest trace of homological development parallel to that of human children. (Leiber 1984, p. 84)

After years of gentle teaching Koko has learned to use American Sign Language—the very same sign language used by the deaf. With her new-found vocabulary, Koko is now providing us with an astounding wealth of knowledge about the way animals view the world. (Patterson 1985a, p. 1)...

There are several sources of the stridency of the debate.

... [L]anguage, at least in the European intellectual tradition, is the quintessential human attribute, at once evidence and source of most that is transcendent in us, distinguishing ours from the merely mechanical nature of the beast. Language is regarded as the *sine qua non* of culture, and its presence in our species is the most salient behavioral difference between us and the other hominoids—with the relinquishing of tool use and, more recently, tool making (Goodall 1971; Beck 1980) as uniquely human capabilities, the significance of language as a separator has grown. And resistance to losing our quintessential attributes is, arguably, itself one of those uniquely human traits. Hence, some ape partisans (Linden 1974; Gysens-Gosselin 1979) have argued, the prevalent reluctance to accord the talking apes their due. An occasional variant of this interpretation is the accusation that those who refuse to recognize ape language are insufficiently committed to the Darwinian perspective or, worse, are anti-Darwinian. Thus Linden (1987) depicts those who question the likelihood of ape–human linguistic continuities as latter-day Wilberforces, averse to investigating "creatures who threaten to paralyze us by shedding light on the true nature and origins of our abilities" (p. 8).

A countervailing vector of our ideology, perhaps peculiar to our culture but possibly pancultural, consists of careless anthropomorphic projection and an irrepressively attractive vision of communication between our own and other species. In fact, it seems correct to observe that, at least until recently in the debate and probably up to the present, the majority opinion, both lay and scientific, regarding the linguistic capabilities of the apes has been positive. People seem not only accepting but positively desirous of the possibility of ape language.

Even if language did not have the sacrosanct status it does in our conception of human nature, the question of its presence in other species would still promote argument, for we are lacking any universally accepted, unassailable diagnostic criteria for language. There is no shortage of candidates for the indispensable attribute of language. For Katz (1976) and Limber (1977), the projective capability is crucial, the provision of language for the articulation of any conceivable new proposition through a novel combination of words. Savage-Rumbaugh (1981) holds the referential nature of individual symbols to be the essence of language, while Premack (1984) and Marshall (1971) see the capacity for representation of real-world situations to be paramount, and so on. The property most commonly invoked as definitive of language is its predication on a system of abstract rules for the production and interpretation of utterances —in other words, grammar. Hockett's (1959, 1960, 1963; Hockett and Altmann 1968) famous list of so-called design features of language—including rapid fading, duality of patterning, and displacement—has provided a useful orientation for those trying to capture the differences between human and nonhuman natural systems of communication. What is wanting, nonetheless, is consensus on what the necessary and sufficient, as distinguished from inessential, property or properties of language are and hence on how we might unequivocally identify language in another species.

This problem of defining features is more severe where the language of the young child is concerned, and it is the child's language that is taken by most parties to the debate to be the proper material for comparison with the apes. If the young child is not, in fact, capable of linguistically encoding anything she can think of, if her production and understanding of utterances do not suggest abstract grammatical constituents and processes, then can it be said that the child has language? Limber (1977) and Lightfoot (1982), at least, would say no.

This is a defensible position, its major problem found in the fact that the young child's language, which may not yet be language, will eventually become language. How is this discontinuity in development to be bridged? The difficulty is not the existence of a discontinuity per se—there are a number of others in human development. The physiological transition from prepubescence to pubescence, for example, poses a similar problem—the two developmental phases are identifiably distinct, yet there are no two adjacent points in time about which it could be said that the child was prepubescent in the first but pubescent in the second.

What makes the transition from "nonlanguage" (. . . early language) to language more problematic is that, unlike the case of puberty, in which the first phase is defined largely by the absence of characteristics of the later one, early language has its own, very salient features. Moreover, there are some striking functional and possibly structural similarities between these features and those of adult language. . . . And, contrary to those who would deny language to the young child, there is extensive evidence for grammatical structure in the earliest word combinations (Bloom 1970; Brown 1973), and, some have suggested (De Laguna 1927; McNeill 1970), in single-word utterances as well. (The proper characterization of this structure, however, is the subject of ongoing debate in developmental psycholinguistics—in fact, this may be the dominant concern of the field. . . .

Language, in summary, is central to our self-definition as a species, even though we have yet to derive an adequate definition of language itself, one that includes the essential but excludes the merely contingent.

Behaviorist Roots of the Ape-Language Experiments

There is an additional source of the contention surrounding the ape-language question. The issues in the debate tend to resonate along the longstanding cleavage within the behavioral sciences between those who advocate study of cognition and/or innately determined behavior, on the one hand, and those, on the other, who are behaviorist in method and theory.

Behaviorism, or stimulus–response psychology, came into being in the early decades of this century as an avowed antidote to the introspectionist trend in turn-of-the-century psychological investigation. Knowledge, thought, intention, affect, and all other unobservable mental phenomena were banished in favor of overt behavior as the only proper subject of a scientific psychology. To explain the behavior of animals, behaviorism, like the eighteenth-century empiricism from which it descends, posits a bare minimum of cognitive apparatus: (1) perception, (2) a capacity to represent in durable format the results of perception, and (3) the ability to form associations among those representations. In the behaviorist paradigm, the acquisition and strengthening of such associations constitute learning.

An association may be formed between a perceptual stimulus and an inborn response if that stimulus consistently accompanies another one that is innately connected to the response, as in the celebrated conjunction of the ticking of a metronome, food, and salivation in Pavlov's dogs. Or an animal may form an association between one of its own actions and a subsequent stimulus, as when a pigeon comes reliably to peck a button because its activation results in the dispensing of food. In this process, an association is created between an action and a following stimulus that "reinforces" that action. To qualify as a reinforcing stimulus, a consequence need not be one that we would regard a priori as satisfying or pleasant—in fact, any stimulus that increases the probability of the organism emitting the behavior that preceded it is, by definition, reinforcing.

In the behaviorist conception, all behavior is determined either by current stimuli or by past consequences. Language is verbal behavior; words function both as responses to stimuli and as stimuli themselves, eliciting further responses. Thus a sentence can be interpreted as a chain of stimulus–response events, each word a response to the preceding one and also a stimulus evoking the next, with the first word elicited by an environmental stimulus or an internal one, a "private event." Or, in some formulations, the entire sentence is regarded as one complex response to a stimulus.

The orthodox behaviorist account of learning has little use for traditional distinctions among types of behavior. Nor are species differences in behavioral mechanisms acknowledged. Although sometimes touted as such, the latter attitude is not an appreciation of evolutionary continuity, with the selectively and historically wrought similarities and divergences in behavior that such a theoretical affirmation entails. Rather, it reflects a commitment to cross-species *homogeneity*, a rejection of the notion that there are important differences across species in the processes that underlie the development and causation of behavior....

Like other contemporary adherents of behaviorism, the ape-language experimenters embraced the various concessions to reality that the most primitive versions of behaviorism were forced to make over the years. The Gardners, for example, acknowledge that some parts of the innate behavioral repertoire of a species are more plastic and hence more readily conditioned than others, and also that species differ in their intrinsic propensities for various behaviors. Thus the chimpanzee's inborn motivation to communicate obviates conditioning as laborious as another behavior might require. That language acquisition in the chimpanzee and in the child are similarly dependent on extensive molding, shaping, and imitation, however, is an assumption that is fundamental to their research, and fundamentally erroneous. Indeed, their suggestion that the linguistic performance of the preschool child requires "intensive training" (1971, p. 188) is the *opposite* of one of the few claims to which virtually all language-acquisition researchers would assent....

Lastly, it may be worth observing that the potential personal rewards of the ape projects have been substantial and emotional commitment commensurately high—the first person or team to give language to another species would certainly attain scientific immortality.

❦

... In describing their aspirations for Washoe, the first of the modern ape-language pupils, the Gardners expressed pessimism about a direct assault on the question "Can an ape talk?" and ... adopted instead an unabashedly behavioristic goal: "We wanted to develop behavior that could be called conversation" (1969, p. 665). And critics ... have maintained that Washoe and her peers, though they may have simulated conversation, acquired neither a human language nor something crucially like one, but rather a system of habits that are crude facsimiles of the features of language.

Refuting the claim that apes have the ability to learn a language logically entails proving that they do *not* have it. This [selection] has not succeeded in doing something that cannot be achieved: proving that something does not exist. The relevant refutable claim, rather, is that one or more of the animals featured in these pages learned a language. Refuting this unequivocally, however, presupposes a set of definitive criteria for language and a demonstration that at least one of them was not met by each of the animals in question.... [S]uch criteria do not yet exist, either for adult forms or for children's forms of language. So it is not possible in principle to show that no ape *could* learn a language, and it is not possible in practice to show that none *has* learned a language....

The ape-language experiments confirmed what students dating back at least as far as the gestalt psychologist Wolfgang Kohler have repeatedly demonstrated, which is that apes are highly intelligent creatures, probably second only to us, on measures of human intelligence. We may wonder how the evolutionary process engendered such a powerful mentality in the midst of the African rain forests, asking, like Humphrey (1976), of what use "conditional oddity discrimination" is to an ape in the jungle. But the cognitive prowess of the apes is a fact regardless of our inability to account for it.

That the apes, too, are reflexive and capable of impressively abstract mentation suggests that at least modest versions of these faculties arose before the ancestral hominoid lineage diversified into the African apes on the one hand and us on the other. Consider a modest assertion: a capacity for culture requires at least ape-level powers of abstraction. And a case could be made for self-awareness, too, as prerequisite to culture. To the extent that Freud's understanding of humanity's cultural creations as "immortality projects" is sound, an ego is presupposed. If the capacity for language, too, had arisen prior to that last hominoid divergence, then linguistics might have been a branch of comparative psychology, the ape-language experiments would never have been conceived, and this [selection] would have been about something else, say patterns of interspecies marriage. But, for that matter, had language arisen prior to the split that produced them and us—had we all spoken the same language—there might not have been a them and an us.

POSTSCRIPT

Can Apes Learn Language?

The two sides on the issue of ape-language ability remain widely separated. At the heart of the issue are several questions about (1) the biological nature of human beings and their nearest primate relatives; (2) the character of language and cognition, particularly among children who are just beginning to acquire language; and (3) the best and most unbiased methods for investigating ape-language abilities.

One of the strongest critics of the ape-language experiments is the cognitive psychologist Steven Pinker, who outlines his arguments in his book *The Language Instinct* (Harper-Collins, 1994). Pinker argues that ape trainers have inadvertently used very subtle conditioning to train their primates. The sequences of symbols produced by even the most talented of the apes are far simpler than normal children's linguistic abilities. His view is that Savage-Rumbaugh and other trainers have overinterpreted the primate symbolic sequences and ignored numerous random "utterances." Chimps and bonobos may be clever animals, he concedes, but their cleverness is conditioned along the lines that Skinner had proposed; it is not linguistic behavior as understood by Chomsky and most linguists. If true, Pinker's criticism suggests that all of the ape-language projects have been failures, and at best trainers have tricked themselves into believing that apes can use symbols in linguistic ways.

Do the ape-language experiments introduce bias by interpreting symbolic strings too broadly and ambiguously? Are detractors of these experiments themselves biased, refusing to believe that apes are capable of any human-like linguistic or cognitive processes? And even if these experiments do not demonstrate an ability to use symbols in ways that precisely parallel child language use, can they not tell us a great deal about general patterns of cognition relevant to both humans and primates?

If Pinker is correct that humans use a different part of the brain for language than do apes when making natural vocalizations, then the efforts to demonstrate language ability in even the brightest of the great apes may ultimately be unsuccessful. Nevertheless, as Wallman and Savage-Rumbaugh suggest, however primitive apes' use of symbols may be, researchers may still learn a great deal about certain kinds of cognitive processes. If research does convincingly show that apes have some kind of language capability, there is still much to be learned about ape cognition in several of the areas that Savage-Rumbaugh has suggested.

Such advances are possible only if ape-language researchers can develop research methods that are completely free from bias and inadvertent human conditioning of their ape subjects. While Savage-Rumbaugh and the other researchers have tried to minimize the possibility of conditioning on their subject animals, as Pinker suggests, the context of the training makes it difficult to exclude the possibility of conditioning.

Up to now none of the ape-language projects have been able to tell us much, if anything, about ape communication in natural settings because all of the projects were conducted in laboratory settings. Even though no language-like communication has been identified among wild chimps or bonobos, there is still much to be learned about how these species communicate. Such studies, particularly if they can be linked to the ape-language experiments, may have a great deal to offer about primate cognition, and they may ultimately offer insights about the process of language acquisition in human children.

For a discussion of Washoe and other early ape-language projects, see R. Allen Gardner and Beatrice T. Gardner's essay "Communication with a Young Chimpanzee: Washoe's Vocabulary" in Rémy Chauvin, ed., *Modèles Animaux du Comportement Humain* (Centre National de la Recherche Scientifique), Herbert S. Terrace's *Nim* (Knopf, 1979), and David Premack and Ann Premack's *The Mind of an Ape* (Norton, 1983). On Kanzi, see Savage-Rumbaugh and Roger Lewin's *Kanzi: The Ape at the Brink of the Human Mind* (Wiley, 1994). On child language acquisition, see Pinker's *Language Learnability and Language Development* (Harvard University Press, 1984). For Skinner's original behavorist model of language learning, see his *Verbal Behavior* (Appleton-Century-Crofts, 1957) and Chomsky's critique *Syntactic Structures* (Mouton, 1957). Students may also enjoy Pinker's most recent analysis of what defines language in *Words and Rules: The Ingredients of Language* (Basic Books, 1999). For recent views about the state of ape-language experiments, see Savage-Rumbaugh, Stuart G. Shaker, and Talbot J. Taylor's *Apes, Language, and the Human Mind* (Oxford University Press, 1998), Barbara J. King, ed., *The Origins of Language: What Nonhuman Primates Can Tell Us* (SAR Press, 1999), and Barbara J. King's *The Information Continuum: Evolution of Social Information Transfer in Monkeys, Apes, and Hominids* (SAR Press, 1994).

On the Internet ...

Archaeology Magazine

This is the Web site of *Archaeology* magazine. This site has a searchable database with links to various articles about recent issues in archaeology, including a number of articles on the goddess cult in Europe and the descent of Polynesians.

http://www.archaeology.org

New Guinea Research Program

This site provides information about the New Guinea Research Program and examines ethnological collections from the South Pacific. It has links to news and current projects in the Southwest Pacific.

http://www.fieldmuseum.org/research_collections/
anthropology/anthro_sites/pacific_web/ngrp.htm

The Maya of Guatemala

This site provides general information on the Maya and contains links to further articles on the Maya of Guatemala, Mayan archaeology, and Mayan languages.

http://mars.cropsoil.uga.edu/trop-ag/the-maya.htm

PART 2

Archaeology

*A*rchaeologists are prehistorians concerned with questions about the unrecorded history of human communities and civilizations. Like other historians, archaeologists seek evidence about how people lived, what they subsisted on, and the kinds of social institutions they established. But, unlike most historians who can turn to documents and papers to detail the life and times of their subjects, archaeologists must find evidence in excavations. Over the past century, archaeologists have developed specialized methods for excavating and analyzing artifacts, stone tools, animal bones, shells, pollen, and carbon from old fires to determine a great deal about the environment, vegetation, subsistence patterns, living arrangements, and also when sites were occupied. At issue is how these varied kinds of data from ancient sources can be interpreted to reconstruct the lifeways of earlier times. A traditional set of questions that archeologists ask is when, why, and how did people first settle different parts of the world, such as the Americas or the Polynesian Islands. They also ask questions about the meaning and significance of certain kinds of artifacts, such as the goddess figures of ancient Europe and the Middle East. Archaeologists also ask questions about why complex civilizations rose and fell.

- Did People First Arrive in the New World After the Last Ice Age?

- Did Polynesians Descend from Melanesians?

- Was There a Goddess Cult in Prehistoric Europe?

- Were Environmental Factors Responsible for the Mayan Collapse?

ISSUE 6

Did People First Arrive in the New World After the Last Ice Age?

YES: Stuart J. Fiedel, from *Prehistory of the Americas,* 2d ed. (Cambridge University Press, 1992)

NO: Thomas D. Dillehay, from "The Battle of Monte Verde," *The Sciences* (January/February 1997)

ISSUE SUMMARY

YES: Archaeologist Stuart J. Fiedel supports the traditional view that humans first reached the Americas from Siberia at the end of the last Ice Age (perhaps 14,000 years ago). He argues that there are currently no convincing sites dated before that time and is skeptical of claims by other archaeologists who date human occupation of sites such as Meadowcroft in Pennsylvania and Monte Verde in Chile significantly earlier.

NO: Archaeologist Thomas D. Dillehay asserts that the site he has excavated at Monte Verde, a complex site in Chile, proved that humans reached the New World well before the end of the last Ice Age, possibly as early as 30,000 years ago. He contends that those archaeologists who are skeptical about his carbon-14 dates and other findings are so entrenched in traditional thinking that they refuse to accept the solid evidence Monte Verde provides.

For more than a century archaeologists have asked, When and how did human beings first arrive in the Americas? The conventional view is that humans arrived from Asia via an ancient land bridge across the Bering Strait, which connected Siberia and Alaska during the last Ice Age. This traditional view has several components that Stuart J. Fiedel analyzes in his selection. First, the land bridge existed because ocean water was trapped in glacial ice. But this same glacial ice would also have presented an impenetrable barrier to human passage until glacial ice began to recede at the very end of the Ice Age. A narrow corridor between two separate ice sheets appears to have opened up about 14,500 years ago. Second, once human populations had passed through this ice corridor, they found large populations of woolly mammoth, saber-toothed tiger, and other megafauna, and these species became extinct soon after the ice pack retreated. Third, the archaeological association of certain kinds of stone projectile points (called Clovis points) with the bones of several of these extinct species has suggested that humans hunted them for food. Some archaeologists have argued that excessive human hunting caused their extinction (the overkill hypothesis).

Convincing radiocarbon dating of many sites on both continents suggests that if humankind first arrived in the Americas at the end of the Ice Age, they had spread throughout both continents within a thousand years or so. For many years, archaeologists have disputed whether or not this was enough time for this sort of human dispersal across many different ecological zones.

In his selection, Fiedel surveys the history of the search for the earliest Americans and focuses on two of the most promising candidates for acceptance as pre-Clovis sites: the Meadowcroft shelter in Pennsylvania and an upland coastal site in south-central Chile called Monte Verde. Fiedel is skeptical that either will prove unambiguously to be pre-Clovis, but he recognizes that, unlike most other sites thought to be early, neither of these can be firmly dismissed as postglacial, although for different reasons. His skepticism emerges from several angles simultaneously, and considers the question: If humans had settled the New World significantly before the last Ice Age, why have archaeologists not identified dozens of pre-Clovis sites before now?

Thomas D. Dillehay is probably best known for his archaeological excavations at Monte Verde, a site he has worked on for more than 20 years. He contends that this site is complex. One part fits what one might expect a genuine pre-Clovis site to look like: It was occupied for a relatively short time by a hunting-and-gathering group, and the tool kit is significantly simpler than that of most Clovis sites. But simple or not, this assemblage has now been dated to significantly earlier than the date that the corridor through the northern glacial ice pack appeared, which means that human settlement of the Americas must have occurred before the last glacial maximum.

Dillehay suggests that skeptics of the quality of his carbon-14 dates are largely reacting defensively to his findings because they would force archaeologists to abandon models about the early settlement of the Northern Hemisphere that they have held for many years. What one can see in these two selections is a clash of paradigms.

Fiedel and Dillehay raise a number of questions of general interest to archaeologists. Are the authors defending different theoretical models of New World settlement, or are the "facts of the case" genuinely problematic? Are early carbon-14 dates sufficient to establish the Monte Verde site as genuinely pre-Clovis, or do Dillehay and his colleagues need to work out the artifact sequences before we can accept their findings? As with other controversies in archaeology, the arguments here seem to be about the facts of Monte Verde, but are these archaeologists actually arguing about their own models? Would it be appropriate for a nonpartisan team of archaeologists to visit Monte Verde and assess Dillehay's findings either to demonstrate problems in the data or to establish the site as an early one once and for all?

Stuart J. Fiedel

 **YES**

The Paleo-Indians

Archaeological Evidence of the First Americans

In the latter part of the nineteenth century, American scholars and amateurs, inspired by Darwin's theories and the Stone Age discoveries made in Europe, sought evidence of early man in the New World. Sure enough, they turned up a great many stone tools. The crudeness of some of these suggested that they were very ancient, belonging either to the Pleistocene or even to some earlier epoch. In addition, human remains were found, and for these, too, great antiquity was claimed. However, the eminent Czech-born physical anthropologist, Aleš Hrdlička, ruthlessly demolished these claims, demonstrating that all the American skeletal finds represented humans of modern type. On the basis of this conclusion, Hrdlička asserted that Ice Age man had not lived in the Americas; he set the initial entry at about 3000 B.C. No one seems to have pointed out at the time that humans of modern type had lived during late glacial times in Europe, where their remains had been found at Cro-Magnon and elsewhere; so the absence of pre-*sapiens* fossils in the Americas did not preclude a Pleistocene occupation. Hrdlička's conservative view prevailed in scholarly circles until an astonishing discovery in 1927 rendered it untenable.

George McJunkin, a black cowhand, had noticed some bones protruding from the side of a gulley near Folsom, New Mexico. This find was brought to the attention of J. D. Figgins of the Denver Museum of Natural History, who excavated the site. The bones turned out to belong to a large, long-horned species of bison (*Bison antiquus*), which became extinct at the end of the Pleistocene. In 1926, Figgins found a stone spearpoint embedded in clay near the bones. This point was initially dismissed by other archaeologists as intrusive. But in 1927, Figgins came upon another point, this time lying between two bison ribs. He left the point in place, and invited several prestigious archaeologists to examine the new find. They agreed that the Folsom site presented an indisputable association of man-made artifacts with the remains of extinct Pleistocene animals. Initially, archaeologists could only guess the age of the Folsom remains; but, since 1950, a series of C14 dates for sites where stone points of the same type have been excavated place the Folsom culture at about 9000 to 8000 B.C.

Many more Folsom sites have been discovered since 1927. At a few of them, artifacts were recovered from geological strata lying *below* those that yielded Folsom points. The distinctive artifact type of these earlier assemblages is the Clovis point. Clovis points were first excavated at the Blackwater Draw site near Clovis, New Mexico; here, and at several other sites, they were found in association with the remains of mammoths. The Clovis or "Llano" culture of the western United States has been dated to about 9500 to 9000 B.C. Clovis-like fluted points have a very wide geographic distribution, having been found throughout the United States and in Canada and Central America. The striking similarity of these points, found over such a vast area, has led many archaeologists to conclude that the points were made and used by closely related hunting bands.

We can envision one or several ancestral bands entering the northern Plains through the ice-free corridor, thus stumbling upon a hunter's paradise, teeming with game that had never experienced the terrible cunning and tenacity of the human predator. In such a favorable situation, the original human population would have grown rapidly: where growth is not constrained by food or space limitations, population can double or even triple in each successive generation. We can estimate, using some speculative yet reasonable calculations, the minimum length of time necessary for the Americas to have been filled to capacity with hunting bands. We start with figures derived from ethnographic studies of extant hunting and gathering groups. These studies indicate that, irrespective of environmental differences, the typical hunting band consists of 25 to 50 people. These studies also reveal a range of population densities, from 0.4 to 9.6 persons per 100 square km (1 to 25 persons per 100 square miles). Pleistocene densities may have exceeded the upper end of this range; we can use a figure of 0.4 persons per square km (one person per square mile). North and South America, south of the glacial margins at 10,000 B.C., contained roughly 26 million square km (10 million square miles). Ignoring for the moment environmental differences that made areas more or less suitable for human habitation, and applying the 0.4 per square km (one per square mile) density figure, we get 10,000,000 as the potential hunting population of the Americas. If we assume that a band of 25 people passed through the corridor into North America, and that this population doubled in each successive generation (every 30 years or so), we reach the 10,000,000 figure in about 500 years. In reality, judging from the scarcity of their typical artifacts, Paleo-Indian populations probably did not reach even one-tenth of this level. In any case, assuming an exponential growth rate, the difference is insignificant; the 1 million level could have been attained in about 350 years.

... It has sometimes been assumed that thousands of years must have elapsed between the initial entry of humans into North America and their arrival at Fell's Cave [in Patagonia]; however, our calculations have shown how rapidly population expansion could have occurred. The distance from the base of the corridor to Tierra del Fuego is about 13,000 km (8,000 miles). If the expansion of human population to the limits of the continents took as little as 500 years, we would have to assume that the rate of migration was about 26 km (16 miles) a year, or 780 km (480 miles) per generation. Such movement is quite feasible, particularly in light of evidence that Paleo-Indians sometimes made tools of flint that they had carried from sources located several hundred kilometers away (as, for example, at the Shoop site in Pennsylvania and the Wapanucket site in Massachusetts). The southward movement was probably wavelike, constantly widening on its southern front. The impact of this human wave on the herd animals of the Americas may well have contributed to their extinction. . . .

So, we see that the presence of man at "the end of the road," Tierra del Fuego, by about 9000 B.C., is consistent with an initial entry through the ice-free corridor as late as 9500 B.C. However, the widespread and easily recognized Clovis culture was not necessarily the earliest in the Americas. The archaeological record offers tantalizing hints of earlier occupation.

Over the years, thousands of crude stone tools have been found in North America. These closely resemble the chopper-chopping tools of East Asia; as you may recall, the latter were produced from hundreds of thousands of years ago until quite recently. Some archaeologists have suggested that the American choppers must be older than the Clovis points, that they in fact represent a "pre-projectile point horizon." The absence of points in the supposedly pre-Clovis industries has been interpreted as evidence of a subsistence pattern involving less specialized hunting of large mammals and greater reliance on small game and plant foods.

However, claims for a preprojectile horizon must be regarded with skepticism. Most of the crude choppers have surface finds, whose age cannot be determined. Others have been found in datable geological contexts, but they are so formless that they are almost certainly not artifacts at all. Still other choppers are definitely man-made, but are associated with relatively late, more delicate artifacts. Such choppers were probably used for tasks that did not require more finely made tools. Some crudely retouched bifaces found in North America superficially resemble the Acheulian handaxes of Europe and Africa; but the American pieces have been shown to be "blanks," stones retouched into rough form at a quarry site with a view toward later, finer modification into a desired tool. . . .

The most convincing evidence of pre-Clovis occupation in North America, south of the Pleistocene ice margins, comes from the Meadowcroft rockshelter in western Pennsylvania. Here, stone tools and waste flakes from the earliest culture-bearing layer (Stratum IIa) have been dated, by eight radiocarbon determinations, between 17,000 and 11,000 B.C. C14 dates for the overlying strata form a consistent sequence, and are appropriate for the Archaic and Woodland period cultural material with which they are associated. However, the geologist C. Vance Haynes has suggested that the early dates from the lowest level might be the result of contamination by old carbon from coal deposits in the vicinity of the site. This attempt to explain away the early dates has been vigorously disputed by the excavator of Meadowcroft, James Adovasio, and his colleagues. But there is other evidence that casts doubt on the dates for Stratum IIa. Flotation of soil samples from this layer yielded abundant remains of plants—pits, nutshells, and carbonized fragments. These remains clearly indicate that the prevailing environment at the time of the Stratum IIa occupation was the same as that which existed during later periods—a deciduous forest including oak, walnut, and hickory trees. But at the time indicated by the C14 dates for Stratum IIa, the front of the Laurentide ice sheet was only 83 km (50 miles) to the north of the rockshelter. It is almost certain that Meadowcroft lay within a band of tundra, bordered by forests of spruce and pine, at about 15,000 B.C. It was not until about 8500 B.C. that the tundra and boreal forest were replaced by deciduous forest, spreading up from the south. An earlier presence of deciduous forest around Meadowcroft at the height of the Wisconsin glaciation would be very surprising. The few animal bones from Stratum IIa do not resolve the apparent contradiction between the radio-carbon dates and the paleo-botanical evidence. Among the highly fragmented bones was a piece of antler that could be confidently assigned to the white-tailed deer. Other identified specimens represent passenger pigeon and southern flying squirrel. All three species usually inhabited temperate deciduous forests. No remains of extinct Pleistocene mammals such as horse, mastodon, or mammoth, nor remains of tundra-dwelling caribou, have been found at Meadowcroft.

The stone tools from the lowest levels of Meadowcroft rockshelter do not appear to be typical of eastern Paleo-Indian assemblages, but neither do they represent a preprojectile horizon. Small blades are common. Also found were a bifacially retouched flake knife (called "Mungai" by Adovasio) and a projectile point. This point is lanceolate in shape like a Clovis point, but it is neither fluted like Clovis points nor as finely retouched as they usually are. Haynes, who questions the pre-Clovis dating of this material, suggests that the point is basically similar to unfluted, post-Clovis Plano points. Adovasio, on the other hand, sees similarities to points from a few western sites, such as Fort Rock Cave, which may be earlier than 10,000 B.C. He suggests that the Meadowcroft point might represent the prototype from which Clovis and Plano points were derived.

The Upper Paleolithic character of the Meadowcroft lithic assemblage is obvious. This is not the first discovery of blades in an early context in North America; well-made blades were reported in 1963 from the Clovis site of Blackwater Draw in New Mexico. These had been detached from a cone-shaped core by striking a bone or antler punch, resting on the core's basal rim, with a stone hammer. The small blades from Meadowcroft were made in the same way. In the Old World, this technique probably developed out of Middle Paleolithic Levallois flaking from prepared cores; but blades, retouched into numerous tool types, first became dominant in Upper Paleolithic assemblages. But, as we have seen, some archaeologists have argued that the first Americans were exclusively users of crude chopper-chopping tools and broken bones; according to this view, they made neither bifacially flaked points nor blades. The development from these simple Lower Paleolithic tools to the elegantly made Clovis point would have been an indigenous process, unrelated to cultural developments in Eurasia. This seems to me a very unlikely course of events. Even if Clovis points were an American innovation—and to date, nothing like them has turned up in Asia—they were products of an Upper Paleolithic technological tradition, incorporating methods of blade production and retouching, which were developed in Eurasia. . . .

Two caves in the western United States may have been occupied before 10,000 B.C. In a deep level of a stratified sequence in Wilson Butte Cave, in southern Idaho, a bifacially worked, bipointed point and a blade have been C14 dated, using samples of associated bones, at about 12,500 B.C. It is conceivable that the dated bone was contaminated by older carbon in the surrounding soil, or that it was brought in from earlier deposits by rodents. At Fort Rock Cave in south-central Oregon, a charcoal concentration lying on Pleistocene lake gravels has been C14 dated at 11,200 B.C. Nearby were two projectile points, several scrapers and gravers, and some flakes, as well as a milling stone and a handstone fragment. These ground stone artifacts are suggestive of the processing of collected seeds, a subsistence activity that is well attested in the Desert Archaic culture of this region after about 8000 B.C. However, grinding stones do not occur at Paleo-Indian sites that are earlier than 8000 B.C. Therefore, some doubt exists as to the association of the dated charcoal and the lithic finds. But since an overlying level was C14 dated at 8200 B.C., it seems indisputable that the artifacts are at least that old.

Clovis

... The Clovis culture ... appears distinctive in several important respects from known Siberian Paleolithic cultures. Cultural change and innovation must have occurred during the migration of the ancestral Paleo-Indians across Beringia and through the corridor. It seems, on present evidence, that the fluted point was invented in North America.

If we accept the evidence from Valsequillo, Meadowcroft, and the few other sites that indicate that man was present in the Americas as early as 20,000 B.C., the rapid spread of Clovis-style lithic industries around 9500–9000 B.C. becomes more difficult to explain. We must choose among several plausible models for Clovis expansion:

1. Pre-Clovis occupation was ultimately unsuccessful; earlier inhabitants vanished or were restricted to a few isolated areas before the Clovis point-makers arrived.
2. Pre-Clovis occupation was widespread and successful. Somewhere in North America, fluted points began to be made. Then, (a) this new technology spread quickly as it was adopted by local hunting groups, who found it useful in hunting big game, or (b) the fluted point gave its inventors such an adaptive advantage that they rapidly expanded, encroaching upon and replacing the original inhabitants of other areas.

Model 2(a) seems the least likely explanation. There are no significant regional distinctions among Clovis tool kits, such as would indicate the addition of point-making to ongoing local flint-working traditions. The known distribution of Clovis points causes problems for model 2(b). It seems unlikely that fluted points would have been decisively advantageous in all of the diverse environments—tundra, grassland, boreal and deciduous forests—that Paleo-Indians occupied at the end of the Pleistocene. Model 1 poses an obvious problem: Why should hunters equipped with a sophisticated Upper Paleolithic technology, including effective stone projectile points (found at most of the convincing pre-Clovis sites), and resourceful enough to have endured a trek through Beringia and the glacial corridor, have been any less successful than the Clovis hunters? The paleontologist Paul S. Martin has wryly suggested an answer to this problem: "Given the biology of the species, I can envision only one circumstance under which an ephemeral discovery of America might have occurred. It is that, sometime before 12,000 years ago, the earliest early man came over the Bering Strait without early woman."

Martin has proposed an elegant model of Paleo-Indian migration. His theory would account at once for the rapidity of occupation of North and South America, the uniformity of Clovis tool kits, and the extinction of many species of large mammals at the end of the Pleistocene. Discounting claims of earlier sites, Martin assumes that the makers of Clovis points were the first humans to pass through the ice-free corridor into North America. Here they encountered herds of animals that had no experience of human predation, and so had developed neither defensive nor reproductive strategies to deal with this new threat. Taking advantage of the seemingly limitless supply of game, the Clovis hunters multiplied rapidly, their numbers doubling with each generation. As their numbers grew, the hunters also pushed southward, their movement taking the form of a great wave of advance, with the greatest density of population at its front. After a brief bottleneck in Central America, the same sort of expansion occurred in South America. Martin calculates that the descendants of an original band of 100 people who emerged from the ice-free corridor could have finished off the large Pleistocene mammals in North America. He estimates that the maximum total animal biomass for unglaciated North America at the end of the Pleistocene was some 230 million metric tons. Human population in North America could have reached a maximum of 600,000, at a density of 0.4 per square km (one per square mile), in about 250 years. If, at the front of the wave of advance, one person did all of the hunting for himself and three others (as might the adult male in a small nuclear family), and if this hunter killed only one animal weighing 450 kilograms (or 992 pounds—about the weight of a young modern bison) per week, the animals at the front would have been wiped out in less than ten years. At this rate, all of the large mammals in the Americas could have been slaughtered in about 500 to 1,000 years—as long as it took for the Paleo-Indians to reach Tierra del Fuego.

Numerous objections have been raised against Martin's "overkill" hypothesis. However, scientists agree that there is a basic fact that requires explanation: at the end of the Pleistocene, some 32 genera of American mammals became extinct. These included the mammoth, the mastodon, the giant sloth, the armadillolike glyptodon, the camel, the horse, the saber-toothed "tiger" and the dire wolf. Clearly, these extinctions must be connected in some way with the major environmental and climatic changes that were caused by the retreat of the Wisconsin ice sheets. However, the ice sheets had retreated before, in previous interglacial episodes, but these events had not resulted in the extinction of so many species. As Martin points out, the unique factor present during the last glacial retreat was human hunting....

Paleontologists have proposed several alternative explanations for the late Pleistocene extinctions. Most have seen climate change as the primary cause. Dramatic shifts in temperature and rainfall patterns led to contraction of the habitats of at least some Pleistocene mammals. Over-specialized animals could not adjust to the new environments, and large animals, with their greater food and space requirements, could not compete with smaller species for which readaptation was easier. But this theory does not account for the extinction of those mammals whose habitats changed very little as the ice sheets retreated....

It has also been suggested that the late Pleistocene opening of the glacial corridor permitted not only human hunters but also an assortment of new parasites and disease organisms to invade North America. But epidemics did not cause widespread extinction during previous interglacials. Generally, after initial high fatality rates, populations became resistant, and more stable disease-host relationships set in before extinction of the host. So diseases are unlikely to have been the critical factor in the Pleistocene extinctions.

The problem of Pleistocene extinctions is a challenging one, and none of the suggested solutions is entirely satisfactory. Many scientists would probably grant that Paleo-Indian hunters might have delivered the *coup de grâce* to several species, but would also emphasize that these and other mammals were already seriously weakened by climatic and environmental stress....

Paleo-Indians in South America

Carbon dates from Fell's Cave in Patagonia indicate that man had reached the southernmost tip of South America by about 9000 or 8700 B.C. As we have seen, these dates are not inconsistent with an initial entry into South America only a few hundred years earlier. However, there have been claims that a few sites demonstrate occupation of the continent before 10,000 B.C. Clearly, if it can be proven that any South American sites are really that old, claims of pre-Clovis habitation of North American will gain credibility....

An extraordinarily well-preserved and apparently very early site has been excavated at Monte Verde, in south central Chile. Twelve wooden structures, abundant plant remains, and bones of butchered mastodon and guanaco, all buried under a layer of peat, have been C14 dated to between 13,650 ± 250 and 11,790 ± 200 B.P. (ca. 11,700 to 9800 B.C.). A lower layer of the site yielded broken stones and charcoal that possibly represent remains of human activity more than 30,000 years ago. The long hiatus between this dubious occupation and the late Pleistocene reuse of the vicinity has not been convincingly explained. The houses, made of planks and small tree trunks, are thought to have been covered with hides. Clay-lined hearths had been excavated outside the houses. Wooden mortars and grinding stones were used to process plant food. Actual plant remains include wild potatoes, medicinal plants, and salt-rich plants that must have been brought from the coast, 30 km distant from the site. The stone tool kit is reported to be a very simple one, consisting mostly of split pebble choppers and flakes. Some roughened stones may have been tied together with leather thongs and used as bolas. Hunting devices of this sort would have been a necessity if stone spearpoints were unknown to this culture. In fact, however, two well-made, thin lanceolate spearpoints, chipped from basalt, have been found at Monte Verde. They bear some resemblance to the El Jobo points of Venezuela, which are associated with comparably early, but controversial, radiocarbon dates. At present, too little is known about the Monte Verde culture to compare it with any others. Apart from the mastodon remains, the lifeway represented seems more Archaic than Paleo-Indian. The 2,000-year range of the radiocarbon dates is surprisingly wide for a site that is thought to have been created during a single brief occupation. Acceptance of the most recent dates would take the site into the period of Clovis immigration. However, the predominantly simple stone tool kit attested at Monte Verde is not very similar to typical Clovis assemblages. Nevertheless, if the early C14 dates are verified by further research, Monte Verde will have provided irrefutable evidence of a human presence in the Americas about 1,000 years before the Clovis migration (or diffusion). If Monte Verde and other South American sites really do predate 10,000 B.C., archaeologists will have to explain the puzzling absence of proven sites of comparable antiquity in North America.

South America was occupied around 9000 B.C. by Paleo-Indians who made fluted points, stylistically distinctive from, yet obviously related to, the Clovis points of North America. In the 1930s, Junius Bird found "fishtail" points, many of them fluted, at Fell's Cave. Similar points have been discovered at El Inga, in the highlands of Ecuador. Unlike North American fluted points, these broad-bodied points taper to markedly thinner stems, which take up more than a third of the points' length. However, some Clovis-like points from the southeastern United States have very similar fishtail-shaped bases, and are constricted just above the base so that they almost appear to have stems. A link between these northern and southern points is provided by several surface finds from Central America. Short, broad fishtail points of the type found at Fell's Cave, are known from Panama (Madden Lake) and Costa Rica (Turrialba). Somewhat thinner fishtail points, more similar to the Clovis-like points of eastern North America, have been found at the same sites, and also in western Costa Rica, Guatemala, and Durango, Mexico. Recently, a Clovis point like those found in the southwestern United States was collected from a site in the Quiche Basin, in the highlands of Guatemala; similar points are reported from recently excavated sites in Belize. Lacking firm chronological controls, we cannot be sure that the more slender of the Central American points represent a transitional phase in the stylistic evolution of fishtail points from North American Clovis prototypes; but this seems to be the best explanation of the existing evidence. The close resemblance of fishtail points from sites in Costa Rica and Patagonia, separated by more than 6,400 km (4,000 miles), implies a very rapid migration of Paleo-Indians along the mountainous spine of western South America. As in North America, such a rapid migration seems to imply that there was no previous human occupation of the region; alternatively, if the pre-10,000 B.C. dates are valid, the earlier population must have been so small and scattered that they could be easily replaced or absorbed by the makers of fluted points.

It should be noted that there have been finds in South America of leaf-shaped and lanceolate points that seem to be as old as the fishtail points. Some archaeologists argue that such points, of which the best known examples are the El Jobo points from Venezuela, may in fact be older than the fishtail type; however, this argument rests primarily on a few dubious radiocarbon dates. The closest North American parallels to the leaf-shaped points are the Lerma points of Texas and Mexico, and the San Dieguito points of California and the Great Basin; these types are dated to between 9000 and 6000 B.C.

Apart from fluted points, other items in the tool kit of the South American Paleo-Indians—scrapers, gravers, and knives—suggest a derivation from North American forms. The probable use of these tools in the processing of meat and hides further implies a continuation of the ancestral North American Paleo-Indians' pursuit of big game.

The South American Paleo-Indians' big game-hunting orientation is confirmed by associations of artifacts with remains of extinct Pleistocene mammals at several sites. There is evidence of the hunting of horse, mastodon, and giant ground sloth. The Paleo-Indians also hunted animals of modern species—deer and guanaco, various rodents, rabbits, and birds, particularly the ground-dwelling tinamou. The Paleo-Indians probably turned increasingly to such small game as the Pleistocene megafauna disappeared. Bones found at Los Toldos, Argentina, and Tagua Tagua in Chile hint at the early domestication of the dog, which would have been helpful in hunting the tinamou. In addition to small animals, plants became more important as a food source after 9000 B.C. There is evidence at Guitarrero Cave that beans and peppers were cultivated, and various tubers and fruits were collected, perhaps as early as 8500 B.C. and certainly before 7000 B.C. This dietary diversification in the Andean highlands is comparable to the broad spectrum adaptations that developed after the extinction of the Pleistocene megafauna in North America and Mesoamerica.

NO ↰

Thomas D. Dillehay

The Battle of Monte Verde

In archeology the simplest questions are often the hardest to answer. Two such questions—who were the first Americans and when did they reach the New World?—have tormented investigators for more than a century. Archaeologists have long believed that Asian immigrants, crossing the Bering land bridge in pursuit of big game, pioneered the New World about 11,000 years ago. Known as the Clovis people, after the site in New Mexico where their elaborate, fluted projectile points were first discovered, the immigrants gradually worked their way south. They were skilled hunters, and when their travels brought them to places teeming with an astonishing variety of prey, the result was a human population explosion. In a matter of centuries Clovis hunters moved throughout the Americas, helping to wipe out bison, woolly mammoths, camelids and other species in the so-called Pleistocene die-off.

Or perhaps not. In recent years a wave of discoveries outside North America has brought nearly every aspect of the migration theory under intense scrutiny. Fresh insights on the peopling of China, Japan and Siberia are redrawing the debate about the first Americans on a much broader canvas, framed by the entire Pacific Rim. And in South America a rash of controversial early dates has suggested that the Americas were settled even earlier than 11,000 years ago. Several sites in Tierra del Fuego, for instance, have been convincingly shown to be about 11,000 years old.

How could people have arrived in North America and at the southern tip of South America at approximately the same time? Did they journey through Alaska before the Clovis hunters, or did they sail across the seas to reach South America just as Clovis hunters were crossing the Bering land bridge? Faced with such questions, New World archaeologists have divided into Clovis and pre-Clovis camps. The dispute between the two has become so emotionally charged that one archaeologist has likened it to the debate between creationists and evolutionists.

Twenty years ago I was drawn into the fray when I began excavating Monte Verde, a site near the town of Puerto Montt, in south-central Chile. Monte Verde had been discovered accidentally in 1976 by some local lumbermen clearing paths for their ox carts. They had been cutting back the banks of a small creek in a marshy area when they literally stumbled on some large bones and

From Thomas D. Dillehay, "The Battle of Monte Verde," *The Sciences*, vol. 37, no. 1 (January/ February 1997). Copyright © 1997 by *The Sciences*. Reprinted by permission. Individual subscriptions are $28 per year. Write to: *The Sciences*, 2 East 63rd Street, New York, NY 10021.

buried wood. The bones were later determined to be the remains of mastodons. In 1977, when the find was brought to my attention, I was head of the anthropology department at the Southern University of Chile in Valdivia. That year I formed an international interdisciplinary team, which eventually grew to eighty members, and we began to excavate the site.

Early on, we knew that Monte Verde was an exceptional site. But we also knew that our finds would provoke a barrage of skepticism, not least because of their age. According to firm radiocarbon dates, the most impressive remains date from 1,500 years before Clovis hunters are said to have discovered North America. The possible remains of human habitation in Monte Verde's deepest levels are nearly 20,000 years older than that.

❧

Archaeologists are, by necessity, masters of inference. From the meanest, most innocuous of things—discarded oyster shells, broken pots, the subtle bands of color and texture in an excavation wall—we try to re-create an entire world and its inhabitants. To the uninitiated, the process may seem as occult as counting the angels on the head of a pin. How does this standing stone signify religion? Why is that "chopper" not just a rock? How can so much be made of so little?

Thanks to some happy accidents of nature, the remains at Monte Verde are of a far more evocative kind. Some 12,500 years ago the site was an open-air settlement on the banks of what is now Chinchihuapi Creek. All around were sandy knolls, small bogs and a cool, damp forest. As the bogs spread into the adjacent creek bed, they buried the abandoned settlement under a layer of fibrous peat, preserving it like an exotic specimen pickled in formaldehyde. The water protected the remains from the wear and tear of changing humidity. It also prevented oxygen from reaching the remains, thereby keeping bacteria from digesting them.

Once it was carefully drained and stripped of its layers of protective peat, the site revealed much more than the usual cache of bones and stone tools. From wood structures to medicinal plants to hunks of meat, it held a wealth of organic debris that normally disappears from the archaeological record. More than any other early site in the Americas, Monte Verde would enable us to reconstruct life in the Ice Age.

❧

At the beginning of the project, we put together a team that included geologists, botanists, forestry scientists and zoologists to study the fauna and flora preserved at the site. Our digging uncovered the remains of a sixty-foot-long tentlike structure sturdy enough to house twenty or thirty people, some of them year-round. The frame was made of logs and planks anchored by stakes, and the walls consisted of poles covered with hides (from mastodons and paleo-llamas, judging by the bones we excavated). The entire structure was bound together with cordage and string made of junco reed. Inside the tent, planks and poles apparently set off individual living spaces, each of which had a brazier pit lined with clay. Hundreds of microscopic flecks of hide, embedded in the dirt, suggest that the floor was probably covered with skins.

Outside the tent we found two large communal hearths, a supply of firewood, and wooden mortars with their grinding stones. Near the hearths, we uncovered two brown, sopping hunks of meat next to some mastodon bones. The most dramatic remains, however, are of a more delicate variety. About 12,000 years ago one of the Monte Verdeans walked across some soft, wet clay brought to the site for refurbishing the hearths. As the clay hardened, it preserved three footprints for posterity. In one print the toes, heel and arch of a foot were clearly visible. On the basis of the print's size and shape, specialists from our team of forensic anthropologists think it was made by a small adult or a large adolescent.

West of the main building, we found a wishbone-shaped structure made of wooden uprights set into a foundation of sand and gravel hardened with animal fat. Mastodon carcasses were butchered inside the structure, hides were prepared and tools were manufactured. Because the medicinal parts of certain plants were found next to those remains, we think the Monte Verdeans may have also gone there to practice healing.

In southern Chile today the Mapuche people use medicinal plants to treat rheumatism, stomach aches, dysentery, infected cuts and pulmonary problems, among other ailments, as well as to induce abortions. The twenty-three kinds of medicinal plants found at Monte Verde are all still used to treat various problems. Boldo leaf (*Peumus boldus*), for instance, is used for intestinal ailments and hallucinations, natre leaf (*Solanum crispum*) reduces fever, and *Lycopodium* (a kind of club moss) gives a natural talcum powder that soothes skin infections. Some of the plants are native to the area, but about half come from the coast, and one is found only in arid regions to the north.

To modern sensibilities, the most intriguing plants preserved at the site are the ones that now seem most commonplace: potatoes. Many explorers and scientists, Charles Darwin among them, have noted the wide variety and abundance of wild potatoes in southern Chile. On the basis of studies done on wild potatoes in the region, Soviet botanists in the 1930s speculated that potatoes originally came from that area and from Peru. The presence of the tuber at Monte Verde, in the cracks and pits of wooden mortars and in food storage pits in the corners of shelters, confirms the Soviet hypothesis and underlines the importance of southern Chile in the evolution of the potato.

The smorgasbord of food scraps the Monte Verdeans left behind suggests that the bulk of their diet was made up of meat from mastodons, paleo-llamas, small animals and freshwater mollusks, together with aquatic plants from freshwater marshes and other areas. Most of those foods are found in ecological zones thirty-five miles from Monte Verde, along the Pacific shoreline and in the Andean mountains. Three varieties of seaweed—a rare occurrence on the southern coast—were probably scavenged some fifty miles to the west or received in trade. Salt, pebbles worn flat and round by ocean waves (ideal for polishing animal hides or grinding food), and bitumen used to attach stone tools to wooden hafts were also found at the site, demonstrating that the Monte Verdeans brought back more than food from the coast.

To make use of so many resources from so many ecological zones, the Monte Verdeans devised a sophisticated division of labor. Residential areas are separate from non-residential areas at the site, and certain areas are associated with specific tools and food remains. In one living space, for instance, quartz artifacts for cutting and scraping were found with the remains of fruits and tubers that grow only in brackish estuaries, which suggests that the occupants specialized in collecting resources from the coast. In another area of the tent, stone scrapers and pieces of skin indicate that people worked animal hides there.

∗∗∗

Our excavations at Monte Verde have revealed a much more complex social and economic organization than archeologists have come to expect of early New World cultures. The excavations also call into question the commonly accepted idea that all Ice Age bands were nomadic. Our evidence shows that some of the people at the site's younger settlement remained there year-round, living off a wide variety of plants and animals. Although few sites contemporaneous with Monte Verde have been found so far, we think the Monte Verdeans probably belonged to a scattered group of colonizers accustomed to temperate wetlands and forests. The fact that they used many river resources suggest that they came from the Maullín River basin, seven miles to the north, into which Chinchihuapi Creek discharges.

For all their surprising sophistication, the Monte Verdeans had fairly crude tools. True, our excavations uncovered some artifacts made of wood, such as digging sticks, as well as some bone artifacts, such as a baton for striking flakes off stones and gouges made of mastodon tusks. But many of the tools we found were simply pebbles from the creek bed or distant ocean beaches. Their damaged edges, coated with residues from food plants, identify them as tools that were picked up, used and then discarded. Other stones were simply split or struck to remove a few flakes. Only a few stone specimens, such as bifacially flaked projectile points and chopping tools, grooved sling stones and grinding stones, would be universally accepted as human tools even if they had been discovered in a different setting with no corroborating evidence.

Our findings should serve as a cautionary tale for archaeologists seeking indisputable artifacts in ancient sites. If, as it sometimes seems, we deceive ourselves by thinking that rocks are tools, we may just as often mistake tools for rocks. The oldest, deepest levels at Monte Verde are a case in point. Four feet below the latest settlement, in another area of the site, we found twenty-four fractured pebbles and three shallow depressions, lined with clay, containing burned wood and seeds. Seven of the pebbles were probably flaked by people; four of the twenty-four pebbles show polish or striations on their sharp edges from the cutting and scraping of meat, hides and plants. Charcoal from two of the depressions has been radiocarbon-dated to about 33,000 years ago.

Were the charcoal and the pebbles around it made by people? The evidence is inconclusive. But if the answer is yes, the faint traces the early Monte

Verdeans left behind suggest that they were probably transient explorers. The paleo-ecological evidence indicates that 33,000 years ago the region was going through an interglacial period. As the climate warmed up and moors and beech forests began to appear, southern Chile would have grown increasingly hospitable to colonists.

⋘◉⋙

[In] January [1997] a multidisciplinary research team will be at the University of Kentucky for two days to inspect the Monte Verde artifacts and to discuss the site in greater detail. The team will then travel to Chile for a three-day visit to examine the site setting and the stratigraphy. I have mixed feelings about the visit. Although we have been calling for a site visit since 1979, no one has accepted our offer. Given that the military government of General Augusto Pinochet was in power throughout the 1970s and 1980s, some archaeologists were understandably reluctant to visit us. Even more of them, however, were put off by the late Junius B. Bird of the American Museum of Natural History.

Dean of paleo-Indian research in South America, Bird was sent to inspect the site in 1979, when the National Geographic Society was funding our excavations. He arrived at the site early, when we were still establishing our base camp and grid system. Bird stayed for just two days, during which time we screened dirt only from the site's sterile upper layers. He later told colleagues in the United States and Chile that he did not see any cultural materials at Monte Verde and that the site was still of questionable value.

As far as artifacts were concerned, Bird spoke the truth. If he had stayed just two more weeks at the site, however, he would have seen us uncover the dramatic 12,500-year-old remains. As a result of that visit, unfortunately, the archaeological community—particularly Thomas F. Lynch of Cornell University in Ithaca, New York, and other strong advocates of the Clovis paradigm—joined Bird in dismissing the site.

⋘◉⋙

Much of the debate about the existence of pre-Clovis peoples in the Americas hinges on standards of archaeological evidence. Clovis advocates maintain, with some justification, that most pre-Clovis sites are nothing more than jumbled deposits of old soil and much younger artifacts and plant remains. Pre-Clovis advocates counter that their opponents are isolationists and chauvinists, that they too often reject sites without proper evidence of disproof. If the same standards were applied to Clovis sites, they go on to say, many of those sites would not be accepted either.

In the years since Bird's visit, Clovis proponents, led by Lynch, have criticized Monte Verde on nearly every count. The site's 12,500-year-old layers, they say, must be contaminated by younger artifacts that worked their way down with burrowing animals, tree roots or through cracks in the ground. The material that was radiocarbon-dated must be contaminated by petroleum. The wood and bone artifacts must have been picked up from another site and washed into Monte Verde by floods.

None of those claims have been backed up by any geological or archaeological evidence. In the fifteen years that our team worked at the site, we did not find a single artifact above the 12,500-year-old level. There is one Archaic site, between 8,000 and 5,000 years old, about a third of a mile upstream from Monte Verde. But those deposits are buried several hundred yards inland, in an intact stratum not subject to erosion or flooding. The artifacts from that site, in any case, are made of raw materials entirely different from those at Monte Verde. Moreover, there is no geological, archaeological or other evidence to indicate that the younger Monte Verde remains were ever disturbed. The footprints, house floors, tied and knotted strings and other materials we found—all of them intact—verify the site's high archaeological integrity.

In recent years, as we have published more data on the site, much of the criticism of it has subsided. Even Lynch, to his credit, has conceded that the younger level of the site is valid, though he and others reserve final judgement until all the archaeological data is published. I can only hope that my second volume of findings from Monte Verde, due to be published by Smithsonian Institution Press [in] February [1997], will put their remaining doubts to rest.

~◎~

Support for pre-Clovis colonization of the Americas is starting to come from other disciplines as well, though each new theory brings its own guesses, loose ends and inconsistencies. The linguist Richard A. Rogers of the University of Kansas in Lawrence thinks native North American languages are too various to have evolved only in the past 11,000 years. Given the rate at which languages diversify, he suggests that people were living in southern parts of the continent substantially more than 18,000 years ago, when the Pleistocene ice sheets had reached their greatest extent.

The bioanthropologist Christy G. Turner II of Arizona State University in Tempe has proposed an alternate scenario. On the basis of a comparison of teeth from 9,000 skeletons discovered in Eurasia and in America, he has proposed that the first immigrants entered Alaska from northern China more than 12,000 years ago. Their descendants then rapidly colonized the Americas, all the way to Tierra del Fuego. Other biological evidence, such as the high incidence of shovel-shaped incisors, the absence of blood group B and the rarity of group A, shows that all Native Americans except the recently arrived Eskimos and Aleuts are closely related to one another and clearly distinct from their Asiatic ancestors.

Some biological anthropologists suggest that Native Americans are genetically similar because the first colonizers were few in number—perhaps only a single band of hunters and foragers. But the diverse lineages indicated by the genetic data also suggests that people arrived in the Americas more than 11,000 years ago, and that more genetic variability exists among members of the Native American population than anyone had previously estimated. It may be that instead of a massive migration of big-game hunters at the end of the Ice Age, between 12,000 and 11,000 years ago, several small bands walked from Siberia to Alaska much earlier. To avoid the massive ice sheets that mantled Alaska until about 13,000 years ago, they may have skirted the Pacific coast on foot or by boat.

The migration to the Americas represents the last step in a worldwide human dispersion. Recent findings of fossil skeletons and genetic data indicate that people physically identical to ourselves lived in Africa and the Near East at least 90,000 years ago. From there they spread out across the face of Europe and Asia in slowly advancing waves, reaching China, Japan and Australia about 30,000 years ago. Many archaeologists believe that only fully modern humans had the skills and tools necessary to adapt successfully to the harsh, arid grasslands of Siberia and, later, to push into the coldest reaches of North America.

The big picture of modern human origins has become clearer, but the debate about allegedly pre-Clovis peoples remains as contentious as it was when the first Ice Age sites were discovered more than fifty years ago. Monte Verde demonstrates conclusively that people were living in the Americas more than 12,000 years ago. But archaeologists still have little solid evidence to suggest that people made it to the New World before 15,000 years ago.

⋅⦿⋅

Although I was braced for some criticism when we first began excavating Monte Verde, I was taken aback by how quickly our work was cast into the middle of the pre-Clovis controversy. Every few months, it seems, a new instant analysis of Monte Verde and other pre-Clovis sites appeared, all without a site visit or a review of all the evidence. Given that many good archaeologists, including the late Ruth Simpson and Louis S. B. Leakey, have lost some of their standing as "objective" scientists by championing failed pre-Clovis sites, the skepticism is understandable. And to be honest, I have been guilty of some instant analysis of my own—for example, when questioning finds at the Pedra Furada site in Brazil, which are said to be between 15,000 and 45,000 years old. Instant-opinion-hurling has become something of a sport in the study of the first Americans—a sport that reveals our arbitrary understanding of little-known sites and of the peopling of the Americas.

Much of the bickering, I believe, has served only to trivialize the processes of scientific proof, criticism and debate. In the case of many early sites, it has distracted archaeologists from the cultural value of their findings and from the interdisciplinary research methods they have employed. More important, it has led to a neglect of questions such as, Why did people migrate to the New World in the first place? And how did they adapt so quickly to environments ranging from the frozen wastes of Alaska to the equatorial rain forests of South America? In archaeology, it sometimes seems, a single priority—the omnipotent radiocarbon date—still overshadows any other information about a site.

Admittedly, the date that people first arrived in the New World is a key to how they managed to do so. Depending on when they arrived, the first Americans might have had to navigate an ocean or traverse glaciers, build snow shelters against the cold or thatched huts against the tropical rains. Yet the dating game has little importance if one cannot assign wider cultural and historical meaning to an archaeological site.

Archaeologists will probably never find the remains of the very first Americans. Even if they do, they may not recognize those remains for what they are. Like the Mapuche's ancestors, those of us who study them are bound to go down many long paths that lead nowhere, and sometimes to turn on one another in frustration. But if we give as much attention to the pattern and process of human dispersion as we do to its timing, perhaps we can get better at choosing the good paths—and at making the journey a joyful one.

POSTSCRIPT

Did People First Arrive in the New World After the Last Ice Age?

Even if one accepts Monte Verde as a genuine pre-Clovis site, how widespread across the hemisphere were such pre-Clovis settlements? Were the Monte Verde settlers with their simple technologies in use 14,000 years ago ancestors of peoples living in the region who had a more sophisticated Clovis technology? Do Monte Verde and Clovis sites represent two distinct migrations into the New World or the rapid cultural evolution of a single people? Moreover, dating Monte Verde to 14,000 years ago does not explain where the Monte Verde people came from, how long they had been in the Americas, or how they got there.

The debate over Monte Verde raises many questions that will continue to challenge archaeologists for many years to come. It will continue to raise issues about the limits of carbon-14 dating and more generally about the standards of archaeological evidence. But it also raises questions about archaeological models. Why have early sites been so difficult to locate? Are archaeologists looking for the right kinds of artifacts? Do we have reasonable models of human settlement patterns that would allow us find occupation sites used by people 30,000 years ago?

Those interested in the early debate about Monte Verde and the question of whether any preglacial sites exist in the New World should consult Dillehay's first report, "Early Rainforest Archaeology in Southwestern South America: Research Context, Design, and Data at Monte Verde," in B. A. Purdy, ed., *Wet Site Archaeology,* (Telford Press, 1988), together with Thomas Lynch's assessment, "Glacial-Age Man in South America? A Critical Review," *American Antiquity* (vol. 55, 1990); Dillehay and Michael B. Collins's "Monte Verde, Chile: A Comment on Lynch," *American Antiquity* (vol. 56, 1991); Ruth Gruhn and Alan L. Bryan's "A Review of Lynch's Descriptions of South American Pleistocene Sites," *American Antiquity* (vol. 56, 1991); and Lynch's "Lack of Evidence for Glacial-Age Settlement of South America: Reply to Dillehay and Collins and to Gruhn and Bryan," *American Antiquity* (vol. 56, 1991).

Students may also find two recent popular articles about the first Americans of interest: *Archaeology* (November/December 1999) published a book review essay by Mark Rose, which outlines the current debate, and *Scientific American's Discovering Archaeology* (February 2000) devoted a special section to "The Puzzle of the First Americans," dealing with a variety of current research problems and theoretical concerns.

ISSUE 7

Did Polynesians Descend
from Melanesians?

YES: John Edward Terrell, from "The Prehistoric Pacific," *Archaeology* (November/December 1998)

NO: P. S. Bellwood, from "The Peopling of the Pacific," *Scientific American* (November 1980)

ISSUE SUMMARY

YES: Archaeologist John Edward Terrell argues that while all indigenous peoples in the Pacific had ancestors who lived in Southeast Asia in the very distant past, Polynesians represent a local stock, which derives itself biologically, culturally, and linguistically from a cultural melting pot in Melanesia.

NO: Archaeologist P. S. Bellwood contends that the Polynesians represent the extreme eastern expansion of the Mongoloid peoples he calls *Austronesians*. He states that Austronesians originally came from Taiwan to Southeast Asia and passed through Melanesia on their way to the Polynesian Islands.

For more than a century anthropologists have debated three questions about the prehistory of Pacific Islanders: (1) Where did the Polynesians come from? (2) What led people to settle the remote islands we now know as Polynesia? and (3) How are the Polynesians related to other Pacific Islanders biologically, linguistically, and culturally?

Archaeologists generally agree that the earliest archaeological evidence of human settlement east of Fiji dates to about 3,500 years ago. Today, there is also a fundamental agreement among Pacific prehistorians that the first settlers in Polynesia came from the west. Yet there is little consensus about who first reached Polynesia and to which cultural groups these settlers were most closely related.

There is an especially vocal disagreement about the significance of a certain distinctive kind of pottery called "Lapita" after the site where it was first found in New Caledonia. Lapita pottery is found in many parts of Island Melanesia, where people have much darker skin than Polynesians, but it is also found in the earliest sites in Western Polynesia, where people now have a lighter skin color and straighter hair than their Melanesian neighbors. Are Polynesians descendants of the Melanesian peoples living immediately west of them, or alternatively, are Polynesians descendants of lighter-skinned Southeast Asians who migrated into and through Melanesia, bringing with them efficient canoes, Lapita pottery, and more complex patterns of social organization?

John Edward Terrell argues that all indigenous peoples in the Pacific ultimately had ancestors in Asia but that ties to Southeast Asia are very ancient. He contends that all of the traits that we use to identify Polynesians can be found in Melanesia. He sees the northern coast of New Guinea and the Bismarck Archipelago as an "ancient voyaging corridor," which served as a great cauldron of cultural interaction. Here the ancestors of today's Polynesians practiced the art of sailing, long-distance canoe building, and pottery making for perhaps two or three thousand years before some eventually colonized the southern island groups of Vanuatu and New Caledonia and probably accidentally reached Fiji and nearer parts of Polynesia.

P. S. Bellwood counters that the Polynesians represent the extreme eastern expansion of the Mongoloid peoples. He contends that these *Austronesians* originally came from Taiwan to Southeast Asia and passed through Melanesia on their way to the Polynesian Islands. Bellwood argues that biologically, linguistically, and culturally Polynesians do not resemble Melanesians. Bellwood believes that when the neolithic Austronesians entered Melanesia, their numbers were too small to have much impact on the older neolithic communities of New Guinea and the Melanesian Islands, so they established colonies in small pockets along the New Guinea coast and in the Bismarck Archipelago. He argues that prior to settling Polynesia, Austronesians lived for a time in Melanesia but had little interaction with the earlier, darker-skinned settlers of Melanesia, who may have been there for 30,000 years. Thus, when Austronesians left their colonies in the Bismarck Archipelago to settle the Polynesian Islands, they brought with them a culture that had evolved in Southeast Asia.

Although this sometimes rancorous debate concerns very specific details primarily of interest only to Pacific archaeologists, the debate hinges on how archaeologists and other anthropologists can and should analyze different kinds of data about human variation in race, language, and culture. Archaeological evidence can tell us certain things about how the earliest Polynesians lived, but what can we infer about biological traits or language from excavated artifacts? What can data about the languages people speak across the Pacific today tell us about either the languages or the racial type of peoples living three or four thousand years ago? Do biological traits, languages, and material culture change at the same rates? Or alternatively, should we be careful in drawing conclusions about one of these dimensions of human variation based on data from another? What kinds of data do we need to be able to reconstruct the prehistory of the Pacific?

John Edward Terrell

 **YES**

The Prehistoric Pacific

Fifty years ago, the war in the Pacific over, America found herself the care-taker of more than 1,400 islands and atolls in the former Japanese mandated territory of Micronesia. And two events in 1947 shaped how an entire gener-ation would think about the Pacific islands. In January, James A. Michener's *Tales of the South Pacific* was published. "I wish I could tell you about the South Pacific," Michener begins. "The way it actually was. The endless ocean. The in-finite specks of coral we call islands." So movingly did he talk about the war and its human stories that for many it is impossible to think about coconut palms and island people without also recalling Bali-ha'i, Nurse Nellie Forbush from Little Rock, First Lt. Joe Cable, Emile De Becque, Bloody Mary, and her daughter, the delectable Liat. Then, on April 28, the Norwegian adventurer Thor Heyerdahl and five companions began their epic voyage of 101 days and 4,300 nautical miles from Peru to Raroia in French Polynesia. The war-weary public soon loved *Kon-Tiki*, Heyerdahl's recounting of his experiences—men against the sea—as much as they loved the human stories Michener brought so vividly to life. Yet the voyage of the *Kon-Tiki* had a larger purpose. The rugged Norwe-gian who masterminded the whole adventure wanted to set the scientific world on fire and prove, contrary to established scientific opinion, that in ancient times Native Americans could have rafted successfully across the savage ocean to colonize Polynesia....

Enter Edward W. Gifford

But life is not without its ironies. On February 24, 1947, the American archaeol-ogist Edward W. Gifford and his wife left San Francisco on the Norwegian motor vessel *Thor I* bound for the Fiji Islands in the western Pacific. The Giffords ar-rived there on March 23, more than a month before the *Kon-Tiki* rafted out from Callao Harbor on the Peruvian coast. While Gifford was not the first to practice modern archaeology in the South Pacific, he was among the vanguard of se-rious postwar archaeological investigators. As *Kon-Tiki* headed toward French Polynesia, archaeology was about to sink any serious academic interest in what Heyerdahl had to say about the peopling of Polynesia.

From John Edward Terrell, "The Prehistoric Pacific," *Archaeology*, vol. 51, no. 6 (November/December 1998). Copyright © 1998 by The Archaeological Institute of America. Reprinted by permission of *Archaeology* Magazine.

Today most experts in archaeology, human genetics, linguistics, and other fields agree that Heyerdahl's thesis about Native Americans settling Polynesia is without foundation. . . . Unfortunately, he had people in prehistoric times moving into the Pacific east to west out of the Americas instead of west to east from Asia—at the exact time that Gifford and, soon, others were discovering solid archaeological evidence of humankind's antiquity and travels in the Pacific.

⋘◉⋙

Fifty years ago Heyerdahl's radical ideas aroused both anger and envy in scholarly circles; today there is no contest. Scholars now know that everything and everyone in the Pacific in ancient times came from the west, not from the Americas, except for an important food plant, the sweet potato, which all agree must have been introduced somehow from South America to some parts of the Pacific in pre-European times.

While Heyerdahl's ideas are history these days, heated controversies and strong academic rivalries in the study of Pacific prehistory are not a thing of the past. Passions still run high when Pacific experts get together. To see why, one needs to understand the agenda for archaeology that grew up in the Pacific after the war. That agenda is now under attack, not so much by young Turks playing the role of modern-day Heyerdahls as by the growing weight of new research findings in archaeology, social anthropology, experimental voyaging, and human genetics.

After the war, there was a small migration of European and American anthropologists and archaeologists to Micronesia, Melanesia, some parts of Polynesia, and to expanding universities in New Zealand and Australia. As they began to cultivate this new frontier, they argued that the remoteness of the Pacific islands was a scientific virtue rather than a research handicap. In the mid-1950s, the renowned American anthropologist Ralph Linton wrote,

> The marginal Malayo-Polynesian cultures which have survived in Oceania and Madagascar have contributed little to the main streams of cultural evolution. However, they have provided students of society and culture with some of their most interesting comparative material. The relative isolation of many of the islands and the general tendency of the Malayo-Polynesians to live in small endogamous tribes, or even villages which avoid outside contacts, has provided an excellent opportunity for the study of the results of independent cultural growth.

Perhaps because of the victory in the Pacific and the United States' stewardship over Micronesia, there was a proprietary tone to much of this new scholarship. As one official government report in 1947 declared,

> Our recent war in the Pacific brought into sharp focus the glaring lack of scientific knowledge and data in practically every field and hampered military operations in many different ways. It has become widely evident that the prosecution of fundamental research in the Pacific area is a matter of vital importance to our national defense.

Before the war, the myths and legends of the islanders had been the basis of everyone's understanding of Pacific prehistory. Given the postwar scientific spirit, it is hardly surprising that scholars began to question the truthfulness of traditional tales and to replace oral history and speculative reconstructions of the past based on the writings of early European explorers, missionaries, and ethnologists with the concrete findings of professional "dirt" archaeology. From the mid-1950s onward, the views promoted by Andrew Sharp, a New Zealand government civil servant and student of languages, in *Ancient Voyagers in the Pacific* (1956) and *Ancient Voyagers in Polynesia* (1963) were widely debated and frequently endorsed. He sought to refute once and for all the romantic claims of the previous generation of Pacific scholars that the ancient Polynesians had been skillful, cosmopolitan voyagers, authentic "Vikings of the Sunrise"—as Sir Peter Buck, a New Zealand Maori, had titled his 1938 book championing this older view. Sharp argued that prehistoric methods of navigation and sailing everywhere in the world had never been good enough for people to find new islands, determine their true geographic location, return home safely, and later either lead deliberate voyages of colonization back to their discoveries or tell others how to reach them. Consequently, he insisted, prehistoric people could only have discovered and colonized islands by one-way voyages in which deliberate navigation to known destinations played no part. If they had been forced to sail more than a few hundred miles from home to find new land, the settlers would have been lost to the world. . . .

Radiocarbon dating was a postwar development, and even after dates for archaeological finds in Oceania started being published, there was a prevailing sense that the Pacific islands had probably been the last place on earth to be colonized by people. It was recognized that migrants had undoubtedly reached Melanesia and Australia long ago, but nobody seemed overly concerned to find out how long ago that was—possibly because the story of the Polynesians and the settlement of Polynesia seemed such a challenging and dramatic achievement; and probably also because the Polynesians were not dark skinned, did not have a reputation for being as nasty, shifty, and cannibalistic as Melanesians, and were reportedly so willing to let foreigners partake in their sexual delights.

Scholars knew that the subdivision of the Pacific into the culture areas labeled Polynesia, Micronesia, Melanesia, and Malaysia or Southeast Asia was more convenient than actual. It is estimated that 1,900 to 2,100 languages— one-third of all the languages in the world—are spoken in the Pacific, and there are literally hundreds of recognizably different island societies. The biological diversity of the islanders is also extraordinary. While the incredible scope of human diversity in the Pacific cannot be pigeonholed into these nineteenth-century culture areas, the prevailing sense of Pacific islands cultural geography remained tied to them. The anthropologist and archaeologist Alexander Spoehr wrote in 1952,

It is largely within this framework that students of Oceanic prehistory have attempted to reconstruct the past movements of peoples, the diffusion of cultures, and the development of regional culture growths.

Dominant ideas about historical change in the Pacific—about cultural evolution—were grounded in the belief that the isolation of islands, combined with local environmental differences, must have led to the remarkable cultural and biological diversity of the Pacific islanders. Spoehr wrote,

> The island environment itself had decidedly limiting influences. Large concentrations of population acting as points of continuous diffusion and interaction over a major region were virtually impossible, at least in contrast to continental areas such as Meso-America or the Near East.

Despite their facility with watercraft, the islanders must have found the ocean to be a barrier to travel, diffusion, and mutual support....

❧

Stated simply, therefore, scholarly thought about Pacific prehistory after World War II was based on a belief in a shallow depth of time, reliance on an outdated cultural framework for research and interpretation, and an acceptance of isolation as the defining feature of life. George Stocking, an historian of anthropology, has noted something else about the postwar era: a resurgence within anthropology of the promise of scientific knowledge as an antidote to the horror of the Holocaust and the universal terror of the atomic bomb. Scholars saw modern, scientific archaeology as a way to give Pacific islanders what they had lost by not knowing how to write things down—their real "culture history."

In our current era of skepticism about science, the postwar research agenda in the Pacific no longer looks as sound as it once did. Scholars now see that 50 years ago they may have been behaving more like colonialists than like sympathetic friends of the Pacific islanders. Scholarly views are now undergoing a major shift in perspective and underlying assumptions, but this shift is being driven as much by new research data as by a new willingness to accept that there are alternative ways of knowing the world. Instead of looking at the islands as remote, undeveloped human colonies scattered across a vast and empty expanse of sea, scholars are now discovering that the Pacific was an early sphere of human accomplishment, on land and sea, where the ocean was more an avenue for exchange and diffusion than a barrier to human affairs. So much is happening today in Pacific archaeology that only a few major trends can be noted here under four themes: time, colonization, voyaging, and survival.

Like many Native Americans, Pacific Islanders are not always glad to be told by academics that their ancestors came from somewhere else in the world. Local oral traditions may claim, "We, the people of this place, have always lived here." It is also not uncommon to hear in these legends that their ancestors originally lived underground near where people currently have their villages and gardens. Astonishingly, archaeologists now realize some of these traditions may be closer to the truth than they would have judged 50 years ago, because the bottom has fallen out of everybody's sense of time in the Pacific. The archaeologist David Harris recalled recently,

> I well remember, as an undergraduate in the early 1950s, being taught that Australia was a laggard among the inhabited continents, not colonized until a mere 5,000 or so years ago when humans, probably accompanied by dingoes, appeared on the scene.

Today just about everywhere archaeologists dig in Australia, New Guinea, and the neighboring islands in the southwest Pacific, at least as far as the northern Solomons, they are finding traces of humankind dating back to more than 30,000 years ago. Thermoluminescence dates from the Northern Territory of Australia suggest human occupation of that continent sometime between 50,000 and 60,000 years ago. Island legends claiming that "we have always lived here" no longer look so far-fetched.

Humankind's antiquity in Australia, New Guinea, and neighboring islands in the southwest Pacific is remarkable. But scholars after the war did not merely misread the chronology of the colonization of the Pacific, they badly misread islanders' place in prehistory. Oceania was clearly not one of the last places on earth to be colonized by *Homo sapiens,* and the early dates for archaeological finds in the southwest Pacific are directly challenging our conventional sense of its ancient geography. Getting off the Asian mainland and out to the islands must have been much easier than anyone had suspected, for people were doing so more than 30,000 years ago. While scholars have normally treated Southeast Asia, New Guinea, and Australia as separate arenas of study, it now looks as if these areas have a shared history.

Ancient Canoe Seaway

Similarly, it seems improbable that people were lost to the rest of the world after the colonization of the southwest Pacific so long ago. There are no real physical barriers to voyaging through the many islands, large and small, between Southeast Asia and the Solomons. It is conventional in archaeological circles to say that New Guinea, Australia, and Tasmania were a single landmass in the late Pleistocene, a geographic entity called Sahul or Greater Australia. Archaeologist and skilled yachtsman Geoff Irwin of the University of Auckland has observed that after people had reached them, island Southeast Asia, New Guinea, and many of the smaller islands in the southwest Pacific were stepping-stones in an ancient "voyaging corridor," or canoe seaway, between Asia and the Solomons. In effect, these stepping-stone islands can be thought of as single "sea-mass," not just in the Pleistocene but afterward, too. While archaeologists once focused their attention on documenting "the date of first colonization" as possibly the most crucial historical event in the prehistory of people in Oceania, it now seems much more important to learn when, how, and how often people living on different islands stayed in contact with one another after they got there. With more than 30,000 years of human settlement in the Pacific, finding the oldest sites in Irwin's voyaging corridor is, literally and figuratively, just one of the countless challenges that archaeologists now face.

In the 1950s Andrew Sharp wanted to put the final nail in the coffin of romantic tales about ancient voyaging prowess in the Pacific. He convinced many people that prehistoric travel in Oceania had been limited to short distances, rarely more than 200 miles of open sea. The islands in the Asia-Solomons voyaging corridor are considerably closer to their neighbors, but those east of the Solomons may be several times that far apart; for example, Hawai'i is separated from Samoa by 2,600 miles and from Tahiti by 2,734 miles. In recent years, archaeologists have learned that the Solomon Islands formed the eastern edge of the inhabited Pacific until the end of the second millennium B.C. On current evidence, deep-sea crossings and colonization of the islands beyond the Solomons started only about 3,000 years ago. This expansion of human settlement in the Pacific was linked to the rapid spread of the earliest pottery so far found in Oceania, an ornately decorated ware called Lapita after an archaeological site in New Caledonia excavated by Edward Gifford in 1952. A generation ago, all you needed to do to get Pacific scholars riled up was to mention the name Thor Heyerdahl. These days, put two or more scholars in the same room, say "Lapita," and see what happens. The reaction is likely to be as heated as anything Heyerdahl inspired.

The current debate about Lapita pottery has a serious side. The excavation of similar types of artifacts at different sites with Lapita pottery has led some scholars to conclude that this ornate ware was the product of an ethnically distinct "people" and that Lapita was a "cultural complex" carried into the Pacific by a migration of racially distinct newcomers from Asia. Those sharing this opinion are likely to suggest also that Lapita pottery was somehow tied to the spread of the Austronesian languages (50 years ago they were called "Malayo-Polynesian" languages) from Taiwan, through the Philippines, and as far east as Hawai'i and Easter Island. Some have likened the impact of these hypothetical Lapita people on life in the Pacific islands thousands of years ago to the impact of Europeans on the Americas.

Others, however, find it easier to accept that Lapita developed right where the oldest Lapita sites have so far been found, in the Bismarck Archipelago northeast of New Guinea. Many of these skeptics, however, are willing to accept that newcomers from somewhere west of New Guinea could have added the art of pottery-making to the cultural stew bubbling in Melanesia in the second millennium B.C. It makes more sense to these scholars to dig prehistoric sites in the Bismarck Archipelago to find out why, around 3,000 years ago, the art of making Lapita pottery moved so quickly from there to islands as far east in the Pacific as Fiji, Tonga, and Samoa than to look for Lapita's precursors somewhere in Southeast Asia.

Pacific archaeologists have not always been conscientious about finishing and publishing their excavation reports, and, unfortunately, there are glaring holes in our knowledge of Lapita pottery and Lapita sites. In fact, Lapita as a cultural complex has never been adequately defined on the basis of shared traits. Most experts agree that sites with Lapita pottery have also produced evidence of arboriculture (e.g., candlenuts, cycads, Canarium almonds), horticulture (inferred from the size of the sites), exploitation of marine resources (including fish, shellfish, turtles, and porpoises), some terrestrial hunting, introduced animals (pigs and chickens), and settled village life, as well as the transfer of raw materials and finished goods, including pottery. What they do not agree on is whether this suite of traits was unique to the earliest Lapita sites in the Bismarcks. Without knowing what life was like at non-Lapita sites, we simply cannot know whether these presumed Lapita traits were new to Melanesia at that time and, equally important, if their joint appearance at archaeological sites truly defines a culturally distinct Lapita complex. At present, no one is even sure how many of these traits must occur at any given site to qualify it as Lapita. All these concerns are critical, for what may actually be important about Lapita is not whether these characteristics originated in Asia or Melanesia but whether they occur together (at least to begin with) only at Lapita sites. Said differently, even if all of these traits were present in Melanesia long before Lapita, their joint appearance at Lapita sites may be telling us that something new—something uniquely "Lapita"—was going on.

ᥱᥣᥩᥬ᥮

For now, it seems that nothing in particular, perhaps not even Lapita pottery itself, can be taken confidently as an indicator that one is digging a genuine Lapita archaeological site. It is just too soon, therefore, to say if Lapita pottery was the hallmark of a single, identifiable archaeological culture or the material expression of a single ethnic group or biologically distinct population. On current archaeological evidence, it may have taken only a few hundred years, maybe less, for the art of making Lapita pottery to travel from the Bismarck Archipelago east to Tonga and Samoa and south to Vanuatu and New Caledonia. The speed at which people and pottery traveled to previously uninhabited islands in the Pacific 3,000 years ago is difficult to explain as merely a predictable human response, say to famine or overcrowding in the older settled parts of the Pacific. It is still anyone's guess what may finally have encouraged people with Lapita pottery to move away from home and risk sailing in deeper waters beyond the Solomons. Significant improvements in canoe-building and navigation, wanderlust, a sense of adventure, a pioneering spirit, and similar motivations have all been suggested.

Some experts have concluded that the domestication of certain kinds of plants and animals—chiefly those thought to be of Asian origin such as dogs, pigs, and chickens—somehow fueled Lapita's expansion in the Pacific. Lapita, they say, was a by-product of what some have described as a "Neolithic Revolution," based on early rice cultivation in Asia, which fueled a population expansion and resulted in migrations. This assessment underplays both the complexity of human subsistence practices and an awkward fact: as far as anyone knows, rice cultivation only made it to the Mariana Islands in western Micronesia in prehistoric times and even there only shortly before the arrival of Europeans in the early 1500s.

Arguing that the islanders needed a Neolithic Revolution to get themselves moving through the Pacific may not even be necessary. By 6,000 years ago, after the end of the Pleistocene, the world's sea levels had reached to within a few feet of their current height and coastlines were near their present position. Pacific archaeologists are only now beginning to appreciate the impact that this stabilization may have had on the availability of naturally productive coastal resources in island Southeast Asia and elsewhere in the voyaging corridor to the Solomons. In my own research area, the Sepik coast of Papua New Guinea, we suspect that by the second millennium B.C., newly stabilized coastal lagoons may have reached a level of natural productivity great enough to support major human population growth fueled mostly, but probably not entirely, by wild foods (notably fish, shellfish, nuts, and edible starch from the pith of the sago palm). Based on pioneering research in East Sepik Province by Pamela Swadling and her colleagues at the Papua New Guinea National Museum, and our own work at Aitape in West Sepik Province, we now think that it was not so much the domestication of certain species, like corn in the Americas, that fueled prehistoric culture change in the Pacific after the Pleistocene, but the increasing abundance of wild foods, somewhat like the remarkable productivity of salmon runs in the rivers of western Canada and the United States. If so, we think population growth supported by these expanding coastal ecosystems would have increased the scope and likelihood of travel and cultural (as well as biological) exchanges in the voyaging corridor. In a word, we now think the successes of the early Lapita colonists and others in the Pacific may have been based on a wide and varying spectrum of food resources, some wild and some, such as yams and taro and pigs and chickens, carefully managed—not just on a handful of recently domesticated species imported from Asia.

A directly related archaeological issue, one that has drawn the attention of environmental conservationists as well as the public, is how rapidly—and how destructively—ancient human colonists disrupted the island ecosystems they moved into east of the Solomons after about 3000 B.P. (before present). Archaeologists, paleobotanists, zoologists, and others have been astonishingly successful in recent years in documenting the impact that forest clearance, the exploitation of wild foods, the introduction of foreign plants and animals, the construction of prehistoric irrigation systems, and the growth of human populations all had on these small ecosystems. There has also been considerable interest in learning how such environmental restructurings led to changes in human social stratification, warfare, and the evolution of complex island polities in Hawai'i and some other parts of Oceania before the arrival of Europeans.

According to popular wisdom, islands are isolated places "entire unto themselves," as the Elizabethan poet John Donne wrote. What is happening today in the archaeology of the Pacific islands may look as marginal to archaeologists elsewhere in the world as the islanders looked to Ralph Linton in the mid-1950s. European exploration and colonization after 1492 fostered a parochial perspective on people, prehistory, and human diversity "beyond Europe" that the anthropologist Alexander Lesser labeled 38 years ago as the "myth of the primitive isolate." This is the pervasive notion that ancient or primitive peoples lived in closed societies, each one out of contact with other human groups. Today this conception still reinforces the elementary claims in popular writings that our human world is a mosaic of distinct societies, cultural traditions, and ethnic groups; that prehistory was a time of isolation, fear, and remoteness; and that the world's cultural diversity is now doomed because television, soda pop, and the Internet are conquering even the most remote corners of the globe. The advances in Pacific islands archaeology and anthropology since the end of World War II are bringing these popular truths into doubt. Even the small island and atoll societies of the vast Pacific Ocean do not fit the comfortable old stereotype of the "primitive isolate." The peoples of the Pacific and their prehistoric past are showing us that the evolution and continuance of human diversity are not a consequence of isolation, and that our present cultural diversity is not doomed as we become ever more connected.

The Peopling of the Pacific

The peopling of the Pacific was the greatest feat of maritime colonization in human history. If one begins at the beginning and chooses to trace all the movements of its major actors, the record spans perhaps two million years in time and extends beyond the Pacific proper as far west as Madagascar and as far north as mainland China above the Tropic of Cancer. Its main arena, however, consists of the islands of Southeast Asia, the subcontinent of Australia and its island neighbors, and the great ocean reaches of what today are called Melanesia, Micronesia and Polynesia. Its first maritime phase was well under way 40,000 years ago. By then certain hunter-gatherers had managed to cross a minimum of 70 kilometers of open water to settle Australia and New Guinea.

Long before the region was known to Europeans it was settled by diverse populations that have maintained their diversity down to the present day. It is impossible to explain this diversity purely on the basis of today's physical, cultural and linguistic patterns; hence the confusion of hypotheses that have proliferated until recently. Advances in archaeology, physical anthropology and comparative linguistics, mainly over the past three decades, now make possible a fresh assessment of the problem. Here I shall present this modern view. It is to some extent my own and one that not all scholars will support. It is, however, at least simple and logical and can be subjected to constant review as new data come to the fore.

To begin, consider the geography of the main arena. With the exception of New Zealand and the southern half of Australia it is a tropical area. On the west the large islands of Borneo, Sumatra and Java lie together on the shallow Sunda Shelf. At times of low sea level during the great continental glaciations of the Pleistocene these islands not only were joined together but also were connected to the mainland of Asia, thereby forming an even larger land mass that has been named Sundaland. The eastern frontier of Sundaland is delimited by the biogeographical divide called Huxley's Line, a variation on a better-known divide, Wallace's Line.

The flora and fauna on opposite sides of this frontier differ markedly from each other. To the east, in the Philippine and eastern Indonesian biogeographical zones, plant and animal life is less diverse and cosmopolitan than it is in Sundaland. Indeed, Sulawesi and the Lesser Sunda Islands in eastern Indonesia have definitely not been linked with Sundaland since at least Lower Pleistocene times, more than a million years ago. The same may be true for the Philippines.

East of this area lie Australia and New Guinea, connected by the shallow Sahul Shelf, which was also dry land at times of Pleistocene low sea level. Here the mammalian fauna includes two primitive forms—monotremes and marsupials—that have been evolving in isolation within Sahulland since continental drift separated the area from Antarctica more than 50 million years ago in Eocene times. It is true that certain marsupials managed to reach eastern Indonesia, perhaps before man first arrived there. It is also true that such advanced mammals as rats and bats reached Australia and New Guinea from Asia. Nevertheless, the basic biogeographical differences between Sahulland and its neighbors imply a high degree of isolation for Sahulland. The deep seas of eastern Indonesia have probably never been bridged.

East of New Guinea lies Oceania, first the large and close-set "black" islands of Melanesia and then the increasingly fragmented island worlds of Micronesia (meaning "small islands") and Polynesia ("many islands") that lie across the Andesite Line. (Andesite, a volcanic rock, is charateristic of the great off-shore arc of active volcanism around the rim of the Pacific basin.) The islands west of the line are large and geologically complex and exhibit such features as sedimentary rocks and mature river valleys. Beyond Fiji (and New Zealand, far to the south) these features are not known; the islands of Micronesia and Polynesia are small, jagged volcanic formations or coral atolls built on mountains long submerged. Many of these islands are ranged in chains. Nevertheless, they tend to be small, isolated and impoverished in their flora and fauna. To cite one example, in order to develop the elaborate societies that greeted Captain James Cook in the 18th century the immigrants who settled Polynesia had to bring all their domestic animals and major food plants with them on their migration eastward.

⋅⟨◉⟩⋅

At some time between one and two million years ago man first entered the western margin of this vast and empty area. The migrants were populations of *Homo erectus;* their remains have been found in central and eastern Java in geological formations of the Lower and Middle Pleistocene. Recently a few simple stone tools have been discovered in associated formations. So far there is no proof of the frequent assertion that these same early representatives of man reached either the Philippines or eastern Indonesia. Faunal evidence suggests the strong possibility that Sulawesi was connected to Borneo by a land bridge in Lower Pleistocene times, but as yet there is no definite evidence that *Homo erectus* was able to take advantage of it to migrate farther eastward.

The most recent fossil traces of *Homo erectus* in Sundaland may date back about 300,000 years. Thereafter information is virtually absent until about 40,000 years ago. Then populations of hunter-gatherers, who must have flourished in Indonesia at the time, somehow succeeded in crossing deep water to settle empty Australia and New Guinea. Perhaps their entry coincided with one of the periods of the lowest Pleistocene sea levels, which are now known to have been some 55,000 and 35,000 years ago. Even so, the immigrants still had a minimum of 70 kilometers of open water to cross; their claim to the title of the first ocean voyagers seems unchallengeable.

Physically these people were the direct ancestors of the modern Australoids. Their own ancestry, in turn, can be presumed to have included a combination of genetic inputs from mainland Southeast Asia and from the earlier *Homo erectus* population of Sundaland. The clearest archaeological evidence of their arrival comes from sites such as Lake Mungo in western New South Wales in Australia and Kosipe in the Papuan highlands of New Guinea; the sites date to between 35,000 and 25,000 years ago.

The significance of this first maritime colonization in human prehistory should be assessed in the light of similar activities elsewhere in the world. For example, major islands in the Mediterranean such as Crete and Cyprus appear not to have been settled before Neolithic times, some 8,000 years ago, even though Cyprus lies within 80 kilometers of the Mediterranean shore. Some island-hopping in the interest of procuring obsidian was going on in the eastern Mediterranean earlier than that, in Mesolithic times, but no colonization resulted.

&<◎>

Where are Australoid populations to be found today? The Aborigines of Australia and the Highlanders of New Guinea are the basic representatives of the group. The so-called Negritos of Malaya and the Philippines are almost certainly Australoid relatives, and the isolated pocket of similar peoples in the Andaman Islands north of Sumatra may also be. The people of Melanesia too are basically Australoid, but they show a genetic complexity stemming from both ancestral and recent Polynesian and Micronesian penetrations. The last two populations are of Mongoloid affinity.

In this connection some physical anthroplogists are unhappy when the term Mongoloid is applied to the people of Polynesia, and it is true that the Polynesians do not present a classic East Asian Mongoloid appearance. Indeed, many Polynesians and many peoples of southern and eastern Indonesia show a high degree of Australoid genetic inheritance. This, of course, is to be expected, given the earlier Australoid dominance in island Southeast Asia. To my mind the Indonesians, Filipinos, Micronesians and Polynesians owe their ancestry to complex patterns of migration and gene flow that originated ultimately on the mainland of East Asia, possibly north of the Tropics. Within the past 6,000 years these populations of Mongoloid ancestry have come to dominate island Southeast Asia and have gone on to settle the empty areas of Micronesia and Polynesia. Why the Mongoloid populations had so little genetic impact on much of Melanesia is a subject to which I shall return.

Having come to within six millenniums of the present, we enter the phase of Pacific settlement that has been the focus of my own research for a decade. In this phase all areas of the Pacific (apart from Australia, most of New Guinea and perhaps some adjacent Melanesian islands) were settled by people who subsisted largely by gardening and who spoke related languages within a large single family: Austronesian (previously known as the Malayo-Polynesian family). Putting aside for the moment these peoples' advanced material culture, the linguistic situation in the region is approximately as follows.

Australia for some reason remained totally isolated from the Austronesian-speakers' expansion into the Pacific, with the result that only languages unrelated to this family are found in the aboriginal population of the subcontinent. That is also true of the greater part of New Guinea, where the many languages belong to the ancient and highly diversified Papuan grouping. Other Papuan languages are found in parts of the Molucca Islands adjacent to New Guinea and in similarly adjacent Melanesian islands. Archaeological and linguistic evidence suggests that Papuan-speaking populations settled the Melanesian islands of New Britain and New Ireland (and perhaps the Solomon Islands) no later than 6,000 years ago and perhaps much earlier. The settlement of the Pacific islands beyond the Solomons, however, was solely the achievement of the Austronesian-speakers and evidently began some 5,000 years ago.

Most linguists today trace the earliest-known ancestor of the Austronesian family of languages, called Proto-Austronesian, to the island of Formosa (Taiwan), where a single such language (or a group of related languages) was probably spoken some 6,000 years ago. The ancestry of the Austronesian family before that stage is difficult to trace. No Austronesian languages are spoken today on the coast of southern China adjacent to Formosa, but it is possible that there is a relationship between Austronesian and the Thai family of languages on the mainland.

⊷⊶

When linguists reconstruct the Proto-Austronesian vocabulary, they can make certain deductions about the material culture of its speakers. Thus it appears that they cultivated rice and millet, and perhaps also yam, taro and sugarcane. Their domestic animals included pigs, dogs and perhaps chickens. Very early in the expansion of Austronesian-speakers into the islands to the south a number of purely tropical crops were added to this inventory: breadfruit, banana, sago, and presumably coconut.

The earliest Austronesian-speakers made pottery, built seagoing canoes of outrigger design and practiced various techniques of fishing. They are unlikely, however, to have known the use of metal. Hence the enormous geographical expansion of the Austronesian-speakers over the following millenniums—westward to Madagascar and eastward to Easter Island, places more than half the earth's circumference apart—was accomplished by an essentially Neolithic group of cultures. The practice of rice cultivation was not carried east of the Mariana Islands. At some time later than 3,000 years ago the peoples of island Southeast Asia acquired metal and possibly domestic cattle as well, but the use of metal did not extend beyond western New Guinea before the time of the first contact with Europeans. One may therefore conclude that the original impetus for one of the greatest colonizations achieved by man arose among people supported by a Neolithic economy and technology.

Recent excavations in coastal areas of China south of the Yangtze indicate a possible cradle area for what later emerged as the Austronesian expansion. Sites assigned to the Ch'ing-lien-kang culture have yielded evidence of rice cultivation, stone reaping knives, the bones of cattle and pigs, and pottery, both plain and red-slipped, that date to sometime between 6,000 and 5,000 years ago. Sites similar to these, some of them perhaps equally old, have been found on Formosa. They are assigned to cultures known respectively as Ta-p'en-k'eng, Lungshanoid (after the site of Lung-shan-chen in Shandong Province) and Yüan-shan. The Ta-p'en-k'eng culture, the earliest of the three, may resonably be equated with the earliest recognizable stages of the Austronesian family of languages.

Here, then, is a crucial point in the prehistory of the Pacific. Populations identified as cultivators of cereals and Austronesian-speakers reached Formosa about 6,000 years ago. If their method of growing rice was the slash-and-burn one, which is particularly prodigal of land, they would have had a good reason to seek more land in the island archipelagos to the south that lay within reach of their technically advanced outrigger canoes. The archaeological evidence suggests that at this time those southern islands were inhabited exclusively by thinly-spread bands of hunter-gatherers, who in the long run were overwhelmed by the expansion from the north.

$\mathbf{\epsilon}$⊙⟩

Little evidence is available at present from Java and Sumatra, but in the Philippines, in northern Borneo, in Sulawesi and as far east as Timor rock-shelters and caves have yielded clear archaeological sequences. Some of these show the sudden appearance of plain or red-slipped pottery between 5,500 and 4,500 years ago. Adzes made of stone shaped by grinding that are quite different from the simpler indigenous flaked stone tools also appear, although in less secure archaeological contexts. There is little alternative at present but to regard these new assemblages of artifacts as a record of a marked cultural change associated with an expanding Neolithic population, exactly as the linguistic evidence suggests.

By combining archaeological, linguistic and ecological information one can fill in the picture a little more. First, as the expanding population moved south through the Philippines, Borneo and Sulawesi its members entered a region of constantly humid equatorial climate where the early cultivated rices did not thrive and where land clearance without metal and a reliable dry season became more difficult. (The peoples of island Southeast Asia do grow rice today, but the practice seems to have spread into many areas only in recent millenniums.) Hence the newcomers' cereal crops gradually diminished in importance and were replaced as major sources of food by the tree fruits indigenous to the south (such as breadfruit, banana and coconut) and by sago-palm starch. Although the indigenous peoples were hunter-gatherers, not horticulturists, they probably exploited the same wild foodstuffs, along with wild taro and some varieties of wild yam.

Pigs, dogs and chickens appear to have adapted successfully to the southern environment. Indeed, native wild pigs are found today in both the Philippines and Sulawesi. Cattle, if the colonists attempted to transport them, did not thrive; archaeological sites of this period in island Southeast Asia hold no cattle bones. As a result when the Austronesian colonists went on to settle the Pacific, their economy was based almost entirely on tubers and fruits and included neither major cereal plants nor herbivorous animals.

By some 4,500 years ago Austronesian peoples had been expanding into the equatorial islands of eastern Indonesia for about a millennium. This expansion, which ultimately encompassed the whole of island Southeast Asia, can be compared to the expansion of Neolithic societies into Mesolithic Europe. The economy of the expanding population had undergone basic changes with respect to food plants, and the colonists themselves had doubtless come in wide contact with the indigenous Australoid hunter-gatherers of the region. One may suspect that as a result of interbreeding many of these Austronesian-speaking colonists had become genetically intermediate between the classical Mongoloid and Australoid norms. Even when allowance is made for a constant Mongoloid gene flow from the north up to the present day, one can still see, moving south from the Philippines to Java or the Moluccas, a gradual increase in the Australoid genetic inheritance. One may perhaps also infer that many of the Austronesian-speaking colonists in eastern Indonesia some 5,000 years ago would have resembled the more recent Polynesians. It must be admitted, however, that human skeletal remains in support of this view have not yet been uncovered.

⌘

By this time—that is, some 5,000 years ago—Austronesian-speaking colonists were probably on the move eastward, establishing footholds on the northern coast of New Guinea and in the neighboring Admiralty, Bismarck and Solomon islands. Here their reception was quite different from the one they had met in moving south, which brings us back to the subject of why the Mongoloid populations had so little genetic impact on Melanesia.

For some time scholars have wondered why Melanesia did not become simply a racial and cultural extension of Indonesia. The progress by the Austronesian colonists might have been slowed by their encounter with malaria, particularly if this parasitic disease was as devastating in Melanesia then as it was until quite recently. A more likely explanation, however, is that the long-established residents, in particular those of New Guinea, may have been able to hold out against the newcomers. Key information in support of this view has recently been supplied by archaeological work in the malaria-free New Guinea highlands near Mount Hagen.

Archaeologists from the Australian National University have found that beginning at least 6,000 years ago and perhaps as early as 9,000 years ago large areas of highland swamp in New Guinea were being drained by quite elaborate systems of ditches. The implication is that the drainage was undertaken to promote horticulture (perhaps the cultivation of taro, although the plant is not known to have been indigenous to New Guinea). This new discovery in the highlands raises numerous questions that are under active exploration. At present it is only possible to point out that horticulture of some kind was practiced in highland New Guinea before, on the basis of any reasonable estimate, there was contact between the Melanesians and the horticulturist Austronesians. Indeed, the Austronesians never did reach the New Guinea highlands.

The implications of early horticulture in Melanesia are great. It is possible to hypothesize that the Melanesians of New Guinea (and probably those of New Ireland, New Britain and the Solomons) had become large, fairly sedentary populations sustained by horticulture more than 5,000 years ago. If future archaeological work supports this hypothesis, then the failure of the Austronesian-speakers to overrun Melanesia may be attributable to their not having the numerical and economic superiority they had once had over the scattered hunter-gatherers of island Southeast Asia. There would have been a standoff between two Neolithic cultures.

❦

The past 5,000 years of prehistory in western Melanesia brought about a degree of cultural, genetic and linguistic complexity that is unparalleled in the Pacific and perhaps in the world. Hundreds of discrete Papuan and Austronesian languages interdigitate as far east as Santa Cruz. Most of them are spoken only in a small area, perhaps in a single valley. Genetic diversity is also enormous, and it is not correlated in any obvious way with the linguistic diversity.

Why should Melanesia be so different? One may perhaps get some answers by reconstructing the prehistory of those crucial past 5,000 years. The earliest evidence for Austronesian-speaking settlers in Melanesia comes from linguistic analysis. There is no coherent archaeological evidence of their presence before the appearance all across Melanesia of the pottery-making Lapita culture (named after the type site in New Caledonia) between 3,500 and 3,000 years ago. But by at least a millennium earlier, according to linguistic reconstructions, Austronesian-speakers had already moved into coastal locations in western Melanesia, where during an ensuing period of isolation from their Indonesian base they developed a number of linguistic peculiarities that today characterize the languages of the eastern Austronesian group. For example, the languages of eastern Micronesia and Polynesia are believed to stem from this earlier matrix in western Melanesia, rather than being transferred directly to those islands from Indonesia or the Philippines.

As for prehistoric social and economic developments in Melanesia, if an initial assumption can be made, the records both of archaeology and of recent ethnography provide some guidance. The necessary assumption is that Melanesian societies in prehistory were no more complex, particularly with respect to political integration, than they are today. If this was the case, then I suggest that the initial hunter-gatherer populations of New Guinea were organized into fairly mobile bands, each consisting of a few families, for at least the first 20,000 years of their residence. Up until the recent past such social systems were characteristic of the aboriginal peoples of Australia and the Philippines.

The next prehistoric phase would have been the initiation of horticulture in New Guinea and perhaps in adjacent islands. Along with horticulture would have come settlement into more or less permanent villages adjacent to the garden areas. As mobility became limited, the Melanesian ethnographic pattern, in which ethnic groups occupy small areas and tend to marry within them, came into existence.

Among these ethnic groups leadership is rarely hereditary. It is usually acquired in adult life by individuals, so-called big men, who are able to build up advantages over their fellow tribesmen in wealth and prestige. Until the recent past active hostilities between geographically restricted groups were frequent. If such has been the social pattern in Melanesia for 5,000 years, it is not difficult to see how genetic, linguistic and societal diversity arose. In recent times peaceful contacts between groups depended on shifting alliances, cemented by occasions of ceremonial feasting and by elaborate and often extensive trading activities. In areas of high population density the trade networks often developed into systems of great ritual complexity. At the time of the first contact with Europeans the Melanesians were the businessmen and traders of the Pacific. In this sense they were quite different from the Polynesians and many of the Micronesians, who formed ethnic groups geographically far more widespread, whose societies were characterized by systems of inherited leadership and for whom trading by individuals was usually subordinated to patterns of communal tribute or of redistribution that were focused on chiefly leaders.

Such, it seems likely, was the prevailing social and ethnic pattern in Melanesia when the first Austronesian colonists arrived. The newcomers were unable to impose their own order on Melanesia; their settlements simply increased the diversity in the region. By about 4,000 years ago cultures of the indigenous Melanesian kind had been planted as far away as New Caledonia and the New Hebrides. It is even possible that these last two areas had been colonized by Melanesians well before the first Austronesian-speakers appeared, although clear archaeological evidence for it is lacking. Meanwhile, elsewhere in the western Pacific, western Micronesia may have been settled by Austronesian-speakers moving directly from the Philippines. The extended archipelagos of eastern Micronesia, of Fiji and of all Polynesia, however, still awaited their first human settlers.

⋘◉⋙

The prehistory of Oceania now reaches its most remarkable and most expansive phase. About 3,500 years ago in western Melanesia representatives of the Lapita culture had established themselves, perhaps in the vicinity of the Bismarck Archipelago, where their distinctive stamped and incised pottery has been found. This population may have entered the area not long before, coming perhaps from eastern Indonesia or from the Philippines. So far there is no archaeological evidence on the precise point of origin of the Lapita culture, and it may even be that the characteristics that distinguish Lapita pottery actually evolved within Melanesia.

Whatever its origin, the new population did not make extensive genetic or cultural contact with the neighboring Melanesians. Instead, as the presence of Lapita pottery at coastal and offshore-island sites makes clear, the Lapita people over the next 500 years went on to colonize Tonga and Samoa, some 5,000 kilometers away in the central Pacific. The Polynesians had at last arrived in Polynesia.

So, perhaps, had the eastern Micronesians arrived in their area, although the absence of true Lapita pottery in those clayless atolls makes that part of the story hard to read. Where archaeological facts are absent, however, the linguistic evidence is suggestive. The languages of Fiji, of Polynesia as a whole and of the archipelagos of eastern Micronesia—the Caroline, the Marshall and the Gilbert islands (now Kiribati, an independent member of the British Commonwealth)—all have a common immediate origin within the Austronesian family of languages. Hence there seems little doubt that the colonizers of eastern Micronesia were also bearers of the Lapita culture.

What, besides a distinctive pottery, were the main elements of this culture? First, like the coastal Austronesian-speakers of the Philippines and Indonesia, the Lapita people practiced horticulture and caught fish. Second, also like their forebears, they were voyagers. They were more than simple sailors; they were skilled mariners who were able to maintain some degree of contact between their widely scattered settlements for several hundred years. On this point the archaeological record affords evidence of their early seafaring feats within Melanesia. Obsidian from volcanic New Britain has been unearthed at Lapita sites in Melanesia up to 2,600 kilometers away. Last of all, the Lapita people were highly successful colonizers of virgin islands.

After its initial phase of successful expansion the Lapita culture was subject to inexorable change. It vanishes from the archaeological record in Melanesia some 2,500 years ago, in the latter half of the first millennium B.C. In Tonga and Samoa, its first Polynesian outposts, the Lapita culture was longer-lived. There during the entire first millennium B.C. the new settlers developed many of the cultural characteristics that were to spread to the farthest corners of Polynesia over the next 1,000 years. Nevertheless, here too change was apparent. For example, these western Polynesians lost the craft of pottery making, possibly as a result of reduced contact with the already waning Lapita societies of Melanesia. In this connection the people of Fiji did maintain contacts with the west and as a result had a more complex archaeological record of cultural development. Today the Fijians are a population that is intermediate between the Melanesians to the west and the Polynesians to the east.

Early in the first millennium A.D. the western Polynesians, whose colonies were now more than 1,000 years old, were ready to undertake their greatest voyages. Large double canoes, able to carry the food plants and the domestic animals required for colonization, sailed off against the prevailing winds and currents to settle the Marquesas Islands in about A.D. 300 and Easter Island, one of the most isolated places on the face of the earth, perhaps a century later. By the end of another five centuries the western Polynesians had also colonized the islands of central Polynesia, the northern outlying Hawaiian chain and finally, by perhaps A.D. 900, the two great southern outliers of New Zealand.

One element that was undoubtedly essential to the success of these long and grueling voyages of discovery was strong leadership. Here the Polynesian social system of hereditary and religiously sanctioned rule must have been a great asset. By the time of Captain Cook this aspect of Polynesian social organization had given rise to the despotic and powerful chiefdoms of Tonga, the Hawaiian Islands and the Society Islands, to mention only the most developed and populous parts of Polynesia.

The Maori, the Polynesians who ended up in temperate and, by island standards, vast New Zealand, were forced into some drastic economic adaptations. They replaced their unsuccessful tropical foodstuffs with the sweet potato (introduced before A.D. 1000 from Ecuador or Peru by means unknown) and the rootlike rhizomes of native ferns. Pigs were not taken to New Zealand but dogs were, and other major sources of meat included marine mammals and moas, species of flightless birds, some of great size, that rapidly became extinct.

Early in the first millennium A.D., at a time when ocean trade between China and India had begun, the Polynesians' Austronesian cousins in the East Indies made an epic voyage of their own and settled in Madagascar, off the coast of Africa. It was not, however, until the second millennium A.D., at some time after A.D. 1100, that the Easter Islanders, some 21,000 kilometers away on the other side of the world, began to quarry and erect their famous stone statues in rows on temple platforms. Although these works have attained more notoriety than any other Polynesian architectural feat, the temple platforms, statues and funerary monuments in other parts of Polynesia are equally impressive.

So ends this reconstruction. Some of my colleagues will disagree with me when I derive the Polynesians from a homeland in Indonesia or the Philippines. There is even a published view that the Polynesians may have arisen directly from a Melanesian genetic and linguistic matrix. There is scope here for complex disagreement, but I can see little evidence in support of that hypothesis, particularly from a genetic viewpoint. At least one thing is now quite certain: the Polynesians are not of American Indian ancestry, in spite of some evidence for minor contacts with the Pacific coast of South America.

Perhaps I may finish with an observation that could have some general anthropological significance. The Polynesians, whose feats of colonization were undoubtedly the most stressful in all Oceania, also developed the largest and most centralized forms of government by hereditary chiefs in the Pacific. The ancestral Polynesians of the period of the Lapita expansion had quite clearly achieved a number of cultural adaptations—social, economic and navigational —without which the settlement of Polynesia would have been unthinkable. The systems of chieftainship, the domesticated food plants and the great canoes did not spring into being fully formed and purely by chance. They evolved partly in the early millenniums of Austronesian expansion and evolved still further as the Polynesians pushed themselves toward ever longer voyages of settlement.

For me Pacific prehistory as a whole provides a record of cultural equilibrium over long periods coupled with advancement toward greater cultural complexity. I see no signs of long-term cultural simplification or degradation, although it is true that some islands, atolls in particular, are so deficient in natural resources that the cultural development of their settlers was necessarily limited. It is also true that some islands, Easter Island in particular, had periods of cultural and demographic decline as a result of either warfare or a reduction in available resources or both. Numerous examples of environmental damage, including the degradation of vegetation and the extinction of animals in prehistoric times, can also be found throughout the Pacific. None of these exceptions, however, implies any irreversible decline in human cultural complexity. Given the many thresholds the migrants of Oceania had to cross in their long period of settlement, it is likely that any groups who slipped backward would have left few descendants to tell the tale.

POSTSCRIPT

Did Polynesians Descend from Melanesians?

We often expect that if people in two communities speak the same language they will probably have the same racial background and have similar cultures. But as anthropologist Franz Boas said many years ago, these three traits do not always co-occur, particularly if a variety of different peoples have been brought together. The United States provides an obvious example since most citizens speak English, but they have ancestors of European, Native American, African, and Asian origin. Similarly, nearly every American home has material goods made in Japan or China even though few Americans can speak Japanese and Chinese, and few Americans would be confused with nationals of those two countries.

Lapita pottery and the question of Polynesian origins raise precisely these kinds of questions about the ancestors of the Polynesians. Does the fact that excavations of early Polynesian sites contain Lapita pots mean that early Polynesians made these pots? When we find Lapita pots associated with places where Austronesian languages are now spoken, does that necessarily mean that the makers or users of these pots similarly spoke an Austronesian language? What happens to a people's language and culture when they are socially and economically linked to many other societies, each with a different mix of biological, cultural, and linguistic traits, as Terrell argues happened in Melanesia 6,000 years ago?

If the ancestors of the first Polynesians lived in a socially and economically interactive Melanesia for 3,000 years, how can we explain the different appearances of Melanesians and Polynesians today? The Fijians are dark skinned like Melanesians, yet their language is routinely grouped with the Polynesian languages. Moreover, if Polynesians are Mongoloid, why are their eyes different from those of most Asians?

Could natural selection and the "founder effect" play a role? Elsewhere Terrell has argued that all Polynesian physical traits are present in Melanesia. He accounts for the larger body type in Polynesia as the result of natural selection; larger stature would be favored in any group cast adrift for some days or weeks without sufficient food and water. Current differences in skin tone and hair texture, argues Terrell, are a random selection of traits from among those found in Island Melanesia today. Once a small group had settled in Polynesia, the founder effect would make these the predominent traits, whereas in Melanesia they are shared by only a minority of people in the original community.

If Southeast Asians brought Lapita pottery into Melanesia and then on into Polynesia, why have no Lapita pots been found in eastern Indonesia?

On the other hand, if pottery was a technology developed independently in Melanesia, why have few unambiguous early sites with pottery been found in New Guinea or the Bismarcks?

Bellwood has elaborated on his theory in several books, including *Man's Conquest of the Pacific* (Oxford University Press, 1979), *Prehistory of the Indo-Malaysian Archipelago*, rev. ed. (University of Hawaii Press, 1997), and *The Polynesians: Prehistory of an Island People*, rev. ed. (Thames & Hudson, 1987). Support for this model of Pacific prehistory can be found in archaeologist Patrick Vinton Kirsch's *The Lapita Peoples: Ancestors of the Oceanic World* (Blackwell, 1997) and in many papers by the archaeologist Roger Green, such as his "The Lapita Cultural Complex," in P. S. Bellwood, ed., *Indo-Pacific Prehistory 1990: Proceeding of the 14th Congress of the Indo-Pacific Prehistory Association* (1991). Jared Diamond's *Guns, Germs, and Steel: The Fates of Human Societies* (W. W. Norton, 1997) provides a popular account of Pacific history and prehistory supportive of Bellwood, Kirsch, and Green's model.

Terrell has developed his ideas more fully in his book *Prehistory in the Pacific Islands: A Study of Variation in Language, Customs, and Human Biology* (Cambridge University Press, 1986); in his essays "Causal Pathways and Causal Processes: Studying the Evolutionary Prehistory of Human Diversity in Language, Customs, and Biology, *Journal of Anthropological Archaeology* (vol. 5, 1986) and "What Lapita Is and What Lapita Isn't," *Antiquity* (vol. 63, 1989); in Terrell and Robert L. Welsch's "Lapita and the Temporal Geography of Pacific Prehistory," *Antiquity* (vol. 71, 1997); and in Terrell, Terry L. Hunt, and Chris Gosden's "Dimensions of Social Life in the Pacific: Human Diversity and the Myth of the Primitive Isolate," *Current Anthropology* (vol. 32, 1997). Jim Allen, who organized the collaborative "Lapita Homeland Project" in the 1980s, has developed a closely related model of Pacific prehistory. See Allen and J. Peter White's "The Lapita Homeland: Some New Data and an Interpretation," *Journal of the Polynesian Society* (vol. 98, 1989); White, Allen, and James Specht's "Peopling of the Pacific: The Lapita Homeland Project," *Australian Natural History* (vol. 22, 1988); and Allen and Gosden's *Report of the Lapita Homeland Project: Occasional Papers in Prehistory, No. 20* (Australian National University Department of Prehistory, 1991). Matthew Spriggs takes a related but somewhat divergent perspective in his book *The Island Melanesians* (Blackwell, 1997).

For a discussion of early navigation in the Pacific, see Geoffrey Irwin's *The Prehistoric Exploration and Colonisation of the Pacific* (Cambridge University Press, 1992). For a review of Austronesian historical linguistics, see Andrew Pawley and Malcom Ross's "Austronesian Historical Linguistics and Culture History," *Annual Review of Anthropology* (vol. 22, 1993) and a very different perspective suggested by Terrell in his "Linguistics and the Peopling of the Pacific Islands," *Journal of the Polynesian Society* (vol. 90, 1981). Biological evidence interpreted largely in support of Bellwood's model is discussed in A. V. S. Hill and S. W. Serjeantson's *The Colonization of the Pacific: A Genetic Trail* (Clarendon Press, 1989).

ISSUE 8

Was There a Goddess Cult in Prehistoric Europe?

YES: Marija Gimbutas, from "Old Europe in the Fifth Millennium B.C.: The European Situation on the Arrival of Indo-Europeans," in Edgar C. Polomé, ed., *The Indo-Europeans in the Fourth and Third Millennia* (Karoma Publishers, 1982)

NO: Lynn Meskell, from "Goddesses, Gimbutas and 'New Age' Archaeology," *Antiquity* (March 1995)

ISSUE SUMMARY

YES: Archaeologist Marija Gimbutas argues that the civilization of pre–Bronze Age "Old Europe" was matriarchal—ruled by women—and that the religion centered on the worship of a single great Goddess. Furthermore, this civilization was destroyed by patriarchal Kurgan pastoralists (the Indo-Europeans), who migrated into southeastern Europe from the Eurasian steppes in the fifth to third millennia B.C.

NO: Archaeologist Lynn Meskell considers the belief in a supreme Goddess and a matriarchal society in prehistoric Europe to be an unwarranted projection of some women's utopian longings onto the past. She regards Gimbutas's interpretation of the archaeological evidence as biased and speculative.

The idea that prehistoric societies were matriarchal and worshiped a supreme Goddess has deep roots in European thought. The Greeks, like the Babylonians, regarded the earth as feminine and associated it with goddesses, a notion preserved in our expressions "Mother Earth" and "Mother Nature." In the nineteenth century some cultural evolutionists, like J. J. Bachofen (*Das Mutterrecht*, Benno Schwabe, 1861) and John Ferguson MacLellan (*Primitive Marriage: An Inquiry into the Origin of the Form of Capture in Marriage Ceremonies*, 1865), postulated that the earliest human societies were woman-centered, but they became patriarchal ("male-governed") before the beginning of written records. Coincidentally some classicists began to see a single great Goddess lying behind the goddesses of classical Greece, and they linked this Goddess to the female figurines ("Venus figures") being turned up in archaeological sites in the Balkans and southeastern Europe. In 1903 the prominent classicist Jane Ellen Harrison drew the threads together, postulating that in prehistoric southeastern Europe there existed a peaceful, woman-centered civilization where people lived in harmony with nature and worshiped a single female deity. This civilization was later destroyed by patriarchal invaders from the north, who brought war and male deities. By the 1950s most archaeologists specializing in Europe accepted the view that a Goddess religion and matriarchal social system had spread throughout Europe before being replaced by the male-centered societies of the Bronze Age. But in the 1960s a young archaeologist, Peter Ucko, challenged this view on the basis of extensive analyses of figurines from throughout eastern Europe and the eastern Mediterranean. He saw that there was great variation among figurines in time and space, and far from all were female. This led the archaeological establishment to retreat to a more agnostic view, once again reserving judgment over the nature of the earliest European religions.

One archaeologist who retained and even elaborated on the theory of the ancient matriarchal society and the Goddess, however, was the late Marija Gimbutas. In the following selection, Gimbutas presents her version of the theory and some of the evidence for it. She bases her interpretation on a large body of archaeological materials, especially the remains of buildings, clay models of buildings, and figurines. She contends that this matrifocal ("woman-focused") culture was destroyed by the invasions of patriarchal, nomadic pastoralists from the steppes of southern Russia, but traces of the earlier culture linger among the non–Indo-European peoples of Europe, like the Basques, and were mixed into the later patriarchal culture.

Lynn Meskell, however, criticizes Gimbutas and her followers for adopting a highly speculative gynocentric ("female-centered") interpretation of the evidence, one that she believes consistently ignores contrary evidence and other possible interpretations. Meskell argues that Gimbutas has allowed her desire to affirm the existence of an ancient feminist utopia to color and distort her interpretation of the archaeological record, leading her, for example, to overlook the large numbers of figurines that are male or ambiguous in gender. She suggests that the current popularity of Gimbutas's view is due to "New Age" feminists hoping to ground their utopian visions in a past that they see as having been unfairly destroyed by men.

These selections raise a number of questions that are important not only for our understanding of the prehistory of Europe, but for archaeological interpretation in general. Are any other interpretations of this evidence possible? If so, how can we choose among the different possible readings? Can archaeologists insulate themselves from social and political currents of their day and provide "objective" interpretations of their findings? What is the proper role of imagination in creating a comprehensive picture of a vanished way of life from the small set of clues that have survived the vicissitudes of time?

Marija Gimbutas  **YES**

Old Europe in the Fifth Millennium B.C.

With the growing realization of the necessity to distinguish the Neolithic and Copper Age pre-Indo-European civilization from the "Indo-Europeanized" Europe of the Bronze Age, I coined, ten years ago, the new term "Old Europe." This term covers, in a broad sense, all Europe west of the Pontic Steppe before the series of incursions of the steppe (or "Kurgan") pastoralists in the second half of the fifth, of the fourth, and the beginning of the third millennium B.C., for in my view Europe is not the homeland of the Indo-European speakers. In a narrower sense, the term Old Europe applies to Europe's first civilization, i.e., the highest Neolithic and Copper Age culture focused in the southeast and the Danubian basin, gradually destroyed by repeated Kurgan infiltrations....

The two cultural systems are very different: the first is sedentary, matrifocal, peaceful, art-loving, earth- and sea-bound; the second is patrifocal, mobile, warlike, ideologically sky-oriented, and indifferent to art. The two systems can best be understood if studied before the period of their clash and mélange, i.e., before ca. 4500–4000 B.C....

Social Organization

Theocratic Monarchies? Old European societies were unstratified: there were no contrasting classes of rulers and laborers, but there was a rich middle class which rose as a consequence of metallurgy and expansion of trade. Neither royal tombs, distinct in burial rites from those of the rest of the population, nor royal quarters, distinguished by extravagance, have been discovered. I see no evidence of the existence of a patriarchal chieftain system with pronounced ranking of the Indo-European type. Instead, there are in Old Europe a multitude of temples with accumulations of wealth—gold, copper, marble, shells, and exquisite ceramics. The goods of highest quality, produced by the best craftsmen, belonged not to the chief, as is customary in chiefdoms, but to the Goddess and to her representative, the queen-priestess. The social organization represented by the rise of temples was a primary centrifugal social force.

The question of government organization is as yet difficult to answer. Central areas and secondary provinces can be observed in each culture group. Some of the foci were clearly more influential than others, but whether centralized

138

government existed we do not know. I favor the theory of small theocratic kingdoms or city-states, analogous to Etruscan *lucomonies* and Minoan palaces, with a queen-priestess as ruler, and her brother or husband as supervisor of agriculture and trade. The basis of such a structure was more social and religious in character than civil, political, or military.

The Matrilinear Society.   There is absolutely no indication that Old European society was patrilinear or patriarchal. Evidence from the cemeteries does not indicate a subordinate position of women. There was no ranking along a patriarchal masculine-feminine value scale as there was in Europe after the infiltration of steppe pastoralists who introduced the patriarchal and the patrilinear systems. The study of grave equipment in each culture group suggests an egalitarian society. A division of labor between the sexes is demonstrated by grave goods, but not a superiority of either. The richest graves belong to both men and women. Age was a determining factor; children had the lowest number of objects.

A strong support for the existence of matrilinearity in Old Europe is the historic continuity of matrilinear succession in the non-Indo-European societies of Europe and Asia Minor, such as the Etruscan, Pelasgian, Lydian, Carian, and Basque. Even in Rome during the monarchy, royal office passed regularly through the female line—clearly a non-Indo-European tradition most probably inherited from Old Europe, Polybius, in the second century B.C., speaking of the Greek colony, Lokroi, on the toe of Italy, says, "all their ancestral honors are traced through women." Furthermore, we hear from Greek historians that the Etruscans and prehistoric Athenians had "wives in common" and "their children did not know their own fathers." The woman in such a system is free to marry the man of her choice, and as many as she pleases (there is no question of adultery—that was a male invention), and she retains control of her children with regard to their paternity. This evidence led George Thomson to the assumption that group marriage was combined with common ownership in prehistoric Aegean societies. Matrilinear succession on some Aegean islands (e.g., Lesbos, Skyros) is reported by written records in the eighteenth century and continues in partial form to this very day. Matrilinear succession to real property and prenuptial promiscuity were practiced in isolated mountainous regions of southwestern Yugoslavia up to the twentieth century. Such customs are certainly unthinkable in present patriarchal society; only a very deeply rooted tradition could have survived for millennia the counter-influence of the patrilinearity of surrounding tribes.

A matrifocal society is reflected by the types of Old European goddesses and their worship. It is obvious that goddesses, not gods, dominated the Old European pantheon. Goddesses ruled absolutely over human, animal, and plant life. Goddesses, not male gods, spontaneously generated the life-force and created the universe. As demonstrated by the thousands of figurines and temples from the Neolithic through the Copper Ages, the male god was an adjunct of the female goddess, as consort or son. In the models of house-shrines and temples, and in actual temple remains, females are shown as supervising the preparation and performance of rituals dedicated to the various aspects and functions of the

Goddess. Enormous energy was expended in the production of cult equipment and votive gifts. Some temple models show the grinding of grain and the baking of sacred bread. The routine acts of daily existence were religious rituals by virtue of replicating the sacred models. In the temple workshops, which usually constitute half the building or occupy the floor below the temple proper, females made and decorated quantities of the various pots appropriate to different rites. Next to the altar of the temple stood a vertical loom on which were probably woven the sacred garments and temple appurtenances. The most sophisticated creations of Old Europe—the most exquisite vases, sculptures, etc., now extant—were women's work (the equipment for decoration of vases so far is known only from female graves). Since the requirements of the temple were of primary importance, production for the temple must have doubled or tripled the general level of productivity, both stimulating and maintaining the level of feminine craftsmanship.

Religion

Temples.   The tradition of temple buildings begins in the seventh millennium B.C. A remarkable series of temple models and actual rectangular temples from the sixth and fifth millennia B.C. bear witness to a great architectural tradition.

At present about 50 models from various culture groups and phases are known. They are more informative than the actual temple remains, since they present details of architecture, decoration, and furnishings otherwise unavailable to prehistoric archaeology. Actual remains of sanctuaries suggest that miniature models in clay were replicas of the real temples. They almost always were found at the altars, probably as gifts to the goddess.

The seventh and sixth millennia temple models seemed to have conceived of the temple as literally the body or the house of the deity. Shrine models from Porodin near Bitola in Macedonia, for instance, have a cylindrical "chimney" in the middle of the roof upon which is modeled the masked features of a large-eyed Bird Goddess, a necklace encircling her neck ("chimney"). Other models have round openings fit for the goddess to enter in the shape of a bird or are made in the form of a bird's nest....

The figurines portrayed (in clay models) and found in actual shrines are shown to perform various cult activities—ritual grinding, baking of sacred bread, attending sacrifices—or are seated on the altar, apparently used for the reenactment of a particular religious ceremony. In the mid-fifth millennium Cucuteni (Early Tripolye) shrine at Sabatinivka in the valley of Southern Bug in the Ukraine, 16 figurines were sitting on chairs on the altar, all with snake-shaped heads and massive thighs. One held a baby snake. The other group of 15 were in action—baking, grinding, or standing at the dish containing remains of a bull sacrifice. In the corner next to the altar stood a life-size clay throne with horned back support, perhaps for a priestess to supervise the ceremony. At Ovčarovo near Trgovište, northeastern Bulgaria, 26 miniature cult objects were found within the remains of a burned shrine. They included four figurines with upraised arms, three altar screens (or temple facades) decorated with symbols, nine chairs, three tables, three lidded vessels, three drums, and several dishes larger than figurines. Such objects vividly suggest ceremonies with music and dances, lustrations, and offerings.

The production of an enormous variety of cult paraphernalia—exquisite anthropomorphic, zoomorphic, and ornithomorphic vases, sacrificial containers, lamps, ladles, etc.—is one of the very characteristic features of this culture and may be viewed as a response to the demands of a theocentric culture where most production centered around the temple. The consideration of these creations is unfortunately beyond the scope of this article. Regarding the technological and aesthetic skills, nothing similar was created in the millennia that followed the demise of Old Europe.

Ceremonial Costume and Mask. A wealth of costume details is preserved on the clay figurines. Deep incisions encrusted with white paste or red ochre affirm the presence of hip-belts, fringe, aprons, narrow skirts, blouses, stoles, a variety of hair styles, and the use of caps, necklaces, bracelets, and medallions. Whether these fashions were commonly worn, or were traditional garb for priestesses or other participants in ritual celebrations, can only be conjectured. The latter was probably the case; most of the figurines seem to have been characters in tableaux of ritual. But, ritual or not, the costumes reflect stylistic conventions of dress and taste characteristic of the period.

In the female costume several dress combinations recur persistently: partly dressed figures wear only a hip-belt, or a hip-belt from which hangs an apron or panels of an entire skirt of fringe, resembling a hula skirt; others wear a tight skirt with shoulder straps or a blouse.

A number of figurines show incised or painted stoles over the shoulders and in front and back. The skirt, which generally begins below the waist and hugs the hips, has a decorative texture of white encrusted incisions, showing net-pattern, zigzags, checkerboard, or dots. The skirt narrows below the knees, and on some figurines wrappings around the legs are indicated. It may be that the skirt was slit in front below the knees and fastened between the legs with woven bands. This type of skirt gives the impression of constraining movement and quite likely had a ritualistic purpose.

The figurines tell little about male attire; males are usually portrayed nude, except for a large V-shaped collar and a belt. In the last phase of the Cucuteni culture male figures wear a hip-belt and a strap passing diagonally across the chest and back over one of the shoulders....

Special attention to coiffure and headgear is evidenced. The Bird and Snake Goddess in particular, or devotees associated with their images, had beautiful coiffures, a crown, or decorative headbands. Vinča and Butmir figurines have hair neatly combed and divided symmetrically in the center, the two panels perhaps separated by a central ribbon. Late Cucutenian figurines, primarily nude, but some wearing hip-belt and necklace, have a long, thick coil of hair hanging down the back and ending in a large, circular bun or with an attached disc, reminiscent of the style favored by Egyptian ritual dancers of the third millennium B.C. A typical item of dress is a conical cap on which radial or horizontal parallel incisions perhaps represent its construction of narrow ribbon-like bands.

Figurines were portrayed wearing masks representing certain goddesses, gods, or their sacred animals, or else they were simply shown as bird-headed (with beaked faces on a cylindrical neck), snake-headed (with a long mouth, round eyes, and no nose), or ram- or other animal-headed. Frequently-occurring perforations of the mask were obviously intended to carry some sort of organic attachment. Plumes, flowers, fruits, and other materials could have been employed in this way....

Deities Worshipped.   In the literature on prehistoric religion the female figures of clay, bone, and stone are usually considered to be the "Mother Goddess." Is she indeed nothing more than an image of motherhood? The term is not entirely a misnomer if we understand her as a creatress or as a cosmogenic woman. It must be emphasized that from the Upper Paleolithic onward the persona of the Goddess splintered the response to the developing economy, and the images of deities portray not only the single maternal metaphor of the deity. Study of the several stereotypical shapes and postures of the figurines and of the associated symbolism of the signs incised upon them clearly shows that the figurines intend to project a multiplicity of divine aspects and a variety of divine functions.

There are, in my opinion, two primary aspects of the Goddess (not necessarily two Goddesses) presented by the effigies. The first is, "She who is the Giver of All"—Giver of Life, Giver of Moisture, of Food, of Happiness; she is also "Taker of All," i.e., Death. The second aspect of the Goddess is connected with the periodic awakening of nature: she is springtime, the new moon, rebirth, regeneration, and metamorphosis. Both go back to the Upper Paleolithic. The significance of each aspect is visually supported on the figurines by appropriate symbols and signs. The first aspect of the Goddess as Giver and Taker of All, that is, as both beginning and end of life, is accompanied by aquatic symbols —water birds, snakes, fish, frogs, all animals associated with water—and representations of water itself in the form of zigzag bands, groups of parallel lines, meanders, nets, checkerboards, and running spirals. The second aspect of the Goddess as Rebirth, Renewal, and Transcendance is accompanied by the symbols of "becoming": eggs, uteri, phalluses, whirls, crescents, and horns which resemble cornucopias. The Goddess often appears in the form of a bee, a butterfly, or a caterpillar. This second group involves male animals such as bulls and dogs.

The Giver of All, the Fish, Water Bird, and Snake Goddess

Hybrids of the human female with bird or snake dominated mythical imagery throughout the Upper Paleolithic, Neolithic, Chalcolithic, and Copper Ages from ca. 26,000 to the end of Old Europe at ca. 3000 B.C., but lingered in the Aegean and Mediterranean regions through the Bronze Age and later—at least 40 percent of the total number of figurines belong to this type. The Fish, Bird, and Snake Goddesses were interrelated in meaning and function. Each is

Creatress and Giver. They are, therefore, inseparable from cosmogonic and cosmogenic myths such as water birds carrying cosmic eggs. She as the Mother or
Source is the giver of rain, water, milk, and meat (sheep, their skin and wool).
Her portrayals usually show exaggerated breasts marked with parallel lines, or a
wide-open beak or round hole for a mouth. Her large eyes are a magical source,
and are surrounded by aquatic symbolism (usually groups of parallel lines).
Beginning in the Neolithic, the ram (the earliest domesticated animal, a vital
source of food and clothing) became her sacred animal. The symbols of this
goddess on spindle whorls and loom weights suggest that she was the originator or guardian of the crafts of spinning and weaving. Metaphorically, as "the
spinner and weaver of human life," she became the Goddess of Fate.

Along with the life-giving aspect of the Goddess, her life-taking or death-
giving aspect must have developed in preagricultural times. The images of
vultures and owls are known from the Upper Paleolithic and from the earliest
Neolithic (in the frescoes of Çatal Hüyük, in central Anatolia, vultures appear
above headless human beings). The figurine type of the nude goddess with large
pubic triangle, folded arms, and face of an owl, well known from Old European
graves, may be representative of the Goddess in the aspect of night and death.

In early agricultural times, the Giver of All developed another function, a
function vital to tillers of the soil—namely, that of "Giver of Bread." Her images
were deposited in grain silos or in egg-shaped vases, where they were indispensable insurance for the resurgence of plant life. She also appears as a pregnant
woman, her ripe body a metaphor of the fertile field. She was worshipped with
her sacred animal, the pig. The fattening of the pig encouraged the growth and
ripening of crops or fertility in general.

Richly represented throughout the Neolithic, Chalcolithic, and Cooper
Ages, still another aspect of the Goddess is, by natural association, that of
"Birth-giving Goddess." She is portrayed with outstretched legs and upraised
arms in a naturalistic birth-giving posture. This stereotypic image appears in
relief on large vases and on temple walls; carved in black and green stone or
alabaster, it was worn as an amulet.

The "Periodic Regeneration" aspect of the Goddess may be as ancient as
the Giver of All aspect, since symbols of "becoming" are present in the Upper
Paleolithic: crescents and horns appear in association with Paleolithic nudes.
To regenerate the life-force was her main function; therefore, the Goddess was
flanked by male animals noted for physical strength—bulls, he-goats, dogs. In
her incarnation as a crescent, caterpillar, bee, or butterfly, she was a symbol of
new life; she emerged from the body or horns of the bull as a bee or butterfly.

The female principle was conceived as creative and eternal, the male as
spontaneous and ephemeral. The male principle was represented symbolically
by male animals and by phalluses and ithyphallic animal-masked men—goat-
men or bull-men. They appear as adjuncts of the Goddess. The figurines of ec-
static dancers, goat- or bull-masked, may represent worshippers of the Goddess
in rituals enacting the dance of life. . . .

Conclusion: The Kurgan Penetration

Old Europe was rapidly developing into an urban culture, but its growth was interrupted and eventually stopped by destructive forces from the east—the steadily increasing infiltration of the semi-nomadic, horse-riding pastoralists from the Pontic steppes. Periodic waves of infiltration into civilized Europe effected the disintegration of the first European civilization. Only on the islands, like Crete, Thera, and Malta, did the traditions of Old Europe survive for almost two millennia. The Bronze Age culture that followed north of the Aegean was an amalgam of the substrate and totally different elements of an eastern culture.

Thanks to a growing number of radiocarbon dates, archaeologists can ascertain the periods of Kurgan penetration into Europe. There was no single massive invasion, but a series of repeated incursions concentrated into three major thrusts:

- Wave No. 1, ca. 4400–4200 B.C.
- Wave No. 2, ca. 3400–3200 B.C.
- Wave No. 3, ca. 3000–2800 B.C.

The steppe (or "Kurgan") people were, above all, pastoralists. As such, their social system was composed of small patrilinear units that were socially stratified according to the strategic services performed by its male members. The grazing of large herds over vast expanses of land necessitated a living pattern of seasonal settlements or small villages affording sufficient pasturage for animals. The chief tasks of a pastoral economy were executed by men, not by women as was characteristic of the indigenous agricultural system.

It was inevitable that an economy based on farming and another which relied on stock breeding would produce unrelated ideologies. The upheaval of the Old European civilization is registered in the abrupt cessation of painted pottery and figurines, the disappearance of shrines, the termination of symbols and signs.

Old European ceramics are readily identified with the rich symbolic signs and decorative motifs that reflect an ideology concerned with cosmogony, generation, birth, and regeneration. Symbols were compartmentalized or interwoven in a myriad combination—meanders and spirals, chevrons and zigzags, circles, eggs, horns, etc. There were a multitude of pictorial and sculptural representations of goddesses and gods, of worshippers, and sacred animals. Kurgan pottery is devoid of symbolic language and of aesthetic treatment in general because it obviously did not serve the same ceremonial purposes as that of Old Europe. The stabbing and impressing technique is quite primitive and seems to focus on only one symbol, the sun. Occasionally, a schematized fir tree occurs which may symblize a "tree-of-life."

Mythical images that were in existence on the Eurasiatic steppe dispersed now over a large part of Europe, and continued to the beginning of Christianity and beyond. The new ideology was an apotheosis of the horseman and warrior. The principal gods carry weapons and ride horses or chariots; they are figures of inexhaustible energy, physical power, and fecundity. In contrast to the pre-Indo-European cultures whose myths centered around the moon, water, and the female, the religion of pastoral, semi-sedentary Indo-European peoples was oriented toward the rotating sky, the sun, stars, planets, and other sky phenomena such as thunder and lightning. Their sky and sun gods were shining, "bright as the sky"; they wore starry cloaks adorned with glittering gold, copper, or amber pendants, torques, chest plates, belts. They carried shining daggers, swords, and shields. The Indo-Europeans glorified the magical swiftness of arrow and javelin and the sharpness of the blade. Throughout the millennia, the Indo-Europeans exulted in the making of weapons, not pottery or sculpture. The touch of the ax blade awakened the powers of nature and transmitted the fecundity of the Thunder God; by the touch of his spear tip, the god of war and the underworld marked the hero for glorious death.

Lynn Meskell

 **NO**

Goddesses, Gimbutas and 'New Age' Archaeology

For a century a notion of a prehistoric Mother Goddess has infused some perceptions of ancient Europe, whatever the realities of developing archaeological knowledge. With the reverent respect now being given to Marija Gimbutas, and her special vision of a perfect matriarchy in Old Europe, a daughter-goddess is now being made, bearer of a holy spirit in our own time to be set alongside the wise mother of old.

Introduction

The field of archaeology, like many others, is prone to fads and fictions within the academic community and general public alike. A recurrent interest since the 19th century has been the notion of an omnipotent Mother Goddess, whose worship symbolizes a cultural continuity from the Palaeolithic era to modern times. The principle advocate for this theory over the past two decades, Marija Gimbutas, is seen to offer archaeological validity to these claims as a result of her recognized academic standing and long history of fieldwork in southeast European sites. From the material particulars of archaeology in her earlier work she moved toward an ideal vision of prehistory (compare Gimbutas 1965; 1970; 1971a; 1973 with interpretations in 1974; 1981; Gimbutas *et al.* 1989; 1989a; 1989b; 1991; 1992). Her widely published theories appeal to those committed to ecofeminism and the 'New Age' range of esoteric concerns, which include ancient religion and mythology. Whilst this vision of the past appears to embrace aspects of cognitive, gender and even feminist archaeologies, the interpretations it presents are simply hopeful and idealistic creations reflecting the contemporary search for a social utopia.

From Lynn Meskell, "Goddesses, Gimbutas and 'New Age' Archaeology," *Antiquity*, vol. 69, no. 262 (March 1995). Copyright © 1995 by Antiquity Publications Ltd. Reprinted by permission of the author.

The concept of The Goddess is entangled within a larger, more complex, political phenomenon that involves regional and nationalist struggles (Chapman 1994; Anthony in press), linguistic aetiology (Renfrew 1987; Mallory 1989: 81), contemporary gender struggles and the feminist cause (Hallett 1993; Passman 1993). However, the revisionist histories on offer (Eisler 1987; Gimbutas 1974; 1989a; 1989b; 1991; 1992; Orenstein 1990; Spretnak 1992; etc.) do not aim for a more complete understanding of ancient societies *in toto*. Rather, they provide altogether alternative historical projections of what certain groups see as desirable. Re-writing the past from an engendered perspective is certainly long overdue, yet re-weaving a fictional past with claims of scientific proofs (e.g. Gimbutas 1992) is simply irresponsible. Such 'new and improved' histories are more telling of contemporary socio-sexual concerns rather than their ancient antecedents.

Why the Goddess and Why Now?

Why has there been a proliferation of studies devoted to the concept of a Mother Goddess in recent years? Why has this appeal been so persistent, particularly to the general public? Whereas the academic study of figurines is usually integrated within regional culture studies, the notion of the Goddess has assumed larger proportions to the wider community. As a result, the literature of the Goddess lies at the interface where academic scholarship meets New Age gynocentric, mythologized interpretations of the past (Eisler 1987; Gimbutas 1974; 1989a; 1992; Spretnak 1992). This is a radically burgeoning field in women's studies and New Age literature, and its books must far outsell their scholarly counterparts. Since achieving icon status, The Goddess has been linked with movements and disciplines as diverse as christianity, feminism and ecofeminism, environmentalism, witchcraft and archaeology. In each of these the Goddess phenomenon is taken as a given rather than one speculative interpretation to be considered with alternative hypotheses. The past is being used in the present as an historical authority for contemporary efforts to secure gender equality (or superiority?) in spiritual and social domains.

... The current interest in the Goddess is not purely academic, but stems from a desire to remedy the results of millennia of misogyny and marginalization (Frymer-Kensky 1992: vii) in both religious and secular spheres. My contention is that the connection has materialized in response to female disempowerment in our own recent history, particularly within religious power bases. The Goddess serves as a vehicle for women's groups and activists to reinforce legitimization of their position by means of an ancient antecedent. Contrary to the bloodied, materialist history and overt androcentrism of the Church, she is earth-centered, offering refuge and a counterbalance to the remote, punitive male god of western religions (Frymer-Kensky 1992; Spretnak 1992).

... Many of these initial gynocentric theories of prehistory share a fundamental commonality to prior androcentric premises since they both employ 'sexist' paradigms in re-constru(ct)ing the past. Thus they do not promote credibility: rather they damage and delimit the positive attributes of gender-based research, due to their poor scholarship, ahistorical interpretations, fictional elements and reverse sexism. I see no detriment to current quests if we acknowledge that inequality was operative in the past, as it was in the historic cultures of the Near East and Mediterranean.

The Figurines as Archaeological Data

Figurines collectively termed Mother Goddesses or Venuses emanate from various regions and span an immense time-depth from the Palaeolithic to the Bronze Age and into historical periods, with considerable variability in form, style, decoration and context. This class of artefact—if that is an appropriate term—appears throughout much of Europe and southwest Asia, primarily southeast Europe and the Mediterranean islands from the Cyclades to Crete, Malta and Majorca (Ehrenberg 1989: 65; Malone *et al.* 1992: 76). The figures are generally accorded the status of 'art', although ethnographic evidence suggests that they do not form a distinct category. In a further tendency to project 20th-century biases of what constitutes 'good art', it has been suggested that carefully made sculptures were produced for important occasions by priestesses or mother figures (Gimbutas *et al.* 1989: 220). Conversely, the simple, schematic examples could have been made by any member of the community (male?). Figurines have been objectified, taken as devoid of spatial and cultural specificity; yet objects do not have inherent meaning divorced from their historically specific context of production and use (Hodder 1991; Dobres 1992a; 1992b).

For many figurines, provenience and context are lost due to poor excavation or non-archaeological recovery (for Cycladic figures see Gill & Chippindale 1993). Runnels (1990) and McPherron (1991) have noted the limits of excavation and recording by Gimbutas for her own site at Achilleion (Gimbutas *et al.* 1989), on which much of the larger picture is reliant. Dating, methodology, testing, typological and statistical analyses have all come under fire, not to mention artistic licence and over-interpretation. Weaknesses in scholarship have prevented Gimbutas' attempts, and the question of gender studies, to be taken seriously in archaeological circles (Tringham 1991: 97; 1993).

As part of a gynocentric agenda, female figurines have been considered largely to the exclusion of male and eferences examples (Gimbutas 1971b; 1974; 1986; 1989a; 1989b; 1992; Gimbutas *et al.* 1989), this selection shaping the vision of a single, omnipresent female deity. Her position is clear: male divinities were not prominent before the Indo-European invasion (see van Leuven 1993: 84). Many are undeniably female. Many are also male, androgynous, zoomorphic or indeterminate (see Marinescu-Bîlcu 1981; Hodder 1990; Milojkovic 1990; Pavlovic 1990; Talalay 1993); these are dismissed.

To her credit, Gimbutas assembled a large corpus of southeast European figurines in English publications, with copious photographs and illustrations. She aimed to investigate figurine attributes such as raw materials, production and form to some degree. However, studies of production have been undertaken more systematically by other scholars (Murray 1970), coupled with analyses of decorative motifs and positioning (Ucko 1968; Marinescu Bîlcu 1981; Pogozheva 1983) and patterns of breakage. It is unfortunate that Gimbutas did not incorporate findings from these studies into her later publications.

Mediterranean Matriculture and the Indo-European Debate

One key debate in 19th-century anthropology, currently experiencing a revival, hinges on the traditional matriarchal view of cultural evolution. Eminent scholars such as Morgan, Engels and Bachofen led the early debate, influenced by their own socio-intellectual biases, though failing to make the distinction between matriarchy, matrilinearity and matrilocality. Bachofen's evolutionist interpretations, long since discredited within academia, have now resurfaced in the Goddess literature....

It has become popular in the past decade to view Neolithic cultures as matriarchal or matrifocal (Hayden 1986: 17), and to depict them as peaceful, harmonious and artistic in contrast to the more aggressive, destructive patriarchal societies that followed (Chapman 1991; Tringham 1991; Conkey & Tringham in press): the overthrowing of matriarchy by patriarchial society was the real Fall which has beleaguered Europe ever since. Childe raised a powerful analogue, arguing that using female figurines to substantiate matriarchal or matrilineal society was as accurate an indicator as the image of the Virgin Mary in the modern patriarchy (Childe 1951: 65). We should not ignore the possibility of matriarchy; rather we are not clear what form such evidence would take.

This line of reasoning ties directly into the polemic debate surrounding Indo-European archaeology and linguistics, in which Gimbutas was a major player (see Renfrew 1987: xiii; Mallory 1989: 182). Briefly, her view of Old Europe in the Neolithic period was characterized by its unfortified settlements (*contra* Marinescu Bîlcu 1981; Anthony in press) where a peaceful existence prevailed without threat of violence or fear of death itself. Within the matriarchy there were no husbands, yet men fulfilled important roles in construction, crafts and trade. Women's lives were liberal, socially and sexually, and inextricably bound to the rich religious system which ensured their prominence (Gimbutas 1992). Old Europe is portrayed as culturally homogeneous (*contra* Pavlovic 1988: 33; Mallory 1989: 22), socially egalitarian (*contra* Tringham 1990: 605; Anthony in press), devoid of human or animal sacrifice (*contra* Marinescu Bîlcu 1981; Anthony in press). Accordingly, this utopian existence was abruptly destroyed by Indo-European invasions: more specifically by the equocentric Kurgan culture from the Russian steppe....

There is a striking congruence between Gimbutas' own life and her perception of Old Europe. Born in Lithuania, she witnessed two foreign occupations by 'barbarian invaders'; however, those from the East stayed. This prompted her immigration to the United States during which time the Soviet occupation of the Baltic states continued almost up until her death in 1994. In her own words, 'history is showing us between eight and ten million women had to die for her [the Goddess]... the wise people of the time... so it reminds me of the same [*sic*] what happened in Stalin's Europe when the cream of the society had to be removed and only fools were left to live. What happened in the twentieth century is the greatest shame of human history' (Gimbutas

1992). This strongly mirrors her view of Old Europe, a creative, matriarchal and *good* society which was invaded by men with weapons from the East.

Other writers (see Eisler 1987; Passman 1993) have run with Gimbutas' theories by stressing the superiority of assumed matristic cultures in Old Europe, Anatolia, Egypt and Minoan Crete on the basis of their peaceful, egalitarian, non-fortified communities and even their predisposition to vegetarianism (?) (Passman 1993: 187). Such a scenario is not borne out archaeologically. Walls and ditches at Nea Nikomedia, Dimini and Sesklo may have defensive functions. Both Neolithic and Chalcolithic sites like Tîrpesti, Ovcharovo, Polyanitsa and Tripolye clearly demonstrate fortification (Marinescu-Bîlcu 1981; Anthony in press: 20). Sites such as Dimini and Agia Sophia (Demoule & Perlès 1993) suggests status differentiation within communities, as does Selevac (Tringham & Krstic 1990: 206), with more evidence of social hierarchy from the cemeteries at Varna, Durankulak and other East Balkan sites (Anthony in press: 20). In addition, there is evidence of human sacrifice at Traian-Dealui, Fîntînilor (Marinescu-Bîlcu 1981: 135) and later from Knossos (Wall *et al.* 1986); animal sacrifices are attested at Poiana în Pisc and Anza. Artefactual evidence from Egypt indicates that weapons, in addition to items displaying battle scenes, were amongst the most common in the predynastic repertoire (see Davis 1992).

Even without the overwhelming archaeological data, historical evidence from Greece (Humphreys 1983; Hallett 1993), Egypt (Robins 1993) and Mesopotamia (Frymer-Kensky 1992) plus numerous ethnographic accounts suggest that cultures with strong female deities—if indeed they are deities—may still regard women in the profane world as a low-status group. The romanticized view of antiquity many feminists and pseudo-feminists present has more to do with creating an idealized past to contrast with our own secular, impersonal and industrialized present than with archaeological facts (Hays 1993: 84). Their visionary work links notions of 'ancient' and 'future', so enabling a richly figured heritage, once lived and lost, to be experienced again (Passman 1993: 182). This political reconstruction of a matristic past furnishes the seed for a return to Edenic conditions, ecological balance, healing the planet and matriculture itself, in opposition to the forecasts of Armageddon and the second coming (Starhawk 1982; Orenstein 1990; Passman 1993).

Cultic Figurines from a Sexist Perspective

Although proponents of post-processualism (e.g. Hodder 1987; 1990; 1991; Shanks & Tilley 1987) aim to understand symbolic systems, they still regard the archaeological record as a polysemous text that can be read (Hays 1993). Some have taken their position as reader to the extreme. Herein lies Gimbutas' attraction for a New Age audience, since she adopts the role of translator (channeller?) for a symbolic language stretching back millennia into the Neolithic mindset. In answer to Onians' claim that figurines represent ancient erotica, Gimbutas argues that 'love-making is clearly far from the thoughts of the ancient artist' (1981: 32). Knowing 'our European prehistoric forefathers were more philosophical than we seem to think' (1981: 39), she understands how they would be stunned to hear these new hypotheses. She further claims that the Achilleion figurines 'represent deities and their sacred animals, witness to continuous ritual performances in temples and at ovens in courtyards' (Gimbutas *et al.* 1989: 335). Her typological analysis was narrowed to fit these criteria, without mention of other functional interpretations. Similarly, she dismissed alternative explanations of Cycladic figures from mortuary contexts in favour of the Great Goddess (or stiff White Goddess) from a deeply rooted European tradition (1974: 158; 1992).

From the 1970s onwards Gimbutas presented arguments, with increasing fervour, to challenge a balanced and complementary view of the sexes in sacred and profane spheres (Hayden 1986; Chapman 1991). Her publications, including site reports (where one experts some attempt to discuss the data without a charged interpretation), were devoted to the Goddess and her manifestations; the gods are overlooked. At Anza 'only one [figurine] can possibly be male' (1976: 200), at Sitagroi 'only 1% can be considered as possibly portraying men' (1986: 226), at Achilleion the divine creatrix does not require male fecundity since 'her divine bisexuality stresses her absolute power' (Gimbutas *et al.* 1989: 196). In these reports every figure that is not phallic—and some that clearly are—are taken as symbols of the Goddess. This includes parallel lines, lozenges, zigzags, spirals, double axes, butterflies, pigs and pillars. Why this miscellany are self-evidently emblems of a female , much less a deity, is never explained. And indeed even the *male* may be symbolically *female:* 'although the male element is attached, these figurines remain essentially female' (1989a: 232). Gimbutas denied that phallicism was symbolic of procreation since Neolithic peoples did not understand the nature of biological conception (1974: 237).

Gimbutas was emphatic that Neolithic mythology was not polarized into male and female, due to the supremacy of the Mother. From this assumption she extrapolated, concomitantly, the role of women was not subordinate to men (Gimbutas 1974: 237; see Chapman 1991; Tringham 1991). Yet male, sexless and zoomorphic figures do exist, which makes the notion of an omnipotent Mother Goddess difficult to support. Ucko's examination of the later Knossos figurines demonstrated that androgynous examples were equal in number to the identifiable female statuettes (1968: 316; see Conkey & Tringham in press). Ucko (1968: 417) further concluded that most scholars treat male figures as exceptions, dismiss the sexless examples and regard female figurines as a singular deity without convincing explanation for their obvious variation.

The Goddess Contextualized

In addressing the archaeological context of finds at Anza, Sitagroi and Achilleion, Gimbutas interpreted partially excavated dwellings as 'house-shrines' and 'cult-places', and benches as 'altars' (1981; 1986; Gimbutas *et al.* 1989). She concluded human activities like grinding grain, baking bread, weaving and spinning were inseparable from divine participation (Gimbutas *et al.* 1989: 213-15). To Gimbutas it was 'obvious that the Goddess ruled over human, animal and plant life' (Gimbutas *et al.* 1989: 220). Perhaps these areas represented dwellings or workshops in view of associated finds like spindle whorls, a needle, awl and pottery discs? Indeed, few artefacts and features from these sites are assigned a mundane status (1981: 198–200; Gimbutas *et al.* 1989: 36–46, 213–15).

... Evidence from Anza, Selevac, Tîrpesti and Achilleion (see Gimbutas 1981; Gimbutas *et al.* 1989; Marinescu-Bîlcu 1981; Hodder 1990; Tringham 1990) indicates that figurines are found in every kind of context—refuse pits included. This would signify, as Gimbutas prefers, that the sacred is everywhere. Conversely, it could demonstrate that these figures are not sacred at all; or they may have multiple meanings which change as a figure is made, used and discarded.

Alternative Hypotheses

Recent work in Kephala (northern Greece) uncovered figurines near graves, which would indicate a possible function as territorial markers to reinforce ancestral ties in the Neolithic period (Talalay 1991: 49). Ethnographic reports from Africa over the past 200 years also suggest this kind of placement may be associated to ancestor cults. Further functions proposed include dolls, toys, tokens of identification, primitive contracts, communication or as part of birthing rituals (Talalay 1993: 40–43). Other plausible interpretations include teaching devices, tools of sorcery, magic, healing or initiation (Ehrenberg 1989: 75). Talalay proposes that clay legs from the northern Peloponnese served to symbolize social and economic bonds among communities like those of marriage contracts or identification of trading partners (1987: 161–2). These alternatives, as opposed to a universal deity, may explain the practice of discard. To assume *a priori* that there is a Goddess behind every figurine is tantamount to interpreting plastic figures of Virgin Mary and of 'Barbie' as having identical ideological significance....

Conclusion: The Goddess, Pseudo-Feminism and Future Research

Whilst the concept of gender as a structuring principle is relatively new to archaeology, many progressive and scholarly studies have emerged in the last few years (e.g. Gero & Conkey 1991; Wylie 1991; Dobres 1992a; 1992b; Bacus *et al.* 1993; Brown 1993; Conkey & Tringham in press). However, many feminists feel that the establishment of an originary myth of the basis of scientific historical reality will facilitate the restoration of women's power. It then follows that the patriarchy will be dismantled and the lost pre-patriarchal culture can be regained (Passman 1993: 187). Matriculture is seen to give feminism the legitimacy the system demands.

Contrary to this position I argue, as feminist and archaeologist, that the approaches of Gimbutas and her advocates contrast markedly to many feminists (Brown 1993: 254), especially those involved in archaeological discourse. This is not to say that Gimbutas claimed to do feminist archaeology; rather that she has been adopted as an icon within the movement, more ardently outside archaeological circles. However, some feminists do not accept her methodology, since she was so steeped within the 'establishment' epistemological framework of polar opposites, rigid gender roles, barbarian invaders and cultural stages (Fagan 1992; Brown 1993) which are now regarded as outmoded. It is unfortunate that many archaeologists interested in gender are drawn to historical fiction and emotional narratives, which either replace or accompany serious archaeological dialogues. At this juncture sound feminist scholarship needs to be divorced from methodological shortcomings, reverse sexism, conflated data and pure fantasy, since this will only impede the feminist cause and draw attention away from the positive contribution offered by gender and feminist archaeologies. Gero & Conkey (1991: 5) assert that we are now in a position to draw from and contribute to emergent theoretical developments within archaeology, particularly post-processual directions that see social and symbolic theories as central. Gender, however, cannot be separated from other archaeological considerations and become the type of speciality area Gimbutas created.

In future studies we should not expect to delineate a rigid and unitary code which holds for all contexts (Hodder 1987), but rather to identify the dimensions of meaning pertaining to particular societies and to comprehend their social locus. It may prove more informative to ask 'how did the social production of this object contribute to its meanings and uses?', 'how did these meaningful objects enhance people's understanding of their lives?' and 'what other associated activities were operative that can inform us about social context?' (Dobres 1992a: 17–18). Naturally the multiplicity of manifestations relative to their archaeological contexts must be considered, coupled with the socioeconomic concerns of their manufacturers.

To conclude, academic and popular audiences alike need to review critically the evidence for a solitary universal Mother Goddess, along with other plausible interpretations. Although the post-processualists have stressed notions of pluralism, most now advocate that not *all* pasts are equal. The gynocentric narratives discussed above reveal more about our relationship(s) with the past and certain contemporary ideologies (Conkey 1992) than how these figurines were deployed in antiquity.

The Mother Goddess metanarrative presents a possible challenge to feminist archaeologies in that solidarity can often prevent us from contesting theories presented by women which seem to espouse pro-female notions: even if the evidence would suggest otherwise. Loyalty to a misrepresented picture of the past and our human heritage by dismissing or misconstruing the archaeological record cannot be supported under the guise of any political standpoint. Needless to say, many men feel that they are not in a position to engage in these issues and that only other women can do so. This exclusivity is not conducive to scholarly development; neither is failing to counter claims of a gendered superiority supported by 'scientific' archaeology that ultimately has filtered into mainstream society. An engendered re-balancing of the scales is long overdue and critically important to the trajectory of the discipline. However, emphasis on one sex to the exclusion of the other is not only detrimental to serious gender/feminist studies, but threatens the interpretative integrity of archaeology.

References

ANTHONY, D. W. In press. Nazi and ecofeminist prehistories: ideology and empiricism in Indo-European archaeology, in P. Kohl & C. Fawcett (ed.), *Nationalism, politics and the practice of archaeology*: 1–32. Cambridge: Cambridge University Press.

BACUS, E.A. *et al.* 1993. *A gendered past: a critical review of gender in archaeology.* Ann Arbor (MI): University of Michigan Press.

BROWN, S. 1993. Feminist research in archaeology. What does it mean? Why is it taking so long?, in Rabinowitz & Richlin (ed.): 238–71.

CHAPMAN, J. 1991. The creation of social arenas in the Neolithic and copper age of SE Europe: the case of Varna, in P. Garwood *et al* (ed.). *Sacred and profane*: 152–71. Oxford: Oxford University Committee for Archaeology, Monograph 32.

— 1994. Destruction of a common heritage: the archaeology of war in Croatia. Bosnia and Hercegovina, *Antiquity* 68: 120–26.

CHILDE, V. G. 1951. *Social evolution.* London: Watts.

CONKEY, M. W. 1992. Mobilising ideologies: the archaeologics of Paleolithic 'art'. Paper delivered to the American Anthropological Association, San Francisco.

CONKEY, M. W. & R. E. TRINGHAM. In press. Archaeology and the Goddess: exploring the contours of feminist archaeology, in A. Stewart & D. Stanton (ed.), *Feminism in the academy: rethinking the disciplines.* Ann Arbor (MI): University of Michigan Press.

DAVIS, W. 1992. *Masking the blow: the scene of representation in late prehistoric Egyptian art.* Berkeley (CA): University of California Press.

DEMOULE, J.-P. & C. PERLES. 1993. The Greek Neolithic: a new review, *Journal of World Prehistory* 7(4): 355–416.

DOBRES, M.-A. 1992a. Re-presentations of Palaeolithic visual imagery: simulacra and their alternatives, *Kroeber Anthroplogical Society Papers* 73–4: 1–25.

EHRENBERG, M. 1989. *Women in prehistory.* London: British Museum Publications.

EISLER, R. 1987. *The chalice and the blade: our history, our future.* San Francisco (CA): Harper Row.

FAGAN, B. M. 1992. A sexist view of prehistory, *Archaeology* 45(2): 14–16, 18, 66.

FRYMER-KENSKY, T. 1992. *In the wake of the goddess: women, culture and the biblical transformation of pagan myth.* New York (NY): Ballantine.

GERO, J. M. & M. W. CONKEY. 1991. Tensions, pluralities and engendering archaeology: an introduction to women and prehistory, in Gero & Conkey (ed.): 2–29.

GERO, J. M. & M. W. CONKEY (ed.). 1991. *Engendering archaeology: women and prehistory.* Oxford: Basil Blackwell.

GILL, D. W. J. & C. CHIPPINDALE. 1993. Material and intellectual consequences of esteem for Cycladic figures, *American Journal of Archaeology* 97: 601–59.

GIMBUTAS, M. 1965. *The Bronze Age cultures in central and eastern Europe.* The Hague: Mouton.

— 1970. Proto-Indo-European culture: the Kurgan culture during the 5th, 4th and 3rd millennium BC in G. Cardona *et al.* (ed.), *Indo-European and Indo-Europeans*: 155–97. Philadelphia (PA): University of Pennsylvania Press.

— 1971a. *The Slavs.* London: Thames & Hudson.

— 1971b (ed.). *Neolithic Macedonia: as reflected by excavations at Anza, southeast Yugoslavia.* Los Angeles (CA): UCLA Institute of Archaeology. Monumenta Archaeologica 1.

— 1973. The beginning of the Bronze Age in Europe and the Indo-Europeans— 3500–2500 BC, *Journal of Indo-European Studies* 1(2): 163–214.

— 1974. *Gods and goddesses of old Europe.* London: Thames & Hudson.

— 1981. Vulvas, breasts and buttocks of the Goddess Creatress: commentary on the origins of art, in G. Buccellati & C. Speroni (ed.), *The shape of the past. Studies in honour of Franklin D. Murphy*: 19–40. Los Angeles (CA): UCLA Institute of Archaeology.

— 1986. Mythical imagery of Sitagroi society, in Renfrew *et al.* (ed.): 225–301.

—— 1989a. *The language of the Goddess: unearthing hidden symbols of western civilisation*. London: Thames and Hudson.

—— 1989b. Women and culture in Goddess-oriented Old Europe, in J. Plaskow & C. C. Christ (ed.), *Weaving the visions*: 63–71. San Francisco (CA): Harpers.

—— 1991. *The civilization of the Goddess: the world of Old Europe*. San Francisco (CA): Harpers.

—— 1992. *The age of the Goddess: ancient roots of the emerging feminine consciousness*. Boulder (CO): Sounds True Recordings. Audio tape #A192.

GIMBUTAS, M., S. WINN & D. SHIMABUKU. 1989. *Achilleion: a Neolithic settlement in Thessaly, Greece 6400–5600 BC*. Los Angeles (CA): UCLA Institute of Archaeology.

HALLETT, J. P. 1993. Feminist theory, historical periods, literary canons, and the study of Greco-Roman antiquity, in Rabinowitz & Richlin (ed.): 44–72.

HAYDEN, B. 1986. Old Europe: sacred matriarchy or complimentary opposition in A. Bonanno (ed.), *Archaeology and fertility cult in the Mediterranean*: 17–41. Amsterdam: B. R. Grunner.

HAYS, K. A. 1993. When is a symbol archaeologically meaningful?: meaning, function and prehistoric visual arts, in N. Yoffee and S. Sherratt (ed.), *Archaeological theory: who sets the agenda?*: 81–92. Cambridge: Cambridge University Press.

HODDER, I. R. 1987. Contextual archaeology: an interpretation of Çatal Hüyük and a discussion of the origins of agriculture. *University of London Institute of Archaeology Bulletin* 24: 43–56.

—— 1990. *The domestication of Europe: structure and contingency in Neolithic societies*. Oxford: Basil Blackwell.

HUMPHREYS, S. C. 1983. *The family, women and death: comparative studies*. London: Routledge & Kegan Paul.

MCPHERRON, A. 1991. Review of Gimbutas *et al.* (1989), *American Antiquity* 56(3): 567–8.

MALLORY, J. P. 1989. *In search of the Indo-Europeans*. London: Thames & Hudson.

MALONE, C., A. BONANNO, T. GOULDER, S. STODDART & D. TRUMP. 1993. The death cults of prehistoric Malta. *Scientific American* (December): 76–83.

MARINESCU-BILCU. 1981. *Tirpesti: from prehistory to history in eastern Romania*. Oxford: British Archaeological Reports. International series 107.

MILOJKOVIC, J. 1990. The anthropomorphic and zoomorphic figurines, in Tringham & Krstic (ed.): 397–436.

MURRAY, J. 1970. *The first European agriculture, a study of the osteological and botanical evidence until 2000 BC*. Edinburgh: Edinburgh University Press.

ORENSTEIN, G. F. 1990. *The reflowering of the Goddess*. New York (NY): Pergamon Press.

PAVLOVIC, M. 1990. The aesthetics of Neolithic figurines, in *Vinca and its world: international symposium. The Danubian region from 6000 to 3000 BC. Belgrade, Smederevska Palanka, October 1988*: 33–4. Belgrade: Academy of Arts and Sciences.

PASSMAN, T. 1993. Out of the closet and into the field: matriculture, lesbian perspective and feminist classics, in Rabinowitz & Richlin (ed.): 181–208.

POGOZHEVA, A. P. 1983. *Antropomorfnaya plastika Tripol'ya*. Novosibirsk: Akademiia Nauk, Sibirskoe Otdelenie.

RENFREW, C. 1987. *Archaeology and language: the puzzle of Indo-European origins*. London: Jonathan Cape.

ROBINS, G. 1993. *Women in ancient Egypt*. London: British Museum Press.

RUNNELS, C. 1990. Review of Gimbutas *et al.* (1989), *Journal of Field Archaeology* 17: 341–5.

SHANKS, M. & C. Tilley. 1987. *Re-constructing archaeology: theory and practice*. Cambridge: Cambridge University Press.

SPRETNAK, C. 1992. *Lost goddesses of early Greece*. Boston (MA): Beacon Press.

STARHAWK. 1982. *Dreaming the dark: magic, sex and politics*. Boston (MA): Beacon Press.

TALALAY, L. E. 1991. Body imagery of the ancient Aegean. *Archaeology* 44(4): 46–9.

—— 1993. *Dolls, deities and devices. Neolithic figurines from Franthchi cave, Greece.* Bloomington (IN): Indiana University Press. Excavations at Franchthi Cave, Greece 9.

TRINGHAM, R. E. 1991. Households with faces: the challenge of gender in prehistoric architectural remains, in Gero & Conkey (ed.): 93–131.

—— 1993. Review of Gimbutas (1991). *American Anthropologist* 95: 196–7.

TRINGHAM, R. E. & D. KRSTIC (ed.). 1990. *Selevac: a Neolithic village in Yugoslavia.* Los Angeles (CA): UCLA Institute of Archaeology Monumenta Archaeologica 15.

UCKO, P. J. 1968. *Anthropomorphic figures of predynastic Egypt and Neolithic Crete with comparative material from the prehistoric Near East and Mainland Greece.* London: Andrew Szmidla.

VAN LEUVEN, J. 1993. Review of Gimbutas (1991). *Journal of Prehistoric Religion* 7: 83–4.

WALL, S. M., J. H. MUSGRAVE & P. M. WARREN. 1986. Human bones from a late Minoan 1b house at Knossos. *Annual of the British School at Athens* 81: 333–88.

WYLIE, M. A. 1991. Gender theory and the archaeological record: why is there no archaeology of gender?, in Gero & Conkey (ed.): 31–47.

POSTSCRIPT

Was There a Goddess Cult in Prehistoric Europe?

Over the past 20 years a popular women's movement, the "Goddess Movement," has grown up, especially in the United States, around the idea that the earliest organized religion was based on worship of a supreme Goddess. This is largely a reaction against the perceived androcentrism and antifemale bias of Christianity, Judaism, Islam, and other world religions and of the civilizations they underpin. Proponents believe that by reviving this religion, they can undo the cultural and psychological harm inflicted on women (and men) by our long history of patriarchal religions and cultures.

Many feminist archaeologists are ambivalent toward the Goddess Movement and Gimbutas's contribution to it. They believe, on the one hand, that Gimbutas's work helps to correct the imbalance in conventional presentations of human prehistory, in which women are usually portrayed as minor bit players. But they are concerned about the quality of her methodology and theories. Feminist archaeologists also worry that Gimbutas's "old-fashioned" ideas, such as the notion of universal stages of cultural evolution and her static view of gender relations, do not contribute to an archaeology in which feminist views are an integral part.

For background on the Goddess Movement's roots in European thought, see Ronald Hutton's "The Neolithic Great Goddess: A Study in Modern Tradition," *Antiquity* (vol. 71, 1997). Also see Jane Ellen Harrison's *Prolegomena to the Study of Greek Religion* (Cambridge University Press, 1903).

For elaboration of Gimbutas's views, see her books *The Language of the Goddess* (Harper & Row, 1989), *The Civilization of the Goddess* (Harper & Row, 1991), and *The Living Goddesses* (University of California Press, 1999).

For critiques of the Goddess theory see Peter Ucko's works: his article "The Interpretation of Prehistoric Anthropomorphic Figurines," *Journal of the Royal Anthropological Institute* (vol. 92, 1962) and his monograph *Anthropomorphic Figurines of Predynastic Egypt and Neolithic Crete with Comparative Material from the Prehistoric Near East and Mainland Greece* (Royal Anthropological Institute, 1968). Also see Anne Baring and Jules Cashford's *The Myth of the Goddess* (Viking Press, 1991) and Margaret Conkey and Ruth Tringham's "Archaeology and the Goddess: Exploring the Contours of Feminist Archaeology," in D. C. Stanton and A. J. Stewart, eds., *Feminisms in the Academy* (University of Michigan Press, 1995). Conkey and Tringham's article also gives an excellent overview of the controversy and discussion of its significance for feminist archaeology.

ISSUE 9

Were Environmental Factors Responsible for the Mayan Collapse?

YES: Richard E. W. Adams, from *Prehistoric Mesoamerica*, rev. ed. (University of Oklahoma Press, 1991)

NO: George L. Cowgill, from "Teotihuacan, Internal Militaristic Competition, and the Fall of the Classic Maya," in Norman Hammond and Gordon R. Willey, eds., *Maya Archaeology and Ethnohistory* (University of Texas Press, 1979)

ISSUE SUMMARY

YES: Archaeologist Richard E. W. Adams argues that while military factors must have played some role in the collapse of the Classic Maya states, a combination of internal factors combined with environmental pressures were more significant.

NO: Archaeologist George L. Cowgill agrees that no single factor was responsible for the demise of the Classic Maya civilization, but he contends that military expansion was far more significant than scholars had previously thought.

T he discovery of vast ancient ruins in the tropical rainforests of lowland southern Mexico and northern Central America in the nineteenth century posed a major question for archaeologists and historians. Spanish explorers discovered major cities and ceremonial centers complete with pyramids that were reminiscent of complexes in ancient Egypt. The explorers realized that these cities were ancestral to the Maya societies they encountered. What caused the disappearance of this pre-Hispanic civilization that had a complex system of hieroglyphic writing, an accurate calendar, elaborate sculpture, and major ceremonial complexes?

Over the past century, archaeologists, linguists, and a variety of other researchers have worked with national and regional governments in Mexico, Guatemala, Belize, and Honduras to excavate and interpret these early sites. Using radiocarbon and other dating methods, researchers have established certain facts: (1) beginning around the fourth century, the preclassic Maya began to form a series of small states, each centered around regional centers; (2) by about 650 C.E. these states began to flourish, with the Maya building enormous architectural complexes and erecting stone monuments to their elites; and (3) soon after 900 C.E. all of the centers in the southern lowlands seem to have been abandoned although cities in the northern lowlands flourished for several more centuries.

Although it is now clear to most researchers that the Maya collapse represents a complex combination of factors, two major theories have emerged. Richard E. W. Adams argues that the Mayan collapse could only have occurred because of a complex interplay of internal factors, culminating in an ecological collapse on a regional scale. He sees the seventh- and eighth-century architectural developments as evidence of the flourishing of Classic Maya civilization. But he argues that this development went too far too fast to sustain the large populations that the grand building programs of the elite required. He contends that crop failures, epidemics, and other environmental factors led to a decline in population from 12 million to fewer than 2 million. Once individual states stopped using their ceremonial centers, a thick, thorny secondary growth jungle covered the sites, making them much more difficult to cultivate. As a result, the Maya abandoned these sites for land that was much easier to cultivate.

While George L. Cowgill accepts that environmental factors played a role in the decline and ultimate collapse of the Classic Maya states, he argues that these factors would probably not have had such a profound impact had the various polities not been so heavily engaged in military activity. He contends that the eighth-century Maya "florescence" was not a time of Mayan prosperity, but instead a period of impending crisis. To understand conditions in the Maya lowlands, Cowgill compares the prehistoric pattern found in the central Mexican highland site of Teotihuacan, which had a strong central authority for many centuries, with the Classic Maya sites. The Maya had many competing local elites. His view is that smaller polities were fundamentally unstable over the long term. He argues that the Maya political development during the preclassic period could survive with many regional elites and no centralized authority. However, once these small city-states grew in population and developed elaborate ritual centers, local leaders sought to become a central authority by defeating their smaller neighbors. Military conflict during the Classic Maya period turned out to be an unsuccessful attempt to meld a single centralized state from many competing centers. As local populations were drawn into local wars, it was only a matter of time before poor crop yields, epidemics, or other regional environmental problems brought an end to these Mayan centers.

The following selections suggest a number of questions for consideration. Is there evidence that the Classic Maya were warlike and participated in conflicts with neighboring Maya groups? Was the local elite so preoccupied with exotic, high-status goods that they were willing to compete with neighbors to get these objects? Did Classic Maya religion encourage local elites to ignore the impending crises that ultimately befell them? Would environmental degradation accompanied by short-term environmental changes have been sufficient to bring about the nearly complete collapse of this civilization?

Richard E. W. Adams  **YES**

Transformations

The Classic Maya Collapse

According to what we now know, Maya civilization began to reach a series of regional peaks about A.D. 650. By A.D. 830, there is evidence of disintegration of the old patterns, and by A.D. 900, all of the southern lowland centers had collapsed. An understanding of the Maya apocalypse must be based in large part on an understanding of the nature of Maya civilization. During the Terminal Classic period, A.D. 750 to 900, cultural patterns of the lowlands can be briefly characterized as follows. Demographically, a high peak had been reached at least as early as A.D. 600 and perhaps earlier. This population density and size in turn led to intensive forms of agriculture and the establishment of permanent farmsteads in the countryside. Hills were terraced, swamps were drained and modified, water impoundments were made by the hundreds, and land became so scarce that walls of rock were built both as boundaries and simply as the results of field clearance. These masses of people were also highly organized for political purposes into region-state units, which fluctuated in size. These states were more than simple aggregations of cities and were characterized by hierarchical and other complex relationships among them.

Society was organized on an increasingly aristocratic principle by A.D. 650. Dynasties and royal lineages were at the top of the various Maya states and commanded most of the resources of Maya economic life. Most of the large architecture of the cities was for their use. Groups of craft specialists and civil servants supported the elite, with the mass of the population engaged in either part-time or full-time farming. Trade was well organized among and within the states. Military competition was present but was controlled by the fact that it had become mainly an elite-class and prestige activity which did not greatly disturb the economic basis of life. Thus, Maya culture at the ninth century A.D. seems to have been well-ordered, adjusted, and definitely a success. Yet a devastating catastrophe brought it down.

Characteristics of the Collapse

It sometimes seems that the accumulation of weighty theoretical formulations purporting to explain the collapse of Maya civilization will eventually, instead, cause the collapse of Maya archaeology. A refreshingly skeptical and clear-sighted book by John Lowe reviews the major theories and tests them as well. We will not be as thorough in the following section but, it is to be hoped, just as convincing. A brief characterization of the collapse includes the following features:

1. It occurred over a relatively short period of time: 75 to 150 years.
2. During it the elite-class culture failed, as reflected in the abandonment of palaces and temples and the cessation of manufacture of luxury goods and erection of stelae.
3. Also during the period there was a rapid and nearly complete depopulation of the countryside and the urban centers.
4. The geographical focus of the first collapse was in the oldest and most developed zones, the southern lowlands and the intermediate area. The northern plains and Puuc areas survived for a while longer.

In other words, the Maya collapse was a demographic, cultural, and social catastrophe in which elite and commoner went down together. Drawing on all available information about the ancient Maya and comparable situations, the 1970 Santa Fe Conference developed a comprehensive explanation of the collapse. This explanation depends on the relatively new picture of the Maya summarized above. That is, we must discard any notion of the Maya as the "noble savage" living in harmony with nature. Certainly, the Maya lived more in tune with nature than do modern industrial peoples, but probably not much more so than did our nineteenth-century pioneer ancestors. As we shall see, some dissonance with nature was at least partly responsible for its failure. More than this, however, data have been further developed since the conference which strengthen some assumptions and weaken others. Therefore, the explanation which follows is a modified version of that which appears in the report of the Santa Fe Conference.

Stresses

Maya society had a number of built-in stresses, many of which had to do with high populations in the central and southern areas. Turner's and other studies indicate that from about A.D. 600 to 900 there were about 168 people per square kilometer (435 per square mile) in the Río Bec zone. The intensive agricultural constructions associated with this population density are also found farther south, within 30 kilometers (19 miles) of Tikal. They are also to be found to the east in the Belize Valley, and there are indications elsewhere to the south that high populations were present. According to Saul's studies of Maya bones from the period, the population carried a heavy load of endemic disease, including malaria, yellow fever, syphilis, and Chagas's disease, the latter a chronic infection which leads to cardiac insufficiency in young adulthood. Chronic malnutrition is also indicated by Saul's and Steele's studies. Taken altogether, these factors indicate the precarious status of health even for the elite. Average lifespan in the southern lowlands was about thirty-nine years. Infant mortality was high; perhaps as many as 78 percent of Maya children never reached the age of twenty. Endemic disease can go epidemic with just a rise in malnutrition. In other words, the Maya populace carried within itself a biological time bomb which needed only a triggering event such as a crop failure to go off.

With population pressing the limits of subsistence, management of land and other resources was a problem, and one which would have fallen mainly on the elite. If food were to be imported, or if marginal lands were to be brought into cultivation, by extensive drainage projects, for example, then the elite had to arrange for it to be done. There were certain disadvantages to this arrangement. Aristocratic or inherited leadership of any kind is a poor means to approach matters that require rational decisions. One need only consider the disastrous manner in which seventeenth-century European armies were mishandled by officers whose major qualifications were their lineages. There is a kind of built-in variation of the Peter Principle in such leadership: one is born to his level of incompetence. Maya aristocracy apparently was no better equipped to handle the complex problems of increasing populations than were European aristocrats. There were no doubt capable and brilliant nobles, but there was apparently no way in which talent could quickly be taken to the top of society from its lower ranks. Lowe's model of the collapse of Maya civilization emphasizes the management-administrative aspects of the problem and essentially considers the collapse as an administrative breakdown.

There are also signs in the Terminal Classic period of a widening social gulf between elite and commoners. At the same time, problems were increasing in frequency and severity. The elite class increased in size and made greater demands on the rest of Maya society for its support. This created further tensions. Intensive agriculture led to greater crop yields, but also put Maya food production increasingly at hostage to the vagaries of weather, crop disease, insects, birds, and other hazards. Marginal and complex cultivation systems require large investments of time and labor and necessitate that things go right more often than not. A run of bad weather or a long-term shift in climate might trigger a food crisis. Recent work on tree rings and weather history from other sources indicates that a Mesoamerica-wide drought may have begun about A.D. 850. In addition, there are periodic outbreaks of locusts in the Maya Lowlands.

These stresses were pan–Maya and occurred to a greater or lesser degree in every region. No matter whether one opts for the city-state or the regional state model, competition over scarce resources among the political units of the Maya resulted from these stressful situations. The large southern center of Seibal was apparently taken by a northern Maya elite group about A.D. 830. Evidence is now in hand of military intrusions from north to south at Rio Azul, at the Belize sites of Nohmul, Colha, and Barton Ramie, and at Quirigua in the Motagua Valley. At least at Rio Azul and Colha a period of trade preceded the raids, presaging the later Aztec *pochteca* pattern. The patterns and nature of the intrusions indicate that the raids were probably from the Puuc zone and that a part of the motivation, as suggested by Cowgill, was to capture populations. Warfare increased markedly along the Usumacinta River during the ninth century A.D., according to hieroglyphic texts and carved pictures from that area.

There are also hints that the nature of Maya warfare may have changed during this last period. A lintel from Piedras Negras appears to show numerous soldiers in standard uniforms kneeling in ranks before an officer. In other words, organized violence may have come to involve many more people and much more effort and therefore may have become much more disruptive. Certainly competition over scarce resources would have led to an increasingly unstable situation. Further, the resultant disorganization would have led to vulnerability to outside military intervention, and that seems to have been the case as well.

There were also external pressures on the Maya. Some were intangible and in the form of new ideas about the nature of human society as well as new ideologies from the Gulf Coast and Central Mexico. The northern Maya elites seem to have absorbed a number of these new ideas. For example, they included the depiction of Mexican Gulf Coast deities on their stelae as well as some Mexican-style hieroglyphs. Altar de Sacrificios was invaded by still another foreign group from the Gulf Coast about A.D. 910. These people may have been either a truly Mexican Gulf Coast group or Chontal Maya, who were non-Classic in their culture.

A progressive pattern of abandonment and disaster in the western lowlands is suggestive. Palenque, on the southwestern edges of the lowlands, was one of the first major centers to go under; it was abandoned about A.D. 810. The major Usumacinta cities of Piedras Negras and Yaxchilan (Bird-Jaguar's City) were the next to go. They put up their last monuments about A.D. 825. Finally, it was Altar de Sacrificios's turn about A.D. 910. Clearly, there was a progressive disintegration from west to east, and it seems likely that it was caused by pressures from militaristic non–Maya groups. These peoples, in turn, were probably being jostled in the competitive situation set up after the fall of Teotihuacan and may have been pushed ahead of peoples such as the Toltecs and their allies. Perhaps the Epi-Classic states discussed above were involved, as well as some mercenary groups. In any case, it appears certain that these groups were opportunists. They came into an area already disorganized and disturbed and were not the triggering mechanism for the catastrophe but part of the following process.

At any one Maya city or in any one region, the "mix" of circumstances was probably unique. At Piedras Negras there is evidence that the elite may have been violently overthrown from within. Faces of rulers on that site's stelae are smashed, and there are other signs of violence. Invasion finished off Altar de Sacrificios. Rio Azul was overrun by Maya groups from the north, perhaps including Toltec allies, as were a number of Maya centers along the Belize coast and down to Quirigua. At other centers, such as the regional capital of Tikal, the elite were apparently abandoned to their fate. Without the supporting populations, remnants of the Maya upper classes lingered on after the catastrophe. At Colha and Seibal, northern Maya acting as new elites attempted to continue the southern economic and political systems, but they abandoned these attempts after a relatively short time. The general demographic catastrophe and disruption of the agricultural systems were apparently too great to cope with.

In short, ecological abuse, disease, mismanagement, overpopulation, militarism, famines, epidemics, and bad weather overtook the Maya in various combinations. But several questions remain. What led to the high levels of populations which were the basis of much of the disaster?

The Maya were much more loosely organized politically during the Late Formative than during the Classic period. The episodes of interstate competition and of Teotihuacan's intervention seem to have led them to try new, more centralized political arrangements. These seem to have worked well for a time, in the case of the Early Classic expansion of Tikal. After the suggested civil wars of the sixth century there seems to have been a renewed and still stronger development of centralized states, which were probably monarchical.

Using general historical and anthropological experience, Demitri Shimkin observed that village-level societies approach population control very differently than do state-level societies. Relatively independent villages are oriented plainly and simply toward survival. There are many traditional ways of population control, female infanticide being a favorite practiced widely even in eighteenth-century England. Use of herbal abortion, late marriage, ritual ascetisicism, and other means keep population within bounds for a village. A state-level society, on the other hand, is likely to encourage population growth for the benefit of the directing elite. The more manpower to manipulate, the better. In the case of the Maya, we have noted a certain megalomania in their huge Late Classic buildings. Unfinished large construction projects at Tikal and Uaxactun were overtaken by the collapse. Such efforts required immense manpower reserves and a simultaneous disregard for the welfare of that workforce. The Maya appear to have shifted gears into a more sophisticated and ultimately maladaptive state organization.

Another question to be considered is, Why did the Maya not adjust to cope with the crises? The answer may lie in the nature of religiously sanctioned aristocracies. Given a crop failure, a Maya leadership group might have attempted to propitiate the ancestors and gods with more ritual and more monuments. This response would have exacerbated the crisis by taking manpower out of food production. Inappropriate responses of this sort could easily have been made, given the ideology and worldview that the Maya seem to have held. On the other hand, if the crisis were a long-term drought, with populations dangerously high and predatory warfare disrupting matters even more, perhaps any response would have been ineffectual.

The rapid biological destruction of the Maya is an important aspect of the collapse. From a guessed-at high of 12 million, the population was reduced within 150 years to an estimated remnant of about 1.8 million. The disease load and the stress of malnutritional factors indicate that a steady diminishment of Maya population probably started by A.D. 830 and rapidly reached a point of no recovery. An average increase of 10 to 15 percent in the annual mortality rate will statistically reduce 12 million to 1.8 million in 75 years. Obviously there was not anything like a steady decline, but the smoothed-out average over the period had to have been something of that order, or perhaps the decline began earlier, at A.D. 750, when Maya civilization reached its peak.

The disruptive nature of population declines can be easily understood if one considers the usual effects of epidemics. In such catastrophic outbreaks of disease, those first and most fatally affected are the young and the old. Even if the main working population survives relatively untouched, the social loss is only postponed. The old take with them much of the accumulated experience and knowledge needed to meet future crises. The young will not be there to mature and replace the adult working population, and a severe manpower shortage will result within fifteen to twenty years. Needless to say, much more work on population estimates and studies of the bones and the general health environment of the ancient Maya needs to be done to produce a really convincing statement on this aspect of the collapse.

A last, although not by any means final, question concerns the failure to recover. This feature may involve climatic factors. If shifts of rainfall belts were responsible for triggering the collapse, then the answer might be the persistence of drought conditions until there were too few people left to sustain the Classic cultural systems. As now seems probable, the Maya were confronted with the situation of having overcultivated their soils and having lost too much surface water. Temporary abandonment of fields would have led to their being rapidly overrun by thick, thorny, second-growth jungle, which is harder to clear than primary forest. Thus, a diminished population may have been faced with the problem of clearing heavily overgrown, worn-out soils, of which vast amounts were needed to sustain even small populations. Second-growth forest springs up overnight and is even today a major problem in maintaining archaeological sites for tourists.

Another possible answer to the question of recovery is that the Maya may have been loathe to attempt the sort of brilliant effort that had ultimately broken them. Just as they preferred to revert to swidden agriculture rather than maintain intensive techniques, they probably found it a relief to live on a village level instead of in their former splendid but stressful state of existence.

The above is an integrated model of the Maya collapse. It explains all the features of the collapse and all the data now in hand, but it is not proved by any means, and in some respects is more of a guide to future research than a firm explanation. If the model is more or less correct, however, it should be largely confirmed within the next ten years of research. Indeed, this process of confirmation has already begun. The 1970 conference which developed the model could explain certain features of the archaeological record only by assuming much higher levels of ancient population than were otherwise plausible at the time. The 1973 Rio Bec work of Turner and Eaton turned up a vast amount of data which indicate that higher levels of ancient populations indeed had been present. Recent work at Colha and Rio Azul has indicated the importance of militarism in the process. All of these findings lend credibility to the model.

Delayed Collapse in the North

The vast and very densely distributed centers of the Puuc area survived for a time. These Puuc cities, possibly a regional state with a capital at Uxmal, appear to have turned into predators on the southern cities. As noted before, part of the motivation may have been for the capture and enslavement of southern populations. Even so, it seems that large centers such as Uxmal, Kabah, Sayil, and Labna lasted only a century longer than the southern cities. Northern Maya chronology is much more disputed than that in the south, but it now seems likely that outsiders, including Toltec, were in Yucatan by A.D. 900 and perhaps earlier, and there are clear indications that Uxmal was absorbing Mexican ideas much earlier. Certain motifs, such as eagles or vultures, appear on Puuc building facades late in the Classic period.

We are now faced with at least three possible explanations of the Puuc collapse: they may have succumbed to the same combination of factors that brought down the southern Maya centers; the Toltec may have conquered them; or a combination of these factors may have been at work. At this time, it appears that the northern florescence was partly at the expense of the southern area.... [E]vidence for Toltec conquest now appears even stronger, and this is presently the favored explanation for the Puuc collapse.

Chichen Itza, in north central Yucatan, is a center which was culturally allied with the Puuc cities in architecture and probably politically as well. Puuc centers have been found even in the far northeast of the peninsula. At Chichen Itza, Puuc architecture is overlaid and succeeded by Toltec architecture. Unmapped defensive walls surround both Chichen and Uxmal. The data available now make it likely that the Toltec and other groups may have appeared in Yucatan by A.D. 800 and thereafter, perhaps brought in as mercenaries, as so often happened later in Maya history. In whatever capacity they arrived, they appear to have established themselves at Chichen Itza by A.D. 950 as the controlling power. As has happened in history elsewhere, the mercenaries became the controlling forces. Toltec raids, battles, and sieges, combined with the internal weaknesses of Classic Maya culture and perhaps with changing environmental factors, brought about a swift collapse in the Puuc.

The aftermath of the collapse was also devastating. Most of the southern Maya Lowlands have not been repopulated until the last fifty years. Eleven hundred years of abandonment have rejuvenated the soils, the forests, and their resources, but modern man is now making inroads on them. Kekchi Maya Indians have been migrating into the lowlands from the northern Guatemalan highlands as pioneer farmers for the past century, and the Mexican government has colonized the Yucatan, Campeche, and Quintana Roo area with dissatisfied agriculturists from overpopulated highland areas. The forests are being logged and cut down. Agricultural colonies have failed in both Guatemala and Mexico, and some zones are already abandoned. In other areas, the inhabitants have turned to marijuana cultivation. Vast areas have been reduced to low scrub jungle, and large amounts of land are now being converted to intensive agriculture. One looks at the modern scene and wonders. Fortunately, in 1988 a movement began to set aside the remnants of the once immense monsoon forests, and it may be that a series of protected zones in the form of contiguous national parks will soon be in existence in Guatamala, Mexico, and Belize.

NO ↵

Teotihuacan, Internal Militaristic Competition, and the Fall of the Classic Maya

In very broad terms, the Teotihuacan civilization, centered in the Mexican Highlands, and the Classic civilization of the Southern Maya Lowlands exhibit a similar developmental trajectory. That is, both enjoyed a period of development, flourished for a time, and then collapsed. But as soon as one looks beyond these gross generalities, the evidence from each region shows striking differences in the pace and timing of events. These differences are of interest in their own right, and one of my objectives is to call attention to them. In addition, however, they help to direct our attention to some of the distinctive features of the Maya trajectory which are relevant for understanding the functioning of Late Classic Maya society and for explaining its collapse. My main concern is to point out difficulties in some recently proposed explanations... and to suggest that escalating internal warfare may have been more a cause than a consequence of serious trouble for the Maya. I do not suggest warfare as a mono-causal explanation for the Maya collapse, but I do think it may have been an important contributing factor, and old evidence should be re-examined and new evidence sought with this possibility in mind.

Emphasis on Maya warfare is part of a widespread recognition that the Maya were not the gentle pacifists that some archaeologists would have them be. But there is a difference between sporadic raiding, with occasional enslavement or sacrifice or captives, and what David Webster calls *militarism*: institutionalized warfare intended for territorial aggrandizement and acquisition of other capital resources, with military decisions part of the conscious political policy of small elite, semiprofessional warriors, and lethal combat on a large scale. Webster and I both argue that the Late Classic Maya may have become militaristic in this sense, but we differ about the probable dynamics and consequences of Maya militarism.

Although it is clear that there were important contacts between the Highlands and the Southern Maya Lowlands, I should stress that I am *not* arguing that either Teotihuacan intervention or the withdrawal of Teotihuacan contacts played a decisive role in the Maya collapse. Direct or indirect contacts with

From George L. Cowgill, "Teotihuacan, Internal Militaristic Competition, and the Fall of the Classic Maya," in Norman Hammond and Gordon R. Willey, eds., *Maya Archaeology and Ethnohistory* (University of Texas Press, 1979). Copyright © 1979 by University of Texas Press. Reprinted by permission. References omitted.

Teotihuacan are important and extremely interesting, but I doubt if they explain much about either the rise or the fall of the Lowland Maya. In any case, my use of the Teotihuacan data here is purely as a contrastive example.

It is often assumed that Teotihuacan developed rather steadily up to a distinct peak somewhere around A.D. 500 to 600, after which it soon began a fairly rapid decline.... [L]argely through the data obtained by the comprehensive surface survey and limited test excavations completed by the Teotihuacan Mapping Project, under the direction of René Millon, evidence for a very different pattern has emerged....

Briefly, it appears that the city of Teotihuacan enjoyed an early surge of extremely rapid growth, followed by a four-to-five-century "plateau" during which growth was very much slower or may even have ceased altogether. Then, probably not before the eighth century A.D., the city collapsed, apparently rather rapidly. This pattern is most clearly suggested by the dates of major monumental construction in the city, but it is also suggested by the demographic implications of quantities and areal spreads of ceramics of various periods, both in the city itself and in all parts of the Basin of Mexico which have been systematically surveyed. Further support comes from data on Teotihuacan obsidian industry.

In contrast, the Maya site of Tikal was settled at least as early as Teotihuacan but developed more irregularly to a modest Late Preclassic climax, followed apparently by something of a pause. There seems to have been a second peak in Early Classic times, and then a distinct recession for a century or so. Then there was a relatively brief burst of glory in the seventh and eighth centuries, immediately followed by rapid decline and very drastic population loss. Tikal population may have been relatively stable from about A.D. 550 until after A.D. 800, or it may have shot up rapidly during the 600's to a short-lived maximum in the 700's. In either case, however, it seems clear that the Late Classic population of Tikal was larger than that at any previous time. Other major sites in the Southern Maya Lowlands had rather different trajectories, but they also generally peaked during the Late Classic and collapsed during the ninth or tenth centuries.

There are also striking contrasts in spatial patterns. The early growth of Teotihuacan is concomitant with rapid and marked decline in the number and size of other settlements in the Basin of Mexico. Teotihuacan quickly achieved, and for several centuries maintained, a size probably twenty or more times larger than any other known Basin of Mexico settlement. Even Cholula, in the Valley of Puebla some ninety kilometers away, does not seem to have covered more than a sixth of the area of Teotihuacan, and other settlements in the Tlaxcala–Northern Puebla area were much smaller. In the Southern Maya Lowlands there were other major centers comparable in size to Tikal, and below these there was a hierarchy of other sites ranging from fairly large secondary centers to small hamlets and individual households. (In contrast to Marcus, Hammond argues that present evidence is insufficient for assigning specific sites to specific hierarchical levels, although hierarchies probably existed. The very fact of the controversy points up the contrast with Teotihuacan, where there is no dispute at all about its primacy in the settlement hierarchy.) There is no suggestion that Tikal or other major centers ever drew people away from other sites or monopolized power to anywhere near the extent that Teotihuacan did in central Mexico....

Implications of the Teotihuacan Evidence

Several implications of the Teotihuacan pattern suggest themselves. The long duration of Teotihuacan seems unreasonable unless economic and political power were quite strong and quite effectively centralized in the city, and much other evidence also suggest this. In contrast, both the more or less concomitant development of many Lowland Maya centers and the dynastic evidence so far gleaned from inscriptions indicate that no single Southern Lowland Maya center ever gained long-term firm political or economic control of any very large region, although there is plenty of evidence for brief domination of one center by another, and of political alliances often bolstered by dynastic marriages.

The obvious next step is to suggest that Teotihuacan was long-lived and highly centralized because it was a "hydraulic" state, based on intensive irrigation agriculture in a semiarid environment, while the Southern Maya Lowlands was politically less centralized and enjoyed a much briefer climax because of critical deficiencies in its tropical forest environment. I do not think that environmental considerations are unimportant, but I do feel that there are extremely serious difficulties with these explanations.

Discussions of Teotihuacan irrigation usually do not deal adequately with its *scale*. Evidence for pre-Toltec irrigation in the Teotihuacan Valley remains circumstantial rather than direct, but it seems quite likely that canal irrigation there does date back to Patlachique or Cuanalan times. But the maximum area available for permanent canal irrigation is less than four thousand hectares. This is not a very large area, nor does it call for large or complex canals, dikes, or flood-control facilities. Assuming a peak population of 125,000, there would have been about one irrigated hectare for 30 people. It is clear that the city grew well beyond any population limits set by irrigation agriculture, and a substantial fraction of its subsistence must have come from other sources, including riskier and much less productive alternative forms of agriculture, and collecting and hunting wild plants and animals. Faunal analyses and paleoethnobotanical studies provide evidence that Teotihuacanos ate a wide variety of wild as well as domesticated plants and wild animals.

It seems unlikely that there were any environmental or purely technical factors which would have made it impossible for the Teotihuacanos to have practiced intensive chinampa agriculture in the southern part of the Basin of Mexico. Chinampas were an important subsistence source for the Aztec population, which was much larger than the Teotihuacan population. Yet there is no evidence for extensive use of chinampas in Teotihuacan times. It is tempting to speculate that technical difficulties in assembling food for more people in one place may be at least part of the reason that Teotihuacan grew so little after Tzacualli times (a point also made by J. R. Parsons). If indeed there were environmental reasons, such as a change in lake levels, which prevented extensive chinampa exploitation in Teotihuacan times, then Teotihuacan is an instance of a population which expanded until it approached a perceived subsistence limit and then stabilized, rather than disastrously exceed that limit. If, as seems more likely, there was no environmental reason why the Teotihuacanos could not have fed more people by simply moving part of the population down to the chinampa area and investing in chinampa developments, their apparent failure to do so must have been for social or political reasons. If so, Teotihuacan population growth in the Basin of Mexico halted at a level well below the number of people it would have been technically possible to feed.

Teotihuacan's behavior has particular significance for the Maya because Culbert suggests that the Maya collapsed because they were unable to control runaway expansion which caused them to "overshoot" disastrously the productive limits of their environment.

Whether or not I am right in suspecting that Teotihuacan population growth leveled off before environmental limits were approached, it is logically inescapable that it was biologically possible for Teotihuacan population to have continued to expand until it "overshot" all technically feasible subsistence possibilities. If it were simply the case that rapid development tends to acquire a sort of momentum which carries it beyond environmental limits and into disaster before it can be stopped, then the ability of the Teotihuacanos to slow down and stop short of disaster would be puzzling.

An extended discussion of Teotihuacan's eventual collapse is not possible here, but I should add that I do not know of any convincing evidence that even the end of Teotihuacan was primarily due to climatic deterioration or other environmentally generated subsistence difficulties. Growing competition from other Highland centers was probably important, and I suspect that Teotihuacan may have collapsed for political, economic, and military reasons, rather than purely ecological reasons.

Proponents of either "population pressure" or "hydraulic" explanations for early states may perhaps argue that Teotihuacan "plateaued" instead of overshooting because the power of the state was very much stronger and more centralized than in the Maya cities, so that when the disastrous consequences of further expansion of the city became evident, the state had the power to intervene effectively and halt further population growth. Possibly this may be part of the explanation, but I do not think this explanation is required. The main reason may have been that there was simply no advantage in further expansion that would have offset attendant inconveniences. There is much evidence that population growth rates are very responsive to shifts in other variables. Assuming the Southern Lowland Maya did indeed "overshoot" their environment, even in the face of growing subsistence difficulties, it is the Maya behavior which is puzzling—far more puzzling than Culbert assumes—and it is the Maya "overshoot" rather than the Teotihuacan "plateau" which is most in need of explanation.

Culbert's "overshoot" explanation of the Maya collapse is one of the least unsatisfactory suggestions made so far. Culbert himself cogently disposes of most previous explanations. And archaeological evidence for the Southern Maya Lowlands in the eighth century does suggest a population so large that, in spite of evidence for terraces, ridged fields, and tree and root crops in addition to swidden, a subsistence crisis seems a real possibility. Nevertheless, there are serious problems with Culbert's explanation. He speaks of many causal factors, but inspection shows that excessive population growth plays a central role in his model. And, in his 1974 book, he offers no particular explanation for the population growth itself. More recently he has attributed population growth to economic development. But the question remains: what would have driven the Maya to expand population and/or environmental exploitation to the point where a subsistence crisis was produced? And if, instead, there was little population growth after about A.D. 550, as Haviland (1970 and personal communication) argues, then the postponement of collapse for some 250 years seems even more puzzling.

A different explanation for the Maya collapse suggests that the eighth-century Maya "florescence" was not, in fact, a time of Maya prosperity at all, but instead an attempt to cope with already serious troubles. This theory, if I understand it correctly, suggests that ability to obtain foreign goods by trade was critical for elite Maya prestige, for the power that derived from that prestige, and as a means of providing incentives for local production. Exclusion of central Peten elites from developing Mesoamerican trade networks supposedly precipitated a crisis for these elites, in which they attempted to offset their sagging prestige by even more ambitious monumental construction projects. But clearly nothing indispensable for subsistence was lacking, and prestige games can be played with whatever one defines as status markers, as Sanders points out. Goods need not be obtained by long-distance trade in order to be scarce and valuable. Furthermore my guess is that the decline of Teotihuacan, if anything, expanded the possibilities for profitable trade by Southern Lowland Maya elites. Webb's postulated development of new Mesoamerican trading networks following the decline of Teotihuacan seems, in very broad outline, a reasonable possibility. But I am much less persuaded than either Webb or Rathje that, at least at first, the Southern Lowland Maya were unable to participate in these new developments. The scale and substance of Late Classic Maya material civilization argues that they *were* able to profit from the situation, at least for a time. To be sure, there is some evidence for poor nutritional status for some Lowland Maya, but the same was probably true for much of the English and Western European population at the height of rapid economic growth in the early decades of the Industrial Revolution. It may well be that Late Classic Maya wealth was very unevenly distributed, and it also may be that the Late Classic Maya of the Southern Lowlands were increasingly "living off ecological capital," but this does not mean that the elites were already badly off, or were doing what they did in order to cope with resource pressures or an unfavorable balance of trade. The argument that the Late Classic Maya were already in serious trouble in the seventh or eighth centuries is unconvincing. Exclusion from trade networks does seem a good explanation for nonrecovery after the collapse, but not for the collapse itself....

It seems likely that in Late Classic times there was general economic development in a number of regional centers in the Southern Maya Lowlands, perhaps at least in part because of the weakening of Highland states such as Teotihuacan and Monte Alban. More speculatively, the elites of the individual centers may have increasingly seen it as both feasible and desirable to extend strong control over a relatively large surrounding area—a control based more on conquest and annexation than on political alliance and elite intermarriage. Population growth may well have been a concomitant of this economic and political development. My argument here and previously is not that population growth rarely occurs, nor that population growth does not have important reciprocal effects on other variables. My objections, instead, are to the idea that population can be counted on to increase for no reason except human procreative proclivities, and to the idea that competition and militaristic warfare would intensify mainly as a response to subsistence shortages. Instead, I suggest that if population was increasing, it was because it was useful either to elites, to peasant households, or to both. And I suggest that intensified militaristic competition is a normal extension of intensified economic competition.

Mayanists are accustomed to assuming that the political institutions of the Classic Maya Lowlands were marginally statelike. I suggest that we should seriously consider the possibility that by the seventh and eighth centuries the combination of economic development, population growth, and social changes was leading to the emergence of more highly developed and more centralized governmental structures—the kinds of structures which would make the incorporation of many small states into a single reasonably stable empire seem a realistic possibility. I would not venture to make further conjectures about the specific forms of these new political and economic developments. However, archaeological and epigraphical evidence promises not only to test the general proposition, but also to shed a great deal of further light on the precise forms of Maya political and economic organization.

What I suggest, then, is that eventually the major Maya centers may have begun to compete for effective political mastery of the whole Southern Lowlands. This postulated "heating up" of military conflict, for which there is some support in Late Classic art and inscriptions, may have played a major role in the Maya collapse. If, indeed, population growth and/or utilization of the environment expanded beyond prudent limits, the spur may have been provided by militaristic competition. And even if population and production did not expand beyond feasible steady-state values (under peaceful conditions), intensified warfare may have precipitated disaster through destruction of crops and agricultural facilities and through disruption of agricultural labor cycles. Clearly, internal warfare is not "the" single cause of the Maya collapse, but I believe it deserves renewed consideration as a contributing factor.

Webster also places new stress on the role of warfare in Maya history, but our views and emphases differ in several important ways. First, he is mainly concerned with Preclassic and Early Classic warfare as one of the causes of the *rise* of Maya civilization. This is a topic I have not discussed here. My feeling is that Webster makes some good points—there is certainly clear evidence for some Maya warfare quite early—but he probably overestimates the explanatory importance of early warfare. Second, Webster tends to see warfare largely as a response to shortages in land or other subsistence resources. I believe that this underestimates other incentives for warfare, especially for large-scale militaristic warfare. Third, Webster places much less stress than I do on Late Classic economic development, and he differs sharply on the matter of political integration. He feels that even the largest autonomous political units were never more than forty to sixty thousand people and that incorporation of further large increments of population, especially at considerable distances, proved unworkable. Presumably, although Webster does not explicitly discuss the matter, he would assume that serious attempts to incorporate many more people and more land and other resources within single states did not play a significant role in Maya history. He does feel that warfare may have contributed to the Maya collapse, but he explains intensified warfare mainly as a consequence of the manipulation of militarism by the Maya elite for bolstering their control of their own subject populations, rather than for any extensive conquests of other states. He says that conflicts may also have intensified over strategic resources, especially capital improvements for intensified agriculture, in the intermediate zones between major centers, but he does not suggest that there may have been major attempts to expand beyond the intermediate zones to gain control of the other centers as well. He does not suggest, as I do, that an important contributory element in the Maya collapse may have been a struggle—violent, protracted, and unsuccessful—to bring into being something like the kind of polity Teotihuacan had succeeded in creating several centuries earlier.

POSTSCRIPT

Were Environmental Factors Responsible for the Mayan Collapse?

Recent archaeological research on the Maya tends to focus on the complex interplay of many variables rather than emphasizing the prominent role of any single causal factor in the collapse of Classic lowland Maya civilizations. In these selections, Adams and Cowgill draw on several factors and differ primarily in the way they interweave these forces into an overall model. At one level, both models are incomplete because they draw on the experiences of different Maya centers. Moreover, as we learn about more Maya sites, archaeologists have begun to recognize regional variations within the Maya lowlands. The decline of some centers may actually be the result of specific local factors. The Mayan collapse increasingly appears far more complex than most early scholars who sought single-factor explanations had suggested.

There is fairly strong evidence that military conquest by neighboring states brought down some centers. Human occupation appears to end abruptly and the memorial stone stelae are defaced, suggesting a hostile takeover by enemies. It is also clear that environmental changes such as heavy soil erosion in some areas were the result of human activities. While there is no question that the Maya population experienced a major decline from 800 C.E. up to the time of the Spanish conquest, it is not clear whether this decline was a sudden response to epidemics or a more gradual reduction that resulted from the combined effects of poorer nutrition, slightly lower fertility rates, and an increase in mortality rates over an extended period. As suggested earlier, each of these factors may have had different local expressions and may have affected different centers in diverse ways. What this means is that there may be no single answer to the question: What caused the Maya collapse?

There are many books and articles about the Maya and their demise. *The Classic Maya Collapse*, edited by T. Patrick Culbert (University of New Mexico Press, 1983) offers a collection of readings by Mayan scholars, each dealing with a different aspect. Charles Gallenkamp's *Maya: The Riddle and Rediscovery of a Lost Civilization* (Penguin Books, 1987); Robert J. Sharer's *The Ancient Maya*, 5th ed. (Stanford University Press, 1994); and John Henderson's *The World of the Ancient Maya*, 2d ed. (Cornell University Press, 1997), offer up-to-date accounts of what we now know about Maya civilization.

Two recent collaborative studies by teams of researchers show how complex the issue of the Mayan collapse continues to be for archaeologists. The first is by a group of scholars working out of Vanderbilt University who have excavated at Petexbatun, a peripheral center in southwestern Peten (Guatemala). In a special section of the journal *Ancient Mesoamerica* (vol. 8, no. 2, Fall 1997),

Arthur Demarest and his colleagues and students report on their excavations at Petexbatun from 1989 to 1995. They argue that interest in the Maya and the Mayan collapse has overemphasized the dynastic histories of the literate Maya elites and has largely ignored the regional impact of Mayan civilization on the environment, demography, and subsistence patterns. A similar collaborative project, based at Pennsylvania State University and headed by David Webster, excavated at the major center Copan in Honduras from 1980 to 1984. A very useful survey of their findings is *Copan: The Rise and Fall of an Ancient Maya Kingdom* (Harcourt Brace, 2000). While this study considers the role of environmental factors, it emphasizes the interplay of political and military factors.

A number of videos about the Maya can be found. *Out of the Past,* directed by David Webster et al. (Annenberg CPB Project, 1993) and *Central America: The Burden of Time,* from Michael Wood's *Legacy* series (Ambrose Video Publishing, Inc., 1991) offer thoughtful analysis about the Maya and the archaeological issues that researchers still face.

On the Internet . . .

DUSHKIN ONLINE

About the !Kung San of Western Botswana

This site provides general historical information on the !Kung San with links to further information pertaining to women and production, marriage, and the current status of the !Kung as their region is encroached upon by outsiders.

http://www.lawrence.edu/dept/anthropology/kungsan/
kungsan.html

The Yanomamö

Created by Brian Schwimmer, this site explores intergroup relations, alliances, and the role of warfare among the Yanomamö. This site also provides links to additional sites on the subject.

http://www.umanitoba.ca/anthropology/tutor/case_studies/
yanomamo/

Margaret Mead's Anthropological Work

This site, created by the American Museum of Natural History, explores Margaret Mead's life and provides a history of her anthropological work. It also includes links to articles that discuss Mead's influence on anthropology.

http://www.amnh.org/Exhibition/Expedition/Treasures/
Margaret_Mead/mead.html

Smithsonian Exhibits

This site, created by the Smithsonian Institution, allows the viewer to see photographs and descriptions of current exhibits at the Museum of Natural History and other museums. The site provides a means for students to evaluate how museums represent ethnic communities.

http://www.si.edu/activity/exhibits/start.htm

PART 3

Cultural Anthropology

*C*ultural anthropologists are concerned with the culture and society of living communities. Like other anthropologists, cultural anthropologists are concerned with developing and testing models about the human condition and the range of human possibilities, such as whether gender inequality or violence are inevitable in human societies. Some anthropologists have asked whether the lives of small hunting-gathering bands resemble the lifeways of early human groups with similar technologies. Other anthropologists have asked about the strength of other people's religious beliefs or whether the amount of sexual freedom offered to adolescents makes a difference in their transition to adulthood. More recently, cultural anthropologists have begun asking about how other cultures are being depicted and represented. But at the heart of anthropological debate today is whether anthropology should model itself on the natural sciences or whether anthropologists should see their role more as interpreters of human cultures.

- Should Cultural Anthropology Model Itself on the Natural Sciences?

- Are San Hunter-Gatherers Basically Pastoralists Who Have Lost Their Herds?

- Do Hunter-Gatherers Need Supplemental Food Sources to Live in Tropical Rain Forests?

- Do Sexually Egalitarian Societies Exist?

- Are Yanomamö Violence and Warfare Natural Human Efforts to Maximize Reproductive Fitness?

- Was Margaret Mead's Fieldwork on Samoan Adolescents Fundamentally Flawed?

- Do Museums Misrepresent Ethnic Communities Around the World?

ISSUE 10

Should Cultural Anthropology Model Itself on the Natural Sciences?

YES: Marvin Harris, from "Cultural Materialism Is Alive and Well and Won't Go Away Until Something Better Comes Along," in Robert Borofsky, ed., *Assessing Cultural Anthropology* (McGraw-Hill, 1994)

NO: Clifford Geertz, from *The Interpretation of Cultures: Selected Essays by Clifford Geertz* (Basic Books, 1973)

ISSUE SUMMARY

YES: Cultural anthropologist Marvin Harris argues that anthropology has always been a science and should continue to be scientific. He contends that the most scientific approach to culture is cultural materialism, which he has developed specifically to be a "science of culture." Anthropology's goal should be to discover general, verifiable laws as in the other natural sciences, concludes Harris.

NO: Cultural anthropologist Clifford Geertz views anthropology as a science of interpretation, and as such he argues that anthropology should never model itself on the natural sciences. He believes that anthropology's goal should be to generate deeper interpretations of diverse cultural phenomena, using what he calls "thick description," rather than attempting to prove or disprove scientific laws.

For more than a century, anthropologists have viewed their discipline as a science of humankind or as a science of culture. But not all anthropologists agree about what being a science should mean. At issue has been the question: Just what kind of science is anthropology?

Nineteenth- and early-twentieth-century anthropologists generally viewed anthropology as one of the natural sciences, and most early theorists, such as Edward Tylor, James Fraser, and Lewis Henry Morgan, saw anthropology as an extension of biology. Like biology, anthropology is a comparative discipline, and ethnographic descriptions of particular societies resemble the systematic descriptions that biologists provide about different species. Most early anthropologists were also attracted to the theories of the naturalist Charles Darwin, whose theory of natural selection attempted to explain how natural species evolved. For anthropologists evolution meant explaining how one social form evolved into another, how one kind of society developed into another.

With the rise of functionalism in the 1920s, evolutionary models became much less important as sociocultural anthropologists made detailed studies of individual societies, conducting ethnographic fieldwork lasting a year or two. Research became a total immersion into the culture, and anthropologists were expected to learn the local language, conduct participant observation, and try to understand the indigenous culture from the "native's point of view."

Although many anthropologists abandoned evolutionary questions in the 1920s, several new kinds of evolutionary models emerged after the Second World War. Leslie White proposed a unilineal model, arguing that cultural evolution could be explained in terms of how much energy a people could capture with their technology. Julian Steward proposed a rather different multilinear model to explain how societies in widely scattered parts of the world respond similarly to environmental and ecological constraints.

Building on these kinds of evolutionary models, Marvin Harris developed an approach he has called "cultural materialism." For Harris cultural materialism makes anthropology a science that parallels the evolutionary and biological sciences. But whereas biologists try to explain the physical evolution of species through natural selection, Harris argues that anthropologists should explain cultural evolution by understanding "cultural selection." Some cultural practices, whether actual behaviors or ideas, directly influence the community's successful adaptation to its material environment. Harris contends that anthropology's research agenda should be to establish regular, predictable, and verifiable laws just as scientists in other scientific fields do.

In his selection, Clifford Geertz argues that anthropologists should not attempt any kind of positivist science at all and that it is futile to seek scientific laws to explain human behavior. He contends that such laws would be either so general as to be meaningless, so obvious as to be trivial, or so specific to particular cultural settings as to have no relevance to other communities. The interpretation of cultures requires "thick description," in which the anthropologist is sensitive to cultural meanings and can provide a nuanced understanding of what he or she has observed, heard, and experienced in the field. Thus, for Geertz, anthropology should develop as a science of interpretation, and by definition such a science of interpretation cannot consist of verifiable laws; instead, it depends on the personal interpretive abilities of each individual anthropologist.

These selections pose several questions that lie at the heart of all sociocultural anthropology. Should anthropologists focus their attention on developing evolutionary theories, such as the kinds of cultural materialist explanations Harris seeks? Or, should anthropology primarily seek a more modest role in the multicultural world of today, attempting to translate and make sense of other people's cultural practices? And finally, is anthropology big enough to hold both of these perspectives and others as well?

Marvin Harris

 **YES**

Cultural Materialism Is Alive and Well and Won't Go Away Until Something Better Comes Along

Cultural materialism is a paradigm whose principles are relevant to the conduct of research and the development of theory in virtually all of the fields and subfields of anthropology. Indeed, it has been guesstimated (Thomas 1989:115) that half of the archaeologists in the United States consider themselves to be cultural materialist to some degree. For cultural materialists, whether they be cultural anthropologists, archaeologists, biological anthropologists, or linguists, the central intellectual experience of anthropology is not enthnography but the exchange of data and theories among different fields and subfields concerned with the global, comparative, diachronic, and synchronic study of humankind: the origin of the hominids, the emergence of language and culture, the evolution of cultural differences and similarities, and the ways in which biocultural, mental, behavioral, demographic, environmental and other nomothetic processes have shaped and continue to shape the human world.

Culture

... The culture in cultural materialism refers to the socially conditioned repertories of activities and thoughts that are associated with particular social groups or populations. This definition of culture stands opposed to the fixed, "essentialist" notions that inspire those who define culture as a realm of pure and uniform ideas hovering over the hub-bub of the daily life of specific individuals. For cultural materialists, culture elements are constructed (more specifically, abstracted) from the bedrock of the immensely variable thoughts and behavior of specific individuals (Harris 1964a).... [C]ultural materialists have long argued that culture is at bottom an unfolding material process (*viz.* the concept of "behavior stream") rather than an emanation of a platonic archetype.... Yet, it would be completely self-defeating to limit the definition of culture and the scope of the social sciences... to the bedrock of individual thought and activity. Although we cannot see or touch entities such as a mode of production or a transnational corporation or a sociocultural system, to the extent that these are logical and empirical abstractions built up out of the observation of individual-level events, they possess a reality that is not inferior to any other reality. Indeed, it is imperative for human survival and well-being that we learn to rise above individual thoughts and actions to the level at which we can begin to examine the aggregate effects of social life and the behavior of such higher-order entities as institutions and whole sociocultural systems. Political economies are as real as the individuals who fall under their sway, and a lot more powerful.

Paradigms

Paradigms stipulate the principles which govern the conduct of research. Principles fall into two classes: rules for acquiring, testing, and validating knowledge (i.e., epistemological principles) and rules for generating and evaluating theories (i.e., theoretical principles). A widely misunderstood aspect of scientific paradigms is that neither the epistemological or theoretical principles nor the paradigm as a whole has the status of a scientific theory. Principles such as creationism, natural selection, or the priority of infrastructure are not falsifiable. This does not mean however that paradigms are "ships that pass in the night." Paradigms can be compared with each other and evaluated from two standpoints: (1) their logical structure and internal coherence and (2) their respective abilities to produce scientific theories in conformity with the criteria discussed below. From this vantage point, the alternatives to cultural materialism presented in this [selection] offer slight hope of safe passage. I see a lot of sunken ships in the muddy waters of post-postmodernism—ships built out of flawed accounts of the history of anthropological theory, parochial agendas, inchoate conceptions of the nature of human society and human cultures, and a lack of well-formed epistemological and theoretical principles or useful substantive achievements that might justify a future—any future—for anthropology.

Epistemological Principles: Science

Cultural materialism is based on certain epistemological principles which are held in common by all disciplines which claim to have scientific knowledge. Scientific knowledge is obtained by public, replicable operations (observations and logical transformations). The aim of scientific research is to formulate explanatory theories which are (1) predictive (or retrodictive), (2) testable (or falsifiable), (3) parsimonious, (4) of broad scope, and (5) integratable or cumulative within a coherent and expanding corpus of theories.

The same criteria distinguish scientific theories which are more acceptable from those which are less acceptable. Scientific theories find acceptance in accordance with their relative powers of predictability, testability, parsimony, scope, and integratability as compared with rival theories about the same phenomena. Since one can only approach, but never completely reach, perfection in this regard, scientific theories are held as tentative approximations, never as "facts."

This view of science derives from the logical positivist and empiricist philosophical traditions.... Note that it makes no claim to being "value free." Rather it proposes to overcome the inevitable biases of all forms of knowledge by methodological rules that insist upon opening to public scrutiny the operations by which particular facts and theories come to be constructed. The oft-repeated charge by postmodernist science-bashers that there is no community of observers who can or do scrutinize anthropological, especially ethnographic operations... is belied by the intense criticisms to which crucial facts and theories are regularly subjected in the pages of anthropology's principal journals. Challenges by other observers to the ethnographic accuracy of the work of Boas, Mead, Benedict, Redfield, Evans-Pritchard, Malinowski, Lee, Vayda, and Chagnon just for starters, whether based on fresh fieldwork or written sources, clearly do fulfill the scientific model for independent testing by other observers.... It may take awhile, but ethnographers working in the same region if not the same village do help to keep each other in touch with basic ethnographic facts. However, I certainly agree... that the future of ethnography lies in greatly expanding the use of field teams and the number of restudies rather than, as Marcus proposes... increasing the number of experimental, personalistic, and idiosyncratic field studies carried out by untrained would-be novelists and ego-tripping narcissists afflicted with congenital logo-diarrhea.

... The reason that cultural materialists favor knowledge produced in conformity with the epistemological principles of science is not because science guarantees absolute truth free of subjective bias, error, untruths, lies, and frauds. It is because science is the best system yet devised for reducing subjective bias, error, untruths, lies, and frauds....

Following the lead of Clifford Geertz and under the direct influence of postmodern philosophers and literary critics such as Paul De Man, Jacques Derrida, and Michel Foucault, interpretationist anthropologists have adopted an increasingly arrogant and intolerant rhetoric aimed at ridding anthropology of all vestiges of scientific "totalizing" paradigms. According to Stephen Tyler, for example, sociocultural anthropologists should abandon

> the inappropriate mode of scientific rhetoric that entails "objects," "facts," "descriptions," "inductions," "generalizations," "verification," "experiment," "truth," and like concepts that, except as empty invocations, have no parallels either in the experience of ethnographic fieldwork or in the writing of ethnographies. The urge to conform to the canons of scientific rhetoric has made the easy realism of natural history the dominant mode of ethnographic prose, but it has been an illusory realism, promoting, on the one hand, the absurdity of "describing" nonentities such as "culture" or "society" as if they were fully observable, though somewhat ungainly, bugs, and, on the other, the equally ridiculous behaviorist pretense of "describing" repetitive patterns in isolation from the discourse that actors use in constituting and situating their action, and all in simpleminded surety that the observers' grounding discourse is itself an objective form sufficient to the task of describing acts. (1986:130)

Tyler's totalizing renunciation of the search for objects, facts, descriptions, inductions, generalizations, verification, experiment, truth, and "like concepts"(!) in human affairs mocks itself so effectively that any attempt at rebuttal would be anticlimactic. I do think it may be useful, however, to point out that the "simpleminded surety" with which positivists and behaviorists are alleged to view human social life flagrantly distorts the entire history of science in general, during which all sureties, simpleminded or not, have been subject to relentless skepticism, and the history of logical positivism in particular, during which the struggle to create objective data languages has constituted the central focus of a vast and continuing philosophical effort.

Anthropology's dedicated science-bashers are not mollified by the assurance that cultural materialists seek probabilities rather than certainties, generalizations rather than laws....

Questions and Answers

The fallacies that embolden these queries are so transparent that one must wonder if the interlocutors really intend to be taken seriously....

Question: Just how often does something have to recur in order for it to serve as the basis for a generalization?

Answer: The more times the better.

Question: If generalizations cannot be expected to be applicable to any specific case, what good are they?

Answer: The better the generalization, the more *probable* its applicability to the particular case, the more useful it is. (It is definitely useful to know that a particular person who smokes four packs of cigarettes a day is ten times more likely to get lung cancer than one who doesn't smoke, even though not all heavy smokers get lung cancer.)

Question: Why must science be equated with generalizing?

Answer: Because science is by definition a generalizing form of knowledge.

Question: Is the mandate to generalize nothing but a "procedural rule"?

Answer: Of course. And anyone is free to ignore the rule but to do so is to cease doing science. (It is also likely to get you killed the next time you step off the curb against the light, or the next time you strike a match to look inside your gas tank.)

Last question: Instead of generalizing, why not consider "all the particularity of the individual case"?

Answer: Because there are no limits to particularity. Any project that proposes to deliver *all* the particularities of any macrophysical event, human or not human, therefore makes a preposterous claim on our time and resources. For this reason, in science endless particularity is the exact equivalent of endless ignorance.

Epistemological Principles: Emics and Etics

In addition to the general epistemological principles shared with other scientific disciplines, cultural materialism is also based on epistemological principles which are specific to the study of human sociocultural systems. These involve: (1) the separation of mental events (thoughts) from behavior (actions of body parts and their environmental effects) and (2) the separation of emic from etic views of thoughts and behavior... The reason for the epistemological distinction between mental and behavioral events is that the operations (observational procedures) used to obtain knowledge of mental events are categorically distinct from those needed to obtain knowledge of behavioral events. In the former, observers depend directly or indirectly on participants to communicate what is going on inside their heads; in the latter observers are not dependent on actors to identify the actor's body motions and the environmental effects of those motions. The reason for the further distinction between emic and etic events is that the separation of mental from behavioral events does not exhaustively specify the epistemological status of the categories (data language) employed in the identification of mental or behavioral events. Observers have the option of describing both kinds of events in terms of categories that are defined, identified, and validated by the community of participants (emics) or by the community of observers (etics). Four types of knowledge stem from these distinctions: (1) emics of thought; (2) emics of behavior; (3) etics of behavior; (4) etics of thought.

To illustrate, consider the practice of indirect infanticide in northeast Brazil: (1) A sample of economically and socially deprived mothers condemns and abhors infanticide. (2) These mothers insist that their own behavior has been devoted to sustaining the life of their infants. (3) Observers note, however, that some of these mothers actually withhold food and drink from certain infants, especially from infants that are first and last born. (4) On the basis of the observed occurrence of maternal neglect and high infant mortality, it can be inferred that these disadvantaged women have thoughts that are contrary to or that modify their elicited emics of thought and behavior.... Emic and etic versions of social life are often but not necessarily contradictory.... But failure to distinguish between emic and etic and between mental and behavior data renders much of the sociocultural literature of cultural anthropology useless by literally preventing researchers from understanding the referential significance of their descriptive discourse (Harris 1968; Marano 1982; Headland, Pike, and Harris 1990).

Despite a persistent barrage of uninformed or malicious assertions to the contrary, cultural materialists insist that the proper study of humankind is both emics and etics and both thought and behavior....

While no cultural materialist has ever advocated making the subject matter of cultural anthropology exclusively etic or behavioral, the postmodernists and their idealist predecessors have relentlessly advocated essentialist exclusions with regard to what cultural anthropologists ought to study....

Theoretical Principles

These rest on the assumption that certain categories of behavioral and mental responses are more directly important to the survival and well-being of human individuals than others and that it is possible to measure the efficiency with which such responses contribute to the achievement of an individual's survival and well-being. This assumption lies at the basis of the "costing" of alternative patterns of behavior which in turn is essential for identifying optimizing behavior and thought . . . and the development of materialist theories of the causes of sociocultural differences and similarities.

The categories of responses whose costs and benefits underwrite cultural selection and cultural evolution are empirically derived from the biological and psychological sciences that deal with the genetically given needs, drives, aversions, and behavioral tendencies of *Homo sapiens*: sex, hunger, thirst, sleep, language acquisition, need for affective nurturance, nutritional and metabolic processes, vulnerability to mental and physical disease and to stress by darkness, cold, heat, altitude, moisture, lack of air, and other environmental hazards. This list is obviously not intended to encapsulate the whole of human nature. It remains open-ended and responsive to new discoveries about the human biogram and population-specific genetic differences . . . .

Infrastructure, Structure, and Superstructure

The components of social life which most directly mediate and facilitate the satisfaction of biogram needs, drives, aversions, and behavioral tendencies constitute the causal center of sociocultural systems. The burden of this mediation is borne by the conjunction of demographic, technological, economic, and ecological processes—the modes of production and reproduction—found in every socio-cultural system. More precisely, it is the etic behavioral aspect of the demo-techno-econo-environmental conjunction that is salient. . . . Infrastructure constitutes the interface between nature in the form of unalterable physical, chemical, biological, and psychological constraints on the one hand, and culture which is *Homo sapiens*'s primary means of optimizing health and well-being, on the other. . . . Cultural optimizations and adaptations must in the first and last instance conform to the restraints and opportunities of the environment and of human nature.

In addition to infrastructure, every human sociocultural system consists of two other major subsystems: structure and superstructure, each with its mental/behavioral and emic/etic aspects. Structure denotes the domestic and political subsystems, while superstructure denotes the realm of values, aesthetics, rules, beliefs, symbols, rituals, religions, philosophies, and other forms of knowledge including science itself.

The basic theoretical principles of cultural materialism can now be stated: (1) optimizations of the cost/benefits of satisfying biogram needs probabilistically (i.e. with more than chance significance) determine (or select for) changes in the etic behavioral infrastructure; (2) changes in the etic behavioral infrastructure probabilistically select for changes in the rest of the sociocultural system. The combination of 1 and 2 is the principle of the primacy of infrastructure.

As a guide to theory-making, the primacy of infrastructure enjoins anthropological researchers concerned with the explanation of sociocultural differences and similarities to concentrate on and to give priority to the formulation of hypotheses and theories in which components of the etic behavioral infrastructure are treated as independent variables while components of structure and superstructure are treated as dependent variables. The practical consequence of such a commitment of research effort is that the search for causal infrastructural variables will be conducted with decisively greater persistence and in greater detail than is likely under the auspices of alternative paradigms. The history of anthropological theory demonstrates that those who lack a paradigmatic commitment inevitably "quit early" when confronted with difficult, puzzling phenomena. . . .

Another aspect of the principle of the primacy of infrastructure that is surrounded by misinformation is the feedback between infrastructure and structure or superstructure. It would be convenient for materialist-bashers if the principle of the primacy of infrastructure meant that cultural materialists regard the mental, emic, and symbolic-ideational aspects of sociocultural systems as mere mechanical reflexes or epiphenomena of infrastructure. ("Harris thinks ideas, symbols, values, art, and religion are unimportant aspects of human life. Ugh!") Again I quote from Murphy's paper: "As for the materialists, they fail to recognize that cultural forms have lives of their own and are not mere epiphenomena of underlying 'infrastructures'" (page 57). The attempt by Murphy and others to portray cultural materialism as a paradigm in which "the ideas by which men [sic] live have no importance for their action" (Bloch 1985b:134) is totally at variance with the prominence of the phrase "sociocultural system" in the specification of cultural materialist principles. Why does one bother to talk about the systemic role of structure and superstructure if infrastructure alone has importance for action? Do cultural materialists propose that people go about producing and reproducing at random and without an idea in their heads? Could sociocultural life as we know it exist if there was nothing but infrastructure? Certainly not. No more than one can imagine people living without an infrastructure, i.e., living on ideas alone. . . . The issue is not whether thought is important for action, but whether thoughts and actions are equally important in the explanation of the evolution of sociocultural systems. Cultural materialism—indeed any genuinely materialist paradigm in the social sciences—says no. The system is asymmetrical. Infrastructural variables are more determinative of the evolution of the system. But this does not mean that the infrastructure can do without its superstructure. . . .

To illustrate, consider the changes in U.S. family life since World War II with reference to the disappearance of the male breadwinner role, the demise of the multiparous stay-at-home housewife, and the rise of feminist ideologies emphasizing the value of sexual, economic, and intellectual independence for women. As I have proposed elsewhere (Harris 1981a), these structural and superstructural transformations are the determined outcome of a shift from goods-producing industrialism to service-and-information-producing industrialism, mediated by the call-up of a reserve army of housewives into low-paying service-and-information nonunion jobs. The infrastructural transformations themselves were related to the use of electronic technologies and to declining productivity in the unionized smokestack industries which had created and sustained the male-breadwinner-stay-at-home-housewife families. The rise of a feminist ideology which glamorized the wage labor market and the intellectual, sexual, and emotional independence of women was the determined outcome of the same infrastructural force. However, it is clear that both the structural and superstructural changes have exerted and continue to exert an amplifying, positive-feedback effect on the infrastructural transformations. As the consequences of the call-up of the female labor force manifest themselves in higher divorce rates, lower first marriage rates, and historically low fertility rates, service-and-information industrialism is in turn amplified into an ever-more dominant mode of production and reproduction. Similarly, as feminist ideologies continue to raise consciousness against the vestiges of male breadwinner sexism, men and women find themselves locked into the labor force as competitors, wages for both are driven down, unions are driven out, and the profitability of the service-and-information industries rises, encouraging more diversion of capital from goods-producing enterprises into service-and-information production....

Power and Cultural Materialist Theories

For proposing that changes in sociocultural systems are selected for in conformity with optimizing principles, cultural materialism has been caricatured as a form of functionalism in which all is for the best in the best of all possible worlds (Diener, Nonini, and Robkin 1978). This accusation cannot be reconciled with cultural materialism's long-standing focus on problems of class, caste, racial, and sexual inequality and exploitation....

The fact that modes of production and reproduction are selected for in conformity with optimizing principles does not mean that every member of a society benefits equally from this selection process. Where marked differences of power have evolved as between sexes and stratified groups, the benefits may be distributed in a completely lopsided and exploitative fashion. Under such circumstances, the costs and benefits must be reckoned not only with respect to individuals in their infrastructural context but with respect to the political-economic decisions of power holders. This does not mean that all changes which benefit ruling-class interests necessarily have adverse effects on everyone else, as Marxists have wanted us to believe. For example, as indicated above, the rise of the service and information sectors in hyperindustrial mixed economies reflects the higher rates of profit to be obtained from unorganized labor. Thus, an increasing portion of the industrial labor force consists of women who have to some extent risen above their previous condition as unpaid housewife-mothers dominated by blue-collar male chauvinist husbands. There is no contradiction involved in holding that the greater advantages accruing to U.S. capitalist interests are facilitated by a lesser but still favorable balance of benefits over costs accruing to women. The behavior of both strata exhibits the predicted optimizations even though one might hold that the gain for most women, especially for minority women, is slight by comparison.

Cultural materialism is thus no less emphatic about the importance of political-economic inequality as a modifier of optimization process than are various Marxist theoreticians who claim to have a monopoly on the defense of the oppressed (Harris 1991).... One can never escape the question of benefits for whom or of costs for whom. Far from neglecting or "covering up" the effects of political factors on optimizations, cultural materialists recognize regular systemic feedbacks from the structural to the infrastructural level which give rise to political economy, political demography, political technology, and political ecology. One cannot for example explain the adoption and spread of technological devices such as shotguns, of new varieties of wheat and rice, tractors, or solar cell generators apart from the interests of trading companies, agribusiness, and petrochemical transnational corporations, local landowners, banks, etc....

Where Is Cultural Anthropology Going?

A popular myth among interpretationist science-bashers is that positive anthropology deservedly collapsed because of its failure to produce a coherent body of scientific theories about society and culture. Marcus and Fischer for example assert that there is a crisis in anthropology and related fields because of the "disarray" in the "attempt to build general and comprehensive theories that would subsume all piecemeal research" (1986:118). This implies that the postmodernists have made a systematic study of the positivist corpus of theories that deal with the parallel and convergent evolution of sociocultural systems. But they have not done this. It was only after World War II that nonbiological, positivist cultural and archaeological paradigms gained acceptance among anthropologists. In the ensuing years unprecedented strides have been made in solving the puzzles of sociocultural evolution through a genuinely cumulative and broadening corpus of sophisticated and powerful theories based on vastly improved and expanded research methods. The cumulative expansion of knowledge has been especially marked within archaeology and at the interface between archaeology and cultural anthropology (see e.g. Johnson and Earle 1987). It is ironic, then, that at the very moment when anthropology is achieving its greatest scientific successes, anthropologists who have never tested the positivist theoretical corpus which they condemn hail the death of positivist anthropology and the birth of a "new" humanistic paradigm. Only those who know little about the history of anthropological theories could hail such a paradigm as "new," much less as "a refiguration of social thought" (Darnell 1984:271).

This raises the question of why antipositivistic humanism has become so attractive to a new generation of anthropologists (and other practitioners of social "science"). One reason may be that the generation of students reared during the 1960s and early 1970s believes that positivist social science is responsible for such twentieth-century scourges as fascism, Stalinism, U.S. imperialism, corpocracies, and the educational-industrial-military complex. No doubt hyperindustrialism, high tech, and the "technological fix" lead to feelings of dehumanization and alienation. But the association between all of this and positivist social science is spurious. The problem is not that we have had too much of positivist social science but that we have had too little (Harris 1974:264ff). The atrocities of the twentieth century have been carried out precisely by people who were ignorant of or vehemently opposed to positivist social science (e.g., Lenin, Stalin, Hitler, Mussolini). Too many anthropologists seem to have forgotten that there is a flip side to relativism, phenomenology, and antipositivism—the side on which relativists who denounce reason and scientific knowledge construct the world in their own image.

Clifford Geertz  NO

Thick Description: Toward an Interpretive Theory of Culture

I

[Here I argue] for a narrowed, specialized, and, so I imagine, theoretically more powerful concept of culture to replace E. B. Tylor's famous "most complex whole," which, its originative power not denied, seems to me to have reached the point where it obscures a good deal more than it reveals.

The conceptual morass into which the Tylorean kind of *pot-au-feu* theorizing about culture can lead, is evident in what is still one of the better general introductions to anthropology, Clyde Kluckhohn's *Mirror for Man*. In some twenty-seven pages of his chapter on the concept, Kluckhohn managed to define culture in turn as: (1) "the total way of life of a people"; (2) "the social legacy the individual acquires from his group"; (3) "a way of thinking, feeling, and believing"; (4) "an abstraction from behavior"; (5) a theory on the part of the anthropologist about the way in which a group of people in fact behave; (6) a "storehouse of pooled learning"; (7) "a set of standardized orientations to recurrent problems"; (8) "learned behavior"; (9) a mechanism for the normative regulation of behavior; (10) "a set of techniques for adjusting both to the external environment and to other men"; (11) "a precipitate of history"; and turning, perhaps in desperation, to similes, as a map, as a sieve, and as a matrix. In the face of this sort of theoretical diffusion, even a somewhat constricted and not entirely standard concept of culture, which is at least internally coherent and, more important, which has a definable argument to make is (as, to be fair, Kluckhohn himself keenly realized) an improvement. Eclecticism is self-defeating not because there is only one direction in which it is useful to move, but because there are so many: it is necessary to choose.

The concept of culture I espouse... is essentially a semiotic one. Believing, with [German sociologist and political economist] Max Weber, that man is an animal suspended in webs of significance he himself has spun, I take culture to be those webs, and the analysis of it to be therefore not an experimental science in search of law but an interpretive one in search of meaning. It is explication I am after, construing social expressions on their surface enigmatical. But this pronouncement, a doctrine in a clause, demands itself some explication.

II

... [I]f you want to understand what a science is, you should look in the first instance not at its theories or its findings, and certainly not at what its apologists say about it; you should look at what the practitioners of it do.

In anthropology, or anyway social anthropology, what the practitioners do is ethnography [the study of human cultures]. And it is in understanding what ethnography is, or more exactly *what doing ethnography is,* that a start can be made toward grasping what anthropological analysis amounts to as a form of knowledge. This, it must immediately be said, is not a matter of methods. From one point of view, that of the textbook, doing ethnography is establishing rapport, selecting informants, transcribing texts, taking genealogies, mapping fields, keeping a diary, and so on. But it is not these things, techniques and received procedures, that define the enterprise. What defines it is the kind of intellectual effort it is: an elaborate venture in, to borrow a notion from [British philosopher] Gilbert Ryle, "thick description."

Ryle's discussion of "thick description" appears in two recent essays of his (now reprinted in the second volume of his *Collected Papers*) addressed to the general question of what, as he puts it, *"Le Penseur"* is doing: "Thinking and Reflecting" and "The Thinking of Thoughts." Consider, he says, two boys rapidly contracting the eyelids of their right eyes. In one, this is an involuntary twitch; in the other, a conspiratorial signal to a friend. The two movements are, as movements, identical; from an I-am-a-camera, "phenomentalistic" observation of them alone, one could not tell which was twitch and which was wink, or indeed whether both or either was twitch or wink. Yet the difference, however unphotographable, between a twitch or wink is vast; as anyone unfortunate enough to have had the first taken for the second knows. The winker is communicating, and indeed communicating in a quite precise and special way: (1) deliberately, (2) to someone in particular, (3) to impart a particular message, (4) according to a socially established code, and (5) without cognizance of the rest of the company. As Ryle points out, the winker has not done two things, contracted his eyelids and winked, while the twitcher has done only one, contracted his eyelids. Contracting your eyelids on purpose when there exists a public code in which so doing counts as a conspiratorial signal *is* winking. That's all there is to it: a speck of behavior, a fleck of culture, and—*voilà!*—a gesture.

That, however, is just the beginning. Suppose, he continues, there is a third boy, who, "to give malicious amusement to his cronies," parodies the first boy's wink, as amateurish, clumsy, obvious, and so on. He, of course, does this in the same way the second boy winked and the first twitched: by contracting his right eyelids. Only this boy is neither winking nor twitching, he is parodying someone else's, as he takes it, laughable, attempt at winking. Here, too, a socially established code exists (he will "wink" laboriously, overobviously, perhaps adding a grimace—the usual artifices of the clown); and so also does a message. Only now it is not conspiracy but ridicule that is in the air. If the others think he is actually winking, his whole project misfires as completely, though with somewhat different results, as if they think he is twitching. One can go further: uncertain of his mimicking abilities, the would-be satirist may practice at home before the mirror, in which case he is not twitching, winking, or parodying, but rehearsing; though so far as what a camera, a radical behaviorist, or a believer in protocol sentences would record he is just rapidly contracting his right eyelids like all the others. Complexities are possible, if not practically without end, at least logically so. The original winker might, for example, actually have been fake-winking, say, to mislead outsiders into imagining there was a conspiracy afoot when there in fact was not, in which case our descriptions of what the parodist is parodying and the rehearser rehearsing of course shift accordingly. But the point is that between what Ryle calls the "thin description" of what the rehearser (parodist, winker, twitcher...) is doing ("rapidly contracting his right eyelids") and the "thick description" of what he is doing ("practicing a burlesque of a friend faking a wink to deceive an innocent into thinking a conspiracy is in motion") lies the object of ethnography: a stratified hierarchy of meaningful structures in terms of which twitches, winks, fake-winks, parodies, rehearsals of parodies are produced, perceived, and interpreted, and without which they would not (not even the zero-form twitches, which, *as a cultural category,* are as much nonwinks as winks are nontwitches) in fact exist, no matter what anyone did or didn't do with his eyelids.

Like so many of the little stories Oxford philosophers like to make up for themselves, all this winking, fake-winking, burlesque-fake-winking, rehearsed-burlesque-fake-winking, may seem a bit artificial.

... In finished anthropological writings, ... this fact—that what we call our data are really our own constructions of other people's constructions of what they and their compatriots are up to—is obscured because most of what we need to comprehend a particular event, ritual, custom, idea, or whatever is insinuated as background information before the thing itself is directly examined.... There is nothing particularly wrong with this, and it is in any case inevitable. But it does lead to a view of anthropological research as rather more of an observational and rather less of an interpretive activity than it really is. Right down at the factual base, the hard rock, insofar as there is any, of the whole enterprise, we are already explicating: and worse, explicating explications. Winks upon winks upon winks.

... The point for now is only that ethnography is thick description. What the ethnographer is in fact faced with—except when (as, of course, he must do) he is pursuing the more automatized routines of data collection—is a multiplicity of complex conceptual structures, many of them superimposed upon or knotted into one another, which are at once strange, irregular, and inexplicit, and which he must contrive somehow first to grasp and then to render. And this is true at the most down-to-earth, jungle field work levels of his activity: interviewing informants, observing rituals, eliciting kin terms, tracing property lines, censusing households ... writing his journal. Doing ethnography is like trying to read (in the sense of "construct a reading of") a manuscript—

foreign, faded, full of ellipses, incoherencies, suspicious emendations, and tendentious commentaries, but written not in conventionalized graphs of sound but in transient examples of shaped behavior.

III

Culture, this acted document, thus is public, like a burlesqued wink or a mock sheep raid. Though ideational, it does not exist in someone's head; though unphysical, it is not an occult entity. The interminable, because unterminable, debate within anthropology as to whether culture is "subjective" or "objective," together with the mutual exchange of intellectual insults ("idealist!" —"materialist!"; "mentalist!"—"behaviorist!"; "impressionist!"—"positivist!") which accompanies it, is wholly misconceived. Once human behavior is seen as (most of the time; there *are* true twitches) symbolic action—action which, like phonation in speech, pigment in painting, line in writing, or sonance in music, signifies—the question as to whether culture is patterned conduct or a frame of mind, or even the two somehow mixed together, loses sense. The thing to ask about a burlesqued wink or a mock sheep raid is not what their ontological status is. It is the same as that of rocks on the one hand and dreams on the other—they are things of this world. The thing to ask is what their import is: what it is, ridicule or challenge, irony or anger, snobbery or pride, that, in their occurrence and through their agency, is getting said.

This may seem like an obvious truth, but there are a number of ways to obscure it. One is to imagine that culture is a self-contained "super-organic" reality with forces and purposes of its own; that is, to reify it. Another is to claim that it consists in the brute pattern of behavioral events we observe in fact to occur in some identifiable community or other; that is, to reduce it. But though both these confusions still exist, and doubtless will be always with us, the main source of theoretical muddlement in contemporary anthropology is a view which developed in reaction to them and is right now very widely held— namely, that, to quote [anthropologist] Ward Goodenough, perhaps its leading proponent, "culture [is located] in the minds and hearts of men."

Variously called ethnoscience, componential analysis, or cognitive anthropology (a terminological wavering which reflects a deeper uncertainty), this school of thought holds that culture is composed of psychological structures by means of which individuals or groups of individuals guide their behavior. "A society's culture," to quote Goodenough again, this time in a passage which has become the *locus classicus* of the whole movement, "consists of whatever it is one has to know or believe in order to operate in a manner acceptable to its members." And from this view of what culture is follows a view, equally assured, of what describing it is—the writing out of systematic rules, an ethnographic algorithm, which, if followed, would make it possible so to operate, to pass (physical appearance aside) for a native. In such a way, extreme subjectivism is married to extreme formalism, with the expected result: an explosion of debate as to whether particular analyses (which come in the form of taxonomies, paradigms, tables, trees, and other ingenuities) reflect what the natives "really" think or are merely clever simulations, logically equivalent but substantively different, of what they think.

As, on first glance, this approach may look close enough to the one being developed here to be mistaken for it, it is useful to be explicit as to what divides them. If, leaving our winks and sheep behind for the moment, we take, say, a Beethoven quartet as an, admittedly rather special but, for these purposes, nicely illustrative, sample of culture, no one would, I think, identify it with its score, with the skills and knowledge needed to play it, with the understanding of it possessed by its performers or auditors, nor, to take care, *en passant,* of the reductionists and reifiers, with a particular performance of it or with some mysterious entity transcending material existence. The "no one" is perhaps too strong here, for there are always incorrigibles. But that a Beethoven quartet is a temporarily developed tonal structure, a coherent sequence of modeled sound—in a word, music—and not anybody's knowledge of or belief about anything, including how to play it, is a proposition to which most people are, upon reflection, likely to assent.

To play the violin it is necessary to possess certain habits, skills, knowledge, and talents, to be in the mood to play, and (as the old joke goes) to have a violin. But violin playing is neither the habits, skills, knowledge, and so on, nor the mood, nor (the notion believers in "material culture" apparently embrace) the violin. To make a trade pact in Morocco, you have to do certain things in certain ways (among others, cut, while chanting Quranic Arabic, the throat of a lamb before the assembled, undeformed, adult male members of your tribe) and to be possessed of certain psychological characteristics (among others, a desire for distant things). But a trade pact is neither the throat cutting nor the desire....

Culture is public because meaning is. You can't wink (or burlesque one) without knowing what counts as winking or how, physically, to contract your eyelids, and you can't conduct a sheep raid (or mimic one) without knowing what it is to steal a sheep and how practically to go about it. But to draw from such truths the conclusion that knowing how to wink is winking and knowing how to steal a sheep is sheep raiding is to betray as deep a confusion as, taking thin descriptions for thick, to identify winking with eyelid contractions or sheep raiding with chasing woolly animals out of pastures. The cognitivist fallacy—that culture consists (to quote another spokesman for the movement, [anthropologist] Stephen Tyler) of "mental phenomena which can [he means "should"]—be analyzed by formal methods similar to those of mathematics and logic"—is as destructive of an effective use of the concept as are the behaviorist and idealist fallacies to which it is a misdrawn correction. Perhaps, as its errors are more sophisticated and its distortions subtler, it is even more so.

The generalized attack on privacy theories of meaning is, since early [Edmund] Husserl and late [Ludwig] Wittgenstein, so much a part of modern thought that it need not be developed once more here. What is necessary is to see to it that the news of it reaches anthropology; and in particular that it is made clear that to say that culture consists of socially established structures of meaning in terms of which people do such things as signal conspiracies and join them or perceive insults and answer them, is no more to say that it is a psychological phenomenon, a characteristic of someone's mind, personality, cognitive structure, or whatever, than to say that Tantrism, genetics, the progressive form of the verb, the classification of wines, the Common Law, or the notion of "a conditional curse" . . . is. What, in a place like Morocco, most prevents those of us who grew up winking other winks or attending other sheep from grasping what people are up to is not ignorance as to how cognition works . . . as a lack of familiarity with the imaginative universe within which their acts are signs. . . .

IV

. . . [T]he aim of anthropology is the enlargement of the universe of human discourse. That is not, of course, its only aim—instruction, amusement, practical counsel, moral advance, and the discovery of natural order in human behavior are others; nor is anthropology the only discipline which pursues it. But it is an aim to which a semiotic concept of culture is peculiarly well adapted. As interworked systems of construable signs (what, ignoring provincial usages, I would call symbols), culture is not a power, something to which social events, behaviors, institutions, or processes can be causally attributed; it is a context, something within which they can be intelligibly—that is, thickly—described. . . .

In short, anthropological writings are themselves interpretations, and second and third order ones to boot. (By definition, only a "native" makes first order ones: it's *his* culture.) They are, thus, fictions; fictions, in the sense that they are "something made," "something fashioned"—the original meaning of *fictiō* —not that they are false, unfactual, or merely "as if" thought experiments. . . .

V

Now, this proposition, that it is not in our interest to bleach human behavior of the very properties that interest us before we begin to examine it, has sometimes been escalated into a larger claim: namely, that as it is only those properties that interest us, we need not attend, save cursorily, to behavior at all. Culture is most effectively treated, the argument goes, purely as a symbolic system (the catch phrase is, "in its own terms"), by isolating its elements, specifying the internal relationships among those elements, and then characterizing the whole system in some general way—according to the core symbols around which it is organized, the underlying structures of which it is a surface expression, or the ideological principles upon which it is based. Though a distinct improvement over "learned behavior" and "mental phenomena" notions of what culture is, and the source of some of the most powerful theoretical ideas in contemporary anthropology, this hermetical approach to things seems to me to run the danger (and increasingly to have been overtaken by it) of locking cultural analysis away from its proper object, the informed logic of actual life. There is little profit in extricating a concept from the defects of psychologism only to plunge it immediately into those of schematicism.

Behavior must be attended to, and with some exactness, because it is through the flow of behavior—or, more precisely, social action—that cultural forms find articulation. They find it as well, of course, in various sorts of artifacts, and various states of consciousness; but these draw their meaning from the role they play (Wittgenstein would say their "use") in an ongoing pattern of life, not from any intrinsic relationships they bear to one another....

A further implication of this is that coherence cannot be the major test of validity for a cultural description. Cultural systems must have a minimal degree of coherence, else we would not call them systems; and, by observation, they normally have a great deal more. But there is nothing so coherent as a paranoid's delusion or a swindler's story. The force of our interpretations cannot rest, as they are now so often made to do, on the tightness with which they hold together, or the assurance with which they are argued. Nothing has done more, I think, to discredit cultural analysis than the construction of impeccable depictions of formal order in whose actual existence nobody can quite believe.

If anthropological interpretation is constructing a reading of what happens, then to divorce it from what happens—from what, in this time or that place, specific people say, what they do, what is done to them, from the whole vast business of the world—is to divorce it from its applications and render it vacant. A good interpretation of anything—a poem, a person, a history, a ritual, an institution, a society—takes us into the heart of that of which it is the interpretation. When it does not do that, but leads us instead somewhere else—into an admiration of its own elegance, of its author's cleverness, or of the beauties of Euclidean order—it may have its intrinsic charms; but it is something else than what the task at hand—figuring out what all that rigamarole with the sheep is about—calls for....

The ethnographer "inscribes" social discourse; *he writes it down.* In so doing, he turns it from a passing event, which exists only in its own moment of occurrence, into an account, which exists in its inscriptions and can be reconsulted....

The situation is even more delicate, because, as already noted, what we inscribe (or try to) is not raw social discourse, to which, because, save very marginally or very specially, we are not actors, we do not have direct access, but only that small part of it which our informants can lead us into understanding....

VI

So, there are three characteristics of ethnographic description: it is interpretive; what it is interpretive of is the flow of social discourse; and the interpreting involved consists in trying to rescue the "said" of such discourse from its perishing occasions and fix it in perusable terms. The *kula* is gone or altered; but, for better or worse, *The Argonauts of the Western Pacific* remains. But there is, in addition, a fourth characteristic of such description, at least as I practice it: it is microscopic.

This is not to say that there are no large-scale anthropological interpretations of whole societies, civilizations, world events, and so on. Indeed, it is such extension of our analyses to wider contexts that, along with their theoretical implications, recommends them to general attention and justifies our constructing them. . . .

It is merely to say that the anthropologist characteristically approaches such broader interpretations and more abstract analyses from the direction of exceedingly extended acquaintances with extremely small matters. He confronts the same grand realities that others—historians, economists, political scientists, sociologists—confront in more fateful settings: Power, Change, Faith, Oppression, Work, Passion, Authority, Beauty, Violence, Love, Prestige; but he confronts them in contexts obscure enough . . . to take the capital letters off them. These all-too-human constancies, "those big words that make us all afraid," take a homely form in such homely contexts. But that is exactly the advantage. There are enough profundities in the world already.

Yet, the problem of how to get from a collection of ethnographic miniatures—. . . an assortment of remarks and anecdotes—to wall-sized culturescapes of the nation, the epoch, the continent, or the civilization is not so easily passed over with vague allusions to the virtues of concreteness and the down-to-earth mind. For a science born in Indian tribes, Pacific islands, and African lineages and subsequently seized with grander ambitions, this has come to be a major methodological problem, and for the most part a badly handled one. The models that anthropologists have themselves worked out to justify their moving from local truths to general visions have been, in fact, as responsible for undermining the effort as anything their critics—sociologists obsessed with sample sizes, psychologists with measures, or economists with aggregates—have been able to devise against them.

Of these, the two main ones have been: the Jonesville-is-the-USA "microcosmic" model; and the Easter-Island-is-a-testing-case "natural experiment" model. Either heaven in a grain of sand, or the farther shores of possibility.

The Jonesville-is-America writ small (or America-is-Jonesville writ large) fallacy is so obviously one that the only thing that needs explanation is how people have managed to believe it and expected others to believe it. The notion that one can find the essence of national societies, civilizations, great religions, or whatever summed up and simplified in so-called "typical" small towns and villages is palpable nonsense. What one finds in small towns and villages is (alas) small-town or village life. If localized, microscopic studies were really dependent for their greater relevance upon such a premise—that they captured the great world in the little—they wouldn't have any relevance.

But, of course, they are not. The locus of study is not the object of study. Anthropologists don't study villages (tribes, towns, neighborhoods . . .); they study *in* villages. You can study different things in different places, and some things—for example, what colonial domination does to established frames of moral expectation—you can best study in confined localities. But that doesn't make the place what it is you are studying. . . .

The "natural laboratory" notion has been equally pernicious, not only because the analogy is false—what kind of a laboratory is it where *none* of the parameters are manipulable?—but because it leads to a notion that the data derived from ethnographic studies are purer, or more fundamental, or more solid, or less conditioned (the most favored word is "elementary") than those derived from other sorts of social inquiry. The great natural variation of cultural forms is, of course, not only anthropology's great (and wasting) resource, but the ground of its deepest theoretical dilemma: how is such variation to be squared with the biological unity of the human species? But it is not, even metaphorically, experimental variation, because the context in which it occurs varies along with it, and it is not possible (though there are those who try) to isolate the y's from x's to write a proper function....

The methodological problem which the microscopic nature of ethnography presents is both real and critical. But it is not to be resolved by regarding a remote locality as the world in a teacup or as the sociological equivalent of a cloud chamber. It is to be resolved—or, anyway, decently kept at bay—by realizing that social actions are comments on more than themselves; that where an interpretation comes from does not determine where it can be impelled to go. Small facts speak to large issues, winks to epistemology, or sheep raids to revolution, because they are made to.

VII

There is an Indian story—at least I heard it as an Indian story—about an Englishman who, having been told that the world rested on a platform which rested on the back of an elephant which rested in turn on the back of a turtle, asked (perhaps he was an ethnographer; it is the way they behave), what did the turtle rest on? Another turtle. And that turtle? "Ah, Sahib, after that it is turtles all the way down."

... Cultural analysis is intrinsically incomplete. And, worse than that, the more deeply it goes the less complete it is. It is a strange science whose most telling assertions are its most tremulously based, in which to get somewhere with the matter at hand is to intensify the suspicion, both your own and that of others, that you are not quite getting it right. But that, along with plaguing subtle people with obtuse questions, is what being an ethnographer is like.

There are a number of ways to escape this—turning culture into folklore and collecting it, turning it into traits and counting it, turning it into institutions and classifying it, turning it into structures and toying with it. But they *are* escapes. The fact is that to commit oneself to a semiotic concept of culture and an interpretive approach to the study of it is to commit oneself to a view of ethnographic assertion as, to borrow W. B. Gallie's by now famous phrase, "essentially contestable." Anthropology, or at least interpretive anthropology, is a science whose progress is marked less by a perfection of consensus than by a refinement of debate. What gets better is the precision with which we vex each other....

My own position in the midst of all this has been to try to resist subjectivism on the one hand and cabbalism on the other, to try to keep the analysis of symbolic forms as closely tied as I could to concrete social events and occasions, the public world of common life, and to organize it in such a way that the connections between theoretical formulations and descriptive interpretations were unobscured by appeals to dark sciences. I have never been impressed by the argument that, as complete objectivity is impossible in these matters (as, of course, it is), one might as well let one's sentiments run loose. As [economist] Robert Solow has remarked, that is like saying that as a perfectly aseptic environment is impossible, one might as well conduct surgery in a sewer. Nor, on the other hand, have I been impressed with claims that structural linguistics, computer engineering, or some other advanced form of thought is going to enable us to understand men without knowing them. Nothing will discredit a semiotic approach to culture more quickly than allowing it to drift into a combination of intuitionism and alchemy, no matter how elegantly the intuitions are expressed or how modern the alchemy is made to look.

The danger that cultural analysis, in search of all-too-deep-lying turtles, will lose touch with the hard surfaces of life—with the political, economic, stratificatory realities within which men are everywhere contained—and with the biological and physical necessities on which those surfaces rest, is an ever-present one. The only defense against it, and against, thus, turning cultural analysis into a kind of sociological aestheticism, is to train such analysis on such realities and such necessities in the first place. It is thus that I have written about nationalism, about violence, about identity, about human nature, about legitimacy, about revolution, about ethnicity, about urbanization, about status, about death, about time, and most of all about particular attempts by particular peoples to place these things in some sort of comprehensible, meaningful frame.

To look at the symbolic dimensions of social action—art, religion, ideology, science, law, morality, common sense—is not to turn away from the existential dilemmas of life for some empyrean realm of de-emotionalized forms; it is to plunge into the midst of them. The essential vocation of interpretive anthropology is not to answer our deepest questions, but to make available to us answers that others ... have given, and thus to include them in the consultable record of what man has said.

POSTSCRIPT

Should Cultural Anthropology Model Itself on the Natural Sciences?

Cultural anthropology is often viewed as a big tent capable of embracing many diverse points of view, as the selections by Harris and Geertz suggest. One can see a number of parallels between anthropology and biology in this respect as well. Biology has always included those who provide systematic descriptions of natural species as well as theoretical biologists who develop and test evolutionary models. Some view anthropology in a similar way, arguing that Geertz's interpretive anthropology is merely the descriptive side of anthropology, while Harris's cultural materialism together with other evolutionary and ecological approaches provide the theoretical grounding. As Harris notes, most biological anthropologists and archaeologists either explicitly or implicitly draw on some form of cultural materialist theory, and it is this shared evolutionary theory that unifies the three main subfields of anthropology.

Geertz strongly disagrees with this view of anthropology, arguing that any positivist, nomothetic anthropology misses the nuance and subtlety that makes human cultures worth studying in the first place. But while Geertz is the most prominent champion of this viewpoint, he is not the harshest critic of efforts to turn anthropology into a law-based science. A number of younger scholars, such as James Clifford, George Marcus, and Stephen Tylor, have been much more vocal in their attacks on positivism in anthropology. Many of their arguments have origins in the interpretive approach developed by Geertz in the 1960s, but they have urged anthropology to become a self-reflective social science, which is often referred to as "critical theory." For these scholars, anthropologists should illuminate the implicit, underlying assumptions that have motivated anthropologists. Sometimes called "postmodernism," this perspective encourages anthropologists to deconstruct the assumptions of Western cultures. Some have suggested that critical theorists are more concerned with studying the culture of anthropology than with understanding anthropology's traditional subjects. In this sense, positivism in anthropology has become one of their most visible targets.

Cultural materialism is one direction for an evolutionary science of culture to develop, but it is not the only kind of "scientific" anthropology that has been proposed. Another evolutionary anthropology is "sociobiology," which takes a somewhat different approach from Harris. Sociobiologists argue that humans, like all animals, are genetically programmed to respond in certain ways, and cultural practices are just an external manifestation of inner biological drives. For example, sociobiologists argue that, like other species, humans are internally driven to pass on their genes to the next generation. Thus, they expect individuals to be altruistic toward their offspring as well as others who are closely related to them and therefore share some of the same genetic material. Increasingly, sociobiologists have developed theories that they claim are both testable and verifiable.

Must all anthropologists have the same perspective, or is the discipline strengthened by having diverse theoretical points of view? Is there some middle ground between cultural materialism and an interpretive (or even a critical) anthropology?

For an extended treatment of Harris's views, see his *Cultural Materialism: The Struggle for a Science of Culture* (Random House, 1979). Two of Harris's other books put his theories into practice: *Cows, Pigs, Wars, and Witches* (Random House, 1974) and *Cannibals and Kings: The Origins of Cultures* (Random House, 1977).

Geertz's *The Interpretation of Cultures* (Basic Books, 1973), for which his selection was written, is the most coherent statement outlining the breadth and scope of an interpretive anthropology. It contains what is probably his best-known interpretive essay, "Deep Play: Notes on the Balinese Cockfight." Students should also consult his *Local Knowledge: Further Essays in Interpretive Anthropology* (Basic Books, 1983) and *Works and Lives: The Anthropologist as Author* (Stanford University Press, 1988). Michael Fisher's review essay "Interpretive Anthropology," *Reviews in Anthropology* (vol. 4, no. 4, 1977) offers a useful overview.

For background on sociobiology, see Edmund O. Wilson's *Sociobiology: The New Synthesis* (Belknap Press, 1975), Daniel G. Freedman's *Human Sociobiology: a Holistic Approach* (Free Press, 1979), and Georg Breuer's *Sociobiology and the Human Dimension* (Cambridge University Press, 1992). For an alternative view, see Marshall Sahlins's critique *The Use and Abuse of Biology: An Anthropological Critique of Sociobiology* (University of Michigan Press, 1976).

Important essays from a critical perspective are contained in two edited volumes: George E. Marcus and Michael M. J. Fisher's *Anthropology as Cultural Critique: An Experimental Moment in the Human Sciences* (University of Chicago Press, 1986) and James Clifford and George E. Marcus's *Writing Culture: The Poetics and the Politics of Anthropology* (University of California Press, 1986).

ISSUE 11

Are San Hunter-Gatherers Basically Pastoralists Who Have Lost Their Herds?

YES: James R. Denbow and Edwin N. Wilmsen, from "Advent and Course of Pastoralism in the Kalahari," *Science* (December 19, 1986)

NO: Jacqueline S. Solway and Richard B. Lee, from "Foragers, Genuine or Spurious? Situating the Kalahari San in History," *Current Anthropology* (April 1990)

ISSUE SUMMARY

YES: Archaeologists James R. Denbow and Edwin N. Wilmsen argue that the San of the Kalahari Desert in southern Africa have been involved in pastoralism, agriculture, and regional trade networks since at least A.D. 800. They imply that the San, who were hunting and gathering in the twentieth century, were descendants of pastoralists who lost their herds due to subjugation by outsiders, drought, and livestock disease.

NO: Cultural anthropologists Jacqueline S. Solway and Richard B. Lee contend that relations between San and other groups are highly variable from place to place. They maintain that while no San group has been entirely cut off from outside contact, some groups, like the !Kung of Dobe in Botswana, were minimally affected by these contacts. The Dobe !Kung followed an autonomous hunting-and-gathering way of life until their land was overrun by pastoralists in the late 1960s.

C an hunter-gatherers (also called "foragers") be economically self-sufficient and politically autonomous even when in contact with more powerful food-producing peoples? This is the basic question behind the "Great Kalahari Debate," which is illustrated by the following selections.

Even in the late nineteenth century, hunting-and-gathering peoples living outside the disruptive influence of complex societies and colonialism were scarce. By then most Native American hunter-gatherers were on reservations or incorporated into the fur trade, and others, like the Veddas of Sri Lanka, had been absorbed and transformed by the dominant societies that surrounded them. The most striking exception was the Australian Aborigines, who were still nomadic hunter-gatherers using stone tools at the time of European contact. By the 1950s, however, most Aborigines, too, had been settled on ranches, missions, or government settlements, and their cultures had been radically disrupted. Anthropologists' waning hopes of studying other "pristine" foragers were suddenly raised when an American family, the Marshalls, found and studied a group of !Kung San living by independent foraging in the Kalahari Desert of Southwest Africa (now Namibia).

In 1963 then-graduate student Richard B. Lee went to northwestern Bechuanaland (now Botswana) in search of an independent foraging San group. He found such a group in the !Kung at Dobe waterhole. Once thought to live in a precarious struggle for survival, he found that the !Kung actually needed to work less than 22 hours a week to get an adequate amount of food. The key to their success was their dependence on plant foods, mostly gathered by women, rather than meat, and the emphasis placed on food sharing. The !Kung became the new model of the hunting-and-gathering stage of human evolution in the minds of most scholars and the general public.

By the early 1970s, however, some anthropologists had begun to question the popular image of San as isolated people with a continuous history of independent foraging since preagricultural times. In their selection James R. Denbow and Edwin N. Wilmsen make the case that the Kalahari San have long participated in the regional economy and political system. They argue that the !Kung and other inhabitants of the Kalahari Desert were agropastoralists (farmer-herders) and commodity traders until the late nineteenth century, when dominating outsiders, drying climate, and livestock diseases caused some of them to lose their herds and revert (temporarily) to full-time foraging.

Jacqueline S. Solway and Lee respond that there is great variation in the degree of integration of San into the wider society. Some groups have become serfs or even slaves of outsiders, but others, like the Dobe !Kung, have been little affected by outside forces until recently. (The unabridged article compares the Dobe !Kung with the Western Kweneng San, who work for Kgalagadi agro-pastoralists most of the year.) Thus, their research suggests that foraging societies can live in rather harsh environments without depending on food-producers or being politically subjugated by them.

This debate raises a number of important questions. Can small-scale, politically weak societies have economic and political ties with powerful outsiders without being dominated and fundamentally changed? Can one generalize from one case like the Dobe !Kung to other foraging peoples? If foragers were herders or farmers in the past, can they still tell us something about the hunting-and-gathering way of life before the advent of agriculture? What kinds of evidence do we need to resolve the question of whether the Kalahari San were, until recently, autonomous hunter-gatherers or a rural underclass?

James R. Denbow and
Edwin N. Wilmsen

Advent and Course of Pastoralism in the Kalahari

It has long been thought that farming and herding were comparatively recent introductions into the Kalahari and that it has been a
preserve of foraging "Bushmen" for thousands of years. Agropastoral
Bantu-speakers were thought to have entered this region only within
the last two centuries. However, fully developed pastoralism and metallurgy are now shown to have been established in the Kalahari from
A.D. 500, with extensive grain agriculture and intracontinental trade
added by A.D. 800. Archeological, linguistic, and historical evidence
delineates the continuation of mixed economies in the region into the
present. Consequences of this revised view for anthropological theory
and for policy planning concerning contemporary Kalahari peoples
are indicated.

When the principal ethnographic studies of southern African peoples,
then called "Bushmen" (1), were undertaken in the 1950's and 1960's, very little
was known of their prehistory or of the history of their association with herding and farming peoples; a similar lack of historic depth characterized earlier
southern Bantu studies (2). At the time, it was universally assumed that Bantu-
speaking farming-herding peoples had intruded into the Kalahari no more than
two or three centuries ago. The region was presumed to have been peopled previously only by San-speaking foragers who had, until then, remained isolated
from external influences.

Before the mid-1970's, only two systematic archeological investigations
had been carried out in Botswana, an area approximately the size of Texas
(575,000 square kilometers); only one attempt had been made to integrate the
history of relations among hunting and herding Kalahari peoples. In addition, the climatic history of the Kalahari and its potential influence on local
economies was entirely unknown. Likewise, linguistic studies, with their implications for revealing the history of social interaction and diversification in
the region, were in their infancy. The assumption that pastoralism and social
heterogeneity in the Kalahari were very recently introduced appeared to be
correct.

Current work in archeology, geology, linguistics, and anthropology renders that assumption untenable. Since 1975, excavations have been carried out at 34 archeological sites in Botswana as well as at other sites in Zimbabwe and Namibia. Seventy-nine radiocarbon dates now delineate the chronology of domesticated food production in Botswana during the past 2000 years. These investigations indicate that cattle (*Bos taurus*) and ovicaprids were introduced along with ceramics into the northern Kalahari in the final centuries B.C. and first centuries A.D. Slightly later, grain cultivation and metallurgy were part of the economic repertoire of Early Iron Age (EIA) pastoralists in the region. By the ninth century, these peoples were engaged in trade networks that brought exotic goods such as glass beads and marine shells from the Indian Ocean into the Kalahari.

Geologic evidence suggests that significantly higher rainfall may have created an environment that encouraged the initial establishment of pastoral economies in the region. Linguistic evidence points to the diversification of Khoisan and southern Bantu languages coincident with this agropastoral expansion. Archival sources from the 18th and 19th centuries as well as oral histories document varying conjunctions of pastoralism and foraging in the economies of both Khoisan and Bantu-speakers that existed in precolonial time and characterize the region to this day. These sources also confirm the continued involvement of these peoples in ancient intracontinental trade networks that were not dominated by European colonial merchants until the second half of the 19th century. As a result of these studies, relations among hunters and herders in the Kalahari are shown to be both of longer duration and more integrated than has been thought.

The Context of Initial Pastoralism

Excavations of Late Stone Age (LSA) sites in the Kalahari reveal forager subsistence patterns differing from those recorded ethnographically among San in the region. Brooks and Helgren report that, in at least some LSA sites in the Makgadikgadi Pans area, fish and other aquatic resources complemented land animals in the subsistence of foragers between 4000 and 2000 years ago. At Lotshitshi, on the southeastern edge of the Okavango Delta, a LSA stratum dating within this period was found to contain fish, bullfrogs, and turtles along with large land mammals. Reconnaissance in the Makgadikgadi complex located over 50 additional LSA sites; two of these include small quantities of Bambata ceramics in their assemblages; eight others contain somewhat later EIA Gokomere or Kumadzulo pottery types. At Bambata Cave, in Zimbabwe, ceramics with remains of domesticated sheep are dated tentatively as early as the second century B.C. Maunatlala, in eastern Botswana, has ceramics and pole-and-clay hut remains at the end of the fourth century A.D.

The middle LSA level of Lotshitshi dates in the third century A.D. Faunal remains from this component indicate a broadly based economy including cattle (*B. taurus*) along with zebra, wildebeest, duiker, warthog, smaller game, and fish. Ceramics from this site are too fragmented for accurate identification, but their thin, charcoal-tempered fabric and finely incised decoration are compatible with Bambata types. Farther westward, in Namibia, ceramics (not Bambata ware) were present before A.D. 400 at Mirabib (with domestic sheep) and Falls Rock. Of the sites mentioned thus far, only Maunatlala has yielded evidence of metal use.

Radiocarbon dates placing sheep, and possibly cattle, but not metal, as far south as the Cape of Good Hope in the first century A.D. have been available for some years, consequently, a gap in data existed between these very early pastoralist manifestations in the far south and older centers north of the Okavango and Zambezi Rivers. The early pastoralist sites in the Kalahari and its margins begin to fill that gap. Consistent association of ceramics and domestic animals with LSA assemblages and their early dates indicate that pastoralist elements were introduced from the north into indigenous foraging economies here before the currently documented beginning of the Iron Age in southern Africa.

Recently acquired geomorphological evidence for fluctuating climates in the region has implications for these changes in LSA economies. At the Cwihaba caverns in western Ngamiland, periodically more humid climatic conditions are indicated by episodes of rapid sinter formation. In order to account for these episodes, Cooke suggests that rainfall in western Ngamiland reached 300 percent of the present annual mean between 2500 and 2000 years ago and again around 750 years ago. In general, these dates parallel those obtained for the sequence of beach levels found around the Makgadikgadi, Ngami, and Mababe basins where a number of higher lake levels with intervening regressions are indicated between 3000 and 1500 years ago.

Although it cannot be assumed that these high lake levels were caused solely by increased rainfall, Shaw argues for generally wetter conditions over the delta at dates congruent with those of Cwihaba. He estimates that rainfall over the Okavango increased between 160 and 225 percent. Under such a regime, many currently ephemeral pans and springs would also have contained more constant supplies of available water. Brain and Brain found evidence, in the form of microfaunal proportions, for episodes of climatic amelioration between about 4000 and 500 years ago at Mirabib in Namibia. Thus, several independent studies indicate higher rainfall during the millennium embracing the initial spread of agropastoral economies through the region 2500 to 1500 years ago.

In recent years, studies of Khoe (Central Khoisan) languages have proliferated in the Kalahari; all lead to an estimate that Khoe diversification in this region began about 2000 years ago. Vossen finds words for cattle and milking with apparent Proto-Khoe roots in the Khoe languages of north central Botswana. Köhler finds such words, along with a Khoe crop vocabulary, among the Kxoe (Khoe-speakers of northern Namibia). Both conclude that pastoralism must have been familiar to these peoples for a long time.

Ehret also argues that the basic separation of Khoi and Central Khoisan languages took place in the Botswana-Angola border region shortly after 500 B.C. He proposed further, from lexical evidence, that the basic pastoralist vocabulary of southern Bantu is derived through a Khoisan intermediary in this area, implying that these Bantu-speakers, but not others farther north, acquired cattle and sheep from Khoisan-speaking peoples. Pfouts suggests diversification of the Bantu languages of Namibia and southern Angola beginning about 1500 to 2000 years ago, whereas Ehret and Kinsman specifically place diversification of Proto-southeast Bantu in the EIA of this time frame. These authors suggest that economic factors contributed to this process of linguistic differentiation; their conclusions are compatible with the archeological evidence regarding initiation of pastoralism and socioeconomic heterogeneity in southern Africa. Elphick reconstructs historical data to reach a similar conclusion.

The Early Iron Age

The western sandveld.   The presence of Iron Age agropastoral communities in the Kalahari by the middle of the first millennium is now attested for Ngamiland as well as for eastern Botswana. At Tsodilo Hills, in the sandveld, 70 kilometers west of the Okavango, extensive excavations have uncovered settlements that span the period from the 6th to the 11th centuries A.D. Ceramics from the earliest (A.D. 550–730) of these sites, Divuyu, indicate that it belongs to an EIA variant, the distribution of which appears to extend northward into Angola. There are no close parallels in known EIA assemblages to the south, either in Zimbabwe or South Africa. Common decoration motifs consist of multiple parallel bands of combstamping separated by spaces that are either blank or filled-in with incised motifs. Divuyu ceramics are charcoal tempered but have substantial inclusions of calcrete.

A wide variety of iron and copper implements and ornaments were recovered from Divuyu but only a single stone tool. The presence of slag and bloomery waste indicates that metal working took place on the site. An amorphous scatter of friable burned clay fragments with stick impressions marks the probable location of a pole-and-clay hut. Fragments of perforated ceramic strainers indicate that salt was extracted from local sources. Unidentified marine shells provide firm evidence for coastal links, possibly through Angolan sites. Local trade with peoples of the Okavango system is indicated by the presence of fish bones and river mollusk shells (*Unio* sp. or *Aspartharin* sp.). Domesticated ovicaprids made up a large portion of the diet at Divuyu; domesticated *Bos* was rare. Large quantities of carbonized mongongo nut shells (*Ricinodendron rautanenii*) attest to the importance of foraging in the economy.

In the second Iron Age site at Tsodilo, Nqoma, a lower stratum contains Divuyu ceramics contemporary with the final dates at Divuyu itself. The major components at Nqoma stratigraphically overlie this material and are dated in the ninth and tenth centuries. Ceramics from these later components are uniformly charcoal tempered with few inclusions of other materials; decoration is most often applied as bands of interlocking triangles or in pendent triangles filled with hatching, combstamping, or linear punctuating. False-relief chevron designs occur frequently. Only a few dated sites are presently available for comparison. We see affinities with Sioma, in southwestern Zambia, and Dundo, in northeastern Angola, dated to the sixth through eighth centuries in the range of Divuyu and the beginning of Nqoma occupations at Tsodilo, but systematic ceramic comparisons of these sites have yet to be undertaken. Nqoma ceramics are similar to those from the ninth century site at Kapako on the Okavango River in Namibia; charcoal-tempered ceramics have been dated to the same period far out in the sandveld at NxaiNxai and are found in adjacent parts of Botswana and Namibia.

Evidence for metal working is attested at Nqoma by the presence of tuyeres as well as slag and bloom. Iron and cooper ornaments are common and include finely made chains and necklaces with alternating links of cooper and iron as well as bracelets with designs sometimes preserved by rust and oxidation. Moderate numbers of stone tools of LSA types are present. Dense areas of burned clay with pole and stick impressions mark the locations of substantial house structures.

Cattle (*Bos taurus*) were paramount in the pastoral economy of Nqoma; preliminary analysis suggests they outnumber ovicaprids by a factor of 2. Bifid thoracic vertebrae indicate that at least some of these cattle were of a hump-backed variety. Carbonized seeds of sorghum (*Sorghum bicolor* caffra), pearl millet (*Pennisetum americannum* thyphoides), and perhaps melons (*Cucurbita* sp.) provide direct evidence for cultivation. Remains of wild game along with carbonized mongongo nuts and *Grewia* seeds indicate that foraging continued to form an important part of the diet of this Iron Age population. Fish bones and river mollusk shells document continuing trade connections with the Okavango to the north and east.

Many glass beads and marine shells, primarily cowrie, along with worked ivory, one piece in the shape of a conus shell, provide evidence that Nqoma was an important local center in an intracontinental trade network extending to the Indian Ocean in the ninth century.

The river systems. Although the origins of the EIA communities at Tsodilo point consistently northward to Angola, contemporary agropastoralist sites on the eastern margins of the Okavango Delta as well as on the Chobe River belong firmly within the Kumadzulo-Dambwa complex documented by Vogel for the Victoria Falls area. This complex forms a regional facies of the widespread Gokomere tradition of western Zimbabwe and northeastern Botswana. Kumadzulo-Dambwa complex ceramics and small clay figurines of hump-backed cattle were found at the eighth century site of Serondela, on the Chobe River, and cattle bones along with LSA lithics and similar ceramics were recovered at Hippo Tooth on the Botletle River dating to the early ninth century. At the island site of Qugana, in the eastern delta, the same ceramic complex with burned, reed-impressed clay hut remains dates to the eighth century; as yet, no domestic fauna have been recovered from this site.

Matlhapaneng, on the southeastern Okavango, is an extensive site dated between the late seventh and tenth centuries, contemporary with the Nqoma sequence at Tsodilo. Ceramics are charcoal tempered with Kumadzulo-Dambwa decoration motifs. Pole-and-clay structures, iron, copper, and ivory ornaments, slag, and bloomery waste mark this as a fully formed EIA community. LSA stone tools are also present. Although this site is not as rich as Nqoma, long-distance trade connections are attested by the presence of cowrie shells and glass beads. Carbonized remains of sorghum (*S. bicolor* caffra), millet (*P. americanum* typhoides), and cow peas (*Vigna unguiculata*) provide evidence for agriculture; cattle and ovicaprids dominate faunal remains. Foraging was important here as it was at Tsodilo; carbonized marula (*Sclerocarya caffra*) and *Grewin* seeds are present and wild animal remains are common.

The eastern hardveld.   Similar developments took place simultaneously in the eastern hardveld where thick kraal dung deposits vitrified by burning have been found at more than 200 sites, indicating that large herds were kept in the region. The same EIA suite of materials already described is present, although ceramics are of Gokomere-Zhizo types with affinities eastward to Zimbabwe and northern Transvaal. East coast trade, documented by glass beads and marine shells, is dated in the late first millennium at a number of these sites as well as at contemporary sites in Zimbabwe and the Transvaal.

Major chiefdoms developed along this eastern margin of the Kalahari at the end of the first millennium, marking a transition to later centralized state development. A tripartite hierarchy of settlement size and complexity is discernible at this time. Large towns of approximately 100,000 square meters, Toutswe, K2, and Mapungubwe, dominated extensive hinterlands containing smaller villages and many small hamlets. Rulers of these chiefdoms succeeded in controlling the Indian Ocean trade into the Kalahari; it is possible that a system supplying valued goods in tribute to these chiefdoms from the western sandveld was instituted at this time, displacing previous exchange relations in which foreign imports as well as local exports had circulated widely.

Supporting evidence for changes in social relations of economic production is found in a comparison of age distributions of cattle and ovicaprid remains at the middle-order sites, Nqoma, Matlhapaneng and Taukome, with those at the capital towns, Mapungubwe and K2. At the first set of sites, a bimodal culling pattern is found similar to that of present-day cattle posts in Botswana, where slaughter is highest in nonreproductive age classes. Such a strategy conserves breeding stock and emphasizes rates of herd growth rather than meat production. Producers and consumers of herd products at these sites probably belonged to the same local social units.

In contrast, at Mapungubwe and K2, both primary centers, the majority of cattle slaughtered were in prime age classes; offtake appears not to have followed the conservative strategy found at the secondary sites. In other studies, this form of distribution has been associated with differential social stratification among occupants of a site. This appears to be the most plausible explanation for the contrasting culling patterns observed in our study. Elites at primary centers appear to have been selective consumers of prime rather than very old animals, many of which would have been produced elsewhere.

The Kalahari in the Second Millennium

These eastern Kalahari chiefdoms collapsed around the beginning of the 13th century. Great Zimbabwe emerged at this time, supplanting the political role played earlier at Toutswe, K2, and Mapungubwe. The extent of this new hegemony is indicated by stone-walled Zimbabwe-Khami outposts found far out in the Kalahari on the margins of the Makgadikgadi Pans. Control of trade became the prerogative of this kingdom. The final component at Toutswe (A.D. 1500) is devoid of exotic goods and no long-distance trade items have been recovered from two rock shelters, Qomqoisi and Depression, excavated at Tsodilo and dated to the 16th and 17th centuries, nor in an upper stratum at Lotshitshi, which, though undated, probably falls in this period.

Glass beads reappear at Xaro in Ngamiland at the beginning of the 17th century. These and cowrie shells are abundant at the 18th century site, Kgwebe, as well as in a probably contemporary (though not yet dated) upper stratum at Nqoma. Portuguese, through their Atlantic trade into the Kongo and Angola, were the probable source of these beads, which reached the interior along trade routes that had functioned since the Early Iron Age. Many of the first Europeans to enter the region from the Cape record that this trade in Portuguese goods was active south of the Orange River and to the east at least as far as the Zambezi by the 18th century. Native peoples including San-speakers, not Portuguese themselves, are specified in these records as the interior agents of this trade.

Archival records as well as oral histories testify to the importance of pastoralism throughout the Kalahari long before Europeans arrived. Every European who first observed the region from the 18th century on reports the presence of peoples of different languages, appearance, and group designation —Bantu and Khoissan—everywhere they went. Virtually every one of these Europeans remarks on the importance of pastoralism in all parts of the region and on the involvement of San-speakers in herding; several specifically mention San owners of livestock. Indeed, the herds of subsequently subjugated peoples were one inducement for Tswana expansion into Ngamiland in 1795. So rich in cattle was the northwestern Kalahari that 12,000 head were exported annually from it alone to the Cape during the 1860's through the 1880's, while unknown but apparently large numbers of interior cattle had been supplied to the Atlantic trade since the late 18th century.

In addition to cattle, 100,000 pounds of ivory along with many bales of ostrich feathers and hides are recorded to have been exported annually from the region as a whole during those decades in exchange for guns, tobacco, sugar, coffee, tea, cloth, beads, and other European goods. These were newly developed markets, but the trade networks they followed were continuations of Iron Age systems. Both Khoisan- and Bantu-speakers are reliably recorded by many observers to have been thoroughly involved in production for precolonial regional exchange networks. When first seen by Europeans in the 19th century, the cooper mines and salt pans of northern Namibia were exclusively under San control; 50 to 60 tons of ore were estimated to be taken annually from those mines and traded to Bantu smiths. Trade routes were linked to wider subcontinental networks. Salt, manufactured into loaves, was traded far into the interior and is reported to have been at least as important an exchange commodity as copper.

In extension of this economic activity, San are credited with producing the bulk of ivory and ostrich feathers exported through Bantu and Nama middlemen during the 19th century. Relations of production and exchange were thus not strictly bounded by ethnic or linguistic divisions but cut across them. More than anything else, it is this negotiable lattice of relations among peoples and production that characterizes the last two millennia in the Kalahari.

Discussion

We have summarized a large body of data pertaining to prehistoric and historic economies of Kalahari peoples, and those surrounding them, which has been accumulated by a number of investigators.... We have concentrated on the early introduction and subsequent local transformations of agropastoralism in the region because these have been the least known aspects of those economies. Pastoralism has been treated in the ethnographies cited at the beginning of this article as if its history in and adjacent to the Kalahari has been recent and separate from that of indigenous foraging. A guiding assumption of these anthropological studies was that 20th-century foraging there is a way of life that has remained unchanged for millennia. Practitioners of these segregated economies have been rather strictly supposed to have had distinct ethnic and racial origins, in contact only for the last two centuries or less. This position can no longer be supported.

Many problems remain to be investigated. Much of the central Kalahari is unexplored archeologically, and the extent to which Iron Age pastoralism penetrated this area is unknown. A hiatus exists in our knowledge of the entire region between the 12th and 16th centuries. While large centralized states with many satellite communities flourished in the east, few if any sites are presently known for this period in the entire western half of southern Africa, with some possible exceptions at the Cape. Drier conditions may have led to shifts in settlement size and location, making detection of sites in the Kalahari difficult under present conditions. A reasonable hypothesis posits a concentration of population along the river systems and permanent springs leaving less densely peopled the drier hinterland, where foraging may have waxed and waned in accordance with changing environmental and regional economic conditions, particularly after European influence penetrated the region. It is unlikely that herders withdrew entirely from the sandveld; more likely, they at least continued to exploit seasonal surface water and grazing. At present, there is no evidence either to support or refute these propositions.

All of the peoples of the Kalahari during the past two millennia have been linked by extensive social and economic networks; thus, during this period of time, the Kalahari was never the isolated refuge of foragers it has been thought to be. It was the vastly intensified extraction of commoditized animal products in the colonial period, abetted by a drying climatic trend and stock diseases, especially rinderpest, which killed 75 percent of all cattle and antelope in southern Africa at the end of the 19th century, that combined to pauperzie the region. These forces became factors leading to increased labor migration to the newly opened South African mines. In the process, the dues and privileges of earlier native states became increasingly translated into private family fortunes of a colonially favored aristocracy, while previously flexible relations among Khoisan and Bantu-speakers were transformed into ethnic categories defined by criteria of race, language, and economic class. The resultant divisions gave, to anthropological observers in the 20th century, the false impression of a Kalahari eternally empty, its peoples long segregated and isolated from each other.

An unresolved problem concerns the presence of Bantu-speakers in the western half of the subcontinent, a presence that now appears to have been more pervasive and much earlier than previously assumed. There is no doubt that the introduction of EIA economies from central Africa brought with it a complex interdigitation of people south of the Zambezi-Okavango-Cunene Rivers. In the eastern half of the subcontinent, it is well established that Iron Age Bantu agropastoralists gained a dominant position over indigenous foragers and pastoralists, ultimately subjugating, absorbing, or eliminating them. This did not happen in the west where, in fact, Khoi-speaking (Nama) herders dominated a large part of the area when first encountered by Europeans. It has been thought that a major reason for this difference lay in the short history of association of these peoples in the west. The perceived isolating severity of the Kalahari environment has been seen as a primary factor protecting San foragers from Bantu pastoralist domination. Neither supposition finds support in the research reported here.

This research has profound implications for understanding relations among contemporary southern African peoples. In particular, those relegated to the ethnographic categories "Bushman" and "hunter-gatherers" are seen to have a history radically different from that hitherto assumed. It is clear that, rather than being static, uniform relics of an ancient way of life, San societies and cultures have undergone transformations in the past 2000 years that have varied in place and time in association with local economic and political alterations involving a variety of peoples.

Two important consequences flow from this new understanding. The first forces reevaluation of models of social evolution based on assumptions brought to the anthropological study of these peoples. At the very least, ethnographic analogies formulated on modern San "foragers" and applied to studies of evolving social forms must be modified to take into account the millennia-long association of these peoples with both pastoralism and Bantu-speakers. Following on this, and more immediately important, is the need to bring the results of this research into the arena of policy planning. In this arena, San are routinely dismissed as rootless "nomads," without legitimate claim to full participation in modern national politics because they are conceived to be unprepared by history to cope with complex decisions involving economic and political alternatives. That this is no more true of them than of any other peoples should be clear in even this brief account of their recent past.

Notes

1. Etymologies of the terms "Bushmen" and "San" are debated; a long-standing derogatory connotation is acknowledged for the first of these, but San, as also "Bantu," has acquired segregating racial and ethnic overtones. To avoid such implications, we use Khoisan and Bantu as adjectives to designate speakers of two different language families, retaining San only where necessary to specify peoples so labeled in ethnographies. We use Setswana spelling, in which *c* and *x* represent the front clicks and *q* the back clicks of Khoissan words.

2. L. Marshall, *The !Kung of NyaeNyae* (Harvard Univ. Press, Cambridge, MA, 1976); R. Lee, *The !Kung San* (Harvard Univ. Press, Cambridge, MA, 1979); J. Tanaka, *The San* (Univ of Tokyo Press, Tokyo, 1980); G. Silberbauer, *Hunter and Habitat in the Central Kalahari Desert* (Cambridge Univ. Press, Cambridge, 1981); I. Schapera, *The Bantu-Speaking Tribes of Southern Africa* (Routledge, London, 1937); W. Hammond-Tooke, Ed., *The Bantu-Speaking Peoples of Southern Africa* (Routledge, London, 1974).

Jacqueline S. Solway and
Richard B. Lee

 **NO**

Foragers, Genuine or Spurious?

One of the dominant themes of critical anthropology in the 1970s and '80s has been the critique of ethnographic models that depict societies as isolated and timeless. Where an older generation of anthropologists tended to see societies as autonomous and self-regulating, the newer generation has discovered mercantilism and capitalism at work in societies hitherto portrayed as, if not pristine, then at least well beyond the reach of the "world system." Thus the Nuer, Samoans, Tallensi, Kachin, Maya, and many other "classic" cases have been the subject of critical scrutiny. These studies have sought to resituate these peoples in the context of wider regional and international economies, polities, and histories.

Studies of hunting-and-gathering peoples have been strongly influenced by this revisionism. It was in the spirit of this endeavor that we produced a critical analysis of the impact of the fur trade on the 19th-century Kalahari San (Solway and Lee 1981). A number of other scholars have focussed on the San, uncovering the early interactions between San foragers and Bantu farmers, herders, and traders within the complex historical dynamics of the Kalahari Desert (Schrire 1980, 1984*a*; Wilmesn 1983; Gordon 1984; Denbow 1984, 1986; Parkington 1984; Denbow and Wilmsen 1986). In their zeal to discover links and to dispel myths of pristinity, however, these scholars are in danger of erecting new straw men and of doing violence of a different kind to the data—imputing links where none existed and assuming that where evidence exists for trade it implies the surrender of autonomy. What is perhaps most troubling about the Kalahari revisionism is its projection of a spurious uniformity on a vast and diverse region....

We challenge the notion that contact automatically undermines foragers and that contemporary foragers are to be understood only as degraded cultural residuals created through their marginality to more powerful systems. We consider the possibility that foragers can be autonomous without being isolated and engaged without being incorporated. And we follow Marx in proposing that exchange can occur in the absence of "exchange value." Further, our argument calls into question any model of social change that implies linearity; the historical record reveals protracted processes, with fits and starts, plateaus

From Jacqueline S. Solway and Richard B. Lee, "Foragers, Genuine or Spurious? Situating the Kalahari San in History," *Current Anthropology*, vol. 31, no. 2 (April 1990). Copyright © 1990 by The Wenner Gren Foundation for Anthropological Research. Reprinted by permission of The University of Chicago Press. Notes and some references omitted.

and reversals, and varied outcomes. While many historical foragers have assimilated to other societies, a number, such as the African Pygmies and the foragers of South and South-east Asia, have developed stable forms of interaction with agricultural neighbours and persisted alongside them, sometimes for centuries. The fact that foragers have coexisted with farmers for so long is testimony to the resilience of their way of life. The position adopted here is that 20th-century foragers are neither pristine nor totally degraded and encapsulated. The historical status of African foraging peoples must be seen as the complex product of the dynamics of the foraging mode of production itself, of long interaction between foragers, farmers, and herders, and finally of dynamics growing out of their linkages with world capitalism.

The Problem

By the mid-20th century, San societies in Botswana exhibited a wide range of "adaptations." Along the Nata, Botletli, and Okavango Rivers there were "black" San who fished, owned cattle, and practiced agriculture; in the Ghanzi freehold zone of western Botswana many San had become farm labourers, dependent squatters on their traditional lands; in the Game Reserve areas of Khutse and the Central Kalahari, the /Gwi and other San groups lived relatively independent lives, hunting and gathering, raising small stock, and gardening; and in the central sandveld many San lived clustered around Tswana cattle posts, where the men were employed as herders.

The historical antecedents of this diversity have been difficult to discern. Until the 1970s the available archaeological evidence indicated that the Kalahari had been a stronghold of hunter-gatherer societies and the diversity was the product of the last few hundred years. Recent excavations, however, have demonstrated a much earlier Iron Age presence, in parts of the Kalahari as early as A.D. 500. Later Stone Age (LSA) sites, commonly associated with populations ancestral to San hunter-gatherers, are present as well and in some areas remain predominant, but a number of these sites have Iron Age materials indicating contact between farmers and foragers. Thus the time depth of contact with non-hunters has increased from a few centuries to a millennium or more, and the presence of "exotic" goods is evidence for regional trade between hunters and non-hunters.

A second line of evidence for the revisionists springs from rereadings of 19th-century accounts of exploration and trade in the Kalahari interior. Gordon, for one, has argued that the interior San were so deeply involved in trade, warfare, and diplomacy that they bore little resemblance to the "autonomous" societies described by 20th-century ethnographers. A closely related issue is the question of San servitude for black overlords. Indeed, many 19th-and 20th-century sources describe the San as living in a condition close to serfdom, a perception that has coloured observations of them.

The revisionists have used these lines of evidence to call into question the claims to authenticity of a number of foraging peoples studied by Marshall (1976), Lee and DeVore (1976), Lee (1979), Silberbauer (1981), Tanaka (1980), and others. Schrire, for example, argues that the San are not hunter-gatherers at all but failed pastoralists who oscillate between herding and foraging from century to century. Labelling recent ethnographies of the San "romantic accounts of Bushman isolation and independence," Denbow dismisses them as "an ahistorical and timeless caricature." He suggests that whatever hunters persisted through the long period of contact did so not as autonomous societies but as "part of long-standing regional systems of interaction and exchange involving neighboring peoples with quite different economic and sociopolitical orientations." Wilmsen, the most outspoken critic, referencing the perspective pioneered by Wolf, challenges the idea that the flexible egalitarian sharing documented for several San groups has anything to do with the dynamics of a foraging mode of production, concluding that "it is more than merely possible that the San are classless today precisely because they are the underclass in an intrusive class structure." In the same vein, Schrire asks,

> Are the common features of hunter-gatherer groups, be they structural elements such as bilateral kinship systems or behavioral ones such as the tendency to share food, a product of interaction with us? Are the features we single out and study held in common, not so much because humanity shared the hunter-gatherer lifestyle for 99% of its time on earth, but because the hunter-gatherers of today, in searching for the compromises that would allow them to go on doing mainly that, have reached subliminal consensus in finding similar solutions to similar problems?

The questions raised by the revisionists are challenging ones, and the claims they make go well beyond the reinterpretation of Kalahari archaeology. Yet it is an open question how much of their revision arises from the data and how much rests on unexamined inference and assumption. It will be useful to set out their claims as a series of propositions in order to clarify the boundary between fact and interpretation. They propose that (1) the Iron Age settlement of the Kalahari is earlier than previously thought, and therefore (2) hunter-gatherers were absorbed into regional economic networks and (3) ceased to exist as independent societies well before the historic period. They go on to argue that (4) if these societies continue to exhibit characteristics associated with hunting and gathering it is because of (*a*) their poverty (Wilmsen) or (*b*) their resistance to domination by stronger societies (Schrire). Of these only Point 1 can be considered well established; Points 2 and 3 draw unwarranted conclusions from scanty data while Point 4 relies heavily on discourses that are as ideological as they are analytical.

What kinds of questions need to be asked in order to evaluate the conflicting claims of the Kalahari ethnographers and their critics? It is necessary, first, for both parties to attend to issues of regional variation. Some foragers certainly were drawn into farming and herding centuries ago, and some of these became part of regional economic systems, but, as we spell out below, both archaeology and ethnohistory contradict the view of a uniform grid of economic interdependency throughout the Kalahari. Second, we need to sensitize ourselves to the assumptions we make about the nature of "contact." For some "contact" appears to be unconsciously equated with "domination." The possibility of trade or exchange *without* some form of domination is excluded from the range of outcomes. When considering the Kalahari we need to ask further whether the conditions for domination existed there before, say, 1850. Were the societies with which the foragers came in contact after A.D. 500 sufficiently powerful to compel San servitude? Again the evidence shows that outcomes were variable and that in a number of areas the foraging life persisted. Third, and related, we need to examine our assumptions about the transformative power of the commodity—the view that when a society is linked to another by trade or tribute that linkage will necessarily transform social organization and create dependency. Are there other outcomes possible in which exchange relations do not undermine existing relations of production? Finally, we need to assess the evidence for San servitude; the contradictions in the literature suggest that appearances may be deceiving and in some cases San subordination may be more apparent than real. We wonder whether the current vogue for projecting unequal tributary and mercantile power relations into the past and for debunking the "myth of the primitive isolate" has not created a climate of scholarly opinion in which contact with domination is accepted as the normative or inevitable condition—thus making it impossible to examine actual cases treating the impact of trade as problematic rather than as given. It seems prudent not to exclude a priori the possibility of societal and cultural autonomy....

The Dobe San

The Dobe area, 700 km north of Dutlwe, was far from the turmoil of 19th-century colonial southern Africa. The Dobe people were not affected by the Difaqane, though they had heard about it, and they were not subject to tribute. More important, the wave of black settlement did not reach them until 1925. Surrounded by a waterless belt 70–200 km in depth, the Dobe area is difficult of access even today; it would have been accessible to Iron Age peoples with livestock for only a few months in years of high rainfall, and even then only after an arduous journey. It would be risky to assume that contemporary patterns of contact (or lack of contact) were characteristic of all periods of prehistory. Fortunately, the data of archaeology can be brought to bear on this kind of question.

The pre- and protohistoric period.   Despite the abundant evidence of Iron Age settlement elsewhere in northwestern Botswana dating from A.D. 500 or earlier and despite concerted efforts to find the same in the Dobe area, there is *no archaeological evidence of Iron Age occupation of the area until the 20th century.* What does exist in Later Stone Age archaeological deposits, along with a classic stone tool kit, is a few fragments of pottery and a few iron implements, items best interpreted as evidence of intermittent trade with Iron Age settlements to the east and north.

!Kung oral traditions reinforce this view. Elders speak of their ancestors' maintaining long-term trade relations with "Goba" while maintaining their territorial organization and subsistence as hunter-gatherers in the Dobe area and to the west of it. Some have gone so far as to insist that the first visitors on a large scale to their area were whites rather than blacks. According to !Xamn!a,

who was born at the turn of the century, "The first outsiders to come to /Xai/
Xai were /Ton [European] hunters.... They used to shoot guns with bullets one
and one-half inches thick. But this was before I was born. My wife's father,
Toma!gain, worked for the /Tons." When asked which of the Tswana ruling
clans had first arrived in the Dobe area in the last century, a !Goshe elder emphatically replied, "None! The /Tons [Europeans] were first." And when asked if
his "fathers" knew of blacks of any origin in the area, he replied, "No, we only
knew ourselves."

The picture that emerges from the archaeological, ethnohistorical, and
oral-historical evidence can be sketched as follows: The Dobe area has been
occupied by hunting-and-gathering peoples for at least several thousand years.
The evidence of unbroken LSA deposits 100 cm or more in depth, with ostrich
eggshells and indigenous fauna from bottom to top, with a scattering of pottery and iron, and with European goods in surface levels supports a picture
of relative continuity. At some point between A.D. 500 and 1500, the interior
!Kung established trade relations with "Goba" to the east and northeast and
carried on trade with them in which desert products—furs, honey, and ivory—
were exchanged for iron, tobacco, ceramics, and possibly agricultural products.
It is unclear whether the Goba made reciprocal visits to the Dobe area or even
whether the ceramics that are found are of outside origin.

Thus, on the eve of the European colonial incursions, the !Kung were evidently occupying the interior on their own as hunter-gatherers and producing
a small surplus of furs and other desert products for barter with agriculturalists on the western margins of the Okavango swamps. The few accounts from
the precolonial era that do refer to the !Kung of the interior—called KauKau
or MaKowkow—treat them with respect as a fierce and independent people (a
reputation that has persisted to the present among neighbouring blacks)....

The fur-trade period.   Two kinds of economic networks were involved in the
San articulation with the "world system": indirect involvement through black
intermediaries—the Goba and later the Tswana—and direct contact with European hunters and traders. The indirect form resembled the precolonial African
trade that the San had carried on for centuries and therefore involved no basic restructuring of relations of production. The direct European trade, while
intense and disruptive, did not last very long. It was not until the 1920s and
'30s, with the arrival of black settlers in the Dobe area, that basic production
relations began to be modified and incorporative processes set in motion....

Agro-pastoralism.   Permanent settlement by non-San came late to the Dobe
area. Starting in the mid-1920s, Herero pastoralists moved into the area at
cattle posts both east and west of the Namibian border. The Herero began to
deepen the waterholes and dig new ones to accommodate increased numbers
of cattle. At first only a handful—about 50—came, but their herds grew rapidly
and created a growing need for labour. After 1954, when an influx of Herero
immigrants increased the area's non-San population fivefold, the demand for
!Kung labour rose still further. Dobe-area Herero remained oriented to subsistence pastoralism rather than moving into production for market; the market

was distant and the price for cattle low. Except for a few cattle sold to pay for special purchases, such as guns, horses, or sewing machines, the Herero preferred to let their herds expand and to draw additional !Kung labour as necessary into the work of managing them. By the late 1950s the job of herdboy had become normative for Dobe-area !Kung men between the ages of 15 and 25. In 1963 there were about 460 !Kung in the Dobe area, 340 Herero and other non-San, and about 2,000 head of cattle. About half of the !Kung young men of the age-category called ≠doiesi (adolescents) were working on the cattle at any one time. Eventually most men returned to their camps to marry and raise families, but some married men stayed on in a semi-permanent arrangement with Herero families.

By the 1960s an alternative economy had begun to crystallize, and the Dobe !Kung were found distributed between two kinds of living groups. About 70% lived in camps—bandlike multifamily units whose members engaged in a mixed economy of foraging, mafisa herding, and some horticulture. The rest lived in client groups consisting of retainers and their families attached to black cattle posts. Despite the variety of economic strategies that supported them, camps continued to exhibit the characteristic patterns of collective ownership of resources and food sharing that have been documented for hunter-gatherers around the world. The client groups offered an instructive contrast, being in effect appendages of the domestic economy of their Herero masters. The men worked alongside their Herero counterparts herding the cattle, while the !Kung women shared in the domestic tasks with the Herero women. Some client groups consisted of a !Kung woman married to a Herero man and her relatives, and a few involved a !Kung man, his (!Kung) wife, and their children and relatives. The camp-living !Kung also maintained ties to the cattle posts; Dobe residents frequently went to Mahopa to ask for milk, meat, or other items. The cattle-post !Kung acted as conduits for the transmission of Herero goods to the population at large.

The stage was now set for the final act in the transformation of the Dobe-area !Kung from a relatively autonomous people with long-standing but non-decisive linkages to the larger regional pastoral, tributary, and mercantile economy to a people bound to the region and the world by ties of dependency. Having survived long-distance trade, contacts with European hunters, Tswana overlordship, mafisa [cattle "on loan" from the Tswana patron] herding, direct employment on cattle posts, even forced resettlement in Namibia, the !Kung became dependent largely as a consequence of the inability of their land to support a foraging mode of production. The bush had always been the backdrop to economic change, giving the !Kung security and a degree of freedom not available to the great majority of the agrarian societies of southern Africa. Tlou speaks of the Tawana's difficulties in exacting tribute or service from the "BaSarwa" (San) and concludes, "The sandbelt BaSarwa rarely became serfs because they could easily escape into the Kgalagadi Desert." By 1970, however, four decades of intensive and expanding pastoralism had begun to take their toll on the capacity of the environment to support hunting and gathering. Cattle grazing and the pounding of hooves had destroyed the grass cover over many square kilometers and reduced the available niches for dozens of species of edible roots and rhizomes. Goat browsing had destroyed thousands of berry bushes and other edible plants. The reduction or removal of these food sources placed added pressure on the remaining human food sources; for example, mongongo nut harvests noticeably diminished in the 1980s. The drilling of a dozen boreholes in Bushmanland, Namibia, just to the west of Dobe, in the early 1980s aggravated these trends by lowering the water table. Hunting remained viable but became subject to much stricter controls by the Game Department, and many men, fearing arrest, stopped hunting. The effect of these changes was seriously to undermine the foraging option and to force the Dobe-area !Kung into dependency on the cattle posts and particularly the state. The latter responded with large-scale distribution of food relief between 1980 and 1987, which further deepened dependency....

Foragers Genuine and Spurious: The Limitations of World Systems

What kinds of socioeconomic arrangements characterized the Kalahari San in the 19th and 20th centuries, and what kinds of explanatory frameworks best account for them? These questions must be approached at two levels: the level of fact, in which the archaeological, ethnohistoric, and ethnographic evidence is set out and interrogated, and the level of discourse, in which the explanatory frameworks themselves become the focus of interrogation.

The archaeological record shows a diversity of economic adaptations in the 19th century and earlier. The interaction of Stone Age with Iron Age cultures resulted in dramatic economic shifts in some areas, while in other areas the effects were more subtle. Kalahari trade was widespread, and in many instances when tributary formations emerged in the 19th century ties of domination/subordination were superimposed on preexisting linkages. But not all San groups experienced this pattern of early linkage and later subordination. Interrelationships were strongest on the river systems and the margins of the desert and weaker as one moved into the interior. Thus there were large areas of semi-arid southern Africa that lay outside tributary orbits, where trade was equal, non-coercive, and intermittent and where independent—but not isolated —social formations persisted into the 20th century.

In attempting to explain this situation, it is important, first, to recognize that trade and exchange cannot simply be equated with domination and loss of autonomy. Exchange is a fundamental part of human life and appears in all cultural settings. Hunter-gatherer peoples have participated in exchange with farming and market societies for hundreds of years (in India, South-east Asia, and East Africa) while maintaining a foraging mode of production. Even with "hunters in a world of hunters," exchange was part of social life.... The evidence for long-established trade relations between foragers and others has been glossed by some as evidence for the fragility of the foraging mode of production. But if it was so fragile, why did it persist?

Throughout these debates about the status of Kalahari and other foragers there has been a lack of attention to the meanings of key terms. Just what is meant by "autonomy," "dependency," "independence," "integration," and "servitude" is rarely made clear. Without consistent, agreed-upon definitions it will be difficult or impossible to resolve the issues with which we are concerned. "Autonomy," for example, has a wide range of uses. Given its currency, it is remarkable how unreflexive its anthropological uses have been. We will confine our discussion to economic autonomy, since much of the debate in hunter-gatherer studies seems to revolve around it. One of the rhetorical devices of the revisionist view of hunter-gatherers is to equate autonomy with isolation —a definition so stringent that no society can possibly satisfy it. But autonomy is not isolation and no social formation is hermetically sealed; we take it as given that all societies are involved in economic exchanges and political relations with their neighbours.

As an economic concept, autonomy refers to economic self-sufficiency, and self-sufficiency in turn hinges not on the *existence* of trade—since all societies trade—but on whether that trade is indispensable for the society's survival. To demonstrate autonomy one must demonstrate self-reproduction. Dependency therefore may be defined as the inability of a society to reproduce itself without the intervention of another....

The camp-dwelling people of the Dobe area were economically self-sufficient during the 1960s. They owned the bulk of their means of production and paid no rent, tribute, or taxes in money or kind. They hunted and gathered for the large majority of their subsistence requirements and for the rest tended *mafisa* cattle or worked as herdboys for their Herero neighbours. The latter tasks provided income that was a welcome supplement but not essential to survival. How can we demonstrate its non-essentiality? First, San *mafisa* holders and herdboys were observed to leave "service" without visible detriment to their well-being. In fact, it was common for young men to work on cattle for a few years and then return to the bush at marriage. More compelling, in the drought of 1964 Herero crops failed and cows were dry yet the San persevered without evident difficulty. In fact, the Herero women were observed gathering wild foods alongside their San neighbours. Since the San carried on through this period without visible hardship despite the withdrawal of Herero resources, it is clear that the latter were not essential to their reproduction....

Difficulties on several levels are encountered when we try to pin down the forms and content of San servitude and dependence. First, it is obvious that terms such as serfdom and chattel slavery, developed in a specific European context, are not easily grafted onto Kalahari social relations. More specifically, the language that is used in the Kalahari itself appears to overstate the degree of dependence. Both Vierich and Solway were struck by the exaggerated descriptions of servitude by San and black alike. The cultural vocabulary of superior/subordinate relations further illustrates the difficulty of translating words that lack cognates in the language of the observer. Silberbauer and Kuper, for example, show that the Sekgalagadi term *munyi*, used for "master" in San-black relations, is also used for the senior in asymmetrical kin relations, i.e., "elder brother." It denotes authority but falls short of our concept of mastership or ownership....

At the level of concrete social relations, there is a puzzling incongruity between the exaggerated degree of inequality described by Kalahari residents and the relative ease (and frequency) with which the San "serfs" disappear into the desert for periods of time, leaving their "masters" high and dry. Vierich has argued that "interdependence" more accurately describes the relationship between San and non-San and that San simply "play the beggar" to get handouts. . . .

Hunter-Gatherer and Agrarian Discourse: Making the Transition

We have traced in some detail the historical pathways followed by the Dutlwe and Dobe San as they changed from autonomous foragers to clients and labourers increasingly subject to and dependent upon local, national, and world economies. In order to understand these processes it is necessary to make a second transition, from discourse about hunter-gatherers to discourse about agrarian societies and the emerging world system.

In agrarian discourse structures of domination are taken as given; it is the *forms* of domination and the modes of exploitation and surplus extraction that are problematic. In the literature on the agrarian societies of the Third World, stratification, class and class struggle, patriarchy, accumulation, and immiseration constitute the basic descriptive and analytical vocabulary. In hunter-gatherer discourse it is not the forms of domination that are at issue but *whether domination is present*. This question is often side-stepped or ignored. . . .

Perhaps the most serious consequences of imposing agrarian discourse on hunter-gatherers is that it robs the latter of their history. What is at issue here is an intellectual neo-colonialism that seeks to recreate their history in the image of our own. This revisionism trivializes these people by making their history entirely a reactive one. Even at its best revisionism grants historical animation and dignity to the San only by recasting their history as the history of oppression. But is their oppression by us the only thing, or even the main thing, that we want to know about foraging peoples? The majority of the world's foragers are, for whatever reason, people who have resisted the temptation (or threat) to become like us: to live settled lives at high densities and to accept the structural inequalities that characterize most of the world. Many former foragers—and that includes most of us—now live in stratified, entrepreneurial, bureaucratic society, but not all have followed this route, and the presence or absence of inequality and domination can be investigated empirically.

Ultimately, in understanding the histories of Third World societies or of our own, we will have to rely on the histories of specific instances and not allow preconceptions to sway us. This caveat applies equally to those who would place the hunter-gatherers in splendid isolation and those who would generalize the power relations of contemporary capitalism to most of the world's people through most of their historical experience.

References

DENBOW, J. 1984. "Prehistoric herders and foragers of the Kalahari: The evidence for 1500 years of interaction," in *Past and present in hunter-gatherer studies.* Edited by C. Schrire, pp. 175–93. Orlando: Academic Press.

———. 1986. A new look at the later prehistory of the Kalahari. *Journal of African History* 27: 3–28.

DENBOW, J., AND E. WILSEM. 1986. Advent and the course of pastoralism in the Kalahari. *Science* 234:1509–15.

GORDON, ROBERT J. 1984. "The !Kung in the Kalahari exchange: An ethnohistorical perspective," in *Past and present in hunter-gatherer studies.* Edited by C. Schrire, pp. 195–224. Orlando: Academic Press.

LEE, R. 1979. *The !Kung San: Men, women, and work in a foraging society.* Cambridge: Cambridge University Press.

LEE, R. B., AND I. DEVORE. Editors. 1976. *Kalahari hunter-gatherers.* Cambridge: Harvard University Press.

MARSHALL, L. K. 1976. *The !Kung Bushmen of Nyae/Nyae.* Cambridge: Harvard University Press.

PARKINGTON, J. 1984. "Soaqua and Bushmen: Hunters and robbers," in *Past and present in hunter-gatherer studies.* Edited by C. Schrire, pp. 151–74. Orlando: Academic Press.

SCHRIRE, CARMEL. 1980. An enquiry into the evolutionary status and apparent identity of San hunter-gatherers. *Human Ecology* 8:9–32.

———. Editor. 1984a. *Past and present in hunter-gatherer studies.* Orlando: Academic Press.

SILBERBAUER, GEORGE B. 1981. *Hunter and habitat in the central Kalahari Desert.* Cambridge: Cambridge University Press.

SOLWAY, J., AND R. B. LEE. 1981. The Kalahari fur trade. Paper presented at the 80th annual meeting of the American Anthropological Association, Los Angeles, Calif.

TANAKA, J. 1980. *The San hunter-gatherers of the Kalahari: A study in ecological anthropology.* Tokyo: University of Tokyo Press.

WILMSEN, E. 1983. The ecology of illusion: Anthropological foraging in the Kalahari. *Reviews in Anthropology* 10:9–20.

POSTSCRIPT

Are San Hunter-Gatherers Basically Pastoralists Who Have Lost Their Herds?

These selections express two radically different worldviews. Denbow and Wilmsen's view—which has been called the "revisionist" view—emphasizes the interconnectedness of societies and the tendency for powerful polities to exert control over their less powerful neighbors. They are skeptical that such small-scale societies as the San groups could have existed within the orbit of powerful Bantu kingdoms without being fundamentally changed by them. Denbow and Wilson emphasize that the San have a history as long as that of any other people and that their history was entwined with that of their neighbors. On the other hand, Solway and Lee's view—called the "traditionalist" view—emphasizes the people's adaptation to their natural environment and sees their relations with outsiders as variable, depending on local circumstances. Because rainfall in the Dobe area was too sparse and unreliable to support continuous herding or agriculture before the advent of man-made wells, hunting and gathering was the most viable economy over the long run. Solway and Lee recognize that the !Kung San of Dobe have had contact and interaction with outsiders for many years, but they see this contact as having had minimal influence on their culture. Most anthropologists recognize that all cultures are influenced by local conditions and by the larger social environment, including, to some extent, the entire "world system." The question is, How much weight should one give to these two types of influence?

The disagreement between these two pairs of scholars and their supporters is not merely a matter of theoretical emphasis. They also disagree about the facts and their proper interpretation. In subsequent publications Wilmsen and Lee, in particular, have argued over such matters as the precise locations of groups and trade routes mentioned in travelers' journals and whether or not the presence of cattle bones, for example, in an archaeological site indicates trade or outside domination. For elaboration of Wilmsen and Denbow's views see "Paradigmatic History of San-Speaking Peoples and Current Attempts at Revision," *Current Anthropology* (vol. 31, no. 5, 1990) and Wilmsen's book *Land Filled with Flies: A Political Economy of the Kalahari* (University of Chicago Press, 1989). For Lee's critique of these sources see his and Mathias Guenther's "Problems in Kalahari Historical Ethnography and the Tolerance of Error," *History in Africa* (vol. 20, 1993) and "Oxen or Onions? The Search for Trade (and Truth) in the Kalahari," *Current Anthropology* (vol. 32, 1991).

The literature on the San is voluminous. Alan Barnard's book *Hunters and Herders of Southern Africa: A Comparative Ethnography of the Khoisan Peoples* (Cambridge University Press, 1992) is an excellent overview of the various

San and Khoi (formerly called "Hottentot") peoples. His annotated bibliography, *The Kalahari Debate: A Bibliographical Essay* (Edinburgh University, Centre of African Studies, 1992), contains over 500 references relevant to this controversy through 1992 alone. Important expressions of the revisionist view include Carmel Schrire's article "An Inquiry into the Evolutionary Status and Apparent Identity of San Hunter-Gatherers," *Human Ecology* (vol. 8, no. 1, 1980) and her chapter entitled "Wild Surmises on Savage Thoughts," in her edited volume *Past and Present in Hunter Gatherer Studies* (Academic Press, 1984). A crucial source on the history of the San is Robert Gordon's *The Bushman Myth: The Making of a Namibian Underclass* (Westview Press, 1992). Works supporting the traditionalist view include Susan Kent's "The Current Forager Controversy: Real vs. Ideal Views of Hunter-Gatherers," *Man* [n.s.] (vol. 27, 1992). Many of the classic monographs on particular San groups—such as Lee's *The !Kung San* (Cambridge University Press, 1979); J. Tanaka's *The San, Hunter-Gatherers of the Kalahari: A Study in Ecological Anthropology* (University of Tokyo Press, 1980); and George Silberbauer's *Hunter and Habitat in the Central Kalahari Desert* (Cambridge University Press, 1981)—focus on their adaptation to their natural environments and implicitly support the traditionalist view as well.

ISSUE 12

Do Hunter-Gatherers Need Supplemental Food Sources to Live in Tropical Rain Forests?

YES: Thomas N. Headland, from "The Wild Yam Question: How Well Could Independent Hunter-Gatherers Live in a Tropical Rain Forest Ecosystem?" *Human Ecology* (1987)

NO: Serge Bahuchet, Doyle McKey, and Igor de Garine, from "Wild Yams Revisited: Is Independence from Agriculture Possible for Rain Forest Hunter-Gatherers?" *Human Ecology* (1991)

ISSUE SUMMARY

YES: Cultural anthropologist Thomas N. Headland hypothesizes that hunter-gatherers could never have lived in tropical rain forests without some access to cultivated foods. He contends that such forests are poor in energy-rich wild foods that are readily accessible to humans, especially starches.

NO: Cultural anthropologists Serge Bahuchet and Igor de Garine and biologist Doyle McKey argue that rain forest foragers harvest far fewer wild foods than the forests actually contain, precisely because they now have easy access to cultivated foods. They present evidence that Aka Pygmies in the central African rain forest can live entirely off of wild foods and have done so in the past.

S ome of the best-documented hunting and gathering peoples live in tropical rain forests. They are generally pictured as small groups living in temporary camps and supporting themselves by gathering wild tubers, fruits, and honey and by killing game with spears, bows and arrows, and blowpipes with poisoned darts. Yet all, or almost all, of these peoples obtain some agricultural produce through trading with nearby farmers, working for farmers in return for food, or growing a few crops themselves. The classic example is the Mbuti Pygmies of the Ituri Forest in the Congo (formerly Zaire). As described by Colin Turnbull in his book *Wayward Servants: The Two Worlds of the African Pygmies* (The Natural History Press, 1965), the Mbuti spend part of each year as nomadic foragers in

226

the forest living off of wild foods and part of each year living in camps near the villages of farmers, with whom they trade meat for cultivated foods, like bananas and manioc (tapioca root). The villagers think of their Mbuti trade partners as their servants or even slaves, but the Mbuti see the villagers as mere resources that they can exploit or ignore according to their own wishes.

During the 1980s a number of hunter-gatherer specialists began questioning just how independent tropical forest foragers like the Mbuti were from their agricultural trading partners. Some scholars began to argue that the foragers' trading for food was not voluntary but was probably a necessity, at least some of the time. This argument was based on the contention that in tropical forests, contrary to appearances, wild foods accessible to humans are scarce, seasonally absent, and time-consuming to obtain and process; in terms of foraging potential such forests are in fact "green deserts."

Thomas N. Headland, a specialist on the Agta of northeastern Luzon in the Philippines, carried this reasoning to its logical conclusion. In his selection, he questions whether or not full-time independent foraging is possible in any tropical rain forest. Drawing on his knowledge of the Agta and their environment and on the literature on other tropical forest foragers, he argues that rain forests contain so few readily accessible carbohydrates that foragers cannot survive there without obtaining supplementary agricultural produce by trade, working for farmers, or growing some crops themselves. Therefore, foragers could not have moved into tropical forests before pioneering farmers with whom they could maintain a symbiotic relationship based on the exchange of forest products or labor for cultivated food.

Serge Bahuchet, Doyle McKey, and Igor de Garine respond to Headland's challenge. They maintain that the fact that tropical forest foragers today obtain carbohydrates from farmers does not mean that they are incapable of living without those food sources or that they have not lived by independent foraging in the past. Using data collected by Annette Hladik and Marcel Hladik on the density of wild yams in the territory of the Aka Pygmies, the authors conclude that there is an ample amount of starch available to support the current Aka population if they choose to live exclusively off of wild foods. They also give linguistic evidence to suggest that the Pygmies had a well-established foraging tradition well before farmers settled in the forest. The authors contend that the Pygmies trade for agricultural produce today because trading for food is more efficient than gathering it from wild sources.

This issue raises a number of important questions for anthropologists. What difference does it make to our understanding of human prehistory and history if people could not have lived in any tropical rain forests before the advent of agriculture? If tropical forest foragers are truly dependent upon farmers for some of their food, can we legitimately consider them hunter-gatherers? What sort of evidence is needed to test Headland's hypothesis decisively? In general, how can we know what a people are capable of doing if they do not actually do it?

Thomas N. Headland

 **YES**

The Wild Yam Question

Introduction

Anthropologists and others have generally represented hunter-gatherer societies found today in tropical forest environments as having always lived in such
biomes, until recently isolated and separated from other peoples, and surviving
solely on wild foods.... Though a number of anthropologists have recently
criticized this view, one still finds what Barnard (1983) calls a "Rousseauian
notion of natural purity and cultural pollution [that] permeates the field of
hunter-gatherer studies" (p. 194).

This [selection] presents an alternative hypothesis. Increasing evidence
suggests that for foraging humans, tropical rain forests are food-poor, not food-
rich. Wild starch foods, and especially wild yams, may be too scarce in such
biomes to sustain independent hunter-gatherers without recourse to cultivated
foods. Prehistoric hunter-gatherers either did not live in tropical rain forests, or
else they lived there following an economy of symbiotic trade with food producers, exchanging forest products for cultivated plant foods. They may even
have practiced cultivation themselves.... Pure foraging, with no iron tools,
no cultivation, and no trade would at best have been a difficult and meager
existence in closed tropical forests.

Tropical Forest Typology

There are two general classes of tropical forest. These are "rain forests" and
"monsoon forests."... Both classes occur in areas with a mean annual temperature of at least 24°C and which are essentially frost-free. "Rain forests,"
however, receive more, and more evenly distributed rainfall, at least 4000 mm
per year, and not less than 100 mm in any month for 2 out of 3 years. "Monsoon forests" usually have less rainfall, but their defining characteristic is in
their having a marked dry season....

In contrast to rain forests, the plant growth in monsoon forests slackens
and may turn brown for want of water during several months of the year. Many
trees lose their leaves, and much more sunlight penetrates to the forest floor
during the dry season. Biomass in monsoon forests is only one-fifth that of

From Thomas N. Headland, "The Wild Yam Question: How Well Could Independent Hunter-
Gatherers Live in a Tropical Rain Forest Ecosystem?" *Human Ecology*, vol. 15, no. 4 (1987). Copyright
© 1987 by Plenum Publishing Corporation. Reprinted by permission. Some references omitted.

rain forests. The implications of this for the ecology of wild tubers will become apparent.

The Case of the Agta Negritos

The Philippine archipelago was once completely covered with unbroken forest of one type or another. The western parts of the Philippines fall generally into the category of monsoon forest, while the eastern sections are classed as rain forest.

. . . In the past, primary lowland dipterocarp forest covered from 80–90% of eastern Luzon, but today much has been cut back. In the 700 km² Casiguran area of Aurora Province, approximately 58% of the area was still dipterocarp forest in 1983. Originally, most of this was "full-closure" primary forest. Today, about 75% of this lowland forest remains primary (about 300 km²), but most of this (about 260 km²) is now "partial closure." The remaining area of lowland forest (about 100 km²) is "secondary forest." . . .

Scattered throughout this rain forest live several nomadic groups of Negrito hunter-gatherers, all of whom refer to themselves as Agta. All of these Agta carry on symbiotic trade relationships with neighboring non-Agta farming populations. The salient characteristic of this symbiosis is the exchange by the Agta of forest products, especially wild meat, for starch foods from the farmers. One aspect of my model hypothesizes that the Agta may never have lived for long periods isolated and independent from agricultural neighbors, following a paleolithic lifestyle. If they ever did, either they must have practiced some type of minor horticulture, or, in past millennia, they lived in a different ecosystem than rain forest. . . .

While wild meat and fish are plentiful at times in areas of eastern Luzon very distant from human residence sites, wild plant foods are not readily available there to humans. Though the Agta sometimes harvest wild tubers, and the starch from the pith of a wild palm (*Caryota cumingii*), the labor they expend to obtain these is quite high for the small amount of starch they get, and the plants are not abundant in any of the five forest microhabitats of eastern Luzon. . . . Caryota resembles the sago palm, but the amount of starch secured per tree is far less than from the true sago. The Agta also eat several types of wild fruits and plants, usually as snack food, and the hearts or buds of some small palms, usually as a cooked vegetable, especially a few species of *Calamus*. These do not, of course, sustain a person for long because of their low caloric content, though they are used as a famine food among indigenous peoples in the Philippines. Honey is an extremely undependable resource, as it is plentiful during only 1 out of every 4–6 years when the dipterocarps blossom.

In late 1985, Clark (in preparation) completed a six-month ethnographic field study among an Agta Negrito group on the eastern coast of Cagayan Province. The expressed purpose of her research was to live among Agta residing in a remote river area who have less access to trading opportunities than most Agta bands. Clark presumed that these Agta would be subsisting on wild roots during periods when trading was not possible. Though she lived with one of the most isolated Negrito groups in the Philippines, she found that roughly

99% of their starch food was cultivated crops, gained by trade with outsiders for forest, riverine, and marine resources. These Agta did dig up wild yams on three occasions, but twice these were at Clark's request....

Of the many ethnographers who have described the Agta..., there are no references to anyone ever observing an Agta band living off wild plant food, even for short periods. These include published and unpublished descriptions written by Europeans who lived in or traveled through Agta areas in the eighteenth and nineteenth centuries. In fact, the earliest Spanish reports of the eastern coast of Luzon describe eighteenth century Agta as trading heavily then with farming populations, and as having swiddens of their own....

This concords with statements by the Griffins who, after several years of field work with the Cagayan Agta, suggest that the Agta environment is plant food-poor (Estioko-Griffin, 1984, p. 211; Griffin, 1984, pp. 96, 100, 117). They also state, "Wild roots and vegetables... are probably not available in quantities adequate to support the present density of Agta" (Estioko-Griffin and Griffin, 1981, p. 143).

In 1984, the Casiguran Agta ate some type of cultivated starch food, usually rice, at 98% of their meals. Almost all of this starch was secured through trade. Wild carbohydrate food was eaten at only 2% of their meals during the same period (in those nine cases, the food was wild yam...).

These data suggest that the energy Agta expend to secure rice is less than it would take to dig up the nutritional equivalent in wild roots. While mere food preference may play a role here, the Agta are far from being affluent foragers. My time allocation study shows that healthy Casiguran Agta men work 6 days a week, 7 hours a day, on the average, much of this as farm laborers for outsiders. Healthy women without suckling children work only slightly less at the same type of labor. The same study presents evidence showing that these Agta suffer chronic undernutrition, with a life expectancy at birth of only 21.5 years, and an alarming death rate which is higher than the birth rate. Securing sufficient rice to sustain themselves is a serious daily problem for the Agta; if wild starch foods are available, why don't they dig them up when they are short of rice or root crops?

I suggest that such wild plant foods are not only not readily available today in Southeast Asian rain forests, but in the distant past they were so scarce and so difficult to secure and process, especially when Negritos did not have iron tools, that early Holocene foragers could have lived only a very marginal existence in such biomes....

The Question of Wild Yam Abundance

... Except for two short preliminary investigations, one by James Eder and one by Douglas Yen, and some data from Karen Endicott from the Malay Peninsula, no empirical data have yet been collected from Southeast Asia which could satisfactorily answer "the wild yam question." The question concerns whether there were, in prehistoric times, enough wild plant foods, specifically wild tubers, to sustain a Southeast Asian (or African or Amazonian) hunter-gatherer population living independently in a tropical rain forest. The argument is that the wild foods necessary to meet human nutritional carbohydrate requirements were so scarce or seasonal in rain forest environments that they could not support human foraging populations year round unless they supplemented their diet by part-time cultivation and/or trade with neighboring farmers. Even a very low population density would not satisfy the conditions, if wild starch foods were not available all year round. As we know from Liebig's "law of the minimum," it doesn't matter how abundant food is for 11 months of the year if there is none during the twelfth. . . .

Rambo (1982, p. 261) has proposed that the Malaysian rain forest is a "virtual desert" for human forager groups, because of the scarcity of edible wild plants and animals. He refers here specifically to the scarcity of wild yams, and to tubers too difficult to harvest because they are buried deep beneath the soil (Rambo, 1982, p. 263). Hutterer (1983) believes that tropical rain forests are "deficient in carbohydrate plant foods for human occupants" (p. 179) because potential plant foods are either out of reach in the forest canopy or are poisonous to humans, and because most rain forest plants store relatively little energy as starch or fat in their fruits, nuts, or seed, or in their underground roots.

Richards (1973, p. 62) makes the more general statement that there is a shortage of edible plants in tropical rain forests, and "this is why jungle hunter-gatherers have very low population densities." . . . Most recently, in a review of Amazonian human ecology, Sponsel (1986) also states, "*Homo sapiens* . . . would have a difficult time obtaining adequate food solely by foraging [in the Amazonian rain forest]" (p. 74). Besides the problem of wild foods being inaccessible or poisonous to humans, Sponsel also points out that "most [neotropical] wild plants are not cost effective in terms of time and energy input/output ratios" (Sponsel, 1986, p. 74). . . .

Evidence Supporting the Wild Yam Hypothesis

In this section, we will review the archeological data, some botanical information concerning the evolution and ecology of yams, the linguistic evidence for Luzon (and for the African rain forests), and the archival evidence for Luzon. These bodies of evidence support the present argument.

The archeological evidence.   Unfortunately, there is little archeological evidence relating directly to the present yam hypothesis, either for or against, although there are three reports on excavations in northeastern Luzon which suggest that Agta Negritos were trading with farmers there during the second millennium B.C. There are no empirical data concerning the use of wild yams by pre-agricultural man anywhere in the tropics, although it is a logical enough deduction that yams were an important food, if not a major staple, at the end of the Pleistocene. . . .

Bellwood (1985), a leading specialist on Southeast Asian prehistory, takes the view that human occupation in equatorial rain forests during the Pleistocene and early Holocene was minimal (p. 161). He suggests that late Pleistocene hunting societies were probably concentrated more in regions of seasonal climates. He bases this idea on the dearth of archeological evidence from rain forest areas, and because most of the flaked stone assemblages come from seasonally dry regions of Java, Sulawesi, the Lesser Sundas, and the Philippines. He notes, however, the "the inland forests of Malaya were widely settled by Hoabinhians from the beginning of the Holocene" (Bellwood, 1985). Dunn (1975) hypothesizes that these Hoabinhian hunter-fisher-gatherers were practicing some cultivation of root crops and other plants by 8000 B.C. (p. 135), and that by 3000 B.C., "root crops probably had assumed an important place in [the] subsistence economy [of Malayan Neolithic people]" (p. 136). In fact, Dunn suggests that Upper Pleistocene peoples 20,000 years ago in the same area "possibly supplement[ed] their diet through some form of incipient root crop cultivation" (Dunn, 1975, p. 132)....

Archeology in northeastern Luzon.   The earliest solid evidence for humans living in today's Agta area is that of Thiel (1980). Thiel's study neither supports nor contradicts the present hypothesis. She does establish that pre-agricultural man was living in northeastern Luzon at the end of the Pleistocene. However, it must be remembered that this area was then probably still a tree savanna ecosystem, not a rain forest....

The earliest established date we have for rice farming in northeastern Luzon, in the same area as Thiel's excavation, is 1400 B.C. (Snow, Shutler, Nelson, Vogel, and Southon, 1986). Cultivation of taro and yam in the same area almost surely predates that by 1000–2000 years. Ceramic manufacturing cultures in northeastern Luzon date back to approximately 3000 B.C. (Snow and Shutler, 1985). Peterson (1974a, b) excavated what he calls an "incipient agricultural site" (Peterson, 1974b, p. 227) in the center of the Palanan Agta area which was probably occupied between 2500–1500 B.C.... I am suggesting that by the second millennium B.C. the ancestors of today's Agta were practicing intense exchange relationships with these non-Negrito populations in Palanan, and certainly with the farmers just 80 km to the northwest who were growing rice in 1400 B.C.

Botanical evidence.   The following botanical information lends some inferential support to the present hypothesis.... Botanists and geographers agree that *Dioscorea* spp. [yams] evolved in the tropical lowlands, but this probably did not occur in rain forest biomes. Coursey (1967) states, "Yams appear to have evolved... in a climate with well marked wet and dry seasons" (p. 32), and "the tuberous development of the edible yams is essentially an evolutionary adaption to a prolonged dry season" (p. 71).... Yams are generally specialized for starch storage, adapted to survive dry seasons, and with roots which grow quickly to maturity each year when the rains return. Botanists point out that varieties of *Dioscorea* in seasonal biomes grow large esculent tubers annually, which gradually wither away as the plants draw energy from them during the dry season. But rain forest varieties in general, and there may be some expectations, have perennial tubers, and these are very small, having no need to store up reserves for survival until the next rains.

Burkill (1951) mentions that many wild yams have evolved in a way which protects their tubers by deep burial in the soil, and others which are not buried deeply protect themselves with much tannin in their tubers or with thorny roots. This hardly speaks in favor of their easy use by stone-age foragers. Referring specifically to the poisonous quality of wild yams, Burkill (1951) states,

> Many wild yams from the forests are eaten [only] after prolonged boiling and others after an all-night boiling along with wood-ashes to mitigate their acridity. Many hold tannin enough to make them unsavoury, yet not prevent the needy from eating them (p. 302).

... The botanical information, then, mostly supports the hypothesis that yams probably did not evolve in rain forests, and most species are not adapted to grow there. Those found in such biomes today tend to be inadequate as a dependable food staple for humans because the plants are widely dispersed, have small roots, are hard to dig up even with iron tools, and are often poisonous. Furthermore, as Hutterer (1982) points out, "Nobody has ever counted the number, or measured the productivity of wild edible roots occurring per hectare in a seasonal rain forest" (p. 135). Endicott (1984, p. 51) makes a similar statement. Two exceptions to this, for the rain forests in Central Africa, have recently been published by Hladik, Bahuchet, Ducatillion, and Hladik (1984) and Hart and Hart (1986). A discussion of this will follow.

The linguistic evidence.   A strong body of support for the argument presented comes from the science of historical-comparative linguistics. These data have been presented elsewhere (Headland, 1986, pp. 17–19, 174–178; Headland and Reid, to appear; Reid, 1987). Philippine Negritos long ago, somewhere around the middle of the second millennium B.C., lost their original languages and adopted those languages of their Austronesian-speaking neighbors, a non-Negrito people who first began migrating into Luzon around 3000 B.C. (Bellwood, 1985, pp. 120, 232). This could only have happened if these two populations were living in intense inter-ethnic symbiosis. The subsequent differentiation today between the languages of the Negritos and those of their non-Negrito neighbors shows that the prehistoric interaction was ancient.

The linguistic evidence defines approximately when the linguistic switch took place, but it cannot tell us why. It is suggested here that the logical reason Negritos established such relationships with these ancient farmers was because of their desire for trade goods, especially carbohydrate foods. The Negritos received food from these farmers in exchange not only for forest products, but for their own labor, just as they still do today....

The archival evidence.   There are a few archival references which tell us that Agta Negritos were practicing some minor cultivation of their own, actually making tiny swiddens during Spanish times.... These mostly eighteenth-century references to Agta agriculture are too many to cite here (see Headland, 1986).... If sufficient wild starch foods were available in the Agta areas, then we may ask why the Agta were going to the trouble to plant gardens in the 1700s.

We may also ask, at this point, how dependent Agta were on food bartered from non-Negrito farmers in eastern Luzon during early Spanish times. There are a good number of references to Agta/farmer interaction in the Spanish archives, most of them indicating that there was intense mutualistic symbiosis between the Agta and local farming populations. These documents show that throughout the Spanish period the Agta were continually exchanging forest products and labor for rice, as well as tobacco, knives, clothing, beads, and pots (see Headland, 1986)....

Examples from Southeast Asia. Ethnographers who studied Negritos early in this century mentioned the importance of wild tubers, that many of the types contained poison, and that a good deal of labor was expended in leaching out the poison (see Garvan, 1964, pp. 55–56 on Negritos in western Luzon; Radcliffe-Brown, 1964 on the Andamanese; Schebesta, 1927, pp. 84, 115–117; Evans, 1937, pp. 58–60 on Negritos in West Malaysia). With the exception of Radcliffe-Brown, all mention that cultivated food was also a major resource among these Negritos.

... Dentan (1968, p. 46) in his "conjectural history" of the Semai (who live in the same general area as the West Malaysian Batek), proposes that in the distant past they probably lived completely off of wild vegetables, roots, and fruits. Yet, he states in the same paragraph,

> Present-day Semai rarely dig up wild roots except in emergencies. Should the crops fail, however, they know where to find patches of yams, especially the giant *takuub* yam (*Dioscorea orbiculata, D. pyrifolia*) whose tuber is often over 6 feet long. It may take all day for a group of men using machetes and dibbles to dig up a single *takuub* tuber and carry it home (p. 47).

... Labang and Medway (1979, p. 56) report that the Penan they observed in Sarawak rain forests secured starch from three species of (wild?) palm, but found and cooked a wild yam only once, when they were requested to do so by one of the investigators....

These reports from Southeast Asia, while not conclusive, do lend support to the wild yam hypothesis. The evidence that yams ever served as more than an emergency "famine food," much less a staple, is absent. I suspect that, in at least some of the ethnographic reports describing wild yam use, what the ethnographers may have observed was the digging up of feral, rather than wild yams, say in long-abandoned swiddens, or the digging of wild yams in secondary forest rather than primary forest. Only a very few Western researchers highly specialized in tropical botany, such as Yen, would be able to recognize the difference between wild vs. ferel vs. cultivated root plants.

Examples from Africa. ... [A] very recent body of empirical ethnographic data has been presented concerning the wild yam question for central Africa. Hart and Hart have challenged the view held by several anthropologists (Hart and Hart, 1986, p. 30) that the Mbuti pygmies lived independently in the equatorial forest prior to its recent penetration by farming immigrants....

The Harts ... argue that there is simply not enough wild food in the central African forests to support a pure hunting and gathering economy year round. Using a large body of data on wild food resources of the area, they demonstrate that none of the calorically important forest fruits and seeds are available in the Ituri forest for 5 months out of the year. Honey is also scarce during this season. Game is available year round, but the main animals caught have low fat content.

Concerning wild yams specifically, Hart and Hart (1986) found that they are widely dispersed, not abundant, small in size, not available year round, hard to harvest and process, poor in taste, and especially, that they do not grow in primary tropical forest, but in secondary forest areas previously cleared by swiddeners. "Most of the important [wild plant] food species gathered by the Mbuti do not regenerate in closed forest environments, but are associated instead with more open habitats" (p. 50). It is their hypothesis that the Ituri evergreen forest was "essentially uninhabited until recently" (p. 51).

The Harts' thesis is supported by a new paper by Bailey and Peacock (in press), which is based on their field work among the Efe pygmies of Zaire. Bailey also challenges the idea that pygmies ever lived in the Congo Basin rain forest independently of agriculture. Though Bailey and Peacock report that there is a 3-month dry season in the Efe forest area, they hypothesize that the Efe do not, could not, and never had lived for more than a few weeks in the forest solely on wild foods. They say this even though they note that wild yams are found in this biome, and that Efe women sometimes forage for them.

The Harts' thesis is also supported by a recent report by Hladik et al. (1984) on the interior forests of Lobaya, Central African Republic. Tubers there are very scarce, as compared to the forest margins and areas of secondary forest growth (97 tuber plants/ha in the former, in contrast to 9400 plants/ha in the latter; Vincent, 1985)....

Examples from South America.   Ethnographies have been written describing Amazonian foraging groups which, at first reading, seem to provide examples contradicting the wild yam hypothesis, since these groups appear to have been isolated hunter-gatherers living independently of cultivated foods or outside trade. A careful reading of such reports, and more recent data, however, provide support for the hypothesis.

For example, Kloos (1977) describes the Akuriyo of Surinam as such an isolate group up to 1968. This was a group he studied for "several months" in 1973, 5 years after they were "(re)discovered," and 3 years after they had moved into villages with other Amerindian farmers. The Akuriyo were a group of only 60 individuals in 1973, former swidden cultivators (pp. 14, 19), who Kloos thinks changed to "a completely nomadic way of life" (p. 7) about 80 years previously. Kloos admits that his reconstruction of their pre-1968 life is only an hypothesis (p. 19), and no empirical data are presented.... Kloos suggests they ate only wild foods, but states that "getting enough food ... requires all their energy for most of their time" (p. 10). He also notes that they suffered from diseases "possibly contracted from visitors" (p. 20), and that they were "acquainted with manioc but not in great quantities" (p. 21). If they had visitors and ate man-ioc, this case supports, rather than contradicts the wild yam hypothesis. Most significant, Kloos (1977) states,

> The Akuriyo distinguish six edible tubers. . . . Most of them are small (many of them not exceeding the size of a finger) and often a day of hard work is rewarded by not more than a pound of tiny tubers (p. 10).

. . . The Ache (or Guayaki) of eastern Paraguay appear to be a hunter-gatherer group who lived independently of trade and cultivated foods. Clastres (1972), the first ethnographer to describe them, said they knew nothing of agri-culture (pp. 140, 142), though the group he studied in 1962 was then living on a plantation under the protection of a Paraguayan farmer (p. 144). Hawkes and Hill believe that the Ache they studied in the early 1980s were formerly "full time hunter-gatherers until the mid-1970s" (Hill, Kaplan, Hawkes, and Hurtado, 1985, p. 30). At the time of their study, the Ache were living on a mission sta-tion, hunting, cultivating several crops, and raising livestock (Hawkes, Hill, and O'Connel, 1982, p. 381). The Ache were, indeed, very successful hunters. If their particular ecosystem really allowed them to live independently of cul-tivation (an hypothesis based on a reconstructed model of their "ethnographic present"), it may be because the area is not a rain forest. Hill and Hawkes (1983) describe many microhabitats (pp. 140–141). The western area is nontrop-ical, with several days of frost every year. Valleys are filled with grasses. Wild foods may be abundant, but Hawkes *et al.* (1982, p. 384) report that the Ache always took manioc or corn with them on their foraging trips from the mission station. . . .

The nomadic Siriono of the Bolivian tropical forest, often used as an illus-tration of extremely primitive Amazonian nomads, grew several kinds of crops in tiny plots (Holmberg, 1969, pp. 67–68, 101–102). Their "digging of [wild] roots and plants . . . are almost negligible occupations" (p. 65). This is true in spite of Holmberg's depiction of them as suffering chronic hunger frustration. The Kaingang Indians in Brazil, a deculturated group studied by Henry in the 1930s, were supposedly forest nomads before 1914 who lived mainly by hunt-ing meat, and did little plant gathering. They are reported as eating pine nuts in season, but wild fruits were of slight dietary importance, and Henry says he *"never heard of the Kaingang using any [wild] roots for food"* (Henry, 1964, p. 161, emphasis added). . . .

Conclusion

. . . This [selection] has presented the hypothesis that wild carbohydrate foods, and specifically wild yams, are scarce in climax tropical rain forests, and that prehistoric foragers attempting to follow a "pure" hunter-gatherer economy could not have survived in such ecosystems without some type of direct or indirect access to cultivated foods. The symbiotic relationships found today throughout the world between tropical forest hunter-gatherers and food producers are therefore not a recent phenomenon. This argument has been illustrated with a case study of the Agta Negritos in the Philippines, as well as data from other areas.

I fully agree with Hart and Hart (1986) that further investigation of the distribution and abundance of yams in tropical forest ecosystems is clearly needed (p. 52). If what they found for central Africa, and what I have observed in eastern Luzon, is general for other areas of the tropical forest world, then we may need to revise our views of human prehistory in the tropics.

References

Bailey, R., and Peacock, N. Efe pygmies of northeast Zaire: Subsistence strategies in the Ituri Forest. In de Garine, I., and Harrison, G. (eds.), *Coping with Uncertainty in the Food Supply*. Oxford University Press, Oxford. In press.

Barnard, A. (1983). Contemporary hunter-gatherers: Current theoretical issues in ecology and social organization. *Annual Review of Anthropology* 12: 193–214.

Bellwood, P. (1985). *Prehistory of the Indo-Malaysian Archipelago*. Academic Press, New York.

Burkill, I. (1951). Dioscoreaceae. *Flora Malesiana* 4: 293–335.

Clark, C. *Trading Networks of the Northeastern Cagayan Agta*. Unpublished Master's thesis in anthropology, University of Hawaii. In preparation.

Clastres, P. (1972). The Guayaki. In Bicchieri, M. (ed.), *Hunters and Gatherers Today*. Holt, Rinehart and Winston, New York, pp. 138–174.

Coursey, D. (1967). *Yams: An Account of the Nature, Origins, Cultivation and Utilisation of the Useful Members of the Dioscoreaceae*. Longmans, London.

Dentan, R. (1968). *The Semai: A Nonviolent People of Malaya*. New York: Holt, Rinehart and Winston.

Dunn, F. (1975). *Rain-Forest Collectors and Traders: A Study of Resource Utilization in Modern and Ancient Malaya*. Monograph 5, Malaysian Branch, Royal Asiatic Society, Kuala Lumpur.

Endicott, K. (1984). The economy of the Batek of Malaysia: Annual and historical perspectives. *Research in Economic Anthropology* 6: 29–52.

Estioko-Griffin, A. (1984). *The Ethnography of Southeastern Cagayan Agta Hunting*. Unpublished Master's thesis in anthropology, University of the Philippines.

Estioko-Griffin, A., and Griffin, P. B. (1981). Woman the hunter: The Agta. In Dahlberg, F. (ed.), *Woman the Gatherer*. Yale University Press, New Haven, pp. 121–149.

Evans, I. (1937). *The Negritos of Malaya*. Frank Cass, London.

Garvan, J. (1964). In Hochegger, H. (ed.), *The Negritos of the Philippines*. Verlag Ferdinand Berger Horn, Vienna.

Griffin, P. (1984). Forager resource and land use in the humid tropics: The Agta of northeastern Luzon, the Philippines. In Schrire, C. (ed.), *Past and Present in Hunter Gatherer Studies*. Academic Press, Orlando, pp. 95–121.

Hart, T., and Hart, J. (1986). The ecological basis of hunter-gatherer subsistence in African rain forests: The Mbuti of Eastern Zaire. *Human Ecology* 14: 29–55.

Hawkes, K., Hill, K., and O'Connell, J. (1982). Why hunters gather: Optimal foraging and the Ache of eastern Paraguay. *American Ethnologist* 9: 379–398.

Headland, T. (1986). Why foragers do not become farmers: A historical study of a changing ecosystem and its effect on a Negrito hunter-gatherer group in the Philippines. University Microfilms International, Ann Arbor.

Headland, T., and Reid, L. Hunter-gatherers and their relationships to agriculturalists from prehistory to the present. To appear.

Henry, J. (1964). *Jungle People: A Kaingang Tribe of the Highlands of Brazil.* Random House (Vintage), New York.

Hill, K., and Hawkes K. (1983). Neotropical hunting among the Ache of eastern Paraguay. In Hames, R., and Vickers, W. (eds.), *Adaptive Responses of Native Amazonians.* Academic Press, New York, pp. 139–188.

Hill, K., Kaplan, H., Hawkes, K., and Hurtado, A. (1985). Men's time allocation to subsistence work among the Ache of eastern Paraguay. *Human Ecology* 13: 29–47.

Hladik, A., Bahuchet, S., Ducatillion, C., and Hladik, C. (1984). Less plantes a tubercule de la foret dense d'Afrique centrale. *Le Terre et la Vie* 39: 249–290.

Holmberg, A. (1969). *Nomads of the Long Bow: The Siriono of Eastern Bolivia.* Natural History Press, Garden City, New York.

Hutterer, K. (1982). Interaction between tropical ecosystems and human foragers: Some general considerations. Working paper, Environment and Policy Institute, East-West Center, Honolulu.

Hutterer, K. (1983). The natural and cultural history of Southeast Asian agriculture: Ecological and evolutionary considerations. *Anthropos* 78: 169–212.

Kloos, P. (1977). The Akuriyo of Surinam: A case of emergence from isolation. IWGIA Document No. 27, International Work Group for Indigenous Affairs, Copenhagen.

Labang, D., and Medway, L. (1979). Preliminary assessments of the diversity and density of wild mammals, man and birds in alluvial forest in the Gunong Mulu National Park, Sarawak. In Marshall, A. (ed.), *The Abundance of Animals in Malaysian Rain Forests.* Department of Geography, University of Hull, and Institute of Southeast Asian Biology, University of Aberdeen, Aberdeen, pp. 53–66.

Peterson, W. (1974a). Summary report of two archaeological sites from northeastern Luzon. *Archaeology and Physical Anthropology in Oceania* 9: 26–35.

Peterson, W. (1974b). Anomalous archaeology sites of northern Luzon and models of Southeast Asian prehistory. Unpublished Ph.D. dissertation in anthropology. University of Hawaii, Honolulu.

Radcliffe-Brown, A. (1964). *The Andaman Islanders.* Free Press of Glencoe, New York.

Rambo, A. (1982). Orang Asli adaptive strategies: Implications for Malaysian natural resource development planning. In MacAndrews, C., and Chia, L-S. (eds.), *Too Rapid Rural Development: Perceptions and Perspectives from Southeast Asia.* Ohio University Press, Athens, pp. 251–299.

Reid, L. (1987). The early switch hypothesis: Linguistic evidence for contact between Negritos and Austronesians. *Man and Culture in Oceania* 3: 41–59.

Richards, P. (1973). The tropical rainforest. *Scientific American* 229(6): 58–67.

Schebesta, P. (1927). *Among the Forest Dwarfs of Malaya.* Hutchinson, London.

Snow, B., and Shutler, R., Jr., (1985). *The Archaeology of Fuga Moro Island: New Approaches for the Isolation and Explanation of Diagnostic Ceramic Assemblages in Northern Luzon, Philippines.* San Carlos Publication, Cebu City, Philippines.

Snow, B., Shutler, R., Jr., Nelson, D., Vogel, J., and Southon, J. (1986). Evidence of early rice cultivation in the Philippines. *Philippine Quarterly of Culture and Society* 14: 3–11.

Sponsel, L. (1986). Amazon ecology and adaptation. *Annual Reviews of Anthropology* 15: 67–97.

Thiel, B. (1980). Excavations in the Pinacanauan valley, northern Luzon. *Bulletin of the Indo-Pacific Prehistory Association* 2: 40–48.

Vincent, A. (1985). Plant foods in savanna environments: A preliminary report of tubers eaten by the Hadza of northern Tanzania. *World Archaeology* 17: 131–148.

NO ↩

Serge Bahuchet, Doyle McKey,
and Igor de Garine

Wild Yams Revisited

Introduction

The Cultivated Calories Hypothesis

At the conceptual core of this new view of subsistence in rain forest foragers is a set of ideas that, for convenience, we will refer to collectively as "the cultivated calories hypothesis." Headland (1987) and Bailey et al. (1989) argue that subsistence based purely on foraging is difficult in tropical rain forest because of the scarcity of energy-rich wild foods, such as fat-rich animals, oilseeds, and carbohydrate-rich tubers and tuberous roots such as those of wild yams. Energy-rich storage organs are scarce in wild plants of tropical rain forest, and those that exist are often chemically defended. Those that can be used as food by humans are too scarce or too uncertain in supply, or the energy too difficult to extract (because tubers are deeply buried, or laborious processing is necessary for detoxification), to supply energy requirements. Animal fat is calorie-rich, but meat is leanest at the same time that plant foods are least plentiful (Hart and Hart, 1986). Thus, tropical rain forests offer only a scarce and uncertain supply of energy-rich wild foods. Access of foraging peoples to starchy staples cultivated by their farming neighbors frees them from a major constraint limiting human use of these environments. Many of the farmer–forager symbioses existing today have a long history, and may have evolved thousands of years ago as an adaptive strategy for exploiting tropical forest.

But Headland (1987) and Bailey et al. (1989) also examine a much bolder hypothesis: Not only are there no peoples currently living independently of agriculture in tropical rain forest, they argue, but subsistence based purely on foraging is impossible in these environments, and humans have never lived in tropical rain forest independently of domesticated plants and animals. This hypothesis appears to be a logically compelling corollary of their ideas, an extension back in time of the ecological constraints they invoke to explain current patterns. We find this extension of their ideas to the past, however, to be much more problematical than their conclusions about contemporary patterns. Lest it be accepted uncritically, the notion that foraging without recourse to cultivated plant foods is impossible in rain forest, and has thus never occurred, must be teased apart from the finding (which we accept) that this mode of subsistence seems not to occur in such environments today. We offer a critique on several grounds. We hope that our constructive criticism will lead to clearer definition and more rigorous tests of a hypothesis that is guiding research on an important question in the history of human adaptation to environment.

Our objectives, however, transcend criticism. Starting from the same observations about ecological constraints on foraging in rain forest as the cultivated calories hypothesis, we propose an alternative hypothesis about the history of subsistence patterns in rain forest foraging peoples, and attempt to test it using ecological and ethnographic data concerning pygmy foraging peoples of the western Congo basin. These data indicate that subsistence based purely on foraging, with wild yams (one conspicuous group of energy-rich wild plant foods) supplying a large proportion of calories, might indeed be possible in this environment....

Critique of the Cultivated Calories Hypothesis

The Argument Is Not Logically Compelling

The argument for the impossibility of subsistence based purely on foraging in rain forest is not logically compelling. The absence of a postulated mode of subsistence among contemporary peoples is not evidence that this mode of subsistence never occurred in the past nor that it is impossible. Were we to conclude that subsistence based on foraging without recourse to agriculture is only possible in environments where this way of life occurs today, then the set of environments that could have been exploited by pre-agricultural people would be vanishingly small indeed! Nowhere in the contemporary world do foragers live independently of other people. But agriculture had definite origins, and before agriculture people lived as foragers. Where did they live? We suspect that in the absence of archeological evidence favoring one position or the other (as in tropical rain forest...), hypotheses could be proposed *post hoc* to explain the impossibility of independent foraging in many of the other environments in which this way of life does not occur contemporarily....

Some Versions of the Hypothesis Are Unfalsifiable

Overly restrictive definitions of "rain forest" render some versions of the cultivated calories hypothesis virtually unfalsifiable. "True rain forest" may be so narrowly defined, along various dimensions, that any one of several escape routes becomes available to avoid refutation of the hypothesis by contradictory data. For example, Headland (1987) proposes a definition of tropical rain forest so restrictive in terms of amount of rainfall ("at least 4000 mm per year, and not less than 100 mm in any month for 2 out of 3 years," p. 464) that his version of the cultivated calories hypothesis effectively removes all of Africa, most of Amazonia, and much of tropical Asia from the discussion. His [selection] includes several examples in which possible exceptions to the cultivated calories hypothesis (e.g., the Batak Negritos of Palawan, Philippines, p. 470, and aborigines in tropical forest of northern Australia, p. 472) are discounted because they seem not to occur in "true rain forest."...

In a similar vein, proponents of the hypothesis sometimes seem to employ a rather too typological distinction between "mature climax forest" and "secondary forest," discounting some examples (of plant species, assemblages of species, or entire ethnic groups) that tend to contradict the cultivated calories hypothesis because they occur in "secondary forest" rather than in "climax forest" (Hart and Hart, 1986, p. 32; Headland, 1987, p. 485). A certain imprecision also creeps into the use of these terms; "secondary forest" is associated with semideciduous forest, "climax forest" with evergreen forest (Hart and Hart, 1986, pp. 30-31). Discussions of the hypothesis have tended not to reflect in full measure the realization that even "mature" tropical forest is a dynamic mosaic of vegetation in various phases of succession, and that it was that way long before human intervention....

Bailey et al. (1989) largely avoid these pitfalls, admitting by their definition of "tropical rain forest" virtually all evergreen and semideciduous forests of the tropics and subtropics. This broad version of the hypothesis, which admits into the discussion an important diversity of environments, is also the most useful, we feel, because it is bold and can be falsified; the escape routes for avoiding refutation are fewer. We suggest that in many cases it will be refuted....

Archeology Is Neutral on the Question

Archeological data could settle this debate, and indeed the absence of archeological evidence for pre-agricultural sites in rain forest has been perceived as supporting the cultivated calories hypothesis. Bailey et al. (1989) state that "it is impossible at present to support the hypothesis that people lived in the tropical moist forest of Africa without the aid of cultivated foods." It must be emphasized that there is no support from archeology for the converse hypothesis, either, because the data are simply too scant. Archeology is neutral on the question.

There is little reason to be sanguine that pre-agricultural sites, even if they existed, might be found in greater numbers. As Bailey et al. (1989) note, tropical forest is not a favorable environment for preserving cultural remains. Furthermore, hunter-gatherers are unlikely to leave distinctive remains, since they leave no agricultural implements, pottery, and the like.... In tropical moist forest, there are many possible campsites, so that concentration of accumulated material at a few particular sites is less likely....

Nevertheless, numerous sites are known from central Africa—although our knowledge of each remains quite fragmentary—and many of these certainly predate the origin of agriculture.... The uncertainty lies in whether the rain forest vegetation that now covers the areas in which these preagricultural sites are found also characterized them during the period of habitation. This uncertainty derives from difficulties of dating of many artifacts, other than typologically, and from uncertainty surrounding the history of climate and vegetation in equatorial Africa.

... The extent to which moist forest vegetation was reduced during the Pleistocene, and the timing of its disappearance and reappearance in different parts of central Africa, are still controversial; but current consensus holds that at 18,000 B.P. the forest was broken into refugia, from which forest re-expanded beginning about 12,000 to 8000 B.P. Even considering the checkered history of the African forest zone, there still existed—as Bailey et al. (1989) duly point out (but not, we feel, with sufficient emphasis)—a span of at least several thousand years during which foraging peoples could have occupied rain forest prior to the advent of agriculture. Again, archeology is neutral as to whether such pre-agricultural occupation of rain forest environments actually occurred.

The Cultivated Calories Hypothesis Lacks Ecological Supporting Data

We have seen that contemporary absence of pure foragers in tropical rain forests does not allow us to conclude that foraging independently of farmers is impossible here, and that archeology is largely silent on whether the world's rain forests were ever inhabited by pre-agricultural peoples. Resolution, however tentative, of the question thus hinges for the present on ecological data. From what we know about the density, distribution, and biological characteristics of wild plant foods in tropical forests, and the subsistence activities and food requirements of foraging peoples, is independent foraging possible in this environment?

This is the empirical core of the cultivated calories hypothesis, and it is much less firm than is generally realized. In only one study (Hladik et al., 1984) has the abundance in rain forest environments of a major group of wild plant foods—in this case, wild yams—actually been measured, and this case... does not appear to offer support for the cultivated calories hypothesis. Although the argument centers on the availability of wild plant foods, data on this point are notably lacking. In those studies that do provide quantitative information of some sort (e.g., Headland, 1987), it usually concerns extent of use, rather than availability. The tacit assumption seems to be that use reflects availability. The current reliance of the cultivated calories hypothesis on inferences about wild plant food availability, rather than actual measures of it, is in fact its principal weakness. As long as availability of wild plant foods is inferred from extent of use, rather than actually measured, a plausible alternative hypothesis cannot be excluded. In the following section, we present this alternative and argue that it provides a better explanation of data concerning pygmy foraging peoples of the western Congo basin than does the cultivated calories hypothesis.

An Alternative Hypothesis

According to the cultivated calories hypothesis, energy-rich wild plant foods make low contributions to the diets of rain forest-dwelling foraging peoples because their availability is low, so low that subsistence based on them would be impossible. However, availability has not been measured; rather, the tacit assumption seems to have been made that low use reflects low availability. For a very simple reason, though, "extent of use" may consistently and grossly underestimate "availability" of wild plant foods, particularly starch-rich roots and tubers such as wild yams. One of the most confident predictions of foraging theory is that a food item will not be used, or will be used sparingly, if qualitatively similar items that give greater net returns are available. Based on everything we know about wild and cultivated starchy plant foods, optimal foraging theory leads us to predict that cultivated plants would be preferred if both are available. Use of wild plant foods may thus consistently underestimate their abundance. Edible wild roots and tubers, sparsely distributed and requiring more effort to remove and process, are likely to be neglected if starch-rich cultivated plant foods are available. Because such cultivated plant foods have long been readily available to foragers through contact with farmers, wild plant foods formerly used more heavily are now neglected. Starting from the same observations about ecological constraints as the cultivated calories hypothesis, it is thus possible, in the absence of direct measurements of resource abundance, to construct an equally plausible but very different hypothesis.

This alternative hypothesis generates two testable predictions: (1) Wild plant foods that are currently used are not used to the limit of their availability. In the absence of cultivated plant foods, they could supply a larger proportion of the diet than they currently do. (2) With long-term access to cultivated plant foods, some low-preference wild plant foods may have been abandoned, some of them so thoroughly that even knowledge about them was lost. Tropical forest habitats may contain potential foodstuffs, used in the past but no longer classified as food....

Ecological Evidence

Biology of Forest Yams

In viewing rain forests as poor in energy-rich wild-plant foods, proponents of the cultivated calories hypothesis argue that yams are principally adapted to environments outside rain forest, and, when present in the forest zone, are found mostly in secondary-forest habitats (Hart and Hart, 1986; Headland, 1987; Bailey et al., 1989). These authors draw upon a literature that has long emphasized species of savanna, savanna-forest ecotone, or anthropogenic clearings in forest, and that has treated the storage tubers of yams as adaptations to strongly seasonal environments (e.g., Coursey, 1976). In such environments, the reserves stored in tubers enable the plants, dormant during the dry season, to produce quickly a new aerial stem at the beginning of each rainy season. If the advantage of underground storage organs is understood solely in terms of seasonability, then it is easy to see why yams and other tuber-bearing plants might be thought not to characterize the relatively less seasonal environments of tropical moist forests.

Contrary to the impression one might gain from this literature, however, distinct forest-adapted species of *Dioscorea* do exist, though only one study has examined them (Hladik et al., 1984). Furthermore, forest *Dioscorea*, as well as a number of other plants (principally vines) of rain forests of the western Congo basin, regularly possess starchy tubers, sometimes quite large (Hladik et al.,

1984). What role do starch-rich tubers play in the biology of yams found in these less seasonal environments?

We believe that the significance of the underground storage organs of forest yams and other vines of western Congo basin rain forest is linked to the successional dynamics of tropical forest (Hladik et al., 1984). In Africa, as elsewhere, tropical forest consists of a mosaic of vegetation in various successional stages following natural disturbances, such as treefalls. In the context of the dynamic mosaic of vegetation, which may for convenience be classified as gap, building, and mature phases, notions like "climax forest" have little meaning. Though human activities have resulted in an increased proportion of forest in relatively young successional stages, in Africa as elsewhere, "secondary forest" and species considered typical of it have been components of tropical forest vegetation since long before human occupation of this habitat.

What we know thus far about rain forest yams suggests that the energy they store in tubers enables them to persist as suppressed juveniles in light-poor environments, and to respond with rapid growth when conditions become favorable....

Is Tuber Density High Enough to Support Subsistence?
Using data on yam abundance, Aka food consumption, size of their camps, and their ranging behavior, we attempted to determine the feasibility of a mode of subsistence in which the cultivated food plants that the Aka currently use as starchy staples—manioc and plantains—would be completely replaced by wild tubers.

We used 2 kg/ha as our estimate of standing crop density of edible tubers in rain forest occupied by the Aka. This was based on a conservative rounding-off of the average density (2.39 kg/ha) found in four C.A.R. plots. An average Aka camp is comprised of seven households and about 26 people, including ten children less than 12 years old (Bahuchet, 1985). Studies of food intake have shown that each Aka consumes 0.5–1.0 kg of starchy plant foods (manioc and plantains) per day. Because food consumption varies in a complex fashion and is difficult to measure, we used two different estimates of the amount of wild tubers that would be required to replace the cultivated starchy staples of the current Aka diet. The minimum estimate is 2 kg/day/household, or 14 kg/day for the entire camp. The maximum estimate is 1 kg/day/person, or 26 kg/day for the camp.

Several factors might determine whether the wild yams in their territory would constitute a resource sufficient for Aka subsistence. First, are there enough tubers there? The territory of an Aka camp covers about 250 km^2, or 25,000 ha (Bahuchet, 1985). At 2 kg/ha, it contains 50,000 kg of edible wild tubers. The camp requires from 5100 kg (based on consumption of 14 kg/day) to 9490 kg (based on 26 kg/day) each year, or ca. 10–19% of the standing crop of yams in its territory each year.

The problem can also be examined on a finer spatial and temporal scale. Aka women gather food within a circle of ca. 2 km radius around a campsite (Bahuchet, 1985). Using our estimate of 2 kg of edible wild tubers/ha, the area within this foraging radius (1250 ha) would contain 2500 kg of edible tubers.

With the minimum estimate of carbohydrate consumption by the camp of 14 kg/day, the area within the foraging radius of a campsite contains enough yams for about 6 months' subsistence (178 days), and even with the maximum estimate of carbohydrate consumption by the camp of 26 kg/day, the quantity of yams around a campsite might support subsistence for up to 96 days. Actual residence times of the Aka in forest campsites between moves averaged ca. 60 days (Bahuchet, 1985). Thus, assuming the Aka can locate them, enough yams are present around each campsite to support the Aka for substantially longer periods than they actually stay.

Second, would tuber density remain high enough to support subsistence in the face of increased levels of exploitation? In the absence of long-term studies of yam population dynamics, it is impossible to know whether the standing crops of edible tubers measured by Hladik et al. (1984) could be maintained under more intense human exploitation. There is reason, however, to suspect that they might.... [T]he Aka move their camps with a frequency that might be high enough to prevent depletion of tubers within the foraging radius of each campsite. Furthermore, the total territory of the camp, 25,000 ha (Bahuchet, 1985), is about 20 times the gathering area around each campsite. Since camps are moved only every 60 days or so, this means that a given area might be exploited for yams less than once every 3 years, and even then may not be greatly depleted of yams.

Third, are the Aka good enough at locating and excavating the tubers that are there? Can an Aka woman locate, excavate, and process wild tubers at the rate necessary to supply her household with 2 kg (minimum consumption) to 3.7 kg (maximum consumption) of edible tubers per day? On this point our data are least satisfactory. We lack estimates of search times. Once yams are located, their excavation is not very time consuming. Data on excavation of a total of 16 tubers of at least four species show that tubers ranging in weight from 0.25–6.70 kg can be dug up by one woman in 10–20 min with a wooden digging stick. Estimating from these excavations, one Aka woman could dig up an average-sized tuber (1.945 kg) in 15 min. Though these data lack precision and only concern excavation time, there are several reasons to suspect that Aka women could supply wild tubers at the rate required. First, Aka population density is such that less than 20% of the yams actually present in their territory must be harvested each year. The Aka may thus be able to concentrate their foraging in areas where tuber density and/or renewal rates are high. They may thus be foraging in areas where yam density is often substantially higher than the average of 2 kg/ha that we are assuming and the returns from their foraging activities might be correspondingly higher. Second, as already noted, yams in rain forests of the western Congo basin generally can be eaten after simple cooking (boiling or roasting)....

Fourth, would edible wild tubers support subsistence throughout the year?... Again, we are hampered by the absence of any long-term studies of yam dynamics. Our view of the biology of rain forest yams suggests that their tubers may show less seasonality in density, size, and composition than those of savanna yam species. Data on the Aka show relatively constant usage of wild yams over the year, but as we have argued, the relationship between use and availability is not simple.

Availability of Other Wild Plant Foods

In our analysis of the feasibility of Aka subsistence based purely on foraging, we have concentrated on one class of wild-plant foods, wild yams, in order to develop a bold alternative to the cultivated calories hypothesis. This has necessarily resulted in some oversimplification. In practice, there are additional ecological considerations that make it even more likely that a purely foraging mode of subsistence is possible in rain forest. [R]ain forest offers other tubers as well as a variety of other energy-rich wild plant foods, including nuts and other seeds. Like wild yams, these could have contributed to the calories now supplied by cultivated plants. . . .

Linguistic Evidence

. . . Data from historical linguistics, in turn, demonstrate that hunting and gathering have long been central components in the economy of these people, and suggest that prior to contact with farmers, they were already living as foragers in rain forest environments similar to ones in which they now live.

. . . The Aka and Baka are geographically separated (found east and west of the Sangha River, in C.A.R. and Cameroon, respectively). Though they share many cultural traits, they speak two different languages, belonging to two different families (Bantu and Oubanguian for the Aka and Baka, respectively). These languages were borrowed by Pygmies from villagers at some earlier stage of their history, and since then have undergone divergence from respective related languages spoken by farmers.

Though they speak very different languages, comparison of their vocabularies shows that 20% of words (identical and/or cognate terms) are common to the two languages. These words shared between Aka and Baka are not present in the languages of any farming group. This fact, and the cultural coherence of this shared vocabulary that will be described [later] allow us to conclude that the Aka and Baka are descended from a common ancestral group of Pygmies termed *"Baakaa"* (Bahuchet, 1989a).

The majority (75%) of the vocabulary shared by Aka and Baka is concerned with forest ethnobiology, tools, and technical skills. This common vocabulary is not just isolated names of many rain forest species of trees (Bahuchet, 1989b), mammals, and other organisms, but—even more informatively—the shared terms form very specific and detailed ensembles. The cultural complexes characterized by common Aka-Baka vocabulary correspond to particular activities that are not only important in the material and symbolic worlds of these two pygmy groups, but also characterize pygmies in the eyes of farmers.

The major cultural complexes for which Aka and Baka share a largely common vocabulary are the following:

1. Honey gathering.   Twenty-four words are shared, including names of several bee species and terms describing their biology, terms for different sounds made by bees, terms for combs, and terms for techniques and implements used in honey gathering (e.g., terms for the axe used for cutting toeholds to climb honey trees and to open the hive, and the bark box used for collecting honey).

2. Hunting.   Forty words are shared, including ethnobiology of prey animals and techniques and tools employed in hunting. Shared terms relating to elephants and their hunting are especially well developed (e.g., shared words for six different "castes" (age-sex groups) of elephants).

3. Yams.   Nine words are shared, including names of three species and terms for growth phases, fruit, and even yam-feeding beetles. There is also a shared term for a specific tool, the special and extremely long wooden digging stick used in extracting the deeply buried tubers of *Dioscorea semperflorens....*

Based on this shared terminology, we conclude that the way of life of the ancestral **Baakaa* was already based upon hunting and gathering in rain forest ecosystems. When the **Baakaa* met the ancestral villagers, they had a characteristic culture, different from that of the non-pygmy villagers. At this time, they were already specialists in rain forest ethnobiology....

Historical Development of Relationships Between Pygmies and Farmers in the Western Congo Basin

The cultivated calories hypothesis and the alternative we present offer two very different perspectives on the historical development of contemporary relationships between pygmies and horticulturists. Bailey et al. (1989) suggest that foraging peoples may only have been able to enter the rain forest together with farmers, who brought along the starch-rich cultivated plants that provided the energy source necessary for specialized hunting and gathering, and whose activities increased the extent of secondary forests, thereby increasing the returns from hunting and gathering.

We suggest that pygmy foraging peoples already occupied the equatorial forests when Bantu farmers began to spread into this environment. Furthermore, instead of the pygmies requiring symbiosis with farmers to exploit the rain forest environment, we argue that dependence may well have been the other way around. The knowledge of rain forest hunter/gatherers about starch-rich wild plants in this environment—plants that could be successfully cultivated in rain forest farms—may have been a key component in the spread of agriculture into African rain forests....

Conclusion

Ecological Evidence for the Possibility of Hunting and Gathering Independently of Agriculture in Tropical Forest Environments

Summarizing the ecological evidence, we find the following: (1) Densities of wild yams and other edible tubers in the rain forest habitat of the Aka are high enough that the wild tubers could be exploited much more heavily than they are by the Aka today. (2) There is evidence that several kinds of wild plant foods, including wild tubers, were formerly more heavily used than they are today, some apparently having been abandoned altogether. These findings support our hypothesis that the limited use of wild-plant foods cannot be attributed to scarcity that prevents any greater use of them, but instead is due to their replacement by cultivated plant foods that became available upon contact (often ancient) of the Aka with farming villagers, a replacement that has continued until the present. Wild plant foods may well have been so extensively replaced by cultivated foods precisely because the latter are more easily available, less seasonal, or otherwise free foragers from ecological constraints. But, we believe, these wild plant foods did allow subsistence in these environments purely by foraging, before the cultivated plants arrived.

References

Bahuchet, S. (1985). *Les Pygmées Aka et la Forêt Centrafricaine, Ethnologie Écologique.* SELAF, Paris, "Ethnosciences 1."

Bahuchet, S. (1989a). *Les Pygmées Aka et Baka: Contribution de l'Ethnolonguistique à l'Histoire des Populations Forestières d' Afrique Centrale.* Thèse de doctorat d'etat es lettres et sciences humaines, Université René Descartes Paris V.

Bahuchet, S. (1989b). Les noms d'arbres des Pygmées de l'Ouest du bassin congolais. *Adansonia, Bulletin du Museum National d'Histoire Naturelle, Série Botanique* (Paris), 11 (4e série): 355–365.

Bailey, R. C., Head, G., Tenike, M., Owen, B., Rechtman, R., and Zechenter, E. (1989). Hunting and gathering in tropical rainforest: Is it possible? *American Anthropologist* 91: 59–82.

Coursey, D. G. (1976). The origins and domestication of yams in Africa. In Harlan, J. R., De Wet, J. M. J., and Stemler, A. B. L. (eds.), *Origins of African Plant Domestication.* Mouton, Paris/The Hague, pp. 383–408.

Hart, T., and Hart, J. (1986). The ecological basis of hunter-gatherer subsistence in African rain forests: The Mbuti of eastern Zaire. *Human Ecology* 14: 29–55.

Headland, T. (1987). The wild yam question: How well could independent hunter-gatherers live in a tropical rainforest ecosystem? *Human Ecology* 15: 463–491.

Hladik, A., Bahuchet, S., Ducatillion,C., and Hladik, C. (1984). Les plantes à tubercule de la forêt dense d'Afrique Centrale. *La Terre et la Vie* 39: 249–290.

POSTSCRIPT

Do Hunter-Gatherers Need Supplemental Food Sources to Live in Tropical Rain Forests?

The hypothesis put forward by Headland and R. C. Bailey, G. Head, M. Tenike, B. Owen, R. Rechtman, and E. Zechenter in "Hunting and Gathering in Tropical Rain Forest: Is It Possible?" *American Anthropologist* (vol. 91, 1989), that foragers cannot live independently in tropical rain forests, has stimulated much new research and careful reanalysis of data already collected. Some research shows that there is great variation from one rain forest to another in the types and amounts of plants and animals suitable for human consumption. One resource not fully recognized in the original formulations of the hypothesis is the starch found in the pith of sago palms, which are abundant in the rain forests of Indonesia and Melanesia. Sago starch is the staple food of the Penan foragers of Borneo, for example. Some scholars have complained that the proponents have defined tropical forest foraging so narrowly that is does not fit the reality of how such foragers live. For example, Peter Brosius criticizes Headland and Bailey for ignoring the fact that foragers both unintentionally and intentionally increase the density of valued plant resources (a point also made by Bahuchet, McKey, and de Garine in the unabridged version of their selection) and that foragers utilize many different microenvironments in the rain forest, including streams and naturally occurring clearings, not just the tree-dominated climax forest. See "Foraging in Tropical Rain Forests: The Case of the Penan of Sarawak, East Malaysia (Borneo)," *Human Ecology* (vol. 19, no. 2, 1991). The debate continues as new research findings appear.

For concise overviews of this controversy see McKey's article, "Wild Yam Question," in the *Encyclopedia of Cultural Anthropology, vol. 14,* (Henry Holt, 1996) and Headland's "Could 'Pure' Hunter-Gatherers Live in a Rain Forest?" at www.sil.org/sil/roster/headland-t/wildyam.htm. The latter contains an extensive and current bibliography, including works both supporting and opposing the hypothesis. Considered the best single source of articles is the special issue of *Human Ecology* (vol. 19, no. 2, 1991) from which the selection by Bahuchet, McKey, and de Garine was taken. It includes an introduction and conclusion by Headland and Bailey and five articles examining the applicability of the hypothesis in various places, including Borneo, the Malay Peninsula, New Guinea, the western Congo basin, and Bolivian Amazonia.

ISSUE 13

Do Sexually Egalitarian Societies Exist?

YES: Maria Lepowsky, from *Fruit of the Motherland: Gender in an Egalitarian Society* (Columbia University Press, 1993)

NO: Steven Goldberg, from "Is Patriarchy Inevitable?" *National Review* (November 11, 1996)

ISSUE SUMMARY

YES: Cultural anthropologist Maria Lepowsky argues that among the Vanatinai people of Papua New Guinea, the sexes are basically equal, although minor areas of male advantage exist. Men and women both have personal autonomy; they both have similar access to material possessions, influence, and prestige; and the activities and qualities of males and females are valued equally.

NO: Sociologist Steven Goldberg contends that in all societies men occupy most high positions in hierarchical organizations and most high-status roles, and they dominate women in interpersonal relations. He believes that this is because men's hormones cause them to compete more strongly than women for high status and dominance.

I n most of the world's societies, men hold the majority of leadership positions in public organizations, from government bodies, to corporations, to religious institutions. In families, husbands usually serve as heads of households and as primary breadwinners, while wives take responsibility for children and homes. Is the predominance of men universal and inevitable, a product of human nature, or is it a cultural fact that might vary or be absent under different circumstances? Are sexually egalitarian societies—in which men and women are equally valued and have equal access to possessions, power, and prestige—even possible?

Some nineteenth-century cultural evolutionists, including J. J. Bachofen and J. F. MacLellan, postulated that a matriarchal stage of evolution, in which women ruled, had preceded the patriarchal stage known to history. Today most anthropologists doubt that matriarchal societies ever existed, but it is well established that some societies trace descent matrilineally, through women, and that in these societies women generally play a more prominent public role than in patrilineal ones, where descent is traced from father to children.

250

Whether or not matriarchal societies ever existed, by the twentieth century European and American societies were firmly patriarchal. Most people considered this state of affairs not only natural but God-given. Both Christian and Jewish religions gave scriptural justification for the predominance of men and the subordination of women.

The anthropology of women (later termed "feminist anthropology"), which arose in the early 1970s, challenged the claim that the subordination of women was either natural or inevitable. The rallying cry of feminists was "Biology is not destiny." Women, it was said, could do anything society permits them to do, and patriarchal society, like any other social institution, could be changed.

Some feminist anthropologists considered male dominance to be universal but attributed it to universal cultural, not biological, causes. The groundbreaking volume *Woman, Culture, and Society,* Michelle Rosaldo and Louise Lamphere, eds. (Stanford University Press, 1974) presents some possible cultural reasons for universal male dominance. Rosaldo and Lamphere proposed that all societies distinguish between "domestic" and "public" domains and that women are always associated with the domestic domain, with the home and the raising of children, while men are active in the public domain, where they have opportunities to obtain wealth, power, and ties with other men.

Some anthropologists contend that sexually egalitarian societies once existed (e.g., Eleanor Leacock's "Women's Status in Egalitarian Society: Implications for Social Evolution," *Current Anthropology* [vol. 19, 1978]). They attribute the scarcity of such societies today to historical circumstances, particularly the spread of European patriarchal culture to the rest of the world through colonialism and Christian missionization.

In her selection Maria Lepowsky argues that in the Vanatinai culture of Sudest Island in Papua New Guinea, the sexes are basically equal. She describes the numerous features of Vanatinai culture, including social practices and beliefs, that make this possible. She contends that matrilineal descent is one contributing factor, but that it alone does not guarantee sexually egalitarian social relations.

Steven Goldberg counters that males have more of the hormones that cause individuals to strive for dominance than women do. Therefore, regardless of cultural variations, men occupy most positions in hierarchical organizations and most high-status roles, and they are dominant in interpersonal relations with women. Goldberg would argue that even in a matrilineal society like the Vanatinai, more men than women would occupy positions of power and prestige.

While reading these selections, ask yourself whether or not the Vanatinai case actually contradicts Goldberg's assertion that all societies are male dominated. Do you know of any other societies in which men and women are apparently equal? Would a single sexually egalitarian society disprove Goldberg's thesis? If you accept Goldberg's contention that males have an innate tendency toward domination, do you think that any cultural arrangements could neutralize this or keep it in check?

Maria Lepowsky  **YES**

Gender and Power

Vanatinai customs are generally egalitarian in both philosophy and practice. Women and men have equivalent rights to and control of the means of production, the products of their own labor, and the products of others. Both sexes have access to the symbolic capital of prestige, most visibly through participation in ceremonial exchange and mortuary ritual. Ideologies of male superiority or right of authority over women are notably absent, and ideologies of gender equivalence are clearly articulated. Multiple levels of gender ideologies are largely, but not entirely, congruent. Ideologies in turn are largely congruent with practice and individual actions in expressing gender equivalence, complementarity, and overlap.

There are nevertheless significant differences in social influence and prestige among persons. These are mutable, and they fluctuate over the lifetime of the individual. But Vanatinai social relations are egalitarian overall, and sexually egalitarian in particular, in that at each stage in the life cycle all persons, female and male, have equivalent autonomy and control over their own actions, opportunity to achieve both publicly and privately acknowledged influence and power over the actions of others, and access to valued goods, wealth, and prestige. The quality of generosity, highly valued in both sexes, is explicitly modeled after parental nurture. Women are not viewed as polluting or dangerous to themselves or others in their persons, bodily fluids, or sexuality.

Vanatinai sociality is organized around the principle of personal autonomy. There are no chiefs, and nobody has the right to tell another adult what to do. This philosophy also results in some extremely permissive childrearing and a strong degree of tolerance for the idiosyncrasies of other people's behavior. While working together, sharing, and generosity are admirable, they are strictly voluntary. The selfish and antisocial person might be ostracized, and others will not give to him or her. If kinfolk, in-laws, or neighbors disagree, even with a powerful and influential big man or big woman, they have the option, frequently taken, of moving to another hamlet where they have ties and can expect access to land for gardening and foraging. Land is communally held by matrilineages, but each person has multiple rights to request and be given

From Maria Lepowsky, *Fruit of the Motherland: Gender in an Egalitarian Society* (Columbia University Press, 1993). Copyright © 1993 by Maria Lepowsky. Reprinted by permission of Columbia University Press. Notes and references omitted.

space to make a garden on land held by others, such as the mother's father's matrilineage. Respect and tolerance for the will and idiosyncrasies of individuals is reinforced by fear of their potential knowledge of witchcraft or sorcery.

Anthropological discussions of women, men, and society over the last one hundred years have been framed largely in terms of "the status of women," presumably unvarying and shared by all women in all social situations. Male dominance and female subordination have thus until recently been perceived as easily identified and often as human universals. If women are indeed universally subordinate, this implies a universal primary cause: hence the search for a single underlying reason for male dominance and female subordination, either material or ideological.

More recent writings in feminist anthropology have stressed multiple and contested gender statuses and ideologies and the impacts of historical forces, variable and changing social contexts, and conflicting gender ideologies. Ambiguity and contradiction, both within and between levels of ideology and social practice, give both women and men room to assert their value and exercise power. Unlike in many cultures where men stress women's innate inferiority, gender relations on Vanatinai are not contested, or antagonistic: there are no male versus female ideologies which vary markedly or directly contradict each other. Vanatinai mythological motifs, beliefs about supernatural power, cultural ideals of the sexual division of labor and of the qualities inherent to men and women, and the customary freedoms and restrictions upon each sex at different points in the life course all provide ideological underpinnings of sexual equality.

Since the 1970s writings on the anthropology of women, in evaluating degrees of female power and influence, have frequently focused on the disparity between the "ideal" sex role pattern of a culture, often based on an ideology of male dominance, publicly proclaimed or enacted by men, and often by women as well, and the "real" one, manifested by the actual behavior of individuals. This approach seeks to uncover female social participation, overt or covert, official or unofficial, in key events and decisions and to learn how women negotiate their social positions. The focus on social and individual "action" or "practice" is prominent more generally in cultural anthropological theory of recent years. Feminist analyses of contradictions between gender ideologies of female inferiority and the realities of women's and men's daily lives—the actual balance of power in household and community—have helped to make this focus on the actual behavior of individuals a wider theoretical concern.

In the Vanatinai case gender ideologies in their multiple levels and contexts emphasize the value of women and provide a mythological charter for the degree of personal autonomy and freedom of choice manifested in real women's lives. Gender ideologies are remarkably similar (though not completely, as I discuss [later]) as they are manifested situationally, in philosophical statements by women and men, in the ideal pattern of the sexual division of labor, in taboos and proscriptions. myth, cosmology, magic, ritual, the supernatural balance of power, and in the codifications of custom. Women are not characterized as weak or inferior. Women and men are valorized for the same qualities of strength, wisdom, and generosity. If possessed of these qualities an individual woman or man will act in ways which bring prestige not only to the actor but to the kin and residence groups to which she or he belongs.

Nevertheless, there is no single relationship between the sexes on Vanatinai. Power relations and relative influence vary with the individuals, sets of roles, situations, and historical moments involved. Gender ideologies embodied in myths, beliefs, prescriptions for role-appropriate behavior, and personal statements sometimes contradict each other or are contradicted by the behavior of individuals.

As Ortner points out, a great deal of recent social science theory emphasizes "the centrality of domination" and the analysis of "asymmetrical social relations" in which one group has more power than the other, as the key to understanding a social system. A focus upon asymmetry and domination also tends to presuppose its universality as a totalizing system of belief and practice and thus to distort analyses of gender roles and ideologies in places with egalitarian relations.

Gender Ideologies

... More men than women are widely known for their wealth of ceremonial valuables and their involvement in exchange and mortuary ritual. Still, Vanatinai is an equal opportunity society where this avenue to prestige and renown is open to both sexes. A few women are well known throughout the archipelago for their exceptional wealth, generosity, and participation in ritualized exchanges. All adult women as well as men are expected to participate in exchange to a certain minimum, particularly when a father, spouse, or close affine dies. Besides the opportunity to be the owner or the eater of a feast, women have an essential ritual role as life-givers, the role of principal female mourner who represents her matrilineage in the ritual work of compensating death to ensure the continuity of life.

Women have a complementary power base as life-givers in other spheres that counterbalances the asymmetry of men's tendency to be more heavily involved in exchange, an advantage that results in part from male powers to bring death. The most exclusive is of course the fact that women give birth to children. These children enrich and enlarge the kin group of the mother and her mothers, sisters, and brothers, ensuring the continuity and the life of the matrilineage itself. Her role of nurturer is highly valued, and the idiom of nurturing or feeding is applied as well to fathers, maternal uncles, and those who give ceremonial valuables to others. In ideological pronouncements she is called, by men and women alike, the owner of the garden, even though garden land is communally held by the matrilineage, and individual plots are usually worked with husbands or unmarried brothers. She is, in verbalized ideology of custom, the giver of yams, the ghanika moli, or true food, with which all human beings are nurtured, whether she grew them or her husband or brother. She is likely to raise pigs, which she exchanges or sacrifices at feasts. She is prominent in the life-giving work of healing, a form of countersorcery. And life-giving, Vanatinai people say, is more highly valued than the life-taking associated with male warfare and sorcery....

An overview of the life courses of males and females on Vanatinai and the ideologies of gender associated with them reveals two more potential sources of contradiction to prevailing ideologies of gender equivalence. One seems clear to an outside observer: men may have more than one wife, if they are strong enough to fulfill multiple affinal obligations and if the co-wives consent to enter into or remain in the marriage. Women may not have two husbands. Even though polygyny is rare, and women need not, and do not necessarily, agree to it, it is a customary and continuing form of marriage and an indication of gender asymmetries. A big man may distribute his procreative power and the strength of his affinal labor and personal wealth to two or more spouses and matrilineages, enlarging his influence and his reputation as a gia. Women may not....

Vanatinai menstrual taboos, such as those prohibiting the menstruating woman from visiting or working in a garden and, especially, from participating in the communal planting of yams, are multivalent cultural markers of female power. The symbolic complexity and multiple meanings of such taboos have been emphasized in recent writings on the anthropology of menstruation. Earlier anthropological constructions have emphasized the relation of menstrual taboos to ideologies of female pollution and thus, directly, of female inferiority or gender asymmetry. In the Vanatinai case there is no ideology of contamination through physical contact with the menstruating woman, who continues to forage, prepare food, and have sexual intercourse. Both men and women who have had intercourse in the last few days are barred from the new yam planting, and the genital fluids of both sexes are inimical, at this earliest and most crucial stage, to the growth of yams. (Later on, marital intercourse in the garden will help the yams to flourish.) Vanatinai menstrual taboos, which bar women from what islanders see as the most tedious form of subsistence labor, weeding gardens, are not regarded by women as a burden or curse but as a welcome interlude of relative leisure. Their predominant cultural meaning may be the ritual separation of the sacred power of female, and human, fertility and regeneration of life from that of plants, especially yams, whose parallels to humans are indicated by anthropomorphizing them in ritual spells. Menstrual taboos further mark woman as the giver of life to human beings.

The Sexual Division of Labor

Vanatinai custom is characterized by a marked degree of overlap in the sexual division of labor between what men normally do and what women do. This kind of overlap has been suggested as a primary material basis of gender equality, with the mingling of the sexes in the tasks of daily life working against the rise of male dominance.

Still, sorcerers are almost all male. Witches have less social power on Vanatinai and are blamed for only a small fraction of deaths and misfortunes. Only men build houses or canoes or chop down large trees for construction or clearing garden lands. Women are forbidden by custom to hunt, fish, or make war with spears, although they may hunt for possum and monitor lizard by climbing trees or setting traps and catching them and use a variety of other fishing methods. Despite the suppression of warfare men retain greater control of the powers that come with violence or the coercive threat of violent death.

Some Vanatinai women perceive an inequity in the performance of domestic chores. Almost all adult women are "working wives," who come home tired in the evening, often carrying both a young child in their arms and a heavy basket of yams or other produce on their heads for distances of up to three miles. They sometimes complain to their husbands or to each other that, "We come home after working in the garden all day, and we still have to fetch water, look for firewood, do the cooking and cleaning up and look after the children while all men do is sit on the verandah and chew betel nut!" The men usually retort that these are the work of women. Here is an example of contested gender roles.

Men are tender and loving to their children and often carry them around or take them along on their activities, but they do this only when they feel like it, and childcare is the primary responsibility of a mother, who must delegate it to an older sibling or a kinswoman if she cannot take care of the child herself. Women are also supposed to sweep the house and the hamlet ground every morning and to pick up pig excrement with a sago-bark "shovel" and a coconut-rib broom. . . .

Vanatinai is not a perfectly egalitarian society, either in terms of a lack of difference in the status and power of individuals or in the relations between men and women. Women in young and middle adulthood are likely to spend more time on childcare and supervision of gardens and less on building reputations as prominent transactors of ceremonial valuables. The average woman spends more of her rime sweeping up the pig excrement that dots the hamlet from the unfenced domestic pigs wandering through it. The average man spends more time hunting wild boar in the rain forest with his spear (although some men do not like to hunt). His hunting is more highly valued and accorded more prestige by both sexes than her daily maintenance of hamlet cleanliness and household order. The sexual division of labor on Vanatinai is slightly asymmetrical, despite the tremendous overlap in the roles of men and women and the freedom that an individual of either sex has to spend more time on particular activities—gardening, foraging, fishing, caring for children, traveling in quest of ceremonial valuables—and to minimize others.

Yet the average Vanatinai woman owns many of the pigs she cleans up after, and she presents them publicly during mortuary rituals and exchanges them with other men and women for shell-disc necklaces, long axe blades of polished greenstone, and other valuables. She then gains status, prestige, and influence over the affairs of others, just as men do and as any adult does who chooses to make the effort to raise pigs, grow large yam gardens, and acquire and distribute ceremonial valuables. Women who achieve prominence and distribute wealth, and thus gain an enhanced ability to mobilize the labor of others, are highly respected by both sexes. An overview of the life course and the sexual division of labor on Vanatinai reveals a striking lack of cultural restrictions upon the autonomy of women as well as men and the openness of island society to a wide variety of lifestyles....

Material and Ideological Bases of Equality

Does equality or inequality, including between men and women, result from material or ideological causes? We cannot say whether an idea preceded or followed specific economic and social circumstances. Does the idea give rise to the act, or does the act generate an ideology that justifies it or mystifies it? . . .

On Vanatinai, where there is no ideology of male dominance, the material conditions for gender equality are present. Women—and their brothers—control the means of production. Women own land, and they inherit land, pigs, and valuables from their mothers, their mothers' brothers, and sometimes from their fathers equally with men. They have the ultimate decison-making power over the distribution of staple foods that belong jointly to their kinsmen and that their kinsmen or husbands have helped labor to grow. They are integrated into the prestige economy, the ritualized exchanges of ceremonial valuables. Ideological expressions, such as the common saying that the woman is the owner of the garden, or the well-known myth of the first exchange between two female beings, validate material conditions.

I do not believe it would be possible to have a gender egalitarian society, where prevailing expressions of gender ideology were egalitarian or valorized both sexes to the same degree, without material control by women of land, means of subsistence, or wealth equivalent to that of men. This control would encompass anything from foraging rights, skills, tools, and practical and sacred knowledge to access to high-paying, prestigious jobs and the knowledge and connections it takes to get them. Equal control of the means of production, then, is one necessary precondition of gender equality. Vanatinai women's major disadvantage is their lack of access to a key tool instrumental in gaining power and prestige, the spear. Control of the means of production is potentially greater in a matrilineal society.

Matriliny and Gender

. . . Matrilineal descent provides the preconditions favorable to the development of female political and economic power, but it does not ensure it. In the cases of Vanatinai, the Nagovisi, the Minangkabau, and the Hopi, matriliny, woman-centered postmarital residence (or the absence of a virilocal residence rule), female autonomy, extradomestic positions of authority, and ideologies of gender that highly value women seem closely connected. Nevertheless matriliny by itself does not necessarily indicate, or generate, gender equality. As earlier comparative studies of matrilineal societies have emphasized, in many cases brothers or husbands control the land, valuables, and persons of sisters and wives....

Gender Ideologies and Practice in Daily Life

... The small scale, fluidity, and mobility of social life on Vanatinai, especially in combination with matriliny, are conducive of egalitarian social relations between men and women and old and young. They promote an ethic of respect for the individual, which must be integrated with the ethic of cooperation essential for survival in a subsistence economy. People must work out conflict through face to face negotiation, or existing social ties will be broken by migration, divorce, or death through sorcery or witchcraft.

Women on Vanatinai are physically mobile, traveling with their families to live with their own kin and then the kin of their spouse, making journeys in quest of valuables, and attending mortuary feasts. They are said to have traveled for these reasons even in precolonial times when the threat of attack was a constant danger. The generally greater physical mobility of men in human societies is a significant factor in sexual asymmetries of power, as it is men who generally negotiate and regulate relationships with outside groups.

Vanatinai women's mobility is not restricted by ideology or by taboo, and women build their own far-ranging personal networks of social relationships. Links in these networks may be activated as needed by the woman to the benefit of her kin or hamlet group. Women are confined little by taboos or community pressures. They travel, choose their own marriage partners or lovers, divorce at will, or develop reputations as wealthy and generous individuals active in exchange.

Big Men, Big Women, and Chiefs

Vanatinai giagia, male and female, match Sahlin's classic description of the Melanesian big man, except that the role of gia is gender-blind. There has been renewed interest among anthropologists in recent years in the big man form of political authority. The Vanatinai case of the female and male giagia offers an intriguing perspective.

In the Massim, except for the Trobriand Islands, the most influential individuals are those who are most successful in exchange and who gain a reputation for public generosity by hosting or contributing significantly to mortuary feasts. Any individual on Vanatinai, male or female, may try to become known as a gia by choosing to exert the extra effort to go beyond the minimum contributions to the mortuary feasts expected of every adult. He or she accumulates ceremonial valuables and other goods both in order to give them away in acts of public generosity and to honor obligations to exchange partners from the local area as well as distant islands. There may be more than one gia in a particular hamlet, or even household, or there may be none. A woman may have considerably more prestige and influence than her husband because of her reputation for acquiring and redistributing valuables. While there are more men than women who are extremely active in exchange, there are some women who are far more active than the majority of men.

Giagia of either sex are only leaders in temporary circumstances and if others wish to follow, as when they host a feast, lead an exchange expedition, or organize the planting of a communal yam garden. Decisions are made by consensus, and the giagia of both sexes influence others through their powers of persuasion, their reputations for ability, and their knowledge, both of beneficial magic and ritual and of sorcery or witchcraft....

Images of Gender and Power

... On Vanatinai power and influence over the actions of others are gained by achievement and demonstrated superior knowledge and skill, whether in the realm of gardening, exchange, healing, or sorcery. Those who accumulate a surplus of resources are expected to be generous and share with their neighbors or face the threat of the sorcery or witchcraft of the envious. Both women and men are free to build their careers through exchange. On the other hand both women and men are free not to strive toward renown as giagia but to work for their own families or simply to mind their own business. They can also achieve the respect of their peers, if they seek it at all, as loving parents, responsible and hard-working lineage mates and affines, good gardeners, hunters, or fishers, or skilled healers, carvers, or weavers....

What can people in other parts of the world learn from the principles of sexual equality in Vanatinai custom and philosophy? Small scale facilitates Vanatinai people's emphasis on face-to-face negotiations of interpersonal conflicts without the delegation of political authority to a small group of middle-aged male elites. It also leaves room for an ethic of respect for the will of the individual regardless of age or sex. A culture that is egalitarian and nonhierarchical overall is more likely to have egalitarian relations between men and women.

Males and females on Vanatinai have equivalent autonomy at each life cycle stage. As adults they have similar opportunities to influence the actions of others. There is a large amount of overlap between the roles and activities of women and men, with women occupying public, prestige-generating roles. Women share control of the production and the distribution of valued goods, and they inherit property. Women as well as men participate in the exchange of valuables, they organize feasts, they officiate at important rituals such as those for yam planting or healing, they counsel their kinfolk, they speak out and are listened to in public meetings, they possess valuable magical knowledge, and they work side by side in most subsistence activities. Women's role as nurturing parent is highly valued and is the dominant metaphor for the generous men and women who gain renown and influence over others by accumulating and then giving away valuable goods.

But these same characteristics of respect for individual autonomy, role overlap, and public participation of women in key subsistence and prestige domains of social life are also possible in large-scale industrial and agricultural societies. The Vanatinai example suggests that sexual equality is facilitated by an overall ethic of respect for and equal treatment of all categories of individuals, the decentralization of political power, and inclusion of all categories of persons (for example, women and ethnic minorities) in public positions of authority and influence. It requires greater role overlap through increased integration of the workforce, increased control by women and minorities of valued goods —property, income, and educational credentials—and increased recognition of the social value of parental care. The example of Vanatinai shows that the subjugation of women by men is not a human universal, and it is not inevitable. Sex role patterns and gender ideologies are closely related to overall social systems of power and prestige. Where these systems stress personal autonomy and egalitarian social relations among all adults, minimizing the formal authority of one person over another, gender equality is possible.

NO ↵

Steven Goldberg

Is Patriarchy Inevitable?

In five hundred years the world, in all likelihood, will have become homogenized. The thousands of varied societies and their dramatically differing methods of socialization, cohesion, family, religion, economy, and politics will have given way to a universal culture. Fortunately, cultural anthropologists have preserved much of our present diversity, which may keep our descendants from too hastily allowing their natural human ego- and ethno-centricity to conclude that theirs is the only way to manage a society.

However, the anthropological sword is two-edged. While diversity is certainly apparent from anthropological investigations, it is also clear that there are realities which manifest themselves no matter what the varied forms of the aforementioned institutions. Because these universal realities cut across cultural lines, they are crucial to our understanding of what society *by its nature* is and, perhaps, of what human beings are. It is important, then, that we ask why, when societies differ as much as do those of the Ituri Pygmy, the Jivaro, the American, the Japanese, and a thousand others, some institutions are universal.

It is always the case that the universal institution serves some need rooted in the deepest nature of human beings. In some cases the explanation of universality is obvious (e.g., why every society has methods of food gathering). But there are other universalities which are apparent, though without any obvious explanation. Of the thousands of societies on which we have any evidence stronger than myth (a form of evidence that would have us believe in cyclopes), there is no evidence that there has ever been a society failing to exhibit three institutions:

1. Primary hierarchies always filled primarily by men. A Queen Victoria or a Golda Meir is always an exeption and is always surrounded by a government of men. Indeed, the constraints of royal lineage may produce more female societal leaders than does democracy—there were more female heads of state in the first two-thirds of the sixteenth century than there were in the first two-thirds of the twentieth.

2. The highest status roles are male. There are societies in which the women do most of the important economic work and rear the children, while the men

From Steven Goldberg, "Is Patriarchy Inevitable?" *National Review* (November 11, 1996). Copyright © 1996 by National Review, Inc. Reprinted by permission of *National Review*, 215 Lexington Avenue, New York, NY 10016.

seem mostly to hang loose. But, in such societies, hanging loose is given higher status than any non-maternal role primarily served by women. No doubt this is partly due to the fact that the males hold the positions of power. However, it is also likely that high-status roles are male not primarily because they are male (ditch-digging is male and low status), but because they are high status. The high status roles are male because they possess—for whatever socially determined reason in whichever specific society—high status. This high status exerts a more powerful influence on males than it does on females. As a result, males are more willing to sacrifice life's other rewards for status dominance than are females.

In their *Not in Our Genes,* Richard Lewontin, Leon Kamin, and Stephen Rose—who, along with Stephen Jay Gould are the best-known defenders of the view that emphasizes the role of environment and de-emphasizes that of heredity—attempt to find fault with my work by pointing out that most family doctors in the Soviet Union are women. However, they acknowledge that in the Soviet Union "family doctoring [had] lower status than in the United States."

Which is precisely the point. No one doubts that women can be doctors. The question is why doctors (or weavers, or load bearers, etc.) are primarily women only when being a doctor is given lower status than are certain roles played mostly by men—and furthermore, why, even when this is the case (as in Russia) the upper hierarchical positions relevant to that specific area are held by men.

3. *Dominance in male-female relationships is always associated with males.* "Male dominance" refers to the feeling, of both men and women, that the male is dominant and that the woman must "get around" the male to attain power. Social attitudes may be concordant or discordant with the reality of male dominance. In our own society there was a time when the man's "taking the lead" was positively valued by most women (as 30s' movies attest); today such a view is purportedly detested by many. But attitudes toward male-dominance behavior are causally unimportant to the reality they judge—and are not much more likely to eliminate the reality than would a social dislike of men's being taller be able to eliminate men's being taller.

◆

Over the past twenty years, I have consulted every original ethnographic work invoked to demonstrate an exception to these societal universalities. Twenty years ago many textbooks spoke cavalierly of "matriarchies" and "Amazons" and pretended that Margaret Mead had claimed to find a society in which sex roles were reversed. Today no serious anthropologist is willing to claim that any specific society has ever been an exception.

It is often claimed that "modern technology renders the physiological differentiation irrelevant." However, there is not a scintilla of evidence that modernization alters the basic "motivational" factors sufficiently to cast doubt on the continued existence of the universals I discuss. The economic needs of modern society probably do set a lower limit on the status of women; no modern society could give women the low status they receive in some non-modern societies. But modernization probably also sets an upper limit; no modern society is likely to give women the status given to the maternal roles in some other matrilineal societies.

Scandinavian nations, which have long had government agencies devoted to equalizing women's position, are often cited by social scientists as demonstrating modernization's ability to override patriarchy. In fact, however, Norway has 454 municipal councils; 443 are chaired by men. On the Supreme Court, city courts, appellate courts, and in Parliament, there are between five and nine times as many men as there are women. In Sweden, according to government documents, men dominate "senior positions in employer and employee organizations as well as in political and other associations" and only 5 of 82 directors of government agencies, 9 of 83 chairpersons of agency boards, and 9 per cent of judges are women.

One may, of course, hope that all this changes, but one cannot invoke any evidence implying that it will.

Of course, there are those who simply try to assert away the evidence. Lewontin *et al.* write, "Cross cultural universals appear to lie more in the eye of the beholder than in the social reality that is being observed." In fact, with reference to the universalities mentioned above, they do not. If these universals were merely "in the eye of the beholder," the authors would merely have to specify a society in which there was a hierarchy in which males did not predominate and the case would be closed.

The answer to the question of why an institution is universal clearly must be parsimonious. It will not do to ascribe causation of a universal institution to capitalism or Christianity or modernization, because many hundreds of societies lacked these, but not the universal institutions. If the causal explanation is to be at all persuasive, it must invoke some factor present in every society from the most primitive to the most modern. (Invoking the male's physical strength advantage does meet the requirement of parsimony, but does not counter the evidence of the central importance of neuro-endocrinological psycho-physiological factors.)

When sociologists are forced to acknowledge the universals, they nearly always invoke "socialization" as explanation. But this explanation faces two serious problems. First, it does not explain anything, but merely forces us to ask another question: *Why* does socialization of men and women always work in the same direction? Second, the explanation implicitly assumes that the social environment of expectations and norms acts as an *independent* variable capable of acting as counterpoise to the physiological constituents that make us male and female.

In individual cases, of course, anything can happen.

Even when a causation is nearly entirely hereditary, there are many exceptions (as tall women demonstrate). Priests choose to be celibate, but this does not cast doubt on the physiological basis of the "sex drive." To be sure, there is also feedback from the environmental to the physiological, so that association of physical strength with males results in more males lifting weights.

However, in principle, a society could find itself with women who were physically stronger than men if women lifted weights throughout their lives and men remained sedentary.

But, in real life, this can't happen because the social environment is a *dependent* variable whose limits are set by our physiological construction. In real life we all observe a male's dominance tendency that is rooted in physiological differences between males and females and, because values and attitudes are not of primary causal importance here, we develop expectations concordant with the male–female behavioral differences.

Most of the discussion of sex differences has emphasized the neuro-endocrinological differentiation of males and females and the cognitive and behavioral differentiation this engenders. This is because there is an enormous amount of evidence demonstrating the role of hormones in fetally differentiating the male and female central nervous systems, CNS response to the potentiating properties of certain hormones, and the thoughts and actions of males and females.

There is not room here for detailed discussion of the neuro-endocrinological mechanism underlying dominance behavior. But a useful analogy is iron and magnet. Iron does not have a "drive" or a "need" to find a magnet, but when there is a magnet in the area, iron, as a result of the very way it is built, tends to react in a certain way. Likewise, the physiological natures of males and females predispose them to have different hierarchies of response to various environmental cues. There is no response that only one sex has; the difference between men and women is the relative strengths of different responses. Males react more readily to hierarchical competitiveness than do females; females react more readily to the needs of an infant-in-distress. Norms and socialization do not cause this difference, but reflect it and make concrete a specific society's specific methods for manifesting the response. (Cleaning a rifle and preparing Spaghetti-Os are not instinctive abilities).

The iron–magnet analogy makes clear the role of social environment. Were there to be a society without hierarchy, status, values, or interdependence of the sexes, there would be no environmental cue to elicit the differentiated, physiologically rooted responses we discuss. But it is difficult to imagine such a society and, indeed, there has never been such a society.

Even if we had no neuro-endocrinological evidence at all, the anthropological evidence alone would be sufficient to force us to posit a mechanism of sexual psycho-physiological differentiation and to predict its discovery. We do, however, possess the neuro-endocrinological evidence and the anthropological evidence permits us to specify the institutional effects—the limits of societal variation that the neuro-endocrinological engenders.

For thousands of years, everyone, save perhaps some social scientists and others ideologically opposed to the idea, have known perfectly well that men and women differ in the physiological factors that underlie masculine and feminine thought and behavior. They may not have known the words to describe the linkage of physiology with thought and behavior, but they knew the linkage was there. (I recently read a comment of a woman in Pennsylvania: "They keep telling us that men and women are the way they are because of what they've been taught, but you can go a hundred miles in any direction and not find a single person who really believes that.") And even the most feminist parent, once she has children, can't help but notice that it is nearly impossible to get small boys to play with dolls not named "Killer Joe, the Marauding Exterminator," or at least with trucks—*big* trucks.

None of this is to deny tremendous variation on the level of roles. Even in our own society, in just a century the role of secretary changed from virtually solely male to virtually solely female. With the exception of roles associated with child nurturance political leadership, warfare, security, and crime, virtually every specific role is male in some societies and female in others. No one doubts that the women who exhibit the dominance behavior usually exhibited by men encounter discrimination. But the question remains: why is dominance behavior usually exhibited by *men*?

The implication of all this depends on context. Clearly the correctness or incorrectness of the theory I present is important to an understanding of human behavior and society. But to the individual man or woman, on the other hand, the universals are largely irrelevant. The woman who wishes to become President has a sufficient number of real-life equivalents to know that there is not a constraint rendering impossible a female head of state. But there is no more reason for such a woman to deny that the motivation to rule is more often associated with male physiology than there is for the six-foot woman to pretend that women are as tall as men.

POSTSCRIPT

Do Sexually Egalitarian Societies Exist?

In these two selections, Lepowsky and Goldberg disagree both on the interpretation of the facts and on the types of forces, cultural or biological, that determine relations between the sexes. Lepowsky argues that Vanatinai culture is basically sexually egalitarian and that this is due to a particular constellation of social and ideological features of their culture. Goldberg contends that men are dominant in every culture—the Vanatinai people would be no exception—and that men's innate drive to dominate would lead them to occupy most of the positions of authority and high status and to dominate women in interpersonal relations.

During the last 30 years, anthropologists have conducted many studies focusing specifically on gender ideas and roles in particular societies, especially in non-Western and tribal societies. Their general finding is that gender relations are much more complicated and variable than scholars thought in the early days of feminist anthropology. For example, studies have shown that not all societies make a simple distinction between domestic and public domains, associate women exclusively with a domestic domain, or evaluate activities outside the home as superior to those inside it. Scholars have also realized that analytical concepts like "male dominance" and the "status of women" are too crude. They have attempted to break them up into components that can be sought and measured in ethnographic field studies.

The question of whether or not males are dominant in a particular society is not as clear-cut as it once seemed. One important distinction now made, and reflected in Lepowsky's excerpt, is that between the actual practice of male-female roles and interactions and the ideologies that contain bases for evaluating the sexes and their activities. Studies show that in some societies women and men have similar amounts of influence over daily life, but the cultural ideology (or at least the men's ideology) portrays women as inferior to men. In some cases men's and women's spheres of activity and control are separate and independent. Some societies have competing ideologies, in which both men and women portray their own gender as superior. And some societies, such as the Hua of Papua New Guinea, have multiple ideologies, which simultaneously present women as inferior, superior, and equal to men (see Anna Meigs's book *Food, Sex, and Pollution: A New Guinea Religion* [Rutgers University Press, 1984]). Despite these complications, it may still be useful to term a culture in which both practice and ideology consistently point to equality or balance between the sexes as "sexually egalitarian," as Lepowsky does in the case of the Vanatinai. Of course Goldberg would say that such societies do not exist.

For more information on the Vanatinai people see Lepowsky's book *Fruit of the Motherland: Gender in an Egalitarian Society* (Columbia University

Press, 1993). A very readable introduction to feminist anthropology is Henrietta Moore's book *Feminism and Anthropology* (University of Minnesota Press, 1988). An interesting collection of articles showing variations in male-female relations is Peggy Sanday and Ruth Goodenough's edited volume *Beyond the Second Sex: New Directions in the Anthropology of Gender* (University of Pennsylvania Press, 1990). For a discussion of gender equality and inequality among hunter-gatherers, see Karen L. Endicott's article "Gender Relations in Hunter-Gatherer Societies," in *The Cambridge Encyclopedia of Hunters and Gatherers*, Richard B. Lee and Richard Daly, eds. (Cambridge University Press, 1999).

For a full explication of Goldberg's theory of innate male dominance, see his book *Why Men Rule: A Theory of Male Dominance* (Open Court, 1993). Other works that argue for a biological basis for male dominance include Lionel Tiger's book *Men in Groups* (Holt, Rinehart & Winston, 1969); Lionel Tiger and Robin Fox's book *The Imperial Animal* (Holt, Rinehart & Winston, 1971); Robert Wright's article "Feminists Meet Mr. Darwin," *The New Republic* (November 28, 1994); and Barbara Smuts's article "The Origins of Patriarchy: An Evolutionary Perspective," in A. Zagarell's edited volume *Origins of Gender Inequality* (New Issues Press, in press).

ISSUE 14

Are Yanomamö Violence and Warfare Natural Human Efforts to Maximize Reproductive Fitness?

YES: Napoleon A. Chagnon, from "Reproductive and Somatic Conflicts of Interest in the Genesis of Violence and Warfare Among Tribesmen," in Jonathan Haas, ed., *The Anthropology of War* (Cambridge University Press, 1995)

NO: R. Brian Ferguson, from "A Savage Encounter: Western Contact and the Yanomami War Complex," in R. Brian Ferguson and Neil L. Whitehead, eds., *War in the Tribal Zone: Expanding States and Indigenous Warfare* (School of American Research Press, 2000)

ISSUE SUMMARY

YES: Anthropologist and sociobiologist Napoleon A. Chagnon argues that the high incidence of violence and warfare he observed among the Yanomamö in the 1960s was directly related to man's inherent drive toward reproductive fitness (i.e., the innate biological drive to have as many offspring as possible). For Chagnon, the Yanomamö provide an excellent test of this sociobiological principle because the Yanomamö were virtually unaffected by Western colonial expansion and exhibited intense competition for wives.

NO: Anthropologist and cultural materialist R. Brian Ferguson counters that the high incidence of warfare and violence observed by Chagnon in the 1960s was a direct result of contact with Westerners at mission and government stations. Fighting arose in an effort to gain access to steel tools that were increasingly important to the community. Ferguson asserts that fighting is a direct result of colonial circumstances rather than biological drives.

Napoleon Chagnon's work among the Yanomamö Indians of the upper Orinoco River basin in Venezuela is one of the best known ethnographic studies of a tribal society. When his books and films first became available in the 1970s, they depicted a society that was intensely competitive and violent.

The Yanomamö, according to Chagnon, saw themselves as "the fierce people." Chagnon views the Yanomamö as a prototypic tribal society that until very recently operated independently of the forces, processes, and events that affect the rest of the world. For him they represent a pristine example of how tribal communities living in rain forest conditions may have functioned at other times and places in the world.

For many years, Chagnon has periodically revisited the Yanomamö, assembling a comprehensive set of data on violence, warfare, movement of local groups, genealogies, and marriage patterns. Since the 1970s Chagnon has championed the cause of sociobiology, which is an effort to bring evolutionary biological theory into anthropology. He uses his database to test whether patterns of warfare and violence can be explained in terms of man's innate desire to reproduce as many offspring as possible, which Chagnon refers to as *reproductive fitness*.

R. Brian Ferguson also studies the Yanomamö; however, he routinely uses the term *Yanomami* when discussing linguistically-related tribes studied by Chagnon. Drawing his data from the voluminous books, papers, films, and field reports of others, Ferguson has written a detailed political history of Yanomamö warfare. Rather than viewing the Yanomamö as innately violent, he interprets the intense violence observed in the 1960s as a direct consequence of changing Yanomamö relationships with the outside world. He rejects the notion that the Yanomamö of this period represent a pristine tribal society that state societies may have emerged from in the past. Although the foreign influences on the Yanomamö may be seen as indirect, Chagnon believes that the Yanomamö were nevertheless part of the global system of economic and political relations. Ferguson looks to the control of the material bases of life rather than to biological urges and explains the violent nature of Yanomamö culture as the result of a desire to obtain Western products.

This pair of selections raises a number of questions about how anthropologists can explain the sociocultural processes that lead humans to violence. Are there biological drives and urges that lead individuals and groups to engage in violent behavior? Does a growing scarcity of key resources lead individuals to protect their access through increased violence? Is it possible to use contemporary societies as ethnographic analogies to suggest how early prehistoric societies operated? Are there any communities that are not linked to the global system of economic and political relations?

In the following selections, Chagnon develops a model to explain the incidence and character of Yanomamö fighting. He asserts that human behavior can be explained in terms of the biological drive to reproduce. This innate drive leads men to maximize their access to women who can bear their children, passing as many of their genes on to the next generation as possible. Ferguson counters Chagnon's position by arguing that the Yanomamö have been thoroughly influenced by the flow of steel tools into the region from the outside world. The desire for steel machetes drives Yanomamö who live in settlements far from where machetes are available to fight with other Yanomamö who have access to this scarce resource.

Napoleon A. Chagnon

 **YES**

Reproductive and Somatic Conflicts of Interest in the Genesis of Violence and Warfare Among Tribesmen

Darwin's view of the evolution of life forms by natural selection is now a standard dimension in social and cultural anthropology, modified, of course, to apply to "cultures" or "societies." It is the modification, however, which is today a major issue, since the changes necessary to extend his original arguments by themselves distorted and changed his arguments. Specifically, problems with the "group" versus the "individual" controversy are now beginning to appear in anthropological discussions of the evolved functions of human behavior. This has long been resolved in favour of the individual or lower levels of organization in the field of biology (Williams 1966, 1971).

Another deficiency in our use of evolutionary theory has to do with our almost exclusive focus on "survival," when, in fact, evolutionary theory is about both survival and reproduction. On the one hand, this is probably related to the difficulty of imagining cultures or societies "reproducing" like organisms. On the other, there is a general bias in materialist/evolutionary anthropology to play down or ignore the issue of the individual's role in shaping societies and cultures. Furthermore, when we deal with survival, our concerns appear to be more about the survival of systems (cultures, groups, populations, etc.) than of individuals. This makes it difficult for us to evaluate and discuss the relationship between societal rules and what individuals actually do. We thereby preclude the possibility of understanding the evolved biological correlates of conventions and institutions.

My proposed approach will treat warfare as only one of a class of conflicts which, in band and village societies, must be examined carefully to determine the extent to which they can be traced back to conflicts of interest among individuals (Chagnon 1988a).... [T]he focus will be primarily on individuals, who will be viewed as expending two basic kinds of efforts during their lifetimes: somatic effort (in the interests of survival) and reproductive effort (in the interest of fitness) (Alexander 1985; Chagnon. 1988a)....

Warfare as a Kind of Conflict

... Conflicts between individuals and groups of individuals break out within many band and tribal societies, but the groups contesting are not always (at the time) politically independent. Indeed, a common consequence of such conflicts is the fissioning of the groups along conflict lines, and an escalation/continuation of the conflict. It is at this point that groups become visibly "independent" of each other and more conveniently fit into categories that enable us to define the *extended* conflicts as "warfare." However, we could not do so initially when the contestants were members of a common group. By insisting that our approach to warfare focus only on conflicts between politically independent groups, we run the risk of losing sight of the genesis of the conflict. We are also tempted to restrict our search for causes to just that inventory of things that "groups" (politically independent societies) might contest over, such as a hunting territory or water hole—resources that may be intimately identified with members of specific local groups.

This is a crucial issue. First, conflicts of interest in band and village societies often occur between individuals within the same group and are provoked by a wide variety of reasons. Second, individuals in kinship-organized societies tend to take sides with close kin and/or those whose reproductive interests overlap significantly with their own (e.g., wife's brothers). "Groups" are therefore often formed on the basis of kinship, marriage, or both, and by definition their members have overlapping reproductive interests. They usually have economic and other interests that overlap as well, but it is theoretically important to keep in mind that, from the perspective of evolution, the ultimate interests of individuals are reproductive in overall scope....

Life Effort

A basic assumption in my model is that the lifetime efforts of individuals can be partitioned into two conceptually distinct categories that incorporate all or nearly all of the activities that an individual (an organism in any species) engages in if it is to be biologically successful. These categories are *somatic effort* and *reproductive effort* (Alexander 1985). The former has principally to do with those activities, risks, costs, etc. that ensure the survival of the organism in a purely somatic sense—seeking shelter from the elements, protection from predators and conspecifics, obtaining nutrients, maintaining hygiene and health, etc. This would include most items we traditionally focus on in studies of technology, economics, settlement patterns, cultural ecology, grooming, ethnopharmacology, curing, etc.

The second category is one that is not normally considered in traditional cultural ecological/materialist approaches to intergroup conflicts, warfare, and cultural adaptation. While the category's overall content is "reproductive," it includes a number of specific variables not normally considered in traditional anthropological studies of reproduction as such (see Figure 1). Herein lies the value and power of theoretical developments in evolutionary biology that can shed new light on conflicts of interest between individuals and, ultimately, intergroup conflicts between politically independent groups such as bands and horticultural tribes.

Figure 1

Model of Individual Life Effort from a Darwinian Perspective

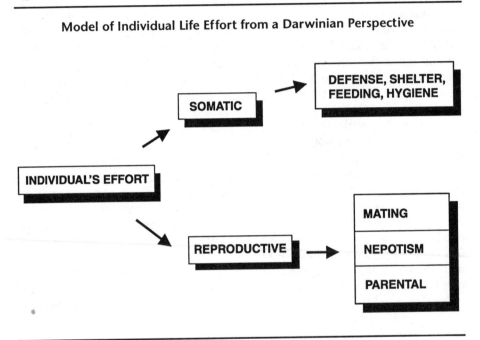

Note: Individuals expend basically two kinds of effort during their lieftimes: Somatic Effort and Reproductive Effort. The former has basically to do with the survival of the organism as such, while the latter has to do with costs, benefits, risks, etc. associated with mating, nepotism (aiding non-descendant kin), and parenting.

A review of the literature pertaining to warfare and conflict in such societies reveals that much of the conflict emanates over such factors as rape, abduction of females, failure to deliver a promised bride, niggardliness in paying bride price or executing bride service, and seduction (Daly and Wilson 1988; Chagnon 1988a). Whereas warfare and conflict in industrialized societies and many "ranked" or "stratified" societies (Fried 1967) can be convincingly shown to be associated with relative scarcity or protection of material resources, the proverbial "means of production," much of the conflict in most band and tribal societies is generated because of contests over the *means of reproduction* (Chagnon 1979).

Let me make one thing perfectly clear at this juncture. I am *not* claiming that all conflicts of interest in band and tribal society derive from conflicts that are reproductive in overall quality, nor am I claiming that conflicts over material resources are not found in such societies. I am simply arguing that conflicts of reproductive interests occur commonly in band and tribal societies and that these often lead, as indicated above, to intergroup conflicts that we traditionally consider to be warfare. I accept (and have always accepted) explanations of specific band and village warfare patterns in which demonstrable and convincing evidence indicates that shortages of material resources are directly implicated in the genesis of the conflicts....

The category "reproductive effort" in my model is advised by and basically derived from the post-1960 theoretical developments in evolutionary biology. Reproduction entails getting copies of one's self into subsequent generations. This can occur in more than the single obvious way we normally think of reproduction: begetting and successfully raising offspring. Since related organisms share identical genes by immediate common descent, organisms can advance their reproductive interests by engaging in activities and behaviours that affect, in a positive way, the reproductive efforts and accomplishments of relatives with whom they share genes. Thus, while the original Darwinian perspective viewed success in terms of fitness measured by numbers of immediate descendants (offspring), the new Darwinian perspective views success in broader, more encompassing terms. What is significant is the number of copies of one's genes that are perpetuated in subsequent generations.

This draws attention to the enormous importance of W. D. Hamilton's now classic papers (1964) defining "inclusive fitness." Individual Egos can pass on their genes by direct acts of reproduction (having children) and by aiding genetic relatives, who, by definition, share genes with Ego in proportion to the degree of genetic relatedness between them. If the aid enhances the relatives' reproduction, Ego "benefits" in a reproductive sense by having more copies of his/her genes enter the gene pool of subsequent generations—through the reproductive accomplishments of those relatives.

The study of "reproduction" becomes, then, more than merely the collection of genealogical facts and reproductive histories of individuals. It entails the study of all social interactions that potentially affect the reproductive success of the individual and those with whom he or she is interacting. Such interactions include, for example, taking risks to protect a kinsman in a mortal duel, sharing a piece of food, tendering aid in clearing gardens, and reclassifying a covillager from the kinship category "sister" to "wife" (Chagnon 1988b).

The study of reproduction also entails the study of both the "rules" and violations of the rules, injunctions, moral prescriptions, etc. (Alexander 1979, 1987), which can and often do lead to conflicts and fighting. Thus, failure to give a piece of food might possibly reflect an immediate shortage of food and have, therefore, relevance in a purely somatic context. At the same time, it can reflect a *reproductive* strategy on the part of an individual to enhance his or her political esteem and authority—to insult a reproductive competitor, for example. It thus has relevance in a purely reproductive context as well, often in the absence of resource scarcities. Such affronts are common in meat distributions among the Yanomamö, for example, where there is a chronic struggle among men to establish individual reputations for authority, prestige, esteem, productivity, generosity, and matrimonial success. The "rule" is to give portions of large game away first to the "big men" and then to the lesser. A meat distributor can strategically conduct his distribution to indicate to the assembled that he doesn't consider a particular individual in the group to be as "important" as he himself and others might consider him to be. This can be done by deliberately giving him an unacceptably small portion, an undesirable portion, or presenting a portion after first acknowledging that others are more important than he by distributing to them first. He might even go so far as to give him no portion. This is, of course, remembered and noted by all... and adds to all those other factors that accumulate eventually into smouldering inter-individual hostilities and conflicts that eventually explode and are expressed in arguments, club fights and, occasionally, homicides.

Reproductive efforts, then, includes a more comprehensive set of variables than traditional anthropological concepts embrace. It can conveniently be partitioned into several broad sub-categories (Figure 1): parental effort, mating effort, and nepotistic effort (Alexander 1985). Parental effort deals primarily with those factors we are familiar with in our more traditional views of reproduction: all those costs and risks required to rear one's children successfully and, by extension, grandchildren and great-grandchildren, i.e., descendant relatives. Mating effort includes the study of all those variables that affect the success that individuals enjoy in attracting (obtaining) a mate; guarding the mate from the seductive attempts of others (cf. Dickemann 1981; Flinn, 1988); and keeping the kin of that mate satisfied in terms of the expectations that they have regarding bride price, bride service, food sharing, etc. Nepotistic effort includes all those social activities entailing costs and risks that are expended in order to aid non-descendant relatives. These individuals, by virtue of receiving such beneficence, are in a position to translate it into reproductive consequences that ultimately enhance the "inclusive fitness" of the original helper, i.e., by producing additional copies of the helper's genes through their own reproductive accomplishments.

Life Effort Model

... By thinking of an individual's life time as a series of efforts entailing costs and risks on the one hand and benefits on the other, one can more clearly identify the factors that are likely to be significant in terms of the individual's attempts to be successful as both a member of society and as an organism constrained by societal rules. One can see how culture and cultural success is relatable to biology and biological success (Irons 1979; Borgerhoff Mulder 1987). The myriad factors that potentially or actually lead to conflicts of somatic and reproductive interests and, ultimately, fighting and warfare can also be appreciated.

By focusing on individual level conflicts of interests, we can more clearly see how the patterns of escalation, found widely in tribal societies, grow in such a way as to enable us to trace the sources of the conflicts back to the individual level and relate them, where possible, to reproductive versus somatic conflicts. This is particularly important for understanding warfare in band and village societies where the initial conflicts are almost always at the level of individuals. The "causes" of specific "wars" in such societies are bound up in complex, often vague, issues that transpired months or even years before the specific raid by "Group A" on "Group B" which we traditionally identify as "war" actually occurs. In contrast, by starting with the "group" as our initial level of analysis (because we usually define warfare as mortal contests between groups), we lose sight of the anterior patterns and are forced to interpret the group level phenomena as having started there.

The focus on individuals not only makes the conflict genesis clearer, it also compels us to consider the history of the conflict and how initial conflicts over one particular cause evolve into newer, more encompassing conflicts that are perpetuated by secondary causes....

Striving for Esteem and Prestige

Kinship and genealogy become significant in understanding conflicts for a variety of reasons. They are as a result central variables in understanding the causes, development and escalation of violence in kinship-organized band and village societies. However, in addition to the variations in one's relative influence in his/her society as determined by the size and structure of one's kinship nexus, individuals are significantly different in their ability to achieve prestige and status through chronic or episodic acts of competition in various arenas of social life. There is marked variation from one society to another in the extent to which there is competition among individuals (viz. Benedict's classic work on patterns of culture [1934]). In some, it is so negligible that ethnographers insist that it is irrelevant or does not occur at all....

This is one area in which we must do more work. Inter-individual conflicts of interest presumably exist in all societies and individuals must therefore resolve them somehow and, we would predict, in fashions that benefit *them* rather than others. In some societies, it might be very difficult to distinguish the effects that kinship power confers on individuals from those attributes of esteem and prestige that are achieved apart from or in spite of the kinship nexus. Among the Yanomamö, virtually every village I have studied is led by headmen who invariably come from the largest descent groups in the village. Yet in a large number of villages there are men from distant, essentially unrelated villages who, through their individual skills and political abilities, rise to high levels of esteem in spite of their comparatively small number of relatives (see Chagnon 1983 [1968b], discussion of the man named Rerebawä). In many societies, competition for or striving for high esteem and prestige is obvious and often spectacular.

The benefits for achieving high esteem in most band and village societies normally entail polygynous marriage and/or a more desirable position in the food/labor exchange networks, which can ultimately be related to differential access to mates and differential reproductive success. Among humans, prestige leads to influence and power, and power appears to lead to high reproductive success. Betzig (1986) has convincingly demonstrated this in her analysis of a larger number of "despotic" societies, but the extent to which this is true, statistically, in a significant sample of egalitarian societies must yet be established. The correlation has been demonstrated for the Yanomamö in several of my own publications (Chagnon 1979b; 1980; 1988a). Large numbers of ethnographic descriptions of tribal societies suggest that polygyny, one spoor of high reproductive success, is usually associated with leadership or other positions of prestige, but none of them document statistical differences in reproductive accomplishments of polygynous versus nonpolygynous males. Indeed, variations in male reproductive success have been documented in only a few instances for *any* species.

Striving for prestige entails taking risks that lead to greater or lesser amounts of success for particular individuals: there will be winners and losers. Those who lose are all the more anxious to establish or reestablish their position. As a result, conflicts and fighting arise, often over issues that appear to have no obvious direct relationship to either somatic or reproductive interests. Whether or not they ultimately do can usually be established by documenting variations in survivorship among the offspring of the successful, as well as differences in numbers of mates and numbers of offspring among the losers and winners, and the comparative reproductive success of the adult offspring of the esteemed (Chagnon and Hames 1983). . . .

A Headmen's Prestige and Reaction to Insult

In about 1980, a particularly devastating war developed between the village of Bisaasi-teri, the group I described in my 1968 monograph *Yanomamö: The Fierce People,* and the village of Daiyari-teri, a smaller. neighboring group described by Lizot (1985) in *Tales of the Yanomami.*[1]

The war was provoked by a trivial incident in 1981 that amounted to a gross insult of the Bisaasi-teri headman, but its ultimate origins go back to the mid-1950s. The Daiyari-teri are members of a larger population bloc that includes a village called Mahekodo-teri. The Bisaasi-teri had just recently fissioned from their parent group, the Patanowa-teri, and were attempting to establish themselves as an independent, viable village. To this end, they were cultivating alliances with unrelated villages to their south. Unfortunately, their erstwile allies invited them to a feast and treacherously massacred many of the men and abducted a number of their young women. The survivors fled to and took refuge among the Mahekodo-teri (Chagnon 1968b). The Mahekodo-teri, acting from a position of strength, took further advantage of them and appropriated a number of their young women. At the same time, they also tendered them sufficient aid to enable the Bisaasi-teri to recover and regain their independence by making new gardens further away from their enemies. The Daiyari-teri, congeners of the Mahekodo-teri, eventually located their village at a site within a day's walk of the Bisaasi-teri. For the next decade or so, relationships between the two groups varied from friendship and amity to neutrality to overt hostility verging on warfare. In 1965, for example, the Bisaasi-teri spread rumors that the Daiyari-teri were cowards. The Daiyari-teri responded by demanding to have a chest-pounding duel with the more numerous Bisaasi-teri to show them—and the world at large—that they were valiant and would not tolerate insults to their reputations. From that point until about 1980, relationships between the two groups were strained, but the Daiyari-teri were not powerful enough to threaten the Bisaasi-teri militarily. Eventually, visiting between them resumed and they became allies, albeit suspicious allies.

In 1980, the Bisaasi-teri headman decided to take his village on a camping trip up the Orinoco river, near the village of Daiyari-teri. Since they were allies, this headman decided to visit their village and ask them for plantains, a commonly expected courtesy between allies under such circumstances. When he reached the village, there were a large number of Daiyari-teri children and youths playing in the water. They began pelting the headman with mudballs and sticks, harassing him in that fashion all the way into the village—an insult of the first order. What apparently made matters serious was the fact that the Daiyari-teri adults neither scolded the youths nor prevented them from continuing their abuse. The Bisaasi-teri headman left, angry, and without plantains. He moved his people back to the village and cancelled the camping trip.

Some time later, perhaps a few weeks, a large number of Daiyari-teri men visited the Salesian Mission at the mouth of the Mavaca river, immediately across the Orinoco from the Bisaasi-teri village. The Bisaasi-teri spotted them immediately, and challenged them to a fight. They attacked them first with clubs and, ironically, pelted the Daiyari-teri men with lumps of hardened cement that had been discarded from a house-construction project on the mission side of the river. Considerable injury to the Daiyari-teri resulted, and they left for home, bleeding from their numerous wounds, threatening to get revenge. They eventually sent word to the Bisaasi-teri that they wanted to settle their dispute in a chest-pounding duel. The Bisaasi-teri enthusiastically accepted the challenge and went to their village to feast and fight. In the ensuing duel, two young men were killed. The Bisaasi-teri departed immediately, but were intercepted by Daiyari-teri archers who managed to wound one of them with an arrow. Shortly after, the Daiyari-teri raided and wounded a Bisaasi-teri man.

Some weeks later, one of the young men in Bisaasi-teri went on a fishing trip with an employee of the Venezuelan Malarialogia service. He was warned not to go on the trip because it was too close to the Diayari-teri village. He went anyway. While they were fishing from their canoe that night, a party of Daiyari-teri men discovered them and killed the young man with a volley of arrows, three of which struck him in the neck. The Bisaasi-teri recovered his body the next day and, in the ensuing weeks, mounted several unsuccessful raids against the Daiyari-teri, who had fled inland to escape retaliation. The Daiyari-teri eventually returned to their village.

The Bisaasi-teri called on their allies to join them in a raid. One of the allied groups, Iyawei-teri, attacked a day before the main group. The Bisaasi-teri raiding party reached the Daiyari-teri village a short time after the Iyawei-teri raiders had struck and fled, leaving two Daiyari-teri men dead. The Bisaasi-teri and their allies, armed with both arrows and shotguns, surrounded the village and set it ablaze, forcing the inhabitants to flee to the bank of the Orinoco river. There they took cover in a large pit they had dug into the ground in the event they were driven from their village by raiders—as they were. They were bombarded with volley after volley of Bisaasi-teri arrows, shot into the air and descending, like mortar rounds, into the open pit. Those who raised up to return the fire were shot with both arrows and shotgun blasts. A number of the adult males were killed; at least two women were deliberately shot as well, and an undetermined number of children and infants were accidentally wounded by the volleys of arrows and random shotgun pellets, some of whom later died. One of the fatalities was a woman who was a sister to the Bisaasi-teri headman and had been appropriated when the Bisaasi-teri took refuge with the Mahekodo-teri in the 1950s.

The survivors fled to an allied village when the raiders left. They solicited aid from the Mahekodo-teri and several other villages to mount revenge raids and eventually managed to ambush a young Bisaasi-teri couple who were on their way to the garden one morning, killing both of them. The Bisaasi-teri were satisfied that they had taught the Daiyari-teri a lesson and have no further interest in raiding them. However, they say they have every intention to exact revenge on the Mahekodo-teri for the two most recent killings and are presently waiting for the most opportune time to do so.

Discussion

In both of the above examples, the notion of prestige and status figure prominently and must be taken into consideration in explaining the conflicts. Moreover, the conflicts are not simply isolated incidents, provoked by a specific single act. They are continuations of smouldering antagonisms that originate in a multitude of previous acts, some involving seduction and male/male competition for women, others involving reactions to insults or testing of resolve and status, and others are purely vindictive and motivated by vengeance. Among the Yanomamö, it is relatively easy to relate all of these variables to reproductive striving, for a village that fails to respond to aggressive acts, even verbal ones, soon finds itself victimized by stronger, more assertive allies who translate their advantage into appropriating reproductively valuable females.

For the leaders, the reproductive rewards for aggressiveness are even more obvious. The above Bisaasi-teri headman, for example, has had 8 wives during his lifetime and has sired 25 children by them (not all survived). At present (1988), he has two wives, one of whom is still young and able to produce his children. Finally, the followers who take risks on behalf of and at the instigation of leaders, benefit in both somatic and reproductive terms as well. By complying with the suggestions and directions of the leaders, they contribute to the reputation of the village, as well as to their own reputations as individuals. By thus establishing the credibility of their claims for being valiant and aggressive, they also manage to prevail in a milieu of chronic aggressive threats and enjoy relatively secure and predictable somatic and reproductive opportunities compared to those who fail to make such demonstrations.

The overall aggregate of groups comprised of competitive status-seeking individuals has its social costs as well. The most obvious one is a domestic condition fraught with relatively constant stress and bickering, particularly in larger groups whose kinship composition might favor factionalism. The chronic fissioning of larger groups along lines of close kinship (Chagnon 1974; 1979a) is a response to this internal social stress and competition whenever external threats are sufficiently low to permit them.

Summary

... Status differentials among individuals are more numerous and dramatic in so-called egalitarian societies than many contemporary theoretical arguments from anthropology assert. These are, in part, inherited in a very real sense. One's fund of kinship power is fixed largely at birth. One cannot, for example, pick his or her parents or descent group, nor alter the reproductive facts of the ascending generations, i.e., how many kin of what kinds or degrees of relatedness he or she will be surrounded by at birth and among whom he or she grows up and must interact socially with on a daily basis. An individual can, as he or she matures, modify the "luck of the kinship draw" (Chagnon 1982) in a number of limited ways, but all of them require the cooperation of others (Chagnon 1980; 1981). One way is to produce children, but Ego must first find a mate, i.e., have elders who will find a mate for him or her. Another way is to "manipulate" kinship classifications and move people in kinship categories that are socially and reproductively more useful, an act that requires the "endorsement" of co-villagers who will go along with the manipulation by altering their own kin usage to conform to that initiated by the original manipulator (Chagnon 1988a). A third way is for particular men to lobby for a village fission that will divide the larger group into smaller ones permitting Ego to surround himself with a mixture of co-resident kin more congenial to his social and reproductive interests (Chagnon 1981; 1982). One's ability to influence others, make demands, coerce, garner cooperation, etc. is often a direct function of the individual's kinship nexus and the kinds and numbers of kin-defined allies he or she can draw on to enforce his or her will. Conflicts of interest emerge and develop in a kinship matrix in most band and village societies, necessitating an understanding of genealogical relatedness, reproductive and marital histories, and other features of kinship and descent. In addition, high status and esteem usually confer advantage in matrimonial striving and, therefore, in reproductive success. It thus should be expected that individuals will compete over and have conflicts about relative degrees of esteem, conflicts that may, on the surface, reveal no obvious relationship to either somatic or reproductive resources. Measurements of relative status and relative degrees of reproductive success should be made to determine if there is a positive correlation between them.

Note

1. Lizot (1989) gives 1979 as the date of this war in a criticism of my 1988a publication where this war is briefly mentioned in a footnote.

 **NO**

A Savage Encounter

The lives of the Yanomami of the Orinoco-Mavaca river confluence of southern Venezuela have been presented in the works of Napoleon Chagnon as a kind of morality play. Embroiled in seemingly endless violence fueled by sexual competition, status rivalry, and revenge, the Yanomami are held to exemplify the Hobbesian condition of " 'Warre'—the chronic disposition to do battle, to Oppose and dispose of one's sovereign neighbors" (Chagnon 1974:77). Moreover, their lifeways are said to represent "a truly primitive cultural adaptation... before it was altered or destroyed by our culture" (Chagnon 1977:xi). Their warfare is portrayed not as aberrant or unusual, but as the normal state of existence for sovereign tribal peoples, seeming atypical only because other war patterns have been suppressed by colonialism (Chagnon 1977:163). It is "an expected form of political behavior and no more requires special explanations than do religion or economy. The conditions Chagnon describes are said to resemble those at the dawn of agriculture. The Yanomami are "our contemporary ancestors"; thus, understanding their "quality of life... can help us understand a large fraction of our own history and behavior" (Chagnon 1983:30, 213–214). The same insecurities that create Warre among the Yanomami account for warfare among modern nation-states, and the same inference is to be drawn: "the best defense is a good offense" (Chagnon 1974:195).

Chagnon's portrayal is persuasive and has been widely accepted. In the Foreword to his *Yąnomamö: The Fierce People,* one of the most widely read texts in the history of anthropology, the series editors write that the "sovereign tribal" politics of these Yanomami is "a product of long-term sociocultural evolution without intervention from outside alien populations and life ways" (Spindler and Spindler 1983: vii). Even scholars who have been the most attentive to the violence-provoking possibilities of Western contact accept the Yanomami's relatively "pristine" character. Students of the Yanomami have been more skeptical, many pointing out that the Orinoco-Mavaca area has undergone extensive contact-related changes. None of the critics, however, has shown in any systematic way how those changes relate to observed patterns of violence.

[T]his paper was written... to explore exactly those relationships, and to challenge the idea that any ethnographic case of indigenous warfare is fully

From R. Brian Ferguson, "A Savage Encounter: Western Contact and the Yanomami War Complex," in R. Brian Ferguson and Neil L. Whitehead, eds., *War in the Tribal Zone: Expanding States and Indigenous Warfare* (School of American Research Press, 2000). Copyright © 2000 by School of American Research Press. Reprinted by permission. References omitted.

understandable apart from the historical circumstances of contact with an expanding state.... I will not dispute that [Yanomami] are less disrupted and transformed by Western contact than most of the peoples for whom we have ethnographic information. Nevertheless, I will argue that after centuries of sporadic contact with outsiders, Orinoco-Mavaca society was undergoing massive change for some two decades prior to Chagnon's arrival, and that this process of change accelerated during the time period described in Chagnon's monographs (1964–72). His statement that "it is not true, as a few of my colleagues believe, that the Yanomamo were described at a particularly 'turbulent' period of their history" (Chagnon 1977:163) is unsupportable. The "fierce people" immortalized by Chagnon represent a moment in history in which Yanomami culture was pushed into an extreme conflict mode by circumstances related to the intensifying Western presence. Their warfare and other conflicts are manifestations of this larger situation. Where Chagnon tells us that the Yanomami provide "an intimate glimpse beyond history, whither we came" (Chagnon 1977:xii), I maintain that they will remain a baffling chimera until they are seen in the light of their own history....

Local History

The ancestors of the Yanomami were raided by slavers, in varying intensity, from probably the mid-seventeenth century to about 1850. The raids drove them deep into the Parima highlands, although some still came down to the rivers to trade. The rubber boom of the latter nineteenth century reached into mountain areas and was accompanied by wars and migrations for the recent ancestors of the Orinoco-Mavaca people. The collapse of rubber production left the region more isolated from Westerners from around 1920 until 1940, a brief interlude which has been misconstrued as a primeval state. For the Orinoco-Mavaca people, this was a time of peace.

Sporadic, sometimes violent, contact began in the area around 1940 and intensified over the decade. The captive woman Helena Valero (Biocca 1971) was in this area, and she describes the intensifying conflicts as new tools and diseases began to filter in. In the late 1940s the Namoweiteri, the population cluster later to host Chagnon's field research, divided into hostile western and eastern (Patanowa-teri) groups. Then, in 1950, the establishment of the first mission near Mahekodo-teri on the Orinoco was followed almost immediately by the slaughter of a western Namowei-teri trading party by the more isolated Shamatari. Interior groups continued to harry the wealthier villages around the Orinoco until, in 1955, the latter demonstrated their military superiority. During the relatively peaceful half decade to follow, a second mission was established by Iyewei-teri at the mouth of the Ocamo River. The Iyewei-teri are an important contrast to other local groups: although only a few hours by launch downstream from Chagnon's field site, they had a more stable and wealthy Western power base than any upstream village, and enjoyed almost unbroken peace while the upriver villages endured several wars.

In 1958, a government malaria control station was set up at the mouth of the Mavaca River. The Bisaasi-teri, the larger of the western Namowei-teri groups, accepted an invitation to settle by the post. (The other western group, the closely allied Monou-teri, was located a short distance up the Mavaca.) Almost immediately, the missionaries at Mahekodo-teri moved their main operation to Bisaasi-teri. The Bisaasi-teri and Monou-teri then set out to establish beneficial alliances with Shamatari groups up the Mavaca, and in one instance demonstrated their willingness to use force against potential adversaries. For the next several years, Bisaasi-teri would be the metropolitan center of the far upper Orinoco, especially in late 1964 to early 1966, when Chagnon lived there, and when another mission was attempting to establish itself directly across the Orinoco. But those years also saw the western Namowei-teri beleaguered by internal factionalism and external enemies. This was the extraordinary fighting described in *Yąnomamö: The Fierce People* (1968)....

Infrastructure

Western contact brings epidemic diseases. In the Orinoco-Mavaca area, epidemics began to occur around 1940, and they continued with devastating frequency (Ferguson [1995] chaps. 9, 10). A major outbreak of malaria in 1960 killed an estimated 10 percent of the area population, and another outbreak is indicated for 1963. Chagnon's initial census established the cause of death of 240 individuals: 130 are attributed to malaria and epidemics, and another 25 to "sorcery." A measles epidemic swept through the area in 1968. Among deaths recorded by Chagnon for 1970 to 1974, 82 (69 percent) were due to all infectious diseases (including "magic"). In a different sample gathered at Mavaca for 1969 to 1979, 53 (39.6 percent) were due to malaria.

A single influenza epidemic that hit three remote villages in 1973 shows how terrible the impact can be. One hundred six people died, 27.4 percent of the combined population. One village lost 40 percent. In this epidemic, and presumably in all of them, the young and old died in disproportionate numbers. The contagion apparently was transmitted by men coming back from a trip downstream to obtain machetes.[1] ...

In sum, in the Orinoco-Mavaca area, a great many families were disrupted by death during the contact period. Only about one-quarter of the children there have both parents alive and coresident by the time they reach the age of 15. For the Yanomami, family, economy, and polity are one, and this many deaths tears at the fabric of society.... The longer-term consequences are described by Chagnon and Melancon (1982:73):

> Disruption of village life and the resulting coalescence or fusion shatters the social organization and creates chaos, conflict and disorder in the newly-constituted village(s).

... [Another] infrastructural consequence of contact is technological change. Of paramount importance is the introduction of steel cutting tools (for details and documentation, see Ferguson [1995]:chap. 2), which are up to ten times more efficient than stone.[2] As with other Amazonian peoples, Yanomami have gone to great lengths to obtain these tools, relocating villages, sending trading parties on long and hazardous journeys, and raiding vulnerable possessors of steel. All known Yanomami had obtained some metal tools long before any anthropologist visited them, yet these highly valued items remained scarce until very recently. And steel tools are only the beginning. New needs develop rapidly for a range of Western manufactures, in a process that can lead to assimilation into the lowest stratum of the expanding state. In the Orinoco-Mavaca area, those with greatest access to Westerners are seen by other Yanomami as having "turned white" (Cocco 1972:377).

Machetes, axes, and knives are unlike anything in the indigenous economy. At least at first, their utility and scarcity makes them more precious than items of native manufacture. Furthermore, they are unequally available, their sources restricted to a few points of Western presence, so procurement is the key problem. It is commonly acknowledged that Yanomami villages have moved out of the Parima highlands in order to provide closer access to sources of steel, and that in the Orinoco-Mavaca area, this is why Yanomami moved from the highlands to the insect-infested rivers. And there is more to it than movement.

> Thus there grew up two types of community—those holding manufactured goods acquired directly at source, and those (isolated ones) which were deprived of them. The entire map of economic and matrimonial circuits, along with political alliances, was transformed and flagrant imbalances appeared. Gradually, though scarcely within twenty years... the economy was disrupted, the society menaced at its roots, and dysfunctional attitudes developed. (Lizot 1976:8-9)...

Structure

The structural effects of contact on war are here separated into three conventional topics: economics, kinship, and political organization.

Economics

A central problem for all Yanomami economies is how to obtain Western manufactured goods (Ferguson [1995]:chap. 2). In different Yanomami areas, these have been obtained by hunting for pelts, traveling to work as farmhands, or producing manioc flour or bananas for sale or trade. In the Orinoco-Mavaca area, the way to obtain Western goods has been to work for the Westerners who come there to live or visit. Missionaries and other resident Westerners regularly give away substantial quantities of manufactures. They make large presentations on special occasions, such as visits to more remote villages, but normally give the manufactures as payment for goods (garden products, meat, firewood), for services (as guides, ground clearers, housebuilders, translators, maids, informants, etc.), and in some instances, for local manufactures with external sale potential. Very few details are available about employment and payments, but one obvious point has important consequences for understanding patterns of conflict: to work for the Westerners in most of these capacities requires that one live close to them.

... [T]he Yanomami generally make great efforts to monopolize access to the Western provider using pleas, threats, and deceptions to keep the distribution of goods within their local group. Beyond the source point, Western manufactures are passed along from village to village through networks of kinship. Often the people in one village use a tool for some time, then pass it along to the next village when they get a new one. The quantities in exchange can only be guessed, but that guess must be high. An incomplete listing of goods distributed from the Catholic mission at Iyewei-teri for 1960 to 1972 includes 3,850 machetes, 620 axes, 2,850 pots, 759,000 fishhooks, and large quantities of other items. Most of these goods were traded to more remote villages. Nevertheless, some villages separated from Western sources by two or three intervening villages are reported as receiving only poor remnants of manufactures....

Most reports indicate that the exchange of Western manufactures is usually without overt contention. A request for an item is made, and that item is given, on the promise of some future compensation. On the other hand, Lizot (1985:184) reports that "the bargaining, however, does not procede without bitter disputes. The partners stay at the brink of rupture." Even the smooth transactions may mask tensions, and the major trading that occurs at feasts is often preceded or followed by violent confrontations. Veiled and not-so-veiled threats are made, as when a man "named the men he had killed on various raids —just before demanding a machete" from Chagnon (1974:1). "In some communities, to declare, 'I will not give anything' or 'I will not give what you are asking' is to risk a clubbing" (Lizot 1985:184)....

In exchange for Western manufactures, more isolated Yanomami make and trade local manufactures. Consistent with the earlier quotation from Lizot, this has led to a clear division of labor between Yanomami communities. All the villages around missions have specialized in the trade of Western items; residents of villages without such access have become specialists in producing specific local commodities which they trade to the mission villages.

But does this general pattern apply to the Bisaasi-teri? Admittedly, it would be difficult to infer its existence from reading *The Fierce People*. Cocco (1972 : 205), however, like Lizot, describes the pattern as applying to all mission villages in the area, which would include Bisaasi-teri. In a letter written during his initial fieldwork, Chagnon (1972a:66) reports the same pattern: "Some villages specialize in making one or another object; others who have special sources of access purvey axes or machetes and pots to the rest." The pattern is also suggested by the captions of two photographs from the same trading session: "Kaobawa trading his steel tools to Shamatari allies" (Chagnon 1974:11), and "Kaobawa... trading with his Shamatari allies for arrows, baskets, hammocks, and dogs" (Chagnon 1983:6); and it is implied in a passing mention of "steel tools and aluminum pots" being the trade specialization of "several contacted villages" (Chagnon 1977:100). But Chagnon follows this point immediately with a discussion that downplays the utilitarian aspect of trade in local manufactures, arguing that trade specialization is to be understood as a gambit to create political alliances....

[T]he material interest in Bisaai-teri trade is apparent in regard to cotton and hammocks. Woven by men in this area, cotton hammocks are scarce and very valuable. They are traded widely, even into the Parima highlands.

The Bisaasi-teri obtain much of their spun cotton and curare arrow points from their Shamatari allies. It takes considerable time and labor to accumulate these items. When the Shamatari are visited by the Bisaasi-teri, the latter make known their desire to have these items, and their hosts promise to produce them. When the items are accumulated, the Shamatari visit the Bisaasi-teri to inform them their cotton and arrow points are ready. A feast is arranged and the items are given over to the Bisaasi-teri after the celebration terminates. The Shamatari then request specific items from their hosts, and the cycle continues. (Chagnon 1966:95)

The Bisaasi-teri export this cotton yarn to another ally, and it is then "brought back in the form of manufactured hammocks, the importer merely contributing labor to the process" (Chagnon 1977:101). In other words, the Bisaasi-teri come to possess a quantity of a very valuable trade item without expending any labor in its production. Curare arrowpoints, not incidentally, are listed by Cocco (1972:378) as the item Bisaasi-teri uses when trading at Iyewei-teri.

In sum, Yanomami with direct access to sources of Western manufactures make great efforts to monopolize them, sharp tensions surround the exchange of Western items, the quality and quantity of Western manufactures diminishes markedly at each step in the exchange network, and outpost villages acquire large quantities of various local, labor-intensive manufactures. My inference is that those groups who control sources of Western manufactures exploit more isolated peoples who depend on them for metal tools. This inference is reinforced by the more obvious exploitation by middlemen in the realm of marriage relationships, discussed in the next section. Later, we will see how all these factors generate warfare.

Kinship

The main focus of this section is marriage patterns and the much-debated "fighting over women." ...

One of the paramount concerns of a senior man is to find wives for his sons, younger brothers, and other coresident agnates. These men comprise his political supporters. But marriage makers are also vitally concerned with the question of bride service. In terms that are negotiated in advance, a groom is required to live with and labor for his wife's parents for a certain period after marriage, usually one to four years in the Orinoco-Mavaca area, before returning to the husband's village. The main duty of a son-in-law is to hunt, but other obligations are involved, including support of the father-in-law in war. The centrality of marriage arrangements is summed up by Lizot (1985:143): "The highest cleverness consists in acquiring wives for one's sons by negotiating the briefest possible marital service and in seeking for one's daughters husbands who agree to settle permanently in the community."

Negotiation of marriage arrangements is made far more difficult by the circumstances of Western contact. In the Orinoco-Mavaca area, there is a well-known scarcity of marriageable females. I argue elsewhere (Ferguson 1989b:253–55) that current evidence supports Chagnon's (1972b:273–74) original observation that the intensity of female infanticide is associated with the intensity of warfare, despite his later assertion that sex ratio is skewed at birth (Chagnon, Flinn, and Melancon 1979). The local scarcity of marriageable women is aggravated by the relative predominance of polygyny. The actual incidence of polygyny is unclear. Some of Chagnon's generalizations, such as "a successful man may have had up to a dozen or more different wives, but rarely more than six wives simultaneously" (Chagnon 1988: 239), appear exaggerated....

This relative scarcity of women would make finding a mate for a young man very difficult, and choosing a mate for daughters very political under the best of circumstances. The Yanomami do not live in the best of circumstances. As noted earlier, marriage arrangements are built up over years of negotiations, and they are reduced to chaos by the death waves of epidemics. Many disrupted families must be reconstituted, and arranging new marriages becomes even more difficult when the youngest generation of women dies off.

Simultaneously, the new ordering principle of access to Western goods enters in. Studies of some eastern Yanomami demonstrate a partial substitution of gifts of Western manufactures for actual bride service (see Ferguson [1995]:chap. 2). The exchange is not a one-time payment. A man who has access to Western goods is expected to obtain them regularly for the wife-giver family. Although most marriages are village-endogamous, intervillage marriages are the firmest basis of alliance. Intermarriage, trade, and political support are all woven together. As noted earlier, the entire map of matrimonial, trade, and alliance networks was redrawn after the introduction of Western manufactures. The basis for this transformation is clear: women flow toward mission and other Western outpost villages. Among the eastern, Brazilian Yanomami, Peters (1973) and others describe a dramatic increase in village exogamy, with women going to the mission residents who could make bride payment with Western manufactures. In the northern reaches of their territory, Yanomami seeking Western manufactures from their well-supplied neighbors the Yekuana, gain access by a one-way ceding of women as brides or sexual partners....

The alliance between Chagnon's main field location, Bisaasi-teri and its Shamatari trade-partners to the south is perhaps the best illustration of this general pattern. In the four or five years after it moved to the government malaria station, Bisaasi-teri managed to obtain from the Shamatari "two dozen or so women... while having given or promised only a half-dozen in return" (Chagnon 1977:80). The chain of trading villages leading out from Bisaasi-teri exhibits a "cline in sex ratios": 0.8, 1.1, 1.2, 1.6 (Chagnon 1966:57–58). Bisaasi-teri has an unusually high rate of exogamic marriages, 53 percent, compared to 15 percent in Patanowa-teri; and the majority of exogamic marriages in at least one of Bisaasi-teri's two divisions are through alliances, while most of Patanowa-teri's are through abductions of women.

Bisaasi-teri has been equally privileged in terms of bride service.

> The men who have obtained Shamatari wives have, as well, managed to cut short their period of bride service in the Shamatari village. Conversely, Shamatari men who have been promised women of Kaobawa's group are pressed into very lengthy bride service. (Chagnon 1977:79)

The bride service of these Shamatari seems particularly difficult. Chagnon (1974:13–14) describes one young man who was "expected to do all manner of onerous tasks... [and] was subject to a considerable amount of ridicule and harsh treatment." His "father-in-law was particularly unpleasant to him. He denied Wakarabewa sexual access to the girl while at the same time he allowed the young men of the natal village to enjoy these privileges."[3]

Viewing access to Western manufactures as the key to obtaining women from allies is a different perspective than that argued by Chagnon, who has consistently attributed success in obtaining wives to physically aggressive measures (e.g., Chagnon 1966:6–10, 198–99; Chagnon 1977:98; Chagnon 1988:239). The relevance of the Western manufactures-for-women connection is, however, indicated in a brief comment at the start of his thesis: "the disposition of desirable trade goods may affect the balance in the exchange of women between two villages" (Chagnon 1966:6). Also, in a coauthored article based on team research in another Yanomami area, Chagnon et al. (1970:343) note that control over steel tools gives Makiratare (Yekuana) the ability to "demand and usually obtain sexual access to Yanomama women," both in affairs and as marriage partners.

Political Organization

Having examined the unequal trade and marital relationships that develop on the basis of unequal access to steel tools and other Western items, we can now understand the nature of the antagonisms that lead to war and other political conflicts in the Orinoco-Mavaca area. Steel tools are essential means of production. In the Orinoco-Mavaca area during the period under discussion, they were available from a few source points. Compared to villages dependent on Yanomami middlemen, those with monopolistic access to Westerners received: (1) more Western items, (2) better quality Western items, (3) many local manufactures, (4) more wives, and (5) better bride service terms....

How is force applicable in this context? (See Ferguson [1995]: chap. 3, and parts 2 and 3.) The most direct application of force is that aimed at obtaining Western manufactures through plunder. That has been done by Yanomami, as by many Amazonian peoples, but it is a high-risk endeavor, and unusual within the Orinoco-Mavaca area. Force is more routinely applied to affect the flow of Western items beyond their source points. This occurs in several ways. Ambush or the threat of ambush is used to discourage travel that would circumvent a middleman village, or raids and surprise attacks at feasts are used to make a village relocate. The latter course can be used by a trade controller against a village that is attempting to move closer to the source of Western goods, and by those without good access to Westerners, in an attempt to make the controlling villages abandon their monopolistic position. Finally, club fights and other violent confrontations are used within established exchange relationships in order to direct the distribution of scarce items, and (more hypothetically) to influence the implicit rates of exchange of Western goods for other valuables.

The Yanomami do not appear at all unusual in this patterning of violence. Very similar considerations shape warfare on the Pacific Northwest Coast (Ferguson 1984).... Conflict over access to Western manufactures fosters intense political conflict not just because of the importance of steel, but because unequal access creates a structured, collective conflict of interest between villages or factions. One man may benefit by capturing a wife, but a whole community benefits by an enhanced flow of machetes, axes, and pots. But turning a community of interest into an action group prepared to do violence is a difficult task, requiring great leadership skills. That brings us to the topic of leaders, and how they too have changed in the circumstances of contact.

Leadership among the Yanomami falls squarely within the general pattern for all recently described Amazonian societies. The headman represents his coresident kin, either a separate settlement or a recognizable cluster of families within a larger village, in interactions with outsiders. He is more likely than other men to be polygynous, and his status relative to other headmen largely depends upon the size of his kin group. In a sense, the group makes the leader, but the leader also makes the group. By his manipulation of marriages and other movements of people, he can gain or lose followers. The headman is the capstone of coresidential group organization, and those groups often dissolve on his death.

Leadership also responds to the changes associated with contact, however. Headmen are the main recipients of Western goods, especially in the more remote villages.... The role of headmen in channeling Western manufactures in outpost villages is less clear, but there are indications that they continue to have special access. To the east, at the Catrimani mission, each mission payment to an individual had to be approved first by the headman. Furthermore, headmen often enjoy the very substantial benefit of explicit backing by resident Westerners....

Another contact-related factor affecting the status of headmen is the intensity of conflict. Increasing danger of war brings an immediate, palpable increase in the authority and jurisdiction of headmen. In a politically charged environment, a leader can be peremptory, even tyrannical, using violence against those who do not obey his orders.

During peaceful times, the need for leadership is limited, but during war and other periods of high tension, the headman has two major responsibilities. One is tending to the necessities of combat, such as organizing raiding parties or checking village perimeters for signs of raiders....

The other responsibility is managing alliances. During peaceful times, political alliances between villages are of limited development and importance. During wartime, they are essential. Allies are needed for survival and success in war, providing both warriors on raids and vital places of refuge. There are often substantial tensions between allies, which the headman must keep under control....

Given the role of the headman as the capstone of the coresidential group, and his centrality in relation to the practice of war and alliance, it is easy to understand a tactic of Yanomami warfare: targeting the headman. Headmen are frequently reported as the intended targets or actual victims of raiders. The effectiveness of this tactic is illustrated by the plight of Monou-teri in 1965, when the killing of their headman by raiders left them adrift and dependent on the leadership of self-interested neighbors....

Superstructure

[Chagnon called the Yanomami "the fierce people."] Fierceness is embodied in a commitment to take revenge, in cultivating an image that retaliation *will* follow any killing. As [one man] reportedly told potential enemies: "We are in this world to avenge ourselves; if you do it to me, I will do it to you" (Biocca 1971:158). This image has obvious defensive value. In a climate of ongoing wars, the failure to retaliate for a hostile act creates the appearance of weakness, and this can encourage future attacks. But it is necessary to distinguish the tactical value of retaliation from the idea that wars are propelled forward by sentiments of blood revenge. In a recent publication, Chagnon (1988:985–87) places great emphasis on blood revenge as a factor itself responsible for raiding and other violence. In a commentary on that article, I argue that the vengeance motivation itself is highly malleable, manipulated to suit political needs (Ferguson 1989c:564).

... [I]ntensifying hostility between political groups is [also] conceptualized in terms of spirit battles, controlled by their respective shamans. An accusation of witchcraft often precedes combat, so that it may appear that these beliefs are the cause of war. But it has been a consistent finding of witchcraft studies in other parts of the world that accusations of witchcraft *express* existing hostilities rather than cause them. Here too, bad relations lead to suspicions of sorcery and villages "linked by trade and feasting ties ... rarely accuse each other of practicing harmful magic" (Chagnon 1977:98).

... [A]ttribution of a death to sorcery is accompanied by a felt need for blood revenge. It may be that witchcraft and revenge are two sides of a coin. Witch beliefs confirm the malevolence of particular outsiders ("them"); vengeance beliefs emphasize the solidarity of the local group ("versus us"). Together, they make up an effective ideological system for the difficult task of mobilizing people for collective violence.[4]

Conclusions

This paper has examined the multiple, interacting effects of Western contact on the war complex of Yanomami of the Orinoco-Mavaca area. Contact both generated war, primarily through conflicting interests in Western manufactures, and led to pervasive reorganization of society and culture, such that all of life became oriented toward violent conflict. Comparing these Yanomami to Yanomami elsewhere, one cannot doubt that they share a fundamental cultural identity. But the "fierce people" represent Yanomami culture in an extreme conflict mode, a mode that is clearly attributable to the exogenous factors of Western contact. These people cannot be taken as "our contemporary ancestors." They do not represent a phase in sociocultural evolution.

No one can say if the Yanomami ancestors made war before they felt any effects of European contact. But their *known* wars are clearly products of the contact situation, and more specifically, of the infrastructural changes wrought by contact, played out through a changing structure and superstructure.

Notes

1. These data support arguments by Whitehead and Abler in this volume that the spread of Western diseases in nonresistant populations is not an automatic process, but is shaped by the character of the contact situation.

2. Moreover, there is some question whether all pre-steel Yanomami even had stone axes (Ferguson n.d.a:chap. 4).

3. Chagnon (1967:123) also notes, but without specifying place, that headmen of particularly strong villages "may even have the bride service waived."

4. The fact that witchcraft suspicions so frequently precede raiding suggests the potential for combining witchcraft and warfare studies.

POSTSCRIPT

Are Yanomamö Violence and Warfare Natural Human Efforts to Maximize Reproductive Fitness?

Although no one can dispute the fact that the Yanomamö were violent in the 1960s, these selections may lead some to ask whether Yanomamö violence was always as pervasive a part of Yanomamö culture as Chagnon describes it. Filmmaker Timothy Asch, who helped Chagnon with some of his films, depicts a much more tender side of Yanomamö life than is typical in Chagnon's films. What seems to be missing from both of these perspectives, however, is the role of basic cultural values in shaping Yanomamö behavior, whether toward violence or toward tenderness. What is also absent in these two accounts is the role of regional patterns of intergroup exchange that may have been disrupted by the introduction of Western machetes.

Ferguson's argument is more fully developed in his book *Yanomami Warfare: A Political History* (School of American Research Press, 1995) in which he draws upon his own research as well as that of many other anthropologists besides Chagnon who have worked with the Yanomamö. Other aspects of Ferguson's argument are developed in several papers, including "Game Wars? Ecology and Conflict in Amazonia," *Journal of Anthropological Research* (Summer 1989) and "Do Yanomamö Killers Have More Kids?" *American Ethnologist* (August 1989).

Chagnon has published several ethnographic volumes about his research with the Yanomamö. These include his original monograph, *Yanomamö*, 5th ed. (Harcourt Brace, 1997), originally published with the subtitle "The Fierce People" in 1968 and *Studying the Yanomamö* (Holt, Rinehart and Winston, 1974). His most recent monograph deals directly with aspects of cultural change and is entitled *Yanomamö: The Last Days of Eden* (Harcourt, Brace, Jovanovich, 1992). He has also published a number of papers supporting his sociobiological interpretations. See "Kin Selection Theory, Kinship, Marriage and Fitness Among the Yanomomö Indians," in G. W. Barlow and J. Silverberg, eds., *Sociobiology: Beyond Natural Selection* (Westview Press, 1980) and "Sociodemographic Attributes of Nepotism in Tribal Populations," *Current Problems in Sociobiology* (Cambridge University Press, 1982).

Two of Bruce Albert's essays, "Yanomami 'Violence': Inclusive Fitness or Ethnographer's Representation," *Current Anthropology* (December 1989) and "On Yanomami Warfare: Rejoinder" *Current Anthropology* (December 1990), deal with the central question of fitness in this issue.

ISSUE 15

Was Margaret Mead's Fieldwork on Samoan Adolescents Fundamentally Flawed?

YES: Derek Freeman, from *Margaret Mead and Samoa: The Making and Unmaking of an Anthropological Myth* (Harvard University Press, 1983)

NO: Lowell D. Holmes and Ellen Rhoads Holmes, from *Samoan Village: Then and Now*, 2d ed. (Harcourt Brace Jovanovich College Publishers, 1992)

ISSUE SUMMARY

YES: Social anthropologist Derek Freeman argues that Margaret Mead was wrong when she stated that Samoan adolescents had sexual freedom. He contends that Mead went to Samoa determined to prove anthropologist Franz Boas's cultural determinist agenda and states that Mead was so eager to believe in Samoan sexual freedom that she was consistently the victim of a hoax perpetrated by Samoan girls and young women who enjoyed tricking her.

NO: Cultural anthropologists Lowell D. Holmes and Ellen Rhoads Holmes contend that Margaret Mead had a very solid understanding of Samoan culture in general. During a restudy of Mead's research, they came to many of the same conclusions that Mead had reached about Samoan sexuality and adolescent experiences. Mead's description of Samoan culture exaggerates the amount of sexual freedom and the degree to which adolescence in Samoa is carefree but these differences, they argue, can be explained in terms of changes in Samoan culture since 1925 and in terms of Mead's relatively unsophisticated research methods as compared with field methods used today.

In 1925, a student of anthropologist Franz Boas named Margaret Mead set off for a nine-month study of adolescent women in Samoa. At only 23 years old, Mead was just barely beyond adolescence herself. Concerned about Mead's safety in a remote and distant place, Boas arranged for her to stay with an

American family. Here she could live in a European-style house and her physical safety would be ensured. For the next several months she studied the culture and lives of young Samoan women by visiting their village.

On her return to New York in 1925, she wrote up her dissertation for Boas, revising this volume for publication in 1928. She titled the book *Coming of Age in Samoa: A Psychological Study of Primitive Youth for Western Civilization*. Mead concluded that because Samoan culture was so much more relaxed about sexuality than Western culture, Samoan adolescents had a much more tranquil transition from childhood to adulthood than was observed in America and other Western countries. *Coming of Age in Samoa* was an immediate best-seller and it earned Mead renown as a scientist.

In 1983 Derek Freeman published his book entitled *Margaret Mead and Samoa: The Making and Unmaking of an Anthropological Myth* (Harvard University Press), an excerpt of which is provided as the Yes-side selection. Freeman argued that Mead was so eager to find support for her model that she blatantly biased her Samoan fieldwork findings and in effect falsified her data.

Freeman had worked in Western Samoa from 1940 to 1943, returning for further fieldwork from 1965 to 1967. During his research he found evidence that challenges some of Mead's published field data as well as a number of her conclusions regarding Samoan adolescence. He contends that his findings call into question Mead's entire project. He also contends that Mead's young Samoan informants perpetrated a hoax on her by making up stories about their promiscuity.

Freeman's selection is countered by a selection written by Lowell D. Holmes and Ellen Rhoads Holmes, who, in the 1950s, had conducted a restudy of the same community that Mead had visited. Holmes and Holmes had expressly intended to test the reliability and validity of Mead's findings. They conclude that while Mead's characterizations of Samoans are in some ways exaggerated, the characterizations are by no means fundamentally wrong.

These selections allow us to ask a number of questions about Mead's research: Did Mead unintentionally exaggerate her findings about sexual freedom? Or did she intentionally falsify her field data, specifically so that she could support Boas's model of cultural determinism? Could Mead's excesses be explained as the consequence of her being a youthful and inexperienced field researcher? Or can differences between Mead's findings and those of the selection authors be explained in other ways?

These selections raise a number of questions about the replicability of anthropological fieldwork, as well. Is it possible to conduct a systematic restudy of another anthropologist's field subjects? Can an anthropologist working in another village or on another island reliably challenge the findings of another anthropologist?

293

Margaret Mead and Samoa

Preface

By far the most widely known of Margaret Mead's numerous books is *Coming of Age in Samoa,* based on fieldwork on which she embarked in 1925 at the instigation of Franz Boas, her professor at Columbia University. Boas had sent the 23-year-old Mead to Samoa to study adolescence, and she returned with a startling conclusion. Adolescence was known in America and Europe as a time of emotional stresses and conflicts. If, Mead argued, these problems were caused by the biological processes of maturation, then they would necessarily be found in all human societies. But in Samoa, she reported, life was easy and casual, and adolescence was the easiest and most pleasant time of life. Thus in anthropological terms, according to Mead, Samoa was a "negative instance"—and the existence of this one counterexample demonstrated that the disturbances associated with adolescence in the United States and elsewhere had cultural and not biological causes. In the controversy between the adherents of biological determinism and those of cultural determinism, a controversy that was at its height in the 1920s, Mead's negative instance appeared to be a triumphant outcome for believers in the sovereignty of culture.

When *Coming of Age in Samoa* was published in 1928 it attracted immense attention, and its apparently conclusive finding swiftly entered anthropological lore as a jewel of a case. Since that time Mead's finding has been recounted in scores of textbooks, and through the vast popularity of *Coming of Age in Samoa,* the best-selling of all anthropological books, it has influenced the thinking of millions of people throughout the world. It is with the critical examination of this very widely accepted conclusion that I am concerned [here].

Scientific knowledge, as Karl Popper has shown, is principally advanced through the conscious adoption of "the critical method of error elimination." In other words, within science, propositions and theories are systematically tested by attempts to refute them, and they remain acceptable only as long as they withstand these attempts at refutation. In Popper's view, "in so far as a scientific statement speaks about reality it must be falsifiable," and rational criticism entails the testing of any particular statement in terms of its correspondence with the facts. Mead's classing of Samoa as a negative instance obviously depends on the adequacy of the account of Samoan culture on which it is based. It is thus very much a scientific proposition, for it is fully open to testing against the relevant empirical evidence.

While the systematic testing of the conclusions of a science is always desirable, this testing is plainly imperative when serious doubts have been expressed about some particular finding. Students of Samoan culture have long voiced such doubts about Mead's findings of 1928.... I adduce detailed empirical evidence to demonstrate that Mead's account of Samoan culture and character is fundamentally in error. I would emphasize that I am not intent on constructing an alternative ethnography of Samoa. Rather, the evidence I shall present has the specific purpose of scientifically refuting the proposition that Samoa is a negative instance by demonstrating that the depictions on which Mead based this assertion are, in varying degree, mistaken.

In undertaking this refutation I shall limit my scrutiny to those sections of Mead's writings which have stemmed from, or refer to, her researches on Samoa. My concern, moreover, is with the scientific import of these actual researches and *not* with Margaret Mead personally, or with any aspect of her ideas or activities that lies beyond the ambit of her writings on Samoa. I would emphasize also that I hold in high regard many of the personal achievements of Margaret Mead, Franz Boas, and the other individuals certain of whose assertions and ideas I necessarily must question in the pages that follow.

... When I reached Western Samoa in April 1940, I was very much a cultural determinist. *Coming of Age in Samoa* had been unreservedly commended to me by [Ernest] Beaglehole, and my credence in Mead's findings was complete.

After two years of study, during which I came to know all the islands of Western Samoa, I could speak Samoan well enough to converse in the company of chiefs with the punctilio that Samoan etiquette demands, and the time had come to select a local polity for intensive investigation. My choice was Sa'anapu, a settlement of 400 inhabitants on the south coast of Upolu. On my first visit to Sa'anapu I had become friendly with Lauvi Vainu'u, a senior talking chief.... I was to become his adopted son. From that time onward I lived as one of the Lauvi family whenever I was in Sa'anapu.

In my early work I had, in my unquestioning acceptance of Mead's writings, tended to dismiss all evidence that ran counter to her findings. By the end of 1942, however, it had become apparent to me that much of what she had written about the inhabitants of Manu'a in eastern Samoa did not apply to the people of western Samoa. After I had been assured by Samoans who had lived in Manu'a that life there was essentially the same as in the western islands, I realized that I would have to make one of the objectives of my research the systematic testing of Mead's depiction of Samoan culture.

Soon after I returned to Sa'anapu its chiefs forgathered one morning at Lauvi's house to confer on me one of the chiefly titles of their polity. I was thus able to attend all *fono,* or chiefly assemblies, as of right, and I soon came to be accepted by the community at large. From this time onward I was in an exceptionally favorable position to pursue my researches into the realities of Samoan life.

By the time I left Samoa in November 1943 I knew that I would one day face the responsibility of writing a refutation of Mead's Samoan findings. This would involve much research into the history of early Samoa. This task I began in 1945 in the manuscript holdings of the Mitchell Library in Sydney and later continued in England, where I thoroughly studied the Samoan archives of the London Missionary Society.

During 1946–1948, while studying anthropology at the University of London, I wrote a dissertation on Samoan social organization.... There then came, however, the opportunity to spend some years among the Iban of Borneo. With this diversion, ... the continuation of my Samoan researches was long delayed.

I finally returned to Western Samoa, accompanied by my wife and daughters, at the end of 1965. Sa'anapu, now linked Apia by road, was once again my center of research. The chiefs of Sa'anapu immediately recognized the title they had conferred on me in 1943, and I became once again an active member of the Sa'anapu *fono*. My family and I remained in Samoa for just over two years, making frequent visits elsewhere in the district to which Sa'anapu belongs, as also to numerous other parts of the archipelago, from Saua in the east to Falealupo in the west.

Many educated Samoans, especially those who had attended college in New Zealand, had become familiar with Mead's writings about their culture. A number of them entreated me, as an anthropologist, to correct her mistaken depiction of the Samoan ethos. Accordingly, early in 1966 I set about the systematic examination of the entire range of Mead's writings on Samoa, seeking to test her assertions by detailed investigation of the particulars of the behavior or custom to which they referred....

[I]n 1967 organized a formal traveling party to [the island of] Ta'ū. We visitors were received as long-lost kinsmen, and in the company of chiefs from both Ta'ū and Sa'anapu I was able to review all those facets of Mead's depiction of Samoa which were then still at issue. In Ta'ū I also recorded the testimony of men and women who remembered the period to which Mead's writings refer. In many instances these recollections were vivid and specific; as one of my informants remarked, the happenings of the mid 1920s were still fresh in their memories.

As my inquiries progressed it became evident that my critical scrutiny of Mead's conclusions would have to extend to the anthropological paradigm of which *Coming of Age in Samoa* was a part....

My researches were not completed until 1981, when I finally gained access to the archives of the High Court of American Samoa for the 1920s. Thus my refutation of Mead's depiction of Samoa appears some years after her death. In November 1964, however, when Dr. Mead visited the Australian National University, I informed her very fully, during a long private conversation, of the empirical basis of my disagreement with her depiction of Samoa. From that time onward we were in correspondence, and in August 1978, upon its first completion, I offered to send her an early draft of my refutation of the conclusions she had reached in *Coming of Age in Samoa.* I received no reply to this offer before Dr. Mead's death in November of that year.

In September 1981 I returned to Western Samoa with the specific purpose of submitting a draft of [my] book to the critical scrutiny of Samoan scholars.... In the course of the refutation of Mead's misleading account of their culture, which many Samoans encouraged me to undertake, I have had to deal realistically with the darker side of Samoan life. During my visit of 1981 I found among contemporary Samoans both a mature appreciation of the need to face these realities and a clear-headed pride in the virtues and strengths of the Samoan way of life....

Mead's Misconstruing of Samoa

... [The] notion that cultural determinism was absolute was "so obvious" to Mead that.... she also avowed it in *Coming of Age in Samoa,* in respect of adolescent behavior.

That this doctrine of the absoluteness of cultural determinism should have seemed "so obvious" to Mead is understandable. Anthropology, when she began its study in 1922, was dominated by Boas' "compelling idea," as Leslie Spier has called it, of "the complete moulding of every human expression— inner thought and external behavior—by social conditioning," and by the time she left for Samoa in 1925 she had become a fervent devotee of the notion that human behavior could be explained in purely cultural terms. Further, although by the time of Mead's recruitment to its ranks cultural anthropology had achieved its independence, it had done so at the cost of becoming an ideology that, in an actively unscientific way, sought totally to exclude biology from the explanation of human behavior. Thus as, [Alfred] Kroeber declared, "the important thing about anthropology is not the science but an attitude of mind"—an attitude of mind, that is, committed to the doctrine of culture as a superorganic entity which incessantly shapes human behavior, "conditioning all responses." It was of this attitude of mind that Mead became a leading proponent, with (as Marvin Harris has observed) her anthropological mission, set for her by Boas, being to defeat the notion of a "panhuman hereditary human nature." She pursued this objective by tirelessly stressing, in publication after publication, "the absence of maturational regularities."

In her own account of this mission, Mead describes it as a battle which she and other Boasians had had to fight with the whole battery at their command, using the most fantastic and startling examples they could muster. It is thus evident that her writings during this period, about Samoa as about other South Seas cultures, had the explicit aim of confuting biological explanations of human behavior and vindicating the doctrines of the Boasian school. By 1939 this battle, according to Mead, had been won....

For Mead's readers in North America and elsewhere in the Western world, there could be no more plausible location for the idyllic society of which she wrote than in the South Seas, a region that since the days of Bougainville has figured in the fantasies of Europeans and Americans as a place of preternatural contentment and sensual delight. So, as Mead reports, her announcement in 1925 that she was going to Samoa caused the same breathless stir as if she had been "setting off for heaven." Indeed, there were many in the 1920s, according to Mead, who longed to go to the South Sea islands "to escape to a kind of divine nothingness in which life would be reduced to the simplest physical terms, to sunshine and the moving shadows of palm trees, to bronze-bodied girls and bronze-bodied boys, food for the asking, no work to do, no obligations to meet."

.... How did the young Margaret Mead come so to miscronstrue ethos and ethnography of Samoa? The fervency of her belief in cultural determinism and her tendency to view the South Seas as an earthly paradise go some way in accounting for what happened, but manifestly more was involved.

The Ph.D. topic that Boas assigned to Mead was the comparative study of canoe-building, house-building, and tattooing in the Polynesian culture area. During 1924 she gathered information on these activities from the available literature on the Hawaiians, the Marquesans, the Maori, the Tahitians, and the Samoans. These doctoral studies did not have any direct relevance to the quite separate problem of adolescence in Samoa that Boas set her in 1925, and, indeed, the fact that her reading was mainly on Eastern rather than Western Polynesia concealed from her the marked extent to which the traditional culture and values of Samoa differ from those of Tahiti. Again, during the spring of 1925 she had little time for systematic preparation for her Samoan researches. Indeed, the counsel she received from Boas about these researches prior to her departure for Pago Pago lasted, she tells us, for only half an hour. During this brief meeting Boas' principal instruction was that she should concentrate on the problem he had set her and not waste time doing ethnography. Accordingly, when in the second week of November 1925 Mead reached Manu'a, she at once launched into the study of adolescence without first acquiring, either by observation or from inquiry with adult informants, a thorough understanding of the traditional values and customs of the Manu'ans. This, without doubt, was an ill-advised way to proceed, for it meant that Mead was in no position to check the statements of the girls she was studying against a well-informed knowledge of the fa'aSamoa [Samoan way of life]

It is also evident that Mead greatly underestimated the complexity of the culture, society, history, and psychology of the people among whom she was to study adolescence. Samoan society, so Mead would have it, is "very simple," and Samoan culture "uncomplex." ...

As any one who cares to consult Augustin Krämer's *Die Samoa-Inseln,* Robert Louis Stevenson's *A Footnote to History,* or J. W. Davidson's *Samoa mo Samoa* will quickly discover, Samoan society and culture are by no means simple and uncomplex; they are marked by particularities, intricacies, and subtleties quite as daunting as those which face students of Europe and Asia. Indeed, the fa'aSamoa is so sinuously complex that, as Stevenson's step-daughter, Isobel Strong, once remarked, "one may live long in Samoa without understanding the whys and wherefores." Mead, however, spent not even a few months on the systematic study of Manu'a before launching upon the study of adolescence immediately upon her arrival in Ta'ū in accordance with Boas' instructions. Thus, she has noted that while on her later field trips she had "the more satisfactory task of learning the culture first and only afterwards working on a special problem" in Samoa this was "not necessary."

... Another problem was that of being able to communicate adequately with the people she was to study. Mead had arrived in Pago Pago without any knowledge of the Samoan language.... In this situation Mead was plainly at some hazard pursuing her inquiries in Manu'a, for Samoans, when diverted by the stumbling efforts of outsiders to speak their demanding language, are inclined not to take them seriously.

Mead, then, began her inquiries with her girl informants with a far from perfect command of the vernacular, and without systematic prior investigation of Manu'an society and values. Added to this, she elected to live not in a Samoan household but with the handful of expatriate Americans who were the local representatives of the naval government of American Samoa, from which in 1925 many Manu'ans were radically disaffected.... Of the immense advantage that an ethnographer gains by living among the people whose values and behavior he is intent on understanding there can be not the slightest doubt. Mead, however, within six weeks of her arrival in Pago Pago, and before she had spent any time actually staying in a traditional household, had come to feel that the food she would have to eat would be too starchy, and the conditions of living she would have to endure too nerve-racking to make residence with a Samoan family bearable. In Ta'ū, she told Boas, she would be able to live "in a white household" and yet be in the midst of one of the villages from which she would be drawing her adolescent subjects. This arrangement to live not in a Samoan household but with the Holt family in their European-style house, which was also the location of the government radio station and medical dispensary, decisively determined the form her researches were to take.

According to Mead her residence in these government quarters furnished her with an absolutely essential neutral base from which she could study all of the individuals in the surrounding village while at the same time remaining "aloof from native feuds and lines of demarcation." Against this exiguous advantage she was, however, depriving herself of the close contacts that speedily develop in Samoa between an ethnographer and the members of the extended family in which he or she lives. Such contacts are essential for the gaining of a thorough understanding of the Samoan language and, most important of all, for the independent verification, by the continuous observation of actual behavior, of the statements being derived from informants. Thus, by living with the Holts, Mead was trapping herself in a situation in which she was forced to rely not on observations of the behavior of Samoans as they lived their lives beyond the precincts of the government station on Ta'ū, but on such hearsay information as she was able to extract from her adolescent subjects....

It is evident then that although, as Mead records, she could "wander freely about the village or go on fishing trips or stop at a house where a woman was weaving" when she was away from the dispensary, her account of adolescence in Samoa was, in the main, derived from the young informants who came to talk with her away from their homes in the villages of Lumā, Si'ufaga, and Faleasao. So, as Mead states, for these three villages, from which all her adolescent informants were drawn, she saw the life that went on "through the eyes" of the group of girls on the details of whose lives she was concentrating. This situation is of crucial significance for the assessment of Mead's researches in Manu'a, for we are clearly faced with the question of the extent to which the lens she fashioned from what she was being told by her adolescent informants and through which she saw Samoan life was a true and accurate lens.

... [M]any of the assertions appearing in Mead's depiction of Samoa are fundamentally in error, and some of them preposterously false. How are we to account for the presence of errors of this magnitude? Some Samoans who have read *Coming of Age in Samoa* react, as Shore reports, with anger and the insistence "that Mead lied." This, however, is an interpretation that I have no hesitation in dismissing. The succession of prefaces to *Coming of Age* in Samoa published by Mead in 1949, 1953, 1961, and 1973 indicate clearly, in my judgment, that she did give genuine credence to the view of Samoan life with which she returned to New York in 1926. Moreover, in the 1969 edition of *Social Organization of Manu'a* she freely conceded that there was a serious problem in reconciling the "contradictions" between her own depiction of Samoa and that contained in "other records of historical and contemporary behavior." ...

Mead's depiction of Samoan culture, as I have shown, is marked by major errors, and her account of the sexual behavior of Samoans by a mind-boggling contradiction, for she asserts that the Samoans have a culture in which female virginity is very highly valued, with a virginity-testing ceremony being "theoretically observed at weddings of all ranks," while at the same time adolescence among females is regarded as a period "appropriate for love-making," with promiscuity before marriage being both permitted and "expected." And, indeed, she actually describes the Samoans as making the "demand" that a female should be "both receptive to the advances of many lovers and yet capable of showing the tokens of virginity at marriage." Something, it becomes plain at this juncture, is emphatically amiss, for surely no human population could be so cognitively disoriented as to conduct their lives in such a schizophrenic way. Nor are the Samoans remotely like this, for.... they are, in fact, a people who traditionally value virginity highly and so disapprove of premarital promiscuity as to exercise a strict surveillance over the comings and goings of adolescent girls. That these values and this regime were in force in Manu'a in the mid 1920s is, furthermore, clearly established by the testimony of the Manu'ans themselves who, when I discussed this period with those who well remembered it, confirmed that the fa'aSamoa in these matters was operative then as it was both before and after Mead's brief sojourn in Ta'ū. What then can have been the source of Mead's erroneous statement that in Samoa there is great premarital freedom, with promiscuity before marriage among adolescent girls, being both permitted and expected?

The explanation most consistently advanced by the Samoans themselves for the magnitude of the errors in her depiction of their culture and in particular of their sexual morality is, as Gerber has reported, "that Mead's informants must have been telling lies in order to tease her." Those Samoans who offer this explanation, which I have heard in Manu'a as well as in other parts of Samoa, are referring to the behavior called *tau fa'ase'e,* to which Samoans are much prone. *Fa'ase'e* (literally "to cause to slip") means "to dupe," as in the example given by Milner, *"e fa'ase'e gofie le teine,* the girl is easily duped"; and the phrase *tau fa'ase'e* refers to the action of deliberately duping someone, a pastime that greatly appeals to the Samoans as a respite from the severities of their authoritarian society.

Because of their strict morality, Samoans show a decided reluctance to discuss sexual matters with outsiders or those in authority, a reticence that is especially marked among female adolescents. Thus, Holmes reports that when he and his wife lived in Manu'a and Tutuila in 1954 "it was never possible to obtain details of sexual experience from unmarried informants, though several of these people were constant companions and part of the household." Further, as Lauifi Ili, Holmes's principal assistant, observes, when it comes to imparting information about sexual activities, Samoan girls are "very close-mouthed and ashamed." Yet it was precisely information of this kind that Mead, a liberated young American newly arrived from New York and resident in the government station at Ta'ū, sought to extract from the adolescent girls she had been sent to study. And when she persisted in this unprecedented probing of a highly embarrassing topic, it is likely that these girls resorted, as [Eleanor Ruth] Gerber's Samoan informants have averred, to *tau fa'ase'e*, regaling their inquisitor with counterfeit tales of casual love under the palm trees.

This, then, is the explanation that Samoans give for the highly inaccurate portrayal of their sexual morality in Mead's writings. It is an explanation that accounts for how it was that this erroneous portrayal came to be made, as well as for Mead's sincere credence in the account she has given in *Coming of Age in Samoa*, for she was indeed reporting what she had been told by her adolescent informants. The Manu'ans emphasize, however, that the girls who, they claim, plied Mead with these counterfeit tales were only amusing themselves, and had no inkling that their tales would ever find their way into a book.

While we cannot, in the absence of detailed corroborative evidence [but see addendum following], be sure about the truth of this Samoan claim that Mead was mischievously duped by her adolescent informants, we can be certain that she did return to New York in 1926 with tales running directly counter to all other ethnographic accounts of Samoa, from which she constructed her picture of Manu'a as a paradise of free love, and of Samoa as a negative instance, which, so she claimed, validated Boasian doctrine. It was this negative instance that she duly presented to Boas as the ideologically gratifying result of her inquiries in Manu'a....

We are thus confronted in the case of Margaret Mead's Samoan researches with an instructive example of how, as evidence is sought to substantiate a cherished doctrine, the deeply held beliefs of those involved may lead them unwittingly into error. The danger of such an outcome is inherent, it would seem, in the very process of belief formation....

In the case of Mead's Samoan researches, certainly, there is the clearest evidence that it was her deeply convinced belief in the doctrine of extreme cultural determinism, for which she was prepared to fight with the whole battery at her command, that led her to construct an account of Samoa that appeared to substantiate this very doctrine. There is, however, conclusive empirical evidence to demonstrate that Samoa, in numerous respects, is not at all as Mead depicted it to be.

A crucial issue that arises from this historic case for the discipline of anthropology, which has tended to accept the reports of ethnographers as entirely empirical statements, is the extent to which other ethnographic accounts may have been distorted by doctrinal convictions, as well as the methodological question of how such distortion can best be avoided. These are no small problems. I would merely comment that as we look back on Mead's Samoan researches we are able to appreciate anew the wisdom of Karl Popper's admonition that in both science and scholarship it is, above all else, indefatigable rational criticism of our suppositions that is of decisive importance, for such criticism by "bringing out our mistakes... makes us understand the difficulties of the problem we are trying to solve," and so saves us from the allure of the "obvious truth" of received doctrine.

Addendum: New Evidence of the Hoaxing of Margaret Mead

In my book *The Fateful Hoaxing of Margaret Mead* (1998) there is an account, based on the sworn testimony of Fa'apua'a, of how Margaret Mead in March of 1926 on the island of Ofu in American Samoa was hoaxed about the sexual mores of the Samoans by her two Samoan traveling companions, Fa'apua'a and Fofoa.

I [have recently discovered] direct evidence, from Mead's own papers, that Margaret Mead was indeed taken in by the "whispered confidences" (as she called them) of Fa'apua'a and Fofoa. This incontrovertible historical evidence finally brings to closure the long-running controversy over Margaret Mead's Samoan fieldwork....

The crucially important direct evidence in question is contained in a little known book entitled *All True! The Record of Actual Adventures That Have Happened To Ten Women of Today* that was published in New York in 1931 by Brewer, Warren and Putnam. The "adventure" by Dr Margaret Mead is entitled "Life as a Samoan Girl". It begins with a wistful reference to "the group of reverend scientists" who in 1925 sent her to study (Mead, 1925) "the problem of which phenomena of adolescence are culturally and which physiologically determined" among the adolescent girls of Samoa, with "no very clear idea" of how she was "to do this." It ends with an account of her journey to the islands of Ofu and Olosega in March of 1926 with the "two Samoan girls," as she calls them, Fa'apua'a and Fofoa. In fact, Fa'apua'a and Fofoa were both twenty-four years of age and slightly older than Dr. Mead herself. Dr Mead continues her account of her visit to the islands of Ofu and Olosega with Fa'apua'a and Fofoa by stating: "In all things I had behaved as a Samoan, for only so, only by losing my identity, as far as possible, had I been able to become acquainted with the Samoan girls receive their whispered confidences and learn at the same time the answer to the scientists' questions."

This account, by Mead herself, is fully confirmed by the sworn testimony of Fa'apua'a (cf. Freeman, 1998, Chapter 11). It can be found on p. 141 of the second and paperback edition (1999) of my book *The Fateful Hoaxing of Margaret Mead: A historical analysis of her Samoan research*. It is definitive historical evidence that establishes that Martin Orans is in outright error in asserting (1996:92) that it is "demonstrably false that Mead was taken in by Fa'apua'a and Fofoa". It is also evidence that establishes that *Coming of Age in Samoa,* far from being a "scientific classic" (as Mead herself supposed) is, in certain vitally significant respects (as in its dream-like second chapter), a work of anthropological fiction.

References

Freeman, Derek, 1999, *The Fateful Hoaxing of Margaret Mead,* Boulder: Westview, 2nd. edition.

Mead, Margaret, 1925, Plan of Research Submitted to the National Research Council of the U.S.A. (Archives of the National Academy of Sciences).

Mead, Margaret, 1928, *Coming of Age in Samoa.* New York: Morrow.

Mead, Margaret, 1931, "Life as a Samoan Girl," in *All True! The Record of Actual Adventures That Happened to Ten Women of Today.* New York: Brewer, Warren and Putnam.

Orans, Martin, 1996, *Not Even Wrong: Margaret Mead, Derek Freeman and the Samoans,* Novato: Chandler and Sharp.

Lowell D. Holmes and
Ellen Rhoads Holmes

 **NO**

Samoan Character and
the Academic World

On January 31, 1983, the *New York Times* carried a front-page article, the headline of which read, "New Samoa Book Challenges Margaret Mead's Conclusions." The book that precipitated this somewhat unexpected turn of events was *Margaret Mead and Samoa: The Making and Unmaking of an Anthropological Myth* by Derek Freeman, an emeritus professor of anthropology at Australian National University in Canberra. This work, which some claim set off the most heated controversy in sociocultural anthropology in one hundred years, is described by its author as a "refutation of Mead's misleading account" of Samoan culture and personality as presented in her 1928 ethnography, *Coming of Age in Samoa.*

The *New York Times* article was of special interest to me because, in 1954, I had conducted a year-long methodological restudy of the Mead data under attack. I had lived in Ta'ū village, where Mead had worked twenty-nine years earlier, and had used many of her informants in a systematic and detailed evaluation of every observation and interpretation she had made about the lifestyle of the people in that Samoan village. A methodological restudy, incidentally, involves a second anthropologist going into the field with the *express purpose* of testing the reliability and validity of the findings of a former investigator. This restudy is made in order to establish what kinds of errors of data collection or interpretation might have been made by certain kinds of people, in certain kinds of field research situations, researching certain kinds of problems. For example, Margaret Mead was a twenty-three-year-old woman investigating a male-dominated society that venerates age. She was a student of Franz Boas and, therefore, went equipped with a particular theoretical frame of reference. She was also on her first field trip—at a time when research methods were crude. My task in this methodological restudy was not only to analyze how my findings might be different from hers (if that would be the case), but I would also attempt to speculate on how differences in the status of the investigators (for example, sex, age, family situation, education) and other personal factors might affect the collection and interpretation of data.

My critique of Margaret Mead's study was presented in my doctoral dissertation, *The Restudy of Manu'an Culture. A Problem in Methodology,* which by

1983 had been collecting dust on a Northwestern University library shelf for some twenty-seven years. I was therefore eager to obtain a copy of Freeman's new evaluation of Mead's work from its publisher, Harvard University Press. In reading the book this is what I found.

In *Margaret Mead and Samoa: The Making and Unmaking of an Anthropological Myth* (1983), Derek Freeman argues that Mead perpetuated a hoax comparable in consequence to that of Piltdown Man when, in 1928, she described Samoa as a paradise where competition, sexual inhibition, and guilt were virtually absent. Refusing to believe that adolescents in all societies inevitably experience emotional crises—storm and stress—because of biological changes associated with puberty (as hypothesized in *Adolescence* in 1904 by psychologist G. Stanley Hall), Mead set out to discover a society where the passage to adulthood was smooth and without trauma. She described such a society in *Coming of Age in Samoa*. In delineating this "negative instance" (which challenged Hall's theory of universal adolescent rebellion and strife), Margaret Mead had in effect established that nurture (culture) is more critical than nature (biology) in accounting for adolescent maturation behavior in the human species. Derek Freeman, on the other hand, rejects the idea that human behavior is largely shaped by culture and believes that Mead and her mentor, Franz Boas (commonly called the "Father of American Anthropology"), were guilty of *totally* ignoring the influence of biological heredity. He believes that Mead's "negative instance" results entirely from faulty data collection and that Mead's Samoan findings have led anthropology, psychology, and education down the primrose path of pseudoscience. Freeman's book, therefore, is an attempt to set the record straight through his own, more accurate, observations of Samoa and Samoans—although his observations of Samoan behavior were in another village, on another island, in another country, and fourteen years later.

Freeman's main theoretical approach in this evaluation of Mead's work derives from the German philosopher of science, Karl Popper, who maintains that science should be deductive, not inductive, and that progress in scientific research should consist essentially of attempts to refute established theories. Thus, Derek Freeman is out to destroy the credibility of what he interprets as the "absolute cultural determinism" to be found in the work of Margaret Mead as well as in much of the work of Boas and his other students. This claim is, of course, spurious, as any student of American anthropological theory knows. For example, in Melville J. Herskovits' biography of Franz Boas, we find the statement that, because of his "rounded view of the problem Boas could perceive so clearly the fallacy of the eugenicist theory, which held the destiny of men to be determined by biological endowment, with little regard for the learned, cultural determinants of behavior." By the same token, he "refused to accept the counter-dogma that man is born with a completely blank slate, on which can be written whatever is willed. He saw both innate endowment and learning—or, as it was called popularly, heredity and environment—as significant factors in the making of the mature individual" (1953:28). Herskovits also points out that "numerous examples can be found, in reports on the various studies he conducted, of how skillfully Boas was able to weave cultural and biological factors into a single fabric" (*Ibid.*).

Marvin Harris concurs: "American anthropology has always been concerned with the relationships between nature (in the guise of habitat and genic programming) and culture (in the guise of traditions encoded in the brain, not in the genes). Neither Boas nor his students ever denied that *Homo sapiens* has a species-specific nature" (1983:26). In his book, *The Rise of Anthropological Theory,* Harris writes, "Boas systematically rejected almost every conceivable form of cultural determinism" (1968:283).

Evaluation of the Mead Data

My restudy experience in Ta'ū village in 1954 led me to conclude that Margaret Mead often overgeneralized; that, in many cases, we interpreted data differently; and that, because of her age and sex, some avenues of investigation apparently were closed to her—particularly those having to do with the more formal aspects of village political organization and ceremonial life. However, her overall characterization of the nature and dynamics of the culture were, in my judgment, quite valid and her contention that it was easier to come of age in Samoa than in America in 1925–1926 was undoubtedly correct. In spite of the greater possibilities for error in a pioneer study, Mead's age (only 23), her sex (in a male-dominated society), and her inexperience, I believe the reliability and validity of the Ta'ū village research is remarkably high.

I look upon an ethnographic account as a kind of map to be used in finding one's way about in a culture—in comprehending and anticipating behavior. Mead's account never left me lost or bewildered in my interactions with Samoan islanders, but I also felt that if one were to come to a decision about the comparative difficulties of coming of age in Samoa and the United States, it would be necessary to know something about what life was like for adolescents in America in 1925–1926. Joseph Folsom's book, *The Family,* published in 1934, but researched about the time Mead was writing *Coming of Age in Samoa,* provided that information. Folsom describes the social environment in which children came of age at that time as follows:

> Children are disciplined and trained with the ideal of absolute obedience to parents. Corporal punishment is used, ideally in cold blood.... All sexual behavior on the part of children is prevented by all means at the parents' disposal.... For the sake of prevention it has been usual to cultivate in the child, especially the girl, an attitude of horror or disgust toward all aspects of sex.... Premarital intercourse is immoral though not abhorrent.... Violations are supposedly prevented by the supervision of the girl's parents.... Illegitimate children are socially stigmatized.... The chief stigma falls upon the unmarried mother, because she has broken an important sex taboo (1934: 10–25)....

While Freeman contends that Mead was absolutely wrong about nearly everything (partly, he maintains, because the teenage girls she used as informants consistently lied to her), I found discrepancies mainly in such areas as the degree of sexual freedom Samoan young people enjoy, the competitive nature of the society, the aggressiveness of Samoan behavior, and the degree of genuine affection and commitment between lovers and spouses.

I saw Samoan culture as considerably more competitive than Mead, although I never considered it as inflexible or aggressive as Freeman does. I observed a great preoccupation with status, power, and prestige among men of rank and, on more than one occasion, was present at fierce verbal duels between Talking Chiefs trying to enhance their own prestige and, incidentally, that of their village....

I also found that Samoan culture was not as simple as Margaret Mead claimed, nor was Ta'ū village the paradise she would have us believe. She often romanticized, overgeneralized, and, on some occasions, took literary license in her descriptions of Samoan lifeways. For example, her very dramatic chapter, "A Day in Samoa," crowds typical activities (some of which occur only at particular times of the year) into a typical day and thereby presents a village scene that was much more vibrant, bustling, and picturesque than I ever encountered in any twenty-four hour period. Mead's chapter is good prose, but is it good anthropology?...

I also did not agree with Mead on the degree of sexual freedom supposedly enjoyed by her informants, but I believe her characterization comes closer to the truth than that of Freeman. Samoans have a very natural and healthy attitude toward sex. Judging by the number of illegitimate children in Ta'ū village when I was there and by the fact that divorce frequently involved claims of adultery, I would conclude that, while Samoans are far from promiscuous, they are not the puritanical prudes Freeman paints them to be. However, I must admit that it was difficult to investigate anything of a sexual nature, primarily because of pressure from the London Missionary Society church. Even today, older Samoans seem more distressed over Mead's claims that they are sexually active than Freeman's claims that they are aggressive with strong passions, even psychopathological tendencies. I would assume, however, that Mead was better able to identify with, and therefore establish rapport with, adolescents and young adults on issues of sexuality than either I (at age 29—married with a wife and child) or Freeman, ten years my senior.

Freeman maintains that Mead imposed her own liberated ideas of sexuality onto the Samoans and that her teenage informants consistently lied to her about these matters solely out of mischief. He has recently made contact with one of Mead's informants, Fa'apua'a Fa'amu, who lived in Fitiuta while Mead was working in Ta'ū village. Freeman believes this informant when she says that she consistently lied to Mead (while also identifying her as a good friend), but Freeman does not seem to consider the possibility that she may be lying to him. The possibility of Mead's informants being successful at such long-term deception is simply not credible considering the fact that Mead was an extremely intelligent, well-trained Ph.D. who constantly cross-checked her data with many informants. Anyone who has studied her field notes in the Library of Congress, as I have, must be impressed with her savvy and sophistication.

I must also disagree with Mead's statements that all love affairs are casual and fleeting, and no one plays for very heavy emotional stakes. Custom dictates that displays of affection between spouses and between lovers not take place in public. However, expressions of love and affection were often observed in the families of my informants. . . .

Although I differed with Margaret Mead on many interpretations, the most important fact that emerged from my methodological restudy of her Samoan research is that, without doubt, Samoan adolescents have a less difficult time negotiating the transition from childhood to adulthood than American adolescents. . . .

Critique of the Freeman Refutation

My objections to Derek Freeman's picture of Samoa are much more substantial than to the picture presented by Margaret Mead. Basically, I question Freeman's objectivity and believe he is guilty of an age-old temptation in science, which was recognized as early as 1787 by Thomas Jefferson—no slouch of a scientist himself. In a letter to his friend Charles Thomson, Jefferson wrote, "The moment a person forms a theory, his imagination sees, in every object, only the traits which favor that theory" (Martin 1952:33).

Not only does Freeman ignore counterevidence, he also ignores time and space and assumes that it is legitimate to assess data obtained by Mead in Manu'a in 1925–1926 in terms of the data he collected in Western Samoa in the 1940s, 1960s, and 1980s.

Time differences.   Freeman plays down the fact that Mead did her study of Ta'ū village in the Manu'a Island group of American Samoa fourteen years before he arrived as a teacher (not as an anthropologist) in Western Samoa and that he did not return to Samoa with the express purpose of refuting Mead's study until forty-three years after her visit. Minimizing this time gap, he arbitrarily states that "there is no . . . reason to suppose that Samoan society and behavior changed in any fundamental way during the fourteen years between 1926, the year of the completion of Mead's inquiries, and 1940, when I began my own observation of Samoan behavior" (1983:120).

However, Freeman did not visit Ta'ū village, the site of Mead's research, until 1968. Having established to his satisfaction that there had been few changes in Samoan culture during this long period of time, Freeman went on to state that he would "draw on evidence of my own research in the 1940s, the years 1965 to 1968, and 1981" (1983:120). I might add that he would draw upon historical sources, some of which go back as far as the early eighteenth century, to prove his points. My own analysis of Samoan cultural change, as published in *Ta'ū, Stability and Change in a Samoan Village* (1958), indicates, however, that while there was relative stability in the culture from 1850 to 1925 and from 1925 to 1954, change definitely did take place, particularly in the twentieth century. There is absolutely no basis for Freeman's dealing with Samoa as though it existed in a totally static condition despite its long history of contact with explorers, whalers, missionaries, colonial officials and bureaucrats, entrepreneurs, anthropologists, and, more recently, educators with Western-style curricula and television networks.

Place differences. It also must be kept in mind that Sa'anapu (where Freeman observed Samoan culture) is not Ta'ū village (where Mead did her study). They are different villages, on different islands, in different countries, and there are great historical and political differences between the island of Upolu in Western Samoa and Ta'ū island in the isolated Manu'a Group of American Samoa. Western Samoa has experienced a long and often oppressive history of colonialism under Germany and New Zealand, while the Manu'a Group and American Samoa in general have been spared this. The U.S. Navy administration (1900–1951) exerted little influence outside the Pago Pago Bay area on the island of Tutuila, and the Department of the Interior, which took over from the Navy, has been an ethnocentric—but still benevolent—force in the political history of the territory. While Sa'anapu is on the opposite side of Upolu from Apia, it has daily bus communication with that port town, with all of its banks, supermarkets, department stores, theaters, bookstores, and nightclubs. Cash cropping has always been more important in Western Samoa than in American Samoa, and today, the economies of the two Samoas are vastly different.... On five separate research trips to Manu'a, I have never witnessed a single physical assault or serious argument that threatened to get out of hand. However, urban centers such as Apia in Western Samoa and Pago Pago in American Samoa have a very different character. As early as 1962, there were delinquency problems in the Pago Pago Bay area involving drunkenness, burglary, assaults, and rapes. Young people who migrate to urban areas such as Pago Pago and Apia are no longer under the close supervision and control of their *matai* [chief of the family] and often behave in very nontraditional ways. It is difficult, indeed, to make a blanket statement that all villages in Samoa are the same and that all behavior within the two Samoas is comparable. I have studied several villages during my thirty-seven-year contact with Samoa, and I find each unique in numerous, social, ceremonial, economic, and political respects.

Freeman's subjective use of literature. A serious scientist considers all the literature relating to his or her research problem. One does not select data that supportive and ignore that which is not. Freeman violates that principle repeatedly.... When [Ronald Rose's book, *South Seas Magic* (1959)] can be used to corroborate or advance Freeman's position, he is quoted; however, where Rose's statements concerning Samoan sexual behavior run contrary to Freeman's claims, and fall in line with Mead's observations, his work is ignored. For example, while Freeman insists that Samoans are puritanical and sexually inhibited, Rose writes that "sexual adventures begin at an early age. Although virginity is prized, it is insisted on only with the taupo.... If a girl hasn't had a succession of lovers by the time she is seventeen or eighteen, she feels she is "on the shelf' and becomes the laughing stock among her companions (1959:61).

With regard to the matter that Freeman believes was Mead's spurious example of a "negative instance"—a culture where coming of age is relatively less stressful—Rose writes (but understandably is not quoted by Freeman) as follows:

> Mental disturbances, stresses and conflicts occur at puberty but, as might be expected. these are not quite as common as in our society where taboos associated with sex abound (*Ibid.*: 164).

One can question the objectivity of a scientist who describes Samoans as "an unusually bellicose people" (1983:157) and attempts to substantiate the claim with citations from the eighteenth century, but fails to quote the favorable impressions of the very first European to come in contact with Samoan islanders from the village of Ta'ū, the very village Mead studied. In 1722, Commodore Jacob Roggeveen anchored his vessel off the village of Ta'ū and allowed a number of the islanders to come aboard. After a two-hour visit, the Commodore wrote in his log:

> They appeared to be a good people, lively in their manner of conversing, gentle in their deportment towards each other, and in their manners nothing was perceived of the savage.... It must be acknowledged that this was the nation the most civilized and honest of any that we had seen among the Islands of the South Sea. They were charmed with our arrival amongst them, and received us as divinities. And when they saw us preparing to depart, they testified much regret (Bumey 1816:576).

Rather than quote Roggeveen, Freeman chooses to discuss, as an example of Samoan bellicosity, the La Perouse expedition's visitation at Tutuila in 1787 that ended in tragedy. It is true that Samoans in the village of A'asu attacked a shore party, killing several crew members, but what Freeman fails to mention is that the attack occurred only after crew members punished a Samoan for pilfering by hanging him by his thumbs from the top of the longboat mast....

It also should be noted that the eminent writer, Robert Louis Stevenson, who lived among Samoans the last four years of his life, recorded in his chronicle of Samoan events, *A Footnote to History,* that Samoans were "easy, merry, and pleasure loving; the gayest, though by no means the most capable or the most beautiful of Polynesians" (1892:148) and that their religious sentiment toward conflict was "peace at any price" (*Ibid.*: 147).

Observers contemporary with Mead in Samoa also record descriptions of Samoan chararacter that do not square with Freeman's allegations or his citations from early literature. For example, William Green, the principal of the government school in American Samoa in the 1920s writes:

> Personal combats and fist fights are rather rare today. I believe there has been no murder case in American Samoa since our flag was raised in 1900. Natives will suffer indignities for a long time before resorting to a fight but they remain good fighters. Boxing contests are held occasionally.... Respect for elders and magistrates has, I suppose, tended to discourage frequent combats. Life is easy, and one's habitual tendencies and desires are seldom blocked (1924:134).

Professional Reactions

... It is questionable whether any anthropology book to date has created such a media circus or produced such a media hero as *Margaret Mead and Samoa, The Making and Unmaking of an Anthropological Myth.* It is also doubtful whether any academic press ever mounted such a campaign of Madison Avenue hype to market a book as did Harvard University Press. The early reviews of the book and feature articles about the controversy were primarily penned by journalists and tended to be highly supportive of Freeman's critique, but once the anthropologists began evaluating the Freeman book, the tide took a definite turn. George Marcus of Rice University called the book a "work of great mischief," the mischief being that Freeman was attempting to reestablish "the importance of biological factors in explanations of human behavior" (1983:2).... Marvin Harris observed in his review that Freeman "seems obsessed with the notion that to discredit Mean's Samoan material is to discredit any social scientist who holds that 'nurture' is a more important determinant of the differences and similarities in human social life than nature" (1983:26).

It is only fair to point out that Derek Freeman had, and continues to have, a cadre of anthropological supporters, mostly in Europe and Australia, and the Samoans are mixed in their support of Mead or Freeman....

Like most American anthropologists, and a few scholarly Samoans, we believe the Freeman book has done a disservice to Samoans and to the memory of Margaret Mead. *Margaret Mead and Samoa* is not an objective analysis of Mead's work in Manu'a, but an admitted refutation aimed at discrediting not only Margaret Mead, but Franz Boas and American cultural anthropology in general. Anthropology has often been referred to as a "soft science" throughout much of this rhubarb over Samoa and nature/nurture. It is little wonder, since Freeman's diatribe, published by a supposedly scholarly press, has been accepted by the media, by a select group of anthropologists, and by a number of distinguished ethologists and sociobiologists as legitimate anthropology. Margaret Mead would have loved to have debated the issues with Derek Freeman, but unfortunately, the book was not published while she was alive. It would have been great sport and good for the science of anthropology. As a friend wrote immediately after the publication of Freeman's book, "Whatever else she was, Margaret was a feisty old gal and would have put up a spirited defense which would quickly have turned into a snotty offense." We would have put our money on the plump little lady with the no-nonsense attitude and the compulsion to "get on with it."

References

Burney, James. 1816. *A chronological history of the voyages and discoveries in the South Seas or Pacific Ocean.* London: Luke Hansard and Sons.

Folsom, Joseph K. 1934. *The family: Its sociology and psychiatry.* New York: J. Wiley and Sons.

Freeman, Derek. 1983. *Margaret Mead and Samoa: The making and unmaking of an anthropological myth.* Cambridge, MA: Harvard University Press.

Green, William M. 1924. "Social traits of Samoans." *Journal of Applied Sociology* 9:129 135.

Hall, G. Stanley. 1904. *Adolescence: Its psychology and its relations to physiology, anthropology, sociology, sex, crime, religion and education.* New York: D. Appleton and Company.

Harris, Marvin. 1968. *The rise of anthropological theory.* New York: Thomas Y. Crowell Company.

_____. 1983. "The sleep-crawling question." *Psychology Today* May:24–27.

Herskovits, Melville J. 1953. *Franz Boas.* New York: Charles Scribner's Sons.

Holmes, Lowell D. 1958. *Ta'ū: Stability and change in a Samoan village.* Reprint No. 7, Wellington, New Zealand: Polynesian Society.

Marcus, George, 1983. "One man's Mead." *New York Times Book Review* March 27, 1983:2–3, 22–23.

Martin, Edwin T. 1952. *Thomas Jefferson: Scientist.* New York: Henry Schuman.

Rose, Ronald. 1959. *South Seas magic.* London: Hale.

Stevenson, Robert Louis. 1892. *Vailima papers and A footnote to history.* New York: Charles Scribner's Sons.

POSTSCRIPT

Was Margaret Mead's Fieldwork on Samoan Adolescents Fundamentally Flawed?

The response to Freeman's *Margaret Mead and Samoa* was quite extraordinary and included books, journal articles, editorials, and conference papers. Special sessions at the annual meetings of the American Anthropological Association were devoted exclusively to the Mead-Freeman debate. The first reaction was largely defensive. But as the initial shock of Freeman's assertions wore off, scholars began to address some of the specific points of criticism. A representative sample of these would include Lowell D. Holmes's *Quest for the Real Samoa: The Mead/Freeman Controversy and Beyond* (Bergin and Garvey, 1987) and Hiram Caton's edited volume, *The Samoa Reader: Anthropologists Take Stock* (University Press of America, 1990).

A number of scholars have pointed out that Samoan life has changed significantly since Mead's fieldwork. The Christian Church now exerts a much stronger pressure over the very same women that Mead had interviewed. Another point is that Mead's informants themselves have become much more puritanical as old women than they were as girls. These women now have reputations of social propriety to uphold that would not have concerned them in their youth. Can we believe that they had the same views so many years ago?

In the 1980s Freeman returned to Ta'u with an Australian documentary film crew, specifically to interview some of Mead's now elderly informants. When asked what they had told Mead 60 years earlier, the women stated that they fibbed continuously and explained that it is a cherished Samoan custom to trick people in these ways. Freeman and the film crew take such statements as incontrovertible evidence that Mead was hoaxed. But if it is Samoan custom to trick others, how can Freeman and his film crew be certain that they are not victims of a similar hoax?

Another Samoa specialist, Martin Orans, approaches the controversy in his book *Not Even Wrong: Margaret Mead, Derek Freeman, and the Samoans* (Chandler & Sharp, 1996). Orans contends that neither Mead nor Freeman framed their research questions about cultural determinism in ways that can be tested. Arguing that anthropologists must frame their conclusions as testable hypotheses, Orans asserts that Mead and Freeman are so vague that neither make their case and are both are so ambiguous that they are "not even wrong." But if Orans is correct, how can anthropologists frame the nature-versus-nurture debate in more specific and testable ways in specific field settings?

ISSUE 16

Do Museums Misrepresent Ethnic Communities Around the World?

YES: James Clifford, from *The Predicament of Culture: Twentieth-Century Ethnography, Literature, and Art* (Harvard University Press, 1988)

NO: Denis Dutton, from "Mythologies of Tribal Art," *African Arts* (Summer 1995)

ISSUE SUMMARY

YES: Postmodernist anthropologist James Clifford argues that the very act of removing objects from their ethnographic contexts distorts the meaning of objects held in museums. He contends that whether these objects are displayed in art museums or anthropological museums, exhibitions misrepresent ethnic communities by omitting important aspects of contemporary life, especially involvement with the colonial or Western world.

NO: Anthropologist Denis Dutton asserts that no exhibition can provide a complete context for ethnographic objects, but that does not mean that museum exhibitions are fundamentally flawed. Dutton suggests that postmodernists misunderstand traditional approaches to interpreting museum collections, and what they offer as a replacement actually minimizes what we can understand of ethnic communities from museum collections.

In the late nineteenth and early twentieth centuries, museums were a major focus of anthropological research. In the United States, for example, until after the First World War more anthropologists were employed in museums than in universities. By 1940, cultural anthropologists had largely moved out of museums as they focused on intensive fieldwork. This change was directly related to a shift in paradigms from cultural evolution to functionalism, which happened in the 1920s and 1930s.

As anthropologists later began to focus on functional questions about how societies and their institutions worked, museum collections became increasingly unimportant. Many anthropologists believed that differences in the bindings of stone axes have little to say about how marriages were contracted or how clans were linked together; objects cannot explain how leadership worked or what role religious ideas might have had in maintaining social order.

The following selections deal with the question of how museums should exhibit and interpret ethnographic collections that were obtained during the "museum period" of anthropology. Both authors are critical of certain exhibitions, particularly art historian William Rubin's "Primitivism" show from 1984, and both feel that a good exhibition should contextualize museum objects historically. But the authors differ profoundly in their approach to the study of museum objects.

James Clifford surveys several different kinds of museum exhibits in New York and asks, Do any of them do justice to the peoples who made and used these objects? For Clifford, objects and the cultures from which they come have histories. He questions how much of these histories are present in the several exhibitions he visited. By definition, each and every non-Western object in a Western museum has been removed from its original ethnographic context, a process often referred to as "decontextualization."

Clifford explains in his selection how museums offer a "representation" of tribal peoples as if these societies were timeless and without history. By focusing on particular features of tribal culture, each exhibition makes statements about the relationship between modern Americans and "primitive" peoples. For him, these are fundamentally misleading representations.

Denis Dutton accepts that exhibitions such as those discussed by Clifford are inevitably incomplete, but the lack of a full context does not completely invalidate the exercise of exhibiting objects from tribal societies. He argues that Clifford and the other postmodernist critics of museum exhibitions go too far in their criticisms and that they, too, have an agenda that is itself misleading. Referring to this postmodernist agenda as a "new mythology" about tribal art, Dutton contends that the new mythologists have exaggerated their interpretations of museum exhibitions.

Dutton argues that museums can never offer complete representations of ethnic communities; but this does not mean that exhibitions cannot be both informative and enlightening even if they are incomplete. He asserts that Clifford's analysis leads us away from any understanding of museum objects; instead Clifford prefers to present his understandings of the culture through museum curators in our own modern culture. For Dutton, the goal should be to discover the meanings and significance of objects from the point of view of their original communities, and such meanings will never emerge from critiques of museum exhibitions like Clifford's.

How serious are the inevitable distortions of a museum exhibit? Does the omission of the current historical and global economic context misinform the public? How much context can a museum exhibition realistically provide? If such misrepresentations do occur, would it be better not to exhibit "primitive" art at all? What solutions to the problem of distortion do Clifford and Dutton propose?

Histories of the Tribal and the Modern

During the winter of 1984–85 one could encounter tribal objects in an unusual number of locations around New York City. This [selection] surveys a half-dozen, focusing on the most controversial: the major exhibition held at the Museum of Modern Art (MOMA), " 'Primitivism' in 20th Century Art: Affinity of the Tribal and the Modern." The... "ethnographic present" is late December 1984.

The "tribal" objects gathered on West Fifty-third Street have been around. They are travelers—some arriving from folklore and ethnographic museums in Europe, others from art galleries and private collections. They have traveled first class to the Museum of Modern Art, elaborately crated and insured for important sums. Previous accommodations have been less luxurious: some were stolen, others "purchased" for a song by colonial administrators, travelers, anthropologists, missionaries, sailors in African ports. These non-Western objects have been by turns curiosities, ethnographic specimens, major art creations. After 1900 they began to turn up in European flea markets, thereafter moving between avant-garde studios and collectors' apartments. Some came to rest in the unheated basements or "laboratories" of anthropology museums, surrounded by objects made in the same region of the world. Others encountered odd fellow travelers, lighted and labeled in strange display cases. Now on West Fifty-third Street they intermingle with works by European masters— Picasso, Giacometti, Brancusi, and others. A three-dimensional Eskimo mask with twelve arms and a number of holes hangs beside a canvas on which Joan Miró has painted colored shapes. The people in New York look at the two objects and see that they are alike.

Travelers tell different stories in different places, and on West Fifty-third Street an origin story of modernism is featured. Around 1910 Picasso and his cohort suddenly, intuitively recognize that "primitive" objects are in fact powerful "art." They collect, imitate, and are affected by these objects. Their own work, even when not directly influenced, seems oddly reminiscent of non-Western forms. The modern and the primitive converse across the centuries and continents. At the Museum of Modern Art an exact history is told featuring individual artists and objects, their encounters in specific studios at precise moments. Photographs document the crucial influences of non-Western artifacts

From James Clifford, *The Predicament of Culture: Twentieth-Century Ethnography, Literature, and Art* (Harvard University Press, 1988). Originally published as "Histories of the Tribal and the Modern" in *Art in America* (April 1985). Copyright © 1985 by Brant Publications, Inc. Reprinted by permission of *Art in America*. Notes and references omitted.

on the pioneer modernists. This focused story is surrounded and infused with another—a loose allegory of relationship centering on the word *affinity*. The word is a kinship term, suggesting a deeper or more natural relationship than mere resemblance or juxtaposition. It connotes a common quality or essence joining the tribal to the modern. A Family of Art is brought together, global, diverse, richly inventive, and miraculously unified, for every object displayed on West Fifty-third Street looks modern.

The exhibition at MOMA is historical and didactic. It is complemented by a comprehensive, scholarly catalogue, which includes divergent views of its topic and in which the show's organizers, William Rubin and Kirk Varnedoe, argue at length its underlying premises. One of the virtues of an exhibition that blatantly makes a case or tells a story is that it encourages debate and makes possible the suggestion of other stories. Thus in what follows different histories of the tribal and the modern will be proposed in response to the sharply focused history on display at the Museum of Modern Art. But before that history can be seen for what it is, however—a specific story that excludes other stories—the universalizing allegory of affinity must be cleared away.

This allegory, the story of the Modernist Family of Art, is not rigorously argued at MOMA. (That would require some explicit form of either an archetypal or structural analysis.) The allegory is, rather, built into the exhibition's form, featured suggestively in its publicity, left uncontradicted, repetitiously asserted —"Affinity of the Tribal and the Modern." The allegory has a hero, whose virtuoso work, an exhibit caption tells us, contains more affinities with the tribal than that of any other pioneer modernist. These affinities "measure the depth of Picasso's grasp of the informing principles of tribal sculpture, and reflect his profound identity of spirit with the tribal peoples." Modernism is thus presented as a search for "informing principles" that transcend culture, politics, and history. Beneath this generous umbrella the tribal is modern and the modern more richly, more diversely human.

❦

The power of the affinity idea is such (it becomes almost self-evident in the MOMA juxtapositions) that it is worth reviewing the major objections to it. Anthropologists, long familiar with the issue of cultural diffusion versus independent invention, are not likely to find anything special in the similarities between selected tribal and modern objects. An established principle of anthropological comparative method asserts that the greater the range of cultures, the more likely one is to find similar traits. MOMA's sample is very large, embracing African, Oceanic, North American, and Arctic "tribal" groups. A second principle, that of the "limitation of possibilities," recognizes that invention, while highly diverse, is not infinite. The human body, for example, with its two eyes, four limbs, bilateral arrangement of features, front and back, and so on, will be represented and stylized in a limited number of ways. There is thus a priori no reason to claim evidence for affinity (rather than mere resemblance or coincidence) because an exhibition of tribal works that seem impressively "modern" in style can be gathered. An equally striking collection could be made demonstrating sharp dissimilarities between tribal and modern objects.

The qualities most often said to link these objects are their "conceptualism" and "abstraction" (but a very long and ultimately incoherent list of shared traits, including "magic," "ritualism," "environmentalism," use of "natural" materials, and so on, can be derived from the show and especially from its catalogue). Actually the tribal and modern artifacts are similar only in that they do *not* feature the pictorial illusionism or sculptural naturalism that came to dominate Western European art after the Renaissance. Abstraction and conceptualism are, of course, pervasive in the arts of the non-Western World. To say that they share with modernism a rejection of certain naturalist projects is not to show anything like an affinity. Indeed the "tribalism" selected in the exhibition to resemble modernism is itself a construction designed to accomplish the task of resemblance. Ife and Benin sculptures, highly naturalistic in style, are excluded from the "tribal" and placed in a somewhat arbitrary category of "court" society(which does not, however, include large chieftanships). Moreover, pre-Columbian works, though they have a place in the catalogue, are largely omitted from the exhibition. One can question other selections and exclusions that result in a collection of only "modern"-looking tribal objects. Why, for example, are there relatively few "impure" objects constructed from the debris of colonial culture contacts? And is there not an overall bias toward clean, abstract forms as against rough or crude work?

The "Affinities" room of the exhibition is an intriguing but entirely problematic exercise in formal mix-and-match. The short introductory text begins well: "AFFINITIES presents a group of tribal objects notable for their appeal to modern taste." Indeed this is all that can rigorously be said of the objects in this room. The text continues, however, "Selected pairings of modern and tribal objects demonstrate common denominators of these arts that are independent of direct influence." The phrase *common denominators* implies something more systematic than intriguing resemblance. What can it possibly mean? ... The affinity idea itself is wide-ranging and promiscuous, as are allusions to universal human capacities retrieved in the encounter between modern and tribal or invocations of the expansive human mind—the healthy capacity of modernist consciousness to question its limits and engage otherness.

... The affinities shown at MOMA are all on modernist terms. The great modernist "pioneers" (and their museum) are shown promoting formerly despised tribal "fetishes" or mere ethnographic "specimens" to the status of high art and in the process discovering new dimensions of their ("our") creative potential. The capacity of art to transcend its cultural and historical context is asserted repeatedly. ...

At West Fifth-third Street modernist primitivism is a going Western concern. ...

Indeed an unintended effect of the exhibition's comprehensive catalogue is to show once and for all the incoherence of the modern Rorschach of "the primitive." ... [T]he catalogue succeeds in demonstrating not any essential affinity between tribal and modern or even a coherent modernist attitude toward the primitive but rather the restless desire and power of the modern West to collect the world.

❧

... If we ignore the "Affinities" room at MOMA, however, and focus on the "serious" historical part of the exhibition, new critical questions emerge. What is excluded by the specific focus of the history? Isn't this factual narration still infused with the affinity allegory, since it is cast as a story of creative genius recognizing the greatness of tribal works, discovering common artistic "informing principles"? Could the story of this intercultural encounter be told differently? It is worth making the effort to extract another story from the materials in the exhibition—a history not of redemption or of discovery but of reclassification. This other history assumes that "art" is not universal but is a changing Western cultural category. The fact that rather abruptly, in the space of a few decades, a large class of non-Western artifacts came to be redefined as art is a taxonomic shift that requires critical historical discussion, not celebration. That this construction of a generous category of art pitched at a global scale occurred just as the planet's tribal peoples came massively under European political, economic, and evangelical dominion cannot be irrelevant. But there is no room for such complexities at the MOMA show. Obviously the modernist appropriation of tribal productions as art is not simply imperialist. The project involves too many strong critiques of colonialist, evolutionist assumptions. As we shall see, though, the scope and underlying logic of the "discovery" of tribal art reproduces hegemonic Western assumptions rooted in the colonial and neocolonial epoch.

Picasso, Léger, Apollinaire, and many others came to recognize the elemental, "magical" power of African sculptures in a period of growing *négrophilie,* a context that would see the irruption onto the European scene of other evocative black figures: the jazzman, the boxer (Al Brown), the *sauvage* Josephine Baker. To tell the history of modernism's recognition of African "art" in this broader context would raise ambiguous and disturbing questions about aesthetic appropriation of non-Western others, issues of race, gender, and power. This other story is largely invisible at MOMA.... Overall one would be hard pressed to deduce from the exhibition that all the enthusiasm for things *nègre,* for the "magic" of African art, had anything to do with race. Art in this focused history has no essential link with coded perceptions of black bodies—their vitalism, rhythm, magic, erotic power, etc.—as seen by whites. The modernism represented here is concerned only with artistic invention, a positive category separable from a negative primitivism of the irrational, the savage, the base, the flight from civilization.

A different historical focus might bring a photograph of Josephine Baker into the vicinity of the African statues that were exciting the Parisian avant-garde in the 1910s and 1920s; but such a juxtaposition would be unthinkable in the MOMA history, for it evokes different affinities from those contributing to the category of great art. The black body in Paris of the twenties was an ideological artifact. Archaic Africa (which came to Paris by way of the future—that is,

America) was sexed, gendered, and invested with "magic" in specific ways. Standard poses adopted by "La Bakaire," like Léger's designs and costumes, evoked a recognizable "Africanity"—the naked form emphasizing pelvis and buttocks, a segmented stylization suggesting a strangely mechanical vitality. The inclusion of so ideologically loaded a form as the body of Josephine Baker among the figures classified as art on West Fifty-third Street would suggest a different account of modernist primitivism, a different analysis of the category *nègre* in *l'art nègre* and an exploration of the "taste" that was something more than just a backdrop for the discovery of tribal art in the opening decades of this century.

Such a focus would treat art as a category defined and redefined in specific historical contexts and relations of power. . . .

Since 1900 non-Western objects have generally been classified as either primitive art *or* ethnographic specimens. Before the modernist revolution associated with Picasso and the simultaneous rise of cultural anthropology associated with Boas and Malinowski, these objects were differently sorted—as antiquities, exotic curiosities, orientalia, the remains of early man, and so on. With the emergence of twentieth-century modernism and anthropology figures formerly called "fetishes" (to take just one class of object) became works either of "sculpture" or of "material culture." The distinction between the aesthetic and the anthropological was soon institutionally reinforced. In art galleries non-Western objects were displayed for their formal and aesthetic qualities; in ethnographic museums they were represented in a "cultural" context. In the latter an African statue was a ritual object belonging to a distinct group; it was displayed in ways that elucidated its use, symbolism, and function. The institutionalized distinction between aesthetic and anthropological discourses took form during the years documented at MOMA, years that saw the complementary discovery of primitive "art" and of an anthropological concept of culture." . . .

Cultural background is not essential to correct aesthetic appreciation and analysis: good art, the masterpiece, is universally recognizable. The pioneer modernists themselves knew little or nothing of these objects' ethnographic meaning. What was good enough for Picasso is good enough for MOMA. Indeed an ignorance of cultural context seems almost a precondition for artistic appreciation. In this object system a tribal piece is detached from one milieu in order to circulate freely in another, a world of art—of museums, markets, and connoisseurship.

Since the early years of modernism and cultural anthropology non-Western objects have found a "home" either within the discourses and institutions of art or within those of anthropology. . . . Both discourses assume a primitive world in need of preservation, redemption, and representation. The concrete, inventive existence of tribal cultures and artists is suppressed in the process of either constituting authentic, "traditional" worlds or appreciating their products in the timeless category of "art."

જ⦿ઝ

Nothing on West Fifty-third Street suggests that good tribal art is being produced in the 1980s. The non-Western artifacts on display are located either
in a vague past (reminiscent of the label "nineteenth-twentieth century" that
accompanies African and Oceanian pieces in the Metropolitan Museum's Rockefeller Wing) or in a purely conceptual space defined by "primitive" qualities:
magic, ritualism, closeness to nature, mythic or cosmological aims. In this rel-
egation of the tribal or primitive to either a vanishing past or an ahistorical,
conceptual present, modernist appreciation reproduces common ethnographic
categories.

The same structure can be seen in the Hall of Pacific Peoples, dedicated
to Margaret Mead, at the American Museum of Natural History. This new permanent hall is a superbly refurbished anthropological stopping place for non-
Western objects. In *Rotunda* (December 1984), the museum's publication, an
article announcing the installation contains the following paragraph:

> Margaret Mead once referred to the cultures of Pacific peoples as "a world
> that once was and now is no more." Prior to her death in 1978 she approved
> the basic plans for the new *Hall of Pacific Peoples*. (p. 1)

We are offered treasures saved from a destructive history, relics of a vanishing world. Visitors to the installation (and especially members of *present*
Pacific cultures) may find a "world that is no more" more appropriately evoked
in two charming display cases just outside the hall. It is the world of a dated
anthropology. Here one finds a neatly typed page of notes from Mead's much-
disputed Samoan research, a picture of the fieldworker interacting "closely"
with Melanesians (she is carrying a child on her back), a box of brightly colored discs and triangles once used for psychological testing, a copy of Mead's
column in *Redbook*. In the Hall of Pacific Peoples artifacts suggesting change
and syncretism are set apart in a small display entitled "Culture Contact." It is
noted that Western influence and indigenous response have been active in the
Pacific since the eighteenth century. Yet few signs of this involvement appear
anywhere else in the large hall, despite the fact that many of the objects were
made in the past 150 years in situations of contact, and despite the fact that
the museum's ethnographic explanations reflect quite recent research on the
cultures of the Pacific. The historical contacts and impurities that are part of
ethnographic work—and that may signal the life, not the death, of societies—are
systematically excluded.

The tenses of the hall's explanatory captions are revealing. A recent color
photograph of a Samoan *kava* ceremony is accompanied by the words: "STATUS
and RANK were [sic] important features of Samoan society," a statement that
will seem strange to anyone who knows how important they remain in Samoa
today. Elsewhere in the hall a black-and-white photograph of an Australian
Arunta woman and child, taken around 1900 by the pioneer ethnographers
Spencer and Gillen, is captioned in the *present* tense. Aboriginals apparently

must always inhabit a mythic time. Many other examples of temporal incoherence could be cited—old Sepik objects described in the present, recent Trobriand photos labeled in the past, and so forth.

The point is not simply that the image of Samoan *kava* drinking and status society presented here is a distortion or that in most of the Hall of Pacific Peoples history has been airbrushed out. (No Samoan men at the *kava* ceremony are wearing wristwatches; Trobriand face painting is shown without noting that it is worn at cricket matches.) Beyond such questions of accuracy is an issue of systematic ideological coding. To locate "tribal" peoples in a nonhistorical time and ourselves in a different, historical time is clearly tendentious and no longer credible (Fabian 1983). This recognition throws doubt on the perception of a vanishing tribal world, rescued, made valuable and meaningful, either as ethnographic "culture" or as primitive/modern "art." . . .

At the Hall of Pacific Peoples or the Rockefeller Wing the actual ongoing life and "impure" inventions of tribal peoples are erased in the name of cultural or artistic "authenticity." Similarly at MOMA the production of tribal "art" is entirely in the past. Turning up in the flea markets and museums of late nineteenth-century Europe, these objects are destined to be aesthetically redeemed, given new value in the object system of a generous modernism.

❦

The story retold at MOMA, the struggle to gain recognition for tribal art, for its capacity "like all great art... to show images of man that transcend the particular lives and times of their creators," is taken for granted at another stopping place for tribal travelers in Manhattan, the Center for African Art on East Sixty-eighth Street. Susan Vogel, the executive director, proclaims in her introduction to the catalogue of its inaugural exhibition, "African Masterpieces from the Musee de l'Homme, " that the "aesthetic-anthropological debate" has been resolved. It is now widely accepted that "ethnographic specimens" can be distinguished from "works of art" and that within the latter category a limited number of "masterpieces" are to be found. Vogel correctly notes that the aesthetic recognition of tribal objects depends on changes in Western taste. For example it took the work of Francis Bacon, Lucas Samaras, and others to make it possible to exhibit as art "rough and horrifying [African] works as well as refined and lyrical ones." Once recognized, though, art is apparently art. Thus the selection at the Center is made on aesthetic criteria alone. A prominent placard affirms that the ability of these objects "to transcend the limitations of time and place, to speak to us across time and culture... places them among the highest points of human achievement. It is as works of art that we regard them here and as a testament to the greatness of their creators."

There could be no clearer statement of one side of the aesthetic anthropological "debate" (or better, *system*). On the other (anthropological) side, across town, the Hall of Pacific Peoples presents collective rather than individual productions—the work of "cultures." At the American Museum of Natural History ethnographic exhibits have come increasingly to resemble art shows. Indeed the Hall of Pacific Peoples represents the latest in aestheticized scientism. Objects are displayed in ways that highlight their formal properties.... While these artistically displayed artifacts are scientifically explained, an older, functionalist attempt to present an integrated picture of specific societies or culture areas is no longer seriously pursued. There is an almost dadaist quality to the labels on eight cases devoted to Australian aboriginal society (I cite the complete series in order): "CEREMONY, SPIRIT FIGURE, MAGICIANS AND SORCERERS, SACRED ART, SPEAR THROWERS, STONE AXES AND KNIVES, WOMEN, BOOMERANGS." Elsewhere the hall's pieces of culture have been recontextualized within a new cybernetic, anthropological discourse. For instance flutes and stringed instruments are captioned: "MUSIC is a system of organized sound in man's [sic] aural environment" or nearby: "COMMUNICATION is an important function of organized sound."

In the anthropological Hall of Pacific Peoples non-Western objects still have primarily scientific value. They are in addition beautiful. Conversely, at the Center for African Art artifacts are essentially defined as "masterpieces," their makers as great artists. The discourse of connoisseurship reigns. Yet once the story of art told at MOMA becomes dogma, it is possible to reintroduce and co-opt the discourse of ethnography. At the Center tribal contexts and functions are described along with individual histories of the objects on display. Now firmly classified as masterpieces, African objects escape the vague, ahistorical location of the "tribal" or the "primitive." The catalogue, a sort of *catalogue raisonné,* discusses each work intensively. The category of the masterpiece individuates: the pieces on display are not typical; some are one of a kind. The famous Fon god of war or the Abomey shark-man lend themselves to precise histories of individual creation and appropriation in visible colonial situations. Captions specify *which* Griaule expedition to West Africa in the 1930s acquired each Dogon statue.... We learn in the catalogue that a superb Bamileke mother and child was carved by an artist named Kwayep, that the statue was bought by the colonial administrator and anthropologist Henri Labouret from King N'Jike. While tribal names predominate at MOMA, the Rockefeller Wing, and the American Museum of Natural History, here personal names make their appearance.

In the "African Masterpieces" catalogue we learn of an ethnographer's excitement on finding a Dogon hermaphrodite figure that would later become famous. The letter recording this excitement, written by Denise Paulme in 1935, serves as evidence of the aesthetic concerns of many early ethnographic collectors. These individuals, we are told, could intuitively distinguish masterpieces from mere art or ethnographic specimens. (Actually many of the individual ethnographers behind the Musée de l'Homme collection, such as Paulme, Michel Leiris, Marcel Griaule, and André Schaeffner, were friends and collaborators of the same "pioneer modernist" artists who, in the story told at MOMA, constructed the category of primitive art. Thus the intuitive aesthetic sense in question is the product of a historically specific milieu.) The "African Masterpieces" catalogue insists that the founders of the Musée de l'Homme were art connoisseurs, that this great anthropological museum never treated all its contents as "ethnographic specimens." The Musee de l'Homme was and is secretly an art museum. The taxonomic split between art and artifact is thus healed, at least for self-evident "masterpieces," entirely in terms of the aesthetic code. Art is art in any museum. . . .

The non-Western objects that excited Picasso, Derain, and Léger broke into the realm of official Western art from outside. They were quickly integrated, recognized as masterpieces, given homes within an anthropological-aesthetic object system. By now this process has been sufficiently celebrated. We need exhibitions that question the boundaries of art and of the art world, an influx of truly indigestible "outside" artifacts. The relations of power whereby one portion of humanity can select, value, and collect the pure products of others need to be criticized and transformed. This is no small task. In the meantime one can at least imagine shows that feature the impure, "inauthentic" productions of past and present tribal life; exhibitions radically heterogeneous in their global mix of styles; exhibitions that locate themselves in specific multicultural junctures; exhibitions in which nature remains "unnatural"; exhibitions whose principles of incorporation are openly questionable. The following would be my contribution to a different show on "affinities of the tribal and the postmodern." I offer just the first paragraph from Barbara Tedlock's superb description of the Zuni Shalako ceremony, a festival that is only part of a complex, living tradition.

> Imagine a small western New Mexican village, its snow-lit streets lined with white Mercedes, quarter-ton pickups and Dodge vans. Villagers wrapped in black blankets and flowered shawls are standing next to visitors in blue velveteen blouses with rows of dime buttons and voluminous satin skirts. Their men are in black Stetson silver-banded hats, pressed jeans, Tony Lama boots and multicolored Pendleton blankets. Strangers dressed in dayglo orange, pink and green ski jackets, stocking caps, hiking boots and mittens. All crowded together they are looking into newly constructed houses illuminated by bare light bulbs dangling from raw rafters edged with Woolworth's red fabric and flowered blue print calico. Cinderblock and plasterboard white walls are layered with striped serapes, Chimayó blankets, Navajo rugs, flowered fringed embroidered shawls, black silk from Mexico and purple, red and blue rayon from Czechoslovakia. Rows of Hopi cotton dance kilts and rain sashes; Isleta woven red and green belts; Navajo and Zuni silver concha belts and black mantas covered with silver brooches set with carved lapidary, rainbow mosaic, channel inlay, turquoise needlepoint, pink agate, alabaster, black cannel coal and bakelite from old '78s, coral, abalone shell, mother-of-pearl and horned oyster hang from poles suspended from the ceiling. Mule and white-tailed deer trophy-heads wearing squash-blossom, coral and chunk-turquoise necklaces are hammered up around the room over rearing buckskins above Arabian tapestries of Martin Luther King and the Kennedy brothers, The Last Supper, a herd of sheep with a haloed herder, horses, peacocks.

NO ⤶

Denis Dutton

Mythologies of Tribal Art

Forty years ago Roland Barthes defined a mythology as those "falsely obvious" ideas which an age so takes for granted that it is unaware of its own belief. An example of what he means can be seen in his 1957 critique of Edward Steichen's celebrated photographic assemblage "The Family of Man." Barthes declares that the myth this exhibition promotes first seems to stress exoticism, projecting a Babel of human diversity over the globe. From this picture of diversity, however, a pluralistic humanism "is magically produced: man is born, works, laughs and dies everywhere in the same way...." The implicit mythological background of the show postulates "a human essence."

Barthes is exactly on target about the philosophic intentions of "The Family of Man." In his introduction to the published version of the exhibition, Steichen had written that the show was "conceived as a mirror of the universal elements and emotions in the everydayness of life—as a mirror of the essential oneness of mankind throughout the world." Such juxtapositions as that which places Nina Leen's *Life* magazine image of an American farm family next to a family in Bechuanaland (now Botswana), photographed by another *Life* photographer, Nat Farbman, are therefore meant to convey the idea that despite all differences of exterior form, of cultural surface, the underlying nature of all families and peoples is essentially the same. This position is what Barthes views as the sentimentalized mythology of "classic humanism," and he contrasts it with his own "progressive humanism," which must try "constantly to scour nature, its 'laws' and its 'limits' in order to discover History there, and at last to establish Nature itself as historical." While classic humanism regards the American and African families as embodying, beneath culture and skin color, abiding natural relationships of kin and affection, progressive humanism would insist that these bourgeois conceptions of the natural are themselves historically determined. Barthes claims that such imperialistic juxtapositions ignore the political and economic roots of diversity.

Although "The Family of Man" had a potently relevant message for the generation that had witnessed the genocidal horrors of the Second World War, it was also worth paying attention to Barthes's claim that Steichen's collection, for all its antiracism and humanist charms, conveyed an implicit illusion

From Denis Dutton, "Mythologies of Tribal Art," *African Arts*, vol. 28, no. 3 (Summer 1995). Copyright © 1995 by The Regents of the University of California. Reprinted by permission of *African Arts*. Notes and references omitted.

of equality of power among the cultures it portrayed. It is now two generations later, however, and critics who accept the importance of exposing cultural mythologies and covert ideologies have new work to do. One area of criticism that especially stands in need of fresh examination is the shell-pocked field where battles have raged over the status and understanding of ethnographic arts. Barthes's reaction to MOMA's "The Family of Man" is particularly pertinent in this regard, because much of what he says adumbrates reactions to another exhibition, " 'Primitivism' in 20th Century Art," which took place over a quarter of a century later in that same museum. That show displayed side-by-side images of Africa and Europe, not photographs of people, but works of art. And it too was denounced as complacently positing, without regard to cultural difference, a specious universalism—aesthetic instead of moral.

But a sea change in academic thinking separates Barthes's critique of "The Family of Man" from the more strident critics of the "Primitivism" show. In the middle 1950s, Barthes was nearly alone in his dissent against a much loved and widely praised exhibition. The generation of critics who questioned (or denounced) "Primitivism" represented a manner of thinking that had become a virtual academic fashion. Some of these later critics were arguing from a set of ideas that had themselves come to embody a virtual mythology in precisely the Barthesian sense. Their views presuppose and constitute, in point of fact, a New Mythology of tribal arts—a prevailing set of presuppositions, prejudices, and articles of political and philosophical faith which govern many discussions of these arts and their relations to European criticism, art, and aesthetics. A contemporary Africanist art historian [Sidney Kasfir] for example, writes in a recent *African Arts* article on the authenticity of African masks and carvings: "That from an African perspective, these objects are *not* art in the current Western sense is too well known to discuss here. The phrase "too well known to discuss here" is symptomatic of a mythology. Barthes claimed his intention to unmask "the mystification which transforms petit-bourgeois culture into universal nature." Today we should be just as willing to deal with those mystifications that transform prevailing conventions of academic culture into validated truth.

This vigorous New Mythology of tribal arts takes on its life against the backdrop of what it posits as the Old Mythology. As with other ideologies, the New Mythology would no more describe its precepts as "mythology" than would the Old: both operate according to the familiar adage "Your views are so much mythology; mine speak the truth." Nevertheless, much contemporary theorizing and criticism about tribal arts are founded on a complacent acceptance of a substrate of givens and unsupported hypotheses which constitute the central tenets of the New Mythology. To be sure, not all of the theses are false. On the other hand, not all of the beliefs the New Mythologists stigmatize as Old Mythology are false either. Independent, critical thinkers should want to choose the component ideas of these mythologies that are worth rejecting, preserving, or reviving.

Providing a disinterested assessment of these ideas is not easy in the present ideologically charged and factious atmosphere. This indeed is part of the problem: so many contemporary theorists of tribal arts posit enemies who have it all wrong, in contrast to themselves, who have it right. This lack of any generosity whatsoever toward one's perceived (or invented) opposition increasingly stultifies writing in this area. The New Mythology finds itself expressed by a wide range of writers, including, for example, the more vociferous critics of the "Primitivism" show such as Thomas McEvilley and Hal Foster; James Clifford in his treatment of museums and ethnographic art; Arnold Krupat in *Ethnocriticism;* Sidney Kasfir in her article "African Art and Authenticity," published in this journal; Sally Price in *Primitive Art in Civilized Places;* Marianna Torgovnick in *Gone Primitive;* and Christopher B. Steiner in *African Art in Transit.*

Mythologies, Old and New

There are actually two phases of the Old Mythology to which these writers tend to react. What I will call *premodernist* or *colonialist* Old Mythology includes the elements of nineteenth-century imperialism—racism, contempt for "childish" artifacts, and regard for "primitive" art as representing a lower evolutionary stage of human development, with missionaries burning "fetishes" and the wholesale looting of indigenous art, as in Benin. The later, more enlightened, *modernist* Old Mythology, exemplified by such figures as Picasso, Roger Fry, and the "Primitivism" exhibition itself, is, from a New Mythological perspective, perhaps even more insidious, because while it pretends to valorize these arts, it perpetuates acts of imperialism, appropriation, and ethnocentric insensitivity toward Third World peoples—all in the name of enlightened, magnanimous liberalism. The grounds for my three-fold distinction—between premodernist/colonialist Old Mythology, modernist Old Mythology, and the New Mythology —can be usefully developed in terms of the following key ideas. Again, some of these notions included within these mythologies are entirely valid, some constitute half-truths, and some are plainly false; no one of these sets of ideas has a monopoly on truth.

> (1) According to the premodernist Old Mythology, at least as the New Mythology likes to imagine it, tribal artifacts weren't works of art at all, but merely "fetishes," "idols," "fertility symbols," "ancestor figures," and the like, which colonialists collected as they might botanical specimens. The later, post-Picasso modernist version of the Old Mythology insists, on the contrary, that they are works of art, embodying universal aesthetic values.

Curiously, the New Mythology frequently sides with the colonialist Old Mythology by aggressively questioning the status of tribal artifacts as works of art: in the New Mythological view, the Old Mythology at least acknowledged difference. This convergence of opinion, however, is complicated. Philistine colonialists often regarded artifacts as demonstrating little skill and no sense of form: the colonialists were applying nineteenth-century European aesthetic criteria to genres of work they did not begin to comprehend, and so were reluctant to call them "art." The New Mythologists' reluctance to identify tribal artifact genres as "art" is based on the notion that this would be hegemonic or imperialistic. Such reluctance is frequently supported by unthinking repetition of the folk legend that pretechnological peoples have no art because they have no word that refers to what Europeans call "art." Patrick R. McNaughton recognizes another aspect of this New Mythologists' doctrine and has stressed the importance of challenging it, "because so many scholars still recite what has become a kind of maxim asserted by outsiders about Africans, that they unlike us treat what we call art as a functional part of life" rather than something for aesthetic contemplation.

(2) The Old Mythology essentialized the primitive, subsuming the endless variety of tribal cultures under a few crude stereotypes.

The New Mythology, on the other hand, while eager to recognize the diverse and frequently unique characteristics that distinguish tribal societies, essentializes "the West," creating, in an inversion of Edward Said's familiar formulation, a kind of Occidentalism. Thus, in the example cited earlier, Kasfir qualifies her discussion of authenticity with the remark that the artifacts in question should not be considered art "in the current Western sense." The quaintness of this last phrase should not go unnoticed: among Praxiteles, Donatello, Rembrandt, Judy Chicago, Duchamp, and Koons—not to mention the myriad genres of European folk craft and popular art—there is no "current Western sense" of art, but various, radically different, and rival senses of the concept, each partially implicated in competing social practices and theories of art. In fact, in its crudity, the very phrase "the West" is the New Mythologists' answer to "the Primitive" as that term might have been used a century ago. The latter was a lazy and misleading way of lumping together such cultures as Hopi, Sepik, Benin, and !Kung—even Aztec, in some understandings of "primitive." In the New Mythology, "the West" refers to twelfth-century French villages, horror movies, the Industrial Revolution, the theology of St. Augustine, New Zealand public education, the international banking system, modern toy retailing, medieval concepts of disease, Thanksgiving dinner, electronic mail, Gregorian chants, Linnaean botany, napalm, the Chopin études, and bar codes —as though the values and ideologies found therein can be the subject of useful generalization. The New Mythology replaces one set of stereotypes with another set, equally banal.

(3) In the Old Mythology, precontact tribal societies were seen as largely isolated, unchanging, coherent, and unbroken in their cultural tradition. Colonialism was supposed to have destroyed their structure and belief base. Their Golden Age of aesthetic and cultural achievement, and hence authenticity, predates European contact. Postcolonial culture and artifacts are culturally "inauthentic."

The New Mythology asserts to the contrary that these societies never were isolated, were not necessarily "unified" or "coherent," and underwent profound breaks in their traditions before European contact. The Old Mythology's "people without a history" view was a convenient colonialist construction. The New Mythology responds to claims of "inauthenticity" by variously claiming

(a) indigenous belief systems were not destroyed but only occulted during the colonial period, and are now coming again into flower; (b) what is truly authentic is now found in the process of mutual appropriation by indigenous and colonial cultures; and in any event, (c) authentic cultural values must always be defined by the people who hold them: therefore, whatever indigenous people claim as authentic is, *ipso facto,* authentic, whether traditional, postcolonial, or merely imported.

Old and New Mythologists for the most part agree that small-scale indigenous societies have been permanently altered or obliterated by the encounter with the West's political systems, media, missionaries, technology, commerce, wage labor, and so forth. New Mythologists, however, are especially keen to emphasize that this has involved imperialist domination and exploitation. What is awkward for them is the fact that less desirable elements of culture change have been enthusiastically (and voluntarily) embraced by many indigenous peoples: cigarettes, soft drinks, movies, pop music, and Jack Daniels. By stressing that tribal cultures were always borrowing and in a state of flux, the New Mythology places in benign perspective the obliteration (or active abandonment) of traditional indigenous values: all cultures, it seems, are in the process of being altered by history.

(4) The Old Mythology, especially in its colonial form, held it unproblematic that traders or travelers might buy or barter for artifacts. Alternatively, artifacts might be accepted as gifts. None of this disturbs their meanings in the Old Mythology, and if anything the native should be thankful for receiving payment for the work before the termites got to it.

The New Mythology sees buying, selling, and trading as essentially Western concepts. Even to accept these objects as gifts is to become, as Kasfir puts it, implicated in "the web of conflicting interests that surround them." There is hence no "noninterventionist" way of obtaining these artifacts, since somewhere in the scheme power relations will obtrude, leading to the exploitation of the indigenous maker or owner of the object. In other words, the native always gets cheated. The New Mythology seems to impute to precontact tribal societies a premercantile edenic state, as though trade and barter (not to mention theft or conquest) of ritual or other valuable artifacts did not occur among these peoples until Europeans came along.

(5) The only reason to collect primitive artifacts, according to premodernist Old Mythology, was as curiosities, examples perhaps of an early stage of Social Darwinist development: they were to be placed in a cabinet alongside fossils and tropical insects. After Picasso & Co., the Old Mythology proclaimed that primitive art embodied the aesthetic sensibilities found in all art, and therefore was as much worth collecting as Constables or Utamaros, and for precisely the same reasons.

The New Mythology displays an oddly ambivalent attitude toward collecting. On the one hand, collecting is persistently disparaged, for instance as a "hegemonic activity, an act of appropriation... a largely colonial enterprise... the logical outcome of a social-evolutionary view of the Other." McEvilley speaks of "captured" tribal objects, a trope suggesting they exist in Western collections as prisoners or slaves. Given the reprehensible nature of collecting, one would expect New Mythologists to demand that the trade in ethnographic art cease, but I have not encountered any such suggestions (except, of course, for the criminal trade in looted antiquities. Even those writers who take moral satisfaction from criticizing collecting appear themselves to have "captured" the occasional artifact.

(6) On puritanical grounds the Old Mythology often forbade taking pleasure in works of tribal art: the sexual element in carvings offended missionary and nineteenth-century colonial sensibilities. In New Zealand, as elsewhere, genitals were hacked off Maori figures, and some overtly sexual carvings were simply burned, lest prurient pleasure be aroused.

The New Mythology replaces this attitude with a new and asexual form of puritanism. Enjoyment of any sort derived from the experience of ethnographic art is considered a cultural mistake at best, a form of visual imperialism at worst: "the colonialist gaze." Angst-ridden New Mythologists are reluctant to record appreciation or enthusiastic emotional reactions to artifacts. Thus Torgovnick heaps contempt on Roger Fry, among many others, for his "insensitive" and "racist" readings in praise of African art, but she never provides, in her own voice, nonracist, sensitive readings to instruct us on how to do it right. Nicholas Thomas is simply bemused: of the museums crammed with indigenous artifacts —"carved bowls, clubs, spears, baskets, pots," etc.—he honestly admits that "I have never understood why people want to look at such things (although I often look at them myself)." Christopher B. Steiner makes the bizarre claim that the objects are valued by Westerners as a way to "celebrate" the loss of the utility they had in their original cultural contexts. Other New Mythologists, such as James Clifford and James Boon (whose article title "Why Museums Make Me Sad" is clear enough), write about ethnographic arts with such a brooding sense of guilt about the historical treatment of conquered cultures that no sense of joy or love for the art is ever allowed to emerge.

(7) Colonialist Old Mythology held that though primitive cultures were to some degree capable of adopting Western technologies and manufactured articles, they could not possibly understand Western culture. In fact, having no adequate comparative perspective, the primitives could not even fully understand their own cultures. Their simple little societies were, however, transparent to the educated, sophisticated Westerner.

The New Mythology, on the contrary, contends that it is the "educated" West which fails to grasp the vast subtleties offered by these cultures, ranging from ethnobotany and folk medicines to spiritual wisdom. Instead, the West ethnocentrically imposes on them its own categories, such as "individual," "religion," or "work of art," when in actuality these concepts have no place in the cultural landscape of the Other. In the matter of borrowing, the New Mythology holds that indigenous artists are, in its preferred parlance, free to appropriate from European culture, infusing their new work with "transformed meanings," fresh associations given to foreign elements introduced into a new cultural context. The reverse—Europeans borrowing from indigenous arts—is to be discouraged. This inversion of the Old Mythology means that an innovative Sepik dancer who incorporates cigarette wrappers in an elaborate headdress is participating in an exciting fusion of cultures, while a Swedish office-worker who wears a New Guinea dog-tooth necklace is implicated in hegemonic, colonialist appropriation.

As a frontispiece for *Gone Primitive,* Torgovnick presents a heavily ironic, not to say sneering, painting (by Ed Rihacek) of a stylish European woman wearing sunglasses and sitting before a zebra skin, surrounded by a collection of "primitive art." In his derisory essay on the "Primitivism" exhibition, Clifford reproduces a 1929 photograph of Mrs. Pierre Loeb, seated in her Paris apartment filled with Melanesian and African carvings. Clifford labels this as an "appropriation" which was "not included in the 'Primitivism' Show" (a curious observation inasmuch as this very photograph appears in the show's catalogue). Both of these images suggest a kind of disapproval of European cultural appropriation that it would be unthinkable to direct toward their cultural inversion —for example, the 1970s posed village photograph Susan Vogel has published showing a Côte d'Ivoire man seated before a wrinkled, painted backdrop of an airplane, a cassette radio proudly displayed on his lap.

> (8) *The Old Mythology at its colonialist worst posited an ethnocentric aesthetic absolutism: advanced, naturalistic European art forms were seen, especially because of their naturalism, as demonstrating a higher stage in the evolution of art. Modernist Old Mythology retained the idea of universal aesthetic standards, but argued that tribal arts fully met these criteria for excellence, which were formalist rather than naturalistic.*

In rejecting both these positions, some New Mythologists urge the abandonment of any idea of transcultural aesthetic criteria (which would be implicitly imperialistic) in favor of complete aesthetic relativism. McEvilley imputes to Kant an epistemology which "tacitly supported the violent progress of 19th- and 20th-century imperialisms" and which justified a view of the Western aesthetic sense as superior to that of non-Western cultures. The New Mythology owes its aesthetic relativism entirely to the climate of poststructural thought rather than to any empirical study of ethnographic and other world arts.

> (9) *More generally, both colonialist and modernist Old Mythologies imply or presuppose an epistemic realism: they both presume to describe the actual, existent characteristics of tribal societies and their arts.*

Under the influence of poststructuralism, the New Mythology often presupposes various forms of constructivism, the idea that categories of human existence are constituted entirely by our own mental activity: we "invent" or "construct" the "primitive," tribal "art," "religion," and so on. The knots into which theorists become tied in trying to introduce such poststructural rhetoric into the study of indigenous arts is illustrated by Barbara Kirshenblatt-Gimblett who writes: "Ethnographic artifacts are objects of ethnography. They are artifacts created by ethnographers. Objects become ethnographic by virtue of being defined, segmented, detached, and carried away by ethnographers." From her first sentence, a dictionary definition, Kirshenblatt-Gimblett deduces a constructivist howler: the trivial fact that ethnographers define the ethnographic status of artifacts does not entail that *they create the artifacts*. Nor do they create the artifacts' meanings; it is the people being studied who determine that, and this awkward reality gets obviously in the way of attempts by New Mythologists to relativize cultural knowledge and meaning. Constructivism is a strong force among New Mythologists most influenced by literary theory, and is less persistent among those who come from a background of academic anthropology. Despite their tendency to toy with the jargon of literary theory, anthropologists generally acquire a robust respect for the independent existence and integrity of the peoples they study.

> *(10) Finally, premodernist Old Mythology, especially in its Victorian colonialist guises, preached the superiority of Western culture. It proposed to bring moral enlightenment to people it viewed as savages, mainly through Christianity, but also with science and modern medicine. In this, it stands starkly apart from modernist Old Mythology, and even from some eighteenth-century explorers of the South Pacific, who claimed that the moral sense and intellectual capacities of "primitive man" were at least equal to those of Europeans.*

The air of smug moral superiority has returned with a vengeance with the arrival of the New Mythology, whose champions patronize, censure, and jeer at any Old Mythology text they find wanting. The New Mythology of tribal arts displays a sense of righteous certitude that would fit the most zealous Victorian missionary.

At Play in the Fields of the Text

In some respects, the New Mythology's frequent borrowing from poststructuralism and the general intellectual climate of postmodernism is healthy and appropriate. For example, the approach to tribal arts must necessarily involve "blurred genres" and fused disciplines, bringing together ethnography, art history, philosophical aesthetics, and general cultural, including literary, criticism. This is fully in the poststructural/postmodern spirit, as is calling into question the peculiarly European distinction between the so-called fine arts and the popular and folk arts and crafts, which normally has no clear application in understanding tribal arts. But there are other aspects of poststructuralism which sit uneasily with the study of tribal arts.

One such notion is the pervasive poststructuralist attack on the authority of the artist or author in aesthetic interpretation. Barthes, whose thinking was again seminal in this regard, proclaimed the death of the god-author, along with the end of the ideologies of objectivity and truth, insisting that the meaning of a literary text is a critical construction instead of a discovered fact. In the theory of literature and the practice of criticism, such constructivist ideas have had their uses, liberating criticism from traditional demands to invoke authorial intention as a validating principle for critical interpretation.

However, the poststructural abandonment of the notion that texts contain meanings placed there by their authors (which it is criticism's job to determine) is only possible in a cultural landscape in which there is enough prior agreement on meanings to allow criticism to become thus freely creative. The poststructural death of the author could only take hold in literary theory because there was already in place an extensive tradition of interpretation of, say, *Madame Bovary* or *Moby Dick*. These novels enjoy a canonical status as works of literary art: they observe the conventions of established genres and were written in European languages by recognized literary artists. The cultural conditions that form the context of their creation and reception are solid enough to enable a generation of critics—notably Barthes, Foucault, and Derrida, but also the New Critics of the Anglo-American world—to declare the hypothetical death of the author and advocate a liberated, creative criticism of *jouissance*.

But do these doctrines and strategies of contemporary theory provide useful models for the critical ethnography of indigenous arts? Hardly. Poststructuralism's image of the free-spirited critic at play in textual fields goes counter to one of the most strongly held (indeed, in my opinion, indispensable) principles of the New Mythology: respect for the autonomous existence of tribal artists, including respect for their intentions and cultural values. Declaring the death of the (European) author may be jolly sport for jaded literary theorists, but an analogous ideological death of the tribal artist is not nearly so welcome in the New Mythology, nor should it be in any anthropology department. The study of tribal arts—indeed, all non-Western arts—cannot presuppose a sufficiently stable, shared background understanding against which one might declare artists' intentions irrelevant or passé. Moreover, the New Mythology gains its sense of identity by pitting itself against what it takes to be the Old Mythology's ethnocentric disregard not only for the intentions of tribal artists but for their very names as well. (Price calls this "the anonymization of Primitive Art," and it was a major complaint lodged against the" 'Primitivism' in 20th Century Art" exhibition. If such ethnocentrism is not to be actively encouraged, the tribal artist's interpretations *must* enjoy special status, defining in the first instance the object of study. In order to respect the cultures and people from which tribal works of art are drawn, the New Mythology must treat indigenous intentions—ascertained or, where unavailable, at least postulated—as constituting the beginning of all interpretation, if not its exhaustive or validating end.

This deep conflict between doctrines of the New Mythology and the poststructuralism it seems so eager to appropriate keeps breaking out despite efforts to paper it over. McEvilley and Clifford enthusiastically adopt the discourse of constructivism, so long as they are talking about how "we," or "the West," or the "omniscient" curatorial mind, construct the generalized primitive, but New Mythologists are not nearly so keen to revert to constructivist parlance when it comes to discussing the actual meanings of works of tribal art. Thus Kasfir asks, "Who creates meaning for African art?," where "for" indicates "on behalf of," implying that Western collectors and exhibitors make a meaning for African art to satisfy the Western eye and mind.

This, however, avoids the more obvious wording of the question "Who creates the meaning *of* African art?" If there is any answer at all to this question, it must begin with the artists and cultures that produce the art. The West can "construct" in the poststructuralist manner to its heart's content, but its understandings will always be about the indigenous constructions of the cultures from which African works derive. It is indigenous intentions, values, descriptions, and constructions which must be awarded theoretical primacy. If an African carving is intended by its maker to embody a spirit, and that is an ascertainable fact about it, then any ethnography that constructs its meaning in contradiction to that fact is false. Of course, ethnography need not culminate with indigenous meanings and intentions, any more than literary criticism comes to an end when an author's intended meaning for a work of fiction has been determined. But ethnography has no choice except to begin with indigenous meanings, which it does not construct, but discovers.

POSTSCRIPT

Do Museums Misrepresent Ethnic Communities Around the World?

Clifford, like many critical theorists, is deeply suspicious of all representations of others. Dutton, in contrast, seems to question both the motives and the logic of this suspicion. He is especially critical of Clifford's lack of historical accuracy when describing the goals and motivations of museums and their curators. Are Clifford's postmodernist conclusions guilty of misrepresenting the museum world in ways that parallel his critique of particular exhibits? Does Dutton's critique of the postmodernists solve the historical problems that are present in both museums and the writings of their critics? Is there a middle ground that would allow for exhibitions with more sensitive context?

Clifford has also dealt with museum exhibits in his book *Routes: Travel and Translation in the Late Twentieth Century* (Harvard University Press, 1997). Related approaches to the problem of representation in museums include Sally Price's *Primitive Art in Civilized Places* (University of Chicago Press, 1989) and Shelly Errington's *The Death of Authentic Primitive Art and Other Tales of Progress* (University of California Press, 1998).

Nicholas Thomas's *Entangled Objects: Exchange, Material Culture and Colonialism in the Pacific* (Harvard University Press, 1991) considers the problem of representation among ethnographic objects in the Pacific. Enid Schildkraut and Curtis A. Keim's *The Scramble for Art in Central Africa* (Cambridge University Press, 1998); Ruth B. Phillips and Christopher B. Steiner's *Unpacking Culture: Art and Commodity in Colonial and Post Colonial Worlds* (University of California Press, 1999); and Michael O'Hanlon and Robert L. Welsch's *Hunting the Gatherers: Ethnographic Collectors, Agents, and Agency in Melanesia* (Berghahn, 2000) provide examples of the rich historical context of museum collections of the sort Dutton seeks.

Both Clifford and Dutton build their arguments on the premise that objects have complex histories, an idea that was originally developed in slightly different ways by anthropological historian George W. Stocking, Jr.'s *Objects and Others: Essays on Museums and Material Culture* (University of Wisconsin Press, 1985) and by anthropologist Arjun Appadurai's *The Social Life of Things: Commodities in Cultural Perspective* (Cambridge University Press, 1986). Both books make two crucial points: objects have histories, and the meanings of objects change when the objects themselves move from one context to another. Also, both argue that objects can take on many different meanings depending on context and viewpoint. Together these books have redefined museological studies and transformed what had been an anthropological backwater into a thriving specialization within the discipline.

On the Internet . . .

DUSHKIN ONLINE

American Anthropological Association Code of Ethics

Created by the American Anthropological Association, the largest organization of anthropologists in the world, this site provides a code of ethics for its members and a handbook on ethical issues faced by anthropologists.

http://ameranthassn.org/committees/ethics/ethics.htm

Kennewick Man

This site contains an article on the controversy following the discovery of the bones of a 8,400-year-old man, now called Kennewick Man. The article discusses whether the bones, which do not appear to be Native American, should be protected under the Native American Graves Protection and Repatriation Act (NAGPRA) and therefore be reburied. Links are provided to previous articles that give further information from both sides of the debate on Kennewick Man.

http://www.archaeology.org/9701/etc/specialreport.html

Female Mutilation Education and Networking Project

This site provides an explanation of female circumcision and gives recent news on the topic. This site also presents a number of perspectives and provides links to further information.

http://www.fgmnetwork.org/index.html

PART 4

Ethics in Anthropology

*T*he ethical treatment of other peoples has come to play an increasingly important role in contemporary anthropology. Ethical issues directly affect how cultural anthropologists should treat their living human subjects. But similar issues also affect archaeologists and biological anthropologists because the artifacts of past communities often represent the ancestors of living communities. A skeleton preserved and ready for study may be the human remains of someone's dead relative. Here the interests of anthropologists and native peoples diverge, and we ask whether such bones should be reburied to respect the dead or if they should be studied for science. Similarly, we may ask what the ethical responsibilites of Western anthropologists should be when they find certain cultural practices abhorrent or unjust. Should anthropologists work to change these practices? All of these issues raise questions about how involved anthropologists should become with the peoples with whom they work. Should anthropologists take a passive, objective, and even scientific position or should they use what they know to support or change these native communities?

- Should the Remains of Prehistoric Native Americans Be Reburied Rather Than Studied?

- Should Anthropologists Work to Eliminate the Practice of Female Circumcision?

- Do Anthropologists Have a Moral Responsibility to Defend the Interests of "Less Advantaged" Communities?

ISSUE 17

Should the Remains of Prehistoric Native Americans Be Reburied Rather Than Studied?

YES: James Riding In, from "Repatriation: A Pawnee's Perspective," *American Indian Quarterly* (Spring 1996)

NO: Clement W. Meighan, from "Some Scholars' Views on Reburial," *American Antiquity* (October 1992)

ISSUE SUMMARY

YES: Assistant professor of justice studies and member of the Pawnee tribe James Riding In argues that holding Native American skeletons in museums and other repositories represents a sacrilege against Native American dead and, thus, all Indian remains should be reburied.

NO: Professor of anthropology and archaeologist Clement W. Meighan believes that archaeologists have a moral and professional obligation to the archaeological data with which they work. Such data is held in the public good and must be protected from destruction, he concludes.

$\mathbf{F}$rom the beginning, the relationship between Native Americans and anthropologists in the United States has been an uncertain one, ranging from mutually cooperative to overtly hostile in which Native Americans deeply mistrust anthropologists and feel that Native American culture is exploited.

Native American activists have invoked concerns about religious freedom, arguing that the excavation of bones is a desecration, a violation of native rights, and a sacrilege against Native American religion. These individuals and organizations demanded the immediate return and reburial of all Native American skeletons currently held in public museums and other repositories. They objected both to the exhibition of the remains and to research on remains by physical anthropologists. Many Native Americans have pointed out that the same museums that exhibit Native American skeletons do not simultaneously display the bones of white Americans.

Responding to the concerns of Native Americans, in 1990 the U.S. Congress enacted the Native American Graves Protection and Registration Act (NAGPRA), which mandates that all public collections of Native American remains must be returned to relatives or descendants for reburial. The return of bones and material culture has come to be called "repatriation."

James Riding In, himself a Pawnee, argues that anthropologists and archaeologists have consistently desecrated graves by excavating and studying the bones of Native Americans. He begins his discussion by outlining the history of many public museum collections of Native American skulls. Many of these, he maintains, were war dead from the Indian Wars of the 1870s, and they should have been reburied on the spot. Riding In says that Native Americans believe that the bodies of the dead must be reunited with "Mother Earth."

Anthropologist Clement W. Meighan counters that the debate over what should be done with bones from archaeological excavations is a conflict between science and religion. In the case of very early prehistoric sites, there is usually no evidence that links living tribes inhabiting the surrounding areas with the early community; many of these groups would either be unrelated to living tribal members or might even be the remains of enemy groups.

For Meighan the requirements of science must be defended, and the unraveling of humankind's prehistory in the New World is of public interest to all Americans, whether Native or not. He contends that the public's right to know about the past is important, and any reburial of archaeological material represents the destruction of scientific data that can never be recovered. Arguing that political motives are at the heart of Native American claims to religious interest in archaeological remains, Meighan views reburial as an attempt to censor archaeological and anthropological findings that conflict with Native American legends and myths.

Although NAGPRA has been the official law of the land for a decade, there remain many contentious concerns about just which bones should be repatriated and how they should be treated both legally and professionally. Riding In and Meighan raise a number of questions about the interests of science and Native American religions. Are Native American religious beliefs more important than those of secular scientists? Do archaeologists desecrate Native American sacred sites whenever they excavate? Should the religious concerns of one ethnic or cultural community override either the professional concerns of another group or the intellectual rights of the general public? Who should control information about the past? Who should control depictions of any ethnic group's past?

James Riding In  **YES**

Repatriation: A Pawnee's Perspective

$\mathbf{M}$y opposition to scientific grave looting developed partially through the birth of the American Indian repatriation movement during the late 1960s. Like other American Indians of the time (and now), I viewed archaeology as an oppressive and sacrilegious profession that claimed ownership over many of our deceased relatives, suppressed our religious freedom, and denied our ancestors a lasting burial. My first encounter with an archaeologist occurred at a party in New Mexico in the late 1970s. After hearing him rant incessantly about the knowledge he had obtained by studying Indian remains, burial offerings, and cemeteries, I suggested that if he wanted to serve Indians he should spend his time excavating latrines and leave the graves alone. Of course, he took umbrage at the tone of my suggestion, and broke off the conversation. While studying history at the University of California, Los Angles [UCLA] in the mid-1980s, I became committed to pursuing the goals of the repatriation movement, which was gaining momentum. Like other reburial proponents, I advocated the reburial of all Indian remains warehoused across the nation in museums, universities, and federal agencies. I also promoted the extension or enactment of laws to protect Indian cemeteries from grave looters, including archaeologists.

While working to elevate the consciousness of the UCLA campus about the troubled relationship between archaeologists and Indians, a few of us, including students, staff, faculty, and community members, took advantage of opportunities to engage in dialogue with the anti-repatriation forces. During these exchanges, tempers on both sides often flared. Basically, the archaeologists were functioning on metaphysical and intellectual planes that differed from ours. We saw their professional activities as sacrilege and destructive, while they professed a legal and scientific right to study Indian remains and burial goods. We wanted the university to voluntarily return the human remains in its collections to the next-of-kin for proper reburial. They desired to protect excavation, research, and curatorial practices. Asserting profound respect for Indian concerns, beliefs, and values, members of the archaeology group offered a host of patronizing excuses for refusing to endorse our calls for repatriation. In this sense, the UCLA struggle mirrored the conflict over human remains ensuing throughout much of the country. In 1989, as the UCLA battle ensued, I accepted an offer to assist the Pawnee government in its efforts as a

From James Riding In, "Repatriation: A Pawnee's Perspective," *American Indian Quarterly*, vol. 20, no. 2 (Spring 1996). Copyright © 1996 by The University of Nebraska Press. Reprinted by permission. Notes omitted.

sovereign nation to reclaim the remains of its ancestors held at the Smithsonian Institution. Being a citizen of this small and impoverished nation of Indians, I welcomed the opportunity to join other Pawnee activists in the repatriation quest. Earlier that year, Congress had enacted a repatriation bill that provided a legal mechanism for Indian governments to reclaim ancestral remains and burial offerings held at the Smithsonian.

Despite the law, obdurate Smithsonian personnel sought to frustrate Indian repatriation efforts with such tactics as stonewalling, deceit, and misinformation. Although Smithsonian personnel claimed that the true identities of six skulls classified as Pawnee could not be positively established, subsequent research on my part uncovered a preponderance of evidence confirming the authenticity of the accession records. This research also showed that, after U.S. soldiers and Kansas settlers had massacred a party of Pawnee men who had been recently discharged from the U.S. army, a Fort Harker surgeon had collected some of the victims' skulls in compliance with army policy and shipped them to the Army Medical Museum for craniometric study

Since that report, I have written articles, given presentations, and, in conjunction with others, conducted research on behalf of Pawnee repatriation initiatives at Chicago's Field Museum of Natural History. I also have written a report from information found in the Native American Graves Protection and Repatriation Act (NAGPRA) summary letters showing the location of additional Pawnee remains, sacred objects, objects of cultural patrimony, and cultural artifacts.

This essay offers some of my views concerning the reburial aspect of the repatriation struggle. It seeks to show the intellectual and spiritual foundations behind the movement as a means for understanding the complexity of the controversy. It also attempts to demonstrate how repatriation advocates managed to effect discriminatory laws and practices. Finally, it conveys a message that, although old attitudes continue to function within the archaeology and museum communities, a concerted effort brought to bear by people who espouse cooperative relations is in place to bring Indian spiritual beliefs in conformity with non-Indian secular values.

At another level, I write with the intent of creating awareness about a pressing need to disestablish racial, institutional, and societal barriers that impede this country's movement toward a place that celebrates cultural diversity as a cherished and indispensable component of its social, political, and economic fabric. Despite the tone of skepticism, caution, and pessimism found within this study, I envision a society where people can interact freely, respecting one another without regard to race, color, ethnicity, or religious creed. Before this dream becomes a reality, however, America has to find ways to dissolve its racial, gender, cultural, and class barriers.

Pawnee Beliefs, Critical Scholarship, and Oppression

The acts committed against deceased Indians have had profound, even harmful, effects on the living. Therefore, as an activist and historian, I have had to develop a conceptual framework for giving meaning and order to the conflict. The foundation of my perspective concerning repatriation is derived from a combination of cultural, personal, and academic experiences. An understanding of Pawnee religious and philosophical beliefs about death, gained through oral tradition, dreams, and research, informs my view that repatriation is a social justice movement, supported by native spirituality and sovereignty, committed to the amelioration of the twin evils of oppression and scientific racism. Yet, I am neither a religious fundamentalist nor a left- or right-wing reactionary. Concerning repatriation, I simply advocate that American Indians receive what virtually every other group of Americans enjoys; that is, the right to religious freedom and a lasting burial.

My training as critical scholar provides another cornerstone of my beliefs about the nature of "imperial archaeology." My writings cast the legacy of scientific body snatching within the realm of oppression. Oppression occurs when a set or sets of individuals within the dominant population behave in ways that infringe on the beliefs, cultures, and political structures of other groups of people. Acts of stealing bodies, infringing on spirituality, and resisting repatriation efforts represent classic examples of oppression.

Although exposed to years of secular interpretations about the nature of the world and the significance of archaeology for understanding the past through formal Euroamerican education, I have continued to accept Pawnee beliefs about the afterlife. To adopt any other perspective regarding this matter would deny my cultural heritage. I cannot reconcile archaeology with tradition because of the secular orientation of the former as well as its intrusive practices. Unlike archaeologists who see Native remains as specimens for study, my people view the bodies of deceased loved ones as representing human life with sacred qualities. Death merely marks the passage of the human spirit to another state of being. In a 1988 statement, then Pawnee President Lawrence Goodfox Jr. expressed a common perspective stressing the negative consequences of grave desecration on our dead: "When our people die and go on to the spirit world, sacred rituals and ceremonies are performed. We believe that if the body is disturbed, the spirit becomes restless and cannot be at peace."

Wandering spirits often beset the living with psychological and health problems. Since time immemorial, Pawnees have ceremoniously buried our dead within Mother Earth. Disinterment can occur only for a compelling religious reason. Equally critical to our perspective are cultural norms that stressed that those who tampered with the dead did so with profane, evil, or demented intentions. From this vantage point, the study of stolen remains constitutes abominable acts of sacrilege, desecration, and depravity. But racist attitudes, complete with such axioms as "The only good Indian is a dead Indian," have long conditioned white society to view Indians (as other non-whites) as intellectually inferior subhumans who lacked a right to equal treatment under legal and moral codes. Complicating matters, value judgments about the alleged superiority of the white race became interlocked with scientific thought, leading to the development of oppressive practices and policies.

Consequently, orgies of grave looting occurred without remorse. After the Pawnees removed from Nebraska to Oklahoma during the 1870s, local settlers, followed by amateur and professional archaeologists, looted virtually every Pawnee cemetery they could find, taking remains and burial offerings. Much of the "booty" was placed in an array of institutions including the Nebraska State Historical Society (NSHS) and the Smithsonian Institution.

We have a right to be angry at those who dug our dead from the ground, those who established and maintained curatorial policies, and those who denied our repatriation requests. Last year, my elderly grandmother chastised white society in her typically reserved, but direct fashion for its treatment of our dead. After pointing to an Oklahoma bluff where many Pawnee relatives are buried, she declared, "It is not right, that they dug up all of those bodies in Nebraska." What she referred to can be labeled a spiritual holocaust. When anyone denies us our fundamental human rights, we cannot sit idly by and wait for America to reform itself. It will never happen. We have a duty not only to ourselves, but also to our relatives, our unborn generations, and our ancestors to act. Concerning repatriation, we had no choice but to work for retrieval of our ancestral remains for proper reburial and for legislation that provided penalties for those who disrupted the graves of our relatives.

Yet our initiatives sought redress in a peaceful manner. In 1988, Lawrence Goodfox expressed our goals, declaring "All we want is [the] reburial of the remains of our ancestors and to let them finally rest in peace and for all people in Nebraska to refrain from, forever, any excavation of any Native American graves or burial sites." In our view, reburying the disturbed spirits within Mother Earth equalizes the imbalance between the spiritual and physical worlds caused by the desecration.

National Challenges to Imperial Archaeology and Oppression

The Pawnee reburial struggle occurred within the context of a worldwide indigenous movement. What beset my people had affected Natives everywhere. In this country, few Indian nations escaped the piercing blades of the archaeologists' shovels or the slashes of the headhunters' knives. These operations infringed on Indian beliefs, burial rights, and sovereignty. The notion that this type of research had validity was so ingrained in the psyche of many non-Indians that rarely did anyone question the morality, ethics, or legality of these practices; that is, until the repatriation movement surfaced in the late 1960s. This movement stands on a paramount footing with the valiant struggles of African-Americans for civil rights and women for equality. Taking a leading role during the early stages of the repatriation movement, organizations such as the American Indian Movement (AIM), International Indian Treaty Council, and American Indians Against Desecration (AIAD) expressed in dramatic fashion Indian concerns about the excesses of archaeology and oppression. Committed to the causes of reburying all disinterred Indians and stopping grave disruptions, these groups often employed confrontational strategies. Near Welch, Minnesota, in 1972, for example, AIM members risked arrest by disturbing a dig site. In addition to burning field notes and tools, they confiscated unearthed artifacts and exposed photographic film. Throughout the 1970s and

1980s, AIAD challenged the human remains collections and curatorial policies of government agencies, museums, and universities. As time progressed,
many college campuses saw a dramatic increase in tensions between Indians
and archaeologists. These actions catapulted the repatriation movement into
the consciousness of sympathetic politicians, newspaper editors, and members
of the general public. Increased knowledge of the issues subsequently spawned
unprecedented levels of non-Indian backing of repatriation.

As the 1980s progressed, more conciliatory Indians, often coming from
the professions of law and politics, surfaced as leading figures in the movement. Unlike the universal reburial advocates, these moderates tended to see
compromise as the most expedient means available to acquire the desired legislation. They often sought a balance between scientific study of Native remains
and the need for Indians to gain religious, burial, and repatriation rights under
the law. Organizations such as the National Congress of American Indians and
the Native American Rights Fund espoused the moderate cause. Realizing that
public sentiments increasingly favored the Indians' views, some archaeologists
and museum administrators endorsed compromise as a means of cutting their
losses and saving face. With common ground beneath their feet, individuals and
organizations waged a series of intense political battles at the state and federal
levels.

With moderates in control, reform transpired relatively swiftly. By 1992,
more than thirty states had placed laws on the books extending protection to Indian cemeteries, including several with repatriation provisions. Congress passed
two pieces of legislation, the National Museum of the American Indian Act in
1989 and NAGPRA the following year. Collectively, these national laws provided
Indian nations a means to obtain human remains linked to them by a "preponderance of evidence" and associated funerary offerings held by institutions
that received federal funding. NAGPRA also provides penalties for individuals
convicted of trafficking in human remains.

Ongoing Reburial Initiatives

With legal avenues now open for Indian governments to reclaim stolen ancestral remains and associated burial objects, some of the old repressive policies
fell by the wayside The change enabled relatives to begin the task of reclaim-
ing stolen bodies and grave offerings for reburial. Collectively, Indian nations
thus far have interred thousands of stolen remains. To date (summer 1995), the
Pawnees alone have placed nearly a thousand bodies back in Mother Earth. The
total number of recovered bodies will surely reach the tens of thousands within
a few years.

Reinterment ceremonies, along with funeral feasts, evoke a gamut of emotional expressions ranging from sorrow to joy. When conducting reburials,
people rejoice at the fact that the repatriated remains are finally being returned
to Mother Earth, but, like modern funerals, an air of sadness pervades the ceremonies. In particular, reinterring the remains of young children causes grieving
and weeping. Mourning is part of the healing process in that reburials seek to

restore harmony between the living and dead by putting restless spirits to rest. At another level, reburials bring closure to bitterly contested struggles.

Future Concerns

Legislation emanating from the repatriation movement has changed the customary ways that archaeologists and museums operate. Most notably, Indian governments now have established a sovereign right to reclaim the bodies of their ancestors from offending museums, universities, and federal agencies. In this capacity, they have the power to grant and deny access to their dead. Additionally, the new laws make face-to-face interaction routine between museums and Indian nations in certain repatriation matters. Several observers have proclaimed that the common ground signals the dawning of a new era of cooperative relations between Indians and museums. Despite changing attitudes and practices, it is too soon to assess the long-term ramifications of the reburial controversy. Six problematic areas cause me concern about the future of repatriation:

First, the laws do not provide for the reinterment of ancient, unclaimed, or unidentified remains. In other words, the fate of tens of thousands of bodies, along with associated funerary offerings, is uncertain. Will those with authority take steps to provide for a proper reburial for these bodies or will they allow the continuance of old practices and policies?

Second, the absence of legislation and aggressive enforcement of burial protection laws in some states may send a message that grave looting can resume without fear of arrest, prosecution, or punishment.

Third, NAGPRA's graves protection stipulations apply only to federal lands and entities that receive federal funding. In states without both progressive reburial legislation and a substantial Indian populace, large-scale acts of grave desecration may continue....

Fourth, and perhaps most significant a pervasive attitude among elements of the archaeology and museum communities keeps repressive and archaic ideas alive. In fact, members of these groups have consistently disavowed any wrongdoing by themselves and their predecessors. Rather, some present their work to the public as neutral, impartial, and objective interpretations of distant Native American cultures. To counter claims that the digging and study is disrespectful, others assert that taking remains for study shows respect for Indian people and culture. In a twisted logic, still others insist that they are the "true spiritual descendants of the original Indians and the contemporary Indians [are] foreigners who had no right to complain about their activities." Like most other repatriation advocates, I reject these pleas as condescending and duplicitous acts of misguided people and lost souls....

Anti-repatriation advocates echoed a common refrain. They viewed their pursuits as being under attack by narrow-minded and anti-intellectual radicals who sought to destroy archaeology. Equating repatriation with book burning, some alarmists often charged falsely that Indians would not rest until they had stripped museums and universities of their Indian collections. These strategies contain elements of self-delusion, arrogance, and racism. A tacit message found in these paternalistic defenses of imperial archaeology was that Indians must, for their own good, learn to respect the work of archaeology. Equally disturbing is the notion that Indians need archaeology. However, the exact opposite is true. Beneath the self-serving rhetoric lay a deceptive ambiance of cultural imperialism that masked the stark reality of how archaeology and museums infringed on Indian religion and burial rights.

Fifth, imperial archaeologists have had substantial levels of support from real and pretend Indians. The phenomena of co-optation and self- interest reverberates loudly here. Usually found working in museums, universities, and government agencies, some of these individuals claim a heritage complete with a Cherokee princess, but they embrace the secular views and values of Western science. Others belonging to this camp clearly have significant amounts of Indian blood, but they rely heavily on the goodwill of their non-Indian colleagues to promote and maintain their careers. Non-institutional advocacy surfaced from some grassroots Indians. At meetings, conferences, and confrontations, archaeologists rarely failed to produce a reservation Indian or two who spoke passionately against reburial in an effort to convince the public and policy makers that Native communities lacked unanimity on the subject. Whatever their motive, degree of Indian blood, or cultural orientation, their willingness to endorse oppressive archaeological practices marks a radical departure from traditional Indian philosophy.

Collectively, "wannabes" and misguided Indians may be able to damage reburial efforts. As the movement pushed for national repatriation legislation in the late 1980s, we found them sitting on committees convened by anthropology and museum associations that issued reports condemning repatriation. In a worst-case scenario, NAGPRA and other committees stacked with them and imperial archaeologists could conceivably frustrate or undermine repatriation requests.

Finally, it seems that archaeologists have launched a campaign to convince the public, tribal leaders, and others that skeletal investigations are necessary for a variety of reasons. According to a recent *Chronicle of Higher Education* article, "More and more of those kinds of opportunities will occur, many scholars agree, when researchers learn to persuade American Indians and others that skeletal remains and artifacts represent something other than a publication toward a faculty member's promotion and tenure." In other words, we are seeing archaeologists adopt less abrasive tactics to get their hands on our dead. Succumbing to subtle pressure, aimed at convincing us to accept a secular view of the dead as research objects, will erode a cherished part of our belief systems and cultures. In any event, some Indian nations have allowed the creation of archaeology programs on their reservations.

Clearly, the repatriation movement has won some major victories, but the war is unfinished. United States history teaches the lesson that individuals who face the threat of losing a privileged status often will devise rationalizations and strategies to resist change. Southern slave owners, for example, argued against abolitionism by making the outlandish claim that involuntary servitude was a benevolent institution that saved millions of blacks from the savagery of Africa. Historians repeated this claim well into the twentieth century.

It is conceivable that at some point someone will challenge the constitutionality of NAGPRA. If this occurs, will the courts respect Indian beliefs and burial rights? America's long history concerning issues of Indian religious freedom and political rights makes the possibility of a legal suit a scary thought. The Supreme Court has occasionally protected Indian sovereignty, as well as hunting, fishing, and water rights, but it also has incorporated such imperialistic notions as the doctrine of discovery and the plenary power doctrine into U.S. law. Its decisions also have eroded the power of Indian self-government by allowing the imposition of federal jurisdiction over certain crimes committed on Indian lands.

In recent years, conservative justices appointed by President Ronald Reagan have endangered Indian religious freedom. In *Lyng v. Northwest Indian Cemetery Protective Association* (108 S. Ct. 1319 (1988)) Justice Sandra Day O'Connor wrote the majority decision stating that the U.S. government had the right to build a road through an area on federal lands sacred to Yurok, Karok, and Tolowa Indians even if such a construction project would destroy the ability of those people to worship. In *Employment Division Department of Human Resources of Oregon v. Smith* (110 S. Ct. 1595 (1990)) the court held that a state could abridge expressions of religious freedom if the state had a compelling reason to do so. In this case, the court paved the way for states to deprive Native American Church (NAC) members of the right to use peyote in connection with their worship. Fortunately, in 1994, Congress addressed the religious crisis caused by the court by enacting a law that sanctioned peyote use for NAC services.

History demonstrates that promises made by white America to help Indians have not always materialized. The administrative branch of the federal government has entered into 371 treaties with Indian nations and systematically violated each of them. The legislative record is another cause of concern. The Indian Reorganization Act of 1934 authorized Indian nations to restructure themselves politically but only in accordance with models and terms acceptable to Department of Interior officials. During the 1970s, Congress declared that Indian government could exercise more powers of self-government. Federal bureaucratic controls over Indian governments, however, actually became more stringent, if not suffocating, in this era. During that decade, Congress also enacted the American Indian Religious Freedom Act of 1978 in a half-hearted effort to encourage federal agencies to accommodate customary Indian worship practices at off-reservation sites. The act provided virtually no protection because federal agencies and the Supreme Court, as we have seen, have followed a tradition that sees nothing wrong with suppressing Indian religious freedom. Although Indians are pursing a legislative remedy to resolve these problems, Congress has yet to enact a true religious freedom law for them.

Conclusion

Facing overwhelming odds, the repatriation movement has achieved many noteworthy successes. United States society, including a growing number of sympathetic archaeologists and museum curators, has finally recognized that Indians are not disappearing, and that Indians are entitled to burial rights and religious freedom. Nevertheless, under the new repatriation laws, many non-Indian entities still "legally" hold thousands of Indians remains and burial offerings. With many archaeologists and museum curators committed to upholding oppressive operational principles, values, and beliefs, the fate of these bodies remains in question. Moreover, others, perhaps best described as wolves in sheeps' clothing, are seeking to gain our cooperation, a euphemism meaning the delivery of another blow to our revered philosophies about the dead.

Given the durability of imperialist archaeology and the new approaches being used to gain access to the remains of our beloved ancestors, we must remain vigilant and monitor their operations. Protecting our dead must remain a moral and spiritual obligation we cannot callously abandon for we cannot allow further erosions of our beliefs and traditions. Thus a need still exists for maintaining the cultural traditions that inspired the repatriation movement.

NO ↩

Clement W. Meighan

Some Scholars' Views on Reburial

[T]here is something inherently distasteful and unseemly in secreting either the fruits or seeds of scientific endeavors.

— Judge Bruce S. Jenkins

Destruction of archaelogical collections through the demands for reburial presents a serious conflict between religion and science. Archaeologists should not deal with these matters by "compromise" alone, but must sustain their rights and duties as scholars.

The above quotation is from a court case having nothing to do with archaeology, yet if we believe that archaeology is a scientific endeavor we must agree that this statement applies to archaeology as well as medicine, chemistry, or other fields of scholarship. The recent increased attention given to the ethics of scientists and scientific organizations, with news accounts almost weekly in such journals as *Science,* requires archaeologists to examine their basic assumptions about the nature of science and their obligations to scholarship. This is brought forward most forcefully in the debate over the past 20 years about the problems of reburial of archaeological and museum collections.

The discussion by Goldstein and Kintigh (1990) is a valiant effort to unravel some of the strands of conflict inherent in the controversy over the destruction of museum collections in the name of Indian religious beliefs. They seek some sort of middle ground in which scholarly and ethnic concerns can coexist in a constructive way. However, in view of the massive losses of scientific data now legislated by the federal government and some of the states, it needs to be made clear that many archaeologists do not agree with some aspects of the philosophical position taken by Goldstein and Kintigh. In particular, their statement that "We must change the way we do business" (Goldstein and Kintigh 1990:589) is not justified, particularly since their suggestions for change involve the abandonment of scholarly imperatives and the adoption of an "ethical" position that accepts the right of nonscholars to demand the destruction of archaeological evidence and the concealment of archaeological data. Of course, changes in the way archaeology is done will inevitably take place, for both internal (professional) and external (social/legal) reasons. This

From Clement W. Meighan, "Some Scholars' Views on Reburial," *American Antiquity,* vol. 57, no. 4 (October 1992). Copyright © 1992 by The Society for American Archaeology. Reprinted by permission. Some references omitted.

does not mean that the basic rules of scholarly obligations to one's data should change as well.

Goldstein and Kintigh fall into the anthropological trap of cultural relativism. In asserting that we must balance our concerns for knowledge with "our professional ethic of cultural relativism," they argue that our values are not the only values or ethics, but only one legitimate belief system. The implication is that all belief systems are of equal legitimacy, therefore one cannot make a clear commitment to any particular values as a guide to action. However, most individuals do make a commitment to the values that will guide their personal action. Recognizing that other people may have other values does not mean that one must accept those values or compromise his/her own ethical standards. Indeed, the dictionary has a word for believing one way and acting another—it is "hypocrisy."

Those who affiliate with organized groups, whether the Church of the Rising Light or the Society for American Archaeology (SAA), supposedly accept the beliefs and goals of the organization as stated in their by-laws or scriptures. The SAA, as an organization dedicated to scholarly research in archaeology, is bound by the general rules of scholarship that require *honest reporting and preservation of the evidence.* If the research data are subject to censorship, how can there be honest reporting? If the evidence (collections) is not preserved, who can challenge the statements of the researcher? Who can check for misinterpretations, inaccuracies, or bias? Once the collection is destroyed, we have only an affidavit from the researcher; we can believe it or not, but there is no way that additional investigation or new laboratory techniques can be applied to the collection to gain a better understanding of the evidence. The astounding new methods for medical and genetic research on ancient populations require a piece of the bone—pictures and notes won't do. Similarly, laboratory advances in dating and determining the source of artifact materials require that the relevant objects be available for study. Since we commonly proclaim that archaeological collections are unique and irreplaceable, how can we ever justify the conscious and acquiescent destruction of our data?

The suggestion of Goldstein and Kintigh that we balance our own values with the professional ethic of cultural relativism by "compromise and mutual respect" is not realistic. Many archaeologists are not going to compromise away their most fundamental scholarly beliefs. Similarly, many Indian activists are not going to compromise away their beliefs (however unsupported by evidence) that every Indian bone of the past 12,000 years belongs to one of their ancestors. There are some instances in which compromise and mutual respect have led to satisfactory results for both sides; there are many more instances in which these valued qualities have been insufficient to prevent or postpone destruction of important archaeological finds.

Those who want to do away with archaeology and archaeological collections are of course entitled to their beliefs, and they are also entitled to use whatever political and legal machinery they can to bring about their stated goals. Originally, the goals were modest, but they have escalated every year since this discussion began more than 20 years ago, as reviewed by me in an earlier article (Meighan 1984). The present-day goals have repeatedly been made clear. For example, Christopher Quayle, an attorney for the Three Affiliated Tribes, stated in *Harpers* (Preston 1989:68–69): "It's conceivable that some time in the not-so-distant future there won't be a single Indian skeleton in any museum in the country. We're going to put them out of business." The "them" refers in this statement to physical anthropologists, but it is also extended to archaeologists. For example, the recent agreement between state officials in West Virginia and a committee representing Indian viewpoints (a committee which, incidentally, includes non-Indians) states that everything in an ongoing study of a 2,000-year-old Adena mound must be given up for reburial within a year—"everything" includes not only the bones of the mythical "ancestors" of the claimants, but also all the artifacts, the chipping waste, the food refuse, the pollen samples, the soil samples, and whatever else may be removed for purposes of scientific study. While the tax-payers are expected to pay for a 1.8-million-dollar excavation on the grounds that it is in the public interest for archaeological data to be preserved, *nothing* of the tangible archaeological evidence is to be preserved. Meanwhile, Indian activists are paid to "monitor" the excavation, and they were given the right to censor the final report and prevent any objectionable photographs or data from appearing.

If there is any doubt about the goals of the anti-archaeology contingent, consider the case of Dr. David Van Horn, charged with a felony in California for conducting an environmental impact study required by law, and being honest enough to report what he found in the site, including some small bits of cremated bone, which required hours of study by physical anthropologists to identify as human. Is the reporting of a legally mandated salvage excavation a felony? It can be in California, and there are many who would like to make archaeology a crime throughout the United States. Archaeologists who accept these situations or treat them as merely local concerns (apparently the position of most scholarly organizations including the SAA), have not just compromised, they have abandoned scholarly ethics in favor of being "respectful and sensitive" to nonscholars and anti-intellectuals. When the current round of controversy is over, this loss of scientific integrity will be heavily condemned.

So there are some situations in which compromise is not necessarily the best approach, and this is one of them. Archaeologists may well be legislated out of business, and museums may well lose all their American Indian collections, and indeed the Indians have been far more successful than the archaeologists in the political arena. Many archaeologists believe, however, that this should not occur with the happy connivance of the scholarly profession of archaeology. Over 600 of them are members of the American Committee for Preservation of Archaeological Collections (ACPAC), which has argued for over 10 years that archaeology is a legitimate, moral, and even useful profession, and that collections that were legally made should remain in museums as an important part of the heritage of the nation. Bahn may have had this group in mind in his news report on the "first international congress on the reburial of human remains," in his reference to "the extremists, who unfortunately did not attend the congress to put the case for rejecting the whole notion of reburial." Who are these extremists? Neither ACPAC nor any individual known to me has stated that no reburial of any kind should take place; everyone agrees that bones of known relatives should be returned to demonstrable descendants. The disagreement is over remains to which no living person can demonstrate any relationship. Museum materials 5,000 years old are claimed by people who imagine themselves to be somehow related to the collections in question, but such a belief has no basis in evidence and is mysticism. Indeed, it is not unlikely that Indians who have acquired such collections for reburial are venerating the bones of alien groups and traditional enemies rather than distant relatives.

If the present attacks on archaeological data were happening in engineering, medicine, or chemistry, they would not be accepted by the general public since destruction or concealment of the facts in those areas of scientific knowledge can lead to disastrous results for many living people. The general lack of public concern about the attack on archaeology arises from the perception that archaeological conclusions really do not matter—if someone's reconstruction of the ancient past is ridiculous or unsupported by evidence, who cares? It will not affect the daily lives of anyone now alive, no matter what we believe about what happened thousands of years ago. However, the principles of scholarship and scientific evidence are the same in all scholarly research, including archaeology and anthropology, and credibility of conclusions is an essential consideration for any field of scholarship, whether or not there are immediate practical effects of the conclusions that are reached.

In one of the polemics put forward by Indian spokesmen in the student newspaper at the University of California (Los Angeles), those of us on the archaeological faculty were accused of participating in an activity that was comparable to the "killing fields of Cambodia." Even allowing for the juvenile rhetoric characteristic of student newspapers, I was dumbfounded at such a statement. How could I harm any person who had already been dead for thousands of years? How could anything that my studies did with the bones of these ancient people harm any living person? The condemnation seems extreme for a "crime" that is merely a failure to invite mythical descendants to control my research and destroy museum collections held in the public interest. When issues of respect and sensitivity are raised, it needs to be pointed out that these work both ways.

Some Legal Issues: Constitutional Requirements

The first amendment states that Congress shall make no laws respecting an establishment of religion. Most state constitutions have similar clauses; that of California says the state will *never* pass such laws. Yet California, other states, and the federal government have numerous laws on the books that are specifically written to favor aboriginal tribal religious beliefs and compel others to act in accordance with them. Religious infringement also occurs when archaeologists are excluded from evaluating claims regarding repatriation because they do not hold particular religious beliefs. Until these statutes are challenged and overturned, they remain an opening for other groups to seek similar legislation making their religious beliefs enforceable by law. Creationists, for example, have been trying for over 60 years to outlaw the teaching of evolution because it is in conflict with their religious tenets.

That there is a science vs. religion aspect is clear in the religious justification for the claiming of bones and "sacred" artifacts, as well as the proclamation of many activists that archaeologists and museums are committing sacrilege in obtaining, storing, and studying archaeological remains. I discuss bone worship elsewhere (Meighan 1990). Tonetti (1990) provides a case study of the situation in Ohio, documenting the religious roots of the anti-archaeology movement. He also reports a survey of Ohio legislators that reveals a frightening ignorance of science in general and archaeology in particular: "As Zimmerman so dramatically stated in his op ed piece in the Columbus Dispatch, he does not want the General Assembly making law dealing with science issues when over 75% do not know what his 5 year old son has known for years—that dinosaurs and humans did not coexist" (Zimmerman (1989), as quoted in Tonetti [1990:22]; recent news reports state that some Indians are now claiming dinosaur bones recovered by paleontologists).

Some Legal Issues: Cultural-Resource Laws

There is a serious conflict between the laws mandating return and destruction of archaeological material (not just bones but also artifacts and anything deemed "ceremonial" by the claimants), and those laws mandating cultural-resource management and the study and conservation of archaeological sites and remains. The Van Horn case previously mentioned put Van Horn in the position of doing an environmental-impact report required by law, only to find himself spending thousands of dollars defending himself against a felony charge for violating laws based on Indian religious beliefs about cremated bones. The judge agreed with defense witnesses that there was no basis for a trial, but the state made its point that archaeologists will be heavily punished if "Indians" request it, regardless of the validity of their complaint.

The legal dichotomy between science and religion as it pertains to archaeology may be related, as Goldstein and Kintigh (1990:589) point out, to the fact that public perception does not include Indian history as part of the history of the United States, even though they recognize that public policy and law include the non-European past as an integral part of the history of the nation. That part of American history that is Indian history is largely the contribution of archaeology; *all* of it prior to 1492 is the contribution of archaeology. This has been recognized and supported by the government since the Antiquities Act of 1906, and it is the basis for all the environmental-impact laws dealing with archaeological remains.

Many opponents of archaeological-resource laws believe that since archaeology has no effect on public health or safety, it ought to be excluded from environmental impact laws. They are given considerable ammunition by laws that state that it is in the public interest to spend a lot of money to get archaeological materials, and then state that such materials are not worth preservation but are to be reburied as soon as possible after they are dug up, in some cases within a few days or weeks of the fieldwork. Further, the belief that archaeology belongs to Indians removes it from the heritage of all of the citizens and makes it less likely that the public will be interested in supporting activities not seen to be in the broad public interest. In these times of stringent budgets, it is hard enough to convince the taxpayers that they should finance archaeological excavations without having to convince them that they should also finance the reburial of the items recovered.

There are major negative results for archaeology in the present situation where not only the federal government, but states, counties, cities, and a plethora of political agencies believe that they should pass regulations controlling archaeological research. These laws and regulations conflict with one another and vary from jurisdiction to jurisdiction. In some states the conduct of archaeological research is a risky business. The smart archaeologist in California does not find certain things. If they are found, they are either thrown away or not mentioned in his/her reports. Field classes are also careful not to expose students or teachers to criminal charges, meaning that students in those classes will never expose a burial or deal with any "controversial" finds. Chipping waste is still a safe area for study.

This chilling effect on research is creating an underground archaeology of ill-trained students, dishonest researchers, and intimidated teachers who are afraid to show a picture of a burial to their classes, let alone an actual human bone. Students, who are often more perceptive than their professors, rapidly catch on and change their major or move their archaeological interests to parts of the world where they will be allowed to practice their scholarly profession. There is an increasing loss to American archaeology, and of course to the Indians whose history is dependent on it.

Some Museum Issues

A negative effect of the ongoing shift to tribalism and the right of anyone to claim anything in museums is already happening. In the past, most of the support for museums came from private donors, who contributed not only money but collections. Donors of collections had the tacit (and sometimes written) agreement that their materials would be preserved in the public interest. Who would contribute anything to a museum if they thought the museum was going to give their material away for reburial or destruction? When even Stanford University and other respected repositories of scientific collections decide that their first obligation is to whatever Indian claimant comes along, the donor who wants his/her material *preserved* will seek a repository in a state or country that is dedicated to that aim. It is a paradox that the National Park Service is busily developing new standards of curation for government collections at the same time the new National Museum of the American Indian is declaring that it will not keep anything that Indian claimants declare that they want.

Reviewers of this article believe that only a very small part of archaeological collections will be taken away from museums and archaeologists. This is a pious hope in view of the escalation of claims previously noted, reaching the apex in the West Virginia case in which *everything* recovered by archaeologists is to be given up for reburial. There are numerous cases in which archaeologists or museum employees have given up entire collections rather than negotiate with Indian claimants; for example, one prominent California case (the Encino excavation) included reburial of a number of dog skeletons, not required by any statute. It is true that the Smithsonian and some other museums now have committees to evaluate claims against their collections; perhaps these will protect scholarly and public interests, but it remains to be seen whether they can withstand the political pressures brought to bear. While I am sure that not all collections will entirely disappear, under current legislation all physical remains, all mortuary associations, and all items claimed to have religious or ceremonial significance are at risk—these are the major sources of information in many archaeological studies. When claimants can get museum specimens merely by using the word "sacred," it should be apparent that anything can be claimed by someone. It does happen, it has happened, and scholars can only hope that it will not happen in the future.

Conclusions

When scholarly classes in United States archaeology and ethnology are no longer taught in academic departments (they are diminishing rapidly), when the existing collections have been selectively destroyed or concealed, and when all new field archaeology in the United States is a political exercise rather than a scientific investigation, will the world be a better place? Certainly the leadership in archaeological research, which has been characteristic of the last 50 years of American archaeology, will be lost, and it will be left to other nations to make future advances in archaeological methods, techniques, and scholarly investigations into the ancient past.

One reviewer of this paper commented that I am engaged in a "futile attempt to resurrect a bankrupt status quo." In this view, not only can nothing be done to improve the present situation, but nothing *should* be done, and we should all meekly accept the regulations, limitations, and restrictions of academic freedom that are brought forward by politicians and pressure groups. For the last 20 years, those who have attempted to change these restrictions in favor of scholarly ethics and the preservation of collections have been dismissed as a small group of outmoded discontents who cannot adapt to a changing world. This is a mistake; I may represent a minority view, but it is not confined to a small number and is growing rapidly as archaeologists see more and more of their basic data destroyed through reburial. ACPAC's 600 members (in 44 states) include a sizeable fraction of the leading archaeologists in the United States as well as physical anthropologists, museum workers, and yes, Indians.

I am, however, triggered by the accusation that my comments lead to nothing but intransigence to offer a few suggestions for action other than "compromise," which so far has mostly meant giving in to political demands. My suggestions:

1. Archaeologists negotiating with Indians or other groups should make an effort to be sure that *all* factions of the affected group are heard, not merely the group of activists who are first in the door. Many archaeologists have been doing this for years, and nearly all of us can report that we had little difficulty in finding Indians who would work

with us in a mutually agreeable and often rewarding relationship that respected Indian interests but at the same time preserved the archaeological collections. Unfortunately, numerous instances can be cited of savage personal attacks on those Indians who agreed to share the archaeologists' task, with attempts to force the archaeologist to use other consultants and claims that the one chosen was not a real Indian (see an example in Tonetti [1990:21]). When money is involved, this is probably inevitable. However, there is no reason for archaeologists to be controlled by enemies of their discipline when they can work with friends. The existence of Indian physical anthropologists, archaeologists, and museum workers, as well as the increasing number of Indian-owned museums with scientific objectives and high standards of curation, should offer opportunities for real collaboration that do not require the destruction of evidence nor the censorship of scientific reporting.

2. Professional organizations should work to amend the legislation dealing with archaeology to get a time cut-off inserted: Remains older than a certain age should not be subject to reburial. The present laws, which ignore time and assume that everything, regardless of age, is directly related to living people, are not scientifically valid, and the scientific organizations are in a position to make this clear, if necessary in court. The recent reburial of an Idaho skeleton dated at 10,600 years ago should never have happened, but as reported by the State Historic Preservation Office of that state, Idaho law requires *no* demonstration of any relationship between Indians and archaeological remains.

3. Professional organizations should point out the disagreements between "preservation" laws and "religion" laws and should try to strengthen the former and eliminate the conflicts. If they are unable to resolve the issue by negotiation, they should support court cases that address the matter.

4. If scholarly organizations are unwilling or unable to make a clear statement of their position with respect to the giving up of archaeological collections and data, it is left to the individual archaeologist to decide his or her own professional ethics in this matter. A clear review of the moral issues is given by Del Bene (1990). This should be considered, particularly by young archaeologists entering the profession, so that they are consciously aware of the decisions they are making and the consequences for their professional future.

References

Del Bene T.A. 1990. Take the Moral Ground: An Essay on the "Reburial" Issue. *West Virginia Archeologist* 42(2):11–19.

Goldstein, L., and K. Kintigh. 1990. Ethics and the Reburial Controversy. *American Antiquity* 55:585–591.

Meighan, C.W. 1984. Archaeology: Science or Sacrilege? In *Ethics and Values in Archaeology,* edited by E.L. Green, pp. 203–233. Free Press, New York.

———. 1990. Bone Worship. *West Virginia Archeologist* 42(2):40–43.

Preston, D.J. 1989. Skeletons in Our Museums' Closets. *Harpers.* February: 66–75.

Tonetti, A.C. 1990. Ghost Dancing in the Nineties: Research, Reburial and Resurrection Among the Dead in Ohio. *West Virginia Archeologist* 42(2):20–22.

POSTSCRIPT

Should the Remains of Prehistoric Native Americans Be Reburied Rather Than Studied?

Since these two selections were written, many Native American groups have requested the return of human remains from museums, and these bones have been reburied. Other groups have expressed little interest in recovering the remains of ancestors or skeletons excavated from their lands because they do not share the same cultural beliefs as those expressed by Riding In. A number of museum curators and archaeologists have taken a much more tempered and conciliatory approach to dealing with these issues than the position expressed by Meighan.

Such possibilities suggest that there are a variety of alternative approaches to the issue of reburial besides the diametrically opposed positions expressed here. Many groups, both from museums and universities, have urged compromise. A number of Native American groups have also tried to find ways to accommodate anthropological interests without sacrificing their own rights. Several contentious issues remain. What should be done with the remains of prehistoric Native Americans who have no known living descendants or cultural groups? Should the religious beliefs of one group of Native Americans stand for the rights of all groups? Should modern Native American communities have rights to rebury any human remains found on their lands? What should happen to the remains of the very earliest settlers in North America who are unlikely to be biologically related to modern tribes?

One recent incident arose in 1996 when a prehistoric skeleton was found along the banks of the Columbia River near Kennewick, Washington. Kennewick Man, as this individual has been called, appears to have lived 9,000 years ago and has been the center of an intense academic, political, and legal debate.

At first the bones were thought to be a white settler's, but carbon-14 dating suggests a much earlier date, which has ruled out ancestry from some early-nineteenth-century settler. When forensic anthropologist James Chatters examined the bones he concluded that the bones were Caucasoid rather than Native American. If true, such a finding would require a revision of North American prehistory. Although archaeologists wanted to examine these bones more carefully, local Native American groups claimed the right to rebury this individual, and the courts have generally supported their motions. These legal wranglings have led some archaeologists to complain that the Native Americans simply want to rebury the evidence that Europeans may have reached the New World at some early prehistoric period and may have predated the arrival of Native American groups coming from Asia. Evidence that Kennewick Man is Caucasoid is slim at best, but without examination by physical anthropologists we will never know.

For a discussion of the Kennewick Man debate, see David Hurst Thomas's recent *Skull Wars: Kennewick Man, Archeology, and the Battle for Native American Identity* (Basic Books, 2000). Other sources on this controversy include Douglas Preston's "The Lost Man: Umatilla Indians' Plan to Rebury 9,300 Year Old Kennewick Man with Caucasoid Features," *The New Yorker* (June 16, 1997) and two articles in *Archaeology*, "A Battle Over Bones: Ancestry of Kennewick Man" (January/February 1997) and "Kennewick Update: Nondestructive Lab Tests on Controversial Skeleton to Begin" (November/December, 1998).

For an excellent summary of anthropological interest in Native American remains, see Robert Bieder's *A Brief Historical Survey of the Expropriation of American Indian Remains* (Native American Rights Fund, 1990). J. C. Rose, T. J. Green, and V. D. Green's "NAGPRA is Forever: Osteology and the Repatriation of Skeletons," *Annual Review of Anthropology* (vol. 25, 1996) provides a useful summary of NAGPRA.

Riding In has also explored the issue of repatriation and the imperialist nature of archaeology in his "Without Ethics and Morality: A Historical Overview of Imperial Archaeology and American Indians," *Arizona State Law Journal* (vol. 24, Spring 1992).

Several essays in Karen D. Vitelli, ed., *Archaeological Ethics* (Altamira Press, 1996), are relevant to this debate. For examples of a more moderate approach, which urges compromise, see Lynne Goldstein and Keith Kintigh's "Ethnics and the Reburial Controversy," *American Antiquity* (vol. 55, 1990).

ISSUE 18

Should Anthropologists Work to Eliminate the Practice of Female Circumcision?

YES: Merrilee H. Salmon, from "Ethical Considerations in Anthropology and Archaeology, or Relativism and Justice for All," *Journal of Anthropological Research* (Spring 1997)

NO: Elliott P. Skinner, from "Female Circumcision in Africa: The Dialectics of Equality," in Richard R. Randolph, David M. Schneider, and May N. Diaz, eds., *Dialectics and Gender: Anthropological Approaches* (Westview Press, 1988)

ISSUE SUMMARY

YES: Professor of the history and philosophy of science Merrilee H. Salmon argues that clitoridectomy (female genital mutilation) violates the rights of the women on whom it is performed. She asserts that this operation is a way for men to control women and keep them unequal.

NO: Professor of anthropology Elliott P. Skinner accuses feminists who want to abolish clitoridectomy of being ethnocentric. He argues that African women themselves want to participate in the practice, which functions like male initiation, transforming girls into adult women.

For more than a century anthropologists have seen cultural relativism as an essential antidote to ethnocentrism, a perspective that evaluates and judges the practices of other peoples according to the standards and sensitivities of one's own culture. This issue raises questions about the boundaries and limits of the anthropologist's cultural relativism. By evaluating cultural practices in a culture's own terms, anthropologists have long defended cultural diversity and the general principle that dominant cultures should not force members of weaker cultures to abandon traditional customs and practices, simply because practices appear peculiar, bizarre, or wrong to those in power. But today the world is increasingly integrated, and a number of international organizations have emerged whose purpose is to defend a single universal vision of human rights. Few anthropologists would object in principle to the notion that human rights should be defended for all people, but universal moral codes also challenge the rights of cultural groups to be different.

In this issue two scholars debate whether or not anthropologists should interfere with the cultural practice, found in many parts of Africa and the Middle East, of clitoridectomy and infibulation, variously called female circumcision or female genital mutilation. The practice is typically part of female initiation ceremonies and takes different forms in different ethnic groups, varying from relatively minor surgery to the clitoris (clitoridectomy) to the complete surgical removal of the clitoris and much of the woman's external sexual organs, after which the vagina is sewn up, leaving only a small opening (infibulation).

Merrilee H. Salmon refers to this practice as female genital mutilation and argues that it is fundamentally wrong, a violation of a woman's human rights. She contends that the practice is part of a male-centered power structure, which allows men to control women. Although Salmon acknowledges that women often control the ritual and even the surgery, it nevertheless supports male dominance within the community. In her view this cultural practice is an immoral one, and anthropological calls for moral relativism in this case are fundamentally ill-founded.

Elliott P. Skinner counters that female circumcision is only found in African societies where male circumcision is also practiced. Both practices involve mutilation of the genitals and are the means of transforming male and female children into adult men and women, respectively. Skinner maintains that not only are the female rituals entirely in the hands of other women, but the practices empower women within a society where men might otherwise dominate them. Feminists who claim that this practice is an example of male power over women, in his view, have got it wrong. Calls for the abolition of female circumcision began with Western missionaries who found the practice repugnant. He argues that Africans supported female circumcision as a form of resistance to white domination, and in Skinner's view current calls from Western people for the abolition of this practice is another example of Western domination of African societies.

At issue here are several key questions: Is female circumcision morally repugnant? Should anthropologists defend it or work to stop it? How should anthropologists deal with such practices when they see them occurring in their village communities where they work?

Although this issue seems very narrowly focused on a particular traditional custom in only one part of the world, it has important general implications for cultural relativism and universal human rights. Should anthropologists defend cultural practices simply because they are traditional? Do anthropologists have a responsibility to help end practices that they find morally abhorrent? If so, whose moral notions should be followed? Is moral relativism fundamentally flawed, as Salmon claims?

Merrilee H. Salmon

Ethical Considerations in Anthropology and Archaeology, or Relativism and Justice for All

Cultural Relativism and Ethical Relativism

Respect for the beliefs, practices, and values of other cultures, no matter how different from one's own, is a hallmark of anthropological wisdom. Franz Boas, the father of American academic anthropology, rejected invidious comparisons between European "high culture" and indigenous American languages, myths, art forms, and religions. Boas, dismissing absolute scales of cultural development such as those proposed by Condorcet and L. H. Morgan, insisted on studying the culture of each group in the context of its own historical development. Boas's work forms the historical basis for the anthropological doctrine known as *cultural relativism*.

Many anthropologists regard *ethical relativism* as an easy corollary of cultural relativism. I show that this view is incorrect. Cultural relativism does not entail ethical relativism; an anthropologist can consistently embrace cultural relativism while rejecting ethical relativism. As most anthropologists understand it, ethical relativism identifies the concepts of good and evil, or right and wrong, with what a particular culture approves or disapproves. Because ethical standards arise within particular cultures and vary from culture to culture, ethical relativists deny any extracultural standard of moral judgments. According to them, moral judgments of good or bad are possible only within a given culture, because such judgments refer only to compliance or noncompliance with that culture's norms.

The fact that a belief arises within a cultural context, however, does not imply that it can have no other basis. Although moral beliefs, like all other beliefs, arise within a given cultural setting, some of those beliefs may transcend the cultures in which they arise. Condemnation of murder and recognition of obligations to help others who are in extreme need, for example, are common to many cultures. Moreover, societies that differ in derivative moral judgments about marriage between close relatives frequently agree about more fundamental moral judgments, such as the immorality of incest. This modicum of moral

From Merrilee H. Salmon, "Ethical Considerations in Anthropology and Archaeology, or Relativism and Justice for All," *Journal of Anthropological Research*, vol. 53, no. 1 (Spring 1997). Copyright © 1997 by The University of New Mexico. Reprinted by permission of the publisher and the author. Notes and some references omitted.

consensus has encouraged some critics to try to refute ethical relativism by identifying a set of universally acceptable moral principles.

Whether universal agreement exists on any specific basic moral judgment is partly an empirical matter and partly dependent on how such terms as "murder," "cruelty," and "incest" are defined. Colin Turnbull's (1962) admittedly controversial studies suggest that the Ik do not embrace the most likely candidates for fundamental moral principles, on any reasonable definition of such principles. In Turnbull's account, the Ik provide a striking counterexample to general views that cruelty to children, for example, is universally condemned. Even if Turnbull's account is rejected, the search for moral principles that are both reasonably specific and universally acceptable is problematic.

The lack of agreement about principles, however, is not sufficient to demonstrate the truth of ethical relativism. What a culture regards as right or wrong conduct depends to some degree on both the members' factual beliefs about the state of the world and their beliefs about the likely consequences of their conduct. The absence of any universally accepted standards would support ethical relativism only if cultures that shared all the same factual beliefs and agreed about the consequences of particular behavior nevertheless disagreed in their ethical judgments. This situation has not been demonstrated. In fact, many apparent differences in ethical matters are resolved by bringing forth pertinent facts about the conditions under which moral choices are made. Even Turnbull (1962) goes to considerable trouble to show that severe hardship and deprivation of material resources in Ik society have altered their perceptions of reality. Whereas lack of universally accepted moral principles does not prove ethical relativism, however, neither would the universal acceptance of some specific moral principles disprove ethical relativism. The agreement could be accidental instead of arising from some feature of the human condition. Berlin and Kay's (1969) refutation of the relativism of color classification was convincing only because they were able to demonstrate the physiological—and thus cross-cultural—basis for color classification.

Ethical relativism apparently accords with anthropologists' determination to reject ethnocentrism and maintain a nonjudgmental stance towards alien cultural practices. Nevertheless, both anthropologists and philosophers have noted a serious problem with relativistic ethics: it seems to rule out condemning even such obviously immoral acts as genocide so long as they do not conflict with prevailing cultural norms. Ethical theories about what constitutes right and wrong behavior are severely tested when they go against our deepest moral intuition in this manner; in such cases one naturally questions the theory rather than giving up the intuition. H. Russell Bernard (1988:117), for example, says that

> cultural and ethical relativism is an excellent antidote for overdeveloped ethnocentrism. But cultural relativism is a poor philosophy to live by, or on which to make judgments about whether to participate in particular research projects. Can you imagine any anthropologist today defending the human rights violations of Nazi Germany as just another expression of the richness of culture?

Bernard's use of "is" in the first sentence shows that he does not distinguish cultural from ethical relativism. If he had done so, his point would be less confusing. *Cultural* relativism, in Boas's sense of trying to understand and evaluate the practices of other cultures in their own historical context, is a good antidote for ethnocentrism. Identifying the practices of any culture as the ultimate moral standard for that culture, however, is a different matter and rightly raises problems for a reflective anthropologist. Bernard in mentioning Nazi Germany has offered the standard counterexample to the claim that morality recognizes no extracultural authority.

Despite its fatal flaw, however, ethical relativism still enjoys wide acceptance among practicing anthropologists. Ethical relativism, for example, played a role in testimony by a French ethnologist in the trial of Bintou Fofana Diarra for complicity in the genital mutilation of her infant daughter. As reported in the *New York Times* (Weil-Curiel 1993), the unnamed ethnologist testified that "Africans should not be punished [for genital mutilation of infant girls] because they act under social pressure." The principle implicit in this statement—that one should not be punished for acts done under social pressure—is uncomfortably similar to the defense offered by Nazi war criminals.

A second problem with making cultural standards the final arbiter of morality is that this practice presumes a uniformity in cultures that current research denies, even for small, isolated, and tightly knit societies, or it gives a privileged moral position to powerful subgroups within the society. In the latter case, for example, the power to set cultural norms may belong to a minority whose control of valuable resources enables it to force others to follow its standards. Conversely, the power to set norms may accrue to those who are members of the majority, while significant minorities have no voice. In either case, one can only refer to the norms of "the culture" by ignoring ethical disagreement within the culture.

Some anthropologists believe that relativism is the only ethical stance that is compatible with a scientific investigation of other cultures. A scientific anthropologist presumably formulates "neutral" descriptions of the culture, reporting such quantifiable information as the frequency of occurrence of behaviors and perhaps the observed attitudes (approval, disapproval) of members of the society, while refraining from judging the culture or interfering with it in any way. Whether such detachment is required to maintain scientific integrity and whether such detachment is even possible are points raised by D'Andrade (1995) and Scheper-Hughes (1995). D'Andrade (1995:399) points to the alleged subjectivity of ethical judgments and contrasts these with the objectivity of scientific judgments. Scheper-Hughes (1995), however, objects to a scientific detachment that would prevent anthropologists from taking an active role in alleviating suffering among their research subjects. This debate is somewhat at cross-purposes because D'Andrade's main concern seems to be with an epistemic relativism that claims that such notions as knowledge and truth have no extracultural basis.... Scheper-Hughes, in contrast, is worried about the behavioral implications of a relativist ethics that takes the existing social arrangements in a culture as the ultimate moral authority.

The strict separation of science and values, a cherished principle of logical positivism, is increasingly difficult to defend in the face of ethical problems raised by scientific advances in many fields. In particular, current biomedical techniques for genetic engineering and research on human embryos raise important problems that tend to blur lines between scientific and value judgments. Bernard (1988) notes that when resources are limited, the very choice of anthropological research topics is value laden. The possibility of an ethically neutral or completely value-free science of human behavior now seems to many scientists both unattainable and undesirable, but recognition of the interrelationships between science and values need not prevent the limited type of objectivity that D'Andrade argues is possible for anthropological research.

Anthropologists may continue to avow ethical relativism despite its difficulties because they have not articulated an alternative ethical theory that is consistent with their distaste for ethnocentrism and their respect for cultural diversity. Nevertheless, maintaining a consistent form of ethical relativism is highly problematic in the present research climate. Facing the loss of valuable anthropological and archaeological resources, anthropologists have re-examined traditional relationships with their subjects, their colleagues, and the general public. To resolve problems and achieve clarity, they are currently debating and revising professional ethical standards. Despite the traditional commitment of anthropologists to relativism, the ethical principles that underlie their professional codes are not relativistic. The codes refer to their duties and responsibilities, and—by implication at least—to the corresponding rights of their research subjects, colleagues, and the general public. The conflict, often unacknowledged, between the avowed relativism of anthropologists and their sincere concern with justice and rights can lead to confusion and ineffectiveness in achieving the important goals of preserving anthropological resources and protecting cultural minorities....

An Anthropological Example—
Female Genital Mutilation

The arguments of feminist anthropologists for altering discriminatory practices of other cultures similarly compromise a commitment to ethical relativism. In some cultures, all females are subjected to genital mutilation. In its severe form, this involves cutting away most or all of the external sex organs (euphemistically called "circumcision") and sewing or sealing (infibulating) the vagina so as to leave only a pinhole opening for urination and menstruation. The practice affects an estimated ninety-five million or more women in at least twenty-five countries, mostly, but not all, in Africa (Lightfoot-Klein 1989). Within the cultures that practice genital mutilation, little disagreement exists about its value, though different groups offer various justifications for the practice. Most, but not all, of the countries that engage in the practice are predominantly Muslim, but it is absent in many other Muslim countries. The operation typically is performed on girls from six to nine years old but also on younger girls and infants. Sometimes when a bride is an "outsider," she is infibulated just before she marries into a group that follows the custom.

Anthropologists have attempted to document, understand, and explain this practice, which, aside from its harshness, strikes most Westerners as extremely bizarre. Why do they do it? What possible benefit do they see from it? How could it be so widespread? In contrast to most accounts in the contemporary press which dismiss the practice simply as a way of oppressing women, anthropologists' explanations are appropriately complex. They refer to the cult of virginity, the cultural association between female purity and the society's honor, and the antiquity of the tradition—Herodotus, writing in the fifth century B.C., obliquely refers to its practice in Egypt, and some mummies show evidence of infibulation. Anthropologists also cite the symbolic role female circumcision plays in distinguishing the Arab-Muslim African societies that practice it from their culturally distinct neighbors.

In places such as the Sudan, where the practice is nearly universal, anthropologists discuss genital mutilation in the context of social practices that involve other forms of mutilation practiced upon both males and females, such as tribal scarring of the face and piercing of body parts. Anthropologists also emphasize the cultural value of enduring pain without complaint. Economic explanations are also proposed. Midwives who perform the operations are sustained by the fees not only from the original circumcision and infibulation but also from treatment of the inevitable medical problems that result. Other explanations are psychological, such as those that refer to the attitudes of older women who say that they have gone through the experience and therefore do not see why the younger ones should be spared.

Besides offering their own historical and cultural explanations, anthropologists report the explanations of the people who engage in the practice. These include such claims as we have always done it, our religion requires it, no one will marry an uncircumcised woman, it makes us clean, it makes us more beautiful, it improves health, it limits the sex drive, it is good for fertility, and—referring to reinfibulation after childbirth—it deters a husband from seeking additional wives.

Some—relatively few—women and men in such societies do question the practice or its supposed benefits, particularly if they have been exposed to modern Western culture. But when asked why they nevertheless have their daughters circumcised, they refer to tradition, or say that their female relatives insisted, or insist that no one would marry the girl unless she were circumcised. Most explanations of female genital mutilation come from women, since few men can be persuaded to discuss the issue, claiming for the most part that it is women's business. Jomo Kenyatta, the revered former leader of Kenya and member of the Kikuyu tribe, who earned a Ph.D. in anthropology under [Bronislaw] Malinowski, however, said, "No proper Kikuyu would dream of marrying a girl who has not been circumcised" (Kenyatta 1938, quoted in Lightfoot-Klein 1989:71).

Women in cultures that practice genital mutilation claim that it is done for the benefit of the men, but women alone are responsible for arranging and performing the operations. Even the question of the acceptability of bridal candidates is largely under control of the women since arranged marriages are the rule, with the groom's mother having a prominent voice. (Recently a young woman from Togo sought and was granted asylum in the United States to avoid genital mutilation. The woman became endangered, however, only after her father had died. Her guardianship then passed to her aunt, who attempted to commit the woman to an arranged marriage.) Thus the practice is unusual inasmuch as it is intended to control women, it affects them almost universally, and they suffer the greatest harm from it; but they manage and control it almost exclusively.

The presence in European cities of sizable African communities that maintain the practice—despite local laws that prohibit it—has brought female genital mutilation to the attention both of the courts and of feminists who see it as "butchery intended to control women" (Weil-Curiel 1993). Anthropologists who claim to be relativists face the ethical dilemma of whether their responsibility ends with describing the practice and placing it in a cultural context, whether they are obligated to protect the practice from outside interference, or whether they should help to end the practice. Relativism might suggest that they have a further responsibility to protect, or at least not interfere with, this culturally sanctioned practice. At the same time, as relativists, they must also consider their responsibility to cooperate with members of their own culture who are trying to end the practice on the grounds that human rights are being violated.

Although relativistic anthropologists are reluctant to try to alter the values of other cultures, many think it appropriate to try to correct mistaken factual beliefs when this would benefit the welfare of members of the culture. Value judgments that are based on mistaken factual beliefs may be revised without undermining the values themselves. Clearly some beliefs of cultures that practice genital mutilation are factually mistaken. Contrary to those who say the practice is beneficial to sanitation or health, mutilation causes severe medical damage in many cases. The operation can cause immediate infection, excessive bleeding, and even death. Delayed common effects of the operation are infections of the urinary tract, menstrual problems, painful intercourse, reduction in fertility, and complications in childbirth. Nor does the Muslim religion command infibulation, as some believe. The practice does not guarantee virginity, since reinfibulation, which simulates the virginal state, is widely practiced. Because sex drive is more a matter of endocrinology than external organs, the claim that infibulation limits sex drive is likewise questionable.

Insofar as genital mutilation is motivated by sanitary or medical considerations, therefore, knowledge of the facts would tend to undermine the practice without reducing the cultural commitment to the values of purity, fertility, or health. Insofar as genital mutilation is motivated by other factors, such as maintenance of cultural distinctiveness and increasing the ability to endure pain, its medical harm could be alleviated by practicing less severe forms of circumcision without infibulation and by performing the operation only in a sterile clinical setting.

Such a medical solution, while it would save lives and preserve health, does not address the ethical question, raised by feminists, of the right to control one's body and whether or to what extent this right is inalienable. Since genital mutilation is usually performed on children, an important issue is whether parents have the right to harm the child in this way. Parents and guardians cannot violate *inalienable* rights of their children even for some supposed benefit.

Parents may, however, subject children to some kinds of discipline, as well as to dangerous and sometimes painful medical treatment, when it is for the good of the child. Erroneous views about the supposed benefits of genital mutilation, of course, cannot justify harming the child.

Unlike mistaken claims about the medical benefits of mutilation, other claims are apparently correct. Marriage within the culture *as things now stand* may not be an option for an uncircumcised woman. Moreover, for females in that culture, marriage is a prerequisite for obtaining any other rights. So being able to marry is a clear benefit and may outweigh the harm of circumcision from the point of view of the girl. (According to principles of justice, the benefit that justifies a harm must accrue to the individual who undergoes the harm, not merely to her extended family. Thus, loss of a bride price for the family would not, without further argument, justify the harm to the child.) Feminist anthropologists, as well as others who are concerned with human rights, want to take both educational and legal means to end the practice of genital mutilation. Their attitude, however, is not consistent with a commitment to ethical relativism....

Individual Rights and the Common Good

... In looking at the question of genital mutilation, the following pertinent questions arise. How fundamental is the right not to have one's body altered? At what age does the girl have the right to decide for herself whether to undergo a mutilation? Young girls in the Sudan who are not circumcised by their eighth year usually ask to have it done. Should we disregard these requests because the children are mere dupes of the culture? If they are, can they ever reach an age of consent? Many Western cultures practice ear piercing on infant girls, and many others accede to the wishes of six or eight year olds to have their ears pierced. Circumcision of male infants is common. Bodily mutilations are as much a part of cultural identity for some cultures as distinctive styles of clothing. Some mutilations we regard as attractive, some as beneficial to health, some as harmless, some as aesthetically offensive, others as brutal. Severe genital mutilation surely falls into the brutal category. Moreover, its rationale is empirically flawed, and because its harms disproportionately affect females, it raises serious questions about violating rights. In cases such as this, anthropological understanding of the practice can legitimately be used to aid attempts to eradicate or modify it for the benefit of the members of the culture where it is practiced. Those who disagree should at least argue for the practice on stronger grounds than the value of cultural diversity....

Anthropologists who work in cultures that withhold fundamental human rights from women, children, or any other subgroup face difficult choices about taking any *action* to restore rights. Some anthropologists would say that their decision to work in such cultures obligates them to alleviate the problem. Others hold that their role as anthropologists is to observe cultural phenomena and record and analyze them as accurately as possible, but not to try to alter conditions. In either case, the anthropologist has a minimal obligation to report the observed and analyzed state of affairs in normal anthropological outlets for publication. Anthropologists do not betray secrets or violate confidences when they describe a custom that is almost universally practiced in the culture. By calling attention to an unjust practice, however, anthropologists at least implicitly invite groups devoted to the protection of rights to take action. By presenting the offensive practice in its full cultural context, which may involve revealing its latent functions in addition to its manifest or stated functions, anthropologists also provide valuable information about how to control or prevent the practice.

After the anthropologist acts to present information in an appropriate way to a suitable audience, his or her responsibility to try to alleviate the injustice seems to me neither greater nor less than that of any person who is in a position to help the victims of an unjust practice. Even if no further action is taken, I think that the anthropologist who refuses to recognize that the value of cultural diversity is morally subordinate to that of protecting rights is on shaky moral ground. The anthropologist who retreats into ethical relativism in such situations, as did the ethnologist at the trial of Bintou Fofana Diana, does not demonstrate tolerance by appealing to social pressures in another culture but instead risks being committed to the same morally untenable position as the "Nazi defense."

Conclusion

I have reiterated some criticisms of ethical relativism, a position which once seemed to offer anthropologists a way to profess tolerance and avoid criticizing the morality of some practices of other cultures. My arguments try to show not so much that ethical relativism is "false" but that its consequences conflict with our deepest held moral intuitions and that it cannot be held consistently while embracing those intuitions. I have tried to show also that anthropologists need not forego tolerance if they abandon relativism in favor of a morality based on principles of justice and fairness. The concern with justice that guides anthropologists' codes of professional conduct can provide the starting point for a more sophisticated analysis of rights, which can be used to analyze cultural practices. (The philosophical literature on rights is vast, but a useful entry for anthropologists is available in Baker 1994.) Ethical judgments of another culture's practices, especially when based on deep understanding of their life, customs, and tradition, are indicative neither of ethnocentrism nor of intolerance. Instead, they show respect for the basic anthroplogical belief in "the psychic unity of humans" and a commitment to justice and fairness for all.

References

Baker, J., ed., 1994, Group Rights, Toronto: University of Toronto Press.
Berlin, B., and P. Kay, 1969, Basic Color Terms: Their Universality and Evolution. Berkeley and Los Angeles: University of California Press.
Bernard, H. R., 1998, Research Methods in Cultural Anthropology. Newbury Park, N.J.: Sage Publications.
D'Andrade, R., 1995, Moral Models in Anthropology. Current Anthropology 36(3):399–408.

Kenyatta, J., 1938, Facing Mount Kenya. London: Secker and Warburg.

Lightfoot-Klein, H., 1989, Prisoners of Ritual: An Odyssey into Female Genital Circumcision in Africa. Binghampton, N.Y.: Haworth Press.

Scheper-Hughes, N., 1995, The Primacy of the Ethical. Current Anthropology 36(3):409–20.

Turnbull, C., 1962, The Forest People. New York: Simon and Schuster.

Weil-Curiel, L., 1993, Mutilation of Girls' Genitals: Ethnic Gulf in French Court. New York Times, November 23.

NO

Elliott P. Skinner

Female Circumcision in Africa: The Dialectics of Equality

Culture and society must, of course, always take account of human biology, but they do so in complex ways. The distinctive characteristics of culture is that it transcends nature; but this does not mean that it has left it behind—rather, it has turned it upside down.

— Robert F. Murphy (1977)

Female circumcision or clitoridectomy, called by the Mossi, the *Bongo*, is [a] not too subtle mechanism of Mossi women to challenge the superiority of men. This was the thought that flashed through my mind, as I watched with amazement, the quiet pride of the women and girls performing the rituals of the graduation ceremonies of their own Bongo. Here were women doing things that they usually never did, and more importantly, should not have been doing. They had procured the drums from men and, much to my surprise and their amusement, were beating them. Where had they learned? Oh yes! They must have practiced these rhythms while pounding millet and sorghum in their mortars. Inexplicable was the source of their knowledge of the songs and dances of the Bongo which were allegedly the sole province of males, but which they performed equally well. True, I had learned both the dances and songs of the Bongo during my numerous visits to the circumcision lodge, but these female graduates did them better than I ever did. Surely some Delilah had tricked a Samson who had then revealed the secrets of arrogant men. During the Bongo ceremony, Mossi women were showing to the men publicly, that they knew male secrets, and moreover, these were not important after all....

The subject of male circumcision and female clitoridectomy and infibulation in African societies has been the source of great speculation and controversy, primarily because it involves the "fundamental ontological differences between the sexes—conditions of simple *being*—based in the first instance on anatomical distinctions" and what flows from these. Questions raised have been: 1. Are these operations cruel? 2. Do they have anything to do with sex? 3. Do they reveal anything about the relative merits of various cultures' sexual sensibilities? and 4. Do male and female versions of the operations differ with regard to the answers to questions 1 and 2? Some anthropologists and some non-anthropologists have already strong views on these questions.

Fran P. Hosken discussing "Genital Mutilation in Africa," severely criticized those "Anthropologists (mostly men) who have studied African traditions have done no service to women by utterly disregarding women's health while they attribute 'cultural values' to such damaging traditions as excision and infibulation." Considering these practices "deleterious to health and indeed dangerous," Hosken lamented that many African groups "subject their female children to genital mutilation for a multitude of 'reasons,' many of which conflict and all of which are based on total ignorance concerning reproduction." She wondered aloud whether it was really in the interest of such populations "that such damaging myths are perpetuated under the cloak of silence and are praised as 'culture' in the literature? I think not. The time has come to face the facts." (Hoskin 1976:6) Hosken is tired of, and angry about those "explanations" of men and of what she calls "brain-washed women" who attribute clitoridectomy "to the fear of female sexuality," and the need to "prevent adultery." (*Ibid.*)

Simon D. Messing, an applied anthropologist, feels that he and his colleagues "cannot evade the issue of such a serious and widespread problem as genital mutilation of females, if they are concerned with public health . . . they should not leave the burden of this task entirely on the shoulders of radical feminists—and the latter in turn should welcome our cooperation." (Messing 1980:296)

Neither the radical feminists nor the anthropologists have considered the possibility that in the frequent dialectics that we find in social life, female circumcision might well be one of the numerous ways in which women challenge the vaunted superiority of men. . . .

Given the contemporary controversy surrounding "female" circumcision (really an interesting misnomer), it is generally ignored that circumcision is predominantly a "male" ritual. Many well-known ancient peoples, such as the Hebrews (who probably adopted this ritual in ancient Egypt as they borrowed other interesting aspects of that culture) limited circumcision to males. The same thing is true for many African populations. As far as I can ascertain, there is not a single African society in which female circumcision exists without its male counterpart. The reasons for this are as intriguing as they are germane to this article. . . .

Initiation ceremonies preparatory to marriage, sexual relations, and the creation of families, are widespread in African societies, but are not necessarily linked to either circumcision or clitoridectomy. . . . Characteristic of this *rite de passage* is the customary withdrawal of the initiates from the world of people; their education into the knowledge and lore of their societies; and their subjection to a great deal of physical pain and other hardships. . . .

The Mossi initiated and subjected their pre-pubescent youth to both circumcision and clitoridectomy. In the Manga-Nobere districts of Burkina Faso (formerly Upper Volta) in southern Mossi country, every three or four years, during December, the coldest part of the year, and depending upon the food supply, the Mossi opened the "Bongo" or the initiation ceremony for boys, in a secluded area in the woods. Here were gathered about twenty to thirty boys, age seven or eight to twelve years old, from the surrounding villages and their helpers. Known as Bankousse, these youths built a camp called the *Keogo*, placing barriers on the paths leading to it so as to warn off uncircumcised children and women. The mothers of the boys brought food daily to the barrier, but did not cross it.

The Mossi considered circumcision to be a simple surgical act which was only incidental to the Bongo—a veritable initiation to life involving a great many hardships. Almost immediately after arriving at the Keogo the boys were circumcised by the head of the camp, known as the *Nane* who used a sharp razor for the operation. As in other parts of Africa, the initiates were not expected to cry, and their wounds were cared for by the Nane. Then came the important post operation period called *komtogo* or "bitter water" by the Bankousse because of the pain involved. Despite the cold nights, they had use of only a small fire and were not permitted to use any covers. Every morning they were forced to bathe in a cold pool, and when they returned, they had lessons to learn involving history, nature study, and life.

The Bongo had its own mystery language whose words turned out on analysis to be synonyms for ordinary More (the language of the Mossi) with the prefix "na." The camp had its own rules on which rank was based, not on those on the outside, but on the order in which the youths were circumcised. What the Nane attempted to do was to forge a link between the boys in opposition to himself, who acted like a veritable ogre. Walking about the camp with a long stick, he whipped the youngsters into line, threw sand in the food brought by the women, and made the Bankousse dance and sing until they were exhausted.

Graduation ceremonies of the Bongo involved going into the woods, cutting grass for the horses of the chiefs, and wood for their fires. Then on the appointed day, the mothers brought new clothes for their sons, hoping that none of them had died during the ordeal of the Bongo. Then on the appointed day the graduates dressed in their new clothing marched through the market place, and visited the chief. Then they engaged in dancing and singing at a public place just outside the market place.

As usual in almost all parts of Africa, the Mossi women were in complete charge of their Bongo from which they excluded all men. Their *Keogo* was not in the woods, but was in the compound of a woman who lived by herself. But as usual for males, I could find out nothing about the nature of the excision that took place. I did hear the drumming and singing that took place there all night until the wee hours of the morning, and did observe the young girls going backward and forward to their homes. Invariably they carried a tufted staff, said to have been given to them by their prospective husbands. The women would say nothing about the symbolism involved, considering the information specific to women alone. The most that they would say about what went on in the female Bongo was that the males have their secrets and so did the women.

Like the graduation exercises of the male Bankousse, the female ritual was a village-wide affair, but strictly within the province of the women. Market days before, the relatives and prospective husbands of the graduates, shopped for the clothes and headties, and makeup for them. Then on the day of the exercise, the young girls went to the home of the female Nane and accompanied by their mothers and sisters who were beating drums and singing, went to the village square where the Bankousse danced and sang the traditional airs of the Bongo. From time to time, male relatives and husbands would detach themselves from the line of spectators and approach the dancers, giving them presents of money. To all intents and purposes, the female Bongo was structurally and functionally quite similar to that of the males. This ceremony demonstrated to all that the Mossi women were just as capable as the men in performing an initiation ceremony whose function was to transform girls into women, as the male version transformed boys into men. Moreover, they had more effectively kept men from knowing their secrets than did the males, whose secrets they had obviously shared. . . .

What is important about the puberty rituals in African societies, whether they involved painful initiation, and whether they involved genital mutilation with recognizable pain, are the emic and etic features involved. The Africans do have their own views of their rituals even though others have ignored these views and insist upon their own interpretations. This is perhaps par for human beings involving as it does relative power. There is no doubt that had they the requisite power, Africans would insist that the world accept their interpretation of their own rituals, as well as their views of the rituals of others. Anthropologists would do well to keep this in mind.

The Mossi are not much given to speculating on the imponderables of social life, or the world in general, judging such ratiocinations quixotic. To them the Bongo for men and for women have the same meaning and serve the same function for both men and women: preparation for marriage and rearing families. Indicative of this equality is that the two genders control their own initiation rituals, even though women have to borrow drums from the males. When badgered about the sexual features involved in genital mutilation, an admittedly chauvinist Mossi male might suggest that since females are inferior to males they are not permitted to touch the male organ during sexual congress, and that clitoridectomy makes sexual congress easier. This may be as good a rationalization as any other, but flies in the face of the anxiety of Mossi men over the conduct of their wives, and their stated axiom: "Women are so important that if a man receives as a wife, either a blind woman or a leper, he should close his eyes, close his mouth, and close his ears, and keep her."

The equally male chauvinist Dogon explicitly associate both circumcision and clitoridectomy with elaborate myths concerning creation and cosmology. Both operations are said to have been instituted as punishments and are indicative of the incomplete state of human beings resulting from the primordial crime of a godling. There is the removal of the opposite sex complement with which all human beings were originally intended to be equipped. Thus for the Dogon there is complementarity in the operation. Mary Daly criticizes the Dogon for what she considered an emic patriarchal obfuscation of the true purposes of the operation, namely the intimidation and humiliation of women. What she conveniently ignores is the fact that the Dogon forbid men to have intercourse with their wives against their will and that the sexual responses of wives are in large part conditioned by the treatment they generally receive from their husbands (Daly 1978).

Somewhat like the Dogon, both the Egyptians and the Northern Sudanese stress the complementarity of circumcision and clitoridectomy. Referring specifically to the Sudanese, [Janice] Boddy asserted that

> Through their own operation, performed at roughly the same age as when girls are circumcised (sic) (between five and ten years), boys become less like women: while the female reproductive organs are covered, that of the male is uncovered, or, as one Sudanese author states, of a child's sex... by removing physical characteristics deemed appropriate to his or her opposite: the clitoris and other external genitalia, in the case of females, the prepuce of the penis, in the case of males. This last is emphasized by a custom now lapsed in Hofriyat wherein one of the newly circumcised boys' grandmothers would wear his foreskin as a ring on the day of the operation (Boddy 1982:687–8).

Paying special attention to the widespread African emic notion of complementarity in the rituals of circumcision and clitoridectomy, Boddy insists that

> By removing their external genitalia, women are not so much preventing their own sexual pleasure (though obviously this is an effect) as enhancing their femininity. Circumcision as a symbolic act brings sharply into focus the fertility potential of women by dramatically de-emphasizing their inherent sexuality. By insisting on circumcision for their daughters, women assert their social indispensibility, an importance that is not as the sexual partners of their husbands, nor in this highly segregated, male-authoritative society, as their servants, sexual or otherwise, but as the mothers of men. *The ultimate social goal of a woman is to become, with her husband, the cofounder of a lineage section. As a respected haboba she is "listened to," she may be sent on the* hadj *(pilgrimage to Mecca) by her husbands or her sons, and her name is remembered in village genealogies for several generations* (italics supplied) (Ibid.:687).

Although Boddy had her own etic views of female genital mutilation among the Sudanese, her ethnographic data support the etic argument of this paper, namely that in this instance of the dialectics of social life, clitoridectomy rather than a ritual performed by women, to demean their already low status in many African societies, is a declaration of equality. What is interesting is that there are few, if any, cases in the ethnographic record where African women (as contrasted to the normally sexist African men) see this ritual as reducing their status. Feminists may consider the African women who defend this practice as "brain-washed," but should be aware that many African women, as well as men, take the same jaundiced view of many rituals of Western Christendom. True, some contemporary African women object to clitoridectomy, but few had dared to confront their mothers and grandmothers over the issue for fear of being taken for "black" white women. The implication here is that these women have failed to assert that cultural equality for which Africans have fought long and hard.

What is important about the controversy about clitoridectomy in Africa is that African women were never part of it. The issue grew out of a Judeo-Christian concern over human sexuality, involved Christian missionaries in Africa, and was used by African men in their struggle for cultural autonomy from Europeans, and ultimately for political independence....

Missionary opposition to clitoridectomy among the Kikuyu was very much linked to their opposition to all aspects of African culture that could frustrate their attempts to impose Western Christendom. We are told that

> The missionaries recognized the significance of the initiatory rites, of which circumcision was the outward physical symbol, and they were appalled at what they saw in them. The physical operation they considered brutal and unhygenic and in the case of girls a barbaric mutilation with permanent ill-effects. *But the atmosphere in which the ceremonies were carried out seemed to them even more evil, with what they took to be the sexual innuendo of the dances and songs, the licentiousness of the old men and women and the gloating cruelty of the operators and their attendants. They taught against the practices and prayed that the people might forego them altogether* (Italics added) (Murray–Brown 1972:50–51).

... What had started out as an issue over clitoridectomy, and a practice which many African Christians were prepared to change, became a cause célèbre over the issue of African cultural and political freedom. Much to the alarm of the colonial government, it became known locally in October 1919 that "John [Jomo] Kenyatta" who had gone to Britain to protest settler colonialism, had been to Moscow and was "in close touch with Communists and Communist Organizations." Songs praising Kenyatta and ridiculing the governor were outlawed as seditious, creating anger among anti-mission Kikuyu....

The problem now was that clitoridectomy had become inextricably linked to the Kikuyu desire for equality in their homeland. The missionaries were insisting that Kenyatta "should tell his people to obey government officers, Kikuyu chiefs, and missions in control of schools....

Kenyatta's subsequent defense of clitoridectomy as an operation in which the operator had "the dexterity of a Harley Street surgeon... with a stroke she cuts off the tip of the clitoris... the girl hardly feels any pain" (Jomo Kenyatta 1962) is only understandable in light of the role that clitoridectomy had played in the drive of the Kikuyu to achieve equality for their institutions in the face of Europe's arrogance. Like Bob Murphy, Kenyatta was very aware of the dialectics of social life. For him colonial tutelage was oppressive and alien. He wrote:

> In our opinion, the African can only advance to a 'higher level' if he is free to express himself, to organize economically, politically, socially, and to take part in the government of his own country. In this way he will be able to develop his creative mind, initiative, and personality, which hitherto have been hindered by the multiplicity of incomprehensible laws and ordinances (*Ibid.*:192).

What the conflict over clitoridectomy did was to bring to "an abrupt close the paternalistic phase of missionary activity; henceforth the emphasis would be on the growth of native churches. The high noon of imperialism... [and the attempt] to extend white dominion over all of East Africa, was over." (*Ibid.*:151)

Kenyatta has been pilloried by many female scholars and feminists, for defending a practice (which he was prepared to see abolished), in the greater interest of political equality for Africans. Few noted, as did Harriet Lyons, that Kenyatta had suggested, perhaps as an after thought, that clitoridectomy may have been practiced to prevent masturbation, a practice condemned in both Kikuyu boys and girls, and that his major emphasis was "largely on social structure." (1981:510) Moreover, he was fully prepared to use education to abolish it. A more intemperate view of Kenyatta's action is that of Fran Hosken who declared that

> An international feminist observer cannot help but wonder why the male African leadership does not speak out about the mutilation of women, a custom that was reinforced by Kenyatta in Kenya and is also supported by the independence movement under his leadership.... It clearly affects the status of women in political affairs (Hosken 1976:6).

Understandably, there are some African feminists who agree with Hosken. Nevertheless, it should be noted that "the resistance of African feminists to anti-clitoridectomy agitation—evident at the United Nations World Conference on women held in Copenhagen in 1980" accords fully with the demand of Kenyatta for African cultural autonomy. Like him, these women realize that African practices must be brought into line with those characteristics of the emerging global civilization. What they insist upon is respect, and the end of European arrogance.

The problem with blaming Kenyatta and other African men for clitoridectomy misses the important point that African women have always been in control of this ritual (until now when male doctors may perform it in modern hospitals), and probably used it, to declare their equality with men. Faced with discrimination for not possessing those characteristics with which dominant social strata have linked their dominance, African women, like other women, and subordinate groups, have striven to acquire the traits viewed as valuable. These practices vary cross-culturally in time and space, and can be as different as Japanese females surgically operating on their eyes to approximate those of American males during the occupation of their country; to certain American females bobbing their noses; other Americans bleaching or darkening their skins; and still others dressing like males, and creating female counterparts of such organizations as Masonic lodges, veteran groups, and institutions of higher learning. In many of these cases, the males or dominant groups whose characteristics were being imitated, were not aware of the attempts to achieve equality with them, or to win their favor. That they were responsible for the behavior in the first place may well have been true, but a dialectician like Robert Murphy, whose eyes were probably opened by his wife, Yolanda, would smile at the irony of it all.

References

Boddy, Janice, 1982. "Womb as oasis: the symbolic context of Pharaonic circumcision in rural Northern Sudan," *American Ethnology,* 9: 682–698.

Daly, Mary, 1978. *Gyn/Ecology: The Metaethics of Radical Feminism,* Boston: Beacon Press.

Hosken, Fran P., 1976. "Genital Mutilation of Women in Africa." *Munger Africana Library Notes,* #36, October, p. 6.

Kenyatta, Jomo, 1962. *Facing Mount Kenya,* New York, Vintage Brooks.

Lyons, Harriet, 1981. "Anthropologists, moralities, and relativities: the problem of genital mutilations." *Canadian Review of Sociology and Anthropology,* 18: 499–518.

Messing, Simon D., 1980. "The Problem of 'Operations Based on Custom' in Applied Anthropology: The Challenge of the Hosken Report on Genital and Sexual Mutilations of Females." *Human Organizations,* Vol. 39, No. 3, p. 296.

Murphy, Robert F., 1977. "Man's Culture and Woman's Nature," *Annals of the New York Academy of Sciences.* Vol. 293, 15–24.

Murray-Brown, Jeremy, 1980. *Kenyatta.* London, George Allen & Unwin Ltd.

POSTSCRIPT

Should Anthropologists Work to Eliminate the Practice of Female Circumcision?

The issue of female circumcision raises important questions about whether or not there are limits to cultural relativism. Critics of cultural relativism have often pointed to the Nazi atrocities during the Second World War as examples of immoral practices that can be understood in culturally relative terms but should not be condoned. Cultural relativists in such cases counter that unlike male or female circumcision in Africa, genocide was never morally acceptable in German society.

At issue here is whether or not an unhealthy practice should be suppressed because it is unhealthy. If anthropologists work to abolish female circumcision, should they also work to prohibit use of alcohol, tobacco, and recreational drugs in our own society because such products are unhealthy? Are there limits beyond which cultural relativism has no power? If anthropologists and international organizations are right to stop female circumcision, would they also be justified in working to abolish male circumcision in Jewish and Muslim communities on the same grounds?

Without dealing directly with issues of cultural and moral relativism, Skinner argues that anthropologists should take seriously the concerns of both African men and women, the majority of whom want to continue to practice clitoridectomy and resent Western attempts to suppress the practice. For another view from a similar perspective, see Eric Winkel's essay "A Muslim Perspective on Female Circumcision," *Women & Health* (vol. 23, 1995).

There are many essays by authors who wish to abolish female circumcision, and nearly all of them refer to the practice as female genital mutilation. A lengthy bibliography can be found at http://www.fgmnetwork.org/reference/biblio.html. Typical examples would include Harriet Lyons's "Anthropologists, Moralities, and Relativities: The Problem of Genital Mutilations," *Canadian Review of Sociology and Anthropology* (vol. 18, 1981) and Anke van der Kwaak's "Female Circumcision and Gender Identity: A Questionable Alliance?" *Social Science and Medicine* (vol. 35, 1992).

For a balanced anthropological view of female circumcision and cultural relativism, see Carole Nagengast's "Women, Minorities, and Indigenous Peoples: Universalism and Cultural Relativity," *Journal of Anthropological Research* (vol. 53, 1997).

For a discussion of issues dealing with cultural relativism and anthropological ethics, see *Ethics and the Profession of Anthropology*, Carolyn Fluehr-Lobban, ed. (University of Pennsylvania Press, 1991).

ISSUE 19

Do Anthropologists Have a Moral Responsibility to Defend the Interests of "Less Advantaged" Communities?

YES: James F. Weiner, from "Anthropologists, Historians, and the Secret of Social Knowledge," *Anthropology Today* (October 1995)

NO: Ron Brunton, from "The Hindmarsh Island Bridge and the Credibility of Australian Anthropology," *Anthropology Today* (August 1996)

ISSUE SUMMARY

YES: Anthropology professor James F. Weiner asserts that anthropologists have a moral obligation to defend the interests of the native communities with whom they work, even if it means halting development projects. In his view, anthropologists have a responsibility to defend traditional native cultures, particularly if secret cultural knowledge is involved.

NO: Applied anthropologist Ron Brunton argues that even when hired as consultants, anthropologists have a moral and professional responsibility to the truth, whether the gained knowledge is considered by the native community as secret or not. This responsibility applies even when such evidence does not support the interests of a native community.

Over the past 30 years anthropologists have increasingly been asked to serve as consultants on various mining and development projects. Anthropologists sometimes work for a government department or developer, but more often work for the native communities whose land will be developed or resources exploited. In such instances, anthropologists are asked to provide expert testimony about traditional native cultures. This testimony can cause government bodies or developers to reshape a project's design or, if matters of serious cultural heritage are involved, may even halt a project. Anthropologists are trained to respect the cultures and traditions of people very different from themselves. However, in legal proceedings involving the development of native lands, they must generally take a stand defending either the native communities or the developers.

The controversy concerning the Hindmarsh Island Bridge in South Australia raises a number of questions about the responsibilities of anthropologists toward the native communities with which they work. Like the United States, Australia has laws intended to protect the sacred sites of native Aboriginal tribes from desecration by developers. Some Aboriginal women of the Ngarrindjeri tribe tried to stop construction of a bridge connecting Hindmarsh Island to the mainland, stating that Hindmarsh Island is a sacred site where women conduct secret ceremonies. The proposed bridge, they asserted, would desecrate this site and threaten the tribe's future prosperity. Until recently, secret women's rites have received little attention from anthropologists studying Aboriginal societies, but some anthropologists have demonstrated that "women's business," as these secret ceremonies are publicly called, are an important part of traditional life. When a female anthropologist working on this case reported that the proposed bridge would indeed desecrate a site sacred to women, the project was halted. Developers raised charges of misrepresentation and the state government established a Royal Commission to investigate whether there had been falsification of anthropological data.

Anthropologists have typically supported the rights of less advantaged communities against exploitation by more powerful individuals and groups. Initially, the Hindmarsh Island Bridge case seemed straightforward—an anthropologist was defending the rights of an Aboriginal group to protect sacred land from desecration. But this case raises a number of other concerns because the knowledge used to support the native community's concerns was secret knowledge that only women should know. The case was further complicated because the Ngarrindjeri are one of the most acculturated tribes in South Australia, and none of its members have lived a traditional lifestyle for more than a century. At issue before the Royal Commission was whether the information that the Ngarrindjeri women gave the anthropologist was based on traditional knowledge of cultural practices or fabrication.

In the following selections, James F. Weiner argues that cultural knowledge is relative and contingent, and that only a few senior Ngarrindjerri women could be expected to know female secrets relevant to "women's business" at Hindmarsh Island. Weiner contends that we should expect all traditions to change, including those of native communities, and it is the anthropologist's responsibility to explain traditional cultures to mainstream society and to defend the rights of less advantaged groups. Recognizing that cultures do change, Ron Brunton asserts that anthropologists have a professional responsibility to find out what traditional beliefs, customs, and practices really are, even if such facts work against the interests of native groups. Brunton maintains that it is simply bad anthropology to accept the statements of any informants without a thorough analysis of all available data.

James F. Weiner

 **YES**

Anthropologists, Historians, and the Secret of Social Knowledge

In the state of South Australia, we are currently witnessing two remarkable things. First, the validity and authenticity of Australian Aboriginal culture and belief are being openly challenged by the State government and the media. Second, the status of anthropological expertise and the procedures used by anthropologists in explicating that culture and belief to Anglo-Australian society are being disparaged, and unfavourably compared with other disciplinary expertise, specifically, that of the historian.

Briefly, the background to these events is as follows. A group of Aboriginal women of the Ngarrindjeri tribe, the traditional indigenous inhabitants of the Lower Murray region in South Australia, claim that there is what they call 'women's business' on Hindmarsh Island, a small island in the mouth of the Murray River. 'Business' is a pan-Aboriginal English word used throughout Australia nowadays to refer to any religious, sacred or ritual knowledge or activities or procedures that pertain to a specific site or landmark.

Hindmarsh Island is the site of a marina development project and the developers, in partnership with the local government councils and the State Government, planned to build a bridge from the mainland to the island. The Ngarrindjeri women who wished to see the plans for the bridge abandoned, claim that the island had to remain separate from the mainland, and that any attempt to compromise the discreteness of the two bodies of land would have an adverse effect on Ngarrindjeri women's ability to reproduce. On the strength of their assertion of this ritual significance, and acting on advice from a professor of law and an anthropologist (both women) who were charged with assessing the nature and extent of this women's business, the Federal Minister for Aboriginal Affairs intervened and placed a 25 year ban on the bridge's construction in May 1994. The ban was subsequently overturned by an Australian Federal Court decision in February 1995.

In May 1995, the Adelaide television station Channel 10 broadcast allegations that the women's secret knowledge which was the justification of the original Federal ban was 'fabricated' by some Aboriginal men and the Anglo-Australian lawyer employed by the South Australian Aboriginal Legal Rights

Movement, who was acting on behalf of the women. Importantly, a group of so-called 'dissident' Ngarrindjeri women also publicly proclaimed shortly afterwards that they had no knowledge of women's business on Hindmarsh Island. This contestation of the existence of women's business by other Ngarrindjeri women encouraged other commentators who sought to discredit the original claim, and ultimately emboldened the State government. In June, a State Royal Commission was appointed to inquire:

> 1. Whether the 'women's business', or any aspect of the 'women's business', was a fabrication and, if so:
> (a) the circumstances relating to such a fabrication:
> (b) the extent of such a fabrication: and
> (c) the purpose of such a fabrication...[1]

It is at this point in the growing controversy, now having achieved national scrutiny, that this criticism of anthropology by a historian took place. In the June issue of the *Adelaide Review,* University of Adelaide emeritus professor of history Austin Gough published an article entitled 'Hindmarsh Island and the Politics of the Future'. He first commented mordantly on the 'remarkable contrast between the scant evidence for "women's business" coming from Aboriginal sources and the positive cornucopia of interpretation, evaluation and embroidery coming from anthropologists and lawyers, always on hand to explain what is culturally appropriate to Ngarrindjeri women'.[2] Gough went on to say:

> Anthropologists have been better placed to find career-building subjects since the spread throughout the social sciences of postmodern relativism, according to which there is no such thing as empirically verified truth, and all belief-systems are of equal plausibility. There is an overwhelming temptation to leave behind the Western bourgeois ideal of the impartial observer, and to adopt the paradigm of the anthropologist as a culture-traveller totally immersed in the beliefs of his subjects, sharing their interests and willing to go to bat for them against the materialist Western world. The principle accepted by the American Anthropological Association and followed by many Australian practitioners is that 'the anthropologist's first responsibility is to those whose lives and customs they study. Should conflicts of interest arise, the interests of these people take precedence over other considerations'.[3]

After this diatribe against the hopelessly non-objective and witlessly committed anthropologist, the author goes on to express his unqualified belief in the documented knowledge of two earlier representatives of the Ngarrindjeri people:

> It is worth noting that Albert Korloan and Pinkie Mack, the greatly respected sources for Ngarrindjeri culture interviewed in the nineteen-forties by Ronald and Catherine Berndt and reported in their magisterial study *A World that Was,* expressed pleasure that their knowledge would now be available for all Australians.[4]

The author did not see fit to comment on the vast difference in relations between Aborigines and Whites in the 1940s—when, apart from people like the Berndts, most Australians lent neither credence, value nor authenticity to any Aboriginal beliefs, secret or otherwise, and when no Aboriginal practice or belief, however important, could have made the slightest difference to the government, graziers, miners, land developers and atomic weapon testers—and the 1990s, when such beliefs are part and parcel of a newly acquired political autonomy and cultural identity and hence of much more urgency and value. This itself is a curious act of disregard by an historian. Finally, the author comments that:

> [the anthropologist] briefed by the [Aboriginal] Legal Rights Movement as a 'facilitator' of evidence . . . should have aroused scepticism when in 1994 she could find . . . women's secrets unknown to Pinkie Mack, who was born in the eighteen-fifties and was revered by all Ngarrindjeri women as the custodian of their culture . . .[5]

Issues pertaining to the nature of social science research are raised by Gough's questioning of the discipline and practice of anthropology. They concern the role and function of secret knowledge in a social formation, the different perspectives that the anthropologist and the (oral) historian must necessarily bring to this phenomenon, and how each is likely to evaluate what we might call the social and epistemological status of such secret knowledge, given the very different notions each has as to what constitutes social life. In addressing more broadly the theoretical and methodological issues that underpin the controversy, I wish to clarify what I take to be the role of the anthropologist (in particular as against that of the oral historian), the role of secrecy in a non-western culture, and the nature of knowledge of sociality in non-western societies.

Although what I have to say applies very widely to non-western societies throughout the world, let me begin with the Ngarrindjeri. The book that Gough referred to in his article, published by Ronald and Catherine Berndt (two of the most renowned anthropologists of Aboriginal society in Australia this century) and entitled *A World that Was*,[6] is not an ethnography strictly speaking: it is a work of oral history. It was an attempt to *reconstruct* a culture from the memories of several surviving members of a tradition that no longer existed in that traditional form. Despite Ronald Berndt's understanding of the fractional nature of his informants' 'data', the assumption behind *A World that Was* is that such a thing as a whole culture exists. It is important to understand that when I say it no longer existed in traditional form. I am not making any claims as to what pieces of secret knowledge have or have not been forgotten by surviving Ngarrindjeri, or how much was still remembered when the Berndts compiled their interviews: I mean that such knowledge was not generated within an intact social system in which it functioned to label and describe people's places and interpersonal relationships in such a system. We must understand at the outset that there is no precise number of secrets or secret knowledge that defines or compiles a culture or society; rather, from the anthropological point of view it is the other way around: the necessity and function of secret or restricted knowledge is generated by the particular strategy or mode of social differentiation of a given community, as I will explain shortly.

But an oral history of the kind approved of by Gough would have to take the content of particular remembered secrets at face value. It must necessarily concede that whatever version of culture one elicits through its methodology, it is confined to the discourse of personal memory, and that such a portrait of culture itself would be exhausted by the sum total of subjective memories of each of its constituent members. As Robert Tonkinson himself remarked in the foreword to the Berndts' book: 'One of the problems with this type of reconstructive research, as the Berndts note . . . , is the intermingling of normative statements about what ideally ought to have been the correct behaviour, with accounts of what actually happened . . .' (p. xix). The Berndts would have had to pretend, along with their informants, that culture was in this instance equivalent to a narratable story or text, and that included in such texts in this case were the particular items of knowledge themselves.

The task of the oral historian is then to transcribe these narrated memories. The resulting texts become the material record of the culture of its narrators, and can be appealed to as documentary evidence.

It may not be surprising that in our current post-structuralist period, where textuality is exalted as a general model of social life, the notion that a culture resides largely in the narrated memories of its members would find a high degree of credibility. Because texts can readily be compared across languages and cultures, and across times and places, such a procedure absolves the oral historian of the difficult and laborious task of accounting for the differences between cultures, social systems and epochs themselves. Gough, though tacitly arguing for the superior empirical grounding of history over anthropology, finds his empirical facts solely in written documents, and thus oddly enough demonstrates his own peculiar adherence to a version of postmodernism in his steadfast belief in the sanctity of the text and its particular form of representation. But many anthropologists would still maintain that this is a narrow view of culture, and could even be pernicious, especially as applied to Aboriginal and other non-western societies, such as those in Papua New Guinea. What are the dangers of such a view, from the anthropologist's perspective?

First, if we see something that we can call 'cultural knowledge' as always unevenly and restrictedly distributed amongst members of a community, then an oral history will always be only a partial account and could never stand as a document of the total repertoire of a culture. Secondly, human social life is not reducible to its narratable form. It is not exhausted by a story one tells about it, or any number of stories, any more than we would say that the history of the Third Reich was accurately or comprehensively given to us in the memoirs of either Albert Speer or Karl Löwith or both together. Social life as I understand it lies in the contrast between the stories we tell in order to represent it to ourselves, and the actual, observable behaviour of those same story-tellers which is often at odds with or contradicts such accounts. It is in the contrast between what we do and what we say we do that some essentially human aspect of life, Aboriginal, Papua New Guinean, Western or otherwise, is revealed to us.

Thus, unlike the oral historian, who interviews the person divorced from any actual social life they are enmeshed in, the ethnographer is obliged to participate in and observe people in such social settings, in order to gauge the contrast between what language avers and what behaviour reveals. The oral historian cannot convey the social situatedness of a narrator's speech and action, because the extent to which we are influenced and constrained in such a way is very often concealed from us. This is the job of the anthropologist, in much the same way as it is the job of the psychoanalyst, to reveal the influences affecting people's behaviour and speech of which they may be unaware.

When it is suggested that 'historians alone have as their preoccupation and responsibility the reconstruction of the past by questioning all the surviving evidence',[7] I would urge that we understand the difference between *historiality* or *historiography,* a western fetishizing of the document and documentary evidence, and *historicity.* The latter refers both to (1) the manner in which the local construction, reconstruction and invocation of the past and the future play a constitutive role in people's discourse and social life, and (2) the phenomenon by which such construction is dialectically related to all those forces and influences which escape our constructionist efforts but which nevertheless impinge upon our perception and motivation. It is this dialectical relation, concerning broadly what we call the role of ideology in culture and human action, which is the anthropologist's subject matter, and apparently not that of Gough, though it is the concern of many responsible and intelligent historians. It is the identification of living history, if I may call it that, which makes the anthropological description of a community's social and cultural life 'historical' through and through, just as it is a concern for the social siting of the historical that makes the discipline of history so necessary to anthropology. From this point of view, those who suffer history often have a very different view of it from those who write it, authorize it and legitimate it.[8]

⋅⦿⋅

It is the anthropologist's understanding that many non-western societies were and continue to be very differently ordered than our own. Let us consider a social world where the point of social life, its rationale, was *not* to reveal, assemble and collate knowledge and information, as is the case in our own, but to prevent its spread, to restrict its transmission and to fashion a system of social statuses out of this variable distribution and restriction of knowledge. In both Aboriginal Australia and Papua New Guinea, there are many occasions in which ethnographers witness people's attempts to both *minimize* and *delay* the amount of information they publicly reveal about things, especially matters pertaining to land ownership, secret names and certain kinds of myth. Papua New Guinea people such as the Avatip and Foi characteristically seek to *not* reveal names and other information in public. The reasons are much the same as those that Aboriginal people give in the same context: if people know what you know, 'proof of ownership could become the opportunity for raids and thefts which could be used against people'.[9] Discursive strategies then become to force others to reveal these names or other items of restricted knowledge. Such an approach to talk and to the act of 'saying' does not then support any simple constructivist approach to knowledge. It also appears that it is precisely this non-constructionist approach to saying and knowing that is the hardest thing to convey to westerners who are not familiar with non-western modes of social and perceptual engagement. *Such an approach would see dispute, contestation and disparity of viewpoint as constitutive of social life, rather than an adventitious and unwelcome by-product of it.*

What we must consider is a social world founded not on consensus, uniformity, solidarity, cohesiveness, collective argument, or law in our sense. We must consider a social world founded on the opposite: relations are made between people by creating and stipulating the gaps and discontinuities between them. By assuming an uneven distribution of sacred knowledge, people create functional relationships of ritual specialization. People with specialized and secret knowledge must be called in to perform ceremonies necessary for other persons who lack such knowledge. Obligations are created between people based on their differences, rather than their similarities.

Under such conditions, knowledge is selectively, differentially and unevenly distributed within a society. It could now be argued that no piece of knowledge, no single datum of cultural information by itself could then 'stand for' the entirety of a culture. What one man or woman knows about the sacred character of a particular locale or piece of territory, and which is not known by other people who are identifiably members of the same community, does not therefore constitute in any direct way the culture or tradition.

But it is my point that *this argument rests on a divorcing of knowledge from its pragmatic, communicative, relational origin.* Let us consider the idea of a dreaming track, one that perhaps stretches the entire length of Australia, from the South Australian coast to the Top End. This track can be considered a single thing, the sum total of the marks and traces left on the landscape during the single journeys of a creator being or beings. We might even concede right at the outset that the track is a culture in and of itself. It certainly seems to be a coherent story of a cultural moment, circumscribed by the beginning and end of a journey of a being or beings. It links what we would at first identify as distinct linguistic and cultural groups: if the creator being passed through the territory of any particular group, then that group is linked to all others through whose territory the being also passed.

Now it is reasonable to assume, as is the case, that even if they were aware of the trans-local nature of a dreaming sequence or track, each local group might only intimately know the parts of the landscape that pertain to the journey of the creator being through their territory. They might not know, or be unable to know in any detail or in their experience, what happened to that being when it left the territory. The local territorial groups are linked by the route of the journey, yet the sum total of the linkages does not make a whole thing. The whole thing is assembled by the anthropologists who have collected the parts of the story from each group along the track and fitted the parts into a whole story with a beginning, middle and end. One would not dispute the wholeness of this story nor its facticity, yet prior to the assemblage by the anthropologist, *it never existed as a whole, complete thing.*[10]

Thus an important point has to be made. If dreamings, or mythical journeys, did not constitute a whole thing between different territorial groups, why should we assume that they performed such a unifying function *within* the group? Could it be that among the different clans and lineages that constituted the local territorial group, knowledge of mythical journeys and linked dreaming sites was similarly discontinuous, fragmented and selectively distributed? The point of social communication would then be to release the evidence of knowledge in a controlled and allusive way, to show the proof that it exists rather than the knowledge itself: *that is, to demonstrate the social implications of the revealed disparities between sites and possessors of knowledge.*

We could say then that Aboriginal and Papua New Guinea cultures seek always to make visible such points of rupture, that this is the supremely creative act for them. We would then find the clearest evidence for the intactness of Aboriginal society, whether it be in South Australia or northeast Arnhem Land, in the surfacing of disputes over possession of secret knowledge and restricted access to territorial and cosmological mythopoeia.[11]

We can now return to the point with which I began. Oral historians believe an account of a culture to be complete when they feel that all the data have been documented. Anthropologists, insofar as they would concede that something as open-ended and ongoing as 'social life' is ever complete, or ever comes to an end, only admit that it does so in the form of the system or theory one devises to describe or model it.

⟞⟡⟞

We have now cleared the way for consideration of what most of us will see as the more important issue in this case, that of the 'fabrication' of secret, sacred knowledge for political purposes by indigenous people. The questions I wish to ask now pertain not to whether some Ngarrindjeri women truly believe in the existence of sacred, secret women's business, but to the social conditions of its elicitation: how and when they acquired those beliefs, under what social and political influences and conditions. From a strictly historical perspective, all beliefs are 'recent' at one stage. The enduring and stable in what we call culture and religion is always negotiated and made visible through the contingent and mutable conventions of the present; to the extent that there is never any perfect instauration of law or convention, then every conventional act or belief is, as Roy Wagner maintains,[12] innovative or 'new' or 'fabricated'.

Thus the perception of antiquity of a belief or custom, in a strict phenomenological sense, can only be negotiated in a present moment. How can we distinguish between the recent acquisition of old knowledge from the recent creation of knowledge per se? The day after the creation of Magna Carta it was already a vital part of the British legal tradition—but we know this only with hindsight, as it might have been retracted on the third day of its life and never heard of again. Now we have had the Magna Carta for centuries. The fact that I may have found out about it at school only two days ago may make my knowledge recent in terms of acquisition, but the knowledge itself is of long duration. The question, again, is thus not one of recentness or antiquity of a belief as a measure of its 'authenticity' or 'truth content', but of the political conditions and motivations for its evocation. A false belief nevertheless can serve a positive social function and be 'true' in the ordinary sense in which we as anthropologists construe such social function.

Peter Sutton, an Australian anthropologist with long experience with a number of Aboriginal communities, remarked to me that he has seen sacred sites 'discovered' by Aboriginal people in the bush where there was absolutely no threat to the site or the land tenure. The site content, from its inception, and the method of 'finding' it, was, according to him, perfectly true to Aboriginal cultural conventions in these cases. To repeat what I suggested earlier, the manifestation of supernatural presence, in particular features of the landscape, is not just a catalogue of religious events; it is a conceptual and a perceptual mechanism with which Aboriginal people make hypotheses about affairs and events in their current life. 'Discovering' sacred sites, including those that have not previously been recorded by anthropologists or anyone else, is a common and inevitable product of such a perceptual and conceptual strategy.

Finally, these strategies of elicitatory fabrication, must be formally situated within a larger system that is now based on a hierarchy of western legal rational authority and Aboriginal traditional knowledge. Within any such hierarchical system, different forms of knowledge preempt and obviate others. The *internal* pre-empting and cancellation of knowledge at work within Aboriginal society is now embedded within a system that encompasses two incommensurable sub-systems (White and Aboriginal) to which it also appears at the same time *external*. There is a new 'inside' (i.e. secret or restricted) and 'outside' (i.e. public) to Aboriginal knowledge now, based on the realization that all knowledge is subtended by western legal canons of verification. This means that the 'question of whether the Ngarrindjeri women 'made up' the knowledge as a ploy to stop the bridge, or whether they knew of it beforehand, might not be as important as tracing the demands made upon Aboriginal knowledge within this larger 'system'. Performatively, knowledge creation and asseveration now serve the function of combating racism and cultural ignorance, and is no less knowledge put to pragmatic situated social use than it had been in its traditional religious context.

⋰⊙⋱

Anthropologists, because they go and live in a community, are both participants in it and yet always an outsider, have the opportunity to see connections which the members of that community do not see, or which are institutionally or otherwise concealed from them. I maintain that such an approach, essential to anthropology, is what is missing in oral history, which inevitably equates a living culture with the set of documents one can reduce it to. For myself, I prefer this more difficult task of reconciling the inevitable slippages between language, assertion, contestation and avowed knowledge through long-term observation and interview. And I would hope that anyone contemplating what must result from such a long-term involvement in people's lives realizes that this implies more than recording people's stories: it means being entailed in and by their lives and bearing the inevitable consequences of having the effects of those lives impinge upon one's own.

The whole rationale of anthropology stems from the constructive dilemma of managing descriptive veracity in the midst of profound engagement in a community's life. It appears as if it is exactly the theoretical and ethical implications of this engagement which are either avoided or denied by Gough. though I hardly think he is representative of many historians these days. But if one admits confronting this dilemma as a sound strategy for understanding people and their social life, then being obliged to them, as our anthropological code of conduct insists we must be, means something much more than the debased and politically self-interested advocacy that some ill-informed opponents of anthropology construe as our true motivation. It means that we are professionally bound to ask awkward questions on behalf of the less advantaged, and to challenge the complacency of the status quo and the so-called rationality of a system which would set indigenous beliefs and culture in amber and deny indigenous communities the possibility of life, transformation and political autonomy that rests on the ongoing invention that is social life.

Notes

1. Terms of Reference, Hindmarsh Island Bridge Royal Commission, 16 June 1995.
2. A. Gough, 'Hindmarsh Island and the Politics of the Future', *Adelaide Review,* June 1995, pp. 8-9.
3. ib. p. 8.
4. ib. p. 9.
5. ib.
6. Milbourne U.P., 1993.
7. Professor Wilfred Prest, in a letter to *The Australian,* 1 June 1995.
8. See *The Past is a Foreign Country,* ed. Tim Ingold, Group for Debates in Anthropological Theory No. 5, 1993. Department of Social Anthropology, University of Manchester.
9. Rose, D. (1994) 'Whose Confidentiality? Whose Intellectual Property?' in *Claims to Knowledge, Claims to Country: Native Title, Native Title Claims and the Role of the Anthropologist.* Canberra: The Native Title Research Unit, AITSIS: p. 6.
10. The Berndts say the following: 'As a rule, no local descent group, clan, or dialect unit owns a complete myth. Even though at first it may appear to do so, what it has is usually only a section, dealing with some actions of a certain being. The men over in the next stretch of country may own another section and can perform the rites associated with that—and so on, all over the country. Members of several local groups come together from time to time to perform their separate, but linked sections. But the myth is never acted out *in toto* because all its owners could not meet, and in fact would probably not even know one another' (*The World of the First Australians,* Adelaide: Rigby Publishers, 1985, pp. 243-44).
11. See Ian Keen's *Knowledge and Secrecy in an Aboriginal Religion,* Oxford U.P., 1994.
12. *The Invention of Culture,* U. of Chicago P., 1981.

NO ↵

The Hindmarsh Island Bridge and the
Credibility of Australian Anthropology

The Hindmarsh Island Bridge affair has become a turning point for Aboriginal heritage claims in Australia. For the first time, Aboriginal objections to a proposed development were denounced as a 'hoax' by another group of Aborigines with no discernible interest in the development itself. As a result of these denunciations by the so-called 'dissident Ngarrindjeri women', the South Australian state government established a Royal Commission to investigate, and in December 1995 the commission found that the original claims had been fabricated to prevent the construction of the bridge. Because of the role that anthropological arguments played in supporting the anti-bridge Ngarrindjeri, the profession has undergone an unprecedented degree of critical scrutiny, and now faces widespread doubts about its credibility.

Unfortunately however, people whose only knowledge of this bizarre case comes from James Weiner's ANTHROPOLOGY TODAY article will have a poor understanding of the matters at stake.[1] Even allowing that Weiner wrote without the benefit of the Royal Commission's findings, his article omits a great deal of vital information. He displays a surprising indifference to the ethnographic particularities of the Ngarrindjeri, and his approach to questions arising out of anthropological involvement in public policy is evasive and naïve.

⁂

Hindmarsh Island is one of a number of islands near the mouth of the Murray River, 70 km south-east of Adelaide. At present, travel to the island is by ferry, and the bridge was necessary for the increased traffic that would result from major extensions to a marina on the island. A state government instrumentality was to build the bridge, and the marina developers would reimburse the costs later. The bridge first received widespread publicity in local and Adelaide newspapers in 1989, and the following year archaeological and anthropological surveys revealed that the Ngarrindjeri were concerned about possible damage to middens and burial sites on the island and the mainland opposite. But these concerns could be met without preventing the bridge's construction, and there

From Ron Brunton, "The Hindmarsh Island Bridge and the Credibility of Australian Anthropology," *Anthropology Today*, vol. 12, no. 4 (August 1996). Copyright © 1996 by The Royal Anthropological Institute. Reprinted by permission of Blackwell Publishers Ltd.

were no Ngarrindjeri objections when preliminary work was undertaken in May 1990. This preliminary work continued over a couple of years.[2]

By late 1992 however, a number of property owners began to complain that the bridge would affect their visual amenity, and that the increased traffic would cause environmental deterioration. Ngarrindjeri opposition first emerged in October 1993—apparently after the anti-bridge group decided that Aboriginal involvement would strengthen their hand. But formal applications in December 1993 to state and federal governments for the prohibition of the bridge were based on the existence of archaeological sites, and nothing else.

In late March 1994 a couple of prominent Ngarrindjeri were visited by an anthropologist, Lindy Warrell, on another matter. When Hindmarsh Island was mentioned, Warrell said she had been working on 'women's business' in the state's north and it would be nice if the Ngarrindjeri had something similar. About two weeks later the first public indications of 'women's business' emerged, perhaps coincidentally, but shortly after it had become clear that the archaeological sites did not provide sufficient basis for the then federal Minister of Aboriginal Affairs, Robert Tickner, to override the state government and prohibit the bridge.

In April the developer and his solicitor were told by the regional chairman of a major Aboriginal organization something to the effect that 'Hindmarsh Island is significant because it is shaped like a woman and there are woman's issues to do with the island associated with, birth'. These claims had supposedly been 'researched' by Doreen Kartinycri, a Ngarrindjeri employee of the South Australian Museum who was well-known for her work on Aboriginal family histories, and who had been involved in other heritage disputes.

On May 9 about 15 Ngarrindjeri women travelled to Hindmarsh Island. There, according to Dorothy Wilson, who was present, and who became a key 'dissident' after she started making her own inquiries into the claims, Doreen Kartinyeri told them about 'women's business'. Kartinyeri also said that neighbouring Mundoo Island was sacred to men as a place where bodies were prepared for burial. Apart from Kartinycri herself, none of the women claimed to have known about 'women's business' before, but all agreed to send a fax to Tickner demanding that he prohibit the bridge. A few days later Kartinyeri also sent a letter to the Minister, which was composed with the help of Steve Hemming, a historian-anthropologist at the Museum.

In response, the Minister commissioned Cheryl Saunders, a University of Melbourne law professor, to inquire into the significance of the region as the relevant legislation required. On June 17, the Aboriginal Legal Rights Movement (ARLM) appointed Deane Fergie, an anthropologist in Weiner's department at the University of Adelaide, to 'facilitate' a meeting between Saunders and the Ngarrindjeri women 'proponents'. Fergie knew Kartinyeri, but she had no particular knowledge of Ngarrindjeri culture. At the time of her appointment she had not even read the major text on the traditional culture, Ronald and Catherine Berndt's *A World That Was*. Little more than a week later however, the ARLM told Fergie that the brief had changed, and that she should write a report within five days.

Fergie's report. which contained two confidential appendices to be read only by women, clearly had a major impact on Saunders' own discussion, and Saunders referred to it many times.[3] Both reports went to the Federal Minister, and on July 10 Tickner announced a declaration which effectively imposed a 25 year ban on the bridge. This decision was widely reported in the Australian media the following day. As a consequence of the ban, the developers' company went into liquidation, and the developers, Tom and Wendy Chapman, are now on the dole.

⚜

Fergie and Saunders both stressed that the bridge would desecrate Ngarrindjeri traditions. In Fergie's words, it would 'form a permanent link between two parts of the landscape whose cosmological efficacy is contingent on separation'. The region around Hindmarsh Island, was 'crucial for the reproduction of the Ngarrindjeri people.' Fergie stated that she had been told that there were 'very strict laws' relating to people's movement on Hindmarsh and Mundoo Islands, and that some Ngarrindjeri women who had made a bus tour of Hindmarsh Island in June 1994 had refused to leave the bus at many places for fear of breaking these laws.

Fergie gave the clear impression that the beliefs were not a recent invention. She claimed that the supposed Ngarrindjeri custodians, two of whom are in their seventies, have had the relevant knowledge 'since their puberty', which was around the time that the Berndts were conducting their field research in the early 1940s. She also stated that the case 'demonstrates the specificity and persistence of womens [sic] tradition in Aboriginal society'.[4] The 'proponent women' themselves claim that it is ancient—40,000 years old'.

Fergie and Saunders both referred to the Berndts' book. Fergie in particular cited it in an apparent attempt to suggest a ready familiarity with the key text, and to point to supposed continuities in nomenclature, mythology, treatment of the dead, and symbolic motifs—although in the last case she actually misrepresented the data.[5] But both Fergie and Saunders chose to omit one crucial piece of information from their respective reports. The Berndts had specifically noted that there was no evidence that the Ngarrindjeri had any gender-based secret-sacred domain. In his summary foreword to *A World That Was*, Robert Tonkinson also noted that Catherine Bernt had previously written that 'gender-based differences, in the sense of inclusion-exclusion, in religious and other affairs, were minimal', and that she had suggested 'this as one of the remarkable features of [Ngarrindjeri] society'. The book even has an index entry, 'secret-sacred issues, absence of'.[6]

During the Royal Commission Fergie said that her findings about the women's secret traditions represented a 'significant anthropological discovery'.[7] But even the loosest canons of research require that a 'significant discovery' should be identified as such, and this was not done in Fergie's report. In his article, Weiner also ignored the Berndts' statements about the absence of gender-based secret traditions. Indeed, Weiner's overgeneralized and ultimately irrelevant discussion of secret knowledge in Aboriginal Australia and

Papua New Guinea gives no indication that there was anything unusual about the Ngarrindjeri. And he invokes Austin Gough's remarks in a manner that implies that Fergie had merely discovered traditions relating to a specific site, rather than a totally unexpected domain of Ngarrindjeri culture.[8]

⋅◆⋅

The professional imperative Fergie—and Sanders[9]—to note a seemingly fundamental conflict between their findings and those of two of Australia's most experienced and distinguished ethnographers is quite separate from the question of whether the Berndts' assessment of the Ngarrindjeri was justified. Of course, the Berndts could have been wrong. Nevertheless, the evidence indicating that the secret women's traditions are a very recent invention is highly compelling.

It is necessary to make the obvious distinction between knowing the content of secrets, as against knowing that secrets exist. By their very nature, and in the light of the restrictions the proponents are demanding, the women's traditions would have had highly significant and visible consequences for the behaviour of all Ngarrindjeri. The possibility that these could have completely escaped the notice of all researchers and other observers until April 1994 is beyond belief, as the region is one of the most intensively studied in Australia, and the records go back over 150 years. When the Berndts carried out their fieldwork, Catherine was fully aware of the possibility of Aboriginal women's secret religious traditions, both from her own work at Ooldea, and from Phyllis Kaberry's work in the Kimberley.[10] The Berndts' major informant, Albert Karloan, was passionately committed to telling them all he could about the traditional culture, seeing his task as a 'sacred trust'. And he and other Ngarrindjeri had no hesitation about telling them specific things that once had been highly restricted.[11]

Even more significantly, when the Berndts were working with the Ngarrindjeri, barrages designed to control the salinity of the Lower Murray were just being completed. The Goolwa barrage joins Hindmarsh Island to the mainland in the south, and a series of barrages—which can carry a single lane of vehicular traffic—form a similar connection to the east. The construction of these barrages between 1935 and 1940 involved major engineering work, some of which, such as the driving of pylons into the river bed, would have been desecrating in itself according to the present claims. Ngarrindjeri workmen participated in the construction, but Betty Tatt, one of the 'dissident' women who was living in the area at the time, told the Royal Commission that there were no suggestions from anybody that the barrages posed any danger of desecration or threat to women's reproductive abilities.[12]

The existence of the barrages was too obvious a problem for Saunders and Fergie to ignore. They attempted to explain it with two different kinds of arguments, neither of which can be sustained. The first involved subtle, but completely uninformed, distinctions between barrages and bridges in terms of permanence, solidity, function and effect on the flow of water.[13] In fact, for some of the supposed distinctions the barrages are far more 'desecrating' than the bridge would ever be.[14] In addition, the subtleties of the distinctions that are now being made would have been extremely difficult to sustain around the time when the barrages were being completed, as the cosmologically damaging effects would not yet necessarily have manifested themselves. At the very least it would have been a period of intense anxiety and widespread speculation, and it is extremely unlikely that any concerns would have been kept from the Berndts or from other anthropologists who were working with the Ngarrindjeri at the time, such as Norman Tindale—who was assisted by his wife Dorothy—and Alison Harvey. Yet as the Royal Commission noted, 'None of the ethnographers and historians working in the area during the period of construction of the barrages and afterwards recorded any indication of desecration.'[15] And had the Berndts heard any concerns about the barrages, it is impossible to see how they would have produced the interpretation of traditional Ngarrindjeri culture that they did.

The second kind of argument advanced by Fergie and Saunders was that when the barrages were built the Ngarrindjeri had no prospect of preventing them. While not specifically addressing the problem of the barrages, Weiner makes a similar point, noting that in the 1940s, 'no Aboriginal practice or belief, however important. could have made the slightest difference to the government,' etc.[16] Certainly any Ngarrindjeri complaints would have been ignored or ridiculed by the authorities. But Ngarrindjeri men and women had no hesitation in conveying their anger and concerns about other matters such as land clearing and archaeological research—which they had equally little hope of preventing—to the Berndts and to Norman Tindale. The Berndts note that older people 'were outspoken about those who excavated burial mounds and camp sites', activities which were seen as desecration of the land.[17] Such protests also show the inappropriateness of Weiner's attempt to dismiss the relevance of the Berndts' work to the present case by suggesting that it is only an 'oral history', based on interviews with 'people divorced from any actual social life they are enmeshed in'.[18] The cultural knowledge' of the older Ngarrindjeri generated certain kinds of responses to circumstances that the ethnographers were able to observe and record, and which contributed to their understanding of Ngarrindjeri culture.

Another obvious problem for those who suggest that it was the Berndts who got it wrong is that it took four years for any Aboriginal opposition to emerge. Fergie and the 'women's business' proponents have attempted to explain this in a number of ways. Some of these are mutually contradictory, and none of them stand up to any examination. For instance, in her report Fergie suggested that the women who knew of the secret traditions were living in different parts of South Australia, and were unaware of the bridge proposal. Elsewhere she stated that Doreen Kartinyeri not heard about the bridge until January 1994.[19] But important information flows readily throughout the Ngarrindjeri community as there is a lot of long distance visiting and attendance at ceremonies, as well as telephone contact.[20] Important information flows readily throughout the Ngarrindjeri community. In any case, in 1990 one of the supposed custodians, Edith Rigney, was a member and attended meetings of the Lower Murray Aboriginal Heritage Committee with a number of other Ngarrindjeri who had been involved in consultations over the bridge.[21] The real implications from Fergie's suggestions are that the custodians of 'women's business' were cavalier about their obligations and did not bother to keep themselves informed of potentially threatening developments.

In her May 1994 letter to Tickner, Doreen Kartinyeri made a different claim, stating 'I have always known about the stories associated with... Women's Business, but until recently I didn't know the exact place that they referred to'. However, two of the three women she named as having passed on the information to her had died many years previously, and the other woman denied knowing anything about women's business'. And in a magazine interview she claimed to have known that the stories referred to Hindmarsh Island in 1954.[22]

The Royal Commission identified many other major inconsistencies and defects in the research and arguments of Fergie and the other supporters of women's business. The transcripts also show that Fergie, her counsel, and other 'proponent' anthropologists seriously misrepresented the texts in attempts to suggest that the existing literature does contain hints of secret-sacred Ngarrindjeri traditions.[23] Certainly, Fergie was given very little time in which to complete her original report. But one of the best ways of compensating for this problem would have been to seek advice from Philip Clarke, a former colleague of hers at the South Australian Museum. Clarke had been studying Ngarrindjeri culture for over a decade, he had just submitted his Ph.D. thesis on the Aboriginal cultural geography of the Lower Murray, and he was married to a Ngarrindjeri. Fergie told the Royal Commission that she had intended to contact Clarke, but that his telephone was not answering.[24] Clarke's office is a couple of minutes walk from Fergie's own office at the University, the Museum has receptionists who take messages, and at the time Fergie was sufficiently friendly with Clarke to ring him at home.

Nevertheless, a few days after the Royal Commission's report was released, Weiner defended Fergie in comments to the press, stating that he 'maintained absolutely', that she 'did the best job she could under the circumstances'. He added that in many ways' the Royal Commission's attacks on her were gratuitous and unwarranted.[25]

&<0>»

But if Fergie was being defended—at least publicly—by a leading anthropologist, the same did not occur for those who helped to expose the fabrication. When the 'dissidents' denounced 'women's business' in May 1995, they were widely attacked as stooges of conservative politicians, and ridiculed by sections of the media. Privately, a great many anthropologists were scathing about the 'women's business' claims, but they kept a public silence. Angered by this silence and the treatment the 'dissident women' were receiving, Philip Jones, then head of the Anthropology Division at the South Australian Museum, told the media that there was 'not a shred of evidence to suggest that secret sacred women's business existed on Hindmarsh Island'.[26]

He was later joined by Philip Clarke, and the two provided the bulk of the anthropological support for the 'dissident women's' position during the Royal

Commission. The only other anthropologist to assist the commission was Bob Tonkinson, who acted as a consultant. Despite its efforts, the commission was unable to obtain the services of any female anthropologist from Australia, and had to engage Jane Goodale from the United States.[27]

Like Weiner, other prominent anthropologists such as Diane Austin-Broos, Julie Marcus and Peter Sutton, criticized the scholars who were publicly complaining about the unconscionable behaviour of the profession in regards to Hindmarsh Island.[28] When, in an attempt to recover some credibility for the profession, Clarke told the Royal Commission that anthropologists were 'appalled by what they believed to be in Deane Fergie's report' and that the report was 'bad anthropology', he too was condemned.[29] Gillian Cowlishaw from Sydney University was introduced on television as stating that Clarke had done an 'immense disservice to his profession'. Cowlishaw also suggested that his comments were at variance with a statement released by the Australian Anthropological Society (AAS), and even implied that Clarke's right to call himself an anthropologist might be questioned, as he was not a member of the AAS. (A line of attack that was also pursued by Fergie and her counsel at the Royal Commission, who attempted to make much of the fact that Clarke's Ph.D. was jointly in geography and anthropology.)[30]

The AAS statement was largely drafted by Cowlishaw, though with her original reference to 'genocidal threat' omitted in an apparent concession to wider Australian sensitivities. While carefully worded, it is a clear attack on those with a 'crudely empiricist understanding of culture' who were arguing that 'women's business' had been fabricated to prevent the bridge. The statement wrongly pretended that the controversy had cast anthropology as having to 'judge the truth or falsity of Aboriginal beliefs'—the frequent refrain of Tickner and the 'proponent women'. This ignores the role that matters of truth or falsity necessarily play in any assessment of the sincerity, contexts and explanations of those beliefs, and indeed—current fashions notwithstanding—in all anthropological work. There are many assertions in the Fergie report, for instance, which are clearly intended to be taken as true, although quite a number of them have turned out to be false. A failure to acknowledge this situation ultimately casts the anthropologist as merely an amanuensis for informants.

Yet at the same time the AAS statement did acknowledge the possibility that deliberate fabrication had taken place, though without offering any plausible means of finding out whether this had occurred—hardly surprising given the expressed attitudes towards 'truth or falsity'—or even accepting that it mattered very much.[31] A similar kind of indifference is apparent in Weiner's article and in his remarks about those who would 'set indigenous beliefs and culture in amber'. From a theoretical viewpoint, the more important questions may well relate to the 'demands made upon Aboriginal knowledge within the contemporary Australian system.[32] (In fact, the most interesting and important theoretical questions are very dependent on whether the beliefs were recently invented. For if the 'proponent's' claims really are of some antiquity, the implications for our understanding of knowledge transmission, the maintenance of what are, in effect, secret conspiracies, and the veracity of anthropological data are very great indeed.)

But anthropologists who accept professional consultancies on heritage matters are being asked for practical assessments, because heritage claims can have enormous impacts on the interests of other people. Are anthropologists really saying that if a group of Aborigines wishes to stop any development, anywhere in Australia, at any time, they should be at liberty to do so, for all that matters is what people currently say they believe? That is certainly how it appears to many observers, and it is an inference not far removed from what the AAS, Weiner, and some other prominent Australian anthropologists have actually stated.[33]

The Hindmarsh Island case also suggests that despite all the moral posturing—the professional obligation 'to ask awkward questions on behalf of the less advantaged' as Weiner puts it[34]—many anthropologists are only comfortable with those of the 'less advantaged' who take an adversarial position in relation to the wider Australian society. The 'dissident women' showed great courage and honesty. They wanted to tell the truth about their history and culture, and to counter what they saw as degrading representations of their past. They were ostracised and subjected to death threats, and a sorceress from Central Australia was brought down to Adelaide—apparently on public money—in order to intimidate them.[35] Yet, when I travelled to South Australia to meet them early this year, I discovered that, apart from Jones and Clarke, I was the only anthropologist who had attempted to contact them and hear their stories.

The Hindmarsh Island saga is far from over. The developers have already initiated damages claims against Tickner and Saunders, and further claims against others involved—including anthropologists—are likely. Two days before the Royal Commission released its report, a group of Ngarrindjeri women and men made a fresh application to Tickner to stop the bridge, using similar claims to those that had been considered by the commission. Instead of dismissing the application as vexatious, Tickner established another enquiry, this time under a judge, Jane Mathews. Soon afterwards, the Labor Government lost power—and Tickner lost his seat in a massive swing against him, at least partly attributable to Hindmarsh Island. However, the new Government appears legally obliged to continue with the enquiry (although Mathews' appointment is currently subject to a High Court challenge). Unlike the Royal Commission, this enquiry is not open to the public, and participants have to sign an undertaking that they will not disseminate any submissions that they receive—conditions that mean its findings, should they differ from those of the Commission, will be widely disbelieved. And also unlike the Royal Commission, the enquiry has encountered no shortage of anthropologists willing to assist Judge Mathews. For this is a 'good' enquiry, established by a man who had made his support for the proponents of 'women's business' abundantly clear, and whose politics are more congenial to most anthropologists than those of the conservative South Australian state government.

Nevertheless, there are some welcome signs. Two anthropologists—Grayson Gerrard and Ken Maddock, renowned for his work on Aboriginal law and religion—have prepared submissions to the Mathews enquiry for the developers' solicitors. And another internationally renowned anthropologist, Les Hiatt, who was outside Australia during the Royal Commission hearings, has offered to make a submission to the enquiry for the 'dissident women's' solicitors, and has indicated his support for Clarke and Jones. It is to be hoped that their actions will encourage more Australian anthropologists to recognize their responsibilities to the wider public and thus help to restore the profession's credibility.

Notes

1. James F. Weiner, Anthropologists, historians and the secret of social knowledge. ANTHROPOLOGY TODAY, October 1995.

2. Except where indicated, information in this section is taken from Iris E. Stevens, *Report of the Hindmarsh Island Bridge Royal Commission.* State Print. Adelaide. 1995: 54–143.

3. Cheryl Saunders, *Report to the Minister for Aboriginal and Torres Strait Islander Affairs on the Significant Aboriginal Area in the Vicinity of Goolwa and Hindmarsh (Kumarangk) Island,* July 1994, e.g. pages 23–24, 27–29, 31–32, 35, 37–39.

4. Dean Fergie, *To All the Mothers That Were, To All the Mothers That Are, To All the Mothers That Will Be: An Anthropological Assessment of the Threat of Injury and Desecration to Aboriginal Tradition by the Proposed Hindmarsh Island Bridge Construction.* July 1994, pages 19, 15, 10, 16, 12.

5. *Ibid.,* pages 13, 15, 6:cf. Stevens, *op. cit.,* page 278; Ronald M. Berndt & Catherine H. Berndt, with John Stanton, *A World That Was.* Melbourne University Press. 1993, 154–155.

6. C. Berndt, Retrospect and prospect, in Peggy Brock, ed. *Women, Rites & Sites,* Allen & Unwin. Sydney, 1989, page 11; *A World That Was, op. cit.,* pages xxix, 621; see also pages 24, 163, 210. One element of the male initiation ritual was supposedly secret-sacred, but the ritual as a whole was not.

7. Transcripts of the Royal Commission into the Hindmarsh Island Bridge, page 5330.

8. Weiner, *op. cit.,* pages 5, 4.

9. Saunders said she had consulted the Berndts' book (*op. cit.,* page 9), and it requires no particular anthropological skills to recognise that the Berndts' and Tonkinson's remarks were very relevant to her report.

10. C. Berndt, *op. cit.,* pages 2–6: P. M. Kaberry, *Aboriginal Women, Sacred and Profane.* Routledge, London, 1939.

11. *A World That Was, op. cit.,* pages 282, 148, 176.

12. Stevens, *op. cit.,* pages 245–246, 261: cf. Fergie, *op. cit.,* page 18.

13. Saunders, *op. cit.,* pages 38–39; Fergie, *op. cit.,* pages 19–20.

14. Stevens, *op. cit.,* pages 245–250.

15. *Ibid.* page 246.

16. Saunders, *op. cit.,* page 38; Fergie, *op. cit.,* page 22; Weiner, *op. cit.,* page 4.

17. Norman Tindale, Prupe and Koromarange: a legend of the Tanganekeld, Coorong, South Australia. *Transactions of the Royal Society of South Australia,* volume 62, number 1, 1938, page 20; R. M. Berndt. Some aspects of Jaralde culture, South Australia. *Oceania,* volume 11, 1940, page 166; *A World That Was, op. cit.,* page 16.

18. Weiner, *op. cit.,* pages 4–5.

19. Fergie, *op. cit.,* page 16; Pamela Lyon, Hindmarsh Island bridge: taking care of women's business. *The Adelaidean,* 1 August 1994, page 6.

20. Foreword, *A World That Was, op. cit.,* page xvii.

21. Stevens, *op. cit.,* page 254.

22. *Ibid.,* pages 134–137; Craig Henderson, Troubled waters. *Who Weekly,* 17 July 1995, page 274. In a telephone conversation, Henderson told me that the words of the interview were checked back with Kartinyeri before publication.

23. Stevens, *op. cit.,* pages 156–162; Chapter 6: Ron Brunton, The False Culture Syndrome. *IPA Backgrounder,* volume 8, number 2, March 1996, pages 6–7.

24. Transcripts *op. cit.,* page 5326.

25. John Kerin, Call for sacred-site index to avert repeat of bridge debacle. *The Australian,* 27 December 1995.

26. Transcripts *op. cit.,* pages 4427, 4431. Although Jones would not have known, Ken Maddock wrote an article for the Melbourne *Herald-Sun* in March 1995 stating his belief that the traditions were a recent invention.

27. *Ibid.,* pages 6667–6668.

28. Dianne Austin-Broos, Evidence that is contemporary. *The Australian,* 16 November 1995; Julie Marcus, Ill-founded in fact and logic. *The Australian,* 22 November 1995; Peter Sutton. Forensic anthropology, expert evidence and legal culture in Australia, paper presented at AAS Conference. Adelaide, 29 September 1995.

29. Transcripts, *op. cit.,* page 3573. Although few anthropologists had seen Fergie's report, its broad thrust could be inferred. When he wrote his article Weiner probably had not seen it, as in February 1996 he asked if I could send him a copy, because legal considerations prevented Fergie from giving one to him. However, by the time of the AAS Conference in September 1996, well before Clarke made his statement, many anthropologists had at least been informed of the crucial omission of the report.

30. ABC TV (Adelaide) *7:30 Report,* 18 October 1995; Gillian Cowlishaw, What really appalled anthropologists, *The Australian,* 18 October 1995; Transcripts, *op. cit.,* pages 3563–3571, 5933–5935.

31. Hindmarsh and anthropology. *Australian Anthropology Society Newsletter* 62, December 1995, page 24.

32. Weiner, *op. cit.,* pages 6–7. Perhaps I should note that I have attempted to deal with these issues, though in a broad-brush way, in *Blocking Business: An Anthropological Assessment of the Hindmarsh Island Dispute,* Tasman Institute Occasional Paper B31, August 1995, pages 22–32, which was based on a submission I made to the Royal Commission. But such discussions are often unwelcome to many Aboriginal organizations, because they raise embarrassing questions.

33. See e.g. Ian Keen, Undermining credibility: advocacy and objectivity in the Coronation Hill debate, A. T. 8.2, April 1992, page 8; Aboriginal beliefs vs. mining at Coronation Hill: the containing force of traditionalism. *Human Organization,* volume 52, 1993, page 344.

34. *Op. cit.,* page 7.

35. Chris Kenny, Witchcraft, *The Adelaide Review,* May 1996.

POSTSCRIPT

Do Anthropologists Have a Moral Responsibility to Defend the Interests of "Less Advantaged" Communities?

Native communities in the United States, Canada, Australia, and New Zealand are increasingly hiring anthropologists to assist them in a variety of public policy concerns. Cases like the Hindmarsh Island Bridge affair show that there are grey areas at the boundaries of established cultural tradition and that anthropologists may not always be able to defend the political and legal positions advocated by native communities.

The Hindmarsh Island Bridge affair has been one of the most divisive controversies in Australian anthropology in recent years. It has been debated in the Australian courts, by a Royal Commission, in newspapers, on television, in several books written for popular audiences, and in anthropological journals. At times the debate has been rancorous and personal both in public discourse and among anthropologists.

Robert Tonkinson's discussion in "Anthropology and Aboriginal Tradition: The Hindmarsh Island Bridge Affair and the Politics of Interpretation," *Oceania* (September 1997) raises a number of questions for academic anthropologists, including: How can secret knowledge that is essential to a society's survival exist yet remain hidden from a general public awareness? How should anthropologists deal with knowledge that is not generally shared within the community, as is the case with most secret knowledge? Building on these concerns, Weiner's essay, "Culture in a Sealed Envelope: The Concealment of Australian Aboriginal Heritage and Tradition in the Hindmarsh Island Bridge Affair," *Journal of the Royal Anthopological Institute* (June 1999), argues that both the state and the anthropologists who were involved with the case have failed to consider the relational nature of social knowledge and culture. An essay that suggests that the Hindmarsh Island Bridge affair has feminist implications is M. Langton's "The Hindmarsh Island Bridge Affair: How Aboriginal Women's Religion Became an Administerable Affair," *Australian Feminist Studies* (October 1996).

Contributors to This Volume

EDITORS

KIRK M. ENDICOTT is a professor and the chairman of the Department of Anthropology at Dartmouth College. He received a B.A. in anthropology from Reed College in 1965, a Ph.D. in anthropology from Harvard University in 1975, and a D.Phil. in social anthropology from the University of Oxford in 1976. He has repeatedly conducted field research among the Batek people of Malaysia. He is the author of *An Analysis of Malay Magic* (Clarendon Press, 1970) and *Batek Negrito Religion: The World-view and Rituals of a Hunting and Gathering People of Peninsular Malaysia* (Clarendon Press, 1979) and is coauthor, with Robert K. Dentan, Alberto G. Gomez, and M. Barry Hooker, of *Malaysia and the "Original People": A Case Study of the Impact of Development on Indigenous Peoples* (Allyn and Bacon, 1997).

ROBERT L. WELSCH is a visiting professor of anthropology at Dartmouth College and adjunct curator of anthropology at The Field Museum in Chicago. He received a B.A. in anthropology from Northwestern University in 1972, an M.A. in anthropology from the University of Washington in 1976, and a Ph.D. from the same department in 1982. He has conducted field research among the Ningerum people of Papua New Guinea, the Mandar people of South Sulawesi, Indonesia, and the diverse peoples of the Sepik Coast of Papua New Guinea. He is the author of *An American Anthropologist in Melanesia* (University of Hawaii Press, 1998) and coeditor, with Michael O'Hanlon, of *Hunting the Gatherers: Ethnographic Collectors, Agents, and Agency in Melanesia* (Berghahn Publishers, 2000).

STAFF

Theodore Knight   List Manager
David Brackley   Senior Developmental Editor
Juliana Gribbins   Developmental Editor
Rose Gleich   Administrative Assistant
Brenda S. Filley   Director of Production/Design
Juliana Arbo   Typesetting Supervisor
Diane Barker   Proofreader
Richard Tietjen   Publishing Systems Manager
Larry Killian   Copier Coordinator

AUTHORS

RICHARD E. W. ADAMS is a professor of anthropology at the University of Texas at San Antonio. He has excavated many sites in Mesoamerica and is the author of numerous books and articles.

SERGE BAHUCHET is Chargé de Recherche at the Laboratoire de Langues et Civilisation à Tradition Orale at the Centre National de la Recherche Scientifique in Paris. He has conducted research among pygmies in the Congo.

P. S. BELLWOOD is a reader in the School of Archaeology and Anthropology at the Australian National University. He has conducted archaeological research in many parts of the Pacific and in Indonesia. He is the author of *Prehistory of the Indo-Malaysian Archipelago*, rev. ed. (University of Hawaii Press, 1997).

RON BRUNTON is a senior fellow of the Institute of Public Affairs at Queensland, Australia. An anthropologist by training, he has conducted research on environmental policies in Australia and Melanesia.

NAPOLEON A. CHAGNON is a professor emeritus of anthropology at the University of California at Santa Barbara. He is best known for his extended work over many years among the Yanomamö Indians of Venezuela, about whom he has written many books, including *Yanomamö*, 5th ed. (Harcourt Brace, 1997) and *Yanomamö: The Last Days of Eden* (Harcourt Brace Jovanovich, 1992).

JAMES CLIFFORD is a professor of the history of consciousness at the University of California at Santa Cruz. He has written many books and articles about postmodern anthropology, including *Routes: Travel and Translation in the Late Twentieth Century* (Harvard University Press, 1997).

GEORGE L. COWGILL is a professor of anthropology at Arizona State University. He is best known for his archaeological research in central Mexico. He is coeditor, with Norman Yoffee, of *The Collapse of Ancient States and Civilizations* (University of Arizona Press, 1988).

JAMES R. DENBOW is an associate professor of anthropology at the University of Texas at Austin. He has conducted field research in southern Africa and was curator of archaeology at the National Museum of Botswana.

THOMAS D. DILLEHAY is a professor of anthropology at the University of Kentucky. He is best known for his excavations at Monte Verde, Chile, and in the southwestern United States. He is the author of *Monte Verde: A Late Pleistocene Settlement in Chile* (Smithsonian Institution Press, 1997).

DENIS DUTTON is associate professor of art theory in the School of Fine Arts at the University of Canterbury at Christchurch, New Zealand. He is a specialist on aesthetics and tribal art and is the author of *The Forger's Art: Forgery and the Philosophy of Art* (University of California Press, 1983).

R. BRIAN FERGUSON is a professor of anthropology at Rutgers University. He has conducted field research in Puerto Rico and among the Yanomamö in South America.

STUART J. FIEDEL is an archaeologist working with John Milner Associates in Alexandria, Virginia. He is the author of many books and papers, including *Prehistory of the Americas,* 2d ed. (Cambridge University Press, 1992).

DEREK FREEMAN is an emeritus professor of anthropology in the Research School of Pacific and Asian Studies at the Australian National University. He has conducted field research among the Iban of Borneo and the Samoans of Western Samoa.

IGOR de GARINE is at the Centre National de la Recherche Scientifique in Gan, France. He writes about topics in human ecology, including a volume coedited with G. A. Harrison, *Coping With Uncertainty in Food Supply* (Oxford University Press, 1988).

CLIFFORD GEERTZ is a professor at the Insitute for Advanced Study in Princeton, New Jersey. He has conducted field research in Indonesia and Morocco. He is the author of *Works and Lives: The Anthropologist as Author* (Stanford University Press, 1988).

GEORGE W. GILL is a professor of anthropology at the University of Wyoming. He is a forensic anthropologist and has examined human skeletons from Mexico, Easter Island, and the Great Plains.

MARIJA GIMBUTAS is a late professor of European archaeology at the University of California at Los Angeles. She was author of seventeen books and some two hundred articles on European prehistory, including *The Civilization of the Goddess* (Harper Collins, 1992).

STEVEN GOLDBERG is chairman of the Sociology Department at City University of New York. He has written many articles and books, including *Seduced by Science: How American Religion Has Lost Its Way* (New York University Press, 1999).

MARVIN HARRIS was a professor of anthropology at Columbia University until 1980, when he was appointed graduate research professor of anthropology at the University of Florida. He is the author of many books on anthropology and anthropological theory, including *Cultural Materialism: The Struggle for a Science of Culture* (Random House, 1979).

THOMAS N. HEADLAND is international anthropology consultant at the Summer Institute of Linguistics and an adjunct professor of anthropology at the University of Texas at Arlington.

ELLEN RHOADS HOLMES has conducted field research in Samoa. She is coauthor, with her husband Lowell D. Holmes, of *Samoan Village: Then and Now* (Harcourt Brace, 1992) and *Other Cultures, Elder Years: An Introduction to Cultural Gerontology* (Sage, 1995).

LOWELL D. HOLMES is an emeritus professor of anthropology at Wichita State University. He has conducted field research in Samoa and in contemporary America. He is the author of *Quest for the Real Samoa* (Bergin & Garvey, 1986).

JAMES RIDING IN is an assistant professor in the School of Justice Studies and acting director of the American Indian Studies Program at Arizona State University. A historian by training, he is also a member of the Pawnee tribe.

RICHARD B. LEE is a professor of anthropology and chair of the African Studies Programme at the University of Toronto. He is best known for his research among the San peoples of the Kalahari Desert. He is the author of *The Dobe Ju/'hoansi*, 2d ed. (Harcourt Brace, 1984).

MARIA LEPOWSKI is a professor of anthropology at the University of Wisconsin. She has conducted field research in Papua New Guinea and is the author of *Fruit of the Motherland: Gender in an Egalitarian Society* (Columbia University Press, 1993).

JONATHAN MARKS is a visiting associate professor of anthropology at the University of California at Berkeley. He researches primate and human evolution, race, and molecular genetics.

DOYLE McKEY is a biologist at l'Université Montpellier II, Montpellier, France, and specializes in the relationship between insects and plants in the tropical rain forest.

ROBIN McKIE is a science writer who has authored and coauthored many popular books about scientific topics, including *The Genetic Jigsaw: The Story of the New Genetics* (Oxford University Press, 1988).

CLEMENT W. MEIGHAN was a professor of anthropology at the University of California at Los Angeles and for many years director of UCLA's Archaeological Survey. He excavated numerous archaeological sites in California and Mesoamerica.

LYNN MESKELL is an assistant professor of anthropology at Columbia University. Her archaeological research is focused on Egypt and the Mediterranean. She is the author of *Archaeologies of Social Life* (Blackwell, 1999).

SCOTT NORRIS is a freelance science writer living in Albuquerque, New Mexico. He has written many articles about biodiversity and biological anthropology.

DALE PETERSON is a professor at Tufts University. He is the author, with Jane Goodall, of *Visions of Caliban: On Chimpanzees and People* (Houghton Mifflin, 1993) and, with Richard Wrangham, *Demonic Males: Apes and the Origins of Human Violence* (Houghton Mifflin, 1996).

MERRILEE H. SALMON is a professor of the history and philosophy of science at the University of Pittsburgh. Her recent research concerns the philosophy of anthropology.

E. S. SAVAGE-RUMBAUGH is a researcher at Georgia State University. She is the author of many articles and books, including *Apes, Language, and the Human Mind* (Oxford University Press, 1998).

ELLIOTT P. SKINNER is an emeritus professor of anthropology at Columbia University. He has conducted fieldwork in Burkina Faso (Upper Volta) where he formerly served as United States ambassador. He is the author of *The Mossi of Burkina Faso* (Waveland, 1990).

JACQUELINE S. SOLWAY is an associate professor of anthropology at Trent University. She has conducted field research in southern Africa and is the author of many articles and reports on the Bakgalagadi people of the Kalahari.

CHRISTOPHER STRINGER is a paleoanthropology researcher at the Natural History Museum in London. He is the author of several books, including, with Clive Gamble, *In Search of the Neanderthals* (Thames and Hudson, 1993).

ROBERT W. SUSSMAN is a professor of anthropology at Washington University in St. Louis and is currently editor of *American Anthropologist*. He is the author of *Lemur Biology* (Plenum Press, 1975), which he coedited with Ian Tattersall.

IAN TATTERSALL is a curator at the American Museum of Natural History and also adjunct professor of anthropology at Columbia University. He is the author of *The Last Neanderthal* (Westview Press, 1999).

JOHN EDWARD TERRELL is curator of oceanic archaeology and ethnology at The Field Museum in Chicago. He is the author of *Prehistory in the Pacific Islands* (Cambridge University Press, 1986).

ALAN G. THORNE is a visiting fellow in the Department of Archaeology and Natural History, Research School of Pacific and Asian Studies, at the Australian National University.

JOEL WALLMAN is a program officer at the Harry Frank Guggenheim Foundation in New York. In recent years he has studied aggression and linguistic ability. He is the author of *Aping Language* (Cambridge University Press, 1992).

JAMES F. WEINER is currently a research associate at the Australian National University. He has written many books and articles about the Foi people of Papua New Guinea, including *The Empty Place* (University of Indiana Press, 1991).

EDWIN N. WILMSEN is a research fellow at the University of Texas at Austin. He has conducted research in Botswana and is the author of *Land Filled with Flies: A Political Economy of the Kalahari* (University of Chicago Press, 1989).

MILFORD H. WOLPOFF is a professor of anthropology at the University of Michigan at Ann Arbor where he directs the paleoanthropology laboratory. He has written many books and articles on paleoanthropology, including a leading textbook *Paleoanthropology*, 2d ed. (McGraw-Hill, 1994).

RICHARD WRANGHAM is a professor of anthropology at Harvard University. He studies primate behavior and ecology and evolutionary biology. He is the author, with Dale Peterson, of *Demonic Males: Apes and the Origins of Human Violence* (Houghton Mifflin, 1996).

Index